Political Thinking, Political Theory, and Civil Society

This new edition of *Political Thinking, Political Theory, and Civil Society* presents a comprehensive overview of the Western tradition of political thought that approaches concepts with the aim of helping readers develop their own political thinking and critical thinking skills. This text is uniquely organized around the theme of civil society – What is the nature of a civil society? Why is it important? – that will engage students and help make the material relevant. Major thinkers discussed in the text are explored not only with the goal of understanding their views but also with an interest in understanding the relationship of their ideas to the notion of a civil society.

New to this edition:

- Visual aids and pedagogy.
- New chapter on black political theory and civil society, including a discussion of protest and #BlackLivesMatter in political theory.
- Expanded discussions of feminism and the LGBTQ movement, as well as an additional discussion of the #MeToo movement from the perspective of its theoretical foundation and its implications for feminist theory.
- Revised chapter on multiculturali̱m, including an expanded discussion of religion, neoliberalism, globalizati

This authoritative text, written by two l̕ turers, is essential reading for all students of p

Steven M. DeLue is Professor Emeritu̱

Timothy M. Dale is Professor of Political Science and Public Administration at the University of Wisconsin – La Crosse.

D1211968

Praise for the New Edition

This is a comprehensive textbook that covers all the historical periods and the most important topics, ideas, debates, and issues in social and political philosophy, as well as many of the dominant and significant theorists or philosophers. The book is well written and easy to read and comprehend, with very clear expositions, analyses, and commentaries.

Polycarp A. Ikuenobe, *Kent State University*

This book provides students with an extremely solid foundation in political theory and political thinking. Within well organised chapters, the authors provide a broad and accessible discussion of political traditions, allowing students to critically engage with a range of issues and apply their thinking to current political developments. There are welcome additions to the new edition, including climate change, racial injustice and civil rights.

Stephen Dixon, *Newman University*

No one committed in any way to the understanding of western tradition of political thought should miss this lucid and engaging piece. The authors use simple language to examine and demystify major traditions and approaches of the West to civil societies, writing with insight, wit, and a striking eye for detail. This edition also offers a lively and readable supplement to undergraduate courses in cognate disciplines, including law, philosophy and public theology.

Olufemi O. Ilesanmi, *Robert Gordon University*

Authors DeLue and Dale capture the essential questions of civil society by providing comprehensive overviews and critiques of some of the most significant thinkers from Plato to Foucault. Technical yet eloquent presentation of timeless debates on topics such as civic virtue lend very well to much larger discussions in the classroom about equality, culture, and politics. This is a vital resource for liberal arts students.

Kristin Matthews, *Assistant Professor of Political Science, Tulsa Community College*

Political Thinking, Political Theory, and Civil Society

Fifth Edition

Steven M. DeLue

Miami University

Timothy M. Dale

University of Wisconsin – La Crosse

Routledge
Taylor & Francis Group

NEW YORK AND LONDON

Fifth edition published 2021
by Routledge
52 Vanderbilt Avenue, New York, NY 10017

and by Routledge
2 Park Square, Milton Park, Abingdon, Oxon, OX14 4RN

Routledge is an imprint of the Taylor & Francis Group, an informa business

First edition published by Allyn and Bacon, 1997
Fourth edition published by Routledge, 2017

Library of Congress Cataloging-in-Publication Data
A catalog record for this book has been requested

ISBN: 978-0-367-54321-1 (hbk)
ISBN: 978-0-367-54319-8 (pbk)
ISBN: 978-1-003-08873-8 (ebk)

Typeset in Times New Roman
by Apex CoVantage, LLC

Brief Contents

Detailed Contents

Preface

It may seem strange that a text on the history of political theory would require a new edition because Plato and Machiavelli have not published additional works since the last edition. From its inception, however, the driving force behind this book has been to invite readers into the discussion that has spanned thousands of years and nevertheless challenges us to think about our own time and the pressing concerns that we confront in our politics and our society. This new edition carries this commitment forward and applies the questions and answers posed by enduring ideas in the history of political thought to our contemporary world.

One of the key questions that has endured throughout the centuries is the issue of the relationship between individuals and society. In what sense does society owe something to an individual? In what sense does an individual owe something to society? How can civic engagement cultivate a better society and an enriched individual? The underlying premise of this book is that these questions are important to ask and that the answers are as relevant today as they have been at any time previous in the history of political philosophy. Hence, the timelessness and timeliness of political thinking: we are asking the same questions across the millennia, and it is incumbent on us to answer these questions because of their continuing, acute relevance to our context and lives.

Indeed, we cannot adequately address any of the challenges that affect us today without the ideas that are contained in the history of political thinking and discussed throughout this book. These ideas both express our aspirations and provide us with a way to talk to each other and reach shared understandings about how to achieve them. For instance, if, among the many things we crave, we want democracy, the rule of law, and political authority that is just and competent, we need to have a shared understanding of what constitutes each of these dimensions, an understanding that cuts across all people from all walks of life. Only then can we partake, together, in the conversations and deliberations by which we bring about as well as preserve these – and many other – important characteristics of political life.

Now, whereas this book discusses a full array of political ideas, the one to which we give a central focus remains, as in the past editions, civil society. We take this route because not only does this approach allow us to elaborate other key ideas in political thinking, but also the idea of civil society enables us to ask if the way we live now represents a way of life that best serves our highest aspirations, and if not, what should we do?

To address these questions better, we have sought to strengthen the book with this edition. In particular, we have added a chapter on the contributions of black political theory to current and pressing discussions about racial justice in the United States. In Chapter 20, "Civil Society, Liberal Democracy, and Racial Injustice: A Political Theory Informed by the Black Experience in America," we detail the significant role the experience of African Americans has in civil society with respect to the goals of inclusion and equality. In this context, the chapter proposes in part that we have a "moral obligation to remember radical injustice toward blacks." Within this conversation, the chapter outlines the contributions of several black voices that manifest in different ways a moral obligation to remember radical injustice.

We have also revised the chapter on feminist political thinking to include additional discussion of the "waves" of feminism, with added consideration of the recent #MeToo movement, and the possibilities of a fourth wave of feminism that calls for increased social accountability. That discussion, as in the past editions, continues to provide a survey of feminist political theorists who offer a range of criticisms and theoretical solutions to the problem of the exclusion of women and gender bias in society.

We also offer in this edition a substantial revision to Chapter 19 on the "21st Century Challenges for Civil Society: Culture, Religion, and Climate Change." In this chapter, we find that in order to pursue its philosophically founded purposes, liberal civil society needs to better address the opportunities within it to account for multiculturalism, religion, and global environmental crises.

We hope these changes, when set alongside the parts of the book which remain from previous editions, will serve the interests of careful, reasoned deliberation about politics, a deliberation that is all the more necessary in the face of the many important issues we face as a global community.

Steven M. DeLue
Petaluma, California

Timothy M. Dale
La Crosse, Wisconsin

Introduction

Historical Timeline of Thinkers in Political Theory

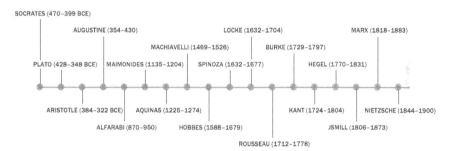

SOCRATES (470–399 BCE)

AUGUSTINE (354–430)

LOCKE (1632–1704)

MARX (1818–1883)

MACHIAVELLI (1469–1526)

BURKE (1729–1797)

PLATO (428–348 BCE)   MAIMONIDES (1135–1204)   SPINOZA (1632–1677)

HEGEL (1770–1831)

ARISTOTLE (384–322 BCE)   AQUINAS (1225–1274)

KANT (1724–1804)

NIETZSCHE (1844–1900)

ALFARABI (870–950)   HOBBES (1588–1679)

JSMILL (1806–1873)

ROUSSEAU (1712–1778)

I. Political Thinking and Political Theory

Individuals engage in political thinking when they seek to determine which political ideas offer more promise, which political solutions best respond to particular challenges, and which political regimes best meet the needs of people. The challenge of this book is to familiarize people with the nature of political thinking in the hope of encouraging readers to engage in this activity themselves. Because we discuss different political theories throughout the book, it is well, before proceeding, to say a few words concerning what political theory is and how we should understand political thinking in relation to it.

We use the term *political theory* interchangeably with the term *political philosophy*.[1] A political theory is constructed as a response to enduring questions that hold the attention of the political theorist. What are some of the questions we have in mind? Plato asked how justice and its important contributions to human life are possible in the face of a society that treats the idea of justice with skepticism. Thomas Hobbes wanted to know why society can become mired in a state of war, and he asked how (or even if) it is possible to overcome this prospect and achieve peace and freedom. John Rawls asked how to construct a society in which people with conflicting but equally reasonable moral perspectives can accord respect to each other's basic rights.

Political theorists are concerned with many other questions as well, and here we list only a few of them. For instance, they seek to demonstrate the nature of the common good and the kind of politics that can best approximate it. Others discuss the definition of the public realm, distinguishing the functions of the public realm from the private realm. Still others want to know what constitutes our obligations and duties as citizens and how obligations and duties are distinct from rights. Throughout political thinking, there is a concern with the role of the family, with religion, and with various structures of government in securing what is commonly referred to as the rule of law. Further, we are treated to many discussions of various types of regimes, including, of course, the nature of democracy and how it is distinguished from other types of political forms. And, finally, as we discuss in this book, others emphasize a quest to preserve civil society in the face of circumstances that threaten its existence.

To address questions such as these, political theorists construct scenarios that are designed to demonstrate the major obstacles that must be faced on behalf of the key objectives that are sought. Thus, if we wish to create a world in which each person is provided the same rights, we must first ask what stands in the way of our doing so. Then, we must ask how best to remove these obstacles so that an equal rights doctrine can be made a central part of society. As we go about this undertaking, we construct a picture of the world that explains why society impedes rights, but, in addition, the picture of the world should explain what factors could help society promote them.

From this enterprise, a political theorist may develop a full-blown theory that explains the relationships among all the significant dimensions of a given issue. To take the example of rights, for instance, a theory would explain what rights are, how they are established and developed in society, and what major obstacles must be overcome to achieve the full attainment of rights. As the theorist engages in this activity, he or she discusses many factors and their relationship to each other, including the role of government, the place of education, the nature of the social and cultural realities that must be in place, and so on.

Now, political theorists can never comprehend all the factors that need to be considered to address the questions at hand. This circumstance arises from the fact that political theorists view the world from a limited and partial point of view. After all, political theorists have their own biases and tendencies to favor one viewpoint over another, and this fact necessarily prevents political theorists from seeing all that must be known about an issue. As a result, all a political theorist can provide is a "vision," to use Sheldon Wolin's term, that describes the possible relationships among the key elements of society, including people and institutions, to address a given question.[2] But possible understandings are not the same as perfect knowledge of social and political events. In consequence, in developing a vision that explains the obstacles that must be confronted to achieve key objectives or answer enduring questions, political theorists inevitably operate from incomplete understandings.

Given that political theorists approach the development of their theories from their own particular experiences and points of view, it is possible that theorists will develop competing theories with respect to the same question. Thus, one theorist may provide a theory that emphasizes certain conceptions of the state that another theorist will reject; a second theorist may define certain cultural conditions that a third theorist would not think are relevant, and so on.[3] In any event, what becomes clear is that any particular theory, when seen from the standpoint of another theory, can be said, in some sense, to lack completeness and comprehensiveness with respect to the question that is asked. As a result, the activity of political philosophy necessarily involves political theorists in arguments with each other over whose theories best explain the world and best help to resolve a particular question.

II. The Link Between Political Theory and Political Thinking

What is the relationship between political thinking and political theory? Both are linked by a common need to address significant and enduring political and social questions. During the course of addressing these questions, political thinking is always drawn back to political theory. For in answering key questions, a person engaged in political thinking often makes use of different visions of political life that various political theorists provide. In doing so, political thinking challenges those who uphold these visions to provide worthy answers to the questions that are being asked.

Political thinking is always fertile ground from which to launch a challenge to a particular vision described in a political theory because, as we just saw, no vision is ever complete, and all visions necessarily include some important elements of reality while downplaying the importance of others. A person engaged in political thinking often highlights this shortcoming by arguing that a particular political vision is just not complete enough to help one understand as fully as necessary a particular social or political reality.

When one vision of the political world does not appear to afford a good basis for addressing a particular question, then a person engaged in political thinking may turn to another theory, with the intention of determining whether the alternative theory does a better job in addressing a given question. While pondering vexing questions, a person may explore as well as compare and contrast many different political theories. For instance, perhaps in addressing the question of justice, we start off with Plato, move on to Aristotle, and conclude with G.W.F. Hegel. In each case, we are comparing different accounts, defending one account against another, shoring up perhaps one vision and demonstrating the weakness of another. Ultimately, we hope to arrive at a conception of justice that we can defend against our critics. During the process, we may reject all known visions of political philosophy on the subject at hand and create a new one instead. As we do, we may create an entirely new political theory to address an important problem that political thinking raises.

Political thinking draws upon political theory. Without the latter, the former cannot take place. Once the process of political thinking begins, though, a person involved in this activity is committed to testing various visions that are articulated in different political theories. And in doing so, a person engaged in political thinking searches for an all-embracing vision of political life that demonstrates in a way never before possible a definitive answer to the question being raised. Of course, we may never reach this point, and thus people who engage in political thinking are often left to ponder the usefulness of different political theories.

III. Socrates of the *Apology* and the *Crito*[4]

Because the classic defense of political thinking is found in Plato's account of Socrates in the *Apology* and the *Crito*, it behooves us to discuss the main themes of these dialogues. This exercise also prepares the reader for the treatment of Plato's *Republic* in Chapter 2.

Before discussing these dialogues, it is important to provide some background about Socrates (470–399 BCE), the individual whom Plato admired and who is, as we see in Chapter 2, his main protagonist in the *Republic*. Socrates lived in Athens during a period when efforts to maintain democracy were displaced by oligarchic and tyrannical rule. After the defeat of Athens in 404 BCE in the Peloponnesian War with Sparta, Spartan forces occupied Athens. At this time, an oligarchic party in Athens, with the help of the Spartans, took this opportunity to undermine Athenian democracy by establishing the rule of what has become known in history as the control of the Thirty Tyrants. These people were to have established a new democratic constitution, but in fact they refused to do so. Instead, they executed not only well-known democrats but also other oligarchs who stood for the rule of law.[5] Eventually, 3,000 citizens deposed the oligarchy, and over a period of several months, democracy was restored in 403 BCE.[6]

Socrates was not popular with the new democratic regime. He taught that politics required a special kind of expertise that ordinary people skilled in other crafts did not necessarily possess. To the average Athenian, Socrates' views seemed to have a great affinity with the positions that oligarchs held. Thus, the Athenians, who at the time harbored the memories of oligarchic terror, wanted nothing more to do with oligarchy. And consequently, the Athenians rejected Socrates as a threat to democracy. Socrates was then put on trial and ultimately condemned to death.[7] Plato in the *Crito* and in the *Apology* as well as in the *Republic* memorializes both Socrates' commitment to truth-seeking and to the view that experts who understand how to use power for moral purposes should run political regimes.

In what follows, we provide an interpretation of the *Apology* and the *Crito* that demonstrates the importance of political thinking.

In the *Apology*, Socrates is accused of not believing in Athenian gods, of "making the weaker argument appear stronger," and of corrupting the youth. Socrates believes himself innocent, and, despite long and convincing defenses of his conduct, a legitimate Athenian court finds him guilty and sentences him to death. Socrates, with the mildest of urgings, allows us, the readers, to conclude that he is guilty merely of engaging in political thinking.

Why did the Athenians find Socrates' use of political thinking so objectionable? To answer this question, it must be clear what Socrates hopes to accomplish with political thinking. He seeks to use political thinking to address key, enduring questions pertaining to the best forms of moral and political life. For instance, he asks questions such as: what is justice? What is piety? What is the nature of law? What is the common good? To answer these questions, Socrates engages in the process called *dialectical* argument.

How does this process proceed? A question is stated, for example, "What is justice?" And various conceptions of justice are presented. From among those conceptions of justice considered, the objective is to find the one conception that is true. To this end, people are asked to provide their own views on each conception, including the reasons that explain why particular conceptions should not be accepted. These reasons are then carefully examined. As telling reasons emerge to deny the validity of certain conceptions, these conceptions are no longer considered, and the list of possible conceptions of justice is narrowed. Ultimately, as one goes through the list, one hopes to find a conception of justice that is comprehensive enough to withstand any further challenge. The remaining conception becomes the basis for answering the initial question, namely: what is justice? Indeed, Plato's *Republic* is modeled along these lines, as we see in Chapter 2.

To engage in political thinking, then, requires a discourse involving others who are willing to have their views tested in public. And this is the approach to political thinking that Socrates takes throughout his life. In the *Apology*, Socrates says, "I still go about testing and examining every man whom I think wise, whether he is a citizen or a stranger."[8] But it is precisely this activity, Socrates believes, that has gotten him into trouble. He tells us that "persons who are cross-examined get angry with me instead of with themselves, and say that Socrates is an abomination and corrupts the youth."[9]

But why did the Athenians get angry with Socrates? Is it that the people associated him with oligarchy, or are there other reasons? We can only speculate, of course, about what the reasons for their anger might be. But the speculation is useful because it demonstrates a general problem that the process of political thinking poses for many even today.

One reason for Athenian skepticism of Socrates' efforts might be that for them to engage in dialectical argument, individuals must accept that existing views and opinions might be wrong and thus subject to revision or elimination. But that outcome could have very adverse consequences for people. Sometimes maintaining the status-quo view of substantial ideas of justice or piety, for instance, is important for protecting what constitutes one's existing way of life.

Another reason for skepticism of Socrates' endeavors might have to do with the fact that his approach requires people to consider their own views in a context of contesting opinions. In this case, for those committed to finding common definitions of key concepts, political thinking suggests a risk much different from the risks presented to those who fear that political thinking will disrupt the status quo. In considering diverse views and in accepting the challenge they represent to one's own opinions, one confronts the possibility that no shared understanding will ever be reached. In this case, the search for the answer to important political questions is ongoing and perpetual, as it becomes clear that good arguments constantly appear to counter reasonable views. Here, what is troubling is discovering that social reality is not necessarily a solidified condition based on acknowledged truth but that it is a condition requiring continuing acceptance of diverse views and opinions, many of which cannot be reconciled or easily combined.

Socrates hopes to avoid this possible outcome of political thinking and to find the comprehensive definitions of key concepts that could ground social reality in truth. He always seems confident that he would. But, still, in approaching the search for truth through the process of dialectical argument, he risks falling into a myriad of unsolvable problems and a world of irresolution.

Socrates is willing to assume these risks. But it appears, however, that the Athenians are not. In consequence, Socrates is sentenced to death, and his sentence symbolizes the Athenians' refusal to engage in political thinking and to tolerate its liabilities. So committed is Socrates to this enterprise that, in the *Crito*, when Crito enters the prison to convince Socrates to accept his (Crito's) offer of escape, Socrates argues that he would not leave unless he could be convinced that leaving was the just thing to do. Socrates says, "If we ought never to act unjustly at all, ought we to repay injustice with injustice, as the multitude thinks we may?"[10]

In raising this question, Socrates takes the moment with Crito to dramatize the importance of political thinking. All major issues must be subject to the analysis pursued in the dialectical form of argument, which undergirds political thinking. This objective is achieved in the *Crito* during the famous imagined discussion with the laws of the society. Here, Socrates engages in a discussion with the laws as if the laws were wise people whom Socrates is cross-examining. A major contention that is implicit in the argument that the laws present is that, by fleeing, Socrates would be violating the laws of Athens. Why is this the case? A legitimate court has convicted him, and the laws require that people who are convicted accept their sentence.

But why, Socrates seems to ask, is it wrong to violate the laws and, as in this case, flee Athens after conviction by a legitimate proceeding? The laws answer that it is wrong to violate *just* laws, and in fact the laws of Athens are on the whole just. Why are the laws just, Socrates seems to ask? In the main, the laws are just because they have provided benefits of critical importance to the moral maturation and intellectual development of individuals in the society. In making their case to Socrates, the laws indicate that they have provided Socrates with an education that has prepared him for life, including a life of political thinking. In fact, the laws demonstrate that they have not prevented him from engaging in political thinking. The laws have permitted him to debate the state's policies and, if and when he disagrees with them, to try to convince the state to change its positions. The laws permit him to leave without penalty if the policies that the state adopts are not ones with which he concurs.[11]

The implication of the arguments the laws make is now clear. Socrates' complaint should not be against the laws because the laws are just. His complaint should be launched against the people of Athens who have acted unjustly toward him. Furthermore, because the laws are just, Socrates owes them his undying allegiance. He must do nothing to harm them. If he were to disobey just laws, he would in fact be acting in ways that are harmful to the laws and, by doing so, compounding the injustice already committed against him. Given these views, Socrates decides that the just thing to do is to accept his execution.

Furthermore, by supporting just laws, Socrates upholds what is one of their central purposes, which as we see, is to protect political thinking. The search for truth demands nothing less. Socrates, were he alive today, would no doubt reinforce this point. Campaign managers and media experts who have little concern for political thinking now conduct contemporary politics. Their objective is not to encourage the dialectical approach to examining ideas that political thinking demands but to incur from the populace the desired, as the campaign managers define, response to various cues that they hope can be used to marshal mass support for particular candidates or issues. Campaign strategists see political thinking as a threat to those like themselves who hope to turn societies into large crowds, where the crowd mind imputes opinions to citizens. As a result, individuals are no longer able to forge their own judgments through the process of comparing and contrasting ideas, a process that is integral to the dialectical mode of thought. Many now are aware that this goes on, and many resent it. But pointing out the problem is not enough. Restoring to the culture an understanding of the art of political thinking is fundamental to securing a democratic politics capable of securing the rights of each citizen. We hope this book makes a contribution to this effort.

IV. The Rest of the Book

Our approach in this book is to provide examples of political thinking, examples that we hope encourage the reader to engage in political thinking him- or herself. To this end, we plan to discuss how one thinker would defend his or her vision of society against other thinkers. In the process of this undertaking, our intention is to ask readers to question our interpretation of the possible arguments that we suggest the respective thinkers would use in responding to other thinkers.

To facilitate this endeavor, we develop the nature and the importance of a civil society as a major theme. As we discuss the different visions emanating from the various approaches to political thinking that this book addresses, we consider how these different visions bear on this central theme. For instance, interwoven throughout the discussions are questions such as: would Plato support a civil society? How would Aristotle have responded to the question of civil society? Why is John Locke's theory likely to support a civil society? But why is Jean-Jacques Rousseau's vision less likely?

Our effort to encourage political thinking is carried out as well by response and rejoinder sections throughout the book, often at the end of a chapter. In these sections, we imagine how the various thinkers would have responded to one another. In particular, we ask how thinkers who come before others would respond to the people who come after them, and, in addition, we try to demonstrate the way later thinkers would respond to critiques by earlier ones. In all cases, the concern is with how certain thinkers would respond to each other on a variety of issues touched on in each chapter. Whereas the civil society question is the central theme, the response and rejoinder sections are designed to develop a discussion across a variety of questions found in the different visions described throughout the book.

In the remaining part of this section, we provide a brief overview of the thinkers we cover. The first chapter is a discussion of civil society. Here, we develop the main conception of a civil society that is referred to throughout this book as we discuss the various visions found in the political theories we address.

In Part I, there is a discussion of classical Greek, Christian, and some non-Christian visions of political philosophy. Regarding the classical Greek dimension, there are chapters on Plato and Aristotle. We address Christian thought with a chapter that includes medieval and Reformation Christian thinkers. We also include a chapter on non-Christian medieval thinkers, including Moses Maimonides, and important Islamic thinkers, such as Averroes, Alfarabi, and Avicenna. These chapters are designed to demonstrate how civic virtue in the classical Greek, Christian, and non-Christian worlds differ from the view of civic virtue found in modern conceptions of civil society. We have written these chapters to demonstrate that, whereas classical Greek, Christian, and non-Christian thinkers are not principally responsible for developing the notion of a civil society, there are still important elements in these writers' views that are made a part of civil society thinking.

In Parts II and III, we turn to early modern, late modern, and contemporary approaches to civil society. In the process, we discuss a host of writers of great importance to the history of political theory. Found throughout these sections are liberal and conservative views of civil society. Liberal views of civil society seek to secure the broadest possible individual freedom by protecting citizens' basic rights. The classical Greek, Christian, and non-Christian traditions envision individuals as part of a society that is subject to the overarching conception of the common purpose that dictates the nature of one's place and one's role in society. In contrast, a liberal view of civil society asserts that individuals should define their own moral purposes, and that political equality, secured by rights, allows them to do so. In addition to the aforementioned Hobbes, Locke, Hegel, and Rawls, some other writers included in the liberal category are Benedict Spinoza, Immanuel Kant, and John Stuart Mill. The chapters on Rousseau and Karl Marx should be viewed as modern critiques of the liberal views of civil society. And the chapter on Niccolò Machiavelli at the beginning of Part II provides a transition from the classical and religious tradition to the liberal conceptions of civil society discussed in some of the writers that come after him.

Conservative writers, while accepting the fundamental importance of human freedom, worry that the emphasis on rights may go so far that the norms and traditions that underscore community life, also necessary for securing freedom, are neglected. In the process of making this mistake, the importance of orienting people to understand the types of social relationships and the basic values needed to secure a rich and full life are denied a place of prominence. Included among writers in this tradition are Edmund Burke, Alexis de Tocqueville, and Michael Oakeshott. Conservatives, not unlike writers in the classical Greek, Christian, and non-Christian traditions, seek to maintain an integrated social order in which each person's identity is part of the larger context of traditions and common ways of experiencing life. For the conservative, when individuals are cut off from such attachments, they are robbed of the real sources of identity, the aspects of experience that give meaning and significance to one's life.

Part IV contains critiques of the modern views of civil society. Here, we discuss feminist critiques as well as the views that Friedrich Nietzsche and Michel Foucault put forward. Why have these people been selected? Their accounts are of great importance because each, from a different perspective, seeks to demonstrate that civil society is merely a mask to hide or to give cover to, in the name of important ideals such as rights and civic virtue, repressive relationships. Each of these ways of thinking discussed here, then, raises the question about whether the idea of a civil society represents a worthy enterprise.

The Nietzschean arguments, for different reasons, would answer this question with a loud and resounding no. For Nietzsche and those who follow him, a civil society blunts the imagination and destroys the creative power of individuals so that, in the long run, individuals are unable to achieve the liberation that civil society promises. Nietzsche would thus hark back to a different social arrangement, one in which society is, in the main, under the dominant power of an aristocratic class that is able to set a new and more liberatory course for society. Michel Foucault will pursue a Nietzschean unmasking of the oppressive dimensions of civil society, also. However, he will update his critique to fit modern organizational life and development, and he will demand a politics that supports those techniques, peculiar to his own brand of political theory, that permit individuals to overcome modern repression. Feminists, however, for the most part, do retain an essential faith in civil society. Feminists take this view so long as major reforms are provided that help to make civil society not just a place where males flourish at the cost of females but where all can flourish in a setting conducive to full human freedom.

In Chapters 19 and 20, we conclude the book by providing an overview of the state of civil society in today's world. In Chapter 19, we discuss the relationship between civil society and multiculturalism, religion, and the struggle to address global environmental crises, as well as the prospects for a global civil society. In Chapter 20, we add the important voices of black political theory to address contemporary issues of racial injustice. We hope readers will find in these discussions the need for civic renewal, a renewed accounting for justice in society, and the overall importance of civil society for a liberal democracy.

One final point: though we discuss the idea of civil society in the context of major political thinkers throughout history, we see our doing so not just as a way to come to grips with important and enduring political ideas, but also as a vehicle for sparking reasoned discussions of many contemporary issues now apparent in the society. Will the politics of present-day America, as well as of world politics, generally speaking, eventuate in an ever-stronger presence of civil society or in a situation in which civil society is only a dim voice in the world?

An example of a group now holding the former view is the grassroots organization referred to as Black Lives Matter, which – in response to the breakdowns of police–community relations in many cities – says that groups historically denied a chance for full participation in society must be accorded the opportunities promised to all citizens. In taking this view, groups like Black Lives Matter have a major role in sustaining the great tradition within civil society thinking of civic engagement on behalf of securing full rights for all citizens. Groups like Black Lives Matter serve to strengthen civil society and its commitment to full toleration and mutual respect for all people, regardless of religious, ethnic, gender, or cultural differences.

Notes

1. In taking this position, we follow Sheldon Wolin. See Sheldon S. Wolin, *Politics and Vision: Continuity and Innovation in Western Political Thought* (Boston: Little, Brown and Company, 1960), 21. For a different view, one that distinguishes political theory from political philosophy, see Nannerl O. Keohane, "Philosophy, Theory, Ideology," *Political Theory* 4, no. 1 (February 1976): 81–82.

2. Wolin, *Politics and Vision*, 18–19.

3. Ibid., 19.

4. Our account is based on our interpretation of Plato's *Apology* and the *Crito* in Plato; Euthyphro, *Apology and Crito*, trans. F. J. Church (Indianapolis: Bobbs-Merrill Company, 1956), 21–67.

5. Irving M. Zeitlin, *Plato's Vision: The Classical Origins of Social and Political Thought* (Englewood Cliffs, NJ: Prentice Hall, 1993), 47–48.

6. Mulford Q. Sibley, *Political Ideas and Ideologies: A History of Political Thought* (New York: Harper and Row, 1970), 44.

7. Zeitlin, *Plato's Vision*, 59.

8. Plato, *Apology*, Church ed., 28.

9. Ibid.

10. Plato, *Crito,* Church ed., 59.

11. Ibid., 60–61.

1

The Importance of a Civil Society

I. Civil Society: The Problem Faced

The term *civil society* has several uses. In one use, a *civil society* refers to a regime committed to secure the rule of law on behalf of the common good. In contemporary society, the common good refers to a variety of possible items, including but not limited to the provision of basic rights, public safety, education, systems of communication and roads, national parks, and so on. But the term *civil society* has another use as well, and it is this second use that will be given a predominant place in this book. The second use of the term refers to a space that exists between the national government and the individual. In that space, there are a variety of different groups and associations, each of which is dedicated to upholding certain values and to achieving particular ends.

As contemporary writer Jean Bethke Elshtain says, a civil society refers to many different forms of associations, often called voluntary groups or secondary institutions, such as families, religious organizations, trade unions, self-help groups, charitable associations, neighborhood organizations, private clubs and organizations, and so on. These organizations, which exist outside the formal structures of government power, point to a separate sphere. In that sphere, individuals are free to pursue a variety of life experiences made possible by the different associations people may join.[1] An important aspect of a civil society is that, as a separate sphere, civil society acts as a buffer against the power of the central government, and, in this role, encourages an atmosphere that allows various groups to follow their own courses without fear of central government intrusions.

Moreover, these groups are also independent of large corporate, business organizations whose power to dominate markets and to influence governments is vast and decisive. Corporations such as Microsoft or General Motors have the power to dictate many of the terms of their workers' lives. A civil society counters this tendency by acting as a buffer against large corporate power, just as it acts as a buffer against the power of the central government. As a buffer, a civil society permits individuals to determine through the associations they make with others what they do with their free time, what religious beliefs, if any, they hold, what friends and life-long partners they choose, what kinds of civic activities they will pursue, and so on.

But, as Nancy Rosenblum says, American political theorists tend to focus less upon the separate sphere as a buffer against the central government and more upon the moral education obtained in the groups that make up the separate sphere.[2] We think there is less focus as well on civil society as a buffer against corporate power than there is on the need to see civil society as a basis for moral education. On this view, then, people enter the separate sphere, participate in groups, and receive from this experience an important moral dimension to their lives. Here, the connections people forge in the various groups of a civil society help them maintain a sense of civic responsibility for the welfare of many others, including one's neighbors, friends, and society. Owing to this important experience in civil society, out-of-control, unlimited egoism is subordinated to the norms of civic conduct.[3] Consequently, a civil society, as it stresses the separate sphere of groups and voluntary associations, points to important civic values that the society expects its members to embrace.

Because civic values are important in discussions of civil society, it is necessary to describe the nature of the moral environment that a civil society as a separate sphere promotes. What is the nature of this moral environment? A civil society is associated with an environment in which individuals are accorded political equality and thus guaranteed the same rights, while at the same time maintaining among themselves a commitment to uphold *civic virtue*. Civic virtue refers to the respect citizens have for the common standards and conception of the common good integral to the life of a community. So, on the one hand, individuals are to be accorded full dignity and respect by being provided the same package of rights that guarantee, among other things, freedom of association, speech, conscience, due process of law, and ownership of private property. With these rights, individuals gain not only the ability to influence the political decisions of the government, but they achieve the capability to pursue reasonable, self-defined life objectives. On the other hand, a civil society encourages people to endorse the common standards deemed necessary to maintain a decent and *civic* life. In upholding the common norms, individuals manifest respect for civic virtue and, in consequence, maintain a commitment to the common good.[4]

This conception of civil society suggests two different approaches to the way we come to understand ourselves as individuals. First, when individuals see themselves as equals, they are likely to think of themselves as independent and self-standing persons whose way of life predominantly derives from their own reflections and choices and not from impositions emanating from outside their lives. However, the civic virtue dimension of civil society proposes that there are common standards that all members of the society are expected to support. Specifically, this means one must manifest allegiance to all the norms associated with good citizenship.

Now, there are many values allied with the civic virtue dimension of civil society. Here, we will give a few examples, but it must be clear that the list we provide is neither determinative nor exhaustive; rather, this list is an illustration of what is meant, generally, when we discuss the civic virtue side of civil society. For instance, there are what William Galston refers to as "general virtues," including both respect for the laws and the basic political principles and institutions of the society.[5] Further, there are the basic civic virtues of *tolerance and mutual respect*, to which we give special emphasis in Section VI.

In addition, as Galston indicates, citizen or civic virtues also include concerns for how people should approach participation in the economic life of the society.[6] Each individual must have a work ethic or an ability to do one's job well while supporting oneself. Furthermore, the work environment requires that individuals learn to adapt to the changing circumstances of economic life by acquiring new skills or updating existing ones. Also, as we discuss in our review of Adam Smith's concept of the modern market economy in Section VII, individuals must be able, in the name of longer-term self-interests, to save certain amounts of their incomes, even when doing so requires sacrifice of immediate short-term desires.

A civil society, at its heart, can be characterized by a tension between an individualist viewpoint that is guaranteed by the provision of basic rights and the communal dimension of society that reflects a need to respect the civic virtue requirements. The goal of a civil society is to permit people to pursue their own concepts of life, while at the same time respecting civic virtue obligations and constraints. In general, there are several approaches to this objective, and each approach establishes baseline values for the society to adopt and for the various groups that make up a civil society to uphold. Here, following Rosenblum, we discuss three different approaches, one suggesting a *democratic* civil society, another suggesting a civil society of *mediating* groups, and a third suggesting a *liberal* view of civil society.[7]

II. The Democratic Civil Society

In this section, we discuss the democratic approach to achieving a setting in which the individualist and the communal perspectives are bridged.[8] A society of this sort expects all citizens to take part in defining the rules and norms by which each will be governed. In a democratic setting, people enter the public deliberation as individuals, with their own interests and needs. But during the deliberation, each person articulates his or her interests in a way that helps create a common, shared policy orientation. For instance, in discussing the best approach to cleaning up the environment, we may enter the political arena with our own particular commitment to protect as many green spaces as possible. Others may seek to clear some of these spaces for building new workplaces. As a result of the deliberation, a way is discovered to achieve a fair accommodation between the opposing views.

Thus, as Rosenblum points out, advocates of a democratic civil society suggest that democratic participation in major institutions – including trade unions, churches, or the professions – would help people develop a capacity for deliberating with others on behalf of determining the common good.[9] In consequence, people would learn to think of themselves as citizens as well as private individuals. And when the two roles were in conflict with each other, the citizen role would always take precedence.

In a democratic civil society, then, individuals, through their trade unions and work associations, should be able to have important influence in shaping their work environment, even to the point of helping determine the nature and purpose of the work they do. At the same time, in the other associations, such as religious groups or charitable organizations, the members should help shape the policies there as well. Furthermore, the experience of democratic life in various group settings orients people to be attuned to the needs of the larger society. Here, as a result of democratic experience in civil society associations, when groups participate in the society's national politics, they will be more capable of considering a broad array of interests on behalf of searching for the common good.

Thus, those who support democratic approaches to civil society seek to make the norms of democratic life a part of all forms of group life. Otherwise, the ability of individuals to learn how to embrace and to consider other views and to make them a part of the deliberation with others would not be possible. For instance, families can conform to democratic norms when there is shared responsibility for parenting and when there is a fair division of labor within the family setting.[10] Similarly, an elite few should not dominate labor unions, but all members should enjoy full participation in making key policies.

Alternatively, the democratic approach suggests that groups not presently democratic should be made so. The democratic approach recognizes that some associations have excluded in the past individuals merely owing to their status as women and minorities. Under the democratic approach, associations should ensure that, in the future, individuals previously excluded merely on the grounds of gender or race are included in the "rational d~~~~~ ~~~~~~~~~ ~~~~~~ should take place in ~~~~~~~~

But the ~~~~~~~~~~ ~~~~~~~~~~~ to all persons a dei ~~~~~~~~~~~ ~~~~~~~~~~ crats, want to spen ~~~~~~~~~~~ ~~~~~~~~~~~ s. To have to spenc ~~~~~~~~~~~ ~~~~~~~~~~~ olicy of one's grou ~~~~~~~~~~~ ~~~~~~~~~~~ from other kinds o: ~~~~~~~~~~~ ~~~~~~~~~~~ more so. Included ~~~~~~~~~~~ ~~~~~~~~~~~ with friends, religi ~~~~~~~~~~~ ~~~~~~~~~~~ gov- ernment can a ~~~~~~~~~~~ ~~~~~~~~~~~ ities

[Handwritten note overlaid on text:] Suggesting that since people are automatically given natural born rights makes them less likely to participate in all aspects of democracy – Suggesting to take rights away? ↑ only true for certain groups of people (women + minorities) don't have these rights

for participation during critical moments such as national elections, the need for participation may become minimized for many.

III. Civil Society of Mediating Groups

The mediating view of civil society suggests that individuals create their own organizations to provide important services, such as education or care for the elderly. Moreover, individuals in these groups manifest a civic commitment to care for the needs of each other, and through this experience, individuals create among themselves a sense of belonging, within an integrated and well-ordered community. Here, as voluntary groups assume many of the functions of government, individuals act in ways that are in keeping with respect for the common good of others.

The problem with this view is that in diminishing the need for government, the basic legal institutions that are necessary for maintaining a civil society may lose their fundamental importance to many people. For instance, some individuals today advocate the use of community organizations to dispense basic welfare benefits to people, such as job training. But do mediating groups that engage in this activity have sufficient resources to provide these services on the massive scales that are necessary? Given that they may not, the government's role becomes all the more necessary.

There is thus a need to recognize the importance of the larger environment in which a civil society exists. This environment includes those political and legal institutions that maintain essential services, which, for instance, secure basic rights, provide protection from criminals, and so on. Without government services of this sort, and in particular without the prospect of maintaining the rule of law, a civil society could not be sustained over the long run.[13]

IV. Civil Society: The Liberal Approach

In the liberal view of civil society, the main objective is to promote respect for the diversity of values and ways of life in society.[14] This goal is made possible only in a society that is designed to permit a person the opportunity to move in and out of the different group settings and affiliations to afford a person the chance to discover and then live a way of life that a person would find most suitable. Indeed, as people are free to enter and to leave groups, they find ways to compensate for the lack of opportunities found in one group with the enhanced opportunities discovered in another.

Thus, if it were the case that we have a need for religious experience, we should be free to enter those groups that would facilitate this need. However, because of a subsequent decision that another way of life might be best for us, we should be able to leave the religious group and enter groups that we believed most suited our needs. People should have the right to enter and to leave groups, always, of course, on terms that the groups themselves determine are acceptable. Still, groups, in establishing their internal norms, must always be supportive of the need to not deny any members their basic rights as citizens.

Moreover, the liberal conception of civil society requires a spirit of openness that permits individuals to create new groups and organizations when individuals find it necessary to do so. Existing groups must not stand in the way of new group formations, and new groups must not trample upon the prerogatives of existing groups. In upholding these requirements, opportunities would be provided for those who want to form groups that secure a democratic or participatory experience. Or, alternatively, it would be possible for individuals to create and join groups performing an important mediating or service role in society.

Finally, the provision of rights should not be based upon whether individuals are members of groups. Instead, each individual must be guaranteed the same basic rights, regardless of which groups he or she might be members of, and each person, regardless of his or her group memberships, must acknowledge the rights of others.[15]

Now, one might ask, how is the liberal view of society likely to promote the idea of civic virtue? Is not the liberal view merely one dimensional, emphasizing for the most part the side that fosters individual choice and excluding for the most part the civic virtue side?

V. Liberal Civil Society: Civic Norms

A liberal civil society, which permits individuals the freedom to enter different groups as the basis for pursuing self-determined ways of life, can survive only when there is respect for shared civic norms. Why is this depiction of reality in a civil society accurate? We will answer this question with an example. If individuals wish to pursue a legal career, they must adhere to the standards of conduct that define the path for success in this arena. Now, to be sure, the norms they uphold in this case are not necessarily all civic norms. Following the protocol required to write a legal brief refers to standards that the legal profession solely establishes. The legal profession, just as any other organization, whether it is a religious group, a trade union, or a charitable group, has its own standards that members must uphold. But these professional or group norms point to the importance of civic norms. To uphold the standards of the legal profession, individuals will have to practice many important civic norms. For instance, individuals will have to display a good work ethic, respect for the laws of the society, acceptance of basic citizen duties, such as paying taxes and performing needed volunteer work, a concern for the larger good of society, and so on.

So, civic norms abound in a liberal civil society. In supporting these civic norms, individuals not only enhance their own opportunities, but they also recognize the need to modify personal goals when they conflict with civic standards. At other times, to practice civic norms, it may be necessary to question the basic fairness of an association of which an individual is a member. On these occasions, it is right to evaluate existing group norms in light of the opportunities they provide or fail to provide. For instance, if a private club excludes certain categories of people because of their race or their gender, and if, as a result, these individuals are denied full rights and opportunities accorded all others in society, then it is necessary to work for reform of these practices. Thus, if a private country club is a setting in which important real estate transactions are made, and if this club denies women realtors entrance, then women, for reasons of gender alone, are denied opportunities provided to men. In this case, advocating reform is an understandable practice.

Because a liberal civil society provides many different kinds of groups, there will be different prospects for people to pursue. In this way, a liberal civil society helps to sustain a diversity of ways of life. But, in doing so, it is inevitable that there will be people with different and competing interests, often in conflict with each other. We witness this fact of life all the time. Lawyers and doctors each have professional associations that advocate different policies with respect to standards pertaining to situations in which patients can sue doctors. Religious groups compete for converts. Neighborhood organizations compete for federal dollars. Charitable organizations compete for the private donor's money. Trade unions fight against business-group-backed laws limiting the conditions of union membership. The list describing the different kinds of competition is long. Furthermore, intense competition may engender attitudes of conniving and cunning. Demeanors of this sort can cause individuals to have little regard for the rights of others.

This situation represents an important danger for people in a liberal civil society whose main concern is to protect the basic rights of individuals. Now, the function of the state in a liberal civil society is to secure rights by affording protection to individuals from those in society who would take away their rights. But, in addition to the state's efforts in this regard, respect for rights is maintained in two other important ways, and each of these ways introduces additional and important conceptions of civic virtue.

Critical to maintaining a civil society is the need to manifest either toleration or mutual respect. Each of these outlooks signifies a demeanor of a different sort, but, as we will argue, mutual respect is more desirable than toleration as a civic virtue. Still, toleration can become the basis for achieving mutual respect, and, because of this fact, toleration is a civic virtue of high importance, also.

VI. The Civic Virtues of Toleration and Mutual Respect

The norm associated with toleration is that individuals agree to live and let live by creating separate places in society where people with various lifestyles can practice their beliefs and ways of life. In classical liberalism, as we shall see in discussing John Locke, religious toleration suggests that in tolerating other religious views, one is not required to understand, to come to grips with, or to even test out another's views on oneself. One is asked, instead, just not to interfere with another's religious practices. As a result of toleration, the right to not be hindered in one's religious beliefs is protected for all.

The conduct we maintain while simply tolerating others may lead us to never know about or understand the values of the others whom we tolerate. The doctrine of toleration encourages us to create walls around others and ourselves, and these walls often make the people we tolerate seem even more alien and strange as time goes on. The problem with this attitude is that it may orient us to believe that people who are different from us and whom we tolerate really do not deserve to be accorded those basic rights that a civil society is committed to provide all citizens. Often, this attitude has led to situations in which the rights accorded the "tolerated" may not have the same worth as the rights accorded other members of the society. This means that, even though all have the same rights, owing to a difference in the worth of rights, some can do far more with their rights than others can.

Many examples of the consequences of this kind of situation abound. In this country, after official segregation of African Americans ended, a doctrine of live-and-let-live toleration, embodied in the idea of integration, was maintained toward African Americans who were now free to participate in society on the same terms as whites. But because of continuing racist attitudes, various barriers remain in place, and these obstacles unfairly limit the opportunities for African Americans. In consequence, they have not enjoyed the full measure of rights granted whites. For some Native Americans, the live-and-let-live approach has meant confinement to reservations. The latter came to symbolize policies that did not work to secure the same worth to their rights as provided to mainstream Americans. For women, historically, the household setting has often been the place where women are subordinated to the needs of men and kept from larger participation in the society, including its workplaces and its public, political structure. Reforms of these practices have led to the passage of laws that deny discrimination in various workplace and educational environments. The impact of these laws has been to require men to live and let live with women in the public settings of work, education, and politics. But still, many barriers exist that stifle the full advancement of women in many settings. These barriers include subtle forms of discrimination predicated upon attitudes that establish an implicit agreement among men that women should not be permitted to advance to the higher echelon of many workplaces. This is what many call the "glass ceiling."

Here, the "tolerated" may find themselves marginalized, as in the cases of many women, African Americans, and Native Americans. In consequence, these individuals may suffer a loss of opportunities, especially when compared to those members of society who are advantaged, owing to their gender, race, or ethnic background. The best way to overcome this situation is to advance beyond toleration by teaching the importance of people's learning to understand, to respect, and to consider the views of others who are different from them. To move in this direction is to embrace the civic virtue of mutual respect.

The mode of interaction required for maintaining mutual respect requires that individuals who share a basic commitment to respect the rights of others, however different others may be in status or outlook, seek to understand each other's interests and perspectives. Here, as X interacts with people with different values from his own, his intention should be to learn about and accord respect for the different ideas, points of view, and attitudes that these individuals may hold on issues of common importance to each of them. In discussing political questions, X not only should be willing to engage the people who are in his own professional or religious affiliations, but he should also engage those who are in professional and religious groups different from his own. X should try to find out why others who live in contexts different from his hold the views they profess, and he should seek to determine the reasons others use to justify their positions. While doing so, X helps to make room for other views differing from his, and he removes the walls that might separate him from others. In this new setting, others are not alien to X, and he would have no trouble according them, in the full measure possible, the rights due to them.

To be sure, we cannot accord to all people in society an effort to understand their views, aspirations, and ways of life. There are just too many people for that. But we can accord respect in the sense just defined to those with whom we come in contact. As we manifest this kind of respect for others, and, indeed, as the bulk of the members of society do so as well, then mutual respect would become a widely held civic virtue.

Still, despite the importance of mutual respect, it may be the case that toleration is the best we can do. Indeed, in some circumstances, toleration may be a first step in the long journey to achieving what is clearly the higher-order condition of mutual respect. At first, for society to have social peace, toleration may be the only practical and appropriate doctrine. Take, for instance, a society that has experienced many years of turmoil between several groups. Here, owing to a long period of hateful conflict, it might be too much to expect that individuals would come to engage in relationships of mutual understanding. Still, at least in learning to live and let live, the violence between groups would be ended, and the way would be set for a future in which mutually respectful discourses might begin to occur between groups who were former enemies. In the Middle East, for instance, the doctrine of toleration, if established today, might lead tomorrow to a new commitment to a form of civic virtue that could cause people, who previously manifested mutual distaste or even hatred, to engage each other in a dialogue of mutual recognition and understanding.

Toleration is important for another reason. Where the state must force people to respect the rights of all members, then the state may use policies designed to intimidate people, such as illegal force or constant surveillance, and these policies would place both the separate sphere and basic rights in jeopardy. This condition is avoided when individuals, through a commitment to toleration, voluntarily respect the rights of others. Here, the state could protect rights and the rule of law through approaches that are not intimidating but that enhance the opportunities for all citizens in the various domains of life, such as work, education, art, or the enjoyment of nature.

Still, a civil society as a separate sphere of groups and associations, when it is at its best, embodies both the civic virtues of toleration and mutual respect. In this circumstance, a civil society can be a setting with many diverse groups, each of which contains members from across the social and political spectrum of society. Here, even though a group is dedicated to a central purpose, such as providing public service or enabling people to come together to discuss great books, a group nonetheless includes people from different racial or religious or class backgrounds or from different political and social philosophies. And thus disagreements within, as well as among groups, are always likely. However, where the civic virtue of mutual respect complements the civic virtue of toleration, individuals become practiced in the art of a give-and-take discourse that is designed to find a common ground among competing views within groups, as well as within the society at large. As a result, the quest for inclusion becomes a primary focus of groups in civil society, and this search makes rights-respecting conduct more likely, thus helping to secure a state and society dedicated to protecting the rights of all its citizens.

VII. The Market Dimension of Civil Society: Adam Smith's Dilemma

What we have highlighted in the last several sections is an environment with a multitude of voluntary groups, each of which exists to facilitate a wide diversity of life choices. Allowing people the freedom to choose their own ways of life and permitting group contexts for realizing the ways of life people may choose is a vision of society modeled along the lines of a free market. As in a free market, each person is to have the freedom to choose the way of life he or she determines is best. But, for some, the idea of the free market as it pertains to economic activities represents severe problems for a civil society and, in particular, for its need to sustain civic virtues such as toleration and mutual respect.

In discussing the implications of the free market for civil society, there is no person more important than the eighteenth-century Scottish economist and moral philosopher, Adam Smith (1723–1790). Smith's *The Wealth of Nations* is, as Max Lerner points out, "the foundation-work of modern economic thought."[16] Smith's view of market relationships suggests a market setting in civil society in which an individual "neither intends to promote the public interest, nor knows how much he is promoting it." Indeed, individuals are concerned only to promote their own "security," but, in the process of doing so, they are "led by an invisible hand to promote an end which was no part of [their] intention."[17] And that end is the common good.

For Smith, the "invisible hand" refers to those free-market rules that indicate the ways of life individuals must adopt as a condition for successful attainment of one's interests. So, individuals, in seeking their own interests within the free-market setting, not only recognize the existence of constraints, but these constraints permit the natural unfolding in society of those activities that realize over the long term the best interest of all members of the society.

Why and on what basis is this outcome possible? Answering this question revolves around what Smith saw was the benefit of the industrial society he described in *The Wealth of Nations*. Smith argued that, in "savage nations of hunters and fishers," all who are able work in useful endeavors, but the total amount of goods produced is not enough to meet the needs of the people. Such nations are so poor that they are forced, at times, to abandon their young, their old people, and their sick to hunger or "to be devoured by wild beasts."[18] In contrast, in a modern, civilized, manufacturing society, not all people perform productive work, but the product from those who do productive work is large enough to supply even the poorest worker who "is frugal and industrious" with a "greater share of the necessaries and conveniencies [*sic*] of life than it is possible for any savage to acquire."[19] So, the answer to our question about how the collective good is realized when individuals act only for their own interests revolves around demonstrating how, in a manufacturing society operating by free-market values, it is the case that there still redounds to society a surplus of wealth sufficient to provide all with a decent life, even when not all perform productive labor. How is this end possible?

Smith answered this question by demonstrating how the productive power of workers has been increased in manufacturing societies. The principal way by which this outcome has been achieved is through the introduction of a division of labor. This method of organizing work allows for the introduction of machinery, it improves the skills and dexterity of workers, and it introduces many efficiencies into the work process.[20] Overall, these factors contribute to the enhanced production of each worker, such that a given worker can produce not just enough for himself of a given good but enough units of that good for many others as well. To be sure, because of these advances in the productive process, the average working individual did not find himself at the same level as the wealthy classes in Europe.[21] Still, the working person, although not at the level of the rich in his own country, exceeded the level of the wealthiest people in the poorest countries during Smith's time.[22]

What prompts a new, more productive division of labor to arise in the first place? The division of labor evolves from the tendency people possess to exchange one "thing for another."[23] Self-interest considerations push us to engage in such exchanges with others. Some people have an interest in producing certain goods, and others have an interest in producing other goods. Moreover, in each case, each person has an interest in possessing or acquiring the goods that others produce. But to be in a position to acquire the goods of others, a person must produce a surplus of goods so that he has enough goods both to supply himself and to sell to others. With the money he receives from selling his surplus goods to others, he can then purchase the different items he has an interest in acquiring.[24] Thus, over time, each person finds that one's interest is best served by specializing in producing one type of good and in finding the best way to produce a surplus of that product.

But to succeed in this endeavor, individuals must accept the values of thrift and parsimony. That is, individuals must learn to practice moderation with respect to personal spending habits as a condition for success in the market setting. Why is this the case? As we have just indicated, it is in our self-interest to produce a surplus of goods. Now, personal consumption is one use of the surplus. Here, we exchange our surplus for money that enables us to purchase other goods that we want and need. But if we want to continue to build up our surplus, we must take some of it and invest it by purchasing those goods that allow us to engage in more efficient forms of production, thus yielding more profit.[25]

At the heart of the manufacturing society stands an individual both willing and ready to acquire more goods, but at the same time this individual is enlightened enough to know that he or she must practice the virtues of frugality and saving money to be successful.[26] This ethos, when made a standard part of society, helps to make clear the origin of capital. A person who has sufficient wealth to maintain him or herself and yet still has enough left over may invest this surplus wealth with the intention of creating additional wealth. In doing so, the person creates capital. Here, capital represents the surplus wealth a person uses to improve land or to further invest in such goods as machines, for the purpose of realizing additional profits.[27] For Smith, self-interest, when placed in the market setting of the manufacturing economy, produces the basis for capital growth in society, a form of growth that helps to supply everyone with the basis for a decent life.

Smith's argument thus explains the way the common good is achieved in an environment in which self-interest-oriented behavior is encouraged. The natural question in this circumstance is whether the civic virtues we have discussed, in particular, toleration and mutual respect, would have any place in Smith's civil society. Smith would certainly contend that these civic virtues are to be a part of his view of society. Indeed, Smith, in *The Theory of Moral Sentiments*, argued that individuals are not simply oriented to their own ends and needs, but, in addition, there is a propensity in persons to sympathize with others.[28] To make his point, Smith said that human beings are conscious of the fact that it is always necessary to view themselves from the standpoint of the way all others would view them, what Smith refers to as the *impartial spectator* point of view. From this standpoint, as a person "views himself in the light in which he is conscious that others will view him," that person understands that he is not to consider himself better than any other person among the multitude of people making up society.[29] Naturally, individuals will always "prefer themselves to the rest of mankind," but that mentality must be balanced against the spectator perspective that exhorts us to "view ourselves not so much according to that light in which we may naturally appear to ourselves, as according to that in which we naturally appear to others."[30] Given this moral point of view, we understand that we are to "humble the arrogance of . . . self-love, and bring it down to something which other men can go along with."[31] Thus, as we pursue our fortunes in life, we must always attempt to interact with others in ways that all consider fair. Smith said:

> *In the race for wealth, and honours, and preferments, he may run as hard as he can and strain every nerve and every muscle, in order to outstrip all his competitors. But if he should jostle, or throw down any of them, the indulgence of the spectators is entirely at an end.*[32]

Here, the natural sympathy Smith described would make the liberal commitment to the civic virtues of mutual respect and toleration matters of great importance.

Finally, as another way to maintain regard for rights, it should be clear that Smith provided, as all civil society theorists do, an important role to the state. Smith did support the presence and importance of civil government. Indeed, for Smith, "the first duty of the sovereign" is defending the society from foreign attack.[33] Furthermore, government has a prime role in protecting each member of the society from "injustice or oppression" inflicted by other members.[34] Here, a major concern is "to prevent the members of a society from incroaching [*sic*] on one another's property, or seizing what is not their own."[35] The government must provide justice to all citizens by protecting what each has a "right to and could justly demand from others."[36] To this end, the civil government must maintain a system that is designed to administer justice. Thus, Smith's commitment to the invisible hand never denied the need for a government that could provide for the essential needs of society. What Smith did disapprove of is the need for government regulation of domestic market activities. For when governments regulate domestic industry through various policies, including placing tariffs on goods from foreign manufacturers, the result is to discourage the development of capital growth in a society.[37] So, Smith hoped to restore "freedom of trade," but he thought private interests as well as public prejudice in Britain opposed this objective, and, owing to these elements, free trade would never be fully revived.[38]

Given Smith's views of civil government and the place of sympathy in his theory, the self-interest orientation of Smith's free-market setting, which is highlighted in *The Wealth of Nations*, would not undermine civic virtue commitments. Still, some would argue that the free-market setting and the cultural attitudes that grow up around it undermine the prospect of achieving Smith's depiction of civil society – a depiction that is no doubt compatible with the civic virtues of both mutual respect and toleration described in the previous section. Indeed, the concern that the market will have a corrosive moral influence on civil society is a major theme throughout this book. This theme is manifested in the work of a wide range of thinkers that we will discuss in the second and third parts, including Jean-Jacques Rousseau, G.W.F. Hegel, John Stuart Mill, Alexis de Tocqueville, John Rawls, and, of course, Karl Marx. A major worry of these writers is that the market may turn civil society into an environment in which individuals pursue their interests selfishly, with little regard for the needs of others and with no concern to maintain the commitment to the virtues of civic life. Here, the hope of sustaining the larger moral environment that promotes both individualist goals alongside a respect for civic virtues that define our citizenship responsibilities is all but lost.

A final problem is that, in a context in which the market dominates, the only important values are materialist or utilitarian ones, and then other values that are critical to full human flourishing are denied a place. But values that have to do with the spiritual or the aesthetic or the intellectual or the moral sides of persons, as well as values that provide a sense of belonging and community, are critically important, too. A civil society must protect these values as well. But where the market dominates, materialist values push other values to the sidelines. Critics as well as supporters of civil society will make these issues central, as we will demonstrate throughout this book.

VIII. The Importance of Civil Society

Civil society is an important subject because it is only in a civil society that individuals develop the moral capacity and awareness that helps to protect the basic freedom that people in modern society value. In general, outside of a civil society environment, citizens have no regard for the standards of citizenship, including toleration and mutual respect, and then, instead of a setting that secures rights and freedom, a society emerges that may well be hostile to them. And without freedom, individuals lack an ability to find lives for themselves that each person considers meaningful, significant, and of enduring value.

Obviously, few would wish to experience this fate for themselves. Yet today, either many do not think that civil society is in danger, or if they recognize that it is, they are not willing to be part of a campaign to save it. Standing by and watching civil society dissolve, a consequence of not having a strong political will to defend it, can lead only to the worst possible outcome in which the goods of civil society, including individual freedom and the norms of civic life, disappear. The result of this tragedy is a life that loses its energy for many, and, instead of the happiness associated with a free and meaningful life, individuals must accept the loneliness of their insignificance.

Notes

1. Jean Bethke Elshtain, *Democracy on Trial* (New York: Basic Books, 1995), 5–6.
2. The view of civil society that we use here is modeled upon Nancy L. Rosenblum's in "The Moral Uses of Civil Society: Three Views," *The Newsletter of PEGS: The Committee on the Political Economy of the Good Society*, Supplement to 3, no. 2 (Summer 1993): 3, now called *The Good Society*.
3. Elshtain, *Democracy on Trial*, 6–7, 13, 19.
4. Rosenblum, "The Moral Uses of Civil Society," 3.
5. William A. Galston, *Liberal Purposes: Goods, Virtues and Diversity in the Liberal State* (Cambridge: Cambridge University Press, 1991). See his chapter on liberal virtues, especially pp. 221, 223–25. Also, Rosenblum, "The Moral Uses of Civil Society," 3.

6. Galston, *Liberal Purposes*, 223–24. Also, Rosenblum, "The Moral Uses of Civil Society," 3.

7. Rosenblum, "The Moral Uses of Civil Society," 4.

8. Ibid., 4. My view follows Rosenblum's understanding of democratic civil society. Also, see Benjamin R. Barber, *Strong Democracy: Participatory Politics for a Democratic Age* (Berkeley: University of California Press, 1984), Ch. 6, especially pp. 117–33.

9. Rosenblum, "The Moral Uses of Civil Society," 4.

10. Ibid.

11. Ibid.

12. Ibid.

13. Ibid.

14. Ibid.

15. Ibid.

16. Max Lerner, "Introduction," in Adam Smith, *An Inquiry into the Nature and Causes of the Wealth of Nations*, ed. Edwin Cannan (New York: Modern Library, 1937), v. From here on, we refer to this volume as *The Wealth of Nations*. In addition to page numbers, we refer to part, chapter, and paragraph in the numbers next to the page.

17. Smith, *The Wealth of Nations,* 423.

18. Ibid., lviii.

19. Ibid.

20. Ibid., 3–12, especially, p. 7.

21. Ibid., 12.

22. Ibid.

23. Ibid., 13.

24. Ibid., 15.

25. Ibid., 26–263.

26. Ibid., 322.

27. Ibid., 262–63.

28. Adam Smith, *The Theory of Moral Sentiments* (Indianapolis: Liberty Classics, 1976), 51, Sect I, Ch.1, Para. 11; also, p. 54.

29. Ibid., 162.

30. Ibid., 161–62.

31. Ibid.

32. Ibid.

33. Smith, *The Wealth of Nations*, 668.

34. Ibid., 669.

35. Adam Smith, *Lectures on Jurisprudence*, ed. R. L. Meek, D. D. Raphael, and P. G. Stein (Indianapolis: Liberty Classics, 1978), 5.

36. Ibid., 7.

37. Smith, *The Wealth of Nations*, 425.

38. Ibid., 437–38.

PART I

Civil Society in the Classical and Religious Traditions

2

Plato: Civic Virtue and the Just Society

I. Introduction

Plato's (428–348 BCE) principal concern in the *Republic* is to define the nature of a just society. Plato's political thinking, as with Aristotle's (whom we discuss in the next chapter), addresses the problems of the chief political unit each knew: the city-state. Plato's Athens, like all city-states, was a small political community of about 300,000 people. In Athens, there were three main groups: slaves, resident aliens, and citizens. Slaves, who represented about a third of the Athenian population, had no role in government. Resident aliens, like the slaves, were not permitted any role in the political life of Athens but were free men, not subject to social subordination as were slaves. Citizenship was granted to about 100,000 individuals whose parents had been citizens. Citizens, including native tradesmen, artisans, and farmers, as well as the wealthy landowners, could participate in public affairs. The extent of their participation depended on the nature of the regime in power at the time. In some Athenian regimes, citizens (and here we are speaking only of males) were eligible for many different public offices, ranging from participation in the courts, to representative bodies, and to executive councils, but, in other regimes, limitations were placed on the public offices a person could hold. Still, in general and regardless of the regime, all male citizens could take part in the Assembly, which operated as a town meeting for all citizens who came together to discuss and to debate matters of public concern. The Assembly, which met about ten times a year, was not a mechanism for direct democracy; rather, policy was devised and carried out by representative bodies who were responsible to the Assembly. The representative bodies were a cross section of the citizens, and to ensure as equal a chance for participation as possible, members to the representative bodies were chosen by lot.[1]

In Athens, and especially during the leadership of Pericles (495–429 BCE), the animating spirit was that citizens should be able to take part in public affairs. Indeed, as George Sabine said, "This ideal of a common life in which all might actively share presupposed an optimistic estimate of the natural political capacity of the average man."[2] Moreover, general participation was designed to encourage individuals to think of themselves as part of the larger community whose interest each individual served.

But this ideal was never fully realized in practice because persistent and severe conflict between citizens who represented different economic interests remained strong.[3] Those citizens with aristocratic backgrounds, who came from old families born to wealth, predicated their economic and social position upon their landholdings. Those citizens promoting democracy, mainly consisting of people who could profit from trade, sought to expand Athenian participation in trade by making Athens a major naval power. The aristocratic group maintained strong opposition to this approach since it would require taxing their property to support a large naval force.[4]

Plato saw these realities and the turmoil associated with them as proof that democracy could not achieve a stable society. His solution was to emphasize the central place of rational intelligence and the wise ruler in predicating stability upon a moral conception of a just society. On this view, Plato did not think that all people were equally capable of holding public office, nor did he think that the experience of participation in public affairs would by itself teach people to work with each other to achieve the common good. In contrast, the basis for moral unity rested with knowledge of what constitutes the just form or model of society.[5]

What is the just form of society for Plato? At this point, it is worth providing an overview of Plato's argument to prepare the reader for the general themes in this chapter.

II. Plato's "Just Society"

For Plato, justice is a condition in which the various parts of human personality (or what he also refers to as the *soul*) are properly arranged and ordered. Individuals are characterized by a rational element, which is the seat of the search for truth. In addition, the soul is motivated by appetite to attain wealth or pursue sexual desire. The third part of the soul is the spirited part, which is concerned with displaying the courage necessary to act for the common welfare and win honor from others for doing so. Finding the proper arrangement among these parts of the soul is critical to achieving justice not only in the personalities of each citizen, but in the society at large. Here, for Plato, the rational part of the soul should rule the other two parts. If the other parts of the soul were to dominate reason, then the soul would be out of balance and the individual would neither deliberate nor act in the best interests of either him or herself or of society. Indeed, in this circumstance, the appetite and the spirited part might even conflict with each other, a situation that would ensure not only personal unhappiness, but also an inability to perform well the various tasks and functions that secure important basic needs for society.

One caveat must be made before proceeding. In developing Plato's views, it must be clear that Plato admired Socrates' dialectical approach to the search for truth and knowledge. What approach did Socrates use? For Socrates, truth-revealing inquiry begins, as we saw in the Introduction, from the standpoint of a reasoned discourse among individuals whose only objective is truth. The *Republic* is a dialogue between Socrates and his compatriots.[6] To avoid confusion, it should be clear that when Socrates is referred to in the *Republic*, as well as in this chapter, it is really Plato who is talking and who speaks through Socrates. It must also be clear that Plato sees himself as emulating Socrates' dialectical method. The basic purpose of Plato's approach, then, is to demonstrate that the main avenue to truth is testing propositions against other propositions to determine which ones have truth and which ones lack truth.

This discourse leads to the development of rational concepts, or what otherwise are referred to as the *forms*, or ideas of good order. These forms should be used as guides in developing the main roles and institutions of society as well as the various parts of the souls of individuals so that each member of society is able to contribute to the common good. In contributing to the common good, which in Plato's case means citizens acting to help maintain the form of a just society, citizens manifest civic virtue.

III. Plato's *Republic*: What Justice Is Not

Cephalus and Polemarchus

Plato began the *Republic* by demonstrating in his various dialogues how far his own society was from holding a valid understanding of the nature of justice. Indeed, as he discussed the views of justice current during his times, Plato always seemed to have in the back of his mind a more authentic version of justice than he believed his contemporaries held. To make his view clearer, he had to first demonstrate to his colleagues why their views were wrong. In doing so, he examined conventional views of justice that, during his times, were taken to be valid and demonstrated why, upon analysis, these views were deficient. To this end, he engaged the arguments of Cephalus and Polemarchus and, in doing so, like Socrates, he challenged those who held those conventional views to defend them against his, that is Plato's, own arguments.

Cephalus is a "money maker" or a man engaged in business that, by Plato's own account, does not seem to "love money too much." Socrates asked Cephalus to explain the "greatest good" he has received from being wealthy.[7] Cephalus responds that men of wealth like him seek a clear conscience; they do not want to cheat or deceive anyone, lest after death they may suffer terrible punishments. Socrates summarized Cephalus's response to what the latter thinks by describing justice as following the principle that the just person is one who always seeks to tell the truth and one who tries to pay his debts. In other words, one must always keep one's agreements with others. But Socrates responded by saying that this principle could not be upheld on all occasions. Socrates asked if one should return a weapon lent to one by a friend when the friend, after going mad, asked for it back. Clearly, in this case, it is necessary to violate an agreement, and Cephalus agreed.[8]

Keeping one's agreements with other individuals, although an important virtue, is not *the* virtue that should be made the basis of all social interactions in the society. More important, by implication, is that one should uphold one's obligations and duties to the larger society. And when one focuses solely on obligations owed to other individuals, it might well be that one overlooks the obligations owed to the larger society. That is what the example of keeping an agreement with a madman shows. Although the madman, in asking for the return of the weapon, may pose no harm to the person who lent it to him, he does pose harm to the society. Thus, owing to the obligation we must protect society from murder and mayhem, we have no duty to return a weapon to a madman. In a similar fashion, wealthy businessmen such as Cephalus should ponder whether their keeping agreements with each other to make possible greater wealth for themselves causes harm to the larger society. Clearly, Plato thought it might.

Next, as a definition of justice, Polemarchus suggested the idea that "it is just to give each person what is owed to him."[9] Socrates, after a series of comments and rejoinders with Polemarchus, concluded that justice as Polemarchus described it involved treating "friends well and enemies badly."[10] Socrates flatly rejected this principle for defining justice. For Socrates, justice is clearly a major virtue, and virtues cannot be used to do harm to others. To put this point differently, for Socrates, to use one's skills and abilities to harm another is to use them in a manner that contradicts their purpose. If we are teachers of music, we should use our skills to make people musical, not unmusical.[11] To do otherwise would suggest a form of society in which people turned virtue into a license that permitted them to use their best abilities and skills to impair human flourishing. But in a just society, people should use their skills to enhance and to enrich the lives of others.

Thrasymachus

But why can it not be argued that helping friends and keeping agreements are important virtues for people to follow? Indeed, are these values not essential to any conception of civic virtue? Plato might certainly answer this question in the affirmative. But his point seems to be that civic virtue is not the same thing as justice, and it is wrong to define the latter in terms of the former. Perhaps, as we will see later, civic virtue contributes to a just society, but in doing so, it contributes to a value of singular importance, one that signals the overall basic good to which all members of society should be oriented. Here, the value of the highest importance toward which all other values must contribute is justice.

Thus, in criticizing certain approaches to civic virtue, Plato did not intend to deny its importance. This fact is best seen in his treatment of Thrasymachus, whose view of justice, as we shall see, would completely deny any respect for civic virtue. Thrasymachus argued that what is just is what the strongest and the most powerful say is just. On this view, there is little room for civic virtue, for civic virtue presumes that people will make sacrifices for the larger good. Thrasymachus's position manifests the arrogance of those who, owing to their extraordinary power, need never contemplate making sacrifices for the larger good. Rather, people who hold Thrasymachus's view just define the larger good to suit their own interests, thus putting themselves in a position where they never have to manifest civic virtue. The following account of Socrates' discussion with Thrasymachus elaborates on this point.

Thrasymachus said that each regime has a ruling group, and the ruling party makes laws in its own interest. Furthermore, the ruling party claims that whatever is in its own interest is also in the interest of the whole society. Socrates responded by saying that the ruling powers are fallible, and, at times, they make mistakes and thus put into place policies that are not to their advantage.[12] On this view, it is not always the case, then, that what is in the interest of the stronger is either in their own interest or in the interest of the society. With these arguments, Thrasymachus is now forced to qualify his view of justice, and he no longer can hold that justice is "what the stronger believes to be to his advantage, whether it is in fact to his advantage or not."[13]

Thrasymachus's approach to recoup his position is to qualify what he meant by saying that justice is the interest of the stronger. In particular, Thrasymachus shows that the ruler is stronger because he is much like any other kind of expert – say, doctors – in that, like them, owing to expertise, a ruler is not likely to make a mistake.[14] The reason for this view is that, in each case, whether we are talking of a ruler or a doctor, each operates by the knowledge that makes one capable of performing with excellence. Given this view, the ruler is stronger because unlike ordinary citizens, rulers are less likely to make mistakes in ruling, including mistakes that would harm the ruler's interest.

This response prompts a discussion of the nature of a craft, such as medicine. Socrates said that a craft suggests an activity in which a person uses his skills to attain only the purposes of the craft.[15] This means for Socrates that a doctor uses his skills not to advance his own interests, such as making money, but to advance the interests of his patients. In the same way, a ruler, by analogy to other crafts, should use his knowledge to advance the interests of the citizens.[16]

In arguing this view, Socrates suggested that rulers must put aside their own interests and make the interests of the community primary. This commitment is the essence of what constitutes a life of civic virtue. Indeed, for Plato, rulers, like doctors, must exercise their skills so that they are in keeping with a commitment to serve the needs of their community. And, thus, rulers must not seek "anything other than what is best for the things it rules and cares for, and this is true both of public and private kinds of rule."[17] In consequence, a person concerned with the interests of the citizens does not enter politics to provide for his or her own advantage or to attain goods such as money and honor, but enters politics to help those who are weaker than him- or herself.[18] In fact, what draws many lesser people to politics is not what draws the good individual to politics. What attracts the good person to politics is fear of those who see politics as a way to promote their own interest at the cost of the society's interest. Good people fear being ruled by "someone worse than [themselves]." This fear "makes decent people rule when they do."[19]

No reasonable person wants to be ruled by someone whose main purpose in ruling is advancing only his or her own interests. But that is what Thrasymachus advocated. For Thrasymachus, those who commit acts of injustice are "clever and good." Indeed, for Thrasymachus, those who "are completely unjust" can "bring cities and whole communities under their power."[20] There is great profit in injustice, then.

Socrates attacked this position, arguing that the desire to act unjustly is a defect in the character of people. And the contention that injustice is a defect is easy to prove. Any society that was designed to act for unjust purposes will never succeed because the society will become riddled through and through with hatred and quarreling, thus making it impossible for people to work together as a unified community.[21] This point is important because the major purpose of any society is to serve the basic needs of its citizens, and a society that is unable to act in a unified fashion cannot possibly achieve this objective. Only people committed to the larger good of the community, those who manifest civic virtue and a concomitant commitment to justice, should be rulers because it is only these people who can create the conditions that make possible the just, well-ordered society that Plato hoped to achieve.

Another important proof that injustice is an undesirable defect arises from the contention that no person would ever be personally happy were he or she to live life outside of a commitment to justice. Why is this? No person wants merely to live, said Socrates, but to live well, and living well means being able to perform well one's functions in society. But one cannot perform one's functions well if one's soul has been deprived of the "peculiar virtue" that allows one to execute one's tasks at the level of excellence required for the good performance of a task. The virtue of the soul that enables one to perform well one's function is justice, and thus it follows that "a just soul and a just man will live well." Moreover, this state is desirable for people because one who lives well leads a "blessed and happy" life.[22]

IV. The Next Question: What Is Justice?

Socrates has demonstrated not only what justice is not, but he has demonstrated, also, that it is far better or advantageous to lead a just life than to lead an unjust one. But Socrates suggested that in making these points he has raised another important question. In particular, he has yet to tell us exactly what justice is. And, since a just life is to be a happy life, if it is not possible to demonstrate the nature of justice and how justice as a virtue contributes to our well-being, it will not be possible to demonstrate the basis for a happy life.[23]

Socrates thus felt compelled to demonstrate to Glaucon the definition of justice, intending to show him not only that justice is a good, but that it is "one of the greatest goods."[24] As one of the greatest goods, what kind of good is justice? Justice is a good that not only provides an important result for its holder, but it is important for its own sake as well. Goods that are good for their own sake do not include money, for instance, but they do include "seeing, hearing, knowing, being healthy and all other goods that are fruitful by their own nature and not simply because of reputation."[25] A good that is good for its own sake, then, is one that is so essential to life that it would be impossible to imagine a worthwhile life in the absence of that good. Such is the case with knowing, seeing, and hearing as well as justice. It is for this reason that justice is the basis for a life "blessed with happiness."[26]

But whereas it is intuitively clear to all what knowing, seeing, hearing, and good health are, it is not intuitively clear what justice is. To make a careful representation of justice, it is necessary to turn to sound, rational argument as opposed to intuition.

So, what is a just society? What arguments defend the conception of justice Plato supports? In the next sections, we will begin to address these questions.

The Basic Dimensions of Society

The early part of the *Republic*, which is a discourse between Socrates and the various individuals we have mentioned, now turns more to a conversation dominated by Socrates. Socrates' intent in this conversation, which involves Glaucon, is to provide a basic lecture on the fundamentals of social organization, and, once he has done that, to build from these fundamentals to develop his conception of justice.

The starting point, then, for describing justice is that, in any society, people have basic physical needs, and thus they desire the material goods that satisfy those needs. Moreover, people by themselves cannot provide for these needs. So, societies are formed for this purpose. In particular, we are told that, to secure the basic requirements of the citizens for food, shelter, and clothing, society needs a class of working people, including farmers, builders, and weavers.[27] There also must be a marketplace where citizens can purchase the various goods that the different groups produce. Money is invented to facilitate exchanges. In the market setting, there are many merchants and retailers or shopkeepers trading their goods for money. These are people "whose bodies are the weakest and who aren't fit to do any other kind of work."[28]

In this setting, all the basic needs that people have are cared for, and people live a long, peaceful, and healthy life in a just society, which they bequeath to their children. But Glaucon suggests to Socrates that Socrates' city is not satisfactory because people will want luxuries as well as having their basic needs satisfied.[29] Socrates thought that the city built on serving basic needs is the "true and healthy city." But he conceded the need to include in his discussion of a model for a just city what presumably some people want: namely, in addition to providing for basic needs, a city must provide luxuries, as well. Socrates called this city the city with a "fever." Here, Socrates described a city in which some people will seek to have fine clothes and good food. In addition, some people seek to have comfortable and decorated furniture, as well as prostitutes for sexual pleasure. Also, there will be people to provide art, music, and dance, as well as goods such as jewelry.[30] To enjoy these goods, people will have to have leisure time, and this dimension is secured by providing them with a class of servants, including tutors and cooks who take care of the day-to-day necessities of life.[31] Finally, and most tragically, the quest for luxuries becomes the main motive for war, as people, in the search for the "endless acquisition of money" for the sake of luxuries, seek to take each other's resources.[32]

In accepting that the pursuit of wealth and money is the essential motivation in society, Plato certainly accepted the notion of private ownership. Being able to have exclusive ownership to property provides one with an incentive to perform the necessary work that produces both basic goods and luxuries. Still, Plato did not intend to make a conception of society that emphasized the pursuit of wealth and luxury the basis for defining a just order. As we can see from his view of the origin of war, which emanates from the constant pursuit of wealth, Plato clearly feared making appetite the main motivating and dominant force in society. To avoid this circumstance, appetite – in this case, the quest for luxuries and wealth embodied in private property ownership – must be limited by the constraints of reason. Here, property ownership need not symbolize the unlimited pursuit of appetite but a willingness to use one's property in ways that support the common good. To achieve a society with this possibility, Plato discussed the role of the guardians.

The Guardians and the Three Parts of the Soul

As we have mentioned, Plato distinguished three parts to the soul. In addition to the rational part that deliberates with the intention to determine truth, there is the part referred to as appetite and the spirited part. The appetite, says Socrates, "is the largest part in each person's soul and is by nature most insatiable for money." Moreover, the appetite is motivated by the "pleasures of the body."[33] Still, the appetite can be made subject to the commands of reason. One basis for this contention is the presence of the spirited part. Socrates views the spirited part as the "helper of the rational part," or as the dimension of soul committed to see that the rational conception of good order is realized.[34] Socrates says, "I don't think you can say that you've ever seen spirit, either in yourself or anyone else, ally itself with an appetite to do what reason has decided must not be done."[35] In resisting appetite but in promoting the goals of reason, the spirited part manifests courage because, in holding steadfast to the "declarations of reason about what is to be feared and what isn't," the spirited part enables individuals to endure the pain of promoting the reasonable course.[36] Here, the spirited part signifies a desire to win honor from others for upholding the common good.

Moreover, for Socrates, the spirited part must be "rightly nurtured," lest instead of courage it manifests itself as "hard and harsh."[37] In this case, as opposed to working for the goals of reason, it might work against them. This view suggests that the spirited element is a fierce sort of passion or emotion that, if improperly developed, harms instead of helps the quest to realize the common good.

There are several other important implications to be gleaned here as well. First, Plato is not saying that the appetite can or should be completely suppressed. Still, however, the appetite must be constrained by reason and the spirited part, lest appetite lead to a situation in which individuals are prone, as Socrates says, to seek to "enslave and rule over the classes it isn't fit to rule, thereby overturning everyone's whole life."[38] Here, those who are motivated by their appetite to acquire wealth and luxuries, for instance, must accept the regimen of a society that requires them to conduct their lives in keeping with the norms established by reason.

The problem, then, for Plato, and this is the second important implication of his three-part view of the soul, is to harness both the appetite and the spirited part so that each serves the goals posited by reason. To this end, Plato emphasized the importance of a special class of citizens, whom he called *guardians*.

Now, there are different types of guardians, and, furthermore, guardians have two major functions, ruling and guarding the city. The "best of the guardians," as Socrates referred to them, are rulers.[39] Those guardians, who have acted both as rulers and as protectors of the city, presumably through military exploits, are referred to as *complete guardians*. Younger people who show promise of being guardians in the future, but who have not yet proved themselves capable of being complete guardians, are called *auxiliaries* who act as assistants to the guardians.[40] The auxiliaries assist the guardians by supporting their objectives and helping to carry them out.[41] The auxiliaries would certainly help the guardians fulfill their military duties. In the latter role, guardians would manifest courage and a desire for honor, as well as the various skills associated with soldiering. For Plato, it is a mistake to believe that people who have expertise in other areas of life, say as farmers or craftsmen, will also have the knowledge and skill needed to be good warriors. In all cases, the complete guardians act from an unstinting commitment to protect the society from "external enemies and internal friends."[42]

Moreover, guardians must be properly educated so that they are able to perform their functions well. Here, Plato's key point is that, without a proper system of training, individuals will not attain the appropriate degree of civic virtue that will enable them to act in the best interests of society. Speaking specifically of the auxiliaries, for instance, who possess military prowess, it is important to make certain that they do not use that power against the best interests of the people they are supposed to protect.[43] Indeed, we are told that guardians will "be gentle to their own people and harsh to the enemy."[44] That is why, to the question "who will guard the guardians?" Plato would certainly answer: no one will have to, because the guardians, owing to proper education, are the model of rational self-command.

Plato, in discussing the guardians, had in mind people who could be trusted with great power and authority, and yet ordinary citizens would never fear that they would harm society. The guardians, as rulers or as soldiers, are the moral saviors of the society because they act always and only for the common good. Finding them will be a society's greatest challenge. Children will have to be watched and monitored to determine whether they demonstrate guardian traits, to be either rulers or auxiliaries.[45] This view suggests that, when proper candidates for a guardian life are found, they must be separated from the rest of the society. This will be necessary to raise these people independently from the ordinary influences that, if not properly controlled, would tend to deny the proper training that makes both the appetite and the spirit subject to reason.

Thus, guardians, unlike ordinary people, own no private property, accumulate no luxury, live in common with other guardians, and are not allowed to have their own families. Within guardian communities, each parent is the parent of all the children. No parent claims a child as his or her own, nor does any parent claim a special status for children he or she helped to conceive.[46] Were people to do so, guardians would identify too closely with *their* own children. And this would cause guardians to define their objectives in a narrower way than would be healthy for society. Guardians are not to place the needs of their own children above those of others and certainly not above the needs of the whole community. The words *mine* and *not mine* for Socrates must have reference only to what the community as a whole defines as mine and not mine. When these words refer to any particular individual's preferences, that person's ability to support the common good will be very weak.[47]

Each person who is a guardian must orient themselves to support the good of the community. Such individuals will not be limited to men but will include consideration of women as guardians also. In support of this position, Plato even suggested that the relationship between the sexes should be different for guardians from what this relationship entails for ordinary citizens. Male guardians should be willing to accept the view that some women can perform all essential guardian functions, and those women who have this ability should be given the same opportunity as men to be guardians.[48] Now, Socrates' position in comparing men and women is to accept the general prejudice of his age and to say that, on the whole, men are superior to women. He says in discussing various life activities that "in all of them women are weaker than men," or, in other terms, women perform them less well than men. However, there will be some women who have guardian natures, and these women, even if weaker than men, are "adequate for the task" and should be allowed to be guardians.[49]

Why, if Plato had such a patronizing view toward women, did he grant them the opportunity to be guardians? Perhaps Plato's actual intention in according women a place in society as guardians was to reduce their sexual importance to men. Here, as men look upon women as partners in a common enterprise, possibly they will not seek to conquer women sexually. In this case, Plato's commitment to sexual equality for guardians was merely a way to check male sexual aggression, which, if unleashed, would make the appetite the primary factor and deny respect for reason. Plato argued on behalf of women's being allowed to be guardians for reasons of securing a society committed to the common good and not because he was principally a proponent of gender equality.

The commitment to the common good and the need to create a special class of people able to bring about this great goal make it necessary for the introduction of manipulative techniques regarding marriage and childbearing. Marriages among guardians will be regulated to match people with the best combination of qualities to each other. To make this outcome possible, there will be lotteries in which people choose their mates, but these lotteries will be rigged so that the best people are matched together. And further, even though the number of children will be regulated by the rulers, those men who are successful in war will be able to have sex more frequently so that they can father as many children as possible. This will ensure a larger and better stock of children.[50] For others, full sexual freedom is regained after they have passed the childbearing age. In this case, people can have sex with anyone they choose to have sex with, but if they should conceive a child by accident, their offspring will be killed.[51]

The Philosopher as King

For Socrates (or Plato, who, as we have said, speaks through Socrates), the "best of the guardians" must be rulers, and, to this end, must train for the life of philosophy, which will be a major part of a ruler's life. Socrates argued that "future rulers" must, in childhood, be offered basic training in geometry and mathematical calculation as well as all other topics needed to prepare them to engage in dialectical thinking.[52]

Not everyone will be permitted to complete the course that leads to elevation to philosopher/ruler. Indeed, Socrates sought individuals who could use dialectical thinking to construct a unified and true picture of the reality under study, or, as in the *Republic*, of a just society. Those individuals with this ability will be screened from the rest, and when they reach the age of 30, they will undergo training in the techniques of dialectical argument. Socrates did not want to have those who are capable of philosophy trained in dialectical argument younger than age 30 because he feared that when people are exposed to the techniques of argument as young persons, they will employ these techniques merely to demonstrate an ability to refute other arguments. Such people merely seek to best others in argument as opposed to using argument to find truth.[53] But Socrates said that "an older person won't want to take part in such madness. He'll imitate someone who is willing to engage in discussion in order to look for the truth, rather than someone who plays at contradiction for sport."[54]

Again, those who are capable of dialectical thinking will be selected for training in the dialectic at the age of 30. After five years of training in this endeavor, in which they learn how to find truth, the future ruler will be sent into the "cave," a term for ordinary society, to live with average people. In the cave, future rulers take part in military matters

> *and occupy the other offices suitable for young people, so that they won't be inferior to the others in experience. But in these, too, they must be tested to see whether they'll remain steadfast when they're pulled this way or that or shift their ground.*[55]

A person will undergo this experience for 15 years, and then at the age of 50, these individuals will be permitted to spend most of their time with philosophy, but, as Socrates said, "when his turn comes, he must labor in politics and rule for the city's sake."[56] These individuals, both men and women alike, will be given the task of putting "the city, its citizens, and themselves in order."[57]

Socrates said that, until "philosophers rule as kings" or until kings act as philosophers, it will be impossible to marry power to philosophy and thus create cities bent upon avoiding evil and achieving good.[58] Why are philosophers especially suited for linking power and morality? The answer lies in their character. Philosophers are gentle people, they are not cowardly or slavish, they are lovers of knowledge, they are not desirous of money or luxuries, and they learn quickly and with ease.[59] When power is placed into the hands of people with these characteristics, we can be assured that it will not be used to advance a quest for personal wealth. Instead, power will be used to support, in a steadfast and courageous way, a desire to make sure that the goods defined by reason are made the main objective of society.

Justice, Civic Virtue, and the Noble Lie

To make possible a society in which an ethical order based on reason can be achieved, the guardians need to provide a basic education that teaches children civic virtue.[60] In particular, children must be taught the importance of law-abiding behavior if they are to mature into law-abiding people. To this end, children must take part in games that teach the importance of respect for law, and music and poetry must be designed for the same reason. Respect for lawfulness is also taught by learning to accept the authority of one's elders and by being taught to care for one's parents.[61] When people are filled with good habits such as these, they are likely, from their own volition, to maintain conduct that contributes to the basic good of the society. Furthermore, these people will know what is best for the city and, in consequence, what laws need to be legislated. Indeed, for Socrates, when right conduct is not a part of the ingrained civic outlook of people, efforts to achieve good ends for the city through legislation will always fall short of the mark. The reason for this is that people who lack the habits of civic virtue are like "sick people" who are prone to the extremes of appetite, and thus they are not likely to listen to those who warn against the harmful effects of lechery, drunkenness, and overeating.[62]

Once a basic commitment to civic virtue or a general respect for the common good of the society is in place, then the city has been properly established and a basis exists for the flourishing of other critical virtues in the city: wisdom, courage, moderation, and justice.[63] It is clear that these basic virtues are linked so that justice, the highest and most important of the four, cannot exist unless the others do. To explain this point, we will describe each virtue in turn.

Wisdom, Courage, Moderation, and Justice

First take *wisdom*. In discussing wisdom, Socrates distinguished between the knowledge possessed by particular craftsmen and the kind of knowledge needed to govern a state. Those who possess the latter kind of knowledge, the philosophers, have the knowledge necessary to understand what is needed to secure a well-ordered city, including how to create good relations internally as well as between the city and other cities.[64] *Courage* is a capacity that enables people to maintain a steadfast commitment to uphold the basic values given to society by those who make the laws. Here, the laws embody fundamental beliefs that society is to protect, and individuals who manifest courage uphold these values, regardless of any particular difficulties or pains such actions may entail.[65] *Moderation* is a third important virtue, and it suggests self-control or the ability to constrain our desires so that they do not rule our lives. Possessing moderation, individuals are not given to extreme modes of behavior, and, consequently, the different parts of the society are more able to coexist in harmonious and cooperative relationships.[66] A city that possesses moderation "makes the weakest, the strongest, and those in between – whether in regard to reason, physical strength, numbers, wealth, or anything else – all sing the same song together."[67] Where moderation is the norm, each is able to contribute to the common needs of the society, and the quest for luxury or any other desire is not allowed to defeat this objective.

These values create the setting that is conducive to *justice*, the fourth essential virtue. Justice is mentioned last because the first three prepare the ground for justice. Indeed, Socrates said that justice would be what was "left over in the city when moderation, courage, and wisdom have been found."[68] Given this view of the relationship among the basic virtues, how would this relationship be rendered into concrete, practical terms to define the vision of a just society? A city with moderation, courage, and wisdom is just because each person has a role for which he or she is best qualified and, in performing that role well, each contributes in essential ways to the community's common good. Socrates' view was that "everyone must practice one of the occupations . . . for which he is naturally best suited."[69] This state of affairs represents the condition of a just society. As Socrates said, "This doing one's own work . . . is justice."[70] Indeed, a just society is one in which "each does his own work and doesn't meddle with what is other people's," and this value, the value of doing one's own work, "rivals wisdom, moderation and courage in its contribution to the virtue of the city."[71]

A society in which each person contributes to the good of the whole, in keeping with one's basic abilities and skills, is a society that manifests what might be called *external justice.* Clearly, for Plato, such a state is predicated upon a *meritocratic principle* of each person's being assigned to those tasks for which one is, as Socrates says, "best suited." Here, the workers should carry out the skills of their respective crafts, the auxiliaries should perform well their warrior role, and the philosophers should be good rulers.

The problem with maintaining this principle is how best to persuade people of its truth. After all, as a consequence of adhering to the norms of Plato's just society, some will be given more important tasks than will others, so how will those at the bottom of society accept this outcome? Socrates' answer was to invoke a lie in the name of securing justice. Here, it would seem that in addition to learning the habits of basic civic virtue to encourage people to contribute to the common good, a citizen must be made to believe a falsehood about the reason that justice is a worthy value. Obviously, then, the habits of civic virtue, such as law-abiding behavior, are by themselves not sufficient to secure support for the ways of life of a just society.

Thus, Socrates referred to a "noble falsehood" that could be used to persuade the rulers and the people in the city of the importance of all people accepting the role in society for which they are most naturally suited. According to the falsehood that Socrates would teach, even though "all in the city are brothers," the god who created people placed a different metal in each person. He put gold into those who would be rulers; silver into those who would be auxiliaries; and iron and bronze into those who would be farmers and craftsmen (workers). Moreover, this god engineered people so that they would, for the most part, produce children like themselves. Still, it is possible that children with silver or bronze metal will be born from a gold parent or vice versa. When this event occurs, it is the god's intention that people be placed into positions in society appropriate to their abilities and coincident with the particular metal of their souls. For instance, if it is the case that the children of rulers are found to have a soul with bronze, then these people should be placed into the farmer or worker class. On the other hand, if the offspring of the worker class have gold in their souls, they should be given training to become rulers.[72]

A lie can be noble and thus worthy if it is used for a good reason. And Plato would no doubt envision several good reasons for his noble lie. The first good reason, as just indicated, is that the lie maintains support for the external justice of a meritocracy. Another good reason for the lie is that it encourages what underlies external justice, namely, the proper ordering or the arranging of the key elements of the soul: reason, appetite, and spirit. We call this condition of the soul *internal justice*, and it represents a condition of mind that is the highest-order possibility of human life, a condition that the just city secures.

What is internal justice or the justice of the soul, and why is it such a valuable condition? Each of the parts of the soul has its own objectives, and, in achieving these objectives, one is able to attain the pleasure associated with that part. Thus, in realizing the objectives of the spirited part, one receives the pleasures associated with manifesting the courage to uphold the common good; in realizing the objectives of the appetite, one realizes pleasures associated with receiving money. But for Socrates, when one's focus is entirely upon either of these dimensions to the exclusion of the direction provided by one's reason, or what Socrates refers to as "those pleasures that reason approves" of, then one does not "attain the truest possible pleasures" associated with the appetite and the spirited part of the soul.[73] For instance, take a situation where either the spirited part or the appetite is made so central in one's life that the importance of reason is downplayed. Here, a person pursuing the objectives of the spirited part of the soul, outside the direction of reason, may become so desirous of success in battle that he or she becomes overly violent and loses the ability to make decisions that would bring about the victory he or she seeks. Or, a person whose only quest in life is to accumulate money may end up having no regard for the goods that reason stipulates, and, in consequence, such a person may destroy all relationships with others who love him or her.

Moreover, when a person allows him or herself to become maniacally dedicated to the objectives of the spirited part and the appetite at the same time, he or she may set in motion two powerful desires, each warring with the other. For instance, individuals desirous of both showing courage and having money may find that to have the former they may have to sacrifice the quest for money. But the appetite may demand that their quest to demonstrate courage and dedication to the common good take a back seat to money. In this case, the quest to serve society is always at war with the urge for money. In contrast, when an individual allows their reason or philosophical part to have the upper hand, this tragedy is avoided. For Socrates, "therefore, when the entire soul follows the philosophic part, and there is no civil war in it, each part of it does its own work exclusively and is just, and in particular it enjoys its own pleasures, the best and truest pleasures possible for it."[74]

Now a well-ordered and balanced soul brings happiness to the individual, but, in addition, such a soul can make an important contribution to maintaining the well-ordered character of society. Here, because the appetite and the spirited part are under the direction of the philosophic part, it follows that individuals maintain an internal balance to their personalities that would permit them to be able to perform well the various tasks for which they are best suited. The internal justice of the soul is linked to and supports the external justice of a meritocratic life.

Given this account of internal justice, for Socrates it is now understandable why it is best for "everyone to be ruled by divine reason, preferably within himself and his own, otherwise imposed from without, so that as far as possible all will be alike and friends, governed by the same thing."[75] It must be clear that, to attain this objective, the real city is not so much the external city in which people live their daily lives, although it is of course that, too. But the real city is the properly arranged soul, and unless this state of mind is possible, there will be no happiness or external justice. As Socrates said:

> It's also our aim in ruling our children, we don't allow them to be free until we establish a constitution in them, just as in a city, and by – fostering their best part with our own – equip them with a guardian and ruler similar to our own to take our place. Then, and only then, we set them free.[76]

When the city reaches this stage, the habits of civic virtue – which contribute to each citizen's ability to support the common good by upholding basic virtues such as moderation, courage, wisdom, and justice – as well as Plato's noble falsehood have both paved the way for not only a good constitution in the state, but an equally good one in the soul of each individual.

V. Democracy and Injustice

The hope for the good city must be contrasted with the reality of the bad ones. For Plato, timocracy, oligarchy, and democracy are corrupted regimes that propel society in the direction of tyranny. The implications for people are severe and tragic. In what follows, we provide a brief summary of Plato's argument. To understand Plato's account, it is important to recognize that regimes are distinguished by the fact that different characteristics of the soul come to dominate them. In the best city, the Republic, the faculty of reason is preeminent. But in the lesser regimes, either the spirited part of the soul or the appetite dominates.[77]

In a *timocracy*, the spirited part dominates and thus the regime is dedicated to make honor, courage, and the love of military victory the main objective.[78] This situation results from the dueling tendencies in a timocracy. On the one hand, there are those who seek to acquire wealth, and on the other, there are those who manifest aristocratic tendencies and who want to govern by virtue. A civil war breaks out between the two groups, but it ends with a compromise that permits private property in land and the enslavement of peasants to work the land. In addition, war-related activities become a main aspect of life. The individuals appointed as rulers will be "spirited and simpler" people who will spend their time engaging in war as a means for gaining honor from others. Further, they will satisfy their own appetites with other people's money, while saving their own. Still, of the two passions – that for money and honor – the latter dominates, and thus there is continual quest for military victory. In this setting, there is no interest in making philosophy and the rational dimension of the soul count for much in society.[79]

The next regime is *oligarchy*, a regime in which "victory-loving and honor-loving people become lovers of making money, or money lovers."[80] Here, the appetite takes over as money is valued more than virtue, and the wealthy people are admired and made the rulers. Indeed, the political system is designed so that only people with property may hold office, and the poor have no opportunity to rule, even if a poor person could do a better job.[81] A major characteristic of this kind of society is that money is not used to support a life of luxury so much as it is used to satisfy necessary needs or appetites, and the rest of the money one accumulates from the profits of one's enterprises is hoarded.[82] Also, in this kind of society in which money is worshipped and virtue is lost sight of, many people avoid responsibility for their own lives. In consequence, some sell all they own, and by doing so many people no longer have the means or are willing to perform essential functions as workers and craftsmen, and, instead, they become poor people without the means to make a living. These people become "drones," who must live off the labor of others. Some do so as beggars and others do so as "evildoers" who commit crimes and become thieves and pickpockets.[83]

Naturally, the poor become resentful of the rich, and the poor see the rich as undeserving of their station. When the poor overthrow the rich, they establish a *democracy*. Here, each person is given a chance to take part in ruling the city.[84] Democracies quickly become societies in which the appetite, in this case not just for basic or necessary needs, but for unnecessary goods (or goods such as luxuries that people could live without), is allowed unlimited freedom. In an atmosphere of "general permissiveness," individuals lack sufficient self-control, and all pleasures are declared to be of equal value. Indeed, the democrat cannot distinguish between "fine and good desires" and those that are "evil." The democrat pursues whatever desire is at hand, and there is no basis for establishing a rational order to life. But the democrat calls this way of life free and happy, when in fact this way of life is a passport to "extreme slavery" or tyranny.[85]

Finally, there is *tyranny*, which evolves from democracy and is associated with a form of appetite that is "lawless" because it promotes desires that, in addition to being unnecessary, will not accept the discipline of reason.[86] The setting that culminates in the rule of the appetite not subject to the discipline of reason is characterized by an "insatiable desire for freedom."[87] Indeed, Socrates blames an extreme desire for freedom for the emergence of tyranny.[88] In this setting, the ruling class consists of people who can make no useful contributions to society – the "drones" who were part of oligarchic life. The ruling drones seek to maintain power by currying favor with the common people. To this end, the ruling class postures as the champion of the people against the rich, and thus the ruling class promises to take money from the rich and give it to the people. However, the ruling drones keep for themselves the largest part of the money that they take from the rich.[89] The rich complain before the common people while the ruling drones accuse the rich of plotting to hurt the ordinary people. The rich, in turn, fearing that the ordinary people will side with the ruling drones, react by becoming like oligarchs and demand rule by the rich. This feuding culminates in both the rich and the drones being charged with crimes and being put on trial.[90] In the midst of this general disorder, the people decide to set up one person as their champion. The latter becomes a tyrant when he dominates the "docile mob" and resorts to violent and coercive tactics, including inciting a civil war against the rich.[91] Ultimately, the people realize they have created a monster, and they thus order him to leave the city, but he refuses and uses violence to retain control.[92]

The story just described demonstrates that when civic virtue is eroded and, in consequence, the virtues of justice, moderation, courage, and wisdom are no longer a part of the life of the city, appetite in its various forms and with its harmful effects rules a city. In the context of what Plato described, it is best for cities to follow a just course.

However, the good consequences of justice and the terrible ones following injustice exist not only for cities, but for individuals as well. Socrates concluded the *Republic* by making clear the nature of the personal advantages of leading a just life and the disadvantages for individuals of leading an unjust life. Thus, Socrates argued that the gods will always help a just person in need "either during his lifetime or afterwards," because the gods "never neglect anyone who eagerly wishes to become just."[93] Socrates asked whether it is not true that just people "enjoy a good reputation and collect the prizes from other human beings?"[94] In contrast, Socrates said the unjust person will become "wretched," and he will be "ridiculed." Indeed, the unjust will be "beaten with whips, and made to suffer those punishments, such as racking and burning, which you rightly described as crude."[95]

This fate awaits the unjust person in the life to come, as well. In his discussion of the Myth of Er, Socrates gave an account of the terror and pain that await unjust individuals in the afterlife. He cautioned Glaucon to practice justice and to act in accordance with reason in every way, so that he will be able to receive the rewards from the gods while on earth and after his death. In this case, Socrates concluded, "We'll do well and be happy."[96]

The account Socrates provided here suggests that, if people cannot be persuaded to act justly through a reasoned discourse as he had provided throughout the *Republic*, then perhaps a picture of the terrible pains they will suffer for acting unjustly will frighten people into a life of justice. Fear, then, may achieve what reason cannot.

VI. Plato, the *Laws,* and Civil Society

Plato's political theory is an account of justice that does not uphold, as in the modern world, the idea that because, morally speaking, people are each free and autonomous, then, legally speaking, they must be accorded, equally, a long list of basic rights, including to speech, conscience, association, and due process of law. Rather, under Plato's idea of justice, society consists of many parts, each of which is organized into a well-integrated whole. All persons contribute to the society in ways appropriate to their abilities and, in exchange, they receive from society the bases for a happy life, including moral education and rule by the best philosophic minds. A well-ordered soul – one with the proper relationship between reason and emotion – is the basis for a just society.

What are the implications of Plato's view of the well-ordered social and political setting for civil society? Plato's answer cannot be adequately described from the arguments made in the *Republic* alone. Instead, a later writing, his *Laws*, complements the teachings of the *Republic* in a manner that helps us to be clear about the contributions of Plato's political philosophy to civil society.

Here is what we mean.

Plato had hoped that reliance on the Socratic dialectic would always lead to a clear statement of the main ideas, or forms, that should guide political judgments. But he came to realize that political leaders, even when they know the forms, might nonetheless use them to undermine the common good. The worst manifestation of this possibility is when political leaders acting in the tradition of Plato's dialectic end up establishing a tyranny that serves only the needs of the tyrant. As we just saw, Plato criticized democracies because too often they became tyrannies. But it is possible that elite rule, even when influenced by Plato's forms, does the same thing. Indeed, Plato saw precisely this outcome take place in one of the places where he had been asked to contribute to the governance of the area, Syracuse.

The temptation to take this route is always present in the philosopher-king, who, because he knows best how to use the dialectic to discern the forms, may lose patience when differences in society exist as to how best to achieve them. In this context, the leader may destroy fealty to the forms and turn society into an organization that instead of contributing to each other's needs defiles them. So, to prevent this from happening, in the *Laws*, Plato replaces the philosopher-king with the political leader able to "reconcile" citizens and secure "friendliness."[97]

Political leaders must use conciliatory approaches to bring "internal concord" among disparate factions of society.[98] To put the point differently, all may know the form of a just society, but there may be many different approaches to achieving it. To serve the form of justice best, political leadership must have a capacity to mediate among people with different views. And the political leader becomes far more important in this mission than the philosopher. Whereas the latter is good at deriving truth, the political leader is far better at applying it. This is the case because the astute political leader is more practical than absolutist. He knows that finding a basis for agreement among people with contesting views of how to apply truth to circumstances is the true art of politics and, when achieved, best serves philosophy as well as justice.

Chief among the conciliatory values is civic friendship. Civic friends with different understandings but who nonetheless share a common commitment to the same core ideas, such as "temperance, courage, nobility and wisdom," display a conciliatory frame of mind that allows them to reach agreement on the best way to achieve shared notions of right.[99] In consequence, the city is a place in which reciprocity flourishes, thus achieving a society in which mutual cooperation is the governing norm. The political leader, and not the philosopher, is better suited to realizing this objective.

Plato's *Republic* will never advance civic rights or individual freedoms as the core mission of society. But Plato will advocate in the *Laws* something that many consider just as important. He will argue that a just society depends on the talents of its leaders to resolve differences and to create a shared vision for how best to achieve Plato's forms. In taking this position, Plato upholds a major value of civil society, which is to say, learning to listen to others, no matter how different, and finding ways to agree on the best approach to realizing ideas with high purposes.

The implication of Plato's political thought for civil society is now clear: civility must complement the dialectic if a just politics is ever to be achieved.

Notes

1. George H. Sabine, *A History of Political Theory* (New York: Holt, Rinehart and Winston, 1963), 4–9, 15. Also, Mulford Q. Sibley, *Political Ideas and Ideologies: A History of Political Thought* (New York: Harper and Row, 1970), 44.

2. Sabine, *A History of Political Theory*, 14.

3. Ibid., 15.

4. Ibid., 23.

5. Ibid., 33–34, 15.

6. In discussing Plato's views in the *Republic*, we will use Socrates' name at times because the latter is the main figure in the *Republic* and, indeed, Socrates can be viewed as reflecting Plato's views. Also, the translation we are using is that by G. M. A. Grube, *Plato's Republic*, revised by C. D. C. Reeve, 2nd ed. (Indianapolis: Hackett Publishing Company, 1992). References are to the standard numbers used in all texts.

7. Ibid., 4–5, 330b–d.

8. Ibid., 5–6, 331c–d.

9. Ibid., 6, 331e.

10. Ibid., 7, 332e.

11. Ibid., 10–11, 335a–e.

12. Ibid., 14–15, 338c–39c.

13. Ibid., 16, 340c.

14. Ibid., 16–17, 340e–41a.

15. Ibid., 18, 342b–c.

16. Ibid., 18–19, 342c–e.

17. Ibid., 21, 345d.

18. Ibid., 22, 346e, 23, 347b.

19. Ibid., 23, 347c.

20. Ibid., 24, 348d, 27, 350c.

21. Ibid., 28, 351d–52a.

22. Ibid., 31, 353e, 354a.
23. Ibid., 31, 354b–c.
24. Ibid., 42, 367d, 33, 357a–c, 34, 358a.
25. Ibid., 42, 367d.
26. Ibid., 34, 358a.
27. Ibid., 44, 369d.
28. Ibid., 46, 371b–d.
29. Ibid., 47–48, 372d–e.
30. Ibid., 48, 373a–c.
31. Ibid., 48, 373c.
32. Ibid., 48, 373d–e.
33. Ibid., 118, 442b. See "Introduction" to Grube, *Plato's Republic*, xv.
34. Grube, *Plato's Republic*, 116, 441a.
35. Ibid., 440b.
36. Ibid., 118, 442c, 50, 375b.
37. Ibid., 87, 410d.
38. Ibid., 118, 442b.
39. Ibid., 89, 412c.
40. Ibid., 90–91, 414a–c.
41. Ibid., 90, 414b.
42. Ibid., 349–50, 374c–75a, 90, 414b.
43. Ibid., 92, 416a–c.
44. Ibid., 50, 375b–c.
45. Ibid., 90, 414a.
46. Ibid., 92–93, 41b–c, 136, 461d–e, 138–39, 464a–e.
47. Ibid., 136–37, 462c–d.
48. Ibid., 130, 456a–b.
49. Ibid., 129, 455c–e, 130, 456a–b.
50. Ibid., 134, 459e–60c.
51. Ibid., 135, 461c. There are other limitations. A man is not to have sex with his daughter, his mother, his daughter's children, or his mother's relatives, and a woman is not to have sex with her son or any of his children or her father and his relatives.
52. Ibid., 208–9, 536d–37d.
53. Ibid., 209, 537c–d, 211, 539b–d.
54. Ibid., 211, 539c–d.
55. Ibid., 211, 539d–e, 209, 537d.
56. Ibid., 212, 540b.
57. Ibid.
58. Ibid., 148, 473d.
59. Ibid., 158–60, 485a, 485e, 486a–d.
60. Ibid., 99, 424a. Our interpretation of civic virtue follows Grube's view, p. 94.
61. Ibid., 100, 424d–25b.
62. Ibid., 100–01, 425–26b.
63. Ibid., 102, 427d.
64. Ibid., 103–4, 428b–29a.
65. Ibid., 104, 429b–d.
66. Ibid., 106–7, 430e–32a.
67. Ibid., 107, 432a.
68. Ibid., 108, 433b.
69. Ibid., 108, 433a.
70. Ibid., 108, 433b, 109, 433e.
71. Ibid., 108, 433c–e.

72. Ibid., 91–92, 414c–15d.
73. Ibid., 257–58, 586d c.
74. Ibid., 258, 586e.
75. Ibid., 262, 590d.
76. Ibid., 262, 590d–91a.
77. Ibid., 214, 544d.
78. Ibid., 215, 545b, 218, 548d.
79. Ibid., 217–18, 547b–48d.
80. Ibid., 221, 551a.
81. Ibid., 221, 551b–c.
82. Ibid., 224, 554a.
83. Ibid., 223, 552d–e, 222, 552a–c.
84. Ibid., 227, 556d, 557a.
85. Ibid., 231–32, 561b–d, 234, 563e–64a.
86. Ibid., 232, 562a, 241–42, 571b–c.
87. Ibid., 232–33, 562c.
88. Ibid., 234, 563e–64a.
89. Ibid., 235–36, 564d–65b.
90. Ibid., 236, 565b–c.
91. Ibid., 236, 565d–66a.
92. Ibid., 240, 569a–b.
93. Ibid., 284, 613a.
94. Ibid., 284, 613c.
95. Ibid., 285, 613d.
96. Ibid., 292, 621d, 287, 615d–16a.
97. Plato, "The Laws," in *Readings in Classical Political Thought*, ed. Peter Steinberger (Indianapolis: Hackett Publishing Company, 2000), 319, Bk. I.
98. Ibid.
99. Ibid., 343, Bk. VIII.

3

Aristotle's Response to Plato: The Importance of Friendship

I. Introduction

Aristotle (384–322 BCE) became Plato's student in 367 BCE and for 20 years continued an association with Plato. During this time, Plato's views heavily shaped Aristotle's thought, and, as John Morrall says, Aristotle "never entirely renounced" Plato's influence.[1] Thus, Aristotle no less than Plato divided the soul into two parts, the rational and the non-rational. The former is the higher part because it is grounded in reason, and the other part, which includes the world of appetite and desire, is nonetheless capable of obeying the requirements of reason.[2] Owing to this basic, shared assumption, both argued that the state must educate its citizens to understand as well as to act in keeping with a view of society that embodies the best achievements of the rational part of life. Indeed, civic virtue, the commitment to the common good, pertains to those habits that enable one to uphold the qualities of a rational life.

Still, over his career, Aristotle did take steps to revise some of the main elements of Plato's political vision. Aristotle's departures from Plato had to do with Aristotle's intention to draw a more comprehensive picture of the rational way of life than he thought Plato had done. Aristotle thus hoped to enlarge Plato's vision of society so that it included what Aristotle thought Plato had omitted.

To provide an overview as to how Aristotle approached this objective, it is necessary to review an essential element of Plato's Republic. Plato's Republic, in establishing the reign of reason in a just society including, of course, the just soul, envisioned a society in which workers, guardians, and philosophers would each have separate but important functions in achieving the overall good of the society. To sustain people's commitment to their roles, Plato advocated ruler manipulation of people through such tactics as regulating the marriages of the guardians or the teaching of a "noble falsehood" that suggests that the god of creation wants all people to be placed in roles that are appropriate to their native abilities. Thus, when the habits of civic virtue are insufficient to secure citizens' acceptance of their roles, modes of subtle force become necessary.

In contrast, Aristotle's approach to ensuring that people perform well the functions for which they are best suited is to emphasize the central place in people's lives of community. For Aristotle, it is precisely this experience that must be at the center of all social and political life if the society is to facilitate all citizens' contributions to the common good. Aristotle thus saw the civic virtue of friendship as having a powerful role to play in society, for when people are friends, they are bound together by common moral values. This experience enables people to collaborate to achieve communal goals by manifesting the individual excellence needed to perform well the various functions in society. Indeed, as Morrall says, for Aristotle, the basis of society is a "communal solidarity springing from an affective friendship towards one's fellow-citizens," and the Greek word for this experience is *koinonia*.[3]

In this chapter, the importance of friendship in Aristotle's thought will orient our discussion of his view of politics and of his possible approach to civil society. Before developing his view of friendship, it is necessary to distinguish his approach to studying politics from the approach Plato took.

II. Scientific Knowledge and Practical Intelligence

For Aristotle, two major forms of knowledge are scientific knowledge and practical intelligence.[4]

Scientific knowledge indicates the possession of "eternal things," which are "indestructible."[5] The latter suggests principles that are considered true on their face and for which no further justification is needed. From these principles, it is possible to construct a deductive system of thought, called a *theory*, which enables us to make predictions about future events pertaining to matters under study in a particular area or domain of investigation.[6] For instance, given a theory that explains the origin of a certain illness, we can be certain that when we apply a treatment sanctioned by the theory, the patient will recover his health.[7]

Whereas scientific knowledge is able to provide universal, precise, and unvarying understanding about what it studies, practical intelligence is unable to provide similar certitude in discussing its field of concern. The difference between what each type of thinking is able to achieve has to do with the different realities each studies. Science studies nature, and practical intelligence is concerned with those actions in the realm of experience that are good, in this case morally and rationally good, for human beings.[8] The world of nature that science investigates is a world in which invariant relationships exist among the various components of a field of knowledge, such as the human body. But constancy among the factors that make up human experience – and the world of ethics and politics in particular– does not exist to the same degree as it does in nature. Aristotle said in his *Ethics* that "what is fine and what is just, the topics of inquiry in political science differ and vary so much that they seem to rest on convention only, not on nature."[9] Consequently, in discussing politics, the concern is to help define the "good" or the basis for a rational life for both the individual and the society, but the method used in finding the rational way of life in society will never have the exactitude found in scientific thinking. For Aristotle, then, we "should not seek the same degree of exactness in all sorts of arguments alike."[10] We will be able to understand the realm of politics and ethics "roughly and in outline" form, only.[11]

As Martha Nussbaum says, practical intelligence manifests an ability to "understand and grasp the salient features, the practical meaning, of concrete particulars."[12] Thus, practical intelligence requires that we remain concerned with the particular facts of ongoing circumstances in which decisions must be made. Focusing upon these particulars, instead of theories that consist of well-developed deductively based systems of rules to explain the ever-recurring structure of nature, practical intelligence can describe only patterns and tendencies that provide general guidelines for how to understand as well as to act in the world. Here, recognition must be given to the fact that the world of experience is subject to unpredictable changes. In consequence, practical intelligence must be able to accept the flux of circumstances and be flexible enough to improvise and change strategies and plans in the face of the unexpected.[13]

Given the importance of focusing on particulars as well as the flux they signify, the person of practical intelligence understands that theories, which derive from deductive systems of reasoning, often will prove useless, and they may be a hindrance to understanding and action. There is a good reason for this conclusion. A general theory will simplify the world too much, and, in consequence, a theory will allow us to see only certain elements of reality; therefore, it may deny us access to crucial elements we should see. For instance, before the fall of the Berlin Wall in 1989, almost no one in the US government, including the intelligence community, predicted this event. Why was this? Almost certainly the answer is that ever since the end of World War II, Americans tended to see communism as a monolithic ideology that united the Eastern bloc countries, including the former Soviet Union, against the West. Thus, even if Eastern bloc nations did have their differences, their ideological solidarity was such that it was not even thinkable that their union would dissolve. Here, the commitment to view the Eastern bloc in a way that reconfirmed a particular theory about communism prevented American policymakers from seeing the other realities – including the persistent

unhappiness with Soviet rule and a desire to pursue a course similar to the West –
that ultimately had the greatest impact in affecting events.

Finally, how does one come to possess practical intelligence? It emerges as a
result of much experience in life in which an individual works, over many years,
at understanding the meaning of events for developing courses of action that are
useful in achieving particular goals.[14] Young people can become accomplished
in deductive systems of thinking, such as geometry, because learning these systems is merely a matter of learning how to apply the rules given in a theory. But
the young cannot be taught the art of practical intelligence because this ability
requires years of experience engaged in the study of human events. The intention
of such study is to develop an ability to grasp the significance of particular events
for devising guidelines that are useful in directing action.[15]

III. Aristotle on Plato's Forms and the Search for Happiness

For Aristotle, a person with practical intelligence seeks the "best good for a
human being that is achievable in action."[16] On this view, one should pursue only
the best goals that are worthy of human life and that are capable of being realized
in practice. Aristotle, in the *Politics*, believed that Plato's theory of the forms
violated this requirement. Aristotle argued that Plato's forms did not enable a
person either to understand what is possible in particular circumstances or how to
act in these circumstances to achieve moral objectives. For Aristotle, then, Plato's
forms, as projecting a "total unity" onto society, signified a comprehensive theory
about how society should be organized to achieve particular goals. When one
approaches society in this way, one may lose sight of the crucial realities that are
critical to making important social reforms, as we saw in the last section.

To take Aristotle's own example, in considering Plato's exclusion of private
property for the guardians, one must not just consider, as Plato did, the evils that
this proposal would eliminate. Aristotle believed that it was necessary to consider
the benefits that would be denied people as a result of this proposal as well. Plato's
quest for "total unity," or a comprehensive theory for establishing a just society,
caused him to consider only the first issue and not the second one.[17]

The major danger of Plato's approach is especially important for someone
such as Plato, who sought to create a system of education that would succeed in
orienting people to respect moral values. To educate people properly, it is necessary to put into place those social factors that properly shape people's understanding so that they can act in ways that uphold moral norms. But if one does
not consider the benefits and disadvantages of proposals for the development of
these social factors, one is unlikely to provide a proper environment within which
to educate people to the civic virtues they should maintain. Thus, Aristotle found
it "surprising" that Plato, whose Republic is predicated on a system of political
and moral education, failed to investigate the impact of his reforms on the actual

factors that help to shape human character, factors such as the "social customs," the "mental culture," and the laws.[18]

Moreover, one must keep in mind, as one changes existing habits, laws, or traditions, what the overriding benefit of any such change should be. For Aristotle, the overriding purpose of the *polis* (Greek word for city-state) is to achieve happiness. Happiness is an end unlike any other end we may seek in life. People may pursue many ends, such as wealth or flute playing, but these ends have as their goal a larger and more complete end, which is happiness. Thus, happiness represents life's highest possibility because it symbolizes for Aristotle a way of life "more than anything else [that] seems unconditionally complete."[19]

What is the happy life for Aristotle? There are many different functions in society, and each function embodies the rational element when it is performed well or excellently. And this situation takes place only when a function is carried out in conjunction with the virtues or standards appropriate to the excellent performance of the function in question. For instance, to use Aristotle's example, a good harp player will play the harp with excellence because he will embody in his playing the "proper virtue." Here, it is not good enough just to play the harp, but it is necessary to play the harp well by exhibiting in one's performance the appropriate standards of excellence. In carrying out, with excellence, the standards associated with harp playing, one's life manifests virtue.[20]

Now, for Aristotle, there are many different activities for people to participate in. In addition to being a harp player, one can be a farmer, a parent, and so on. In each case, there are particular standards appropriate to the activity in question. Clearly, the activity of being a harp player does not require adherence to the same standards as being a parent. But in each case, the objective of a person's life should be to perform a given function in a way that exhibits virtue. Here, a person is not just a parent, but a good parent, not just a harp player, but a good harp player. The good life, then, is a life that expresses "the best and most complete virtue. Moreover, [the good life] will be in a complete life." And a person who lives in this fashion throughout his life is "blessed and happy."[21] Happiness emerges for individuals who, throughout their whole lives, attempt to master the various standards of performance associated with the excellent achievement of the different activities that they engage in.

For Aristotle, human beings are "good," and thus happy, when they perform well their functions in society, and people can perform them well only when they uphold the virtues or standards of excellence associated with these functions.[22] How does Plato compare with Aristotle on this issue? Plato's just society has many things in common with Aristotle's, to be sure. For instance, for Plato, each person must perform his or her function in keeping with the standards associated with the good performance of that task. Guardians, workers, and philosophers each operate in terms of the values allied with the tasks they are to perform. And because the good performance of one's various functions is so critical to acting justly, and because performing these functions well requires that one adhere to the standards associated with good performance, it would seem that Plato and

Aristotle differ very little on what constitutes the primary activity of people in society. For both Plato and Aristotle, individuals must, if they are to lead happy lives, perform well their functions by doing all that is necessary to uphold the standards associated with those functions.

But could Plato have as full and as complete an understanding of what constitutes our functions, or the larger environment in which they occur, as would Aristotle? Aristotle would answer this question negatively. And the reason once again is that Plato conceptualized the nature of a just society from the standpoint of a comprehensive theory, and, by doing so, he was bound to miss important factors that he should consider. From the standpoint of practical intelligence Aristotle used, however, we are in a better position to mine human experience for a fuller understanding of its rational character.

As an example of this last point, it is well to mention Aristotle's discussion of moral virtue. For Aristotle, not unlike Plato, habituation to proper forms of conduct forges moral character. People, starting as children, learn virtue through practice and not through reasoning and argument about the nature of virtue. But what does habituation to virtue teach? For Aristotle, moral education habituates people to avoid either excess or deficiency while pursuing the middle ground between both. For instance, to be brave, one should neither be afraid all the time nor become rash from the absence of fear. To manifest the virtue of temperance, one should neither be a glutton who seeks pleasure all the time nor a complete ascetic who avoids all pleasure. And to practice the virtue of truth-telling, one should neither be a braggart who "overstates" issues nor be "self-deprecating" by understating the truth.[23] In each case, there is a proper middle ground, and knowledge of that dimension allows one to be courageous, temperate, and truth seeking. It would seem that without these general moral virtues, one would not be able to be a good worker, a good family member, or a good citizen.

Knowledge of these general moral virtues, which are not apparent in Plato, arises from learning the important lessons of experience, lessons that speak to how a person achieves a virtue in any number of activities throughout life. Implicit in Aristotle's view, then, is that existing ways of life already contain or embody rational characteristics. He worried that, if changes were made in these practices without due consideration to this fact, then some of the rational dimensions of existing practices might be annihilated. As we will see in Section IV with Aristotle's defense of private property and the family, Aristotle believed that there were rational reasons for maintaining these practices. And he believed that Plato, owing to his theory of justice, was unable to understand how these practices contributed to the overall rational structure of society and thus to people's happiness. Aristotle, along these lines, will also discuss friendship as a basis for communal solidarity as well as his conceptions of the good constitution and public deliberation.

Thus, whereas Plato starts from an ideal of justice and constructs a theory of a rational society based on this ideal, Aristotle starts from existing ways of life and finds the bases for a rational order to life contained in the ongoing practices of society. Armed with this understanding, Aristotle seeks to build upon the rational characteristics that are already a part of existing experience. To describe Aristotle's political vision, then, we start at the ground level and discuss his view of society contained in his concept of the polis.

IV. The Nature of the Polis

The polis is made up of several associations – most important are families and villages – and its purpose is to make possible the "good life." The polis arises from the fact that individuals could not by themselves create the bases for happiness, for what is necessary are not only those goods that contribute to the material well-being of people, but goods that contribute to people's moral development as well. And only the polis can provide all the goods associated with material and moral well-being. Because of this, the polis is called "self-sufficient."[24]

For Aristotle, then, it is clear why human beings are social and political animals. Human beings, unlike animals, are provided by nature with a moral capacity, but, at the same time, they also are born with proclivities to shun the obligations associated with their moral natures.[25] In the polis, individuals are taught how to live morally, and thus the polis is arranged so that humankind is freed from the domination of "lust and gluttony."[26] Aristotle said that "man, when perfected, is the best of animals, but if he is isolated from law and justice he is the worst of all."[27] And individuals are only perfected when they shed any tendency toward isolation and join into political association with others. Here, relationships with others teach important moral values that orient individuals to uphold the common good. Outside of political association with others, there would be no recognition of values such as courage, moderation, generosity, and justice.[28]

The distinctive character of the polis, then, is that it is organized so that the rational or moral dimension always dominates the nonrational element. Indeed, Aristotle argued that there is a natural course of events taking place that ensures the priority of the rational. First, male and female unite from a "natural impulse" and not from a "deliberate intention" to reproduce human life. Next, there must be forms of association that permit the rational element. The latter makes possible the capacity of "forethought," to rule over other elements in society, which lack a capacity for rationality.[29] The family, which provides for "satisfaction of recurrent daily needs,"[30] is arranged so that the male, the ruling or the rational element, rules the female, the children, and the slaves.[31] Now, the male rules his wife "like a statesman over fellow subjects"; his children like a king; and a slave like a master.[32] This means that the male can make decisions for his slaves and his children without consulting them, but in making decisions that affect his wife and the family, he should consult her.

The statesman model also suggests a difference in status between those who rule and those who are ruled. The latter should manifest both high regard and respect for those who have ruling authority. In a similar way, the wife is to maintain respect for the authority of her husband. This is the case because only the male in the household, like the statesman who possesses practical intelligence, has full rational capacities that permit him to deliberate intelligently about important matters. "The slave is entirely without the faculty of deliberation; the female indeed possesses it, but in a form which remains inconclusive; and if children also possess it, it is only in an immature form."[33] This statement suggests that women, although having some dimension of the rational capacity, do not have as fully developed a rational capacity as men do. Women, like others who are of lesser stature than the husband in the household (slaves and children), have only that amount of rational capacity that permits them to perform their functions in the family. Thus, whereas women may have sufficient rational quality to help run the family, they do not have the full rational quality evidenced in men and that men use in making judgments about important issues, either in the public setting or in the family. Aristotle quotes, with approval, Sophocles, who said that "a modest silence is a woman's crown."[34]

As Susan Moller Okin argues in *Women in Western Political Thought*, central to Aristotle's account of society is the view that women are merely to be caretakers of the household and the "bearers" of new citizens, but women can never be citizens themselves. Only the male is allowed to perform the active citizen role, and the household provides the support for him to take part in this role by removing from his shoulders responsibility for the family and placing it upon women.[35] The clear implication of this view is that women must remain in the home because they are inferior to men, or, as Aristotle said, because they lack full deliberative powers. Obviously, this view of women becomes the basis for excluding any consideration of the unjustness of preventing women from participating with men in the public arena where decisions about laws are made.

After the family, the next form of association is the village, and it provides for "more than daily recurrent needs."[36] The village is a grouping of different families into a unit that facilitates exchanges among various families of necessary goods, goods that each family might not be able to provide by themselves. The first method for exchanging goods in the village was through a straight barter of goods for goods. The barter system was too cumbersome for exchanges that involved transactions between people in different villages, and so money was instituted and made the basis for exchanges.[37] With the introduction of money, severe problems emerge that threaten the moral environment of society. Money makes possible retail trade, which, because it is conducted for profit, permits some individuals to acquire large fortunes. Indeed, in the retail atmosphere, individuals may become so preoccupied with money that they use all their abilities and capacities to secure for themselves ever-larger fortunes. Such individuals hold the view that there is no limit to the amount of wealth they can be permitted to acquire. Thus, for Aristotle, the retail experience is unhealthy for society because, instead of orienting people to the morality of the good life, it orients individuals to think that money is "the one aim and everything else must contribute to that aim."[38]

Aristotle's view of the polis, as in Plato's view of society, is that it is organized to provide basic needs. Furthermore, like Plato, Aristotle worried that the mentality of the endless acquisition of money would overwhelm citizens and thus undermine the commitment to make reason the basis for society. But the approach to avoiding this outcome was not through a civic virtue orientation as well as a noble lie that would enable a guardian class of auxiliaries and wise rulers to protect the common good, as Plato had done, but through an effort to create the grounds for community.

Citizenship and Friendship

For Aristotle, friendship is a virtue "most necessary for our life." Without friendship, life would be missing a major dimension, and consequently, our lives would lack real significance. Moreover, as a virtue, friendship is only possible among people who practice the moral virtues discussed earlier, such as courage, truthfulness, and temperance.[39] People who practice virtues like these make the search for the middle ground a common feature of their lives. This trait is more likely to enable people to find ways to accommodate each other's needs and thus to become friends. Most importantly, by pursuing the middle ground, people maintain friendships because together they find ways to achieve shared objectives.

Friendship is thus a source of community because it suggests a basis for people to collaborate for common purposes. Indeed, the experience of friendship for Aristotle contributes to concord among people with respect to the major questions facing society. For Aristotle, then, concord, a "feature of friendship," is a condition in which the citizens in a city "agree about what is advantageous, make the same decisions, and act on their common resolution."[40] Concord suggests agreement not just on "anything" but on what Aristotle referred to as "large questions" or when, as a result of the agreement, the members of the society all "get what they want" on issues of critical importance to the society.[41] Here, Aristotle, in talking about "large questions," referred to issues such as whether to make alliances with other city-states or whether to make all offices elective. In our society, an important question about which there must be concord if there is to be a sense of community would include the need to secure the same rights to each member of society so that each member can determine his or her own purposes in life.

What makes possible agreement or concord on large questions of this sort is that, underlying these agreements, are shared moral values. For instance, underlying our contemporary commitment to provide rights to all is the moral commitment to respect equally the full dignity and worth of each individual. Without this shared moral value, we could not agree that providing rights to all is an important good, and society would be filled with extreme conflict between those who advocated rights for all and those who did not. But because our society presumably supports respect for the dignity of each person as a shared moral value, the people in society can agree that a policy to accord rights to everyone is a good policy. Indeed, such a policy, when it has been developed, would confirm in an even stronger sense the place of the shared moral value of equal regard for the dignity of others, and, in doing so, would make an even stronger basis for maintaining friendship and a concomitant sense of community.

Because there exist shared moral values, there can be agreement on important questions so that the society is not torn apart by differences over major issues. It is for this reason that "political friendship" that "is concerned with advantage and with what affects life [as a whole]" is possible.[42] Moreover, people who are friends, politically speaking, contribute to securing the society's continuing stability. The existence of political friendship helps us understand why Aristotle could say as he did that friendship "would seem to hold cities together, and legislators would seem to be more concerned about it than about justice."[43] As friends, people avoid all forms of "civil conflict" that are associated with "enmity," and the members of the society are able to work together to achieve a common end.[44] Indeed, in this setting people "have no need for justice" or, in other terms, no need for a system of laws or rules that impose a just order because, in maintaining the ties of friendship, people act as they should to each other without external prompting of any sort.[45]

But maintaining friendship, especially the type that holds together a community, is possible only among "decent people." Who are decent people? They have an enduring commitment to "what is just and advantageous, and also to seek it in common."[46] Decent people, then, are individuals who are committed to maintaining those common moral values that are critical to making possible a rational way of life in society. Such people make the search for the middle ground a common characteristic of their lives. Thus, decent people "are in concord with themselves and with each other, since they are practically of the same mind; for their wishes are stable, not flowing back and forth like a tidal strait."[47]

It follows from the preceding account that "base" people cannot find concord with others except in minor ways because "base" people are those who seek only their own gain and have no regard for the common good, including the search for the middle ground. Now, "base" people understand what constitutes the common moral values, and thus these individuals know what a life of justice entails. Yet, "base" people want others to live such a life, even though they themselves do not want to have to do so. Thus, "base" people are always engaged in conflict with the rest of the society.[48] Obviously, these people represent a threat both to friendship and to the ability of a society to maintain community.

To overcome the threat that this situation poses to society, Aristotle pointed out the importance of institutions that are part of the encompassing social and political environment, such as "marriage, kin-groups, religious gatherings, and social pastimes." These practices help produce a basis for a "common social life" by reinforcing through the socialization process the importance of common moral values, and, when these shared moral values are in place, a basis for maintaining friendship among the members of the society exists. Aristotle said that "institutions [such as marriage and religious associations] are the business of friendship. . . . It is friendship . . . which consists in the pursuit of a common social life."[49] In this atmosphere, people maintain a fundamental decency and civility and, as a consequence of this demeanor, they are more likely to perform their respective functions in ways that contribute to the common good of the society.

Friendship, as the ground of community, would permit different people who perform different functions to continue to maintain their commitment to the common good. On this view, then, an important defect of Plato's argument was his failure to make friendship a central civic virtue in the development of a just city and in providing the foundation for other virtues Plato identified, such as moderation, wisdom, and courage. As we saw in the last chapter, however, Plato, in the *Laws*, remedied this deficiency by making friendship a central element of political community.

Slavery and Friendship

One consequence of citizenship is that, to support its practice, there will have to be a class of noncitizens who perform all the drudge labor so that the citizens, freed from such labor, can perform, fully, their citizenship duties. Aristotle allowed men time for citizenship duties by transferring to women and slaves the job of raising families and maintaining the household. Ordinarily, this situation might create enmity and rebellion on the part of the subordinate class toward the superior class. But, friendship, which can occur among those who are not equals, or citizens and noncitizen members of society (women, children, and slaves), enables individuals who are unequal in status to share a sense of community with those who are citizens and thus of higher stature. Characteristic of friendship among those who are not equal in status is that each party in the relationship has a different function to perform with respect to the other party. And in performing that function, each person receives something he or she needs through cooperation with others, and this experience is the basis for different kinds of "love" between people.[50] Again, even among people with unequal status there can be shared moral values, and these values help to justify the inequality in status. It is on this basis that there can be friendship between master and slave.

Aristotle's discussion of slavery indicates what slaves do, how people are justifiably made into slaves, and what he considers to be the moral justification of slavery. For Aristotle, a slave is a person who does not produce goods but who serves the needs of the household. Slaves are needed to perform many of the activities associated with household life, and, in performing them, presumably, individuals (in this case, the adult male members of the household) are provided with the leisure time needed to take part in political affairs and public activities.[51]

There are two justifications for slavery, conventional or natural, and only the latter form is acceptable to Aristotle. In making people slaves by convention or legality, the powerful subjugate the less powerful to their control, as, for instance, when one nation invades another and makes the citizens of the invaded nation into slaves. Aristotle believed conventional slavery to be unjust. There are several reasons for his position. First, a war in which one nation invades another and takes the invaded nation's citizens as slaves may, in fact, not be conducted on just grounds. In this case, enslaving others would be unjust. Second, it is possible that people enslaved even in just wars may not deserve to be enslaved at all. Aristotle condemned the practice of enslaving people as a result of a war because one may be enslaving persons with a capacity for reason.[52]

From this account, it is clear who can be enslaved and who should not be. Enslaving another is legitimate only under a condition in which there is a *natural* relation between master and slave, a relationship in which the slave, lacking in deliberative qualities, is ruled by the person who possesses those qualities.[53] It would not be appropriate to place into slavery a person who possessed deliberative qualities; such a person would be held back from making full use of his or her powers, and clearly this could not be good for the slave or for the society. Still, slaves have a degree of rationality, however small, that permits them to follow the commands of those who have full rational powers and who by virtue of this fact are properly placed in authority over slaves. Those who naturally lack a *full* rational dimension benefit from slavery; such people are provided with necessary goods to ensure their survival and, further, they can take part in work that is beneficial to society. And the master benefits because slavery allows him the leisure to contribute to public affairs. Here, slavery is a natural or a moral relationship because it provides mutual benefits to the master and to the slave. Thus, for Aristotle, "there is a community of interest, and a relation of friendship, between master and slave, when both of them naturally merit the position in which they stand."[54]

Slavery is justified to make possible the rule of those who have rational capacities and who are in a position to make good use of practical intelligence. Slavery is a means to a higher end; it is itself not an indication of an unjust and immoral state of affairs. The reason it cannot be for Aristotle is that he had no conception of individual rights, which, itself, requires that all individuals be accorded the same dignity. Notwithstanding Aristotle's efforts to reform slavery by denying a right to enslave people with deliberative skills who may have been captured in war, the fact is that his acceptance of slavery remains abhorrent to the modern proponent of civil society.[55]

Citizenship and Differentials in Contribution

A polis is a form of society in which the chief goal is "true felicity and goodness."[56] Individuals find in the polis the common goods all people share, the means for physical security as well as the basis for a moral and virtuous life. However, the common ends of polis life can be obtained only so long as everyone accepts that different citizens contribute disproportionately to the ends of polis life, and those citizens who contribute more should be honored more. In particular, some citizens, owing to their superior "civic excellence," do more than other citizens to achieve the "good" life for all members of the society. Because of this fact, these individuals are to be accorded "a greater share in the polis."[57] Here, even if citizens are equal in social status or wealth, a person who contributes more to the well-being of the society should receive greater recognition for his or her contributions to society. Similarly, among people unequal in social status and wealth, it is the person who contributes the most to "civic excellence" who should be rewarded the most.[58]

Disproportionate awards, based on meritorious contributions, although necessary to maintain the polis, may have harmful effects, also. Citizens who are accorded such high regard might engender among other less highly respected citizens envy and contempt. Were this to happen, the concord so necessary for good order would be undermined. But this grim prospect would be averted by the existence of political friendship, which suggests a shared commitment to common moral values. This commitment is the basis for a community in which each citizen learns to respect the accomplishments and contributions of other citizens and to see these contributions as essential to the well-being of the society. Thus, friendship is an important civic virtue because it permits citizens to accept, without rancor, differences in recognition resulting from differences in contributions to the welfare of the society.

Family and Private Property

Aristotle's account of citizenship and friendship would contribute to limiting the damage from envy, but so would his conception of the family and private property. Both institutions are needed in order to enable individuals to feel that their lives have value, and both are necessary dimensions of a well-organized polis that secures a sense of communal solidarity among diverse people – citizens and noncitizens, women and men.

For Aristotle, Plato's guardian community is a "watery sort of fraternity."[59] Aristotle particularly rejected the idea of common families, where the children are the children of all. Aristotle said:

> *Men pay most attention to what is their own: they care less for what is common; or, at any rate, they care for it only to the extent to which each is individually concerned. . . . The scheme of Plato means that each citizen will have a thousand sons: they will not be the sons of each citizen individually: and every son will be equally the son of any and every father; and the result will be that every son will be equally neglected by every father.*[60]

Plato's scheme would dilute family bonds so much that no father would have any strong feeling to treat all the other "sons" in the guardian community with very much care and concern. Similarly, in Plato's commune, no son would ever feel any filial relationship to the father figures.[61] This unfortunate outcome would surely contribute to a sense of resentment among many parents toward the community.

Regarding private property, Aristotle said that when people have their own "separate sphere of interest" they are more likely to avoid quarrels and disagreements with each other. Moreover, it is likely that people's interest and intensity in their activities will be increased where private property is permitted "because each will feel that he is applying himself to what is his own."[62] Furthermore, for Aristotle, there is no reason why private property cannot be used to support common communal purposes, as he thinks Plato implied it could not do. People can make use of what they own in ways that benefit the society in general. For Aristotle "the better system [than Plato's] is that under which property is privately owned but is put to common use; and the function proper to the legislator is to make men so disposed that they will treat their property in this way."[63]

At first glance, owing to the fact that private property accords people with a separate sphere, it might seem that Aristotle was laying the ground for a civil society. But Aristotle, in linking people to the need to make common use of one's property, ensures that the separate sphere of a civil society would not emerge. What Aristotle really means by a separate sphere is just a place that property holders can call their own. But it is not a place that allows individuals autonomy and a wide range of private choices, as would be the case in a civil society, especially a liberal one, as described in Chapter 1.

Furthermore, given Aristotle's view of Plato, it might appear that Aristotle tended to think that Plato advocated a scheme of collective ownership of property for all people in society and not just for the guardians. But, in fact, that was not the case. As we saw, Plato would have accepted private property for many people outside the guardian category. Further, Plato accepted, as did Aristotle, the idea that appetite could be properly harnessed and controlled by moral training. In this case, as Aristotle said, "Moral goodness . . . will ensure that the property of each is made to serve the use of all, in the spirit of the proverb which says 'Friends' goods are goods in common."[64] For Aristotle, then, no less than for Plato, in fact, the concept, "this is mine," should be seen as contributing to the understanding that one is permitted to have personal wealth on the condition that one use it to promote community goals.

V. Constitutions: Just and Unjust

The constitution of a polis pertains to several important characteristics of the political community. A constitution is organized into offices, each of which has certain powers in relation to the common ends and values of the community.[65] A constitution, then, is "an organization of offices in a state, by which the method of their distribution is fixed, the sovereign authority is determined, and the nature of the end to be pursued by the association and all its members is prescribed."[66]

Moreover, any constitution is to a large extent influenced in its character by the social and economic classes that dominate the society.[67] Thus, because different classes will predominate, there will be different constitutions. Further, given the variety of constitutions, it is natural to ask what makes a constitution worthy. Aristotle is clear that only those constitutions that promote the common interest can be considered "right constitutions." All others that promote the personal interests of the ruling classes are "perversions."[68]

Aristotle used both the categories of class and of respect for the common interest as a basis for evaluation and description of various constitutions. The three good kinds of constitutions, those based on respect for the common interest, are kingships, aristocracies, and polities. The predominant class in the first is the king, in the second it is the few who are meritorious, and, in the third, it is the many, later referred to as the *middle class*. The perversions of these forms are tyrannies, oligarchies, and democracies. Tyranny is rule by a corrupt single ruler, oligarchy is rule by the wealthy who define the public good in a way that benefits only itself, and democracy is rule by the many, which in this case is the poor.[69] We will discuss each form of constitution in turn as we distinguish the good from the bad.

The "most nearly divine" of the right kind of constitution is kingship.[70] A kingship is closer in nature to an aristocracy because it is the rule of the "better classes," and thus, as in an aristocracy, merit is the basis for ruling others. Further, a kingship protects the wealth of property owners from "unjust treatment" arising from those who might otherwise take their property. At the same time, the king protects the rest of society from "arrogance and oppression."[71] Aristotle also said that it is best for kings to accept, as the basis of their regime, the rule of law. "The rule of law is therefore preferable . . . to that of a single citizen." Aristotle went on to say that the "law . . . trains the holders of office expressly in its own spirit," and thus the rule of law enables rulers to settle issues justly.[72] In a society governed by the rule of law, "God and reason rule." But where men alone rule, society falls under the authority of the "beast."[73] When men rule without regard for the rule of law, appetite and out-of-control emotions, and not reason, are the main political forces in society.

The perverted form of kingship is tyranny. The tyrant makes the pursuit of his own interest primary, and he has no concern for the public interest. The tyrant, like the oligarch, amasses great wealth so that the tyrant is in a position to provide himself with an army as well as with luxuries. The tyrant does not trust the masses, and he makes every effort to deny them weapons.[74] Either he can try to stay in power by sowing distrust among the people, so there is no united opposition to him, or he can take a higher road and become more like a king. In the latter case, he dedicates himself to upholding the public interest, and through displays of moderation, he can win the favor of the masses as well as of the aristocrats.[75]

An aristocracy, as already indicated, is rule by the meritorious few.[76] A perverted aristocracy is an oligarchy, a way of life in which the wealthy rule the rest of the society on behalf of their, the wealthy class's, own interest and without respect for the rule of law principle. An oligarchy is distinguished from a democracy by the fact that, in the former case, the rich rule, and in a democracy the poor are in control.[77] Aristotle argued that oligarchies, if they want to continue, should reform themselves. This they can do by allowing all property holders a chance to hold political office. Further, oligarchs should be willing to occupy the most important public offices without pay so that it appears to the rest of the citizens, who are excluded from office, that the public officials are concerned with making the public good a priority.[78]

Next, Aristotle turned to a discussion of the polity, "the best constitution and way of life for the *majority* of states and men."[79] In a polity, there is a middle ground between competing forces in society, in this case, between contrasting class perspectives.[80] Thus, in a polity, the middle class acts as a moderating force between two divergent classes in competition with each other, one representing the interests of an oligarchy and the other of a democracy. Generally, some polities show greater tendencies to be like democracies, while others incline in the direction of being like oligarchies.[81]

In any case, a polity is considered the basis for a moderate form of politics. Aristotle said that individuals who are favorable to leading a moderate life are "most ready to listen to reason."[82] Such people manifest the quest to avoid extremes and instead base life on the middle ground, the heart and soul of a virtuous life. Indeed, this moderate way of life is mirrored in the society through the fact that the polity is predicated upon a middle class, a class midway between the rich and the poor. People, who are in either camp, rich or poor, are fanatical with respect to promoting their respective causes, and neither can follow the rule of reason. The rich tend to be more violent and are likely to engage in "serious crime," and the poor are given to "roguery and petty offenses."[83]

Obviously in both these settings, citizens would not be ruled by just laws. The rich, because they have too many advantages, never acquire the discipline needed to respect and to uphold just laws. The poor, who lack all advantages, become resentful and mean in spirit, and thus they too would not be able to establish just laws. Where these two classes predominate, the state becomes nothing more than the poor constantly fighting with the rich, a setting "only of slaves and masters: a state of envy on the one side and on the other contempt." Aristotle went on to say that "nothing could be further removed from the spirit of friendship or the temper of political community. Community depends upon friendship; and when there is enmity instead of friendship, men will not even share the same path."[84]

On the other hand, the members of the middle class "suffer least from ambition," and thus they are most capable of ruling in a setting that promotes the common good and a basis for good laws that should be sovereign throughout society. The middle class would seem most able, then, to establish common moral values that could be the basis for friendship and community among the different classes in society.

The common moral values that a polity, through the middle class, promotes are clear as well. "A state aims at being . . . a society composed of equals and peers [who, as such, can be friends and associates]; and the middle class, more than any other, has this sort of composition. It follows that a state which is based on the middle class is bound to be the best constituted."[85] A polity strives toward equality by the way it distributes property. Indeed, a major reason for the success of the polity is that it is based upon a "moderate and adequate [distribution of] property."[86] In a society in which property is distributed unfairly and some have most of it and the rest have nothing, there will be little chance for community. Instead, society will either turn into an oligarchy (the rule by small segments of society who own most of the property) or become an "extreme democracy" (the rule of the poor over the rest). Moreover, a reaction against either of these forms of unjust regimes may end up turning the society into a tyranny.[87]

Unfortunately, polities are generally rare because one of the two tendencies, oligarchic or democratic, ultimately comes to dominate. This happens in large part either because the middle class is too small or because there is intense animosity between the mass of people and the rich.[88]

VI. Democracy and Public Deliberation

Whereas tyranny is the most perverse of the unjust regimes and oligarchy is next to tyranny, democracy is the "most moderate" among the worst regimes and thus the "least bad."[89] Democracy is a form of government based upon the rule of the poor and the "free-born," the vast bulk of the people.[90]

Further, a democracy highlights two views of liberty. The first conception is that individuals should share in being ruled and in ruling.[91] This means that the citizens should each have an opportunity to take part in public office. Furthermore, the collective view of the citizens should prevail on issues such as the nature of law. Here, unlike Plato, who argued in the *Republic* that only philosophers should rule, Aristotle thought it quite possible that citizens deliberating together might make the best decisions. Aristotle believed that even if it were the case that an individual by him- or herself will not be a better judge than an expert, still when individuals meet together and make judgments as a result of deliberation, their judgments are better or at least no worse than those of the so-called experts. Aristotle said that "each individual may, indeed, be a worse judge than the experts; but all, when they meet together, are either better than experts or at any rate no worse."[92]

Furthermore, there are many areas of interest in which the experts on particular subjects are not better judges than nonexperts, or what could be called *average citizens*. Aristotle said that "a house . . . is something which can be understood by others besides the builder."[93] Extending this analogy to politics, it is likewise possible that ordinary citizens who deliberate together are just as good, if not better, in making judgments about domestic or foreign policy matters as the experts in these respective fields. Perhaps one reason for this view stems from Aristotle's treatment of practical intelligence. As the reader will remember, practical intelligence is not concerned with providing a theory, with a well-developed system of rules to explain events, but, rather, practical intelligence describes patterns and tendencies that provide guidelines for how to formulate and to think about the law or other public questions. Now, defining these tendencies is a very imprecise science, to be sure. Because events are fluid, it is often difficult to determine the pattern in a series of events. But when people share this endeavor together, they can compare and contrast views, and, in the process, they are more likely to create a more accurate picture of events as the basis for the laws they ultimately accept. Thus, when Aristotle said that in a democracy the majority must determine the outcome and that their view is "the expression of justice," it should be understood that the majority decision is to emerge from a process of public deliberation. The latter is to inform the views of people so that their resulting judgment is based on an intelligent assessment of the issues, as opposed to an emotional reaction.[94]

Moreover, this approach to ruling is more likely to avoid political instability. For Aristotle, Plato's approach to ruling, which makes one group of citizens the state's perpetual rulers, denies opportunities for all citizens to take part in holding office. And this situation would "breed discontent and dissension even among the elements which have no particular standing, and, all the more, therefore, among the high-spirited and martial elements."[95] For Aristotle, Plato would thus be unable to maintain among citizens the shared moral values that could bridge the different interests in society and create the bonds of community and friendship Aristotle believed were necessary for a healthy and just political society.

Aristotle's view of common deliberation is certainly made possible by a moral perspective that highlights the search for the middle ground as a critical feature of public and of community life. Further, this approach to common deliberation anticipates civil society thinking discussed throughout this book. In particular, when we discuss the prospect of public reason in our chapters on Rousseau, Hegel, Kant, and Rawls, we will be discussing a form of reasoning in which individuals learn to consult the views of others as the basis for developing both their own views and the consensus of the society on a given issue. This experience is fundamental to promoting what we have called in the first chapter *mutual respect*, or the ability of people to understand the views and opinions of those who differ from them.

The second conception of liberty in a democracy is that individuals should have the freedom to "live as they like." "Such a life, the democrats argue, is the function of the free man, just as the function of slaves is *not* to live as they like."[96] Under this form, individuals are to be free from interference from the government. Moreover, this view contributes to a system of liberty that incorporates equality, in which freedom, if made possible for one person, must be made possible for all persons. It would seem that living as one liked, however, would always conflict with the first view of liberty, which emphasizes that individuals should partake in public deliberation of issues. To accomplish this objective, people must accept the fact that, at times, they must forgo living as they might want to live, to help make possible a consensus on important public issues. Only then would it be possible to maintain those shared moral values that are the basis for continuing the bonds of friendship.

Aristotle provided advice on how to improve democracy and move it in the direction of a good, stable regime. He argued that it is necessary to ensure a permanent level of prosperity for the lower classes. "Poverty is the cause of the defects of democracy." Prosperity could be achieved by distributing surpluses in the form of "block grants to the poor."[97] In taking this view, Aristotle would hope to make democracy more like a polity because this setting would be likely to maintain friendship and thus preserve the community experience that is so essential to securing a good society. Indeed, in this setting, it would be possible to imagine a sufficient degree of trust to permit the kind of public deliberation that democracy demands of its citizens.

Aristotle's discussion of public deliberation in making the law reinforces the view, manifested in his discussion of kingships, that government in a society should be based upon the rule of law and not upon the personal authority of particular rulers. Personal authority, whether exercised by a single person or a body of people, should be used only where, owing to the difficulty in framing general rules that cover all contingencies, there exist no laws to cover a particular matter. In making a strong case for the rule of law over the rule of particular individuals, Aristotle demonstrated his conviction that "the final sovereign" should be the rule of what he called "rightly constituted laws." What are rightly constituted laws? That is a difficult question because, given that different constitutions rest upon particular social classes, laws may be biased in the direction of one class or another. Still, to answer this question, Aristotle suggested the importance of good constitutions to producing good laws. Indeed, he said that just laws are laws that must be "in accordance with right constitutions."[98]

It would seem, given Aristotle's emphasis on allowing experts to be replaced with ordinary citizens in the processes of public deliberation, that one important criterion, among others, for defining just constitutions would be a provision that permits the laws to emanate from the common deliberation of the citizens. And thus, Aristotle, in promoting the idea of the rule of law, advocated the rule of citizen deliberation as one important basis for a just polity. In doing so, he demonstrated once again a vision of political life that enlarges upon the one found in Plato.

VII. Aristotle and Civil Society

Still, despite the emphasis on common deliberation among citizens, it should be clear that Aristotle's view of society excluded a great many from full participation in public life, as we saw already with respect to women and slaves. In addition, Aristotle said that "mechanics" and "shopkeepers" engaged in activities that were "ignoble and inimical to goodness," and, in "a state with an ideal constitution," these individuals cannot be citizens taking full part in the government. Work tasks of this sort, just as farming, must be performed by a separate class of people so that others – those who are permitted to be citizens – have the full leisure necessary to participate in government. "Leisure is a necessity, both for growth in goodness and for the pursuit of political activities."[99]

For Aristotle, the people who perform the necessary work of society will not be able to be given access to the type of opportunities that lead to the development of their rational faculties. And thus, even in the best city, the most that human life has to offer will not be open to all. These views suggest that Aristotle believed that for society to achieve its collective purposes, there would be some people denied the same justice afforded to others. Now, ironically, there is a virtue to be gained from defining social circumstances in this way. Indeed, such an approach permits Aristotle to define clearly the limits placed on human action, and, with these limitations in mind, the legislator knows the kinds of limitations he must work against to bring about a more just society.[100]

What would give Aristotle cause to challenge the limitations of his views of society? It would seem that his commitment to friendship would encourage him to rethink his view of class hierarchy. As we have seen, without friendship there is no basis for community. Now, friendship for Aristotle is predicated upon shared moral values among the different members of the society. But where the moral values in question are ones that cause serious and deep strains and conflicts in society, one could ask whether these values really have moral and rational validity. For how can values that divide people along lines that suggest a lack of fairness be considered morally worthy? Moreover, if one were to conclude that the values in question have no moral validity, then society would lack both shared moral values and the friendship that these values make possible. Aristotle, who wished to make friendship the basis for society, would have no choice, then, but to reform the moral values of society so that just values could be provided. If he were successful in this endeavor, both friendship and community could be restored.

If he took this route, he would be following, after all, Plato. As we saw in the last chapter, Aristotle criticized Plato for his tendency to impose a philosophical conception of truth on to all of society. In contrast, Aristotle would build a just society from the bottom up, not top down. But in pursuing this course, he is actually following the Plato of the *Laws*. Remember, there, in a change of approach from the *Republic*, Plato had made the main actor the political leader, not the philosopher-king. He did so because he realized that in the hands of powerful individuals, his philosophy might well be a hindrance to justice. Those who impose truth on society, regardless of the costs, are fueled by a constant need for control over all facets of society. The more control they seek, the more they must have, and the more power they employ, the more likely that they make decisions that initiate outcomes that run counter to justice.

The political leader of Plato's *Laws*, in contrast, is the embodiment of Aristotle's practical wisdom. He recognizes that achieving justice requires making judgments that conciliate differences on behalf of the society's shared values.

Judgments of this sort are achieved by consulting experience – one's own and that of others – in the hopes that useful approaches to comity among differences can be achieved. A politics based on this approach establishes the pursuit of justice on civic friendship. In this context, people employ principles of a just order common to their society in a way that advances the mutuality of society. Then and only then does it become clear why we have society, which is to make possible many reciprocal exchanges among people so that each not only gets what one needs, but that from each person society gets what each person can give, for the sake of the larger good.

This view resonates with civil society thinking. Diverse ways of life are drawn together into a unity that benefits all citizens. This is what politics, a just politics, is always about. And this is why there is a strong basis for civil society in Aristotle.

Notes

1. John B. Morrall, *Aristotle* (London: George Allen and Unwin, 1977), 43.

2. Aristotle, *The Politics of Aristotle*, ed. and trans. Ernest Barker (New York: Oxford University Press, 1965), 317, Bk. VII, Ch. XIV, Para. 9. From here on, in citing from the *Politics*, we will cite the numbers using colons for separation. Thus, the quote just cited would be VII:XIV:9.

3. Morrall, *Aristotle*, 100.

4. Aristotle, *Politics*, 317, VII:XIV:9, and Barker's commentary on p. 320.

5. Aristotle, *Nicomachean Ethics,* trans. Terence Irwin (Indianapolis: Hackett Publishing Company, 1985), 151, 1139b23–25.

6. Ibid., 156, 1140b30–41a; as Aristotle says, "scientific knowledge is supposition about universals." Also, p. 152, 1139b33–35.

7. This example comes from Martha C. Nussbaum, *The Fragility of Goodness* (New York: Cambridge University Press, 1986), 94–97. In this example, we follow Nussbaum, who uses the word *theory* in the way we use it here.

8. Aristotle, *Ethics*, 154, 1140b5.

9. Ibid., 3, 1094a15–18. Here, political science is equated with practical intelligence, and both are distinguished from scientific knowledge; Ibid., 157, 1141aa20–30.

10. Ibid., 3, 1094b13.

11. Ibid., 4, 1094b21.

12. Nussbaum, *The Fragility of Goodness*, 305; Aristotle, *Ethics*, 158, 1141b15–18.

13. Ibid., 302–5.

14. Ibid., 305.

15. Aristotle, *Ethics*, 160–61, 1142a14–20.

16. Ibid., 158, 1141b13–15.

17. Aristotle, *Politics*, 51, II:5:13–14.

18. Ibid., 51, II:5:15.

19. Aristotle, *Ethics*, 13–14, 1097a27–b5.

20. Ibid., 17, 1098a10–15.

21. Ibid., 17, 1098a20.

22. Ibid., 42, 1106a15–25.

23. Ibid., 33, 1103a15–20, 36, 1104a20–25, 44, 1107a35–40, 48, 1108a20–25.

24. Aristotle, *Politics*, 5, I:II:8.

25. Ibid., 5–6, I:II:10–14.

26. Ibid., 7, I:II:16.
27. Ibid., 7, I:II:15.
28. Nussbaum, *The Fragility of Goodness*, 344–46, 352.
29. Aristotle, *Politics,* 3, I:II:2.
30. Ibid., 4, I:II:5.
31. Ibid., 13, I:V:6, 32, I:XII:1–2.
32. Ibid., 32, I:XII:1.
33. Ibid., 32–33, I:XII:2, 35, I:XIII:7.
34. Ibid., 36, I:XIII:11.
35. Susan Moller Okin, *Women in Western Political Thought* (Princeton, NJ: Princeton University Press, 1979), 90–92.
36. Aristotle, *Politics*, 4, I:II:5.
37. Ibid., 23–24, I:IX:5–9.
38. Ibid., 24–27, I:IX:9, 12–18.
39. Aristotle, *Ethics*, 207, 1155a; Nussbaum, *The Fragility of Goodness*, 306.
40. Aristotle, *Ethics*, 249, 1167a25.
41. Ibid., 249, 1167a30–33.
42. Ibid., 250, 1167b.
43. Ibid., 208, 1155a23–25.
44. Ibid.
45. Ibid., 208, 1155a25–28.
46. Ibid., 250, 1167a38–40, 1167b5. See Nussbaum, *The Fragility of Goodness*, 354–56.
47. Aristotle, *Ethics*, 250, 1167b5–10.
48. Ibid., 250, 1167b10–15.
49. Aristotle, *Politics*, 120, III:IX:13.
50. Aristotle, *Ethics*, 220, 1158b15–20. Here, Aristotle talked about friendship between a man and a woman, between a son and a father, and between any kind of ruler and those whom he rules, and this clearly includes the master and the slave.
51. Aristotle, *Politics*, 10, I:IV:4–5. Also see Barker commentary on p. 11.
52. Aristotle, *Politics*, 15–16, I:VI:5–9. Also, Nussbaum, *The Fragility of Goodness*, 348.
53. Aristotle, *Politics*, 16, I:VI:9–10.
54. Ibid., 17, I:VI:9–10, 35, I:XIII:7 and Barker note 3.
55. On this point, see Nussbaum, *The Fragility of Goodness*, 348.
56. Aristotle, *Politics*, 120, III:IX:14.
57. Ibid., 120, III:IX:15.
58. Ibid.
59. Ibid., 47, II:IV:7.
60. Ibid., 44, II:III:4–5.
61. Ibid., 47, II:IV:7. "A father would be very little disposed to say 'mine' of a son, and a son would be as little disposed to say 'mine' of a father."
62. Ibid., 49, II:V:6.
63. Ibid., 50, II:V:8.
64. Ibid., 49, II:V:6.
65. Ibid., 110–11, III:VI:1–6.
66. Ibid., 156, IV:I:10.
67. Ibid., 108–9, III:V:5–7.
68. Ibid., 114, III:VII:2.
69. Ibid., 114–15, III:VII:3–5.
70. Ibid., 158, IV:II:2.
71. Ibid., 236, V:X:9.
72. Ibid., 146, III:XVI:3–5.
73. Ibid.

74. Ibid., 236–37, V:X:9–11.
75. Ibid., 246, V:XI:16–17, 249, V:XI:33.
76. Ibid., 175–76, IV:VIII:7.
77. Ibid., 115–16, III:VIII:4.
78. Ibid., 272–73, VI:VII:4–5.
79. Ibid., 180, IV:XI:1. Italics in text.
80. Ibid., 180–81, IV:XI:4–8.
81. Ibid., 175, IV:VIII:3.
82. Ibid., 181, IV:XI:5.
83. Ibid.
84. Ibid., 181, IV:XI:7, IV:XI:6.
85. Ibid., 181, IV:XI:8.
86. Ibid., 182, IV:XI:11.
87. Ibid.
88. Ibid., 183, IV:XI:16–17.
89. Ibid., 158, IV. 11:2.
90. Ibid., 164, IV:IV:6.
91. Ibid., 258, VI:II:1–2.
92. Ibid., 126, III:XI:14.
93. Ibid.
94. Ibid., 258, VI:II:2.
95. Ibid., 54, II:V:25.
96. Ibid., 258, VI:II:3. Italics in text.
97. Ibid., 268–69, VI:V:8.
98. Ibid., 127, III:XI:19–21.
99. Ibid., 301, VII:IX:3–4.
100. On this point, see Nussbaum, *The Fragility of Goodness*, 347.

4

Christian Conceptions of Civic Virtue

I. Introduction

In this chapter, we survey different Christian perspectives on civic virtue, starting with St. Augustine (354–430 CE) and then moving to the late medieval thinker St. Thomas Aquinas (1225–1274). We conclude the chapter with a discussion of Reformation Christianity, including Martin Luther (1483–1546) and John Calvin (1509–1564). Common to all views of Christianity we discuss here is acceptance of the importance of Christian religious institutions to the welfare of individuals in society. In this chapter, we review the different views of Christianity provided here as we develop the respective conceptions of civic virtue, as well as the implications of these different approaches to Christianity for civil society.

This chapter is all the more relevant in a time when religious belief is used to support various political positions in US politics, such as with respect to gay marriage and abortion, and when religious belief is used to support extremist political movements. A healthy dialog among people of different approaches to issues based on religious beliefs requires understanding the foundations of these beliefs, and this chapter is dedicated to this effort. Now, to a discussion of these thinkers.

II. Introduction to Augustine: Cicero

The Roman emperor Constantine, in 313 CE, established by edict the toleration of Christianity. By the end of the fourth century, the Empire had moved to support

Christianity by destroying its competitors.[1] In particular, Constantine's period marked the beginning of the Empire's effort to destroy what had been the official Roman religion, paganism. The latter, which included worship of many gods, was subjected throughout the fourth century to various decrees of condemnation, all designed to deny paganism a place in the Empire. Some of the supporters of paganism strongly resisted this endeavor.[2]

In this context, Augustine wrote the *City of God* to defend the Christian religion against the pagan accusation that Christianity deserved the blame for the decline of the Roman Empire and, in particular, for the "sack" of Rome itself by the Goths in 410 CE.[3] In his book, Augustine defends Christianity by arguing that the actual cause of the misfortunes that the Romans have experienced is not Christianity but the absence of moral restraint on the part of the citizens and leadership of the Empire. "The lust that burned in their [Roman] hearts was more deadly than the flame which consumed their dwellings."[4] Moreover, Augustine says that pagan gods did nothing to "prevent the degeneration of traditional morality."[5] Augustine challenges Roman critics of Christianity "to quote injunctions against luxury and greed, given by their gods to the Roman people."[6] In contrast to pagan teachings, Augustine says Christian holy books are filled with "those uniquely impressive warnings against greed and self-indulgence, given everywhere to the people assembled to hear them, in thunder of oracles from the clouds of God."[7]

In further support of his case that Christianity is not the cause of the downfall of the Roman Empire, Augustine refers to the writings of Cicero (106 –43 BCE). Cicero's account of the Roman state, in *On the Commonwealth*, was written during the time of Julius Caesar, 60 BCE to 52 BCE.[8] Cicero wrote from his experiences as a prominent lawyer and elected public official. He also lived during the political upheaval and power struggles recurrent during the time of Caesar.[9] In the *City of God*, Augustine shows that Cicero's *On the Commonwealth* argues that the Roman commonwealth is predicated upon "a common sense of right and a community of interest."[10] But Cicero's view of the Empire refers to an image of its past greatness, and Cicero laments that, during his time, Roman life has not met the standards that the past set. Augustine demonstrates that Cicero feels that owing to the moral degradation of Roman life, the magnificence of the past might no longer be obtainable in the present. Augustine notes that Cicero makes this argument before Christ appears, and during a time when pagan gods show "no concern to prevent the ruin and loss of that commonwealth."[11]

The Roman Empire that Cicero hopes to restore embodies the vision of an ancient morality based on long-standing traditions that have been the basis for uniting the diverse cultures and territories of the Empire.[12] Indeed, the ancient standards, if restored and made a part of current practice, would permit a commonwealth based on the rule of law whose origin is universal reason and whose objective is liberty. Liberty, for Cicero, means the absence of external impediments that keep people from doing as they choose. But this situation is possible only when individuals voluntarily subject themselves to the limitations of law and moral principle. People then uphold these standards of civic virtue, because doing so is advantageous to securing their freedom. Freedom means more than just individual choice, however. In addition, freedom permits citizens to take part in the political affairs of the regime, and in this realm, too, individuals are to display respect for the norms of civic virtue. Cicero's view of freedom, then, is occasioned by his concept of justice. Justice is a way of life that directs us to manifest consideration for the interests of all others, and, further, Cicero expects the state to translate this concern into laws that are fair and that are applied impartially. And good laws, when implemented evenly, extend liberty to all.[13]

Lest one think Cicero is the founder of modern, liberal conceptions of civil society, it must be made clear that Cicero's vision of freedom and justice has never been used to critique the rigid class hierarchy that favors the aristocratic few against the rest of society. The Roman Empire is based on an agricultural economy with most of the wealth derived from the arduous labor of a large peasant class. Peasant-generated wealth is transferred to the aristocracy who use it to maintain a life of privilege, leisure, and control of a vast Empire. In addition, there is a large class of urban workers who perform various jobs in Rome. Some of these people are citizens, others are freedmen who have been released from slavery, and still others are freeborn. Freeborn males, often peasants forced from their homes, provide the necessary labor for building, for hulling materials, and for working on the docks and the nearby farms. Some of the freedmen are skilled craftsmen, tradesmen, teachers, doctors, or artists, and a few are well-educated men of letters. Many freedmen serve as household superintendents and civil servants, while some are confidential secretaries. Urban workers live in impoverished conditions and are subject to the power and needs of the ruling class. The lowest class consists of slaves, many of whom perform the same functions as urban workers. There is no powerful middle class of prosperous businessmen or professionals.[14]

Cicero's discussion of justice is never designed to provide reforms, which would have addressed the misery and injustice inflicted upon peasants and urban workers by the class structure that dominated Roman life. Indeed, Cicero is part of an aristocratic class who took for granted the benefits of life the other classes made possible. By appealing for a restoration of traditional values, he seeks to secure what he understands to be a civilized life, which in his case means the preservation of the socially and politically better-off class.[15] He does so despite the fact that in the abstract, at least, his concepts of justice and liberty, if applied to those on the bottom rungs of society, would have suggested social reforms to bring about a fairer and more just circumstance for all people.

Augustine does not take Cicero to task for failing to question the existing class structure and asking how it supports Cicero's ideal of a just commonwealth. Instead, Augustine takes issue with Cicero's view that there was a time, a golden age, when Roman life embodied Cicero's conception of civic virtue.[16] Augustine argues that the Roman commonwealth of Cicero's description never in fact existed. He said that "there never was real justice in the [ancient Roman] community."[17] Augustine does not deny that Rome is better ruled by the "Romans of antiquity than by their later successors."[18] Moreover, Augustine could accept that the Roman republic is a commonwealth in the sense that the citizens of Rome are united by a common agreement on behalf of shared objectives. But, for Augustine, the moral character of a commonwealth depends upon the objectives of its common efforts. "The better the objects of this agreement, the better the people."[19] But the objects of Roman commonwealth never include a love and respect for God, and consequently, there is never in place a commitment to maintain the canons of a virtuous life. "Because God does not rule there [in Rome], the general characteristic of that city is that it is devoid of true justice."[20]

That condition awaits humankind in the world to come, the kingdom beyond this world, the Kingdom of God. True justice is a condition in which everyone receives his or her due when each acts in accordance with the rational or "just order of nature." Whereas Augustine could accept that such an order exists, he argues that true justice is an objective that is not possible in the human world. And this is because individuals, owing to human frailty, are incapable of conduct in keeping with a rational order that requires people to subordinate themselves, body and soul, to God. Augustine asks, "Does not justice demonstrate . . . that she is still laboring at her task, rather than resting after reaching its completion?"[21] As Herbert Deane says:

> *Only in that city "whose founder and ruler is Christ" is mutual love the ruling principle, so that there is no need for coercion, punishment, or repression. In that city alone can men realize the noble aims proclaimed by the philosophers of Greece and Rome – complete and unbroken peace, perfect concord and harmony, true self-realization, and perpetual happiness.*[22]

Augustine's position suggests that while he retains the Platonic ideal of a just society, he does not accept that justice could ever be attained in the earthly condition. Rome is not alone in failing to achieve true justice; this outcome is common to humankind.

What, then, should we hope for in this world? What kind of commonwealth is within our grasp? For Augustine, we can only expect a society that makes possible sufficient order to ensure peace.[23] But why is this the case, or, in other terms, why does Augustine deem the hope of Plato impossible? Moreover, what are the implications for civic virtue of Augustine's political realism?

The Problem of Sin

For Augustine, the fall of man, which occurred in the Garden of Eden, is the basis for the inability of society to achieve true justice. When the first man and woman disobeyed God, sin was introduced into the world, and all humankind for the rest of time was punished. The most significant consequence of this event, according to Augustine, is that individuals lost the ability to conduct their lives in keeping with the rule of a rational will, which originally, before the fall, was able to make appetite follow a moral course. Sexual desire is perhaps the most important example of this circumstance. Before the fall, for Augustine, Adam and Eve possessed, as Anne Pagels says, "mental mastery over the procreative process: the sexual members, like the other parts of the body, enacted the work of procreation by a deliberate act of will."[24] But after the fall, Augustine believes, individuals lack the ability to control and guide their sexual urges and to subject these urges to the moral authority of the individual's rational will.

Thus, Augustine says that "had there been no lust," then "sexual organs could have been the obedient servants of mankind, at the bidding of the will."[25] For Augustine, the special casualty of lust is happiness between men and women and love within the family. For instance, owing to the presence of sin, marriage cannot bring about genuine happiness, but, instead, marriage is suffused with conflict. Had it not been for sin, "marriage would have been worthy of the happiness of paradise, and would have given birth to children to be loved, and yet would not have given rise to any lust to be ashamed of."[26]

This condition seems to imply that even though we may know what constitutes rational conduct, we are forever hampered in our ability to do what is right. Needless to say, this condition would produce for humankind a continuing sense of frustration and unhappiness. Indeed, as Pagels says, "The commonest experiences of frustration – mental agitation, bodily pain, aging, suffering, and death – continually prove to us our incapacity to implement the rule of our will."[27]

What hope, then, are we left with? For Augustine, God can release us from the pain of sin through His granting of grace.[28] Heaven and eternal happiness await those to whom God accords grace. Not all are granted grace, however. God has predestined only a few to receive this gift. As Deane points out, for Augustine, "this minority, the elect, were chosen to receive the gift of faith and, as a consequence, salvation and exemption from the just punishment of sin, without any regard to their future merits or good works." For Augustine, God has condemned the whole human race, now and into the future, to be denied salvation as a result of the fall, but it is through His mercy that a few are saved.[29]

Putting aside the theological implications of this doctrine, the social and political ones are clear enough. People who lack the knowledge of their ultimate fate live with a great degree of fear and inner turmoil. And this fact has favorable consequences to those who wish to rule them. How is this possible? In Augustine's world, people live with the great anxiety and frustration associated with uncertainty. The uncertainty is caused not only by the absence of true justice in society, but also by the fact that individuals have no certain knowledge that they are accorded God's grace. The uncertainty can become paralyzing to such an extent that a person, lacking all hope, can never have a moment of happiness or release from the ever-present painfulness of doubt. The only solution is to refuse to let uncertainty take hold in one's life. And having faith in God is one way by which to achieve this objective. But for faith to work to this end, it must be total.

Consequently, the quest for faith means individuals must place themselves into the hands of those who articulate the articles of faith, as well as those who maintain the order of society in which the faithful are protected. In each case, there are institutions of major importance placed in charge of people's lives. In one instance, the institution of importance is the church and in the other it is the state.

The Two Cities: The Earthly City and the Heavenly City

For Augustine, there are two cities, each based on a different kind of love. "The earthly city was created by self-love reaching to the point of contempt for God, the Heavenly City by the love of God carried as far as contempt of self."[30] In the earthly city, the major objective is to glorify the acts of man, but in the heavenly city, the objective is to live for the glory of God. In the earthly city, those who rule have a "lust for domination" that is manifested in the love of strength and power. In the heavenly city, all look for guidance from God, who manifests the strength of goodness and conscience.[31] Our focus for the rest of this section is the earthly city.

Given the prevalence of sin in the world, the best that any state can achieve is, as we indicated, peace and order. This means that, whereas it is possible to achieve concord among the citizens, a concord that makes peace, stability, and order possible, it is never possible to achieve true justice, a situation in which each person is given his or her due.[32] Eternal peace and justice are to be found only in the heavenly city.[33] As mentioned already, true justice awaits individuals only in the world to come.

If peace is all that people can hope for in this world, what kinds of social arrangements are prescribed to achieve peace? Peaceful relationships begin with the "ordered harmony" among those who live in the same house. Here, a wife obeys her husband, children obey their parents, and servants obey their masters. Those who give commands must manifest concern for the welfare of those to whom they give the commands.[34] Ultimately, there is a ruler who provides commands to citizens. Moreover, the ruler's main means of maintaining order, fear of punishment, is not used, as Deane says, to "make men good or virtuous, but only less harmful to their fellows."[35]

Indeed, so committed must the state be to maintaining its ability to punish, the fact of the matter is that to achieve this end it must on many occasions punish innocent people. A review of Augustine's descriptions of the plight of citizens in the court system will help make this point clear. Judges, because they cannot see "into the consciences of those on whom they [must] pronounce [guilt or innocence]," are often "compelled to seek the truth by torturing innocent witnesses in a case which is no concern of theirs."[36] But the innocent witness is not the only victim of a trial. In addition, to get at the truth, it may be necessary for a judge to torture the accused, too. In doing so, Augustine indicates that the judge acts with good intention; in particular, he is, after all, seeking the truth so his verdict can be just. He does not want to execute an innocent man. Yet, ironically, the judge may end up killing an innocent victim anyway, during the course of torturing him, to determine the accused person's guilt or innocence. "Consequently, he [the judge] has tortured an innocent man to get to the truth and has killed him while still in ignorance [as to his guilt or innocence]."[37]

Would intelligent, thinking people take their seat on the bench, given that outcomes of this sort are always inevitable? Augustine says that a "wise man" would take his seat as judge; it would be "unthinkable to him that he should shirk [his duty]."[38] To refuse to participate in the legal system as a judge demonstrates a failure to confront and to accept the "wretchedness of man's situation" that causes this dilemma in the first place.[39] In this instance, it must be accepted that people commit crimes and that proving beyond any doubt that they have is often difficult. Sometimes witnesses do not tell the truth, and at other times, defendants refuse to confess, even after being tortured. Moreover, the accusers may not be able to prove their charges. Yet, judges must decide on a defendant's guilt or innocence, even in the absence of the kind of perfect knowledge judges need to prove either one. That is their job. To do that job, at times he, "through unavoidable ignorance [on the judge's part of the defendant's guilt or innocence] and the unavoidable duty of judging . . . tortures the innocent." No judge likes to be put into this situation because no judge wants to cause harm to the innocent. Still, no judge can turn away from the fact that taking part in judging is "necessity," which arises from "human wretchedness."[40]

Augustine's discussion suggests that participation in the legal system as a judge is an unhappy obligation, needed to maintain order. Without institutions in place to mete out punishment to people, there would be complete and total chaos. What holds down the chaos is the existence of a state that strikes terror into the hearts of people. And what strikes more terror than the thought of a system that uses irrational means (torture) to achieve rational results (proof of innocence)? If innocent people are tortured, then others who are prone to commit crimes might not do so on the assumption that for certain they will be caught and tortured, too. The legal system that Augustine discusses is the opposite of ours. While we bend over backwards to protect the rights of the accused, thus allowing some guilty people to go free and unpunished, the legal system in Augustine's time moves to the other extreme, demonstrating a readiness to punish the innocent as well as the guilty. In a world in which most people are ruled by sin, heavy punishment applied indiscriminately both to the guilty and to the innocent is the only means to maintain order.

Implications of Augustine's View for Civic Virtue and Civil Society

Augustine's depiction of the earthly city demonstrates that civic virtue does not have the same significance for him that it had for Plato. As we see in Plato, civic virtue refers to the habits, such as respect for the law, that orient people to uphold the common good. These habits are the basis for enabling individuals to develop within themselves the proper arrangement of the different parts of the soul, so that overall, each can contribute to the needs of the society. Here, civic virtue suggests a basis for perfecting our souls by making our lives conform to the rational order of a just life. In this context, reason rules the appetite and subjects it to the demands of a rational life.

However, Augustine rejects this view entirely. For Augustine, even a person committed to make reason the controlling element over appetite falls short of achieving a virtuous life. And the basis for this view is that a rational faculty that is not dedicated to serving God is a rational faculty that can never bring people freedom from vice.[41] Moreover, even when people have a belief in God, the peace that faith brings only secures "solace for our wretchedness rather than the joy of blessedness."[42] In this situation, people may hope to receive only forgiveness for their sins but never perfection in the development of their virtues, as Plato had hoped for. In the earthly city, even for the faithful, it will always be the case that no matter how hard people try to subdue sin and appetite with their reason, sin reappears and undoes their best efforts. We can never attain "perfect peace" because, even for the Christian, a life dedicated to the rule of reason always runs afoul of the weaknesses that permit sin to gain the upper hand. Real happiness and true justice await entrance into the heavenly city after we pass from this life. The "ultimate peace," a life in which people are finally "healed" or cured of sin so that they can live as Plato had hoped, in keeping with their reason, awaits us in the life to come, when we have achieved "immortality."[43]

This position should not be construed to exclude the prospect of good rulers. The latter not only benefit those whom they rule by providing some degree of justice, but they also benefit themselves because, unlike the wicked, they do not destroy their souls.[44] Thus, as with Plato, there is the hope that the good will rule, but given Augustine's view of the depraved quality of human nature, it is likely that there will be few people who can make justice the main objective of their lives. In this event, true justice, where everyone receives his or her due in a rationally ordered society, is a value that would seem for Augustine to be beyond the reach of all states or what he called kingdoms. This outcome is terribly unfortunate, for where justice does not exist, a state is nothing more than a criminal organization. Augustine said:

> *Remove justice, and what are kingdoms but gangs of criminals on a large scale? What are criminal gangs but petty kingdoms? A gang is a group of men under the command of a leader, bound by a compact of association, in which the plunder is divided according to an agreed convention.*[45]

But even in the absence of true justice, the earthly city, by maintaining peace, can still at least avoid the chaos just described, and this possibility is important for Christians, who in Augustine's period lived among cultures and traditions that often had no appreciation for Christian teaching. A Christian in this setting is often like a "pilgrim in a foreign land."[46] The earthly city, although not based on love of God, can protect peace and, by doing so, permits diverse cultures to coexist in a way that does not interfere with Christians' ability to practice their religion. Christians, as members of the heavenly city during their sojourn on earth, have every interest in working for peaceful coexistence with alien cultures. Indeed, it is peace that enables Christianity to survive and to teach that the real peace "of the perfectly ordered and completely harmonious fellowship in enjoyment of God," awaits the faithful. Christians, then, are engaged in a "pilgrimage," which manifests a deep faith in God's message that the perfect peace and justice of "rational creation" and eternal life can and will ultimately prevail.[47]

Here, Christian civic virtue symbolizes the ability of people to sustain belief in a possible, happy future in a time marked by a personal struggle with sin as well as by societal conflict. The pilgrimage to the better world is merely the experience of a person who must undergo great tests to his or her faith. In addition, civic virtue suggests that, during the pilgrimage to the better world, individuals will work to maintain peace and order. Of course, order is not true justice, which can be realized only in the next world. But as long as there is peace, there is some resistance to sin, and thus there remains the hope that Christianity will remain a strong force in the world.

Augustine's world does not accommodate the civil society experience described in Chapter 1. Augustine's faithful live in fear of sin, and thus they are likely to be frightened of their own freedom; indeed, they tend to see their own freedom as a manifestation of sinfulness. It is not likely, then, that a separate sphere of associations could emerge in Augustine's society, within a larger moral environment committed to those civic virtues, like toleration and mutual respect, that are the basis for people's securing the rights of all individuals. For this situation to emerge, individuals must be first freed from the terrors that Augustine describes in the earthly city. Aquinas seems to move in this direction.

III. St. Thomas Aquinas: Justice Restored

For Augustine, faith and not reason offered a truer picture of our possibilities. For Aquinas (1225–1274), reason is restored as an important resource for understanding the nature of the world. Why is this? During Aquinas's time, largely as a result of Muslim thinkers, Aristotle's writings were rediscovered, and they inspired debate and discussion among philosophers and theologians.[48] At first, the Roman Catholic Church resisted Aristotle, even banning his work at the University of Paris. But later, the Church accepted those, such as Aquinas, who attempted to create a reconciliation between Christianity and Aristotle. In the new synthesis, both reason and faith are co-partners in understanding the just or rational structure of society.

Aquinas accepts Aristotle's view that there is a rational order to society. The farmer contributes food, the religious leaders make possible chances for spiritual awareness, and the rulers provide necessary leadership. Embodied in this view is the notion that God establishes the foundation of a rational order, and the ruler of society must contribute to maintaining the rational order of society and thus help to uphold the common good.[49] Aquinas, unlike Augustine, holds a concept of Christianity open to the view that a just, or rationally ordered, society is feasible. In taking this position, Aquinas's view of society provides the hope that a rational unity undergirds society and makes possible Aristotle's communal solidarity. But, unlike Aristotle, he believes that central to this endeavor is acceptance of God as the source of the laws that ground both the community and the authority that rulers hold over the community.

It should be noted, before proceeding to a discussion of Aquinas's view of law, that his commitment to replicating Aristotle's approach to political community in the Middle Ages provided justification for sustaining medieval Christian societies as well. Medieval societies were smaller units than what had been the experience in the Roman Empire and what would be the experience with the nation-state in modern times. These small units were centered on a king who, as the only landowner, granted his barons rights to land in exchange for their services. The barons, in turn, had under them serfs, upon whose toil the entire system was based. The serfs worked the land in exchange for food and a place to live.[50] The revenues, which arose from the tenants, barons, and serfs alike, were used to maintain an army as well as to secure order within the kingdom. In these communities, the kings were owed obedience by barons and serfs. The king was obligated to provide the barons and serfs with protection and to uphold those local customs that defined their rights and prerogatives.[51]

Obviously, then, wide differences in status existed between the king and those who worked for him. Does this mean that these communities lacked common values? Not at all. Feudal societies were Christian, and, furthermore, these societies believed that there were to be two authorities, one that was temporal – to maintain social order – and the other spiritual – to teach the lessons of faith. Neither was to interfere with the work of the other, but each was to support the other in keeping with the laws of God and reason.[52]

Aquinas upholds these common standards as well, and he seeks to strengthen them and the medieval society that embodies them. To this end, he argues that the political unit is a community making possible collaborative efforts that contribute to the common good and the moral unity of society, much as Aristotle did. Central to the success of this endeavor is the existence of civil law, whose actual foundation rests with God. Thus, the basis for community is not merely rational laws and common moral values that such laws embody, as Aristotle argues, but also the realization that the basis for this law, as the Church taught, is God. Without respect for the Church that teaches God's truth, a community among people is not be possible on earth.

In taking this position, the two realms of king and church are viewed as complementing each other, and people, by upholding the law and fulfilling their civic virtue obligations, act not only as good citizens but as good Christians, too. This combination is the basis for sustaining community even in a society in which there are wide differences in entitlements and privileges.

We turn now to a discussion of Aquinas's view of law.

The Natural Law in Aquinas

Aquinas says that there are four forms of law. Each form represents a different dimension of reason, and yet all forms of reason are integrated under the divine plan of God. The four forms of law are eternal, natural, divine, and human. *Eternal law* refers to the unchanging, timeless relationships that God creates among all things in the universe.[53] The eternal law – when manifest as natural, divine, and human law – guides human beings and the working of society. For instance, *natural law*, which is known through reason, is concerned with defining the standards of good and evil, just and unjust, by which all individuals in the society are to act.[54] *Divine law* arises from revelation, not from reason, and the content of this revelation is the morality described in Scripture.[55] Divine law's importance derives from the fact that natural law, while stating the nature of good and evil, does not by itself make clear the true end to which God directs people. By contrast, divine law makes clear that the true end of life is "eternal happiness." And, further, divine law indicates that to achieve this end, it is necessary not only to do as the natural law requires, but it is also necessary to act according to the "divine" laws given by God's command.[56]

Further, Aquinas's view of divine law is important in achieving Aristotle's communal setting. Community, as we see in Aristotle, depends upon the possibility of forms of friendship in which there is a basic understanding among individuals as to what constitutes the common moral values that are vital to the well-being of all members. These values enable people to formulate common opinions about what is best for society with respect to the way people should conduct their lives. Without a conception of the common moral values that ground the community, there might be many contradictory views as to what constitutes proper conduct, and in the face of this situation, it would be impossible to clarify the laws all should uphold. Thus, for Aquinas, "different people form different judgments on human acts," and, owing to this fact, "different and contrary laws result."[57] As a result, society finds itself torn by conflict, and consequently, this situation is antithetical to maintaining community.

To avoid this situation, it is necessary to approach matters involving human judgment from the standpoint of the shared understanding of morality found in God's words, and then each person can "know without any doubt what he ought to do and what he ought to avoid."[58] Here, because the laws given by God "cannot err," the ambiguities associated with differences in judgment are fully overcome.

In transcending these differences and in defining the common norms of conduct all share, individuals are able, as for Aristotle, to maintain a basis for the affective ties of community.

Finally, divine law suggests that, when people act virtuously, they do so not from the presence of external force alone but from right motives and choice. Here, the presence of human laws alone will not engineer virtuous conduct; individuals must, from their own volition, deny the influences of evil. Individuals who make divine law a primary basis for their lives, will, from choice and not from external force, act against evil and in keeping with what natural law requires. This is an important element of Aquinas's argument. If we have to rely upon external human laws threatening force as the basis for conformity with all natural law principles, then the law becomes so all-pervasive that it ends up threatening "many good things" and thus hindering the "advance of the common good." For Aquinas, when people do not uphold the canons of moral right from their own volition, then creating a basis for community becomes difficult. But community, based on recognition of the common good, is necessary, says Aquinas, for "human intercourse."[59] Again, as for Aristotle, the basis for community requires that there be shared moral values. In the case of Aquinas, the shared moral values include not only natural law, but divine law, or that law given to us directly from God through the Scripture. Together, these moral values form the basis for the affective ties of community.

The *human law* embodies the principles of right conduct, or natural law, in rules that govern daily life. Indeed, Aquinas says that "every human law has just so much of the nature of law as it is derived from the law of nature."[60] Since natural law provides the principled foundations of human law, it is well to discuss natural law in some detail.

The main or primary natural law principle is that the "good is that which all things seek after." Hence, "good is to be done and ensued, and evil is to be avoided."[61] For Aquinas, all other precepts of the natural law stem from this primary principle. This means that we are to do what is good and to avoid doing what is evil. What are the good things we should do? And just as important, how do we distinguish the good from the bad? For Aquinas, there are natural inclinations that our reason interprets as good, and, in following these inclinations, we do what is morally permissible. Alternatively, we should avoid pursuing ends that are contrary to our natural inclinations, for these ends are evil.

So, what are the good things we have natural inclinations to do? First, each of us wants to preserve his or her life, and, by virtue of this inclination, "whatever is a means of preserving human life and of warding off its obstacles belongs to the natural law." Second, there is an inclination to do those things that nature ingrains in all animals including human ones; in particular, we have an inclination to engage "in sexual intercourse, education of offspring, and so on." These activities, too, fall under the natural law. Third, there is a natural inclination in human beings to pursue their natures as rational persons, and this inclination exhorts us to "know the truth about God and to live in society." What pertains to this inclination falls under natural law, and this includes an obligation to "shun ignorance, to avoid offending those among whom one has to live, and other such things regarding the above inclination."[62]

Now, the primary natural law principle of always seeking to do good and the precepts that follow from it, such as those just mentioned, we will, following Aquinas, refer to as "common natural law principles" that are used as guides when determining the basis for conduct. Here, it is necessary for people to search for a correct application of these principles, and Aquinas refers to the resulting norms as *secondary principles*. When differences arise over how to interpret the common natural law principles, what is the best way to resolve them? Aquinas believes that "as to certain proper or derived norms, which are, as it were, conclusions of these common [natural law] principles, they are valid and so recognized by all men only in the majority of cases."[63] Because people would be approaching such matters from the perspective of divine law, finding acceptable and valid applications of common natural law principles should not be difficult. Once again, as for Aristotle, having common moral values in the community is the basis for establishing concord among the citizens on important questions, such as in Aquinas's case, providing interpretations of common natural law principles. The only hindrance to achieving acceptable secondary principles emerges during those times when people's reason has been "distorted by passion."[64]

But how useful is Aquinas's natural law doctrine? Those who argue that natural law is not very helpful might point out that too often natural law principles are so vague they can provide little guidance to us as we try to determine the best route of conduct. For instance, take the natural law principle that requires us to do good and to avoid evil by preserving human life and removing whatever might injure life. What does this principle suggest for how one should determine one's position on abortion? The answer to this question depends largely upon factors other than the principle itself. After all, both those for and against abortion might use this principle to justify their respective positions, but, in the end, each party's decision is based on other considerations, such as one's view of privacy, of the status of the fetus, and so on. One might use this case to make the claim that natural law principles are not really useful guides in resolving key moral dilemmas, such as the abortion dilemma.

On the other hand, some proponents of natural law might argue that authentic natural law principles provide in a clear and definitive way the moral course we should take on various key issues. If natural law fails in this regard, it is not so much the fault of natural law, it is the fault of the natural law theorist who has failed to compose the natural law in a way that makes it useful. Indeed, the proponent of natural law can argue that great progress has been made in the modern world to draw up principles that, in unambiguous ways, prescribe the course of proper conduct. For instance, the contemporary principle that says individuals should respect the rights of others is clear as to what kinds of actions are entailed by this principle. From this principle, we know that we should eliminate all slavery as well as remove from society all obstacles that stand in the way of equal rights and fair opportunities for all people, regardless of race, gender, sexual preference, and so on. In this case, natural law is a great help in achieving not only a just society but also a society that seeks to balance the quest for freedom with the need to secure the basic needs of people.

Human Law and Civic Virtue

Given these competing views of natural law, which one, it might be asked, does Aquinas subscribe to? Clearly, it is his hope that natural law should represent the precise moral framework for the members of a community. But how is this achieved? Of course, one way would be to teach people the importance of divine law. But another important approach to this objective is to emphasize civic virtue. For Aquinas, people who lack a commitment to make the community's good their own will naturally interpret the natural law in any way they wish, and they will not likely see natural law as providing the precise moral boundaries of life. It is for this reason, for instance, that Aquinas worries that, whereas primary natural law principles cannot be "blotted out from men's hearts," the power of reason to understand the precise significance of these principles for particular actions is compromised by the presence of lust and appetite. In this case, the general principle to be followed is known, but reason is "hindered from applying the general principle to a particular point of practice, on account of concupiscence or some other passion."[65] Moreover, knowledge of the correct secondary principles that individuals should follow can be "blotted out from the human heart by evil persuasions."[66]

Human law is an important instrument in overcoming both of these problems and in giving natural law its recurring importance as a precise set of moral boundaries for determining the nature of conduct. Human law, which embodies natural law principles, must teach virtue and accustom individuals to uphold the teachings of natural law. Through the shaping influence of "training" and, in particular, the "fear of punishment," individuals learn the "discipline of laws" and are reminded that they must accommodate their lives to the proper course of conduct laid out by both primary and secondary natural law principles.[67] A major function of the community is to teach the important civic virtues that orient people away from tendencies to selfishness and a lack of regard for the common good. In this regard, as in Plato's and Aristotle's views of a rational society, human law helps to clarify the particular roles in the society and what the expected contributions of people to each of those roles should be. For instance, soldiers should defend the nation, priests should provide spiritual knowledge, and rulers should govern justly.[68]

But Aquinas warns us to adopt a practical set of expectations pertaining to what we can hope to achieve through human law. It must be clear that, since the majority of people do not manifest moral perfection, it is impossible to create human laws that will be able to eradicate all vices. The best the human law can do, then, is to eliminate the grosser vices, those actions that, if permitted, would undermine human society, and for this reason there must be laws against murder, theft, and so on.[69]

This point of view suggests as well that it would be wrong to try to create human laws that eradicated all vices. Were such an objective to be embodied into human law, there would have to be morals police on every corner questioning each person about the moral nature of their intentions, and each of us would have to check with these police to see if our proposed activities were morally sanctioned. This situation would hardly be a place receptive to building the affective ties of community. In this spirit, for instance, Aquinas says at times "it is right for those who are in authority to tolerate some evils so as not to prevent other goods or to avoid some worse evil from occurring."[70] Following this line of argument, Aquinas cites with approval Augustine, who says, "Suppress prostitution and the world will be torn apart by lust." Further, unbelievers may be tolerated for Aquinas, "because a greater good may come of it or some evil may be avoided."[71]

Aquinas on the Question of Civic Virtue and Civil Society

Nonetheless, the major purpose of Aquinas's view of human law is to teach people the habits of civic virtue, which enable people to uphold the common good. But unlike Aristotle, Aquinas believes that the habits of civic virtue, which teach respect for the moral boundaries embodied in the natural law, can be sustained over the long run only when individuals share a belief in the Catholic Church's teachings of the nature of divine law. Here, when individuals understand that they are part of a common world ordained by God, they not only understand the origin of morality and natural law, but they also experience as the source of morality the same religious inspiration that helps to bind people together communally. Certainly, Aristotle hoped for a political community predicated upon friendship and communal solidarity, but Aquinas would argue that that hope is best realized when the members of society hold in common a commitment to divine law and faith in the teachings of the Catholic Church.

But from the standpoint of modern civil society thinkers, a significant problem with Aquinas's view of civic virtue would remain. For Aquinas, individuals must make the teachings of the Catholic Church the centerpiece of their lives. Aquinas, in discussing heresy, says that "if it is just for counterfeiters or other criminals to be executed immediately by secular rulers, it is all the more just for heretics once they are convicted of heresy not only to be excommunicated but to be put to death."[72] He qualifies this harsh statement by saying that the Church hopes for conversion of "those who are in error." Here, there is no question that Aquinas is protecting society from all those who might undermine belief and with it the benefits of community. Still, in taking this view, Aquinas demonstrates that a single institution, the Church, must have a powerful role to play in the moral and intellectual lives of each citizen. Given this fact, individuals, in reasoning about what is best for society, are not to question the Church's authority in matters of truth.

Now, as we have seen, a civil society suggests the need for a separate sphere in which individuals can move among different groups and from this experience determine the way of life that is best for themselves. But for Aquinas, this view of society might pose a threat to the autonomy of the Church and, in particular, to its ability to determine the nature of moral order in the society. We now turn to Reformation thinking to discuss the approach to Christianity found there.

IV. Luther and Calvin: An Introduction

For Martin Luther and John Calvin, the central target is the authority of the Roman Catholic Church. Luther argued, as Sheldon Wolin points out, that "religious experience was located around an intensely personal communication between the individual and God."[73] Individuals must have a direct relationship with God, which is built upon faith. Faith cleanses the soul and allows us to love God. By virtue of faith, our souls desire that "all things" and (most importantly) our bodies will become morally pure so that we will be able to love God. As a result of faith, then, a person comes to obey the commandments of the Scripture and to repress "lasciviousness and lust." For Luther, "faith alone and the Word of God rule in the soul. Just as the heated iron glows like fire because of the union of fire with it, so the Word imparts its qualities to the soul."[74]

Given this view, Luther seeks to remove as much as possible the various structures of established Church authority. These structures only serve to impede the direct relationship that individuals must have with God.[75] Moreover, in removing these structures, Luther hopes to accord people greater spiritual freedom. Luther says that an individual is to be "responsible for his own faith, and he must see to it for himself that he believes rightly."[76] In Luther's community of believers, faith is a matter to be left to each individual, and no one is to force another to believe doctrines that individuals do not embrace from their own volition and conscience. "Faith is a free work, to which no one can be forced."[77]

In contrast, as Wolin says, Calvin does not accept that the religious community could exist as a freely subscribed-to setting, governed by persuasion and not force, but that it could exist only if there were maintained a strong structure of authority to secure the "coherence and solidarity of the group." The church community, without restoring a pope, should be governed by a strong leadership group.[78] Thus, Calvin believes that a church, in this case, his church, must establish a regimen of discipline to limit and constrain all people so that they are capable of accepting the teachings of God. Without the discipline the church can provide, human beings stray from the teachings of the church, and this consequence "promote[s] the entire dissolution of the Church."[79] Here, the church is right to lay down rules pertaining to people's sex lives, their leisure, and their relationships within families.[80]

Ironically, as individuals are weaned away from the authority of the Roman Catholic Church, they are placed under a new church authority whose purpose, as Wolin argues, is to "mould the members to a common outlook and instruct them in the lessons of the common good."[81] For Calvin, the impact of the new church on individuals is to make people subject to the requirements of order and discipline or to the norms of civic virtue. And the consequences of this policy are to ensure that each person is a good contributing member to society, while at the same time a strong and committed believer.[82]

Luther and Calvin: Morality and Civic Virtue

Both Luther and Calvin require citizens to have allegiance to the state and to respect its efforts to maintain order. For Luther, for all people to be motivated by God's Word, there would be no need for a state to impose order and maintain constraints. Luther says that Christ acknowledges a sword, but he does not need to use it in His Kingdom. But Luther believes that those who live by the Word of God, Christians, are in the minority, and thus most people are not motivated by Christian piety.[83] There is a need for the state, therefore, to use its force to ensure compliance with the law and thus to maintain order sufficient to protect the lives and property of individuals.[84]

Given that Christians' piety makes the use of force as the basis for good conduct unnecessary for them, should Christians submit to a state that uses force to secure compliance with the laws? Luther answers in the affirmative. A true Christian subordinates him- or herself to the state and does all he or she can "to further government, that it may be sustained and held in honor and fear."[85] In the secular world, the Christian must manifest civic virtue by upholding two contradictory moral systems. Christian morality requires that individuals be concerned to labor "on earth not for himself" but for others. Christian morality "impels him to do even that which he need not do." Thus, the Christian helps the sick, and does what is "necessary for his neighbor."[86] But, in addition, the good Christian must contribute his or her share to the order-keeping dimension of society, and this means that at times he or she may have to kill for the state. "Therefore, should you see that there is a lack of hangmen, beadles [macebearers], judges, lords or princes, and find that you are qualified, you should offer your services."[87]

Calvin holds a similar view of the moral responsibilities of citizenship. He indicates that, in the political world, a major concern of government is with the ongoing needs of physical existence, including the provision of food and clothing, as well as enacting laws for the purpose of regulating society by the "rules of holiness, integrity, and sobriety."[88] Thus, it is necessary to recognize the importance of a civil government that supports the worship of God, to preserve "pure" religious doctrines, "to defend the constitution of the Church," and to maintain among people peace and civil justice.[89] To accomplish these purposes, it is necessary for the state to use methods of severe punishment so that the innocent are protected from the activities of the "wicked." In doing so, however, the state is not acting in a way that is at "variance" with the reign of Christ. For the truth is that there are some people so wicked and evil that without the authority of the state to crush them there is no basis for a civil, Christian life.[90] Here, it will be necessary, as in Luther, for those who are asked to carry out the state's commitment to civil order, to resort to practices that appear to be contrary to Christian morality, such as killing. Indeed, unless the state resists evil, there is no way to provide a sphere that can preserve Christian teaching. Thus, in acting as the state requests, even if this means killing others in the name of resisting evil, one is sustaining the basis for a Christian state, and, actually, then, maintaining a commitment to Christian principles.

Still, for Calvin, Christians are warned not to adopt the ways of those from whom the state must protect them. "God not only enjoins the preservation of the mind chaste and pure from every libidinous desire, but prohibits all obscenity of language and external lasciviousness."[91] Also for Calvin, as for Luther, living a life at peace with God requires that individuals demonstrate charity and service to their neighbors.[92] In living day-to-day life, Christians must manifest civic virtue by being able to "bear injuries and reproaches" and to "do good to them from whom they experience injuries."[93] At the same time, as part of what it means to maintain civic virtue, Christians must obey the state and carry out those policies that promote order and civility.

The State and Intellectual Freedom in Luther and Calvin

In discussing the role of the state, neither Luther nor Calvin sees the state as a protector of intellectual or moral freedom. Initially, it might appear otherwise for Luther, who says that the state must not use its authority to interfere with the church teachings and "prescribe laws for the soul."[94] In taking this position, Luther makes clear that a state seeking to maintain Catholic doctrines is not to bully citizens. Thus, he says that "if then your prince or temporal lord commands you to hold with the pope, to believe this or that, or commands you to give up certain books, you should say, it does not befit Lucifer to sit by the side of God."[95] The view that the state must not impose Catholic doctrines is in keeping with the previously stated position Luther has that individuals should derive their faith from their own conscience and volition.[96]

Luther is concerned not only with protecting people from the Catholic Church, but also with securing political order. Wolin says that Luther believes that, in the face of the many evils facing society, the political order is very fragile. To prevent the destruction of the fabric of society, the state is given a divine mission to uphold order, and, if successful, the state would then help to secure the prospects of the newly reformed church Luther advocated.[97] In taking this direction, Luther believes that the state must protect the doctrines of the reformed church, and thus he contends that the government can deny a right to a person to question the main ideas of the Christian creed. Luther's view would not support ways of life and basic rights for individuals whose conduct conflicts with church teachings.[98] Ironically, then, Luther, who in the spiritual realm argues for intellectual freedom, must in the political realm argue against it. As Wolin says, "The divine element in political authority was inevitably transformed from a sustaining principle into a repressive, coercive one."[99]

Calvin suggests a repressive state, with respect to freedom of beliefs, too. Quoting scripture, Calvin says that "rulers are ministers of God, revengers to execute wrath upon him that doeth evil."[100] Christian civil magistrates are the "vice-gerents" [deputies] of God, and, as such, they must always defend God's "honor."[101] Thus, the state must not only protect people's property, maintain peace, and secure justice, but it must also make sure that the "law of God be not violated and polluted by public blasphemies."[102] The state holds power to promote religious purposes and doctrine. Moreover, both the church and the state are to be partners in maintaining sufficient control and power over individuals to ensure that they maintain civil conduct as well as respect for the religious creed. As Wolin says, "In both worlds Calvin conceived man to be a creature of order, subject to restraints and controlled by power."[103] In holding this view, Calvin does not accept that individuals can be permitted to challenge the moral premises upon which their view of the state and church rests, and thus Calvin denies intellectual freedom in the same way Luther does.[104]

Because Luther's church is to be a community of believers, not subject to repressive church structures, it seems that Luther more than Calvin promotes the goals of a civil society. But given that Luther's state is as repressive as Calvin's, Luther no more than Calvin could support a separate sphere, independent of the power of the state. Nor would it be the case that Luther any more than Calvin could make possible a moral environment that made a full doctrine of rights a mainstay.

V. The Implications for Civic Virtue and Civil Society

The doctrine of Christian civic virtue for Luther and Calvin requires individuals to support the state in its effort to thwart sin and protect, as we just demonstrated, the integrity of Christianity, especially against its detractors. Thus, in upholding the habits of civic virtue, citizens make their contributions to the state, maintaining even those functions that might appear to be opposed to Christian beliefs, such as killing. This view of civic virtue, which suggests that citizens must support the state's efforts to maintain peace and civil justice, accepts Augustine's realism that most people will not live lives that minimize the need for the state to use force to ensure the peace. Given that there will be those who always threaten good order, it would be difficult to imagine how, for Luther and Calvin, Aquinas's communal solidarity based upon a rationally organized and structured society would be possible. On this score, Luther and Calvin seem to share with Augustine the same perspective on society.

Still, an important civil society aspect might be said to emerge from the Luther and Calvin Reformation effort. The Reformation's call for autonomy from external institutions, such as a government-sponsored Catholic Church, points in the direction of a civil society with a separate sphere, as discussed in Chapter 1, in which people can exercise their freedom of conscience and determine their own religious commitments. Of course, the Reformation thinkers we have discussed here did not demand this kind of environment, and, admittedly, each of them would have rejected it. Nonetheless, what laid the basis for establishing an independent sphere of life not subject to state interference was the thrust of the Reformation in arguing that an individual's faith should govern him or her rather than external, controlling institutions.

Thus, in uniting the need for autonomy from the Catholic Church with charity and with a concern for others, as Luther and Calvin both did, a basis is created to move in the direction of a civil society. All that is needed to complete the project is to replace the repressive form of state that both Luther and Calvin advocate (as well as the repressive religious community that Calvin advocates) with a state whose foundation is a moral environment that protects rights. Now, some might argue that the writings of Thomas Hobbes, Benedict Spinoza, John Locke, and Immanuel Kant, whom we discuss subsequently, move in this direction by taking the central Christian ideas of autonomy and charity and rendering them in secular form. If this is the case, then, in an indirect way, Christian thinking has helped to make possible the experience of a civil society.

Notes

1. Mulford Q. Sibley, *Political Ideas and Ideologies: A History of Political Thought* (New York: Harper and Row, 1970), 170.
2. John O'Meara, "Introduction," in St. Augustine, *City of God*, trans. Henry Bettenson (London: Penguin Books, 1972), x.
3. Augustine, *City of God*, 49, Bk. II, Ch. 2; George H. Sabine, *A History of Political Theory* (New York: Holt, Rinehart and Winston, 1961), 189.
4. Augustine, *City of God*, 49, Bk. II, Ch. 2, 50, Bk. II, Ch. 3.
5. Ibid., 51, Bk. II, Ch. 4.
6. Ibid., 70, Bk. II, Ch. 19.
7. Ibid., 75–76, Bk. II, Ch. 22.
8. George H. Sabine and Stanley B. Smith, "Introduction," in Cicero, *On the Commonwealth*, trans. George H. Sabine and Stanley B. Smith (Indianapolis: Bobbs-Merrill, 1929), 44–45.
9. Ibid., 2.
10. Augustine, *City of God*, 73, Bk. II, Ch. 21.
11. Ibid., 74, Bk. II, Ch. 21.
12. Neal Wood, *Cicero's Social and Political Thought* (Berkeley: University of California, 1988), 206–7.
13. Sabine and Smith, "Introduction," 49, 55–56.
14. Wood, *Cicero's Social and Political Thought*, 16–21.
15. Ibid., 207, 211.
16. Sabine and Smith, "Introduction," 47.

17. Augustine, *City of God,* 75, Bk. II, Ch. 21.
18. Ibid.
19. Ibid., 890, Bk. XIX, Ch. 24.
20. Ibid., 891, Bk. XIX, Ch. 24.
21. Ibid., 854, Bk. 19, Ch. 4.
22. Herbert A. Deane, *The Political and Social Ideas of St. Augustine* (New York: Columbia University Press, 1963), 11.
23. Augustine, *City of God,* 872, Bk. XIX, Ch. 14.
24. Elaine Pagels, *Adam, Eve, and the Serpent* (New York: Random House, 1988), 111; see also, pp. 108–10.
25. Augustine, *City of God,* 585, Bk. 14, Ch. 23.
26. Ibid.
27. Pagels, *Adam, Eve, and the Serpent,* 110.
28. Augustine, *City of God,* 513, Bk. XIII, Ch. 3.
29. Deane, *The Political and Social Ideas of St. Augustine,* 19.
30. Augustine, *City of God,* 593, Bk. XIV, Ch. 28.
31. Ibid., 593–94, Bk. XIV, Ch. 28.
32. Deane, *The Political and Social Ideas of St. Augustine,* 125–26.
33. Augustine, *City of God,* 872, Bk. XIX, Ch. 14.
34. Ibid., 873–74, Bk. XIX, Ch. 14.
35. Deane, *The Political and Social Ideas of St. Augustine,* 134; see also pp. 117, 125.
36. Augustine, *City of God,* 859, Bk. XIX, Ch. 6.
37. Ibid., 860, Bk. XIX, Ch. 6.
38. Ibid.
39. Ibid.
40. Ibid., 60–61, Bk. XIX, Ch. 6.
41. Ibid., 891, Bk. XIX, Ch. 25.
42. Ibid., 892, Bk. XIX, Ch. 27.
43. Ibid., 893, Bk. XIX, Ch. 27.
44. Ibid., 138–39, Bk. IV, Ch. 3.
45. Ibid., 139, Bk. IV, Ch. 4.
46. Ibid., 877–78, Bk. XIX, Ch. 17.
47. Ibid., 878–79, Bk. XIX, Ch. 17.
48. Sabine, *A History of Political Theory,* 247–48; Paul E. Sigmund, "Introduction," in *St. Thomas Aquinas: On Politics and Ethics,* ed. Paul E. Sigmund (New York: Norton, 1988), xvi–xix.
49. Sabine, *A History of Political Theory,* 249.
50. Ibid., 214–15.
51. Ibid., 216.
52. Ibid., 225.
53. St. Thomas Aquinas, *The Summa Theologica,* ed. Dino Bigongiari, in *The Political Ideas of St. Thomas Aquinas* (New York: Hafner, 1965), 12.
54. Ibid., 13–14.
55. Sabine, *A History of Political Theory,* 253.
56. Aquinas, *The Summa Theologica,* 17.
57. Ibid.
58. Ibid.
59. Ibid., 17–18.
60. Ibid., 58.
61. Ibid., 45.
62. Ibid., 45–46.
63. Ibid., 50, 52.

64. Ibid.

65. Ibid., 54.

66. Ibid.

67. Ibid., 56.

68. Ibid., 63.

69. Ibid., 68.

70. Aquinas, *The Summa of Theology*, in Paul E. Sigmund, *St. Thomas Aquinas: On Politics and Ethics*, ed. Paul E. Sigmund (New York: Norton, 1988), 62.

71. Ibid.

72. Ibid., 63.

73. Sheldon S. Wolin, *Politics and Vision* (Boston: Little, Brown and Company, 1960), 149.

74. Martin Luther, "On Christian Liberty," in *Three Treatises: Martin Luther* (Philadelphia: Fortress Press, 1960), 282–84, 294–96.

75. Wolin, *Politics and Vision*, 152.

76. Martin Luther, "Secular Authority: To What Extent Should It Be Obeyed?" in *Great Political Thinkers: Plato to the Present*, ed. William Ebenstein and Alan O. Ebenstein (Chicago: Holt, Rinehart and Winston, 1991), 351.

77. Ibid.

78. Wolin, *Politics and Vision*, 167–68.

79. John Calvin, "Institutes of the Christian Religion," in Ebenstein and Ebenstein, *Great Political Thinkers*, 357.

80. Sibley, *Political Ideas and Ideologies*, 322.

81. Wolin, *Politics and Vision*, 179.

82. Ibid., 190, 172, 182.

83. Luther, "Secular Authority," 347.

84. Ibid., 350.

85. Ibid., 348.

86. Ibid.

87. Ibid., 349.

88. John Calvin, "On Christian Liberty," in *On God and Political Duty* (Indianapolis: Bobbs-Merrill, 1950), 41.

89. Calvin, "Institutes of the Christian Religion," 359, 361.

90. Ibid.

91. Calvin, "On Christian Liberty," 43.

92. Ibid., 37.

93. Calvin, "On Civil Government," 69.

94. Luther, "Secular Authority," 350.

95. Ibid., 353.

96. Ibid., 351.

97. Wolin, *Politics and Vision*, 156–57.

98. Sibley, *Political Ideas and Ideologies*, 318–19.

99. Wolin, *Politics and Vision*, 157–58.

100. Calvin, "On Civil Government," 49.

101. Calvin, "Institutes of the Christian Religion," 360.

102. Ibid.

103. Wolin, *Politics and Vision*, 173.

104. Sibley, *Political Ideas and Ideologies*, 323.

5

Elements of Islamic and Jewish Medieval Political Thought

I. Introduction: Alfarabi's Legacy

Aristotle remained outside of philosophical and religious discourse during most of the medieval period in the West, until, as we address in Chapter 4, he was rediscovered in Aquinas's time. How did Aristotle and classical Greek thought, including Plato, once again become central to Western thought after so long an absence? The rediscovery of Plato and Aristotle in the Western medieval world was made possible by Islamic culture. As early as the ninth century, the study of Greek contributions in science and philosophy were brought into Islamic society through the monetary support of several Islamic political authorities.[1] And as Islamic society made its way through North Africa and Spain it brought along its intellectual and religious culture, including Greek philosophy.

However, within the Islamic medieval world itself, philosophy faced difficulties surviving. Philosophy, with its origins in Greek culture, often was viewed as a foreign intrusion into Islamic societies and thus was resented by religious leaders in the Muslim world. Many Islamic religious leaders thought Islamic approaches to discovering truth should be followed on all occasions. Those who held this view argued that Islamic sources could best provide an understanding of the structure of nature as well as how to construct a good society based on interpretations of Islamic law in local circumstances.[2]

Of course, in classical Greek philosophy, issues such as the structure of nature and the way to achieve a good society were approached from the perspective of reason, and religious arguments had little place. But in Islamic societies, the Koran, the Muslim holy book, as well as the sayings of the Prophet Muhammad and his followers, gave clear answers to vexing questions. As Oliver Leaman says, from the standpoint of Islamic religious leaders, the information from these sources provides "unambiguous answers to the important questions concerning how people ought to live, how the world was created, what sort of state should be constructed, which types of behaviour are valid and which wicked, and so on."[3]

Further, Islam was buttressed by a history of mysticism, which permitted particular individuals with special qualities to claim a direct understanding of God. In the face of this prospect, it was natural that many Islamic religious leaders thought that philosophy was unnecessary. Islamic philosophers disagreed, and to support their arguments, they invoked the name of Aristotle. For Islamic religious leaders, however, if Aristotle, a non-Muslim, could evoke truth without Islam, what, then, would be the value of Islam?[4] And, thus, Islamic religious leaders often argued against philosophy's methods, suggesting that these methods produce not only flawed reasoning but also wrong-headed conclusions. In contrast, Islamic philosophers persisted in believing that their methods were the best path to truth.[5]

Despite these complaints from Islamic religious leaders, Greek philosophy had a strong foothold in Islamic societies. The Islamic philosopher who played a substantial role in furthering the study of Greek philosophy in Islamic culture was Alfarabi (870–950 CE).[6] Charles Butterworth says that "it is now generally conceded that Alfarabi deserves to be recognized as the one who first introduced political philosophy into Islamic culture and that Avicenna . . . and Averroes all take their bearings from him as much as from Plato and Aristotle."[7]

Of Turkish descent, Alfarabi became known in Baghdad as a principal authority on philosophy and logic.[8] He lived during a time of political and social instability. Yet, despite this circumstance, strong support continued during Alfarabi's time for studying Greek philosophy. Indeed, Miriam Galston says that he was part of a period that could be called the "renaissance of Islam." Baghdad had a rich cultural life punctuated by public debates among opposing schools of thought on such subjects as logic and grammar. There were also vigorous discussions as to whether religious writings should be understood literally or were to be interpreted by the methods of philosophy. In addition, Baghdad was a center for philosophers who worked to translate and to comment on the writings of Aristotle, as well as other Greek thinkers. In this setting, Alfarabi had a productive career, during which he wrote on Aristotle's ethics, physics, and metaphysics. He also wrote a commentary on Plato's *Laws*, and he prepared summaries of both Aristotle's and Plato's political thoughts.[9]

Alfarabi, as Galston says, thought that "religion is an imitation of philosophy."[10] Alfarabi believed that religion and philosophy both seek to know answers to similar questions, but that philosophy provides a superior account of knowledge than does religion.[11] Nonetheless, religion must not be discounted in importance. For Alfarabi, the truths of philosophy are well beyond the grasp of ordinary people to comprehend. But these truths can still be conveyed through religious concepts and symbolism.[12]

A central concern in this chapter is to explain the place of political philosophy in medieval Islamic and Jewish thought. To do so, it is necessary to discuss what we mean by reasoning, the chief function of philosophy. Reasoning is composed of two essential activities. In the first place, reasoning requires us to define the basic assumptions and definitions that are the starting points and building blocks of an argument. Further, once these assumptions are determined, the next question pertains to their accuracy. Indeed, a large part of philosophical analysis involves questioning the validity of basic assumptions by determining if evidence can support them.

Secondly, there is the question of the argument's form. In this regard, it is essential to see if the conclusions of an argument follow logically from the argument's basic assumptions and definitions. The form of the argument thus starts with assumptions X and Y and then moves from them logically to conclusion Z. For instance, in religious arguments, the basic starting point is often the assumption that God exists. The conclusions are what follow logically from that assumption. Once one posits a definition of God and describes God's characteristics, for instance (as we see in Maimonides), the rational ends God makes necessary, then logic is used to construct a fuller, more comprehensive vision of the world that is built from these assumptions.

Political philosophers embrace the techniques of philosophy throughout discussions of political, religious, or ethical matters. Overall, political philosophy, employing well-grounded assumptions and flawless logic, seeks to construct visions that define approaches to enhancing the best prospects of human life. A dominant vision in the works we discuss in this chapter embraces the enterprises of classical Greek thinkers such as Plato and Aristotle. In this regard, a main concern of political philosophy is to build communities that satisfy humankind's need for a happy and contented life through a society that teaches moral virtue to its citizens. Moral virtue orients individuals to restrain desires in ways that make possible respect for the common good, as embodied in the laws of a community.

Further, the different writers we discuss in this chapter use political philosophy to define the proper relationship between faith and reason. In this regard, the Islamic and Jewish traditions highlighted in this chapter did for Islamic and Jewish thought what Aquinas did for the Christian tradition, as we discuss in Chapter 4. And in doing so, it is necessary to create a secure place for philosophy in society. Moreover, from the standpoint of the main theme of this book, creating a place in society for philosophy helps to pave the way for civil society in future generations. For, to sustain philosophy – and the intellectual inquiry it demands – a space that makes possible toleration and mutual respect for diverse ideas and ways of life is necessary. And that space is called a civil society.

II. Avicenna: The Philosopher and the Lawgiver

Avicenna (980–1037 CE) lived in the eastern Middle East in Persia, or the area that is known now as Iran. His world, like each of the Islamic thinkers discussed here, was feudal, and, as such, it was filled with diverse power centers, governed by local monarchs, each of whom was grounded in Muslim law and tradition. Avicenna served several of these rulers, first as a physician, but later and for the bulk of his career as a high administrative official in government. As a person of great skill, local rulers could count on him to help manage the state effectively.[13] He performed this role in a context characterized by a tendency of Muslim monarchs to bring to their courts a thriving intellectual culture. As Peter Heath says, "Rulers [during Avicenna's times] were perfectly aware that the attendance of eminent poets, noted scholars, and learned theologians at their courts added an aura of cultural glory that reinforced their shaky claims to legitimacy."[14]

Thus, rulers needed philosophers. And the rulers' need for philosophers was matched by the philosophers' need for patrons. Without a patron, a philosopher lacked the financial means needed to continue philosophy. In fact, during the last 15 years of his life, Avicenna found a benefactor who permitted him to devote himself to philosophy.[15] His efforts in this regard yielded important results. Heath says that Avicenna's main contribution was to forge Aristotle's work into a cohesive and insightful whole for future generations in both Islamic and Western societies.[16]

Avicenna, in addressing major issues, seeks to accommodate the truth made available through reason with the worldview that is central to Islamic religious thought. To this end, he begins with the view that the elements constituting life – whether in nature or in the human world – need to be explained in terms of cause-and-effect relationships.[17] Avicenna depicts the cosmos as a unified whole, governed by a first principle, also referred to as a first cause, which is known as God. Using the first cause as the main starting point in any argument, all events can be logically understood in terms of a chain of cause-and-effect relationships. As Shlomo Pines says, "In fact, Avicenna's system is strictly deterministic. And this determinism extends to God and His activity."[18] Given this viewpoint, he could conceptualize a unified system that included all elements of the universe, including all things in nature, the solar system, and human life. Reason, when used in this manner, helps to explain the cosmos as well as some of its essential components, including human society.[19]

How did Avicenna conceptualize society? Avicenna believed that individuals are, as Aristotle says, social by nature, and because of this, people need to be part of a political community if they are to have happy, contented lives. In this community, individuals learn, in keeping with the directive of moral virtue, to discipline their own desires to support the common welfare. Ironically, ordinary people are not by themselves capable of forging a political community that achieves this end. Why is this the case? For Avicenna, because each person seeks to make his or her interests primary, people are hostile to each other, and moral virtue seems beyond the grasp of most people. As a result, people accept only laws that benefit themselves while harming others. This approach to life guarantees that ordinary people are incapable of forming a political community based on laws that embody the needs of all people.[20]

How can political community, which is so necessary for a decent human life, be formed if ordinary people are incapable of forming it? Avicenna believed that special people or great leaders – called lawgivers or legislators – form political community. Lawgivers are political leaders with special abilities to shape a community, subject to a law common to all. Lawgivers accomplish this purpose even among people who, because of their self-serving demeanors, manifest extreme hostility toward each other.[21] In achieving community among people who are so much at odds, lawgivers are like prophets. As Pines says in speaking of Avicenna's views on lawgivers, "Only a prophet, i.e., a man endowed with certain faculties not found in the common run of people, can create a social bond between them and thus preserve them from the calamities and the destruction that wait upon the solitary."[22]

What produces lawgivers in a situation that seems so hostile to them? After all, if ordinary people are incapable of creating political community, why would special leaders, with the ability to construct political community based on respect for the common good, emerge among them? Avicenna's answer is that such leaders and their successes in obtaining common laws and political community are an inevitable development of nature.[23] The lawgiver is thus a natural product of a world designed to achieve rational ends, such as political community, despite the proclivities of individuals to act otherwise.

An equally important question pertains to what role the philosopher would have in a situation where political community depends for its existence upon the prophetic-like quality of a special leader. Avicenna suggests that true prophets must have the qualities of philosophers.[24] In fact, philosophers naturally inherit the mantle of prophets. As James Morris says, for Avicenna, "the true 'knowers' and rightful 'heirs of the prophets' are the accomplished philosophers."[25] Now, since lawgivers manifest the character of prophets, then the special political leaders that make possible political community would also be expected to demonstrate the highest qualities of philosophers. Indeed, true leaders are not only the heirs of prophets, but these leaders also embody the best contributions of philosophers. In consequence, to establish political community, there must be political leaders/ philosophers who can help people realize the moral qualities of their social nature, even when ordinary people are not capable of doing so themselves.

In providing such a prominent place for philosophy, Avicenna puts a premium on what philosophy must have to be useful – a place of respect in society. This circumstance helps to set the stage for a civil society, if not in his own time, at least in subsequent generations.

III. Averroes: The Importance of Democracy

Averroes (1126–1198) of Cordoba (in Muslim Spain and Muslim North Africa) maintained his intellectual independence in settings not always receptive to his philosophical activities. Indeed, at the end of his career at the age of 70, he and his followers were banished from Cordoba by the Muslim ruler and forbidden, along with everyone else, from engaging in philosophy. Moreover, after Averroes's death a year later, a ban on philosophy by the ruling authority remained in place.[26]

A distrust of philosophy characterizes Averroes's circumstances. Muslim Spain and North Africa were the frontiers of Islamic advances into the West, and unlike the eastern Muslim world, which was more settled, Spain and North Africa had to confront traditions hostile to Islam. In the face of this reality, Islamic authorities exhorted people to accept literal teachings, or the exact meaning of the words, of religious texts.[27] Averroes rejected this approach, and according to Fred Bratton held the view that "the philosopher could view it [the Koran] in the light of reason and make his own interpretations."[28] Philosophers, as well as philosophy, survived in many local settings of Muslim Spain and North Africa because the state lacked the total control necessary to prevent philosophy.[29] Thus, in this context, Averroes produced important commentaries on Aristotle and on Plato's *Republic*, the main work discussed in this section.[30]

Averroes, while arguing for the importance of reason as the Greeks had done, still accepted the notion of revealed religion. He held the view that even though philosophy and religion teach the same truth, because reason is fallible, religion, which emanates from an infallible God, must be allowed to set the limits as to what constitutes the acceptable topics for philosophical inquiry.[31] In this regard, Averroes was a precursor of Aquinas because, like Aquinas, Averroes sought to establish the appropriate relationship between faith and reason.[32] What is the basis for reconciling the two?

Philosophy, through the use of reason, seeks to know the purposes of life, and to attain this goal, it is necessary to have an understanding of the intentions of the world's creator, or God. Religion seeks the same information, not through reason but through direct knowledge from God. Further, both religion and philosophy, in focusing on the same questions, also seek to know, in light of the knowledge pertaining to God's intentions in creating the world, how God expects people to conduct their lives.[33] Here, both religion and philosophy can be reconciled on the basis that each seeks knowledge of the good life.

How does Averroes define the vision of the good life that both religion and philosophy should embrace as the preeminent guide for society? As Leaman says, Averroes maintained, like Aristotle, that people are social animals by nature and, as such, need political community to satisfy not only basic physical needs but to live in keeping with moral virtue, or those moral rules that enable people to live justly.[34] Life is only worth living as long as people can be part of communities that contribute to these purposes and that enable people to embody them in their lives.

This view of society is found in Averroes's treatment of Plato's *Republic*. Averroes's commentary on the *Republic* is a summary of Plato's views of politics, which includes his visions of the just society and of the Ideal State.[35] The essence of the just society is that individuals are taught moral virtues appropriate to their place in society, with the intention of making possible a just society. Indeed, Averroes reminds us, as we learned in Chapter 2, that Plato's just society embodies four central moral virtues, including wisdom, courage, temperance (or modera-tion), and justice. For Plato, justice is the main virtue, and it is manifested in a just society, where individuals perform well the function for which they are best suited by nature.[36] And central to the notion of the just society is the prominent role of the philosopher. Indeed, the best or Ideal State is one in which the philosopher is the "prince and ruler."[37] What are the qualifications of the philosopher who is also, upon possessing these qualities, referred to as a king?[38] The philosopher/ king studies all domains of science, loves truth, has no desire for wealth, is not ruled by sensual pleasures, manifests courage, seeks the good for society – which includes justice – and is capable of being a good speaker in matters having to do with philosophy.[39]

After the Ideal State, Averroes discusses the other types of states that Plato notes, and which we described in Chapter 2. Averroes recounts Plato's descrip-tions of timocracy, a state based on honor. Then, there is oligarchy, where a few with wealth are rulers. Finally, there is democracy, followed by tyranny. Aver-roes also adds to Plato's list of different states the notion of a state formed from necessity, which we address later in our treatment of Averroes's view of Plato's discussion of democracy.[40]

In general, for Leaman, Averroes, in his commentary on Plato, is merely describing elements of Plato's *Republic* and allowing the reader to determine if Plato's ideas are a good statement of "the just society and the just citizen."[41] How-ever, in our view, Averroes is doing more than just describing Plato's ideas with the intention of allowing readers to determine the validity of Plato's notion of justice as it pertains to the society and to the individual citizen. Averroes is also defending one of Plato's key ideas and criticizing another. In one case – that of enlarging the role for women in society – he makes a strong defense of Plato's ideas on this subject. In the second case, Averroes defends democracy against Plato's own tendency to associate it with the evolution of tyranny. In each case, whether he is defending or criticizing Plato, what Averroes seems to be doing is advocating positions that would not be supported by the leading traditions of his own times. And if our interpretation is valid, then Averroes could be construed, through his commentary on Plato's *Republic*, as seeking to reform his society.

Here, we explain this argument further by first discussing Averroes's defense of Plato's effort to enlarge the role of women in the *Republic*. And then we discuss Averroes's critique of Plato's view of democracy.

Averroes, in his discussion of Plato's guardian class, interrupts his descrip-tion of this dimension and says he wants to investigate if women and men have different natures.[42] Averroes says that men are better at most activities, though women might be better at some others. For instance, men are better at creating music, whereas women are better at performing it.[43] Or, women are said to be better at crafts such as weaving and sewing.[44]

The tendency to ascribe different talents, and thus roles, to men and women should not blind people to the fact that there are women who have the same capacities that men have, as Plato said, to be philosophers, rulers, and guardians.[45]

(Guardians are rulers or protectors of the community, and they must manifest military prowess, as we discuss in Chapter 2.) Yet, it is clearly the case that the possibility of women assuming roles as rulers, philosophers, or guardians would be overlooked in many societies, according to Averroes. Here, Averroes seems to be suggesting that the understanding of women's possibilities is unnecessarily limited by a tendency to reinforce traditional role divisions between the sexes. Indeed, this perspective, when carried out in full, tends to limit women to male-dominated households, where they are consigned to tasks such as procreation, rearing children, breastfeeding, and serving their husbands.[46] Here, women are not allowed to contribute fully to all aspects of society. As a result, women appear to be nothing more than "plants."[47]

Identifying women as plants means that they are passive, nonassertive people, incapable of fighting like men on behalf of protecting the state from its enemies. Were this description true, then women could never be guardians. And if women cannot be guardians, as explained in Chapter 2, they are denied a chance to be philosophers and rulers, too, since people must prove themselves to be among the best of the guardians before they can become rulers and philosophers.

But Averroes says emphatically that women can be guardians just like men. He indicates that a look at animal behavior demonstrates that, in many cases, both males and females have a capacity to fight enemies. By extension, to the human species, it follows that women – just like men – are capable of protecting a state from its enemies.[48] It is a mistake to relegate women to a passive role, one in which they are subordinated to men, based on the idea that women cannot fight and protect the state like men, because they can!

Moreover, when women are placed only in inferior positions to men, great damage is inflicted on society. Why is this? Averroes refers to societies in which women, who vastly outnumber men, are forced to stay at home in a male-dominated setting, producing and caring for children. As a result, women are not taught many of the basic tasks, as well as the requisite virtues, that allow women to contribute fully to the economic base of society. And because men alone cannot in these societies provide what is needed to satisfy basic goods – such as shelter, food, and so on – society is thrown into poverty. Averroes says that the fact that women

are a burden upon the men in these States [where they are not taught many basic tasks and requisite virtues] is one of the reasons for the poverty of these States. [Women] are found there in twice the number of men, while at the same time they do not, through training, support any of the necessary activities, except for the few which they undertake mostly at a time when they are obliged to make up their want of funds, like spinning and weaving. All this is self-evident.[49]

In his description of Plato's view of women, then, Averroes says that the problems raised for society by the limited role allowed to women, as well as the obvious need to enlarge women's role in society, are "self-evident." In saying that Plato's views are self-evident, especially as they pertain to actual settings, Averroes is suggesting that the truth of Plato's views is contained in their mere assertion, and, thus, further evidence to substantiate them is unnecessary. Averroes, by taking this position, has interspersed in his description of Plato's views his own favorable opinions about the benefits of Plato's advocacy of an expanded role for women. Given this to be the case, it seems acceptable to take these views as Averroes's critique of his society and of those societies with which he is familiar.

We turn now to what we take to be Averroes's defense of democracy. Averroes's embrace of democracy rings clearest when he refuses to associate democracy with a necessary slide into tyranny, as Plato did. Averroes tells us people want democracy because they wish to be free. He says of democracy:

> *Thus most of those States existing today are democratic. . . . This is the State which the great mass of the people think is the ruling one; since everyone is of the opinion at first thought that he deserves to be a free man.*[50]

Yet, for Plato, as we saw in Chapter 2, the longing for freedom as the motivation for democracy did pose a threat to a just arrangement of the Ideal State. In Plato's view, freedom led to an excess of desire, and this circumstance, by undermining the rule of reason, spawned the social instability that could be overcome only through the imposition of order from a powerful ruler. This ruler for Plato, after he had established himself, would manipulate the population into allowing him to have total power, and he would thus become a tyrant.[51]

Now, Averroes uses firsthand experience to substantiate Plato's point that, at times, democracy can lead directly to tyranny. Averroes tells us that his native Cordoba turned to tyranny after having been almost exclusively democratic.[52] Still, as we begin to explain in the next paragraph, for Averroes, democracy need not always turn into tyranny. Indeed, democracy can be an important first step to the Ideal State.

Averroes relates in his commentary on Plato's *Republic* that democratic societies are places where people are free from restraint to do whatever they desire and where each can move in any direction that a person's "soul leads him."[53] Further, in a democratic society, the existence of freedom permits all the qualities that are peculiar to Plato's other types of states. Thus, in a democracy, uniformity of outlook is replaced with a variety of ways of life, each of which embodies different values and perspectives. There are some people who love honor, others who love owning property, and still others who love tyranny. Also in a democracy, there are those who possess as well as act from a commitment to the various moral virtues.[54] Owing to these many differences that exist in a democracy, there is bound to be a broad flourishing of "all arts" and ways of life.[55] In consequence of this prospect, Averroes says it is possible for an Ideal State, run by philosophers, to emerge from democracies.[56]

Why would democracy help to spawn an Ideal State? Averroes seems to answer this question by saying that a democracy is like a multicolored "garment." And just as many youth and women find a multicolored garment good for its array of different colors, many people find democracy admirable for its hodgepodge of different ways of life.[57] But why would the fact that democracy contains many differences be attractive to people? Here, we can only speculate. But it would seem that a democracy – just like a multicolored garment that blends many colors into a useful fabric – manifests the possibility of integrating various ways of life into a working whole. And this situation in a democracy could support a rich intellectual life in which a host of perspectives would be assessed while finding the best arguments on any issue under discussion. This setting could contribute well to a culture that supports an interest in philosophy and an appreciation for the Ideal State.

Still, there is a downside to a democratic state containing many differences, and the principal problem is that these differences might produce a destructive fragmentation of society. For Averroes, experience with democracies in his own time as well as in earlier periods demonstrates that, unless there is a commitment to moral virtue, there will not be sufficient self-restraint to unite the different elements into a community or association built upon respect for the needs of the whole society. And then democracy – like a multicolored garment whose main threads have been ripped – will lose its common fiber and soon perish.[58] In this event, tyranny, or any of the other states that fall short of an ideal society run by philosophers, might well result from democracy. Indeed, Averroes says that because of the diverse tendencies that are allowed expression in a democracy, all the different types of states – including timocracy, oligarchy, and tyranny – are "destined" to arise from democracy.[59]

Here, we focus only on the question of whether democracy is the precursor to tyranny. Plato thinks that this connection is inevitable because democracy is associated with the pursuit of excess freedom. This circumstance opens the door to seeking freedom in larger and larger amounts, all in the name of securing unlimited desire, a situation in which one desire leads to people having many others, seemingly without end.[60] Indeed, for Averroes, political leaders in a democracy cater to this tendency by providing citizens with what they most desire, as part of what is meant by securing people's freedom.[61] What are the objects of people's desires? Averroes tells us that, in democracies – especially newly founded ones – the thirst for acquiring property grows.[62] Plato would no doubt say that this situation encourages people to give a higher place of importance to their desires than to the collective needs of society. And then, to stop the chaos that follows, a single, powerful strong man may be called upon to rule over the society.

As this scenario demonstrates, freedom pursued to excess turns to its opposite, which is tyranny.[63] Here, democracy will fail to survive, unless people are able to constrain desire (or what, to use modern terms, we will call self-interest) as a result of their possessing a strong enough sense of moral virtue.[64] Now, Plato argued that the acquisition of these moral qualities as the basis for stability in his just or Ideal State arises from the fact that people "agree by conviction to keep that which the laws demand."[65] To act from this conviction means that a person would not have a longing for what a person "does not possess."[66] Plato's Ideal State avoids this situation and thus is able to teach moral virtue because it focuses people's attention not on pursuing their self-interest but on doing the jobs for which they are best suited, thus serving society's interest.[67]

But Averroes seeks to demonstrate that the pursuit of self-interest does not necessarily cause society to slide from democracy to tyranny. He says that, in a democracy, people may recognize that it is in their self-interest to protect freedom by accepting moral constraints on desire. In this case, for the sake of securing freedom, people will accept a democratic form of authority that is designed to uphold limits on how far people can promote self-interest. This argument anticipates liberal conceptions of the state, as we discuss in the next section, where freedom is made possible only when individuals accept moral constraints on the pursuit of their interests. What is Averroes's basis for making this claim?

Governments have authority in a democracy only when the governed accept that authority.[68] But in a democracy, a government's authority will not last very long if people, because of their lack of self-constraint, always place their own interests ahead of the interests of society. This understanding is at the core of Averroes's view of democracy. Evidence for this contention arises from Averroes's statement that "in view of the character of this [democratic] State [which provides freedom for each citizen to pursue his or her interests]," it is considered improper "that everything should be permitted to everybody" in a democracy.[69] Indeed, Averroes says that in a democracy people must understand that they cannot have all they desire, or otherwise "a point would be reached when they would murder and plunder one another."[70] Here, people in a democracy could have an interest in a form of authority that makes possible, for the sake of freedom, the moral constraints necessary to avoid the chaos arising from unrestrained self-interest.

Democratic societies in which people have an interest in freedom – as the occasion for moral constraint – may arise from a series of circumstances, beginning with what Averroes refers to as states of "necessity." Indeed, for Averroes, the first states to come into existence emanate "naturally" from necessity, a type of state not discussed by Plato.[71] This means that states initially come into existence as a result of people *naturally* joining together to satisfy basic, necessary needs – such as food, shelter, and so on. Further, for Averroes, democracy is the first type of state to emerge from states that originate from necessity: for once, people have their necessary needs taken care of, they are likely to seek a variety of desires well beyond basic needs, and the new desires are for things such as property and wealth.[72] In this setting, democracies are formed for the sake of providing people with the personal freedom they need to obtain what they desire.

But, as we have seen, a democracy will take a turn toward chaos unless it can be an association with a government whose authority binds people to upholding moral restraints on their desires. Now, for Averroes, an association of people that limits desire is a result, not of design, but of "chance."[73] Indeed, in a democracy, a governing authority that necessitates moral constraints on desire is merely "acci-dental."[74] Why is this the case? As we saw earlier, democratic states in which people seek freedom are filled with diverse people, some supporting honor, some property, and others moral virtue or even tyranny. It is possible that, owing to chance, the makeup of the state will emphasize every other tendency but moral virtue. If this outcome were to take place, then democracies would be unable to maintain a commitment to self-restraint and, consequently, democracies could turn toward tyranny. But if, by chance, there are enough people who recognize the need for moral virtue, then a democratic government's authority can be predicated on people's acceptance of the need to limit desire for the sake of freedom. In this case, people would be more likely to understand that it is in their self-interest to place limits on their desires, lest society become a place in which overzealous commitment to desire destroys all freedom.

Moreover, the tendency to support democracies from self-interest is strengthened in the face of the need to combat tyranny. Averroes says that Muslim kings of his time become tyrants when they plunder the property of the common people. Indeed, at times, a king may tax people and distribute property gained in this manner inequitably. In doing so, a king may display this property before the bulk of the population as a symbol of his power, and this circumstance angers most people. In response, the mass of people hopes to free themselves from these kings. And kings react by attempting to impose a tyranny on ordinary people.[75] In seeking their freedom from corrupt kings as well as in pursuing protection from tyranny, the masses of ordinary people would necessarily share a collective interest in democracy. "Therefore this [democratic] State is in utmost opposition to the tyrannical State."[76] For Averroes, democracy is humankind's ultimate protection against tyranny. And this lesson has strong personal meaning for Averroes, who laments tyranny that takes place "in our own time and in our own State."[77]

Further, Averroes warns that, in tyrannies, the "priestly part" – or, in other terms, religious authority – becomes tyrannical,[78] and when this happens, great "disrepute" accrues to the priestly class. Averroes says that this circumstance, which contradicts the expectation that the priestly parts of society should advance moral excellence,[79] is commonly found in his own time.[80] Thus, insofar as democracy opposes tyranny, democracy helps to ensure a religious authority that promotes, as it should, an Ideal State in which the best – those with philosophical and moral excellence – rule. Certainly, Averroes understands that reason is fallible and that it must work within an Islamic framework, which emanates from an infallible God.[81] But he knows that this outcome could never be realized where tyranny prevailed. And, thus, democracy has an important role to play in securing the proper relationship between religion and philosophy.

Averroes's commentary on Plato's *Republic* is an important statement of social reform for his own times. Of course, from the way Averroes was treated at the end of his life, as mentioned in the beginning of this section, it is also clear that the ruling, including the religious, authorities of his time, rejected his views for reforming society. Still, his thought contributes in important ways to the modern world because it helped to set the stage for civil society in our own times.

IV. Maimonides: The Limits of Reason and Religion

Moses Maimonides (1135–1204) – a medieval Jewish philosopher, physician, and rabbi – was born in Cordoba. Maimonides and his family had to leave Cordoba to escape the intolerance of orthodox Islamic believers who sought to force Jewish and Christian conversion to Islam.[82] Maimonides traveled to Morocco, where intellectual openness did exist. There, he met Islamic scholars who introduced him to Arabic translations of Aristotle. He went from Morocco to Alexandria and settled in Cairo, another city that tolerated intellectual vitality.[83]

Liberal climates tolerating intellectual inquiry, like what existed in Cairo, were, in part, made possible by the great Muslim leader Saladin, who took back Jerusalem in 1187 CE from the Christian Crusaders who had previously taken it from the Muslims. When the Christian Crusaders conquered Jerusalem in 1097 CE, they slaughtered Jews and Muslims alike. Jews were burned to death in their synagogues where they had sought protection, and Muslims were beheaded with impunity.[84] After retaking Jerusalem, Saladin refused to take revenge for Christian cruelties. He allowed Christians and Jews to leave the city without harm, and Christian priests were permitted to conduct religious services in Jerusalem, Nazareth, and Bethlehem. Later, he opened Jerusalem to Jews, ensuring them complete freedom to rebuild their synagogues and schools. When he became the sultan of Egypt, he supported practices that respected people from other religious faiths, and this circumstance contributed to Cairo becoming a city that welcomed intellectual flourishing.[85]

Studying Maimonides is helpful in addressing one of the central questions that emanated from the experience of the Jewish Diaspora, which took place after the Babylonian captivity during the sixth century BCE. As a result, Jews were scattered to countries outside of Palestine.[86] (The word *Palestine* refers here to the ancient country of biblical times or to what is now often called the Holy Land.)[87] In the face of the Diaspora experience and its continuing impact on Jewish life at the time of Maimonides, how did Jews manage to survive as a people, even as they were dispersed across different cultures?

Maimonides maintained that the Jewish people, also referred to in biblical texts as the nation of Israel,[88] survived as a unified community because of the continuation of a strong presence of what Jews considered to be God's law. Adherence to God's law helped to bind Jews to the core values contained in that law, as well as to the Jewish community that revered it. The law is found principally in the Pentateuch, the first five books of the Old Testament, which are contained in the Torah. In Jewish tradition, the Torah was handed down from God to the Jewish people through Moses, the great liberator of Jews from slavery in Egypt.[89]

For Maimonides, Jewish tradition divides God's law into two essential parts. The Torah contains the written law that Jews are to follow. But the written law has always been supplemented in Jewish tradition by oral commentary designed to demonstrate how that law should be interpreted. In Maimonides's view, Moses, "our master, wrote down the entire *torah* before he died . . . and gave a scroll to each tribe [of Israel]."[90] In addition, for Maimonides, Moses provided an explanation of the written Torah, which he did not write down but which he told the elders in the Jewish community, as well as all of Israel, to follow. And Maimonides calls this verbal explanation the "Oral Torah."[91]

For Maimonides, the most important adherents as well as implementers of the Oral Torah are the members of the Jewish Sanhedrin of Jerusalem, the supreme council of the Jews. The Sanhedrin, which existed from the fifth century BCE to the fall of the Second Temple in 70 CE, acted as a supreme legislature and as the highest court of justice for the Jewish people.[92] The Jewish people, even as they lived under the rule of others, had their own courts to resolve disputes. Each court sought to settle disputes in keeping with its particular traditions. Matters that could not be resolved went to the Sanhedrin for resolution.[93] To perform this job, the Sanhedrin used the oral tradition to apply the written Torah law in resolving disputes. Maimonides says, "The Great Sanhedrin of Jerusalem is the root of the Oral Law. The members thereof are the pillars of instruction; out of them go forth statutes and judgments to all Israel."[94] Indeed, through their authority, Jews were given a common source of law and identity.

But the Sanhedrin came to an end when the Romans destroyed the Second Temple and dispersed Jews from Jerusalem. After this event, there was no longer in place an authoritative source for interpreting the law to all Jews and for ruling over their affairs. So an alternative source of authority emerged to provide a basis for continuity among the dispersed Jewish people. The new authority emphasized the Torah and its laws as central elements in a covenant between the Jewish people and God. A special group of legal scholars, called either sages or rabbis, was trained in rabbinic academies to interpret the Torah and to explain and to determine what the law meant, not just literally but when applied to actual circumstances during the Jewish people's dispersal throughout various cultures.[95]

These legal scholars –hereafter called rabbis – were different from prophets. Prophets, and of course the great lawgiver Moses, were viewed as possessing wisdom and authority, owing, in part, to their direct relationship to God.[96] But in Jewish tradition, God does not talk through rabbis to the people as He did through Moses. Instead, rabbis, as learned men with wisdom, were to make applications of God's law to particular circumstances and thereby instruct Jews on how to uphold God's law and, in the process, maintain the covenant with God.[97]

Maimonides builds upon this tradition when he says that rabbis could make interpretations of divine law in the Torah, so long as they did not change it.[98] Rabbis have similar roles to judges in the US court system. Judges, in making rulings, must uphold the sacred principles of the US Constitution. Similarly, rabbis must apply the law without violating the Torah. And both rabbis and judges must often defend themselves against the charge that their interpretations violate the basic law – the Constitution in the case of judges, the Torah in the case of rabbis.[99] Further, rabbis, like contemporary judges in US courts, create, over time, an accumulated body of knowledge that helps to give authority to their interpretations. This knowledge, as opposed to divine revelation, is the basis for subsequent decisions by rabbis. Here, "specialists," the rabbis, as opposed to ordinary individuals, make the law that gives continuity to the Jewish community.[100]

Rabbis, while never attempting to supersede the Torah law, seek to apply it to practical circumstances with compassion.[101] When there are disagreements on how best to do so, decisions are often made by a majority vote among the rabbis.[102] Prior to reaching a decision, however, discussions are marked by an intense respect for all views, including ones that dissented from majority positions. Indeed, dissenting positions are given as much legitimacy as accepted ones.[103] Speaking of the rabbinic dynasty that emerged from the followers of first-century CE Hillel the Elder, David Shatz says that members of this group emphasize tolerance and patience toward those who disagree with them. Indeed, for the followers of Hillel, often, as David Shatz says, "a rejected view may reflect greater legal acumen and cogency than the accepted one!"[104]

The work in Jewish tradition that contains rabbinic interpretations of the law is the Talmud. Dating from 375 CE, it was written by sages and rabbis across Jewish history. It is a collection of Jewish laws and, as such, contains the oral laws as well as commentaries on them.[105] Maimonides says that the bulk of legal rulings since the days of Moses are contained in the Talmud.[106] Often, a reading of the Talmud provides a full rendering of the various points of view that should be considered in interpreting a particular issue of law but less clarity in specifying the nature of the law itself. Indeed, as one writer said:

A bright student, they say, could give forty-nine reasons for deciding a point of law one way and forty-nine reasons for deciding it the opposite way – and this sort of thing was never seen within the Jewish tradition as mere sophistry. God's word really was open-textured, available for study, discussion, disagreement, even a kind of intellectual play.[107]

Further, if there were no dire need to decide on a matter, Talmudic arguments would avoid reaching a conclusion so that subsequent generations could take up the matter later without being bound to earlier decisions.[108]

From the foregoing account, it is clear that the rabbinic tradition contains two radically different approaches to understanding the Torah. On the one hand, the Torah embodies the eternal laws of God that could not be changed. As we have seen, Maimonides says that rabbis could interpret the law but should not change its basic essence. Yet, in interpreting the law, the Torah can be perceived as a document that could be adapted to new circumstances. Seen in this light, the

Torah is an ever-changing document, as opposed to being a symbol of eternal and absolute laws.[109]

Maimonides, often referred to as the most prominent of the medieval rabbis, hoped to overcome this dualism by writing a legal code that sought to end all the arguments – as found in the Talmud – about the nature of the law for the Jewish people.[110] The book, which was written with this purpose in mind, is entitled the *Mishneh Torah*. As one writer says, in the *Mishneh Torah*, Maimonides presents both the Talmudic and "the Oral law in what was meant to be definitive form, without proof texts, disagreements, and alternative views that marked the Talmud itself and all the commentaries and compilations that followed upon it."[111] Maimonides says that those who want to know the law can discern its nature by reading the *Mishneh Torah* alone.[112]

For Maimonides, only a few people can understand the Talmud, and those who can understand this work require "a capacious mind, a wise spirit, and a long time."[113] The *Mishneh Torah* would thus help ordinary people comprehend what only a few could know intimately. Moreover, the effort to craft a work that enabled ordinary people to live in keeping with God's law manifests the view that learned rabbis have great responsibility in society. Indeed, Maimonides is like Avicenna in suggesting that whereas ordinary people need political community, only superior leaders can provide it.[114] Why is this the case for Maimonides?

For him, there are many differences among people with respect to their moral commitments and character. There are cruel people, and there are those who would not even hurt an insect. Many other differences are evident as well. Given these differences, it will be difficult to find a way to achieve a community in which each person is willing to submit him- or herself to the same law.[115] Nonetheless, this objective must be achieved if a decent society is to be at all possible. And as Pines says, Maimonides thinks this task can be handled well only by learned men with special abilities, as opposed to ordinary people.[116]

Still, Maimonides says that at times learned men – and we say men, since women had no social or political parity with men – may not be available in particular towns, and, in this case, Maimonides would concede decision making to townspeople and tradesmen.[117] Here, as Amy Gutmann says, for Maimonides, the rule of ordinary men, though not as good as rule by experts, is acceptable as a matter of necessity and not as a matter of morality.[118] However, in the best of circumstances, as just stated, for Maimonides, excellence in determining the law arises not from ordinary men but only from those sages and rabbis who spend a lifetime dedicated to developing expert knowledge of the law.[119]

We wish now to turn to another of Maimonides's concerns. As we have just seen, for Maimonides, biblical texts are important for understanding God's law. But, in addition, these texts, for Maimonides, contain understandings with respect to some of life's enduring questions – such as the fundamental nature of people (are people born good or evil?), the implications for human life of reason's limitations, and the nature of justice. In addressing matters of this sort, Maimonides demonstrates the importance of reason and thus of the philosopher to society.[120]

How Maimonides approaches this objective occupies the remaining part of this chapter, as we discuss the way he treats matters such as the nature of people, the limitations of reason, and justice.

As Leo Strauss points out, for Maimonides, the Torah has a literal meaning and a hidden meaning, and the worst errors with respect to understanding the complexities found in the Torah arise from approaching the Bible merely from the standpoint of its literal meaning.[121] So, to rectify this problem, in *The Guide of the Perplexed*, Maimonides sought to explain the "secrets of the Law" in the Bible.[122] In doing so, Maimonides moves from what, on a surface reading, the Bible appears to be saying to what, on a deeper reading, it actually says. Yet, as he undertakes this task in *The Guide*, he must determine how to confront an ancient legal prohibition arising from Talmudic sages who forbid the explanation of these secrets to the public at large. The secrets of the Bible can be explained only in private to those with political and scientific wisdom.[123] Leo Strauss points out that, in *The Guide of the Perplexed*, where Maimonides "embarked upon the explanation of the secrets of the Torah, he was confronted with the apparently overwhelming difficulty created by the 'legal prohibition' against explaining those secrets."[124]

How does Maimonides confront this prohibition? He makes his explanation of the biblical secrets difficult for the average reader to grasp. In this way, the secrets remain hidden from most people. Indeed, Maimonides's intention was that only a few astute and shrewd readers would ever be able to fathom Maimonides's words.[125] For instance, Maimonides contradicts himself at various points throughout *The Guide* to force the reader to stop constantly and reflect on what meaning should be attributed to these contradictions. Readers would devote a great deal of time to addressing these matters, making the experience of reading *The Guide* too tedious for most people.[126] Moreover, *The Guide* was written to provide many hints of the truth, and the reader must make use of each clue to reveal the secrets.[127]

Perhaps one of the most important discoveries of the Bible Maimonides articulated in this arcane manner is that reason has significant limitations. Indeed, Maimonides, while having great reverence for reason, still for the sake of maintaining a moral vision of life, which we describe next, hopes to note its limitations. Thus, for Maimonides, it is important to understand that reason or the "intellects of human beings have a limit at which they stop."[128]

Building upon this point, Marvin Fox says Maimonides understands that "reason has its limits and an intelligent man should recognize these limits."[129] Often, in facing important issues, we rely upon our reason to help provide knowledge and critical judgments. Just as often, we discover that reason can provide neither. Still, the issues in question do not disappear. They remain important to others and to us, and, thus, we are forced by virtue of this fact to take positions on these matters, using grounds other than reason to do so. For instance, in many public debates about controversial moral issues, we realize that with the employment of reason, we cannot achieve consensus on the nature of the best course. The lack of consensus does not eliminate these issues from public concern, however.

Still, we must decide our stances on them. We must do so as citizens, as parents, and as professionals. And, often, when we decide, we discover that reason cannot provide an adequate explanation, and then we may resort to arguments that emanate from religion.[130]

And this approach is what Maimonides takes with respect to many issues of his day. As Fox says, Maimonides's method is to see first if reasoned inquiry can resolve a matter, and, if not, then he resorts to explanations based in religion. And he is honest about what he is doing. He does not try to mask a religious argument as emanating from reason. And when he resorts to religious views to support a position, he makes clear the nature of the religious grounds he is using as well as why he chose them. Moreover, he does not reject a better argument, in this case one that arises from reason, if such an argument emerges at a subsequent time. In particular, he does not allow himself to be limited to Scripture if a good argument from reason can be found in the discussion of an issue.[131] Thus, he does not permit religious belief to sabotage reason and the knowledge derivative from it. But if reason were incapable of helping to discern truth, he does not allow reason to mask or to subvert this fact, especially in the face of religions' possible helpful contributions.

To provide an example of this approach, we now comment on Maimonides's view of the nature of humankind; in particular, we address the question from Maimonides's perspective as to whether human beings are, by nature, good or evil. For this purpose, we start with Augustine's position found in Chapter 4, that human beings are driven by sin, and we demonstrate the possible critique Maimonides would make of Augustine's view. Maimonides would have demonstrated the frailty of Augustine's position by first resorting to reason, and then, when the limits of reason became obvious with respect to concluding his critique, he would turn to religious tradition. First, we establish the argument from reason that Maimonides would use against Augustine.

In Augustine's doctrine, it is said that as a result of the fall of man in the Garden of Eden, the stigma of sin follows humankind for all time. Maimonides would have rejected this view because he believed that each human being is born with a potential for perfection that can and should be actualized. Maimonides says that "man is not granted his ultimate perfection at the outset; for perfection exists in him only potentially."[132] Achieving perfection is a possibility because, in Maimonides's view, human beings have a "noble form," or an overall disposition, which has been created in *"the image of God and His likeness."*[133]

But how should we characterize the "ultimate perfection" that is enshrined in our noble form and that defines our possibilities? Maimonides describes human potential in terms of the rational ends that we can and must pursue if we are to realize the true possibilities inherent in our noble form. Rational ends are those universal purposes that all human beings should seek, regardless of their place in the world. Maimonides clarifies these ends when he says, "For example, man's apprehension of his Creator, his mental representation of every intelligible [aspect of the world], his control of his desire and anger, his thought on what ought to be preferred and what avoided, are all consequent upon his form."[134] Owing to our noble form, then, we should seek, through the proper use of reason, knowledge of the human and natural worlds. In addition, we also realize that we must, as human beings with reason or as people created in God's "likeness," seek to live in accordance with moral virtue, or what constitutes a morally right way to live.[135]

For the moment, we wish only to focus on the moral virtue dimension that our human, noble form promotes. We do so to address an important problem: namely, that the fact that our noble form orients us to pursue moral virtue does not mean that we in fact do live in keeping with what is morally right. For it is also true that individuals have a capacity for sin, and this fact might contradict as well as stifle the possibilities embodied in our virtuous disposition. The possibility of sin follows from the desires that emanate from the human body, or what he refers to as human "matter." Maimonides says, "His [man's] eating and drinking and copulation and his passionate desire for these things, as well as his anger and all bad habits found in him, are all of them consequent upon his matter [body]."[136]

Nonetheless, sin need not be our destiny. Rather, we can live in accordance with moral virtue. And this is because, as just indicated, our lives are overshadowed by a higher capacity in life – a disposition to moral virtue located in our human form. Maimonides says:

> *[God] granted it – I mean the human form – power, dominion, rule, and control over [the body], in order that [form] subjugate [the passions of the body], quell [the body's] impulses, and bring it back to the best and most harmonious state that is possible.*[137]

Thus, whereas individuals, owing to their bodies, have a capacity for sin, people, owing to their form, have a fundamental need, as well as potential, to live in accordance with moral virtue.[138]

Here, Maimonides's position against an Augustinian darkness at the center of each human being is built upon a rational argument. Given the assumption that God has given humankind a form that orients people to rational ends, including the need to live a morally virtuous life, then it follows logically that individuals are not forever driven to sin. Rather, individuals can in fact live in keeping with God's hope that people will find themselves in a "harmonious state."

To achieve this possibility, God's law for Maimonides promotes the welfare of the soul and of the body. The welfare of the soul "consists in the multitude's acquiring correct opinions corresponding to [the multitude's] respective capacity."[139] How should we understand this statement? The term *soul* is merely another word for what Maimonides referred to as our noble form. As such, the soul, like the noble form, contains two rational ends: the necessary quest for knowledge and the need to live in keeping with moral right. It is in light of these rational ends that we can understand what Maimonides means by the term, *correct opinions*. Here, it seems that this term refers to each person understanding a requirement to pursue the rational ends embodied in our noble form, or soul.

Now, from Maimonides's discussion of the welfare of the soul, what is clear is that not all people can be taught correct opinions in the same way. People have different abilities when it comes to learning, and for this reason, some must be taught differently than others. This view is suggested by the statement that people acquire "correct opinions corresponding to their respective capacity." Thus, Maimonides says that some people, presumably because of their higher capacity for understanding, can be provided with correct opinions through explicit explanations or explanations that are reasoned. Other people, however, with less capacity for understanding – what Maimonides refers to as the "common multitude" – must be taught through "parables," or stories, that provide down-to-earth examples as the basis for acquiring an understanding of the rational ends of the soul.[140]

What does Maimonides mean when he discusses the welfare of the body? The welfare of the body is an idea signifying that people should not act wrongfully to each other. To accomplish this objective, people must not put the pursuit of their own capacities and objectives above the need to do what is "useful to the whole." Indeed, Maimonides argues that each person must be "forced" to do his or her part to maintain the community as an environment that serves the shared needs of all members of society. To accomplish this end, Maimonides says that each person must acquire the "*moral qualities* that are useful for life in society so that the affairs of the city may be ordered."[141] As a result of these moral qualities, or what can be called moral virtues, people limit their desires and by doing so help to make possible a community that provides for the common needs of all people.

Why is meeting this objective so important? Only if the goods of a community are made available will people be able to pursue the perfection of the soul, or the fullest development possible of their reason.[142] If people are hungry and without shelter or if they are in pain and filled with suffering, they are not likely to be reflective people able to engage in rational inquiry. Indeed, without the acceptance of basic moral qualities, the welfare of the body is not possible, and without the welfare of the body, there is no basis for securing the advancement of the rational ends of the soul.[143] Thus, the welfare of the body, which symbolizes the possibility of a moral community, contributes to the welfare of the soul or human-kind's "ultimate perfection" – what is "indubitably more noble [than the welfare of the body] and is the only cause of permanent preservation."[144]

But a problem with profound consequences emerges at this point in Maimonides's discussion. His view of the soul points to serious shortcomings in human ability that we must address and, in some way, compensate for, if we are to achieve the rational ends postulated by the ultimate perfection made possible by our noble form. To illustrate this point, we first explain the dilemma in Maimonides's own words, and then we follow his statement with our own description and elaboration of the ideas contained in his words.

For Maimonides, human beings seek to realize their full rational potential by knowing all that can be known "within the capacity of man to know in accordance with his ultimate perfection."[145] This statement suggests that, through our reason, we cannot know all that we might have a longing to understand because reason is limited in its capacity to know all things. Indeed, Maimonides says that "it is clear that to this ultimate perfection [of the soul] there do not belong either actions or moral qualities and that it consists only of opinions toward which speculation has led and that investigation has rendered compulsory."[146] Thus, from intellectual activity – that is, from the use of our reason to explore the world – we do not obtain definitive answers to many of the questions that our quest for knowledge obligates us to ask. We neither solve all controversies with respect to attaining a perfect understanding of the way the human and natural world works, nor do we acquire a precise and definitive understanding as to what "moral qualities" we should embody in our actions so that we act in morally correct ways.

This outcome has important consequences for each of our attempts to live a moral life. For Maimonides, even as reason, as the manifestation of our noble form or soul, tells us to do right and to live virtuously, it cannot clearly delineate right from wrong. As Fox says, "Maimonides teaches explicitly that morality is not derived from reason and that moral statements are neither true nor false."[147] To use a contemporary issue to provide an example of this point, when discussing the death penalty, we will be in favor of this punishment if we think that it is a deterrent to people committing murder, but we will be against it if we think that killing others is always wrong, no matter who does it. One perspective emphasizes the social good of the death penalty and the other manifests the public harm caused by it. The perspective one takes and the assumptions one employs to address this question will determine one's position on the issue. Can rational inquiry help to transcend these two competing perspectives and allow us to find a resolution to this conflict that can be accepted by all sides in the debate? Or is this example an instance, like many others, of Maimonides's claim that reason, while urging us to find the morally correct path in deciding the best approach to critical issues, is unable to demonstrate in a definitive way the nature of that path?

If Maimonides is correct and reason cannot determine the morally right course of action from the wrong one, how can we understand the nature of moral virtue, and moreover, how can we live virtuous lives? Maimonides's answer is to turn to another source for determining moral right. And that alternative source is religious tradition. How does Maimonides support his position?

Following Aristotle, Maimonides says that human beings are social animals and thus seek community and friendship. Indeed, Maimonides says:

> *It is well known that friends are something that is necessary for man throughout his whole life. Aristotle has already set this forth in the ninth book of the "Ethics." For in a state of health and happiness, a man takes pleasure in their [friend's] familiar relations with him; [and] in adversity he has recourse to them [friends].*[148]

Why are community and friendship so important? As we have seen already, the notion of the welfare of the body suggests the importance of those moral virtues that help to make possible a community in which individuals are able to secure the welfare of the soul. And clearly, for Maimonides, religious traditions – as a continuing foundation for securing moral virtue in society – have a great role in maintaining friendship and community. Thus, religious traditions in helping to secure community and friendship make possible an environment in which people can realize the rational ends of the soul.

Maimonides would thus suggest that individuals be taught many of the moral virtues embodied in these traditions. For instance, people should avoid bad habits, such as gambling, but be taught good ones, such as loving one's fellow Jews as well as strangers and helping those who commit sins in order to understand the best way to live. In helping people who commit moral mistakes, we should not shame them publicly but only talk to them in private, using a "gentle language," which communicates an interest in the other's good.[149] In addition, religious traditions contain a host of lessons with respect to sexuality, all in the name of protecting people against the temptation to stray from a morally virtuous course in life, thus making it difficult to create and to maintain community.[150]

Other illustrations of the way in which religious traditions teach moral virtues to limit excessive desire are given in *The Guide*.[151] In this regard, one last example is in order. The concern to maintain justice is a natural expression of the rational end to pursue moral right, or as we saw earlier in discussing the welfare of the body, to not wrong others and to do what is useful for the community. Indeed, justice requires "granting to everyone who has a right to something, that which he has a right to and giving to every being that which corresponds to his merits."[152] But how do we carry out this principle in the different circumstances that we face? Or, to use other terms, how should we practice justice – which means not harming others and doing what is useful to the community by granting everyone that which he or she has a right to expect – in the context of particular issues and cases? Rational inquiry by itself may not always be able to answer this question. In the face of this, Maimonides turns to the moral virtues found in religious practice. He takes this path to provide the rational soul with what it has a right to expect. And, thus, Maimonides says, "For when you walk in the way of the moral virtues, you do justice unto your rational soul, giving her the due that is her right."[153]

Finally, how do we know that particular religious practices best serve the interests of justice? For instance, take the issue of the death penalty again. Suppose a religious practice justifies its use for those who murder. How can we be sure that we are acting justly by invoking the death penalty, even when its use is sanctioned by a religious tradition? Maimonides would say that this question highlights the importance of knowledge. For only as we acquire knowledge about the death penalty, in its many facets, can we be in a position to make compelling judgments about the justness or unjustness of its use. Of course, as we saw earlier, individuals are limited in their ability to acquire knowledge. Perfect knowledge is beyond our reach. Still, despite this fact, it is possible to obtain sufficient knowledge to render good judgments about how best to achieve justice in the death penalty question, as well as in many other issues of morality and politics.

Thus, communities that seek to serve the rational end obligating us to moral conduct cannot do so unless they permit the relentless pursuit of knowledge – the other rational end of the soul. Here, just communities, which enable us to unite knowledge with moral right, make possible the greatest achievement of human flourishing – wisdom.

V. Conclusion: The Implications for Civil Society

Where would Maimonides and the Islamic thinkers we discuss here, stand on the need for a civil society? Certainly, these writers would not have created a separate sphere independent of the state. Nonetheless, we think Maimonides, like the Islamic thinkers, can be seen as creating, in the medieval non-Christian world, an opening to civil society.

After all, in providing a place for reason alongside a respect for religious tradition, Maimonides and these Islamic philosophers make clear the limits of both. Reason cannot by itself achieve the moral right it demands, and religious tradition may, at times, fall short of the expectations for moral right commanded by reason. In this circumstance, we have no choice but to search for the knowledge that helps us ensure that religious traditions truly work for realizing justice. And, in the face of the need for knowledge that can help establish the proper relationship between faith and reason, it becomes clear that social and political settings that frustrate or deny this pursuit become viewed as archaic and as lacking legitimacy. Such becomes the fate of the medieval world.

And what advances to the forefront is the need for a social and political setting that gives centrality of place to knowledge and to moral right, the two rational ends of Maimonides's view of the soul – thus making clear the need for civil society.

Notes

1. Miriam Galston, *Politics and Excellence: The Political Philosophy of Alfarabi* (Princeton, NJ: Princeton University Press, 1990), 15–16.
2. Oliver Leaman, *Averroes and His Philosophy* (Oxford: Clarendon Press, 1988), 5.
3. Ibid., 6.
4. Ibid.
5. Ibid., 7–8.
6. Galston, *Politics and Excellence*, 14.
7. Charles E. Butterworth, "Introduction," in *The Political Aspects of Islamic Philosophy*, ed. Charles E. Butterworth (Cambridge: Harvard University Press, 1992), 3–4.
8. Galston, *Politics and Excellence*, 14.
9. Ibid., 14–19.
10. Ibid., 43.

11. Ibid.

12. Ibid., 43–44.

13. Peter Heath, *Allegory and Philosophy in Avicenna (Ibn Sînâ)* (Philadelphia: University of Pennsylvania Press, 1992), 21–24.

14. Ibid., 19.

15. Ibid., 21–24.

16. Ibid., 25.

17. Leaman, *Averroes and His Philosophy*, 52.

18. Shlomo Pines, "Introduction," in Moses Maimonides, *The Guide of the Perplexed*, trans. with notes by Shlomo Pines, with introductory essay by Leo Strauss (Chicago: University of Chicago Press, 1963), xciv.

19. Heath, *Allegory and Philosophy in Avicenna*, 37–41.

20. Pines, "Introduction," xcix.

21. Ibid.

22. Ibid.

23. Ibid.

24. James W. Morris, "The Philosopher-Prophet in Avicenna's Political Philosophy," in Charles E. Butterworth, ed., *The Political Aspects of Islamic Philosophy*, 183–87.

25. Ibid., 192.

26. Leaman, *Averroes and His Philosophy*, 4. Also see, Fred Gladstone Bratton, *Maimonides: Medieval Modernist* (Boston: Beacon Press, 1967), 4–8.

27. Leaman, *Averroes and His Philosophy*, 1–3.

28. Bratton, *Maimonides*, 8.

29. Leaman, *Averroes and His Philosophy*, 1.

30. Ibid., 8–9.

31. Ibid., 127–28.

32. Bratton, *Maimonides*, 7.

33. Leaman, *Averroes and His Philosophy*, 144.

34. Ibid., 120.

35. Averroes, *Averroes' Commentary on Plato's Republic,* ed., intro., trans. and notes by E. I. J. Rosenthal (Cambridge: Cambridge University Press, 1966), 111.

36. Leaman, *Averroes and His Philosophy*, 120; Averroes, *Averroes' Commentary on Plato's Republic*, 115, 156–63.

37. Averroes, *Averroes' Commentary on Plato's Republic*, 178.

38. Ibid.

39. Leaman, *Averroes and His Philosophy*, 121; Averroes, *Averroes' Commentary on Plato's Republic*, 178–79.

40. Averroes, *Averroes' Commentary on Plato's Republic*, 209–49. Also, see Leaman, *Averroes and His Philosophy*, 121. In support of our view that Averroes defends democracy, see Rosenthal's comment in Averroes, *Averroes' Commentary on Plato's Republic*, 294, where Rosenthal suggests it is possible that Averroes's favorable view of democracy arises from Aristotle, who saw democracy as the least bad of the unjust regimes. This aspect of Aristotle's thought is discussed in Chapter 3, Section X, of this book.

41. Leaman, *Averroes and His Philosophy*, 127.

42. Averroes, *Averroes' Commentary on Plato's Republic*, 164.

43. Ibid., 164–65.

44. Ibid.

45. Ibid.

46. Ibid., 166.

47. Ibid.

48. Ibid., 165–66.

49. Ibid., 166. Italics added.

50. Ibid., 214.
51. Ibid., 232.
52. Ibid., 235.
53. Ibid., 212–13.
54. Ibid.
55. Ibid.
56. Ibid.
57. Ibid., 229–30.
58. Ibid., 230.
59. Ibid., 213, 230.
60. Ibid., 232.
61. Ibid., 214.
62. Ibid.
63. Ibid., 232.
64. Ibid., 230.
65. Ibid., 160.
66. Ibid.
67. Ibid.
68. Ibid., 213.
69. Ibid.
70. Ibid.
71. Ibid., 214, 230.
72. Ibid. See note by Rosenthal in *Averroes' Commentary on Plato's Republic*, 286, describing states of necessity, which provide for the necessities of life.
73. Ibid., 214. See note by Rosenthal in Averroes, *Averroes' Commentary on Plato's Republic*, 287, suggesting that the use of the term *association* refers to a political community, which seems to bind people to morality.
74. Ibid.
75. Ibid., 214–15.
76. Ibid., 215.
77. Ibid., 214.
78. Ibid., 215.
79. Ibid., 205.
80. Ibid., 216–17.
81. Leaman, *Averroes and His Philosophy*, 127–28.
82. For background, see the following: Bratton, *Maimonides*, 28–59; Abraham J. Heschel, *Maimonides: A Biography* (New York: Image Books, 1982), 3–24; Rev. A. Cohen, "Introduction," in *The Teachings of Maimonides*, with a prolegomenon by Marvin Fox (New York: Ktav Publishing House, 1968), 7–29.
83. Cohen, "Introduction," 7–11.
84. Bratton, *Maimonides*, 51.
85. Ibid., 52.
86. Laurence Urdang, Stuart Berg Flexner, and Jess M. Stein, *The Random House College Dictionary* (New York: Random House, 1988), 98, 367.
87. Ibid., 957.
88. Ibid., 710.
89. Michael Walzer, Menachem Lorberbaum, and Noam J. Zohar, eds., *The Jewish Political Tradition. Volume One: Authority* (New Haven: Yale University Press, 2000), 553–54. Note that the Torah consists of the Pentateuch, or the first five books of the Old Testament, as well as the whole body of Jewish law, including the Talmud, which we discuss later.
90. Moses Maimonides, "Introduction to the *Mishneh Torah*," in Walzer et al., *The Jewish Political Tradition*, 255. Italics appear in text.

91. Ibid.

92. Urdang et al., *The Random House College Dictionary*, 1167.

93. From a section of a Talmudic discussion entitled "Defining the Elder's Rebellion," in Walzer et al., *The Jewish Political Tradition*, 326.

94. Moses Maimonides, "MT Laws of Rebels," in Walzer et al., *The Jewish Political Tradition*, 285.

95. Michael Walzer, "Introduction to Chapter 6, Rabbis and Sages," in Walzer et al., *The Jewish Political Tradition*, 247.

96. Ibid.

97. David Hartman, "Commentary. Expanding the Covenant," in Walzer et al., *The Jewish Political Tradition*, 26–68.

98. Walzer, "Introduction to Chapter 6, Rabbis and Sages," 249–50.

99. Ibid., 250

100. Ibid.

101. Noam J. Zohar, "Commentary. The Oral Law: Celebrating Radical Reinterpretation," in Walzer et al., *The Jewish Political Tradition*, 278–79.

102. Walzer, "Introduction to Chapter 6, Rabbis and Sages," 250.

103. David Shatz, "Commentary, Interpretive Pluralism," in Walzer et al., *The Jewish Political Tradition*, 340.

104. Ibid., 341, 533.

105. Walzer et al., *The Jewish Political Tradition*, 547, 550, 553.

106. Maimonides, "Introduction to the *Mishneh Torah*," 256.

107. Michael Walzer, "Introduction to Chapter 7, Controversy and Dissent," in Walzer et al, *The Jewish Political Tradition*, 314. Also, Shatz, "Commentary, Interpretive Pluralism," 340.

108. Walzer, "Introduction to Chapter 7, Controversy and Dissent," 314.

109. Ibid., 315.

110. Ibid.

111. Ibid. Also see author's introduction to Maimonides, "Introduction to the *Mishneh Torah*," 254.

112. Walzer, "Introduction to Chapter 7, Controversy and Dissent," 315.

113. Maimonides, "Introduction to the *Mishneh Torah*," 355.

114. Pines, "Introduction," xcix.

115. Ibid.

116. Ibid.

117. Maimonides, "MT Laws of Sales," in Walzer et al., *The Jewish Political Tradition*, 419.

118. Amy Gutmann, "Commentary, Who Should Rule?" in Walzer et al., *The Jewish Political Tradition*, 422.

119. Ibid.; Maimonides, "MT Laws of Sales," 419.

120. Pines, "Introduction," cxvii.

121. Leo Strauss, "How to Begin to Study *The Guide of the Perplexed*," in Maimonides, *The Guide of the Perplexed*, xiv.

122. Ibid. The quotation marks are found in the text.

123. Ibid. Also Leo Strauss, *Persecution and the Art of Writing* (Glencoe, IL: The Free Press, 1952), 46.

124. Ibid.

125. Strauss, "How to Begin to Study *The Guide of the Perplexed*," xiv–xv.

126. Ibid., xv.

127. Strauss, *Persecution and the Art of Writing*, 53–55.

128. Maimonides, Pines edition, *The Guide of the Perplexed*, 70, I.32.

129. Marvin Fox, "Prolegomenon," in Rev. A. Cohen, *The Teachings of Maimonides*, xl.

130. Ibid., xl–xli.

131. Ibid.

132. Maimonides, Pines edition, *The Guide of the Perplexed*, 73, I.34.

133. Ibid., 431, III.8. Italics in text.

134. Ibid.

135. We realize that Maimonides, in addition to the two rational ends cited, notes a third – "apprehension of the Creator." But we emphasize the two mentioned in this paragraph because it seems that, in seeking knowledge of the natural and human worlds, and in doing as moral right requires, humankind would in Maimonides's view, receive an understanding of the Creator. This means that to understand the Creator is to comprehend the nature of the Creator's world, including the way the Creator wants people to live in that world.

136. Maimonides, Pines edition, *The Guide of the Perplexed*, 431, III.8.

137. Ibid., 432, III.8.

138. Ibid., 431, III.8.

139. Ibid., 510, III.27.

140. Ibid.

141. Ibid. Italics are added.

142. Ibid.

143. Ibid., 511, III.27.

144. Ibid., 510–11, III.27.

145. Ibid., 511, III.27.

146. Ibid.

147. Fox, "Prolegomenon," xli.

148. Maimonides, Pines edition, *The Guide of the Perplexed*, 601, III.49.

149. Moses Maimonides, "Commentary on the Mishnah, and Mishneh Torah," in Rev. A. Cohen, *The Teachings of Maimonides*, 296–97.

150. Maimonides, Pines edition, *The Guide of the Perplexed*, 602–12, III.49, 77, I.34.

151. Ibid., 433–36, III.8. Maimonides advocates shaming people for their anger; promoting drinking and eating only for nourishment, not for pleasure; and avoiding obscene language, as well as discussions about copulation. There is no space available here to discuss the implications and wisdom of Maimonides's views on subjects of this sort for the modern world.

152. Ibid., 631, III.55.

153. Ibid.

PART II

Early Modern Approaches to Civil Society

6

Niccolò Machiavelli: Civic Virtue and Civil Society

I. Historical Setting and Introduction

Niccolò Machiavelli (1469–1526) was a political realist, unlike others we discuss in this book, who approached politics from philosophical, moral, or religious perspectives. As such, his main concern was learning how to get and keep power. Still, it would be wrong to conclude that "Machiavellianism" is a doctrine radically divorced from morality and thus from a conception of civic virtue. Even though his arguments reflected the view that political authority could no longer be justified based on ecclesiastical or religious grounds, he still understood the importance of maintaining among the members of the society a commitment to the common good. Without the habits of civic virtue, which include respect for the rule of law and which exhort people to promote the common good, societies might be undermined by the natural selfishness found in humankind. As one writer said, for Machiavelli, "men are apt to behave toward one another worse than most savage beasts."[1]

Prior to discussing Machiavelli's doctrines, it is necessary to provide some historical background. Throughout the fifteenth century, a single family, the Medicis, had run Machiavelli's Florence. They had governed Florence as a ruling elite while making it appear that they were maintaining a republic as opposed to a monarchy. A republic is different from a monarchy in the sense that the latter is governed by a king whose authority derives from family background. A republic, on the other hand, is a political regime united around promoting a conception of the common good, but it is also presumed that the authority of the government in a republic rests upon citizen participation in determining the common good and the laws that enshrine it.

In 1494, the Medici's dominance came to an end, and there followed a series of republican and Medicean regimes until the Medici family was fully restored in 1512. During this period, Machiavelli assumed various roles, including advisor, bureaucrat, and diplomat. But after 1512, Machiavelli, who had always been committed to republican rule and who had always been anti-Medici, lost all chances for political office, and he was accused of treason, arrested, and even tortured. Eventually, he was cleared of all wrongdoing, and he went to live on a Florentine suburban farm. During this time, he wrote *The Prince* and *The Discourses on the First Ten Books of Titus Livius*, both of which we discuss in this chapter.[2] The former work was written to provide advice and to win back favor from the Medicis, and it is thus dedicated to one of the Medici sons.[3]

Central to Machiavelli's analysis of politics was the revolution in circumstances taking place during his life. Machiavelli wrote during the fifteenth century, when Italy was divided into five large states – Florence, Milan, Venice, Naples, and the papal state.[4] During this time, opportunities for economic and cultural growth were abundant. Owing to new trade opportunities, to the breakup of the feudal system, and to the establishment of new crafts, the Italian states became a part of the world economy, participating in international trade and business. But at the same time, the political structures of the Italian states could not accommodate themselves to the challenges that the new trading opportunities presented. These states were constantly involved in various conflicts, and they could not unite to form a single Italian state.[5] Machiavelli believed that the states of the Italian peninsula needed to overcome these conflicts and to form unified states like Spain, France, and England. He also believed that the pope was both too weak to unite Italy and too strong to prevent others from doing so. Machiavelli, who lived during a time that was at the earliest stages of the present-day Western nation-state system, hoped for a form of Italian government that could provide a basis for economic expansion and for eliminating divisiveness.[6]

For Machiavelli, Italy was marked, then, to cite George Sabine, by "arrested political development."[7] To move the Italian states into the modern world, there needed to be a new kind of political ruler who could create political structures that met the challenges of the changing social and economic conditions. Machiavelli's prince would have the responsibility of recasting society and creating a government with sufficient power to achieve prosperity in the new-world setting. The new ruler would help create a republic, backed by the people and institutions that secure some form of citizen participation. And the shared goal of the republic would be to advance the material progress and power of Italy as a whole.

For our purposes, Machiavelli is especially important because, in discussing the agenda for the new ruler, Machiavelli helped to pave the way for a civil society that works to secure the rule of law on behalf of protecting basic individual freedoms. As our discussion of *The Prince, The Discourses on the First Ten Books of Titus Livius*, and *Mandragola* in the rest of this chapter demonstrates, Machiavelli is a transitional figure in this book. For even as he accepted an old-world commitment to promote the traditions of civic virtue that secured respect for the common good, he, at the same time, realized that the civic virtue orientation had to be made compatible with the quest, found in the new world, for individual liberty. Now, Machiavelli did not engage in writing the political theory of civil society, demonstrating how to define constraints that at the same time secured liberty. That task awaited those who followed him, such as Thomas Hobbes, Benedict Spinoza, and John Locke. Still, Machiavelli set the stage for those whom we discuss in the next section.

One final point. Machiavelli approaches his subject from the standpoint of two types of regimes: monarchies and republics. In *The Prince*, he is concerned with discussing monarchies, especially new ones, and in *The Discourses*, he is concerned with republics.[8] In discussing new monarchies, Machiavelli demonstrates how to use power to create a new political regime within a newly conquered territory. In *The Discourses*, republics are referred to as a form of mixed government, or a government based upon established traditions that include monarchical, aristocratic, and democratic elements. His hope is that these three elements, when allowed to share power together, would help to sustain a commitment to the common good among citizens. Such a regime would permit citizen input on behalf of defining the common good and on behalf of making possible a society dedicated to the rule of law. Owing to the inherent corruptibility of humankind, however, Machiavelli worries that respect for the traditions of civic virtue, including respect for law, would be hard to maintain. This pessimism emanates from his view that human nature, as indicated earlier, is in large part characterized by selfishness and greed, and these tendencies are likely to be exacerbated in a world that more and more emphasizes individual freedom. The portrait he paints of human nature in the modern world can be found in his play *Mandragola*, which we discuss at the end of this chapter.

II. *The Prince*

Monarchy

The Prince is a treatise on how to get and keep power, and, in this work, Machiavelli addresses how these objectives could be achieved in monarchies. In discussing monarchies in *The Prince*, Machiavelli does not dwell on hereditary ones because these states can be sustained merely by retaining allegiance to "ancestral usages."[9] For Machiavelli, "the difficulty of maintaining hereditary states accustomed to a reigning family is far less than in new monarchies."[10] The monarchies that require special attention, then, are those in which a prince is trying to establish sovereignty over a new territory or, in effect, to place himself in control of a regime previously ruled by another. "It is in the new monarchy that difficulties really exist."[11] Securing a prince's power in this situation is fraught with difficulty because partisans of the old regime who resent the new order are always still present in society.[12] Machiavelli says:

> *It must be considered that there is nothing more difficult to carry out, nor more doubtful of success, nor more dangerous to handle, than to initiate a new order of things. For the reformer has enemies in all those who profit by the old order, and only lukewarm defenders in all those who would profit by the new order, this lukewarmness arising partly from fear of their adversaries, who have the laws in their favour [sic]; and partly from the incredulity of mankind, who do not truly believe in anything new until they have had actual experience of it.*[13]

Every prince must face the uncertainties associated with *fortune*. No one can know in advance of a proposed action what the consequences of an intended action might be. For a prince who takes over a previously governed regime, this problem is exacerbated by the hostile environment he faces. There are those who want to restore the old order, as well as so many others who expect the new prince to deliver on all his promises. There are external enemies who will seize upon any weakness they see to invade and overthrow the new regime. For these reasons, it is foolish for a prince to think that he can ever master fortune completely. Still, a prince should be able to master fortune at least partially. Machiavelli says that "fortune is the ruler of half our actions." But, nonetheless, fortune allows "the other half or thereabouts to be governed by us."[14]

Thus, despite the obstacles it presents, Machiavelli thinks that fortune could be mastered, but only certain people are capable of doing so: in particular, those who are both bold and sagacious. Machiavelli says that "fortune is a woman, and it is necessary, if you wish to master her, to conquer her by force; and it can be seen that she lets herself be overcome by the bold rather than by those who proceed coldly."[15] Indeed, for skilled political leaders, fortune merely represents an opportunity to show how capable they are at mastering events. Machiavelli says that great leaders "owed nothing to fortune but the opportunity which gave them matter to be shaped into what form they thought fit."[16]

Leader virtue, or what Machiavelli calls *"virtù,"* refers to the ability of the prince to carve from the disorder and uncertainty of fortune a political order that incurs people's continuing support for the prince's regime. To this end, the prince manifests *virtù* when he satisfies the yearning of people for the security of their material interests, including such things as people's property and families. Machiavelli holds up for high praise leaders who are successful in the effort to secure for people their possessions, in the face of those potential enemies who would take them away.[17] Such leaders become heroes to their people, and they deserve to be accorded glory and fame. In this regard, Machiavelli approves of leaders such as Moses, who helped the people of Israel escape from slavery in Egypt.[18]

At the same time, Machiavelli attacks leaders who use their abilities to gain power at great cost to their fellow citizens. Leaders in this category are people such as Agathocles, who betrayed his friends and killed his fellow citizens, and these actions cannot be called virtuous. People such as Agathocles, to paraphrase Machiavelli, "gain power, they do not gain glory."[19]

Still, to master circumstances in a manner that wins the people's support, a prince who demonstrates *virtù* may show little regard for traditional moral ideas, such as keeping agreements. These conventional moral norms may be essential in conducting relationships within the family or among friends, but they often have no place in a public setting that calls for a prince to manifest the boldness and daring needed to control public events on behalf of creating lasting benefits for people.

The prince, then, must destroy, at times, to make available important goods for his people, and thus it is not always possible or likely that the prince can sustain moral values traditionally considered essential in normal day-to-day settings. Indeed, the science of politics for Machiavelli is derived neither from studies in moral philosophy, nor from theoretical inquiries into natural law, nor from an understanding of theology. Rather, the science of politics evolves from a study of people whose main objective is to acquire power and to use it to create orderly societies that serve people's vital interests.

Moreover, Machiavellian approaches to the discussion of the science of politics always presume that there are only certain people who should become a prince. These people must face the uncertainty of fortune, never knowing in advance the consequences of their actions. To weather the storms associated with this reality, princes must be capable of doing whatever is necessary to survive, including committing violence against their enemies. Those who wish to lead more normal lives, in accordance with traditional moral categories, need not apply. On the other hand, those willing to use whatever means are needed to create regimes that serve people's lasting needs are ideal candidates. What is a prince's reward? Of course, there is the attainment of power that attracts would-be princes. But, in addition, people who succeed in creating regimes that protect people's vital interests are remembered favorably for generations to come. In effect, the prince's greatest reward is to be remembered fondly by his nation for his willingness to be bold, daring, and ruthless in the face of great danger. Such people stand against a people's archenemies and survive, and their victory is the nation's triumph.

Innovation Through Violence

To provide an understanding of how a ruler with *virtù* might behave, it is well to give an example of a Machiavellian role model, Cesare Borgia. Initially, fortune smiled on Borgia, who gained control of Romagna, a former province in the papal state, with the help of his father, Pope Alexander. Yet, the same fortune that gave him power later took it away when his father died. Machiavelli says that Borgia "acquired the state by the influence of his father and lost it when that influence failed."[20] Still, during the time that Borgia ruled, he demonstrated a masterful control of events. For instance, once he had gained power, Borgia sought to consolidate his grip over Romagna by various means that Machiavelli finds praiseworthy. Borgia made friends with those aristocrats who had formerly supported other political elites by giving them new offices and privileges in exchange for their support. Those people whose loyalty could not be bought were forcibly crushed with the help of French troops. Finally, before Borgia gained power, Romagna was ruled by weak people who could not protect the citizens from "every kind of disorder." But once in power, Borgia gained the support of the citizens by giving them "good government" and by bringing peace and ending instability.[21]

To end disorder, it was at times necessary to rely upon extreme cruelty. For this reason, Borgia appointed Remirro de Orco, "a cruel and able man, to whom he gave the fullest authority."[22] Once de Orco had succeeded in bringing order and stability, Borgia, fearing the citizens would begin to despise him as a result of de Orco's cruelty, removed him from power and established a civil court "under an excellent president, to which each city appointed its own advocate."[23] Now, order would be maintained through public legality as opposed to official violence. Still, Borgia feared that de Orco's actions might arouse toward him hatred from the citizens. To avoid this possibility, Borgia sought to distance himself from de Orco. Thus, Borgia murdered de Orco in a way that would draw public approval as well as dissociate Borgia from de Orco's cruelty in the public's mind. So, Borgia, in a solemn and sanctimonious moment, had de Orco "cut in half and placed one morning in the public square . . . with a piece of wood and bloodstained knife by his side. The ferocity of this spectacle caused the people both satisfaction and amazement."[24] The people saw Borgia as their protector once again, this time against his own hired murderer.

Ultimately, fortune finally triumphed over Borgia and caused his downfall. Upon the death of his father, Borgia was unable to install as pope the person Borgia wanted, but he at least prevented a person whom he did not want. Thus, Julius II, while not Borgia's choice for pope, was still a person with whom Borgia thought he could live. Still, despite the appointment of Julius II, Borgia was unable to maintain power. Borgia blamed fortune for this outcome. Machiavelli reports that Borgia told him he had a good plan to keep his power, but, owing to his ill health, he was not able to execute it. From Borgia's perspective, then, as Machiavelli describes the situation, had Borgia been well himself at the time of his father's death, "everything would have been easy." But Borgia told Machiavelli that, at the time of his father's death, he (Borgia) was dying, too.[25] And this supposedly ended his hope for continued rule.

However, as Machiavelli knew, Borgia lived another three years, and, ultimately, he lost his life in a war.[26] So, what is the real reason for Borgia's downfall? Machiavelli believes Borgia made some tactical errors regarding his father's successor. In particular, Borgia, in allowing the elevation of Julius II to pope, "made a bad choice."[27] If Borgia could not have the person as pope whom he wanted, he should have prevented

*any one individual being made pope, and he ought never to have per-
mitted any of those cardinals to be raised to the papacy whom he had
injured, or who when pope would stand in fear of him. For men commit
injuries either through fear or through hate.*[28]

Still, Machiavelli views Borgia as a person who used "force and fraud, to make himself beloved and feared by the people."[29] Whoever wants to destroy one's enemies, introduce innovations, and, in general, use deception and violence to manipulate circumstances for achieving power "can find no better example than the actions of this man."[30] Well-used power and toughness, just like well-designed deception, are acceptable means for securing power. These tactics are acceptable especially when they are used to establish a political order that is based on public legality.

Techniques of Power: Maintaining Appearances

The Borgia case study in addressing fortune is supplemented by Machiavelli's advice to princes on how to regard their subjects. Here, his interest is in demonstrating to a prince how, once he has gained power, he should act to keep it.[31] Machiavelli's advice is clearly designed to emphasize that the appearance and the style of a prince are critical to his winning the confidence of the citizens. Now, this means that he must often appear to be what he, in fact, is not. He must appear to be "faithful, humane, sincere, religious, and also to be so; but you must have the mind so disposed that when it is needful to be otherwise you may be able to change to the opposite qualities."[32] The prince must be careful, then, when portraying himself, to depict himself in public in ways that make him appealing to the citizens. He must "take great care that nothing goes out of his mouth" that makes it appear that he is not wedded to the qualities just listed, and this point is especially true with respect to religion.[33] People are swayed by the image projected by a prince, and most people do not care to look beyond that image to the real person.

Besides the characteristics just mentioned, there are other qualities that the prince should display. Machiavelli believes a prince should be considered liberal as opposed to miserly, generous as opposed to rapacious, trustworthy as opposed to a man unable to keep his promises, courageous as opposed to cowardly, serious as opposed to frivolous, and humane as opposed to haughty. Now, no prince can embrace all these good qualities and at the same time avoid all the bad ones, but he should avoid any particular vices that "would lose him the state." Yet, when it is necessary for him to manifest particular vices for the sake of preserving his power, he should do so.[34]

Machiavelli's emphasis on a prince's maintaining proper appearances is a point certainly by now well taken by most people who manage modern campaigns and who use television to project the images that entice citizens' support for candidates. Clearly, Machiavelli, like today's campaign manager, had a cynical view of the body politic and its tastes. Thus, Machiavelli says:

Let the prince therefore aim at conquering and maintaining the state, and the means will be judged honourable and praised by every one, for the vulgar is always taken by appearances . . . and the world consists only of the vulgar, and the few who are not vulgar are isolated when the many have a rallying point in the prince.[35]

The emphasis on maintaining a proper appearance before the people suggests that, if one approach to resisting the slings and arrows of fortune is unsuccessful, the prince must be flexible enough to change directions. He cannot be an ideologue who is dedicated to one and only one course of action. Moreover, if, in modifying a previous policy direction, a prince finds it necessary to break a promise, then he should do so. "A prudent ruler ought not to keep faith when, by so doing, it would be against his interest."[36] To be sure, while it is best to appear morally good and upright, the circumstances may dictate that one be like Borgia, ruthless and bold. That is why a prince must "learn how not to be good, and to use this knowledge and not use it, according to the necessity of the case."[37] Maintaining the right appearance, then, is in large part a function of a prince's making the right choices pertaining to how he should act in a given circumstance. If he is humble when he should be bold, he appears to be unable to carry the mantle of power. He then appears bumbling and incompetent, and, in consequence, he opens himself up to numerous attacks from his enemies and is overtaken by fortune.

Still, even when the prince makes the right decisions and maintains an aura of control and competence, this fact by itself does not secure a prince's position. Indeed, if maintaining good appearances is all that is needed, then all a prince would have to do is that which would win him the love of all his citizens. Now, certainly all princes do best when they can maintain the faith and love of their people. For Machiavelli, "the best fortress [to protect one's power] is to be found in the love of the people."[38] But Machiavelli makes clear that a prince must accept that, for the most part, people will always find fault with him, even when he appears in control of circumstances and maintains the right appearances. Why is this? For Machiavelli, all princes are faced with the age-old question citizens ask politicians: "Yes, you did well by me yesterday, but what have you done for me lately?" Although Machiavelli is not the originator of this question, he might have been. Machiavelli is well aware, then, that most citizens are "ungrateful"; they are "dissemblers"; they are "covetous of gain"; and they are not reliable; in short, "as long as you benefit them, they are entirely yours; they offer you their blood, their goods, their life, and their children . . . but when [any unfortunate circumstance that disadvantages them] approaches, they revolt."[39]

So, how is the prince to maintain his power in the face of this type of problem? Machiavelli is clear that, at times, if a prince cannot be loved, then it is best for him to be feared.[40] People must be acquainted with the prince's toughness and with the knowledge that he can use the same force against them that he uses against the enemies of the society or against his own enemies. Still, the prince must recognize his limits to making the general population fear him. He cannot go so far that he invokes the people's hatred.[41] To avoid incurring people's hatred, a prince must not be "rapacious, and [usurp] the property and women of his subjects. . . [nor may he] attack the property or honour of the generality of men."[42] Here, Machiavelli makes clear that the prince must recognize that he can survive only as long as he serves well the vital interests of the citizens. If people do not fear conditions that threaten those interests, they do not need a protector, and thus if the prince is perceived as a part of the conditions they fear, they do not need the prince. It is clear that a vital interest for people is security for those things people find most dear, and, in consequence, people expect the prince to create a society that protects their families and properties.

Now, Machiavelli lists different ways by which the prince can protect the vital interests of people. One way is to engage in "great enterprises." Examples of great enterprises include successful military campaigns, which "astonish" the public and which in consequence would presumably engender in the public a sense of national pride. A prince may also engage in domestic actions that serve the public's interest in important ways. Here, a prince seeks "fame for being great and excellent."[43] In each case, a prince's doing good for the society brings admiration from the people, who are grateful to him for the benefits he has bestowed on the society.

Perhaps the most important way to promote people's vital interests is to create a society in which individuals can receive those things from life that make their lives pleasing and satisfactory. The prince must work for conditions that ensure the material prosperity of his citizens, and these conditions must permit individuals to take part in ways of life of their own choice. Machiavelli says:

> *Moreover, he must encourage his citizens to follow their callings quietly, whether in commerce, or agriculture, or any other trade that men follow, so that this one shall not refrain from improving his possessions through fear that they may be taken from him, and that one from starting a trade for fear of taxes; but he should offer rewards to whoever does these things, and to whoever seeks in any way to improve his city or state.*[44]

Machiavelli's prince realizes that people are never free if they live in fear that the fruits of their best efforts will be taken from them. This means that people are free to promote a way of life of their own choice only when they are convinced that others will not rob them of their gains. It would seem, then, that the prince must put in place a system of laws that protect people's basic interests. Furthermore, for Machiavelli, it is not enough that people be protected from the loss of those goods they acquire from pursuing their own ways of life, but, in addition, people must understand a corresponding responsibility to pursue ways of life that enhance the society as well. So, Machiavelli's prince realizes that people, as they follow their own interests, must become wedded to the need to contribute to the larger good of society, and thus the importance of civic virtue remains. To this end, Machiavelli's prince will provide people with rewards for acting in ways that benefit not just themselves but the entire society. Machiavelli builds upon this idea in his discussion of republics, as we see in the next section.

III. *The Discourses* and Republican Forms

In *The Prince*, the leader with *virtù* creates an order that is the basis for people's support for his regime. In *The Discourses*, a leader displays *virtù* when he creates lasting institutions that transcend his own reign and that secure people's vital needs for generations to come. Here, the basis for assessing a leader's contributions is not, as in *The Prince*, how a leader such as Borgia had mastered fortune to maintain a regime in his own lifetime but whether a leader's regime continues to exist long after he dies.[45] For Machiavelli, "the welfare, then, of a republic or a kingdom does not consist in having a prince who governs it wisely during his lifetime, but in having one who will give it such laws that it will maintain itself even after his death."[46]

But creating an enduring political system, in this case a *republic*, which is the topic of *The Discourses*, is difficult because governments, while initiated for reasons of securing justice, are constantly undermined by corruption. Indeed, for Machiavelli, the rise and fall of governments are attuned to a cycle in which just governments, owing to corruption, are turned into unjust ones, and then citizens rebel on behalf of restoring justice, but then, corruption once again returns. This cycle is ongoing throughout history. To explain this recurring cycle, Machiavelli discusses six different types of governments. First, there are the three good or just types of regimes: monarchy, the rule of the single best man; aristocracy, the rule of the few best men; and democracy, the rule of all. Each of these has a corresponding perverted or unjust form. The corrupt form of monarchy is tyranny, the rule of the single unjust man; the corrupt form of aristocracy is oligarchy, the rule of the few unjust men; and the corrupt form of democracy is anarchy, the rule of the mob.[47]

In the following discussion, we outline the parade of government types that appear throughout the "just to unjust cycle" to demonstrate Machiavelli's affinity for mixed governments, or a republic. The latter, which orients people to the common good, contains elements of each of the just kinds of government. The republic is Machiavelli's model regime, which he believes existed in ancient Rome.[48]

The cycle of regime types starts with a discussion of the first governments. Before there were many people, there was no need for government. But as the number of people increased, people found it necessary to unite for the purpose of securing the common welfare. To attain their common objectives, the people chose the best and strongest to lead them. At the same time, people began to distinguish between those among them who were honest and those who were "bad and vicious." The latter were selfish people who could not be trusted with power. These sentiments led to establishing laws to ensure punishment for those who committed wrongful acts against others. "Such was the origin of justice," says Machiavelli. Further, "this caused them [the people], when they had afterwards to choose a prince, neither to look to the strongest nor the bravest, but to the wisest and most just."[49] Thus, the first governments, or monarchies, were founded by great and wise men who symbolized government by the single best person.

When power was transmitted to the next generation, non-elective, hereditary approaches were used. But with the transition, problems arose, and these problems made maintaining a just regime difficult. The children of the first good leaders were spoiled by a life of ease, and consequently, they lacked all recognition of the importance of excelling through displays of virtue and believed, instead, that they should be accorded every possible luxury. "The prince consequently soon drew upon himself the general hatred."[50] And because the people's hatred frightened the prince, the prince decided to protect himself by turning into a tyrant who subdued the people to maintain his own rule over them.

The people rebelled against these conditions, and those who led the rebellion became known as "liberators."[51] The latter constituted a government with a new ruling class of the nobility and thus created an aristocratic government. Here, the government of the few best men remembered the terrors of tyranny and hoped not to reinstitute them. Consequently, the nobility promoted laws that had as their main objective the public interest. But their children, who succeeded them, were ignorant of what their fathers had tried to accomplish, never having "experienced [tyranny's] reverses" and, not content "with this civil equality, they in turn gave themselves up to cupidity, ambition, libertinage, and violence and soon caused the aristocratic government to degenerate into an oligarchic tyranny, regardless [or heedless] of all civil rights."[52]

Thus, the oligarchs created the same tyranny that the people had experienced under the first tyrant. The people revolted against this situation and sought the protection of a new prince. But the latter's reign was also tyrannous. So, the people, remembering the failures both of the prince, who had replaced the oligarchy, and of the aristocracy, decided to set up a democracy with the intention that "the authority should not again fall into the hands of a prince or a small number of nobles."[53] But the new form of government remained in place only as long as those who helped establish that government lived. When the new generation came into power, it lacked a good memory of the past, and, as in the past, it fell into all the bad habits that brought about oppression. "Each individual only consulted his own passions, and a thousand acts of injustice were daily committed." Democracy turned into anarchy, necessitating the restoration of the prince, the single leader, who could restore order. But, once again, the same cycle was repeated, and the society fell into anarchy.[54]

Throughout, it would appear that the enemy of all regimes, especially good regimes, is corruption. Thus, "a legislator who gives to a state which he founds, either of these three [good] forms of government, constitutes it but for a brief time; for no precautions can prevent either one of the three that are reputed good, from degeneration into its opposite kind."[55] However, this pessimism is somewhat chastened by Machiavelli's choice of a mixed regime, which is more likely to withstand the cancer of corruption than the ones just mentioned. In a mixed regime, the three elements, the king, the nobility, and the people, share power. Lycurgus, the great lawgiver of Sparta, suggested this approach for Sparta, and Sparta lasted more than 800 years in general tranquility. Rome did not have a great leader like Lycurgus, but it did have Romulus and other kings who gave it laws "suited to a free people." Initially, Roman leadership had as its objective a monarchy and not a republic, but, after many years, the monarchy was transformed into a republic when "royal authority" came to share power with the aristocratic elements of society, as well as with the people. This combination "rendered the constitution perfect."[56]

In a mixed government, or republic, the three classes share power, and each will watch and check the other, preventing any single class from dominating the rest. But even in a mixed regime, the responsibility for protecting liberty must be placed, predominantly, into the hands of one class. And for Machiavelli, liberty is best protected when it is placed into the hands of the common people. Why is this? Whereas the nobility has a great desire to dominate, the ordinary people want only to be free from domination. Thus, the ordinary people have a greater desire than anyone else to

> live in the enjoyment of liberty; so that when the people are entrusted with the care of any privilege or liberty, being less disposed to encroach upon it, they will of necessity take better care of it; and being unable to take it away themselves, will prevent others from doing so.[57]

Given the importance of the people to maintaining liberty, it is critical that the people not become corrupt themselves. "When corruption has taken possession of the whole people, then it cannot preserve its free condition even for the shortest possible time."[58] Indeed, the importance of avoiding corruption among the people is critical to preserving the integrity of the law-making process. Referring to the Roman republic, Machiavelli says that, as long as people are not corrupt, the law-making process is a setting in which citizens propose what they think is in the public interest. Here, all citizens are allowed to express their opinions on the proposals, and citizens make their judgments about what is best only after having heard all sides. But when the people become corrupt, the entire process is destroyed. Machiavelli says that

when the citizens had become corrupt, this system [for law-making] became the worst possible, for then only the most powerful proposed laws, not for the common good and [for] the liberty of all, but [for] the increase of their own power, and fear restrained all others from speaking against such laws.[59]

Protecting liberty is difficult, if not impossible, once this course of events takes place, and the only hope of doing so rests with the emergence of a political strong man, such as Machiavelli discusses in *The Prince*. Here, the state must be reduced to "a monarchical, rather than a republican form of government." Machiavelli says that "for men whose turbulence could not be controlled by the simple force of law can be controlled in a measure only by an almost regal power. And the attempt to restore men to good conduct by any other means would be either a most cruel or an impossible undertaking."[60]

But this remedy is not necessary in a society in which there is strong commitment to the canons of civic virtue. For in this context, people do not become corrupted, but instead they develop the habits associated with what is of central importance in Machiavelli's republic, respect for the law. Here, citizens are willing to put aside the temptations to follow their own self-interests, to secure the place of the law in the society. But for citizens to follow this path, it is necessary that the laws in the society be good or just. Otherwise, people will not develop the habits necessary to uphold them.

Thus, Machiavelli thinks that to maintain support for laws, people must develop those habits that make such a commitment possible. However, in the absence of good laws, these habits will not emerge. Machiavelli says, "For as good habits of the people require good laws to support them [good habits], so laws, to be observed need good habits on the part of the people."[61]

Now, in stressing good laws, what Machiavelli has in mind is the central importance of the rule of law. Good laws have as their objective the common good, but that good cannot be achieved if there are some people who think they are above the law and thus, owing to their higher social status, not subject to it. Machiavelli says:

[A] well ordered republic [should never] cancel the crimes of its citizens by their merits; but having established rewards for good actions and penalties for evil ones and having rewarded a citizen for good conduct who afterwards commits a wrong, he should be chastised for that without regard to his previous merits. And a state that properly observes this

principle will long enjoy its liberty; but if otherwise, it will speedily come to ruin.[62]

Thus, Machiavelli has contempt for those who are not likely to think of themselves as subject to the same law as everyone else. In particular, he has in mind a situation in which a corrupt ruling group dominates, as the traditional feudal landowning class had done. These individuals live off their inherited wealth and do no useful work, yet they seek to maintain relationships of command toward the rest of the society. Their interest is not the public good, only their own good. "Such men are pernicious to any country or republic."[63] These men have no respect for the rule of law, because the ordinary people's interest is of a lesser concern than their own. Governed by a corrupt aristocracy, the ordinary people would always fear for their liberty because neither their property nor their lives nor the lives of their families would be safe.

In contrast, Machiavelli holds up for praise the new aristocracy, who earns their wealth from "commerce and movable property, and moreover none of them have castles or jurisdiction over subjects."[64] Presumably, these individuals respect ordinary people and work to make possible the rule of good laws that work for the common interest. Indeed, in Venice, where this class is prominent, the ordinary citizens, who are excluded from various offices and honors reserved for the new aristocracy, are still able to find with them a basis for social stability and concord. This situation suggests that the new aristocracy of commerce and business poses no threat to the liberty of ordinary people, but, instead, through their industry and commerce, this new class provides a basis for greater opportunities for all.[65] In such situations, society thrives, there is happiness and prosperity, and the republic is secured.

Other elements than good laws can contribute to maintaining those good habits of civic virtue that act as a deterrent to the corruption of the citizens. In particular, religious practices and institutions can engender a sense of respect for the traditions of civic virtue that help maintain a commitment to the common good. Thus, Machiavelli says that "as the observance of divine institutions is the cause of greatness of republics, so the disregard of them produces their ruin." And, later, Machiavelli says that "there is no greater indication of the ruin of a country than to see religion contemned."[66] But Machiavelli does not seem to believe that religious institutions can be the main source of civic virtue any longer, owing to what he believes is the corruption of the Catholic Church. The Church has "destroyed all piety and religion in Italy."[67] More importantly, the church cannot be a force for helping to unify the nation and for teaching citizenship on a nationwide basis. For Machiavelli, the Church is a source of "our ruin" because it "has kept and still keeps our country divided."[68]

Finally, for Machiavelli, in great cities or republics, there is a "great affection for liberty,"[69] an affection that grows from the fact that people understand that prosperity and wealth emerge only for a city in which there is liberty. But prosperity alone does not make a city great. In addition, there must be a commitment to the common good by the citizens. Rome's greatness, in fact, is a product of this understanding. Machiavelli says that

> *the cause of [Rome's greatness] is manifest, for it is not individual prosperity, but the general good, that makes cities [or republics] great; and certainly the general good is regarded nowhere but in republics, because whatever they do is for the common benefit.*[70]

A republic at its best would possess important characteristics of a civil society. There would be a chance for individuals to pursue their own conceptions of what is best, but in a setting governed by an overarching conception of the common good. The latter would manifest itself in the form of good laws that secure a basis for equal treatment to all citizens, no matter what class they might come from. But Machiavelli fears that even this way of life would be continually threatened. His fear emanates from the real reason he believes the habits of civic virtue and good law are needed in the first place. The problem that threatens republican life for Machiavelli is the inherent selfishness of human beings. We turn now to a discussion of this dimension in his play *Mandragola*.[71]

IV. *Mandragola*

Machiavelli's *Mandragola* has a simple plot. A young man, Callimaco, is smitten by a young, married woman, Lucrezia. She is a devout Catholic, desirous of pleasing her husband, Nicia. Nicia is a much older man who wants to have children, but he is impotent. Now, Nicia will not admit to his impotence and will not accept responsibility for his wife's inability to become pregnant. He insists there is something wrong with her. Using this information, Callimaco constructs, with the help of his servant, a plot to get into Lucrezia's bed. The idea is to convince Nicia that the only way for Lucrezia to become pregnant is if she drinks a medicine called mandragola. Callimaco tells Nicia that the first man who has intercourse with his wife after she has drunk the potion dies within a week. Naturally, Nicia does not like this idea, but Callimaco has a way to address his fears. Callimaco suggests that after Lucrezia has had the potion she sleep with a low-life, whom Callimaco has kidnapped and placed in her bed.[72] Naturally, the low-life will be a disguised Callimaco.

Nicia is easily convinced by Callimaco to take part in the scheme. Deceiving his wife is of no importance to Nicia, since his first goal is to manifest his manhood by having children. (When asked if he is impotent, Nicia says, "Me? Impotent? Oh, you'll make me laugh. I don't think there's a man more vigorous and virile to be found in all Florence."[73]) He is too simple-minded to realize he is being inveigled by Callimaco into allowing his wife to sleep with another man.

But convincing Lucrezia is a more difficult task. After all, she is a religious woman and does not believe in adultery. She says at one point:

> But of all the things that have ever been tried, I think this is the strangest – that I should have to submit my body to this outrage, and to be the cause of a man's death for outraging me. For I couldn't believe it, even if I were the last woman left in the world, and the whole human race had to start all over again from me – that I would be expected to do such a thing.[74]

To change her mind, her priest, Friar Timoteo, is asked to be a part of the plot and agrees to participate for money. The good Friar tells Lucrezia that sleeping with a strange man for the sake of conceiving a child would not be a sin. After all, there is a positive good that would come from it, namely, creating another "soul for our Good Lord."[75] And this good far outweighs the fear of committing two evils, in this case, the possible death of another and adultery. Regarding the first evil, the Friar says that it is not certain that the man who gives Lucrezia the mandragola will die because not all men who engage in the activity of adultery die. About adultery, the Friar says that it would be sinful for Lucrezia to displease her husband by not doing as he asks. Moreover, because she takes no pleasure in sleeping with another man, there is no sin in what she is about to do. The Friar tells her that only the "will sins, not the body."[76] Indeed, there is biblical precedent for her actions. She is acting like the daughters of Lot, who "believing themselves to be the sole surviving women in the world, mated with their father, and because their intention was good, they did not sin."[77]

So Lucrezia accedes to the wishes of her husband. After all, the Friar, who is the religious authority, has condoned it, and she is only a fearful woman, whose main objectives in life are to please her husband and to ensure her salvation. The Friar has no problem lying to her because he thinks little of women (they are all "short on brains," he says[78]) and because he wants the money.

In the end, everyone *appears* to get what each wants: Callimaco gets in bed with Lucrezia; Nicia gets his child, a son, without having to think of himself as impotent; Lucrezia remains in good standing with her husband and her conscience; and the Friar gets his money. Moreover, while in bed with Lucrezia, Callimaco confesses his love to her, and she, in turn, indicates her belief that the whole event had been "heaven's will," so she asks Callimaco to stay on and become her "protector" and her "father." Indeed, she decides to maintain the relationship to Callimaco by making him the godfather and allowing him free access to the house and to her. Nicia even gives Callimaco a key to the house so he can enter whenever he wishes.[79]

V. The Moral of *Mandragola* and Civil Society

Machiavelli, in this play, demonstrates that early modern society, without the tradition of moral restraints that civic virtue requires, can become nothing more than a place for people to victimize each other. The Catholic Church, for Machiavelli, no longer has much of a role in teaching people to treat one another with basic decency. Instead, people approach one another, as they do in the free-market setting, from the standpoint of the need to promote their own naked self-interests. From this perspective, people pursue to the fullest extent possible, regardless of the standards of traditional virtue, whatever pleases them. So, if money pleases, one should find a way to gain the sufficient power to obtain money. And, similarly, with women. For Callimaco, then, if a woman provides pleasure, why not find a way to buy her, just as one would buy anything else that gives one pleasure?

The play suggests that a new kind of society is needed, one that permits people to pursue objectives that give them pleasure in life but without endangering or injuring others. People can advocate their own interests without denying to others basic dignity and self-respect, as was the case for Lucrezia. *The Prince* and *The Discourses* promise precisely this possibility. From the accounts in these works, individuals are permitted to pursue their own happiness in an environment that protects the liberty of all citizens. To accomplish these ends, there must be regard for the habits of civic virtue, which promote respect for the common good and the rule of law. Where these standards are not preserved, society becomes an environment in which the laws protect the interests of a few. This situation gives license to a favored group to exploit the rest of the members of society, as Callimaco had Lucrezia. Lost in this setting are the habits of the civic virtue that promote the common good and the standards of basic human decency and civility.

In promoting these views, Machiavelli advances the idea of civil society, but, in doing so, he does not identify the formal doctrines that undergird such a society. Later thinkers devise theories that demonstrate the kind of relationship that must occur to secure a civil society. Thus, even if Machiavelli does not write the political theory of the new civil society, he helps define the vision upon which that theory is constructed. In arguing for a regime that seeks to secure the happiness of citizens within the context of respect for civic constraints, he moves society into the modern world, and he opens the door to the type of civil society theorizing to which we now turn.

Notes

1. Henry Paolucci, "Introduction," in Niccolò Machiavelli, *Mandragola*, trans. Anne and Henry Paolucci (Indianapolis, IN: Bobbs-Merrill, 1957), xiii.

2. In the rest of this chapter, references to *The Prince* and *The Discourses on the First Ten Books of Titus Livius* are from Niccolò Machiavelli, *The Prince and the Discourses*, intro. Max Lerner (New York: Modern Library, 1950).

3. Max Lerner, "Introduction," in Machiavelli, *The Prince and the Discourses*, xxv–viii. Also see J. G. A. Pocock, *The Machiavellian Moment: Florentine Political Thought and the Atlantic Republican Tradition* (Princeton, NJ: Princeton University Press, 1975), 86; Mulford Q. Sibley, *Political Ideas and Ideologies: A History of Political Thought* (New York: Harper and Row, 1970), 296–97. See Machiavelli, *The Prince and The Discourses*, 3–4 for his dedication of this book to a Medici son.

4. George H. Sabine, *A History of Political Theory* (New York: Holt, Rinehart and Winston, 1963), 336.

5. Lerner, "Introduction," xxxiii. This book also has important critical essays by Isaiah Berlin and Sheldon Wolin, among others.

6. Ibid., xxxiii–iv. Also see Sabine, *A History of Political Theory*, 337.

7. Ibid., 336.

8. Machiavelli, *The Prince and the Discourses*, 5–6, Chs. 2–3.

9. Ibid., 5, Ch. 2.

10. Ibid.

11. Ibid., 6, Ch. 3, 18–21, Chs. 5–6.

12. Ibid. "Thus you find enemies in all those whom you have injured by occupying that dominion, and you cannot maintain the friendship of those who have helped you to obtain this possession, as you will not be able to fulfill their expectations. . . ."

13. Ibid., 21, Ch. 6.

14. Ibid., 91, Ch. 25.

15. Ibid., 94, Ch. 25.

16. Ibid., 20, Ch. 6.

17. See Sheldon S. Wolin, *Politics and Vision, Continuity and Innovation in Western Political Thought* (Boston: Little, Brown and Company, 1960), 230.

18. Machiavelli, *The Prince and the Discourses*, 21, Ch. 6.

19. Ibid., 32, Ch. 8.

20. Ibid., 25, Ch. 7.

21. Ibid., 26–27, Ch.7.

22. Ibid., 27, Ch. 7.

23. Ibid.

24. Ibid.

25. Ibid.

26. John T. Scott and Vicki B. Sullivan, "Patricide and the Plot of *The Prince:* Cesare Borgia and Machiavelli's Italy," *American Political Science Review* 88, no. 4 (December 1994): 896.

27. Machiavelli, *The Prince and The Discourses*, 30, Ch. 7.

28. Ibid.

29. Ibid.

30. Ibid.

31. Ibid., 56, Ch. 15.

32. Ibid., 65, Ch. 18.

33. Ibid.

34. Ibid., 56–57, Ch. 15.

35. Ibid., 66, Ch. 18.

36. Ibid., 64, Ch. 18.

37. Ibid., 56, Ch. 15.

38. Ibid., 81, Ch. 20.

39. Ibid., 61, Ch. 17.

40. Ibid.

41. Ibid., 61–62, Ch. 17.

42. Ibid., 66, Ch. 19. Also see p. 62, Ch. 17.

43. Ibid., 81–82, Ch. 21.

44. Ibid., 85, Ch. 21.
45. Wolin, *Politics and Vision*, 231.
46. Machiavelli, *The Prince and the Discourses*, 148, Bk. I, Ch. 11.
47. Ibid., 111–12, Bk. I, Ch. 2.
48. Ibid., 111, Bk. I, Ch. 2.
49. Ibid., 112, Bk. I, Ch. 2.
50. Ibid., 113, Bk. I, Ch. 2.
51. Ibid.
52. Ibid.
53. Ibid., 113–14, Bk. I, Ch. 2.
54. Ibid., 114, Bk. I, Ch. 2.
55. Ibid., 112, Bk. I, Ch. 2.
56. Ibid., 115–17, Bk. I, Ch. 2.
57. Ibid., 122, Bk. I, Ch. 5.
58. Ibid., 161, Bk. I, Ch. 16.
59. Ibid., 170, Bk. I, Ch. 18.
60. Ibid., 171, Bk. I, Ch. 18.
61. Ibid., 168, Bk. I, Ch. 18.
62. Ibid., 181, Bk. I, Ch. 24.
63. Ibid., 255, Bk. I, Ch. 55.
64. Ibid., 257, Bk. I, Ch. 56.
65. Ibid., 256–57, Bk. I, Ch. 55.
66. Ibid., 148, Bk. I, Ch. 11, 149, Bk. I, Ch. 12.
67. Ibid., 151, Bk. I, Ch. 12.
68. Ibid.
69. Ibid., 282, Bk. II, Ch. 2.
70. Ibid.
71. Paolucci, "Introduction."
72. Ibid., 22–23.
73. Ibid., 18.
74. Ibid., 35.
75. Ibid., 36.
76. Ibid.
77. Ibid.
78. Ibid., 34.
79. Ibid., 56–59.

7

Thomas Hobbes and Modern Civil Society

I. Historical Context

Thomas Hobbes (1588–1679) designed a new relationship between citizens and their state in the face of the intense conflicts that permeated his society. Before explaining the particular dimensions of these conflicts and of the new citizen–state relationship, it is well worth discussing why Hobbes can be properly called a major architect of modern liberalism.

Hobbes's political thinking emanates from the demands of some people for the opportunity to chart a course in life previously denied expression. Traditional medieval order was predicated upon a way of life that gave prominence to certain classes, including the nobility, the landed, church officials, and, of course, the king. Those left without power were people who worked the land as peasants and serfs, as well as people drafted into the king's and noblemen-led army. Also left without power was a new bourgeoisie or middle class of tradesmen, merchants, and small farmers who owned their own land. The middle class made demands on the political system for inclusion. In effect, this new middle class sought opportunities for a space in which a person could pursue activities previously denied in the old order.

In practical political terms, the provision of rights provided opportunities for the new middle class to express as well as to pursue its own interests. What did these rights guarantee? Rights in Hobbes's political thinking provided people with the chance to make decisions about what they wanted to do with their own lives, within certain limits that the culture of the times established. This means that people would be permitted more leeway than in the past but not so much leeway that they would violate all the norms of the society. Thus, whereas individuals should be given the freedom to become merchants, if that is what they want to be, they could not expect to be admitted to the nobility if that is what they hoped for.

The political system fashioned from this vision is the basis for liberalism. Liberalism makes possible individual freedom by enabling people to have rights, which provide both opportunities and protections, but at the same time, liberalism requires individuals to observe those obligations linked with the new opportunities and protections. There are several important implications of this view. In the first place, the history of liberalism will always be associated in public memory with the need for critiquing in the name of freedom existing traditional ways of life, as was the case in Hobbes's time, while accepting the need for certain culturally established limits on that freedom. And this questioning will always create conflict in society, which will often be resolved in the name of freedom, and less so in the name of retaining restrictions on freedom for the sake of protecting tradition.

For conservatives, as we see in the chapter on that subject, liberalism is criticized for always seeking to make people justify tradition in the name of freedom. And doing so for conservatives can lead to the betrayal of important value – such as religious or longstanding cultural ones – needed to maintain social order and community. For liberals, however, freedom is not corrosive of society because, for them, freedom is always associated with necessary and reasonable constraints needed to secure freedom. Hobbes discusses the constraints of natural law, Spinoza emphasizes the limits on authority by the majority in a democratic society, and John Locke describes what we refer to as the constrained majority. Each writer understands these constraints as necessary for securing freedom. As we shall see, John Stuart Mill argues that people should be free to do what they wish as long as they do not harm others. Immanuel Kant maintains the presence of coercive laws that are formed in keeping with universal moral standards that secure individual freedom. G.W.F. Hegel gives the state the job of enforcing the law for the sake of freedom. John Rawls discusses the place of an overlapping consensus as the basis for necessary constraints on freedom. In short, what liberals suggest is that if tradition denies the freedom that takes place within reasonable constraints, then tradition should be reformed, as, for example, was the case with traditions of segregation that denied freedom to African Americans.

Thus, the view of liberalism provided here explains why liberalism is both a history of the expansion of the number of rights made available to protect people's freedom as well as a history of the need to extend the coverage of rights to those heretofore not protected by them. In Hobbes, there is to be a basic right to personal freedom, and this right is to permit one to choose one's own occupation and core beliefs. To these ends, the right to own property will be a central concern. Later, as we move beyond Hobbes, we see that the number of rights is expanded to include political rights, such as freedom of conscience, speech, association, thought, and so on. Further, those covered under those rights are expanded to include more and more groups not previously accorded rights. Indeed, the history of our own society follows the pattern of liberalism. We have seen the list of rights grow to include, in addition to basic rights in the first ten amendments of the US Constitution and the Supreme Court–endorsed right to privacy, the evolving presumption of a right to health care and to an education. And we have seen the scope of rights expand to include previously excluded groups, such as women, African Americans, Native Americans, LGBTQ+ people, and so on.

Another important implication of liberalism is the liberty interest that is central to the liberal project, which no doubt Hobbes bequeathed. By this, we mean that in demanding a space for persons to pursue conduct or to hold beliefs previously denied to them, individuals are said to have a prime interest in liberty. This means that other values – such as autonomy, privacy, equality, and community are important insofar as they aid that interest. Let us briefly discuss each in turn.

Autonomy suggests that individuals should have the freedom to make major decisions about their lives, including such matters as choice of career, religion, or friendships. Without liberty, there can be no autonomy of choice with respect to major issues such as these. Privacy refers to a sphere outside the reach of others or the state, a sphere in which individuals can live as they choose. Privacy in the context used here suggests that the state or others must allow individuals to think their own thoughts, have their own feelings, and partake in relationships of their own choice – without interference. Equality is a value of high importance in this setting, too. Equality is seen as providing all citizens with like rights and, in consequence thereof, with equal liberty.

Finally, what liberalism emphasizes is that freedom for the individual is more important than community. This does not mean that community is incompatible with liberalism. It means only that the common good of community must be defined so as not to smother liberty. Indeed, communities are acceptable to the extent they practice norms conducive to a broader liberty.

In taking this view, Hobbes, as one of the founders of liberalism, is advocating the interests of a new class, the bourgeoisie, or what is the new middle class. This class has been both celebrated and scorned. Those who celebrate it are writers such as Hobbes, Locke, and Kant, each of whom sees it as the phalanx of freedom. Those who attack the bourgeoisie see the new middle class as mostly interested in material self-gratification and greed, rejecting in the process respect for all that is sacred. The bourgeoisie is viewed in Jean-Jacques Rousseau as the source of the undermining of community. In Karl Marx, it is the basis for a cruel form of capitalism, and in Friedrich Nietzsche, it is the foundation of herd-like, conformist thinking.

All in all, Hobbes, Spinoza, Locke, and Kant as leading forerunners of liberalism represent the quest of the Enlightenment to further the interests of a society based on the teachings of reason. Reason is how individuals can best determine the basis for a good life. And in taking this position, reason emphasizes the importance of liberty as it defends the latter against all that may stand in its way, including well-worn traditions.

In this chapter, we wish to emphasize the liberty interest dimension and ask how well Hobbes makes this interest compatible with civil society in the separate sphere sense of the term. To that end, we describe now the historical context of liberalism in Hobbes.

On the one hand, there are those who believe that the monarch should remain the pivotal political force, not subject to challenge. But, on the other hand, there are those arguing for greater autonomy and independence from the king's power. The English civil wars of Hobbes's lifetime are in part fought over the issue of who should have greater authority, the king or the parliament. Hobbes supports the idea of an absolute monarchy.[1] In doing so, however, he predicates the king's power upon the idea of a social contract to which the people in society consent. A chief condition of this contract is that the government exists to protect the freedom of individuals. This freedom is used ultimately by the evolving merchant or new commercial class seeking independence to pursue its own interests in a society where a medieval structure historically dominated.

In Hobbes's new social contract, then, people would consent to a powerful monarch ruling them, in exchange for the personal freedom that the monarch would guarantee and protect. This new social contract symbolizes that the medieval order in society is no longer the basis for establishing social obligations. Instead, obligations grow out of the desire for individual freedom. Central to this objective is the need to maintain a respect for civic virtue. What role does civic virtue play in the setting that Hobbes describes in his writings? When people have the freedom to determine the way of life that is best for them, they are bound to face conflicts and disagreements. Still, different people holding conflicting interests can live in peace if there are common ground rules or civic virtues all can accept and abide by while promoting their interests. Hobbes's effort to provide rules that secure rights and freedom is the basis for the *liberal* view of civil society that we discuss throughout this part of the book.

II. Hobbes's Method

The method Hobbes uses to find those rules that provide a common basis for politics among disparate groups derives from his fascination with geometry. Geometry was the "only Science that it hath pleased God hitherto to bestow on mankind."[2] In geometry, one starts with simple, but self-evident, propositions, definitions, and axioms and uses deduction to build complex systems from these simpler starting points. This approach is used to explain relationships in the physical world, and Hobbes thinks the political world can be studied in the same manner. The only hindrance to doing so is in determining the correct or valid, simple but self-evident, propositions that are the basis for explaining the general characteristics of human conduct. Once one finds these, one can use them as the starting points for analysis and for building a logical system for the political world similar in nature to the one that geometry constructs for the physical world.

Hobbes approaches this objective by making use of the method Galileo employs, the resolutive–compositive approach, and applying it to the political world.[3] Galileo uses this approach to understand complex motions. He does so by first, in the resolutive part, hypothesizing there to be simple forces. These simple forces cannot be directly observed, but their existence is merely a creation of the imagination. He postulates these simple forces as a necessary ground for the more complex motions he wants to explain. When these simple forces, with the use of logical reasoning, are combined into a composite, he is able to demonstrate why the complex motions he studies take place.

To take this method into the study of humankind, we can start with the whole arena of human conduct as we know it and ask: what are the basic elements from which the whole is built? Hobbes starts his discussion of politics by first saying that the whole, or society when viewed as a composite, is characterized by a state of war. He then asks what the basic elements of this system are and how they are interrelated to create a world characterized by war. Moreover, with the understanding he gains about how the whole is constituted, he can ask how the whole system of interrelations in society might be reconstituted in a new way to avoid war and to make peace possible.

So, Hobbes's questions are clear. What forces in the human world contribute to war, and how might they be rearranged to achieve a peaceful world? Now, no one can know the mind of humankind for certain, but we can imagine or hypothesize what the forces are that motivate humankind, given what we know of human conduct already. Thus, if reality in general is such that individuals are prone to engage in war with others, we have a basis for explaining our general situation in terms of what can be hypothesized as self-evident and basic truths that explain these circumstances. Further, once we know why human relationships lead to a general condition of war, it should be possible to define those common rules and norms that all should uphold to make possible a society committed to peace.

In our discussion of the state of nature in the next section, we describe the basic forces that suggest the potential for war and under what conditions it is possible to achieve peace. Before turning to this endeavor, it is important to note the practical political implications of Hobbes's method. In discussing society, Hobbes had to confront some difficult conflicts. We have already referred to the one pertaining to the role of the king in relation to parliament. But as we elaborate upon more fully in Section VI, there are grave differences in Hobbes's society pertaining to the role of religious institutions in their relationship to both society and the state. It would appear, given the nature and the depth of the differences permeating Hobbes's society, that there is no common basis upon which to establish the state's role in society.

Seen from the perspective of the particular parties in any of these conflicts, this conclusion would be understandable and inevitable. Hobbes, of course, cannot accept this outcome. He believes it is possible to find a basis for avoiding war in his society. And to do so it would be necessary to discover a common viewpoint that stands above the partisanship found in his society and that can be used to establish the common rules all could accept for securing peace. To this end, Hobbes suggests that the reasons for conflict are quite simple in nature. As a consequence, because the real basis for conflict is uncomplicated, the differences that separate people are not that large at all, and peaceful solutions to resolve people's differences are likely to be easier to identify. In effect, when people understand that the basis for their conflicts is no longer actually located in particular religious or philosophical differences but in simpler explanations about human nature, then it is more likely that individuals will be able to find a common set of rules for organizing political and social life in a way all can accept.

As people comprehend the real roots of conflict, they can attain a basis for overcoming once and for all the conflict everyone loathes. In place of a society filled with war and strife, there can emerge a new civil society that is committed to protect, in the name of the rule of law, the individual freedom of each person. Here, a new doctrine of civic virtue emerges, one that is seen as the basis for supporting notions of individual private freedom, or the freedom to make choices about the way of life that seems best for oneself. In the new civic virtue, the rules that all must accept are rules that are used to avoid destructive forms of conflict while protecting each person's private freedom. In this case, civic virtue is no longer defined in terms of a need to support a particular conception of the common good, a conception that defines for each person his or her fixed and permanent place in society, as in Plato's republic, Aristotle's polis, or Aquinas's form of medieval society. Instead, civic virtue permits each person to have the freedom to determine which way of life is best for him- or herself and, in demanding that all should have this freedom, civic virtue becomes a doctrine that embraces a moral order based upon providing each individual the same basic rights.

Still, the main problem with Hobbes's argument is that his concept of civil society embraces a powerful state that threatens the freedom that his view of civil society defends. Explaining the reasons for this situation is one of the main objectives of this chapter.

III. Hobbes and the State of Nature

What, then, is the enduring source of conflict? To explain the reasons for human conflict, Hobbes describes his view of the state of nature. Hobbes's view of the state of nature represents what he thinks human interactions were like before there was organized society, before there was government, and before there were any formal laws. Hobbes's views are his own imagined description of human life, and his picture of this condition demonstrates why conflict was inevitable. Moreover, given the view he provides, it is also possible to understand why it is likely that individuals will find an acceptable resolution.

In the state of nature, Hobbes argues that people are continually motivated to realize the objects of their desires. People not only want to achieve their present desires, but they have a strong need to be in a position that allows them to achieve whatever future desires they may have as well.[4] It is only when people are successful in these regards that they can attain a "contented life." People differ only in the sense that they may have different passions, but because all want to realize them, all people share a common hope of achieving contentment in their lives.[5] To obtain one's desires, however, one must have sufficient "power," or the necessary means, to acquire whatever one may need to satisfy a particular passion. Thus, given the constancy of the urge to realize one's desires, the search for power is a continual enterprise that "ceaseth onely in Death."[6]

Why, one might ask, is the search for power continual? After all, once one has acquired sufficient power to attain one's objectives, why would one want to seek more power? In the state of nature, people find themselves in a situation in which they never can truly relax and enjoy whatever they are able to acquire with the power they have. People are always looking over their shoulders, wondering when and if the person next to them will cause them harm. To avert this possibility, people always feel the need to find ways to acquire more and more power. As they do, their purpose in acquiring power changes somewhat. They still need power to acquire the goods that enable them to enjoy life, of course. But, in addition, they discover that it is necessary to secure power for its own sake, so they can free themselves from the constant fear that others will cause them harm. Man, Hobbes says, "cannot assure the power and means to live well, which he hath present, without the acquisition of more."[7]

Moreover, the fear that others will take from us what we currently possess creates a condition of mutual violence on the part of each person toward the other. If each person thinks that everything one has may be taken from him or her by another, each person can never trust the other person, and each person thinks that the other person is always scheming to do harm. Naturally, this condition of mutual distrust leads to the development of some very destructive tendencies among people. Here, "the way of one Competitor, to the attaining of his desire, is to kill, subdue, supplant or repell the other."[8] In the state of nature, competition among people leads to the need to gain, at the expense of others, to employ violence against others, and thus people seek "to make themselves Master of other men's persons, wives, children and cattell."[9] It is not surprising that life in the state of nature is "solitary, poore, nasty, brutish, and short."[10]

Hobbes's account of the state of nature seems to describe the ramifications for civil society of the market mentality in its most destructive form. Here, people compete for the financial resources that enable them to obtain the power, or the material means, to acquire the things that give them happiness and contentment in life. Thus, Hobbes had the influence of the market context in mind when he argued that our power as individuals is associated with our "worth," that is, the "price" others would pay for our services. We can acquire more power, or the means to achieve our ends, if we can enhance our worth, or the price we can charge others who want to make use of our services. Our worth, however, always depends upon the judgments and needs of others.[11] If others find that what we offer no longer has any value, we would lose our ability to acquire what brings us contentment and happiness. Hobbesian persons, not unlike many today, live in constant dread and fear that, in the eyes of the market, they will have nothing of value to contribute to the society.

Given this composite picture of humankind in the state of nature, it is understandable why society becomes a dog-eat-dog world, where each is engaged in trying to dominate and subjugate the other before the other dominates and subjugates him or her. If this picture is accurate, it would appear impossible for humankind to avoid war and to establish a civil society. But Hobbes suggests otherwise. For if one looks closely at the nature of human relationships, one can understand how the basis for conflict among persons, the constant need to obtain more and more power, can be turned into a direction favorable to peace, instead of war. How is this possible?

Hobbes said that, in the main, even though most people think they are superior to others and are thus characterized by a "vain conceit,"[12] the fact of the matter is that most of us are equal in ability and capacity.

Nature hath made men so equall, in the faculties of body, and mind; as that though there bee found one man sometimes manifestly stronger in body, or of quicker mind than another; yet when all is reckoned together, the difference between man, and man, is not so considerable.[13]

How does this fact explain the basis for transcending destructive behavior and creating the basis for a new social contract, where cooperation replaces war? In the rest of this section, we address this question.

Our equality of ability suggests an equality of hope that we will be able to attain the ends that bring about contentment.[14] And when, as a result of this equality of ability and now hope, two people seek the same thing, they naturally become enemies, because it is impossible for both of them to have that thing. Hobbes says:

From this equality of ability, ariseth equality of hope in the attaining of Ends. And therefore if any two men desire the thing, which neverthelesse they cannot both enjoy, they become enemies; and in the way to their End . . . endeavour to destroy, or subdue one an other.[15]

Here, in a world where people are equal in ability and where there are not enough of the things we all desire to go around to everyone, it is highly likely that each of us will seek to control and dominate others. The reason for this is that we realize the thin line between success and failure. What differentiates me, the successful person, from you, the unsuccessful person, may just be luck. I got to the cherished job opportunity we both sought before you did, so I got the job. If you had arrived before me, you would have had the job, not me. The problem here is that there is only one job and two people competing for it. And, because each of us is equal in ability, the prospective employer does not have to wait for the more talented person to show up, but, instead, he or she will take the first person in line. Knowing this to be the factual context of life makes those who lose out very jealous and hateful toward those who succeed. The loser feels that the winner wins only because of luck, not because of ability. And because each of us thinks of ourselves, with all our "vain conceits," as better than the other, we think that we should have gotten the job, instead of the other who is "less deserving." So, we are very bitter, and our bitterness propels us to treat others with contempt and violence.

Furthermore, the successful person is no better off, either. He knows that others are jealous and harbor violent feelings toward him, so he worries that everything he has gained will be taken from him at some point in the future. He may have won the job, but if he ever lets his guard down, even for a minute, he will find himself on the street. He can never rest easy at night because he is always insecure about losing everything to someone else. Moreover, in this setting, there are no standards of justice that could be appealed to as the basis for assuaging one's fear.[16]

In this situation, then, people are driven by a need to gain permanent advantage over each other, and we are prone as well to use violence to make ourselves the masters of others. But Hobbes argues that we are not destined to live like this, and, again, the primary reason seems to be the essential equality of our basic capacities. We are all commonly in possession of central passions – the fear of death and a desire to live comfortably. "The Passions that encline men to Peace, are Fear of Death [and the] Desire of such things as are necessary to commodious living."[17] These passions become center stage for us when we realize that the constant quest for power by each of us threatens to destroy all hope for social peace, for comforts, and for release from the fear of death.

At this point, people discover that the ongoing warfare they are engaged in with each other is harmful to creating the conditions that make prosperity possible. Where war is ever-present, there is little industrial development, there is no art or advances in knowledge, there is no trade among nations, and so on.[18] Again, then, as part of the common equality in ability of humankind, a cause of peace is the realization that individuals generally share a common set of expectations for life. Were people's expectations to be wildly different, there would be no basis upon which to establish a peaceful social and political order, but for Hobbes, this is not the case because people want what secures their prosperity and ensures their happiness.

Thus, our common fear of death, as well as a shared commitment to have what makes possible a prosperous life, moves us to seek a new basis for society, and our reason aids in this endeavor by defining the "Articles of Peace, upon which men may be drawn to agreement." The Articles of Peace that all can accept and make the basis of the new civil society are referred to as the laws of nature.[19]

IV. Hobbes's Civil Society: The Laws of Nature and Civic Virtue

What is the nature of the new social contract or civil society, embodying the "Articles of Peace" that Hobbes's citizens accept? The answer to this question revolves around what people understand to be the common element that each would accept as the basis for society. The key element is liberty or the right, ordained by nature or reason, of each person to use his or her "power," to prepare "for the preservation of his own Nature; that is to say, of his own Life; and consequently, of doing any thing, which in his own Judgment, and Reason, hee shall conceive to be the aptest means thereunto."[20] Here, each person is to have the personal freedom to chart his or her own course in life, in accordance with what his or her goals and desires are.

Furthermore, this kind of liberty, for Hobbes, is made possible only when we observe certain limits and constraints on conduct. By observing these limits on our liberty, we move from the state of nature to the state of civil society. The limits on conduct suggest for us the need to follow rules that facilitate the individually defined objectives that individuals may choose. In the state of nature, of course, liberty was defined as the right to all things, and people would never accept the kinds of limits prescribed for civil society. But the right-to-all-things doctrine of the state of nature, that is, freedom without limits, signifies only continual war.[21]

This condition cannot continue if human beings are to create a society committed to peace, a goal made necessary by the constant fear as well as the continual threat of death. In consequence, individuals are led to embrace certain laws of nature, or what can be called *civic virtues*, and to make them the basis for establishing the rules of conduct for all citizens in the society. The first and most fundamental law of nature is that all persons ought to seek peace. At the same time, it is also a law of nature that individuals may use any means, including violence, to defend themselves from harm.[22] In following a peaceful course of conduct, however, people do not have to resort to force. As a result, they move from the state of nature, where the only constant is the tendency to harm others, to a civil society.[23] In a civil society, the new constant is the second law of nature that says no one should seek any more freedom for him- or herself than he or she would accord to others. This law of nature is summed up in the Bible as the Golden Rule or the following idea: "*Whatsoever you require that others should do to you, that do ye to them.*"[24]

Here, Hobbes has in mind a cooperative framework for society, the essence of which is acceptance by each person of the need to mutually accommodate one another's liberty for the sake of securing each person's freedom. Hobbes says that only "in consideration of some Right reciprocally transferred to himselfe; or for some other good he hopeth for thereby"[25] will individuals ever accept the constraints associated with recognizing the liberty of others. No person will abide by a need to respect the liberty of others, unless in doing so one's own rights and basic security are assured. To get people to respect one another's liberty, then, conditions must be created that enable people to feel that when they do so, their basic interests, including the need for self-preservation and contentment, are in no sense placed in danger.[26] When these conditions can be met, then each individual is in a position to respect the liberty of others. Hobbes's new social contract, and the view of civil society that flows from it, suggests the notion of mutual respect, or the idea that each person will act to promote the liberty of others when all people attempt to make a place for all other people's interests.

In the cooperative setting that Hobbes's social contract makes available, avenues are created that permit individuals to be engaged in relationships of mutual exchange. Here, people make contracts with other people whenever they exchange one thing for another, such as when they buy or sell with money.[27] A covenant is another form of contract. In a covenant, two people make an agreement, the provisions of which will be carried out in the future.[28] The idea of the covenant, however, brings up a serious problem that a civil society must address. What is to prevent one party to an agreement, say X, from getting what X contracted for, and then not performing, at some future date, as the contract requires with respect to the other party, Y? This question suggests that the urge to subdue others is never quite removed from individuals, even in the context of a society governed by natural law. This problem can be averted only if there is a common power that can enforce the covenants and punish those who do not comply with them. Hobbes says:

> If a Covenant be made, wherein neither of the parties perform presently, but trust one another; in the condition of meer Nature (which is a condition of Warre of every man against every man,) upon any reasonable suspition, it is Voyd: But if there be a common Power set over them both, with right and force sufficient to compell performance; it is not Voyd. For he that performeth first, has no assurance that the other will performe after; because the bonds of words are too weak to bridle mens ambition, avarice, anger, and other Passions, without the fear of some coercive power.[29]

Based on this position, then, another important law of nature is justice. Justice is the idea that "men [must] performe their Covenants made: without which, Covenants are in vain, and but Empty words, and the Right of all men to all things remaining, wee are still in the condition of Warre."[30] A just society is one in which individuals uphold their agreements with others; when people do not, there is no basis for anyone to obtain from others the cooperation they need to achieve their personal goals and objectives. Moreover, justice is possible only when there is a common power, that is, a commonwealth, or what can be called a state, with coercive power to compel people to uphold their agreements.[31] In the absence of a state that can enforce agreements, society returns to the state of nature, or a condition of continual warfare.

Further, Hobbes's discussion of natural law suggests that, in addition to a common power that each person is to respect, there are other forms of civic virtue (or additional laws of nature) that are useful in protecting the freedom of each person. For instance, people must display gratitude when others give them something without expecting anything in return.[32] Hobbes hopes to create a civic culture in which people no longer perceive each other as potential enemies. Gratitude helps to achieve this end because it requires people to see the bearers of gifts as acting from a sense of goodwill.[33] If we always refuse to attribute goodwill to those people who bestow gifts upon us, there is no basis for initiating trust or benevolence among people. In this regard, we should manifest toward others the virtue of "compleasance," or the idea that an individual should "*strive to accommodate himselfe to the rest.*"[34] This virtue will enable people to understand and to accept the vast diversity of interests and needs that make up society. Moreover, individuals must learn to pardon others for past offenses and to overcome the temptation to extract revenge for past wrongs. Otherwise, there would be no peace.[35] Further, people can secure peace in society only when everyone agrees to treat everyone else as equals. A violation of this principle is the vice of pride.[36] To secure the conditions of equality, individuals must avoid "arrogance," or the tendency to attribute rights to themselves that are not accorded to all others.[37] Instead, all must recognize the basic rights that belong to everyone, like the "right to governe their owne bodies; enjoy aire, water, motion, waies to go from place to place; and all things else without which a man cannot live, or not live well."[38]

These laws suggest that people must learn to deal fairly with each other. When people are not treated fairly, they resort to violence to resolve disputes. But when people are treated fairly, disputes are resolved through peaceful means, such as by impartial judges and arbitrators. In observing this commitment, individuals maintain respect for the natural law or civic virtue called "equity."[39] To achieve equity, which includes fairness in the distribution of basic goods, such as property, additional natural laws or civic virtues are needed, and these pertain to the way that property is divided and how disputes among citizens are settled.

Regarding property, Hobbes argues that there are natural laws pertaining to the distinction between private and public property. With respect to public property, goods that cannot be divided must be shared, and no one can be denied access to them. Hobbes has in mind basic goods needed for survival, such as the air we breathe, the water we drink, and so on. But for things that can be neither divided nor enjoyed in common, it is necessary to find a fair procedure for distribution. In this case, Hobbes has in mind private property. He suggests that the latter be distributed by lot so that each person, presumably, believes there is a fair chance of acquiring his or her share. The principle of distribution by lot is nothing more than the notion that goods that cannot be enjoyed by all in common be distributed on the basis of according entitlement of something to the person who possesses it first.[40]

Further, in situations in which individuals have differences of opinion and fall into controversy about whether certain actions are permitted under the law, it is a law of nature that a citizen must accept that he or she cannot properly be an arbitrator in cases involving him- or herself. And, thus, each must put his or her faith in a neutral third party, certainly the state, which can act fairly and justly toward each individual.[41]

If the laws of nature were naturally a part of each citizen's outlook, then each citizen would respect the rights of others by his or her own volition. But the fact is that people will not embrace even these virtues unless there is the "terrour of some Power, to cause them to be observed." For Hobbes believes that the laws of nature are "contrary to our naturall Passions, that carry us to Partiality, Pride, Revenge, and the like."[42] Hobbes hopes to neutralize these powerful passions and to create a society based on the fair rules of the laws of nature by establishing a powerful state whose sole function is to use its power to promote these laws. As Hobbes says, "Covenants without the sword, are but words,"[43] and so the state in a civil society must have a sword. Nonetheless, as we demonstrate in the next section, the power of the state is allowed to grow to the point at which it is quite likely that it will end up threatening the freedom a civil society seeks to preserve.

V. The Role and Structure of the State

How is what Hobbes calls the commonwealth, or the Leviathan, which is the predominant governing authority with the power to provide for the peace and defense in a civil society, created?[44] Hobbes says the commonwealth, or what also could be referred to as the state, is created when all the members of the community agree to place authority for governing the community in either one man or one assembly of men. In doing so, all agree to submit themselves to the will of a single authority. The act of consent that makes possible a state with great powers to secure peace and to protect the society from external enemies signifies, for Hobbes, a basis for societal unity, predicated upon each person's entering into an agreement with all others to permit only one governmental authority in society. In doing so, Hobbes indicates that it is as though each individual has said to all others:

> *"I Authorise and give my Right of Governing my selfe, to this Man, or to this Assembly of men, on this condition, that thou give thy Right to him, and Authorise all his Actions in like manner."*[45] *The state or commonwealth, also called the sovereign, is vested with sovereign power over the citizens who are called the subjects. We use the words state and sovereign interchangeably.*[46]

Does this act of consent give the state or the sovereign unlimited authority over citizens? Hobbes certainly claims not. Indeed, Hobbes seems to suggest that the state's objectives are defined in a manner that limit the state's authority. What are the state's objectives? Given Hobbes's views of natural law, the state would have to follow a path that promotes justice and equity, and in doing so the state would make as its priority the protection of citizens' rights. Thus, the act of consent to create a sovereign authority, if it means anything, clearly would mean that the citizens, in consenting to the state's authority, do so only on the condition that the state protects their rights.[47] To this end, the state, as it arbitrated conflicts between citizens, or as it sought to maintain and uphold agreements between citizens, would have to stand above politics and attempt to render fair and impartial publicly binding decisions. In all cases, the state would have to uphold the law with equal force for all. To achieve these objectives, the state could not allow its actions to be extensions of one private interest over another, for then public power would be used to promote specific private interests, and, in this case, the rights of all could not be protected.

But the actual state Hobbes describes appears to compromise the state's main objective of protecting basic rights. For Hobbes, the state is defined as an authority with sovereign power over citizens, and that authority is vested in either a single monarch or an assembly of citizen representatives. Here, once citizens give their consent to be subject to a monarch (or to an assembly), citizens cannot, without the permission of the monarch (or the assembly), return the power to themselves for the purpose of transferring it to another.[48] Nor is there a right to revolution. Hobbes says that "protestation against any of their Decrees [of the state], he does contrary to his Covenant, and therefore unjustly.[49] In this regard, a citizen who the sovereign kills for trying to depose the sovereign is really the "author of his own punishment."[50] For after all, in agreeing to be governed by the sovereign, each person agrees to abide by his authority.

But how far are we obligated to the sovereign by our agreement to be governed by him? For Hobbes, we are given extreme obligations that limit our conduct quite severely. Indeed, subjects cannot even accuse the sovereign of wrongdoing. For once the state has been created, the state acts with the full authority of those who have authorized it, that is, the people. And if the state, now that all members of society have authorized it, does wrong, the people need blame only themselves, not the state.[51] Further, the sovereign has a right to determine which doctrines and opinions citizens will be permitted to hold, and no doctrine that is a threat to the general peace of the society can be allowed.[52]

This account suggests that the state's powers are likely to be so great that the state could act with unlimited authority and in doing so threaten the rights of citizens. Further, there are no institutional constraints that would prevent the state from taking this path. For instance, Hobbes argues that all law-making, all judicial powers, and all executive powers pertaining to making war and peace are to reside in a single sovereign authority.[53] These powers, as we have seen, may be located in a single person, such as a monarch, or in an assembly of citizens.[54]

In either case, Hobbes argues for a unitary form of government in which the governing power is either an assembly or a monarch but not both. This view suggests that it would be wrong for the two governing types to share power, and based on this view, it is unlikely that Hobbes would have supported a separation of powers concept of government that is typical in our times. The only result of separated government is divided government, and what divided government eventuates is a return to the state of war.

> *For that were to erect two Soveraigns; and every man to have his person represented by two Actors, that by opposing one another, must needs divide that Power, which (if men will live in Peace) is indivisible; and thereby reduce the Multitude into the condition of Warre, contrary to the end for which all Soveraignty is instituted.*[55]

In all cases, the government is considered a representative of the people. When the representative is one man, the government is a monarchy; when it is an assembly of all, then the government is a democracy; and when the assembly is only a part of the people, then the government is called an aristocracy.[56] Hobbes favors monarchy for several reasons. First, he argues that the monarch is more likely to understand, to articulate, and to work to realize the public interest. The monarch has no interest in harming the citizens because his authority rests with their success and prosperity.[57] Second, the monarch has only to listen to those who are experts and who, as a result, are most likely to make significant contributions in solving public problems. The assembly, on the other hand, is filled with those whose main concern is their own wealth rather than actions based on knowledge of the public interest.[58] These comparisons suggest that the monarch, unlike the assembly, does not have to try to please this group or that group; all he must do is make the best decision possible, using the best information available. As a result, the monarch can maintain consistency of policy directions over time.[59]

The assembly, on the other hand, must try to please many different interests, each of whom has a different conception of the public good. And because it cannot always succeed in doing so, the assembly opens itself and society up to the prospect of civil war.[60] Hobbes dismisses the main problem he identifies with monarchy, namely, that at times flatterers may inveigle their way into the king's counsel. But, for Hobbes, this is a mere inconvenience that is experienced in all governments,[61] and when this problem is weighed against the advantages of the monarchy, it is clear to Hobbes that the monarchy remains the best form of government.

To those who fear the state's power, Hobbes argues that the sovereign cannot command a person to kill or maim him- or herself. Further, if the sovereign interrogates a person, the latter is under no obligation to incriminate him- or herself.[62] Still, one might today ask, once the state has been allowed as much power as Hobbes grants it, what real basis exists to protect citizens from the state's own abuse of its power? This is not a question Hobbes is interested in addressing, but we, of course, are. It would seem in this regard that a benefit of the separation of powers concept is that it suggests various points of access for citizens. The latter may use their access to help define the political agenda or influence government decisions about particular issues on that agenda. Hobbes, in denying a place to the separation of powers approach, took a step in the direction of creating a state that would deny citizens a chance to challenge its policies. How ironical a position for citizens to be in, given that the state itself emanates from their consent!

Important implications for the concept of a civil society arise from Hobbes's view of the state's role. As we have seen, his civil society protects freedom by maintaining regard for civic virtues, such as justice, gratitude, and the provision of rights for all. The state will have a central role in promoting these virtues. The state's necessary role arises from the fact that Hobbes does not trust people to uphold a commitment to civic virtue on their own, and he believes that individuals will do so only when the state compels them through fear.

But, given this view, could there be a separate sphere of voluntary groups that exists to provide a buffer against the prospect of governmental encroachment upon individuals? There is no question that values such as gratitude, justice, and respect for rights could make possible a separate sphere. Why is this the case? These values would contribute to a society in which individuals manifested toward others mutual respect, or the commitment to find ways to make room for each other, no matter how different each person might be. And one such important way to attain this objective would be to make possible a separate sphere that protected individual freedom against government encroachment. Still, even if, for Hobbes, a separate sphere is feasible, it would exist in tension with a state whose powers could become so vast that individuals would not be able to challenge its decisions. Certainly, this tension would not necessarily deny the possibility of a separate sphere, but it would make such a sphere difficult to achieve. Hobbes's treatment of religion demonstrates this problem of his view of civil society very well.

VI. The Christian Commonwealth

The establishment of an English Christian church, in the aftermath of the secession from Rome, mandated that the king should be the head of the church. The church and state should not be two distinct realms, but they should form one common union.[63] Those who supported this view believed that religious life should be promoted, not as Aquinas had argued by an all-embracing Catholic Church, but by a national government in charge of a national church. In this case, the king and, where the king permitted parliamentary participation in these matters, the parliament would be in a position to determine religious doctrines and beliefs.[64]

Some groups met this perspective with opposition, of course. The Anglican or English Christian church faced demands from religious groups – Catholics,

Calvinists (also called Presbyterians), and Independents – each of whom wanted autonomy from state interference for their own churches. The Catholics advocated spiritual autonomy from the state, so they could acknowledge papal jurisdiction in religious matters.[65] The Calvinists did not accept a secular head of their church, either. The Calvinists advocated a separation between the church and the state, but not in the present-day sense that makes the state a secular institution that must avoid promoting a particular religion. Instead, the Calvinists believed they should be free from state interference to determine the doctrines for a moral and religious life, and they expected the state to make these doctrines mandatory.[66] The Independents argued for noninterference in religious affairs by the state and by the national church, so they could establish their own religious communities. As George Sabine says, the Independents wanted to ordain their own clergy and establish themselves as a "voluntary association of like-minded believers," and they did not want the civil authority to promote, as the Presbyterians had wanted, religious doctrines to people of a different religious persuasion. The Independents adopted a doctrine of religious toleration that would have to apply both to themselves and to others who did not believe as they did, although, in practice, the Independents were more likely to support toleration for themselves than for others.[67]

Hobbes argues that there should be one national church and that the civil sovereign, which as indicated earlier can mean either the king or an assembly, should have authority over the religious life of society. Indeed, the church should be subordinate to the power and the authority of the civil sovereign. The latter can make laws that pertain to both the realm of government and the realm of religion. Thus, the civil sovereign can determine the kind of church organization and arrangement that will be put in charge of the religious life of society, and whatever organization is chosen for leading the religious life of society must realize that the civil sovereign has supreme authority over its affairs. For instance, the civil sovereign may commit the state to Catholicism, but, if it does so, the pope must still be subordinate to the civil sovereign. Or, when the civil sovereign establishes a central church under a "supreme pastor or assembly of pastors," the civil sovereign maintains overall control of the church. The civil sovereign maintains control by designating interpreters of the scripture, defining the offices and powers of church officials, and determining how people will be taxed to support the church.[68] The civil sovereign may even define religious doctrine, with the intent especially of providing doctrines that help secure peace in society. And, further, the civil sovereign may appoint the pastors.[69]

Justification for this view derives from the "Laws of God." For Hobbes, the latter are nothing more than the laws of nature. And one of the key laws of nature that the "Laws of God" sanction is that individuals must not violate a "commandment to obey the civil sovereign" that citizens through their own consent have created. This suggests that the "Laws of God" have permitted the civil sovereign to be the primary authority not only for civil law but for religious doctrines and for the management of the church. And, thus, by the "Laws of God," citizens are to obey the precepts of the Bible in those places where the civil sovereign mandates such conduct.[70]

Given this view, it is clear that only the civil sovereign can define the basis for excommunication and for salvation. What doctrines does Hobbes's civil sovereign establish in these regards? First, Hobbes refuses to accept that a believing Christian who obeys the laws of his or her commonwealth can, in any way, be harmed by being made subject to excommunication. To paraphrase Hobbes, the person who believes in Christ is free from all the dangers threatened to persons by excommunication.[71] This suggests that the civil authority has the right to minimize any church's effort to excommunicate a person who is a Christian believer. And to receive salvation, all one need do is maintain two important civic virtues, namely, faith in Christ and the need to uphold the civil law during one's daily conduct in society. Upholding the civil law would have been basis enough for salvation, were it not for original sin and the likelihood that, owing to a lack of perfection, we will at times transgress the law. Given human frailty and the hope for eternal salvation, we do best for ourselves, then, when we seek "remission" for our sins, and this we can attain when we maintain faith in Christ.[72]

Hobbes, in arguing for the supremacy of the civil state over religious matters, does not deny the importance of religious life but suggests that, in his newly constructed civil society, religion must be made subject to civil control. In this setting, all Christian believers were to share a common commitment to maintaining the civil law and the natural law principles of a civil society, principles that secure respect for individual freedom. When placed in its proper relationship to the state, the religious life can help sustain the new civil society and the individual freedom it promises.

But at the same time, because Hobbes's civil authority would determine the content of religious life, his state would always live in tension with any religious organizations seeking independence from state control. Owing to this kind of state–society relationship, creating a separate sphere for groups to exist independently of the state so they could act from their own self-determined doctrines would be discouraged at some points and perhaps disallowed at others. Thus, Hobbes would not be a strong supporter of a civil society that contained a separate sphere of groups that would act as buffers and restraints on the state's power.

VII. Response and Rejoinder

In suggesting that a separate sphere would have difficulty being constituted in Hobbes's civil society, it should be understood that Hobbes is not diminishing the importance of individual freedom. Indeed, Hobbes certainly contends that one of the objectives of his thought is to protect individual freedom with the kind of state he advocates. Hobbes claims that his system provides individuals all the private freedom they want and need. Here, individuals are given the ability to make their own choices about the life they want to lead. The laws are designed to remove impediments to freedom and not themselves be impediments to freedom. It is for this reason, for instance, that individuals can act as they want when the laws are silent.[73] And because the laws are designed to maximize personal freedom, the laws do not dictate to people how they should live their lives in many areas of life. This approach is necessary if diverse people with different values are able to pursue those values in peace.

But problems with Hobbes's view remain. Some might claim that a terrible trade-off is taking place in which individuals gain freedom only if they permit a state with absolute power. Hobbes might respond by saying that, after all, government, in particular his form of government, is based upon the consent of the governed to be ruled by a particular regime. In this case, the state operates within some important limits since the state can do only that which the citizens prescribe for it to do. Now, it is true that Hobbes does have a doctrine of citizen consent to government. But once the act of consent to be ruled by a government whose main objective is to protect private freedom and rights has occurred, it appears that people are forced to forfeit a right to challenge state policies that the citizens do not agree with. In this case, how are citizens going to protect those rights that the state is empowered to secure but which it may decide not to safeguard in the name of shoring up its own authority?

The question, then, is whether Hobbes can maintain security for the freedom he promised when the state is as powerful as Hobbes made it. Hobbes's answer might be that all he is attempting to do is to provide a fair and objective state that can enforce the law for all and prevent the reemergence of a state of war. If he is successful, equality of rights and liberty would be provided to all. Hobbes would claim that the modern state, as it is presently constituted, is often perceived as failing to be a fair and impartial force in society, working to protect the rights of each individual. Hobbes might argue, then, that very often the modern government, built upon the separation of powers model and the provision of access to all interests, falls into paralysis, unable to achieve even basic objectives for its citizens. In the modern state, government invites many private interests, each with its own view of the good, to enter government and to lobby for their own objectives. With so many different interests pushing for their own respective ends, the state is unable to achieve general, broad policies that are in the interest of all. Of central concern in this regard is that the state is unable to realize even those policies that protect the individual, private freedom of each person.

What would fuel this tendency for Hobbes is an attitude on the part of ordinary citizens to think that he or she can be the sole determiner of what is right and just.

From this false doctrine, men are disposed to debate with themselves, and dispute the commands of the Commonwealth; and afterwards to obey, or disobey them, as in their private judgments they shall think fit.[74]

Hobbes argues that, whereas this doctrine might be acceptable in the state of nature, it is not acceptable in a civil society. Indeed, Hobbes considers this view to be a poisonous doctrine that weakens civil society.[75] How is the commonwealth weakened by this kind of activity? In the first place, the only measure of right and wrong should be the laws sanctioned by the commonwealth. But where people think they can determine good from bad themselves, they are encouraged to debate with each other the decisions of the state and to decide whether they want to obey them. Hobbes would no doubt contend that when people enter debates of this sort, they seek to promote their own interests with the intention of getting the state to support them. But in this case, the state would no longer be the fair, neutral arbitrator among interests that Hobbes hoped for. When the sovereign is a strong, independent, and powerful voice for equity and fairness, however, private interests cannot capture public power and use it for their own designs.

But is Hobbes right? Would individuals be so willing to allow an unlimited form of power to the state in order to have the personal freedom and the protections from the intrusions from others that Hobbes offers? Remember that even Machiavelli's realism was tempered by a republican, mixed form of government that protected liberty by avoiding the concentration of power into the hands of a few. We turn now to Spinoza and then to John Locke, each of whom challenges Hobbes's claims about civil society and the role of the state in significant ways.

Notes

1. George H. Sabine, *A History of Political Theory* (New York: Holt, Rinehart and Winston, 1961), 455–56.
2. Thomas Hobbes, *Leviathan*, ed. C. B. Macpherson (New York: Penguin Books, 1981), 105, I:4. For ease in finding sources, we include the Roman numeral that signifies the part, and the next number is the chapter.
3. C. B. Macpherson, "Introduction," in Hobbes, *Leviathan*, 25–30.
4. Hobbes, *Leviathan*, 160–61, I:11.
5. Ibid., 161, I:11.
6. Ibid., 150, I:10.
7. Ibid., 161, I:11.
8. Ibid.
9. Ibid., 185, I:13.
10. Ibid., 186, I:13.
11. Ibid., 151–52, I:10.
12. Ibid., 183, I:13.
13. Ibid.
14. Ibid., 184, I:13.
15. Ibid.
16. Ibid.
17. Ibid., 188, I:13.
18. Ibid., 186, I:13.
19. Ibid., 188, I:13.
20. Ibid., 189, I:14.
21. Ibid., 190, I:14.

22. Ibid.
23. Ibid., 190, I:14, 214, I:15. Hobbes states that the laws of nature that dictate peace are the basis of a "Civil States Society."
24. Ibid., 190, I:14. Italics are Hobbes's.
25. Ibid., 192, I:14.
26. Ibid.
27. Ibid., 193, I:14.
28. Ibid.
29. Ibid., 196, I:14.
30. Ibid., 201, I:15.
31. Ibid., 201–2, I:15.
32. Ibid., 209, I:15.
33. Ibid.
34. Ibid. Italics are Hobbes's.
35. Ibid., 210, I:15.
36. Ibid., 211, I:15.
37. Ibid.
38. Ibid., 212, I:15.
39. Ibid.
40. Ibid., 212–13, I:15.
41. Ibid., 213, I:15.
42. Ibid., 223, II:17.
43. Ibid.
44. Ibid., 227–28, II:17.
45. Ibid., 227, II:17.
46. Ibid., 228, II:17.
47. On this point, see Frank M. Coleman, *Hobbes and America: Exploring the Constitutional Foundation* (Toronto: University of Toronto Press, 1977), 91.
48. Hobbes, *Leviathan*, 228–29, II:18.
49. Ibid., 231–32, II:18.
50. Ibid., 229, II:18.
51. Ibid., 232, II:18.
52. Ibid., 233, II:18.
53. Ibid., 234–35, II:18.
54. Ibid., 237, II:18.
55. Ibid., 240, II:19.
56. Ibid., 239, II:19.
57. Ibid., 241–42, II:19.
58. Ibid., 242, II:19.
59. Ibid.
60. Ibid., 243, II:19.
61. Ibid.
62. Ibid., 269, II:21.
63. Sabine, *A History of Political Theory*, 438, 441–42.
64. Ibid., 441–43.
65. Ibid., 443.
66. Ibid., 443–44.
67. Ibid., 445–46.
68. Hobbes, *Leviathan*, 575–76, III:42.
69. Ibid., 567–68, III:42.
70. Ibid., 612, III:43.

71. Ibid., 540, III:42.
72. Ibid., 610–11, III:43.
73. Ibid., 271, II:21.
74. Ibid., 365, II:29.
75. Ibid.

8

Benedict Spinoza and Liberal Democracy

I. Introduction

Benedict Spinoza (1632–1677), born in Amsterdam and a descendant of Jews who fled to Holland to escape the Inquisition in Portugal, is one of the forerunners of a secular-based, liberal democracy. His view of liberal democracy is designed to advance among citizens the free use of reason as the basis for their determining judgments of personal and public matters. And it is on these grounds that he makes the protection of freedom of thought and speech central to his conception of the liberal democratic state. Under this doctrine of freedom, Spinoza rejects the practices employed either by the state or by the church to impose opinions on citizens. Instead, the state is to protect each citizen's free and uninhibited use of reason in forming their own opinions of political, religious, and social matters.[1] As Spinoza says

> *The object of government is not to change men from rational beings into beasts or puppets, but to enable them to develop their minds and bodies in security and to employ their reason unshackled; neither showing hatred, anger, or deceit, nor watched with the eyes of jealousy and injustice. In fact, the true aim of government is liberty.*[2]

Further, Spinoza's view of a just politics includes the notion that, in a democracy, the majority must have supreme power, but he thinks this poses no danger to the minority because each citizen is given full civic equality. Only in this context do people exercise the free use of their reason, undeterred by emotions designed to deny it. And, within the contemporary political arena, many who advocate for citizen participation in their government in the name of extending democracy, such as found in the Occupy Wall Street movement and the loud voice attack on unlimited spending in presidential political campaigns, make the same case. Now, to Spinoza.

Before discussing his political theory in more detail, a few words about the historical context, which helps to explain Spinoza's determination to support a secular, liberal democracy.

II. Historical Setting

The Inquisition of the sixteenth century, wherein people were forced, often at the hands of the torturer, to prove fidelity to Catholic Church doctrine or suffer death, caused many Jews from Spain and Portugal to flee to other regions of the world. Spinoza's father escaped the Inquisition by relocating to Amsterdam, where Jews, unlike in most places in Europe during this time, were allowed to live in peace, so long as they practiced their religion in private. To do otherwise would be to violate the Calvinist Protestant's view of the time, which held that Judaism – in not upholding the divinity of Christ – was blasphemous.[3]

During this period, two major political forces competed to rule Holland. William II's House of Orange and the official Calvinist Protestant Church advocated a quasi-monarchy with a strong central government. The other group, composed of a union of provinces, each of which sought to guarantee their sovereignty, sought a republic. The republicans objected to concentrating governmental power in a quasi-monarchical figure and advocated instead a regime that diffused power across the various provinces in the society.[4] In addition to the struggle over the form of government, there was strife over religious toleration, and the lines of difference on this issue ran parallel with the schism between monarchy and republicanism. Those who supported the monarchist position – the Orthodox Calvinists – were not sympathetic to instituting the doctrine of religious toleration throughout society and instead preferred, as Steven Nadler says, a "theologically regimented state."[5] On the other hand, the "Collegiants," who consisted of various groups of Christian believers disaffected from the orthodox Protestant Church, were a major proponent of the republic, and they opposed the imposition of a religious doctrine onto citizens by a state-supported, clerical class.[6] For the religiously tolerant Collegiants, people did not need the official Protestant Church of Holland to tell them the meaning of Scripture, but people, from their own reflection and discussion with others in settings where each was an equal to the other, could determine that meaning for themselves. In support of this view, they believed that true Christianity rested on the idea, as Nadler says, of "love for one's fellow human beings . . . and obedience to the original words of Jesus Christ, unmediated by any theological commentary [and thus not interpreted through the eyes of an official state clergy]."[7]

Spinoza's commitment to religious toleration is aligned closely with the Collegiants. He believes that a state-backed church uses fear to paralyze reason, and through this tactic denies citizens their liberty to form their own judgments and to advocate them in public. Indeed, as he says in the preface to *A Theologico-Political Treatise*, the "specious garb of religion," which, for Spinoza, is nothing more than superstition since it cannot be substantiated by fact or justified by reason, is often used to "hoodwink the subjects, and to mask the fear which keeps them down."[8]

III. Philosophy and Religion

None of the aforementioned should be construed, however, to mean that Spinoza objects to religion because, for him, it is a fundamental part of a decent culture, along with philosophy. To support this view, Spinoza seeks to demonstrate the complementary relationship between religion and philosophy. Indeed, the moral teaching of Scripture for Spinoza can be summed up in the commitment to treat others with charity, and, moreover, this teaching should not be disqualified because it arises from religious texts largely upheld through faith as opposed to reason. And the basis for this judgment is that Spinoza, who relies on reason to determine truth, and thus is dedicated to the practice of philosophy, argues that the moral teachings of reason are definitely in sync with the moral lessons of biblical tradition in that each seeks to advance the idea of "charity towards his neighbors."[9]

Still, it is not possible to understand the structure of nature from biblical texts. That task is left to reason and by way of reason to philosophy. Unlike the biblical tradition that communicates through faith and belief, philosophy makes use of reason to understand the structure and laws of nature. Thus, philosophy, as distinguished from other methods of discovery, is the route to knowledge in the fullest sense.[10] And what does philosophy make clear to us about God? God is synonymous for Spinoza with the order inherent in nature and known to humankind by reason. As Nadler says, for Spinoza, nature is a unity of all the attributes that constitute it, and because God is "the immanent [that is, inherent] and sustaining cause of all there is" in nature, then "nature is God."[11] Thus, Spinoza tells us in the *Ethics* that comprehension of the unity of nature is always "accompanied by the idea of God as cause."[12] Further, this understanding brings about a sense of "*delight*" before the truth made available to us by reason, and this delight is not only a basis for an "*intellectual love of God*,"[13] but through this love a rejection of emotions, like envy and jealousy, that threaten the prospects for a decent society.[14]

For Spinoza, the love of God, since it resists hateful passions, provides an opening to those emotions that make it possible for human beings to live as free citizens in a democracy. How this works is that initially people who become friends interact together "with [a] mutual zeal of love," an emotion that enables people to "confer benefits on each other."[15] Moreover, people who act toward each other in this way are "free men" whose lives are mutually guided by reason. As people guided by reason, they conclude that what is good for sustaining friendships among people who know each other well should be equally good for creating a basis for all relationships in society among free people, including friends and strangers, alike. Indeed, it is the mutual commitment to sustain freedom that occasions free men to use their reason to create and then place themselves under a system of laws by which each is required to observe the norms and rules of good citizenship. In this setting, living as the "dictates of reason" propose, citizens ensure the protections of the "general rights of citizenship" and the "greater freedom" made possible by these rights.[16] Thus, knowledge of nature, which is the same as knowledge of God, by resisting hateful passions like envy and jealousy, opens the door to friendship, which is integrally linked with democratic citizenship and the full use and development of one's reason and freedom.

Even so, Spinoza's philosophical perspective on religion implies views of religious belief that were far out of sync with believers in his own times. Indeed, Spinoza's religious perspective, in arguing that knowledge of God is the same as knowledge of the impersonal laws of nature, denies that God should be viewed as possessing characteristics to which people can appeal – through prayer – for assistance and strength.[17] Since both the Christian and Jewish conceptions of religion attributed such qualities to God, Spinoza disagreed with the premises of both faiths, thus he rejected the dominant religious doctrine of his period. More significantly, he stood in conflict with the state, which embodied this doctrine into law. In consequence, his political and philosophical writings were censured, and he was never able to publish his work under his own name during his lifetime.

The term *enlightenment*, when used in this context, thus should be taken to signify Spinoza's strong resistance to state-imposed religious doctrines, in deference to the free and unhindered use of reason. Democracy, which embraces Spinoza's preference, can only be considered a progressive step away from a "dark" period. For Spinoza, then, there is direct link between the use of reason to discern knowledge – a basic principle of the Enlightenment and of modern science – and the achievement of democratic citizenship.

IV. The Social Contract of a Democratic State

In constructing his conception of the state, Spinoza starts from the view of social contract theorists of his time that individuals in the state of nature – that hypothetical time before the invention of civil society – have a natural right to all resources that ensure them as much power as they can acquire over others for the sake of realizing their desires.[18] As a consequence, the state of nature for Spinoza is similar to that of Thomas Hobbes. It is a place of continuous strife guided by the constant presence of "force" and the sense that anyone standing in one's way is an enemy who must be defeated.[19] No doubt, then, fear and uncertainty permeate the state of nature. To overcome these conditions, individuals by mutual agreement decide to live together in accordance with the terms of a social contract or "compact" by which the rights of each person will be protected. In this situation, reason, rather than "force and desire," governs their circumstances.[20] Here, by mutual consent, individuals leave the state of nature and form a civil society where all "enjoy as a whole the rights which naturally belong to them as individuals."[21]

Now, in choosing to form a new "compact" to escape the uncertainty of the state of nature, the citizens construct a new state with its own power.[22] But will the power be used for the stated purposes embedded in the social contract? Spinoza's Machiavellian realism reflects the fact that placing power into the hands of anyone, even when good intentions are to guide the use of that power, always evokes worry about whether the power will be used well or poorly. Faced with this uncertainty, people must ponder the options before them and choose among the alternatives, placing the highest priority on the greatest of the several goods while shunning the least of the evils.[23] In this case, people choose the new social contract because it represents the hope that a democratic state will, on the whole, use power more in keeping with people's vital needs than would be the case were such a social contract not in place.

Why should we place such hope on a social contract that embraces democracy? Why not a social contract that is more in keeping with the absolutist form of government that Hobbes propounded? Spinoza's answer is that democracy is "consonant with individual liberty."[24] In saying this, Spinoza makes the achievement of liberty the main objective of a decent society, and not just security as some might say is Hobbes's objective. Additionally, liberty is best protected in a democracy.

The main reason why this is the case is that democracy establishes, as the basis of governmental power, an obligation to ensure that it is used for common purposes deemed necessary by the majority. But what is to prevent the majority from establishing a tyranny of its own, one that denies regard for the rights of the minority? The answer, for Spinoza, is that all citizens help constitute the majority, so when the majority speaks, it speaks for each citizen. Now, of course, it is possible that a minority might claim that the majority fails to properly represent the needs of the minority. But even when this happens, the members of a minority always retain the right to convince the majority to encompass minority approaches. As Spinoza says, in a democracy, individuals do not give up "natural right[s] so absolutely," or, in other terms, their power to govern themselves so completely, that they have "no further voice in [public] affairs."[25] What makes it possible for the minority to appeal to the majority on behalf of making changes in its dispositions is that each citizen is an equal, politically and civilly speaking, to everyone else.[26] Indeed, each person's political or civil liberty is never denied, no matter what the policy of the majority may be. In consequence, each person retains both the right and the ability to effect changes in the positions the majority holds.

In support of this position, as indicated at the beginning of this chapter, Spinoza seeks to provide all people with the opportunity to realize the free use of their own reason in the determination of both personal and public matters. To this end, there must be full freedom of thought and speech, a major subject that we address in our discussion of John Stuart Mill in Chapter 14. With freedom of thought and speech, citizens are not forced to acquiesce in their opinions to predominant religious or political authorities, but, instead, people rely on their own reason-formed judgments. Moreover, since the free use of reason requires an environment in which people listen to diverse views and seek the best arguments among them, individuals come to appreciate the wide diversity of views on the issues before them. Thus, freedom of thought is the basis for richly textured openness to and toleration of difference, not just of ideas but of diverse ways of life.

V. Spinoza and Civil Society

Spinoza is greatly influenced in his political thinking by his experience in Amsterdam, a progressive city at this time in which "religion and sect is [*sic*] considered of no importance: for it has no effect for the judgment in gaining or losing a cause."[27] The toleration found there is aided by two important realities that characterized Amsterdam for Spinoza – prosperity in commerce and a civil religion. Each of these dimensions helps to advance the possibility of a secular state in which public policy is not the handmaiden of religious doctrine. As Mathew Stewart says, when people are involved in commerce, their passions for religion are cooled. This circumstance allows them to pursue religious belief without creating deep conflict and instability, both of which would threaten commerce and toleration.[28]

Spinoza also advances a notion of a civil religion by which people manifest religious belief in ways consistent with the commitment of the state to maintain a majority rule–based democracy, which promotes democracy without violating the basic rights of any individual, including freedom of thought and speech. In this, religious belief is made to serve larger civic goals, and this approach completely reverses the relationship between the state and religion common in Spinoza's time, where the state and its laws are designed, in part, to serve the interests of religion. But for the civil religion to achieve this purpose, it must be under the control of the state, in this case, not a religiously based theocracy, but a secular democratic state dedicated to ensuring full toleration, full freedom of thought and speech, and government by the rule of the majority.[29]

Spinoza's liberal democracy would encourage as well as benefit from a civil society that maintained itself as a separate sphere of groups and associations. In this setting, individuals would cultivate their own ways of life. But at the same time, owing to the presence of the civil religion and to material prosperity, they would know the importance of maintaining the common and overlapping beliefs that maintain democracy. Differences would be accommodated by a majority that is dedicated to the widest and deepest promotion of reason, consistent with the commitment to freedom of thought and speech – the bellwether values of a liberal democracy.

Notes

1. Benedict Spinoza, *A Theologico-Political Treatise*, trans. R. H. M. Elwes (New York: Dover, 1951), 258. Spinoza says that the state "can never prevent men from forming judgments according to their intellect."
2. Ibid., 259.
3. Steven Nadler, *Spinoza: A Life* (Cambridge: Cambridge University Press, 1999), 85.
4. Ibid., 83–85.
5. Ibid., 85.
6. Ibid., 139, 85.
7. Ibid., 139.
8. Spinoza, *A Theologico-Political Treatise*, 5.
9. Ibid, 261; also p. 187.
10. For accounts of his view of philosophy in its pursuit of knowledge of nature, see Roger Scruton, *Spinoza* (New York: Oxford University Press, 1986), 67–79; Stuart Hampshire, *Spinoza* (London: Faber and Faber, 1956), 12–16, 67–73.
11. Nadler, *Spinoza*, 187.
12. Benedict Spinoza, *The Ethics*, trans. R. H. M. Elwes (New York: Dover Publications, 1955), 263.
13. Ibid. Italics in text.
14. Ibid., 256.
15. Ibid., 234.
16. Ibid., 235.
17. Nadler, *Spinoza*, 186–87.
18. Spinoza, *A Theologico-Political Treatise*, 200.
19. Ibid., 201–2.
20. Ibid., 202–3.
21. Ibid., 202.
22. Ibid., 203.
23. Ibid.
24. Ibid., 207.
25. Ibid.
26. Ibid.
27. Ibid., 264.
28. Mathew Stewart, *The Courtier and the Heretic: Leibnitz, Spinoza, and the Fate of God in the Modern World* (New York: Norton, 2006), 103.
29. Ibid.

9

John Locke, Civil Society, and the Constrained Majority

I. Introduction

John Locke's (1632–1704) *The Second Treatise of Government*, published in 1690, can be construed, as Thomas Peardon claims, as an argument against Thomas Hobbes's call for an absolute monarchy based upon citizen consent. Locke supported the "Glorious Revolution" of 1688, which symbolized that the King of England should exercise his powers in keeping with the dictates of the parliament. Indeed, Locke's own political thought accepted the view that follows from the experience of this revolution, namely, that the parliament is the main source of authority in government. However, as we will demonstrate, Locke did provide a role for an executive branch but in a setting in which the power of both the legislative and the executive branches is limited by virtue of the precise functions each is given.[1] Locke thus rejected Hobbes's view that would place absolute power in either the legislative or executive branches of government. Furthermore, Locke's concept of government in a civil society was undergirded by the view, as Richard Ashcraft argues, that productive labor, the development of land, and commercial activities all benefited society. In taking this position, Locke favored the new bourgeoisie or middle class. This class consisted of merchants, tradesmen, artisans, and small farmers who owned their own land. Locke saw this group as comprising the most productive members of society and thought their interests should supersede the interests of the traditional and, for Locke, unproductive landed aristocracy.[2]

Before proceeding, it is well to point out that Locke no less than Hobbes held the view that, in a civil society, individuals have rights contingent upon acceptance of necessary constraints or what we have referred to as civic virtues. How did Locke approach the definition of such constraints? For Locke, as Charles Taylor says, we are to follow "the law laid down by God, which he [Locke] also calls at times the Natural Law."[3] Moreover, this law, which suggests a rational order to our existence and which, therefore, can be known by rational individuals, represents God's intention to secure to each of us certain basic, natural rights. With these rights, we are able, as individuals, to determine our own intentions and courses of conduct. But it must always be clear that the presence of basic rights, supported by natural law, places limits on what we can choose and how we can act.[4] Indeed, in discussing the state of nature, as we do in Section II, Locke outlines the constraints on freedom, or those rules that individuals must observe while pursuing their own self-defined interests. These constraints secure the rights of all citizens. In upholding these constraints, individuals can be said to be maintaining regard for the civic virtues that protect the rights and the basic liberty of each person.

In the remainder of this chapter, we intend to discuss Locke's view of civil society by pointing out the basic natural law constraints that help to govern and shape it. Locke's central concern is to contest Hobbes by arguing that the state in a civil society must have limited powers, so it does not threaten the very basic rights the state is supposed to protect for each society member. In seeking a state with limited powers, Locke wanted to locate the state's power in what can be called a *constrained majority*. Locke's conception of the *social contract*, or basic agreement upon which to predicate the authority of government, highlights the rule of the majority. But the majority's will must always be grounded in the natural law principles, or notions of civic virtue, that require that the majority never acts to undermine the natural rights provided to all citizens.

II. The Concept of Political Authority

Political authority is unlike any other kind of authority. For Locke, political authority is not the same as the authority that husbands hold in the family, the master holds over the servant, or the lord holds over the slave.[5] The scope of political power is far wider, and its coercive abilities to ensure compliance are far more extensive. Political authority enables the state to make laws that bind the whole of society. Governments even can punish those who violate the law with death. And most importantly, governments may use their power only for the public good.[6] Thus, political power is the *right of making laws with penalties of death and, consequently, all less penalties for regulating and preserving of property, and of employing the force of the community in the execution of such laws and in the defense of the commonwealth from foreign injury; and all this only for the public good.*[7]

The use of power to promote the public good is the most distinguishing feature of political authority. But what is the public good? Or, in other terms, what is the just basis for political authority?

Before answering this question, we need to describe the definition of the public good that Locke rejects. For Locke, the public good has not one thing to do with maintaining monarchical absolutism. Advocates of absolute monarchy argue that the monarch does in fact promote the public good. On behalf of this claim, proponents of monarchy point out that monarchies provide a legal system as well as opportunities to appeal to judges to decide cases of controversy. Locke grants that these uses of authority are good. But Locke argues that it is never in the interest of the public for a government to claim absolute power to achieve even good purposes such as these. Indeed, sensible people would never support permitting a ruler to have unlimited amounts of power while everyone else is made subject to the rule of law. Locke says that the supporters of monarchy "think that men are so foolish that they take care to avoid what mischiefs may be done them by polecats or foxes, but are content, nay, think it safety, to be devoured by lions."[8] Rulers must be made subject to limits, too. And this means that there must be good reasons to justify their authority. But what are these good reasons? That answer is provided in Locke's conception of the state of nature, which in discussing, we will consider his view of the common good that is the basis for defining the legitimate grounds of political authority.

The State of Nature I: Justification for Political Authority

The rational grounds for political authority are located in the original intentions and understandings of people in the state of nature. The latter is a hypothetical situation that describes, for Locke, the natural condition of humankind prior to the entrance of individuals into formal society. Locke thinks people in the state of nature are, in large part, rational individuals who are able to determine the reasonable constraints that should govern each person's conduct. Locke thus describes in his discussion of the state of nature a perspective that can help us understand the true purpose and basis for political authority.

For Locke, the state of nature is a state of "perfect freedom" in which individuals are entitled "to order their actions and dispose of their possessions and persons as they think fit, within the bounds of the laws of nature, without asking leave or depending upon the will of any other man."[9] In this context, people treat each other as equals because "power and jurisdiction is reciprocal, no one having more than other." Further, Locke's state of nature is not a "state of license,"[10] as in Hobbes's version of the state of nature as a state of war, and so Locke's state of nature is not governed by Hobbes's view of people seeking to dominate and control the lives of others. Instead, the state of nature is a place in which each knows that one is not permitted to "destroy himself, or so much as any creature in his possession."[11]

On this view, then, the state of nature is a place where people treat each other in a civil way, in keeping with norms all regarded as reasonable. Locke says:

> The state of nature has a law of nature to govern it, which obligates every one; and reason, which is that law, teaches all mankind who will but consult it that, being all equal and independent, no one ought to harm another in his life, health, liberty, or possessions; for men being all the workmanship of one omnipotent and infinitely wise Maker – all the servants of one sovereign master, sent into the world by his order, and about his business – they are his property whose workmanship they are, made to last during, his, not one another's pleasure; and being furnished with like faculties, sharing all in one community of nature, there cannot be supposed any such subordination among us that may authorize us to destroy another, as if we were made for one another's uses as the inferior ranks of creatures are for ours. Everyone, as he is bound to preserve himself and not quit his station wilfully, so by the like reason, when his own preservation comes not in competition, ought he, as much as he can, to preserve the rest of mankind, and may not . . . take way or impair the life, or what tends to be the preservation of life, the liberty, health, limb, or goods of another.[12]

It is well to concentrate for a brief time on this important paragraph. Several critical dimensions are revealed concerning the justification for political authority. First, Locke argued that from the rational perspective of men in the state of nature, there is a clear understanding of a law of nature, taught by reason and sanctioned by God, which all are obligated to uphold. And the principal teaching of the law of nature is that no one is to harm another. In particular, we are to act positively to protect and to preserve the lives of others by maintaining, when one's own preservation is not at issue, the "life, the liberty, health, limb, or goods of another." This idea suggests that it is reasonable to assume that individuals have *natural* rights, or rights provided to all individuals by virtue of being human beings, and no one may take them from another.

Support for this position ultimately derives from the fact that God, the "Maker" of all people, sanctions natural rights. For Locke, God created individuals as equals and furnished all people with "like faculties." By "faculties," we take Locke to mean the capacities for reason, understanding, and freedom. Had God intended that some should have more rights than others, he would have created individuals with "unlike faculties" and made them unequal to each other. But this was not God's intention.

It is now possible to answer the question asked at the conclusion of the last section: what are the proper or rational grounds of political authority? The main lesson of the state of nature is that no one is to be under the arbitrary will of another, for, otherwise, individuals would lose their freedom and their rights. Political authority is legitimate when it encompasses this lesson, and it does so when individuals are under a form of authority that they have consented to establish. And the only government that citizens will consent to is one whose laws are made by a legislative power that protects people's freedom and rights or a regime that allows "a liberty to follow my own will in all things where the rule prescribes not."[13] Here, no person is to "be subject to the inconstant, uncertain, unknown, arbitrary will of another man." A political regime that embodies these values permits individuals to live as if they were in the state of nature, governed by "no other restraint but the law of nature."[14]

State of Nature II: Constraints for Freedom

Regarding Locke's view of political authority, it is important to understand the various constraints that individuals must accept if they are to maintain the basic rights that secure the freedom of each person. Locke, in arguing for individual liberty, realizes that essential to securing liberty in his natural law framework is the need for citizens to accept the presence in their lives of certain moral restraints or what we have otherwise referred to as civic virtues. Thus, further discussion of the state of nature is needed to help outline these constraints. Moreover, in doing so, we demonstrate, at the conclusion of this section, the problems that Locke's conception of life in the state of nature faces, when it appears he embraces, as part of the state of nature, certain assumptions of market life.

To discuss this subject, it must first be clear that possessing freedom is contingent upon being able to own property. Thus, any discussion of the constraints on freedom arises from Locke's conception of property in the state of nature and the constraints that are associated with owning property. So, it is first necessary to explain the basic dimensions of Locke's concept of property and then move from there to a discussion of the constraints he associates with both holding property and having freedom.

Locke argues that God, and here he quotes King David in Psalm 115, "has given the earth to the children of men."[15] But if God has given the earth to men in common, how is private property ever justified? Locke's answer is that "though the earth and all inferior creatures be common to all men, yet every man has a property in his own person; this nobody has a right to but himself. The labor of his body and the work of his hands, we may say are properly his."[16] Here, what individuals are able to acquire through their own work is theirs, subject to the limitation that enough is left for others as well, or, as Locke says, "Where there is enough and as good left in common for others."[17]

There seems to follow from the preceding argument two major justifications for property rights. The first is fairness. Fairness suggests that people have a right to what they produce through their own labor. People who do not work, and who expect to receive the benefit of others' work, are violating the freedom of others. Thus, Locke argues that God gave the world to those who are "industrious and rational," or individuals who through labor and work contribute something of use to the society.[18]

Second, Locke, in saying that each of us has property in our own person and that nobody has a right to this property but oneself, attaches to the idea of private property a right to make choices about the direction and purposes of one's life. Locke's conception of private property suggests that the property in the person, one's personality, one's choices and decisions about the course one determines for life, are not subject to the arbitrary power of others. "This freedom from absolute, arbitrary power is so necessary to, and closely joined with, a man's preservation that he cannot part with it but by what forfeits his preservation and life together."[19] Certainly, there will be some who cannot or will not act in ways respectful of the rights of others, and these individuals use "force without right," and in doing so fail to observe the natural right to life, liberty, and property of all people. Such individuals enter into a Hobbesian state of war with others. But unlike Hobbes, Locke refuses to characterize the state of nature as a state of war, since the state of nature is a condition in which people act "according to reason," and thus the constraints that protect the freedom of each person are respected.[20] Thus, those who violate the freedom of others in the state of nature represent aberrations from the general tendency to act in ways that are respectful of others' freedom.

What prevents private property from becoming a source of social instability and discord? For, clearly, some will, as a result of their efforts, end up with more property than others. When this occurs, will not private property itself be seen as a threat to freedom? Locke argues that there are common, rational constraints that legitimize differences in wealth across the society. First of all, Locke says that, even though God gave the world to all people to enjoy and to achieve satisfaction and pleasure with, God did not want individuals to take any portion of the earth that people could not "make use of to any advantage of life before it spoils."[21] Here, whereas we have every right to utilize the external world in ways that bring us happiness, we do not have a right to take more than we can make good use of. For, in that case, much of what we accumulate would spoil, and then we would render large portions of the world of no use to anyone. Locke makes reference to the following example. If in enclosing land and calling it our own we can use the grass on that land to feed the cattle we own, we can keep the land. But, if the grass on the land rots, then we have violated a basic natural law constraint of the state of nature and that land can become "the possession of any other."[22]

But even in taking only enough so that one does not cause precious materials or resources to spoil, certain individuals may still become wealthier than others. Locke's response to this likelihood is to justify the types of wealth accumulation that are highly beneficial to society. This means that there are certain categories of individuals who in accumulating wealth are not causing important resources to spoil, but in fact they are adding to the stock of resources that others enjoy. What aids this prospect is commercial trade and finance, which permit owners of land and materials to organize the laboring efforts of people to create products that others need, and through this effort to expand the material wealth of society. Money symbolizes this activity.

Locke says that with the invention of money, it is possible for individuals to exchange perishable goods for durable and nonperishable metals, such as gold. And if an individual were able to exchange consumable items, such as nuts or wool – as Locke specifically lists – for durable goods that do not spoil, such as diamonds, then there is no limit to the amount of wealth that one could in fact accumulate.[23] Here, a person can exchange his or her wool for diamonds, and "he might heap as much of these durable things as he pleased."[24] The possession of durable goods, such as diamonds or gold, symbolizes activity that is useful to the entire society. Locke has in mind the development of productive labor that increases the total wealth of society. It is for this reason that, for Locke, individuals accept, by a form of "tacit and voluntary consent," the fact of the "disproportionate and unequal possession of the earth."[25] This view suggests that, in the state of nature, people who succeed will have more wealth than others, and this provides an incentive for people to work hard to provide the goods that all need.[26]

Based on these constraints, from the standpoint of natural law in the state of nature, individuals are given freedom on the condition that they do not use it in ways that harm the freedom of others. On this view, then, Locke can be interpreted as making the claim that the standard of a civil society is fairness. However, other writers, in particular, C.B. Macpherson, have argued that Locke's treatment of property in the state of nature places his commitment to fairness in doubt.[27] As part of the evidence in support of this claim, Macpherson points to the place in *The Second Treatise of Government* where Locke contradicts his own principle that the fruits of each person's labor belong to the person performing that labor. Locke indicates that an owner of property who employs servants or workers has a right to the wealth that these servants or workers produced.

Thus the grass my horse has bit, the turfs my servant has cut . . . become my property without the assignment of consent to anybody. The labor that was mine, removing them, out of that common state they were in, has fixed my property in them.[28]

For Macpherson, this statement indicates that Locke had incorporated into his view of property in the state of nature a market setting in which a few would end up controlling both land and labor for the purpose of obtaining ever-larger amounts of land and labor. The land and labor so acquired would be used in both the agricultural and manufacturing sectors of the economy to produce goods that could be sold for a profit by the owner class. As a result, for Macpherson, Locke accepted as natural and rational the idea that owners could control as well as own the labor of others. The effect of accepting this view is that, over time, large numbers of workers would end up transferring authority over their lives to those who claimed a right to own their labor. In this situation, the owners could pay the workers only the necessary amount to maintain the workers' self-sufficiency, and the rest of what the workers produced could be transferred to the owner for his, the owner's, own use. Not only would this situation create great social divisions in society between the workers and owners, but it would also lead to a politics of class rule in which the owner class dominated the workers, denying them their liberty.[29]

The Nature of Civil Society and Constrained Majority Rule

Putting aside for the moment Macpherson's arguments, if we take the standards of Locke's view of the state of nature as he enumerates them and make them the basis for a civil society, as Locke does, then a civil society would be a setting in which individuals have rights, conditioned upon the need to uphold the various constraints Locke outlines. Given this view of civil society, then, the purpose of government in a civil society is clear. Locke argues that people unite into a commonwealth and form a government to protect their property, which signifies citizens' basic rights and freedom.[30] Moreover, to support this objective, the state or government in a civil society, as we demonstrate in the next section, is one with limited powers.

This view of the role and powers of government suggests that Locke believes the level of conflict in society would not be severe. Were it the case that the disputes were extreme, then, the state would have to become as powerful and as absolute as Hobbes suggested the state must be in order to protect the rights of all citizens and not just the most powerful ones. In fact, as we indicate at the conclusion of this section, it is likely that the conflicts will be intense and deep in Locke's state of nature. Locke accepts this fact himself when he describes in a "second" view of the state of nature a picture at variance with the view just discussed. Unlike the "first" view that indicates, owing to the rational character of people, a commitment to fairness, the "second" view suggests something more like a Hobbesian state of war. Perhaps the reason for this deviation from the first view is that Locke himself accepts, without saying so, some of the implications of market life that Macpherson ascribes to Locke. Before moving to a discussion of this point, however, let us first describe Locke's conception of the state in a civil society as well as his understanding of the state's origins in consent.

Again, the purpose of a state in a civil society is clear: "The great and chief end . . . of men's uniting into commonwealths and putting themselves under government is the preservation of their property."[31] The state protects everyone's property by providing a system of "settled" and "known law" that becomes the basis for resolving "all controversies between [people]." Further, the state must act as an "indifferent judge" in deciding controversies. Finally, the state has the power to back up its decisions and to ensure their "due execution."[32]

How does the state in a civil society arise? Or, in other terms, what is the nature of the *social contract* or agreement people strike with each other and make the basis for the state's authority? Locke argues the state arises from the unanimous consent of the people for the majority to rule. In this regard, then, Locke says that the political society, or the government of a civil society, is created

> *when any number of men have, by the consent of every individual, made a community, they have thereby made that community one body, with a power to act as one body, which is only by the will and determination of the majority.*[33]

Further, there is a major proviso that needs to made clear here, and this proviso indicates that the rule of the majority is really the rule of a *constrained majority*, or a majority that must respect the rights of all. Although people, in entering civil society, leave behind the state of nature, and thus give up complete and full autonomy over themselves, they do not authorize the state that they constitute in a civil society to violate or to threaten their liberty. Locke says that "the power of the society, or legislative constituted by them [the people], can never be supposed to extend farther than the common good, but is obliged to secure every one's property."[34] Consequently, the majority and those who speak for it, in this case either the executive or legislative arms of government, cannot violate the terms of the original agreement people make when they enter civil society, namely, the requirement to protect "the peace, safety, and public good of the people."[35]

Any majority opinion formed in response to a public issue must make policies that are respectful of the need to treat citizens as equals, that is, as individuals entitled to the basic protections that secure their liberty. Thus, for instance, in discussing taxation, Locke made clear that the legislative branch of society cannot tax people without their consent, that is, without the consent of the majority, who give consent either "by themselves or [through] their representatives chosen by them."[36] But the majority must be constrained by always recognizing the commitment to protect the rights of all. To take a contemporary example, the losing side in a Senate debate might not prevail on an issue pertaining to taxation. But just the fact that it loses on the issue does not mean that it must lose all its basic rights as well, including rights guaranteeing participation in government, due process of law, and so on. The state complies with this objective by maintaining a commitment to the rule of law, which means that the state governs by "laws, promulgated and known to people, and not by extemporary decrees."[37]

In the next several paragraphs, we discuss the implications of this view for practical politics and for citizenship obligations. With respect to the former, Locke suggests, as we argued, that, in having property, people have sufficient autonomy to pursue their interests. But it must be presumed that, at times, and owing to the fact that society will be composed of people with different interests, it is likely that people will have disagreements as to what the law means and how it should be applied in their own cases. The state in a civil society, in operating by known laws, assumes the role of an "indifferent judge" and, thus, acts as an umpire. As an umpire, the state does not dictate to any individuals what way of life is best for them, as would be the case in classical or medieval thought, where the good for each person was defined by virtue of the role a person is given. Instead, Locke's state, in its indifferent judge role, would resolve differences with an intention to protect the basic rights of each person to define his or her own way of life.

Regarding citizen obligations, it is Locke's view that citizens living in a state that protected their liberties are expected to uphold the laws of that state. Citizens give their tacit consent to this arrangement. Locke says:

> *Every man that has any possessions or enjoyment of any part of the dominions of any government does thereby give his tacit consent and is as far forth obliged to obedience to the laws of that government, during such enjoyment, as anyone under it; whether this his possession be of land to him and his heirs for ever, or a lodging only for a week, or whether it be barely traveling freely the highway; and, in effect, it reaches as far as the very being of anyone with the territories of that government.*[38]

In developing the notion of tacit consent, Locke hopes to overcome a problem central to all consent theory, such as the one Locke provides. Where there is no way to demonstrate explicit consent by the people to a regime, how can one maintain that the people have consented to the regime? Locke's answer to this problem is quite simple. The notion of tacit consent suggests the conditions under which rational people *would* consent, were they given a chance to do so.[39] What are the conditions that must be obtained for citizens to give their consent? Rational individuals would say that they would consent to any regime that provided them with essential benefits. Thus, Locke, in saying that we are obligated to the state's authority simply for using a highway, is really using the highway as a metaphor. And the metaphor suggests that when we live in a society that provides us with essential goods, such as protection of our basic liberty, we are clearly obligated to obey the laws of that state.

Finally, Locke's doctrine of tacit consent indicates as well that citizens are aware of a responsibility on their part to uphold, faithfully, the rights of others who, like themselves, own property. Without this sense of obligation to support constraints on freedom, the state would have to become as powerful as Hobbes's state, entering society in ways that threaten the commitment to protect the rights of all citizens. But, given the rights-respecting mentality of citizens, the state can have a more limited role in Locke's society than it would have in Hobbes's society. Here, the idea of civic virtue would have a powerful place in Locke's civil society.

For there to be freedom and rights, individuals must identify as the common good the need to defend both rights and the constraints needed to preserve them, even when doing so at times requires one to accept limits on the extent to which one is able to pursue one's interests. Locke's concept of a constrained majority would seem to assume that this understanding is a necessary part of people's outlook.

Given this view of a constrained majority, then, a civil society would not experience great conflict, and the state could avoid the absolutist state of Hobbes. But this view presumes that the basic peace Locke describes in the state of nature would find its way into civil society. And there is some question as to whether this view is realistic, given Locke's "second" view of the state of nature. Thus, there is another more Hobbesian view of the state of nature to appear in Locke. The "second" view casts doubt on the prospects of a constrained majority perspective, along with the hope of limited government, and, in place of both, the second view suggests a Hobbesian form of absolute government.

Locke's "second" description of the state of nature seems to suggest that the differences between people are not as low level and as harmless as Locke might otherwise suggest. To support this point, we quote from the second part of *The Second Treatise*. It would seem that when Locke wrote the following words, he was not aware of what he had written in the first part where he said the state of nature is a place of "perfect freedom" and mutual respect for rights. But, in contrast, in the second part of *The Second Treatise*, Locke said in reference to why individuals leave the state of nature:

> *The enjoyment of it [freedom] is very uncertain and constantly exposed to the invasion of others; for all being kings as much as he, every man his equal, and the greater part no strict observers of equity and justice, the enjoyment of the property he has in this state is very unsafe, very insecure.*[40]

Locke also said that there are many "privileges" found in the state of nature, but there are many "inconveniences," too, and these inconveniences stem from the "uncertain exercise of the power every man has of punishing the transgressions of others."[41] These words indicate a Hobbesian state of nature as the backdrop of society. If this is so, the potential for intense conflict in society would be strong, and to protect the rights of all people, even Locke would need a Hobbesian absolutist state.

How can we account for this "second," more Hobbesian view of the state of nature? There is no doubt that Macpherson would explain this second view by pointing out that it emerges from Locke's acceptance of market life, which permits a few to dominate and to control both the land in society and the labor of others for their, the owner's, own economic advantage. Further, if the second view of the state of nature, as defined in Macpherson's terms, were the basis for developing both society and government, what kind of experience would typify social life? Society would be characterized by class conflict, between those who own most of the wealth and those who do not. In this case, the majority rule process would only be a majority of a small minority of people. Here, the likelihood of social discord and instability would be ever-present because those outside the policy process, the non-propertied, would demand the same rights accorded to others. Still, Locke's notion of the state of nature, as we saw in his first account of this concept, says that no one is to take away the "life, liberty, health, limb, or goods of another." This suggests that Locke is committed to extending liberty to more than just property owners. But his view of a constrained majority would have little relevance to this project were it merely oriented to protecting the property of a few against the great majority of the non-propertied people.

What would Locke's response be to this problem? We can only provide several conjectures. One response might be a demand for the government to suppress the non-propertied. But, in this case, the state would have to assume unlimited powers for itself, a consequence that Locke rejects. On the other hand, it is possible that Locke envisions that more and more people, due to advances in the economy, would acquire property so that eventually the majority would include all the citizens in the society. Here, where all people own property, any decision by the majority must be designed to protect the rights of all citizens. In that case, the potential for intense conflict would be minimized, making possible both a constrained majority, which sought to extend to all basic liberties, as well as the need for and the possibility of the limited form of government Locke advocates. Were this view to prevail, the main question, then, would pertain to how to maintain a government with limited powers, a government that did not become so powerful that it threatened the rights it is supposed to protect. In the next several sections, we discuss the approaches to this problem that Locke recommends.

III. Locke's Limited Government

In this section, we discuss the concept of limited government that Locke proposes. Locke rejects Hobbes's refusal to entertain a government based upon a separation of powers. Locke does so in large part because he believes that a government based upon the concept of separated powers can institute limitations on the authority and actions of government so that, in the long run, the people's liberty is protected.

There are three functions in Locke's government: the legislative, the executive, and the federative. Federative functions have to do with making foreign policy and using the power of war and peace to this end. Federative powers are ensconced in the executive branch, so, in effect, the power to enforce the law with respect to domestic matters and the power to make foreign policy are placed in the same office.[42]

At the heart of his view of government is the legislative branch, which, for Locke, is "the supreme power of the commonwealth."[43] He says, in this regard, that the "first and fundamental natural law which is to govern even the legislative itself is the preservation of the society and, as far as will consist with the public good, and every person in it."[44] The legislature, which makes the laws, is the supreme authority, but, even so, it must not abuse its authority. The legislature cannot act in an arbitrary fashion "over the lives and fortunes of the people," nor can it do anything other than "decide the rights of the subject [citizens] by promulgated, standing laws, and known authorized judges."[45]

To prevent legislative misuse of power, several remedies are provided. First, since the legislators hold authority only on the basis of the continuing trust of the citizens who elect them, the people have the right "to remove or alter" the legislature if it violates the trust the citizens place in it.[46] A second way to prevent legislative misuse of power is to establish a "separate" executive branch that is to carry out the laws the legislature passes.[47] If the legislature were to have executive functions as well as legislative or law-making ones, then it might be the case that legislators would be more likely to make laws that serve their own interests and less likely to make laws that serve the needs of the whole society.[48]

Now, it should be clear that, in discussing the executive, Locke indicated that the legislative and executive are separated only when it comes to enforcing laws that the legislative branch makes. But, on other occasions, when matters of law enforcement are not at issue, Locke argues that the executive is a part of the legislative branch. Thus, Locke says that the executive should be viewed as having "a share in the legislative." This arrangement permits the legislature to make the executive subordinate to its, the legislature's, power because the latter can change the executive at its, the legislature's, "pleasure."[49]

The executive, however, has special responsibilities that the legislature does not have. In particular, the executive must, as the constitution requires, call the legislature into session to deliberate about the laws and make sure, again in keeping with the constitution, that regular elections are held for the legislature. At other times, it is left to the executive's "prudence" to call for new elections and establish a new legislature when it appears that old laws no longer are relevant to meeting current challenges that threaten the public interest.[50] Regarding the issue of elections, Locke says that, over time, population shifts may occur, and, thus, some districts may need more representatives and others may need less. The executive must examine matters of this sort and distribute representatives proportionately.

For it being the interest as well as intention of the people to have a fair and equal representative, whoever brings it nearest to that is an undoubted friend to and establisher of the government and cannot miss the consent and approbation of the community.[51]

Still, Locke is well aware that the executive may abuse its power, and this problem grows out of the practical necessities of governing. Often, when political problems confront a nation, either the legislature is not in power, or it is too slow to act. In these situations, the executive assumes the power of "prerogative" and makes decisions on behalf of the public interest.[52] Hobbes, of course, also sees this power as inevitable. The difference between Hobbes and Locke on this issue is that the latter does not see this power as placed, without limits, into the hands of the executive (or king, as in Hobbes), and, further, Locke believes that the executive should be held accountable for misusing it. Hobbes places no such limits on the monarch. But Locke presumes that people, acting through their legislators, would allow the executive the use of its prerogative as long as good judgments are made, and, when poor judgments result, the public will seek to limit the executive use of its power of prerogative.[53]

Now, the hope of this view of separated government is that each branch will balance the other, so that, in the long run, the government will continue to make and to enforce fair laws that protect the liberty of the citizens. However, as in our times, we have come to realize that a practical consequence of a separation of powers view of government is intense competition between the branches. Moreover, when this happens, one branch or the other of government may grow in power to such an extent that the government threatens, rather than protects, the rights of its citizens. What is the remedy in this case? Locke says that all people can do is "appeal to heaven; for the rulers, in such attempts, exercising a power the people never put into their hands [and] do that which they have not a right to do."[54]

The Right of Revolution

The right to revolt against the central government arises from the fact that, in cases in which there is abuse of power and no remedy from within constituted authority, citizens always reserve for themselves the option of deciding to revolt against the rulers. Indeed, this option can never be given up by citizens, since it is not within a citizen's "power" to "submit himself to another as to give him a liberty to destroy him, God and nature never allowing a man so to abandon himself as to neglect his own preservation."[55] God ordains, on this view, that each of us has a duty to ensure that our freedom is not taken from us. In the face of errant executive or legislative power, then, Locke reaffirms not just a natural right to liberty, but both a right to revolution as well as a duty, mandated by God, to recreate the conditions of liberty.

The right to revolt, for Locke, would not be a recipe to encourage continual disorder and social instability. The reason for this view is that Locke sees this right as principally exercised by the majority, and, thus, for a revolution to take place, there would have to be a wholesale denial of people's basic rights. Locke says when the majority is "persuaded in their consciences that their laws, and with them their estates, liberties, and lives are in danger, and perhaps religion, too, how they will be hindered from resisting illegal forces used against them I cannot tell."[56]

The power of the majority, in this case, seems to be manifested more in the threat of revolution than in the act of revolution itself. What would most keep public officials from engaging in corrupt activities would be the fear that if they did, and if as a result the majority felt that their liberty was threatened, there would be a revolution that would sweep all public officials from power. Not wanting this situation to arise, public officials must maintain among themselves a modicum of honesty in their dealings with themselves and with the citizens.

Toleration and Civil Society

Locke's view of civil society, as we have seen, provides a concept of limited government to protect the general societal principle that the rights of each person should be protected. This principle was built into his conception of the constrained majority, as well. But there is another approach to rights protection in Locke. His view of civil society includes a space, outside the formal structure of government, where individuals would be protected from infringements of their rights either from others or from the government. An important element that helps create this dimension of civil society is the civic virtue of toleration.

In discussing the civic virtue of religious toleration, Locke understands that people hold their religious beliefs with extreme conviction, and, when they do, others who do not believe as they do are inevitably perceived as less deserving of respect. How, in the face of this problem, will it be possible for individuals to extend rights protection to all, including those whose religion is different from their own?

Locke's solution is found in his *Letter on Toleration.* Locke argues that the state is to preserve "civil interests," such as "life, liberty, health . . . and the possession of outward things, such as money, lands, houses, furniture, and the like."[57] The state's powers extend only to matters such as these, but they do not extend to matters pertaining to religious belief. Thus, the state cannot use its powers to advocate certain religious beliefs. Indeed, the power of the state cannot be used to promote the "salvation of souls."[58]

In this view, a church is a private association that can determine its own doctrines without interference from the state. Individuals who join these associations agree to accept the doctrines that these associations teach. Moreover, whereas these associations may declare their belief of what constitutes proper religious doctrines, they cannot, in the name of religion, invade and thereby threaten or take away the "rights and worldly goods" of others.[59] Locke also says that moral attitudes contrary to certain religious doctrines such as idolatry, covetousness, idleness, and uncharitableness cannot be punished by the state. This is the case so long as these modes of conduct are not harmful to the rights of another or so long as such forms of conduct do not threaten the "public peace."[60]

Locke's doctrine of toleration suggests a live-and-let-live attitude. Locke says that people, who in their practice of religion cause no harm to others, should be tolerated. "This caution and temper they ought certainly to use toward those who mind only their own business, and are solicitous for nothing but (whatever men think of them) they may worship God in that manner which they are persuaded is acceptable to Him, and in which they have the strongest hopes of eternal salvation."[61] All individuals are free to believe as they wish, just so long as they do not deny the basic civil rights to others.

What are the implications of the live-and-let-live mentality for extending rights protection to all citizens? Possibly, members of the same church may want to maintain respect for the rights of other church members. Possibly, members of a church may maintain respect for the rights of nonmembers. But their doing so may not be because they believe in the priority of rights when it comes to matters of religious truth but because they want to avoid the social instability that might arise where various people to try to impose their respective religious views onto others.

The consequence of the attitude of toleration, which exists as a civic virtue of the highest importance, is to secure indirectly the rights of others, including strangers, who believe differently from us. Here, people support the rights of others for a reason other than a clear commitment to make the protection of rights the main priority. People may still harbor the view that the others whom they tolerate really do not deserve the same rights accorded their co-religionists. The live-and-let-live attitude helps to prevent one from acting on these views for the sake of peace and stability. Still, a deep, underlying sense of difference may remain with each side thinking the other side lacks a grasp of the truth and, because of this fact, ultimately poses a long-term threat to each person's religious choice.

A dimension of this attitude is manifested in Locke's views toward Catholics, atheists, and agnostics. Locke says that no "opinions" that are contrary "to the preservation of civil society, are to be tolerated by the magistrate."[62] On this view, Locke barely tolerates Catholics, claiming that there is no requirement to tolerate those (presumably Catholics) who say that "kings excommunicated forfeit their crowns and kingdoms."[63] Could Locke, then, extend rights to Catholics who believed in papal infallibility? Maybe he could, so long as he is assured that the Catholics in question are not subversive of civil society. But it is not clear that he would. For atheists, a more categorical denial of rights is provided. Locke says, "Lastly those are not at all to be tolerated who deny the being of God. Promises, convents, and oaths, which are bonds of human society, can have no hold upon an atheist."[64] Finally, it is not clear that even an agnostic would find a full plate of rights in Locke's civil society. Locke says that all men are to believe in God, and, consequently, all should "enter into some religious society."[65]

Locke's doctrine of toleration, then, suggests that people who, in all respects, uphold the civil laws may still fall outside their protection and thus be denied the same rights guaranteed to all. Because a live-and-let-live view allows people to live side by side without interacting with each other for the purpose of creating common bonds of understanding, bonds that help them to appreciate others' beliefs, individuals may live side by side but with a growing sense of distrust and suspicion. As a result, real barriers to communication would exist between people, and these barriers might lead individuals to form majorities that work to deny basic rights to others for no other reason than that others have different religious beliefs.

However, the civic virtue of toleration suggests a space in society where individuals can meet and form associations and enter into relations of their choice. In these spaces, freedom of conscience would be afforded protection. But the problems we have just enumerated with respect to Locke's view of toleration suggest that this space in a civil society, what we referred to in Chapter 1 as the separate sphere of voluntary associations, might have difficulty enduring where the civic virtue of toleration is not buttressed by the civic virtue of mutual respect. The latter symbolizes a willingness on the part of individuals to manifest goodwill to others, even to those with whom they do not agree, so that persons at least learn to understand views different from their own. As a result of this way of understanding, people create conditions that afford others a place in society where they can be protected as they go about their lives, pursuing particular religious or moral views that in no sense threaten the rights of others. But when mutual respect does not exist in a strong sense, individuals who do not threaten others' rights may still be denied a secure place in society to practice their own views. This problem can be overcome, and the separate sphere of voluntary groups in civil society secured, only when mutual respect is made a preeminent part of the practice of the civic virtue of toleration.

Mutual respect would have particular importance for Locke, whereas, we have seen, class conflict arising from market relations could be an obstacle to securing the rights of all. Still, the existence of the civic virtue of toleration, when coupled with the commitment to constrained majority rule and limited government, goes a long way to maintain both the possibility of mutual respect and a separate sphere. Thus, the prospect of mutual respect is not to be ruled out for Locke. Indeed, it would seem that, owing to this fact, the potential for avoiding destructive class conflict might well be conceivable.

IV. Response and Rejoinder

Hobbes might argue that Locke's second view of the state of nature really is close to Hobbes's own view, the doctrine of toleration notwithstanding. Thus, for Hobbes, Locke would need the same kind of state Hobbes advocated to secure the freedom that his philosophy promises. Locke might respond, however, that the doctrine of toleration is a civic virtue that would minimize conflict over religion, thus making the need for a Hobbesian form of government unnecessary. Moreover, perhaps over time, the intensity of feeling for religion would diminish. In Locke's society, what would take center stage would be the pursuit of material goals, such as wealth and property, and, in this context, religious issues might lose their fervor. Indeed, as Benedict Spinoza had hoped, perhaps religious issues would be less important and less divisive as freedom became more and more associated with material acquisition in a commercially based society.

Also, even if interest in material matters did not diminish the strength of religious concerns, practicing the doctrine of toleration might make people more prone to establish, as the basis for interacting with others, a sincere commitment to understanding the viewpoints and arguments of those who differ from theirs. Were this situation to arise, then, individuals would be able to engage each other in discussions that reached for, and even achieved at times, a common ground. For instance, the religious fundamentalist in discussing public issues might realize that it is best not to broach in such a discussion elements of fundamentalist religious views that tend to threaten and to turn away those who reject fundamentalist religious doctrines. Spinoza would have taken the same position, arguing that, in a society where the majority advances freedom of thought and speech, people will come to appreciate differences and to learn to make room for them. People in a tolerant society thus might learn how to maintain many differences, but still live together without conflict.

Of course, Hobbes might have the same hope that fundamentalists and non-fundamentalists would become more conciliatory to each other over time, but he probably would not believe that this outcome was realistic. Given this fact, the only way to protect the rights of all citizens is with the state Hobbes would contemplate. In this case, Hobbes would argue that the doctrine of toleration would not be sufficient to protect citizens' rights. This is the case because in a situation in which people are strongly committed to a particular view, the only way they will be stopped from interfering with others is when the state uses its considerable power to compel compliance with the laws. Locke, on the other hand, would, as would Spinoza, maintain that Hobbes's approach would end up threatening people's basic rights. Hobbes would no doubt argue in response that threatening rights is not the same thing as denying them. Hobbes would further add that, to protect rights, it may well be necessary to create an atmosphere of fear so that those likely to attack the rights of others would be less prone to do so.

In contrast, Locke would argue that his view of the state that limits the powers of the various branches, in this case, the legislative and the executive branches, is more inclined to achieve a political setting that can protect the rights of individuals. Hobbes's unified state works to hand it so much power that the state itself will likely become an enemy of rights. Locke, on the other hand, would recognize that to offset this problem, it is necessary to secure conditions within the society and the state that limit the powers of the various branches of government, lest the government become the main enemy of the rights it is supposed to protect. Hobbes would have responded that it is impossible to achieve the goals of a fair and just state when the state is constantly made the target for various political opportunists who attempt to take it over and use the state's power for their own purposes. And that is just what Locke's form of state invites when he allows the power of the state to be subdivided into different branches of authority.

Finally, others might claim that Locke's main problem in maintaining a civil society that can secure the rights of citizens has to do with the difficulties of securing a constrained majority. Those who make this argument might claim that Locke failed to address adequately the impact of market realities in his view of the state of nature. This lapse places in jeopardy a majority rule conception, which at the same time is committed to not infringe the rights of any citizen. In particular, it could be argued that Locke's citizens become so concerned, as they pursue their rights, with their own private interests, that they reject any concern for a larger, more embracing common good. Jean-Jacques Rousseau will discuss these problems in the next chapter.

Notes

1. For some historical background, see George H. Sabine, *A History of Political Theory* (New York: Holt, Rinehart and Winston, 1961), 517, 534; Mulford Q. Sibley, *Political Ideas and Ideologies: A History of Political Thought* (New York: Harper and Row, 1970), 373–74; Thomas P. Peardon, "Introduction," in *The Second Treatise of Government*, ed. John Locke (Indianapolis: Bobbs-Merrill, 1952), x–xi.

2. Richard Ashcraft, *Revolutionary Politics and Locke's Two Treatises of Government* (Princeton, NJ: Princeton University Press, 1986), 280–81.

3. Charles Taylor, *Sources of the Self* (Cambridge: Harvard University Press, 1989), 171.

4. Ian Shapiro, "Gross Concepts in Political Argument," *Political Theory* 17, no. 1 (February 1989): 56–59.

5. John Locke, *The Second Treatise of Government*, ed. Thomas P. Peardon (New York: Bobbs-Merrill, 1952), 3–4, Para. 2–3.

6. Ibid., 4, Para. 3.

7. Ibid.

8. Ibid., 52–53, Para. 93.

9. Ibid., 4, Para. 4.10.

10. Ibid., 5, Para. 6.

11. Ibid.

12. Ibid., 5–6, Para. 6.

13. Ibid., 15, Para. 22.15.

14. Ibid.

15. Ibid., 16, Para. 25.

16. Ibid., 17, Para. 27.

17. Ibid.

18. Ibid., 20, Para. 34. See also pp. 98–99, Para. 173, where Locke says that "by property I must be understood here, as in other places to mean that property which men have in their persons as well as goods."

19. Ibid., 15, Para. 23.

20. Ibid., 12–13, Para. 19.

21. Ibid., 19, Para. 31, 22, Para. 36.

22. Ibid., 23, Para. 38.

23. Ibid., 28, Para. 46.

24. Ibid.

25. Ibid., 29, Para. 50.

26. Ibid., Para. 48. Locke sees the profit motive as a main incentive for people to engage in work that would benefit the society. He says in relation to commerce in agriculture, for instance,

"What would a man value ten thousand acres or a hundred thousand acres of excellent land, ready and cultivated and well stocked, too, with cattle, in the middle of the inland parts of America where he had no hopes of commerce with other parts of the world to draw money to him for the sale of the product?"

27. For a good discussion of this aspect of Locke, see C. B. Macpherson, *The Political Theory of Possessive Individualism* (Oxford: Clarendon Press, 1962), 204–17.

28. Locke, *Second Treatise of Government*, 18, Para. 28.

29. Macpherson, *The Political Theory of Possessive Individualism,* 215–16, 220.

30. Locke, *Second Treatise of Government*, 71, Para. 124–25.

31. Ibid.

32. Ibid., Para. 124–26.

33. Ibid., 55, Para. 96. Italics added.

34. Ibid., 73, Para. 131.

35. Ibid.

36. Ibid., 80–81, Para. 140.

37. Ibid., 73, Para. 131.

38. Ibid., 68, Para. 119.

39. Our view is based upon that of Hanna Pitkin, "Obligation and Consent," in *Philosophy, Politics and Society,* ed. Peter Laslett et al. (New York: Barnes and Noble, 1972), 62. Pitkin says that legitimate authority is "precisely that which *ought* to be obeyed, to which one ought to consent, which deserves obedience and consent, to which rational men considering all relevant facts and issues would consent, to which consent can be justified."

40. Locke, *Second Treatise of Government*, 70, Para. 123.

41. Ibid., 71, Para. 127.

42. Ibid., 83, Para. 145–47.

43. Ibid., 75, Para. 134.

44. Ibid.

45. Ibid., 77, Para. 136, 76, Para. 135.

46. Ibid., 84, Para. 149.

47. Ibid., 82–83, Para. 144.

48. Ibid., 82, Para. 143, 86, Para. 153.

49. Ibid., 86, Para. 152.

50. Ibid., 87, Para. 154.

51. Ibid., 90, Para. 158.

52. Ibid., 92, Para. 160.

53. Ibid., 92, Para. 161.

54. Ibid., 95, Para. 168.

55. Ibid., 96, Para. 168.

56. Ibid., 117–18, Para. 209; also, p. 96, Para. 168.

57. John Locke, *A Letter on Toleration* (Indianapolis: Bobbs-Merrill, 1955), 17.

58. Ibid.

59. Ibid., 27.

60. Ibid., 26, 42.

61. Ibid., 28.

62. Ibid., 50.

63. Ibid., 50–51.

64. Ibid., 52.

65. Ibid., 35.

10

Jean-Jacques Rousseau: Community and Civil Society

I. Introduction

Jean-Jacques Rousseau (1712–1778) can be read as a critique of the arguments found in Thomas Hobbes and John Locke, as well as the doctrines found in the period referred to during Rousseau's times as the French Enlightenment. The French Enlightenment tracks heavily the thoughts of Hobbes and Locke. Both writers sought to use reason to explore ways to advance liberty. This quest often meant revising and, when necessary, discarding traditions that impeded liberty. Indeed, liberalism as a comprehensive political vision advances from the view that a rational life must be predicated upon expanding both the number of rights and the scope of their coverage in society. As we have seen, in promoting this position, liberalism can be viewed as the philosophy of the bourgeoisie. The latter is the new class of merchants and traders as well as individuals who make money from banking and finance. This class clamored for changes in society so its members could carve out for themselves opportunities to engage in new ways of life not permitted in medieval settings.

Liberalism's commitment to reason, over and against the traditions of the past, was designed to advance the cause of liberty. But in doing so, Rousseau viewed liberalism and the bourgeoisie supporting it as attacking both community and equality. Community is built upon sacred values such as respect for the common good and religious traditions. Equality suggests the opportunity for each person to participate in helping to define the common good. But liberals advanced the cause not of the community and the common good for Rousseau but that of individual self-interest and selfishness. Further, liberals supported equality only insofar as equality before the law meant the enhancement of individual freedom, as opposed to the fostering of community life through full citizen participation by each member of the society.

In Rousseau's thinking, the Enlightenment fostered a civil society setting that equated the rule of law with the rule of materialism and greed, as well as the undermining of respect for the norms of civility and the common good. In what follows, we provide a more detailed introduction to Rousseau's rejection of the Enlightenment as developed by Hobbes and Locke.

For Hobbes and Locke, the main objective was a civil society that could advance the liberty and thus the rights of each citizen. Of course, as shown in previous chapters, the quest for rights did not mean that individuals were to shed all regard for constraints. Indeed, for Hobbes and Locke, civil society was a place where the pursuit of individual freedom could be made consonant with certain rational constraints that secured the freedom of all persons. This viewpoint suggested that individuals did not have to accept traditional medieval roles as the sole basis for determining their identities. Here, it would appear that the effect of Hobbes and Locke was liberatory, for it fostered the need to free people from traditional, medieval structures. But for Rousseau, the contribution of either writer is extremely destructive. Rousseau believes that both Hobbes and Locke put in the forefront of all social experience the desire for rights, and this approach gave people license to seek their own personal happiness, often at great cost to those canons of civic virtue associated with the common good.[1]

The philosophers of the French Enlightenment, whom Rousseau despises, believed that the ruling powers were wedded to archaic religious, moral, and political traditions, and thus France was under the domination of powerful people who were driven by both prejudice and small-mindedness. Still, these philosophers believed that the great bulk of the people could be freed from this mentality. Through education, people could be "enlightened" or provided with a capacity for good reasoning, which would allow them to rise above existing prejudice and establish a progressive and more just and happy society. Rousseau, however, believes that this attitude damages the prospect for civic virtue on the part of citizens. The result of the Enlightenment is to make the pursuit of wealth and luxury more important than respect for those virtues that secure the common good of the whole community.[2]

In taking this view of the Enlightenment's impact, Rousseau harks back to the previous era of classical philosophy and looks with fondness on that period's commitment to teach the canons of civic virtue, which both the traditions of Hobbes and Locke and the new Enlightenment were destroying. As Rousseau says in his famous essay on the contributions of the sciences and arts, an essay that emphasizes the failures of the Enlightenment, "Ancient politicians incessantly talked about morals and virtue, those of our time talk only of business and money."[3]

For Rousseau, then, Enlightenment-inspired education, or education in the sciences and arts, emphasizes a belief in progress through science and reason. Rousseau believes that, whereas progress in knowledge has increased luxury and material comforts, at the same time, this so-called progress has produced a demise of the moral quality of life.[4] This fact is best seen in the system of education that accompanies the Enlightenment spirit. For Rousseau, education in his times, which embodies the highest regard for material progress, "adorns our minds and corrupts our judgment" by de-emphasizing respect for the great civic virtues, such as courage and love of country. Rousseau says:

> *I see everywhere immense institutions where young people are brought up at great expense, learning everything except their duties. Your children will not know their own language, but they will speak others that are nowhere in use; they will know how to write verses that they can barely understand; without knowing how to distinguish error from truth, they will possess the art of making them both unrecognizable to others by specious arguments. But they will not know what the words magnanimity, equity, temperance, humanity, courage are; that sweet name fatherland will never strike their ear; and if they hear of God, it will be less to be awed by him than to be afraid of him.*[5]

Reversing the Enlightenment mentality became a main part of Rousseau's political agenda. Politics must help restore citizenship and all that citizenship thrives on; in particular, a common respect for the needs of the community and for the corresponding traditions of civic virtue. Attaining this outcome for Rousseau requires a certain kind of political association, one that permits individuals to feel as well as to believe themselves to be part of a community with others. In this setting, each member serves the needs and interests of the common good and, as a result, each individual subordinates private interests to the larger needs of one's community.

Thus, Rousseau would not have accepted either Locke's or Hobbes's view of government, including the latter's Leviathan or the former's conception of limited government. In both cases, these forms of government serve only to support a civil society experience in which the primary objective is to facilitate the priority of private interest over respect for the common good. For Rousseau, Locke's and Hobbes's civil society, while arguing that it supports a common good, in this case a commitment to secure the equal liberty and rights of all persons, really promotes a society that is only designed to facilitate each person's pursuit of his own private interest. Rousseau would reverse this tendency by creating a civil society that is predicated upon the experience of direct citizen participation in shaping the law by which all live.

II. Selfishness and Self-Love

As a prelude to discussing Rousseau's view of the state of nature in the next section, it is necessary to explain Rousseau's notion of self-love and how the latter differs from selfishness. In *Émile*, Rousseau's major work on education, Rousseau says that selfishness is the state of mind in which we constantly compare ourselves to others in the hopes that others will look upon us and want to be like ourselves. "Selfish-ness, which is always comparing [one]self with others, is never satisfied and never can be; for this feeling, which prefers ourselves to others, requires that [others] prefer us to themselves, which is impossible."[6] Still, despite the impossibility of the enterprise, selfish people try to make others want to be like themselves anyway. To do so, selfish people will often have to resort to various forms of deceit and trickery. So, it is understandable that such individuals will become puffed up with self-importance as they manifest toward others "grand ostentation, deceptive cunning, and all the vices that follow in their wake."[7] Here, we try to convince others how important we are by showing them all our wealth, luxuries, and status, in the hopes that if they see these things, they will want to become like us.

But the more genuine condition Rousseau calls self-love, which is

always good, always in accordance with the order of nature. The preservation of our own life is specially entrusted to each one of us, and our first care is, and must be, to watch over our own life; and how can we continually watch over it, if we do not take the greatest interest in it.[8]

By eschewing a life in which we try to be other than whom we are to make others be like us, we focus upon the development of our native feelings and natural tendencies. As the latter emerge, we understand fully our real natures. Here, we would understand that "the tender and gentle passions spring from self-love," whereas the "hateful and angry passions spring from selfishness."[9] We receive from Rousseau a clear understanding of the intent of people's natural feelings when Rousseau describes male adolescence prior to it becoming corrupted by the temptations of a form of wanton sexuality. An uncorrupted young man exhibits "tender and affectionate passions" and a "warm heart . . . touched by the sufferings of . . . fellow creatures." The natural self is moved by "pity, mercy, and generosity."[10]

Rousseau's argument is that these natural sentiments, which give important moral guidance, are denied full expression in a corrupted, modern society. In developing an explanation for why this tragedy occurs, Rousseau, like Hobbes and Locke, uses a method that starts from what is presumed to be an accurate depiction of pre-social man. But Rousseau's view of pre-social man in the state of nature differs radically, as we show in the next section, from the views of Hobbes and Locke.

III. *The Second Discourse on the Origin of Inequality Among Men*

Rousseau's depiction of the source of the betrayal of our natural self revolves around his discussion of political inequality. So, what is political inequality? Political inequality, unlike natural inequality that refers to differences in ability and capacity, emanates from the consent of people. Political inequality "consists in the different privileges enjoyed by some at the expense of others, such as being richer, more honored, more powerful than they, or even causing themselves to be obeyed by them."[11] In discussing political inequality, Rousseau wants to demonstrate how it came to pass that the bulk of people in society end up ceding a right to a few to predominate over the rest, even though the few use their power for promoting their own interests at a cost to the common good. Not only is a politics of the common good impossible in this context, but also impossible is a society based upon respect for those natural instincts and feelings that enable people to have a continuing sense of compassion for others.

To understand how this situation evolves, it is necessary to retrace the steps of humankind, starting with people as they are in the state of nature and then demonstrate their progress from the state of nature to modern society. Along the way, we demonstrate what causes people to turn away from pursuing the truths of their inner selves and what helps launch a regime of political inequality that Rousseau despises. Thus, Rousseau's quest in the *Second Discourse* is to explain "the sequence of wonders by which . . . the people . . . buy imaginary repose at the price of real felicity."[12]

In Rousseau's state of nature, primitive people are not motivated by an urge for power as was the case in Hobbes, nor are they rational, subject to rules created by reason, as was the case in Locke. They live only for the present, and they do not possess a rational plan for their future. They have no social entanglements or dependencies upon others. Their natural instincts dictate their feelings and their needs.

Rousseau says that people are driven by two basic natural urges, a natural drive for self-preservation (the need for food, shelter, clothing, and sex) and "a natural repugnance to seeing any sentient being, especially our fellow man, perish or suffer," or an urge not to harm another.[13] People, then, must pursue their basic needs without causing harm to others. Why would people be disposed not to harm others? People are moved by the sentiment of pity; thus, the compassion people display to others arises not from any sort of "subtle arguments" on the nature of right and wrong but from people consulting their own hearts. Here, there is no need for laws against murder, theft, and rape because there is no motivation to do such things. Owing to this natural disposition, we are to "do what is good for you with as little harm as possible to others."[14]

To make this maxim a part of day-to-day activities requires no complex moral inquiry into proposed courses of action. Primitive people do what seems most natural for them. When they are hungry, they eat; when they need shelter, they find some; and when they have sexual urges, they satisfy them. But in all cases, they approach the satisfaction of their urges from a sensibility that exhorts them not to harm others. Here, personal conduct, then, is merely a consequence of one's true and most basic needs.[15] Rousseau says, "Each man peacefully awaits the impetus of nature, gives himself over to it without choice, and with more pleasure than frenzy; and once the need is satisfied, all desire is snuffed out."[16] In contrast, the modern person achieves one desire only to find him- or herself wanting to satisfy another. Each life is a never-ending series of desires, not one of which, were they to be fulfilled, would make a person happy. Primitive humans, however, reflect the peace of their simplicity.

His soul, agitated by nothing, is given over to the single feeling of his own present existence, without any idea of the future, however near it may be, and his projects, as limited as his views, hardly extend to the end of the day.[17]

As already indicated, primitive people are free from any kind of social dependency. Initially, primitive people live alone, independent of lasting relationships. They form associations with each other only to satisfy mutually desirable ends. Sexual liaisons take place on the basis of an urge for mutual sexual gratification. Once the latter is achieved, people separate and go in different directions, perhaps never to see each other again. Mothers nourish their children until the children can care for themselves and, once they can, mother and child each go their own ways, and, after a while, neither recognizes the other.[18]

Transient relationships end and permanent ones begin when primitive people discover that it is in their interests to work with each other to secure common survival needs.[19] During this phase, people work together without the need for formal language, and they learn to communicate with "inarticulate cries, many gestures, and some imitative voices."[20] In addition, primitive people invent tools, such as hatchets and sharp stones, that allow them to provide for their basic needs. At this stage as well families are formed for the first time and private ownership of property is introduced. Owning property at this point does not create conditions hostile to primitive people's overall happiness because each person is forced to respect the property of others or face a fierce struggle with those from whom they might take it.[21] Furthermore, there is no need to engage in such a struggle since there is enough property for everyone anyway. In effect, because everyone has as much property as they can use, no one has any need for the property of others, so no one desires to take another's property.

Thus, the first permanent relationships founded by primitive people, while part of the road to modern life, are not the sources of moral decay and political inequality. Rousseau describes this condition in idyllic terms. The family setting represents a "habit of living together," which gives "rise to the sweetest sentiments known to men: conjugal and paternal love."[22] Moreover, this condition is associated with sufficient leisure time and conveniences. These new dimensions make people less self-sufficient and sturdy mentally and physically than they had been in the past and more prone to believe that when or if they are deprived of these advantages, they will think life cruel to them.[23]

Still, this experience is not a major factor in revolutionizing the life of humankind. More fundamental causes are at work. Rousseau envisions people initially living on one continuous piece of land, but after floods and earthquakes, the main living area is broken up into many different islands – forcing people to live together in these diverse areas and develop separate languages and distinct and diverse communities. In these new settings, people unite into permanent communities and form nations united by shared traditions and customs.[24]

These new forms of permanent living arrangements have important impacts on the lives of people. People develop "ideas of merit and beauty," and because people begin to compare themselves and each other with these public standards that the whole nation values, those who come out the best arouse envy in others.[25] But even this situation does not usher political inequality into existence. For it is still the case that individuals live in accordance with the common moral standards of the community. No one, not even those who are the highest in ability and achievement, are exempted from them. Rousseau says that it is "necessary for punishments to become more severe in proportion as the occasions for giving offense become more frequent."[26] Primitive community life symbolizes the existence of a strong sense of civic virtue that demands that each person serve the larger good of the society. Individuals are not allowed to claim that because they have superior ability, they can avoid this obligation. Rousseau says that "this period of the development of human faculties, maintaining a middle position between the indolence of our primitive state and the petulant activity of our egocentrism, must have been the happiest and the most durable epoch."[27]

The structure of work in the primitive community does not represent the fatal step that plunges the community into political inequality, either. In the primitive setting, each person is engaged in all phases of the production of any good. There is not yet a division of labor that segments work into simple tasks and that forces the worker to discard whatever skills he or she might have to fit into a production line. Work remains an endeavor by which individuals can demonstrate their skills and contributions to the society and, from these acts, have others recognize and respect them.

As long as they applied themselves exclusively to tasks that a single individual could do and to the arts that did not require the cooperation of several hands, they lived as free, healthy, good and happy as they could in accordance with their nature, and they continued to enjoy among themselves the sweet reward of independent intercourse.[28]

The fatal step for humankind emerges with the invention of metallurgy and agriculture, "the two arts," Rousseau says, that have turned society in the direction of political inequality by changing the nature of work and introducing destructive forms of private property. Rousseau, in describing these events, depicts the evils of a commercial, market society.

With the invention of metal, new industries are built. These industries can be maintained only if populations are shifted to manufacturing centers in cities. But as the number of workers increases, there are fewer people left to perform agricultural functions to feed the rest of the society. To meet this problem, metals are used to create tools to help people farm more efficiently. Now, fewer men can produce larger amounts of food, enough to feed the growing population of the cities.[29] Private property rights emerge from this experience, too. Farmers, who work their land to produce food, are said to create value from their labor, and thus they have a right not only to the products of their work but also to the property on which the farmer toils. Similar to Locke, then, Rousseau says that society is required to protect the property rights of all persons.[30]

These circumstances suggest that accompanying the economic advances made possible by progress in metallurgy and agriculture are growing disparities in power and influence among people. Cities grow in size as factories are built in and around them. And those who own the factories and control the labor of those who work in them become wealthy. The farming areas lose population, but those remaining in this activity become prosperous property owners. In short, "the strongest did the most work; the most adroit turned theirs to better advantage: the most ingenious found ways to shorten their labor."[31] What of the rest? The latter, because they lack the skills or the luck to qualify them as either factory owners or successful farmers, lose their importance and dignity in society. In this setting it is easy to understand that natural differences will be translated into political ones. Rousseau says that "if talents had been equal, and if the use of iron and the consumption of foodstuffs had always been in precise balance,"[32] society would have remained in balance and no political or social inequality would have emerged. Rousseau is moved to say:

Thus it is that natural inequality imperceptibly manifests itself together with inequality occasioned by the socialization process. Thus it is that the differences among men, developed by those circumstances, make themselves more noticeable, more permanent in their effects, and begin to influence the fate of private individuals in the same proportion.[33]

A powerful class emerges to dominate the rest of the society, resulting in a civil war between the rich and the poor.[34] But the rich cannot enjoy their gains when they are always placed in jeopardy by war, and the lot of the poor can never be improved so long as class war is a constant reality. The rich scheme to create a new peace, which diffuses the anger of the poor, without requiring any sacrifice on the part of themselves. The poor are tricked into believing that, as a result of peace, there would be justice and a new social order that would protect their interests and provide them with rights and justice. So, the rich talk about achieving justice through the introduction of a civil society that would provide freedom to all individuals. Of course, the rich have no intention to provide for the needs of the poor. The rich only intend to make it appear as if they do. Still the poor, without sophistication and filled with greed themselves, lack an ability to create their own solutions, so they consent to "chain themselves [to the rich], in the belief that they secured their liberty." As a result, the poor end up agreeing to a social contract that continues the injustice of the past, except that now the poor have given their consent to it. The rich can then rule through institutions that the poor are tricked into supporting, and it appears that the rich no longer have to resort to naked force to justify their authority.[35]

Rousseau says, in summarizing this experience:

> Such was . . . the origin of society and laws, which gave new fetters to the weak and new forces to the rich . . . established forever the law of property and of inequality, changed adroit usurpation into an irrevocable right, and for the profit of a few ambitious men henceforth subjected the entire human race to labor, servitude and misery."[36]

Political inequality that ordinary people consent to is nothing more than ordinary people consenting to their enslavement to the rich.

The Loss of Civic Virtue

The picture Rousseau paints in the *Discourse on the Origin of Inequality* suggests that the economic context of modern society allows those with superior skill to acquire control over others and to use that control to continue to enhance wealth and political power in the society. A new form of class rule emerges, one no longer based on traditional class hierarchy found in the medieval world but one based on one's ability to manipulate the processes of production to one's own advantage.

Private property in this setting comes to symbolize, for Rousseau, not only this new type of class rule but also a way of life that tramples the traditions of civic virtue. More to the point, the new systems of production make money the most important good. For without money, it is impossible to purchase the machines and other materials necessary for gaining an advantageous position in the new industrial-based market contexts. So, systems of finance are established to permit investors access to money that is used to expand the industrial base of a society. All attention is then riveted to the profit-and-loss sheet. Indeed, nothing else matters except profit.

But Rousseau believes that the "systems of finance are a modern invention; they have produced nothing."[37] The preoccupation with money has turned ordinary people into luxury-seeking, "scheming," "violent," and "knavish" individuals.[38] People with these attitudes have no love for the larger good of the community, nor do they wish to be acknowledged for their contributions to the needs of the community. Indeed, the quest for money has all but destroyed the prospect of civic virtue in the society.

When this happens, the politics of society become corrupted, too. Political leaders are more concerned to promote this or that version of the private interest, and they have no ability to conceptualize the public good. All who enter politics do so with the intention to loot and steal from the ordinary people.[39] Votes are bought, elections are rigged, and the government is unable to advance the public interest as a whole. In contrast, in a society wedded to the idea of civic virtue, the leaders are forced to show respect and regard for the larger common good. Indeed, the leaders in this setting become true servants of the people.

How, it might be asked, can a corrupt politics be turned into a new politics of civic virtue? Rousseau believes that the new economic system's worst tendencies can be countered. The key to doing so is through a form of civic education that teaches individuals their duties and teaches them to make love for their country primary.[40] Rousseau believes that this objective, when properly taught, has tremendous power to reverse the ill effects of the money mentality. Once people possess a love for their country, they are able to put the needs of the country ahead of self-interest. And then, civic virtue will finally "reign."[41] Thus, if the objective of a corruption-free politics is to make people virtuous, the best avenue for doing so is to teach people to maintain the canons of civic virtue, and this objective will be a major idea of the new social contract.

The New Social Contract and the New Civil Society

How does Rousseau expect to accomplish this goal? In his discussion of his new social contract in *On the Social Contract*, he hopes human beings will be transformed by becoming a part of a community that is predicated upon common goals and values. Once in this community, individuals will no longer make their own private interests primary, but they will make the pursuit of the common good the most important dimension in their lives. What is the nature of this new community Rousseau has in mind? In this section, we describe its central aspects in some detail.

That Rousseau is discussing a fundamental transformation of individuals from self-seeking individuals to community-minded citizens is made clear when Rousseau raises the following question. He asks:

> *[How does one] find a form of association which defends and protects with all common forces the person and goods of each associate, and by means of which each one, while uniting with all, nevertheless obeys only himself and remains as free as before?*[42]

Rousseau's answer is a new social contract that suggests that each individual must be willing to "alienate" (or turn over) all of one's rights to the community. And "since this condition is equal for everyone, no one has an interest in making it burdensome for the others."[43] Why would individuals embrace this kind of social arrangement? It is because they wish to define themselves as part of a collective organization and, as such, they are willing to submit, like all others, to the organization's common rules and objectives. What advantage would individuals have in doing this? Rousseau says that each person, "in giving himself to all, gives himself to no one"; that is, each person becomes governed by the same idea of the common good that is seen as benefiting all people, including, of course, oneself. No longer is any individual subordinated to the arbitrary power of another, but instead, each person falls "under the supreme direction of the general will."[44]

Here, in making the general will the ground of one's life, individuals act toward each other as the natural moral feelings of primitive society originally dictated they should. The general will symbolizes the commitment of individuals to give priority to the "general interest" or to the common good, as opposed to private interest.[45] Indeed, to maintain a community that is concerned for the needs of each person, each person must make his or her own private interests subservient to the general interest. What is required for this enterprise to work, however, is acceptance of certain understandings about society and politics, outlined in the rest of this section.

First, the general will is associated with the rights that people are to be provided. For Rousseau, rights emanate from the community's own definition of its needs. Locke had argued that each person had basic rights to life, liberty, and property. These rights were attached to each person by virtue of a person being a human being. For Rousseau, this view of rights tends to encourage individuals to think of themselves as empowered to do whatever they please. But when individuals realize that their rights emanate from the community in which they live, they then understand not that the community only defines the nature of the rights they have, but associated with each right are the obligations, duties, and limits they must observe as a condition for having these rights. Rights signify not just individual freedom but individual freedom in the context of civic virtue. Awareness of this fact is the basis for our being able to accord to others protection for their rights.

Also important is what the general will suggests for the nature of the political realm and the approach people should take to issues there. It is in this realm that the common needs are defined with respect to those issues that broadly affect the lives of all persons. Rousseau's argument is that, because certain issues impact the lives of all citizens in major and significant ways, it is best to find a common approach to those issues, thus providing individuals with the same moral direction. Not all issues are general will issues, to be sure. Whether to put a stoplight on a certain street is not an issue that the whole society should consider because this issue affects only a small part of society. On the other hand, general will issues touch upon those things that all individuals understand to involve a common good. For instance, they include matters such as how we define education policy, what should constitute our approach as a society to agriculture, what is the role to be given to the police, what kind of national health care should we have, if any, and so on.

Citizens determine the nature of the common good by deliberating together in a legislative setting. Here, the citizens can make the laws that define what rights citizens will have and what corresponding duties citizens must uphold. The function of the executive is to carry out the will of the legislature and to make decisions pertaining to the application of legislative policies and principles to particular circumstances. This means, then, that the legislative power, "which belongs to the people and can belong to it alone,"[46] while it establishes the general policies and defines the common good in each issue area, leaves questions of implementation to the discretion of the executive.[47] Of course, the people acting as the legislative body can always respond to executive decisions they disagree with. Thus, if the executive determines that a general right established by the legislative power should be applied in a certain way that the legislative power does not accept, the latter can rescind the actions of the executive.

Determining the stance on the major and most important issues rests with the people acting in their legislative function. For Rousseau, then, the "laws are merely the condition of the civil association. The populace that is subjected to the laws ought to be their author."[48] As people make their own laws, they become transformed from people who are exclusively and only accumulators of property and wealth, into people who, as property holders, are citizens, also. It is this transformation that creates a civil society. Rousseau says that the "passage from a state of nature to the civil state," or a *civil society*, "produces quite a remarkable change in man, for it substitutes justice for instinct in his behavior and gives his actions a moral quality they previously lacked."[49] In a civil society, each person learns to subordinate his or her own interests to the interests of the larger society, and this conduct is the basis for treating individuals as equals, with full respect and dignity. Real freedom is what Rousseau calls "civil liberty," which emerges when individuals are equally willing to accommodate all aspects of life touched by the general will, to the general will.[50]

Unless people can make their own laws, Rousseau's transformation of property-holding individuals into citizens who respect the norms of the common good during the course of pursuing their own interests cannot occur, nor can civil society truly exist. For this reason, then, Rousseau does not accept, as did Locke, the laws that the people's deputies or representatives made, and thus, for Rousseau, "any law that the populace has not ratified in person is null; it is not a law at all." For Rousseau, in a well-run society, "everyone flies to the assemblies."[51]

Still, Rousseau is aware that public deliberation might not, on all occasions, produce a consensus on the nature of the common good with respect to a particular area of concern. For instance, where people radically disagree with each other, as in the case when, as we have seen, society becomes divided between the rich and the poor in Rousseau's account of inequality, it is possible that no matter how long people deliberate, they cannot produce an agreement that serves the needs of all members of the community. Where this kind of experience is pervasive, the deliberation might cause people to manifest destructive and hurtful passions toward each other, destroying any hope for a sustained general will.

Rousseau avoids this outcome because he envisions deliberation as occurring in a much simpler context in which the variations in opinion are reduced in number and in degree of difference. People who approach matters from the common-sense perspective of ordinary persons, for Rousseau, do not hold widely divergent points of view; thus, they are never far from agreement. This is what Rousseau means when he says, "peace, union, equality are enemies of political subtleties. Upright and simple men are difficult to deceive on account of their simplicity. Traps and clever pretexts do not fool them."[52] Rousseau has in mind peasants and simple, or ordinary, people making the law.

When, among the happiest people in the world, bands of peasants are seen regulating their affairs of state under an oak tree, and always acting wisely, can one help scorning the refinement of other nations, which make themselves illustrious and miserable with so much art and mystery?[53]

But why is agreement likely among the people Rousseau describes? Rousseau's society, as Charles Taylor says, is "bound together by a sentiment which is an extension of the joy that humans feels in each other's company."[54] In such a society, people share certain fundamental values, which create a unity of understanding and a basis for community. Owing to this fact, people do not approach life from widely diverse and contradictory moral perspectives. Society is not a setting in which some advocate a strong commitment to religion and others do not; where some promote a rural view of life and others an urban one; where some advocate an education in classical literature for all with the intention of making people into critical thinkers who question every tradition and where others prefer to remain uncritically obedient to existing traditions. These differences in viewpoint would shape the way people make judgments about public questions, and consequently, as people approach such questions from these different and radically opposed perspectives, their deliberations would likely always end in either stalemate or unhappy compromises.

We experience this problem quite often in contemporary society. There are many issues in today's world that cannot be resolved in a way that is satisfactory to all sides, and individuals on either side of these issues must tolerate outcomes they do not morally accept. This situation often leads to social and political discord that is destructive of community feeling. Examples of issues that produce discord of this type include, for instance, gun control, abortion, affirmative action, and prayer in schools. But in Rousseau's society, because citizens have shared sentiments and values, they hold in common moral positions that are not far apart or contradictory; therefore, when these people discuss public questions, agreement is more likely. Thus, Taylor is correct when he says that Rousseau's citizens are not destined to engage in "elaborate debate and deliberation."[55]

But Taylor's view should not be construed to suggest that Rousseau denies importance to *all* forms of deliberation among citizens as they engage in the practices of self-government. That deliberation would not be elaborate does not mean it would not occur at all. Deliberation is the basis for citizens making their own laws and, in the process of doing so, manifesting and maintaining the necessary civic virtue that allows individuals to uphold the commitment to the public good. But, still, as Taylor's argument seems to require, for the kind of deliberation to take place that Rousseau describes, it is necessary to continue to maintain a basis for community among people by removing from society whatever prevents them from sharing common values and sentiments. Direct citizen involvement in determining the laws, the experience of democratic participation, can only succeed, then, if what causes a demise of a sense of solidarity among people can be eliminated. To this end, Rousseau discusses the conditions that are essential for the creation of the general will and continued citizen self-government.

Under what conditions are people ready for law-making, Rousseau asks? Rousseau describes conditions that encourage the prospect of a strong sense of community among the members of the society, so that the members are able to make laws that all can support. Conditions that contribute to such a setting would include, for instance, a situation in which each member of the society is known to other members, where existing customs and superstitions are not so deeply rooted that they cannot be modified to support a common basis for community, where no person is asked to shoulder a burden larger than he or she can handle, and where the society is free from foreign attack.[56]

Further, one of the most important conditions that contributes to creating a sense of community sufficient to ground law-making activity among citizens would be the need to prevent divisions arising from differences in wealth and property. Otherwise, the trust, so necessary to reaching agreement in a deliberation, would not be possible. To this end, individuals must learn to approach property acquisition from a standpoint of the need to use it to contribute to the interests of the whole community. Rousseau says:

> *in whatever way this acquisition is accomplished, each private individual's right to his very own store [of property] is always subordinate to the community's right to all, without which there could be neither solidity in the social fabric nor real force in the exercise of sovereignty.*[57]

Were people to hold the view that their property entitles them to an amount of political influence proportionate to their property holdings, then a regime based on political inequality would once again become a primary factor in social life, citizens would lack trust in each other, and there would be no basis upon which to sustain public deliberations to determine the common good. Private interest would become the paramount concern, and it would deny any place of importance to the general will. And this perspective would promote policies that would no doubt maintain political inequality. "For by its nature the private will tends toward having preferences, and the general will tends toward equality."[58]

To make possible an attitude toward private property that permits individuals to act not only as property holders but also as citizens, it is necessary that property or wealth holdings among people be moderate in amount. Here, Rousseau takes a cue from Aristotle who, as we saw earlier, in his conception of the polity advocated moderation in wealth. Rousseau says that no individual should be so wealthy that they can buy another, nor so poor that another can buy them.[59] Moderation in wealth will limit the extent to which individuals will always focus upon achieving material success in the market. Rousseau's views of accumulation of wealth would be in direct contrast to the Lockean position that permitted wide and disproportionate distributions of wealth. For Rousseau, in the Lockean context, people become preoccupied with acquiring ever-larger amounts of wealth. Such a mentality would destroy all chances to establish the general will.

The context for the kind of community that made possible a deliberation to define the common good depends upon a society's ability to maintain the possibility of political equality. This is a situation in which all citizens, regardless of their social and economic backgrounds, would have an important say in determining the laws. But political equality depends upon more than the attitudes toward property or its distribution as just described. In addition, there is a need for leadership in the society, a leadership that helps citizens understand the essential issues at stake and to ponder them from the perspective of the need to find solutions that promote the common good or the general will.

For Rousseau, the general will is always right and tends to the "public utility." The problem, however, is that "the deliberations" among the people to make the laws do not always have "the same rectitude."[60] The average citizen is often tricked into taking actions that are harmful to the collective needs of the society. To avert this prospect, there is a need for leadership, in this case from the seasoned political veteran, the wise legislator. The legislator is an extraordinary individual who, with his or her powers of persuasion as opposed to compulsion, tries to frame the law-making deliberation in such a way as to convince people to embody into the laws that govern a community the idea of the common good. In undertaking this role, the legislator has the task of "changing human nature" and transforming

each individual (who by himself is a perfect and solitary whole) into a part of a larger whole from which this individual receives, in a sense, his life and his being; to alter man's constitution in order to strengthen it; to substitute a partial and moral existence for the physical and independent existence we have all received from nature.[61]

Maintaining the political equality that is so essential to citizen participation in government depends upon the possibility of a society in which citizens are capable of searching for the public interest as they discuss the issues before them. Where people do not have this capacity, then politics is turned into private-interest conflicts, with the winners using public power to promote their own goals at a cost to the rest. Avoiding this outcome depends upon many things as we have seen, but, clearly, the leadership of the legislator is among the most important.

IV. Rousseau's Threat to Civil Society

As just indicated, democratic participation requires that the various factors causing divisiveness be eliminated. To this end, Rousseau institutes practices designed to maintain a strong sense of civic virtue and respect for the common good. But in doing so, does Rousseau provide sufficient protection for people from falling into a situation in which the demand to support the common good would become so strong that individuals would find themselves subject to a tyrannous community that defied the demands of individual liberty? Or, in other terms, does Rousseau's approach to civil society eliminate any prospect of it? In this section, we describe some of the factors that make attaining a civil society difficult for Rousseau.

Regarding voting, individuals may exercise their vote in determining the law, and the majority determines the outcome. Rousseau recognizes, however, that people may not all agree before or during the voting process. Still, after the vote has been taken, each individual who disagrees with the outcome must change his or her view so that it supports the winning side.

> *Each man in giving his vote, states his opinion on this matter, and the declaration of the general will is drawn from counting the votes. When, therefore, the opinion contrary to mine prevails, this proves merely that I was in error, and that what I took to be the general will was not so. If my private opinion had prevailed, I would have done something other than what I had wanted. In that case, I would not have been free.*[62]

In a society filled with diverse associations, many groups, owing to their independent status, might disagree publicly with the result of the vote. In fact, groups that do disagree might want to challenge the results by fostering further discussion of the issues in question in the hope that, at a subsequent time, after further argument and after the introduction of more facts, the opinion of the citizens might be changed. But Rousseau finds this destructive of the general will. And in taking this position, Rousseau argues against private associations having an independently powerful political role in the society. But more importantly, his argument seems to prevent individuals from demanding a reconsideration of a question, in the light of new facts or arguments. By taking this position, Rousseau's view allows a majority to crush minority expression of opposing views.

Censorship is an important practice in Rousseau's civil society. In this case, censorship has to do with maintaining citizens' support for the appropriate public moral conceptions that support the philosophy of the general will. Rousseau says that the "opinions of a people arise from its constitution."[63] But where citizens become fascinated with ideas that take them away from the grounding moral conceptions of their society, the result is lack of commitment to citizen duties. Thus, Rousseau would have no trouble supporting the censorship of those kinds of materials that turn people into highly subjectivist, self-serving, and private individuals no longer concerned with maintaining the common requirements of citizenship. For Rousseau, censorship is a necessary task, and those who lack the will to establish it certainly lack the toughness needed to maintain a sense of civic virtue and a concomitant dedication to the common good of the community. Moreover, once a sense of citizenship is lost, it is difficult, if not impossible, to restore. "It follows from this that the censorship can be useful for preserving mores, but never for reestablishing them."[64]

This does not mean that Rousseau outlaws, entirely, the private realm and the individual liberty associated with it; he merely hopes that the private realm will not kill in people a civic sensibility. Thus, individuals may think as they want to think, and they do not have to account for their views, but when their lives are touched by the requirements of the common good, they must accommodate their personal views to public needs. This point of view has a particularly important place for Rousseau in his discussion of religion. Rousseau says:

> *the dogmas of . . . religion are of no interest either to the state or its members, except to the extent that these dogmas relate to morality and to the duties which the one who professes them is bound to fill toward others. Each man can have in addition such opinions as he pleases, without it being any of the sovereign's business to know what they are.*[65]

This viewpoint is part of what Rousseau refers to as the doctrines of a "civil religion," which all people, no matter what their particular religious affiliation might be, are asked to support. The civil religion defines common values that help maintain a sense of community and cohesion among the members of the society. What are the articles of a civil religion? Rousseau permits certain basic religious doctrines such as the possibility of an afterlife, happiness for those who are just, and a benevolent deity. There is to be respect for the laws and the need to maintain the social contract. Also, Rousseau excludes religious intolerance. He says, "Those who distinguish between civil and theological intolerance are mistaken. . . . These two types of intolerance are inseparable. It is impossible to live in peace with those one believes to be damned."[66] Individuals should be accorded freedom of religious belief, subject to the proviso that no one should treat another with intolerance based on differences in religious views.

Rousseau's conception of the values associated with a civil religion on the surface appear acceptable, in part, to Locke. But Rousseau's approach to religious differences is not designed to support the live-and-let-live view of Locke as it is to make possible a basis for common values that could sustain a community's quest to define and to maintain the general good. Rousseau does not want religious differences to get in the way of this objective, so he hopes to take religious quarreling off the public agenda.

Now, this concern certainly informs the way Rousseau would treat people who continue to define the general good in ways different from the way the society defines it. People who persist in this regard violate the shared beliefs that help create social unity, and such people can and should be banished. Here, for Rousseau, a society in creating a "civil religion" takes the view that the society "can banish [a person who violates citizen norms] not for being impious but for being unsociable, for being incapable of sincerely loving the laws and justice, and of sacrificing his life, if necessary, for his duty."[67] This viewpoint makes it acceptable to excoriate those who, for matters of conscience, do not accept the concept of the general good. Instead of making a place for such persons, a place that allows them to continue to question society's policies, it appears that Rousseau removes them from society.

Given the foregoing, a separate sphere of associations, typical of civil societies (as we discussed in Chapter 1), do not seem to be secured in Rousseau's society. Of course, it is possible that the common good of the whole society might be defined in such a way as to make such a sphere a reality. But what makes this arrangement unlikely is that Rousseau does not see a need for individuals to come together for the purpose of understanding radically different points of view on important moral questions. In a civil society, people from diverse backgrounds join groups and work together within them for common purposes. Here, individuals come to appreciate difference. But this outcome of civil society is not acceptable to Rousseau. He seeks a society where difference is minimized in the name of creating a context that supports the common good and the general will that flows from it. A civil society, in promoting difference, undermines the new social contract. Indeed, when people come together in Rousseau's society, they do so to define common policies that all can and should adhere to, and, if they are not willing to make this activity the main priority of their lives, they can then be called bad citizens and subject to banishment.

Making room for wide differences of lifestyle and ideas would get in the way of this project for Rousseau. But respect for difference is fundamental to the freedom Hobbes and Locke sought, and respect for difference is pivotal to civil society. As we have seen, under the civic virtue of mutual respect (as we discussed in Chapter 1), people who hold quite different, but nonetheless reasonable, moral viewpoints must create ways for these different views to flourish side by side. In this setting, a shared approach to policy that all can uphold on the issues in question, say, abortion, prayer in schools, and so on, is not likely to emerge. Still, it is possible for people with different values and understandings to live together in peace when there is a sense of mutual respect among them strong enough to permit each to work with others to make possible an atmosphere that is respectful of all views.

But whereas Rousseau has a strong commitment to maintaining the elements of civic virtue that can help sustain among people a willingness to maintain support for the common good, he does not include in his view of civic virtue the notion of mutual respect as defined here. The reason is that he does not need to. As we have seen, for Rousseau, deliberation is based on shared beliefs that would eliminate radical differences in moral outlooks among people. And because such differences are not present, mutual respect as a civic virtue is never necessary. Further, if people manifest values widely different from those that society generally holds, these people are excluded from the society. Rousseau's view of civil society does not support a liberal version (as discussed in Chapter 1), which tolerates wide diversity.

V. Response and Rejoinder

For Rousseau, the main problem of modern life is that society has been so corrupted by a conniving mentality, designed to obtain status and wealth, that the basis for fairness, located in a natural, moral sensibility for the welfare of others, has been lost. Rousseau, thus, wants to re-create the ground of society in a general will or a conception of the common good that each individual in the society agrees to uphold. In maintaining the common good, individuals in the new social setting act by a commitment not to harm others, just as they did in the state of nature. The difference between the state of nature and the new society Rousseau hopes to create is now clear. Unlike in the state of nature where individuals show concern for each other from a natural, moral sensibility, in the new society of Rousseau's social contract, such concern is a by-product of citizenship activity on behalf of the common good.

But if society has destroyed the natural, moral sensibility in individuals, how is respect for the new social contract and for the general moral will upon which it rests ever to be regained? In other terms, Locke might have asked Rousseau to explain the basis for supporting the general will in a society in which a natural, moral sensibility is lacking. Rousseau could argue in response that support for the general will emanates from realistic, practical reasoning. Individuals recognize that, in the absence of supporting a society based on the general will, society would be torn to shreds by civil war and strife. But individuals need society to supply them with the myriad goods that satisfy basic and fundamental needs. Given both these understandings, individuals realize there is no alternative but to support the general will and make it the mainstay of their common lives. Here, it would seem that Rousseau echoes Hobbes, who argued that the basis for civil society, predicated on the rule of law, was the need to achieve peace so that society was able to function in ways that served the needs of individuals.

But this argument suggests a motivation that stands at the center of Locke's thought, also: namely, the desire for happiness. Given that this was the case, how, Locke might ask, did Rousseau differ from himself? In response, Rousseau would argue that happiness is never achieved except in a society governed by the strong commitment to civic virtue, a commitment represented best in the general will. Here, a happy life is one in which individuals learn to constrain their self-interested pursuits so that their lives conform to the needs of the community. Rousseau would argue, then, that happiness is not denied a place in his society, but that he has in mind a different sort of happiness than that found in Locke. The latter's happiness, for Rousseau, derives solely from self-interested pursuits. Rousseau celebrates, on the other hand, the type of happiness that evolves from participation in and a sense of contribution to upholding the common good of a community. And the importance of the idea of the general will is that it symbolizes this distinction, and thus the general will is a powerful statement for it.

Locke may have responded by arguing that the idea of the general will was really not as commanding as Rousseau thinks. In fact, many people would not trust it. Locke would have argued that what he tried to do was to give people the freedom to choose their own course in life, within the context of rational norms and rules that we have referred to as civic virtues. This type of freedom leaves with each individual the question as to what one wishes to do with one's life. But Rousseau in contrast, by making people subscribe to the norms of the common good, must dictate to each person what one's life is to be about. The type of liberty advocated by the general will was, for Locke, prescriptive of what people should do, and it suggested the need for an authoritarian state that can force people to be "good."

Rousseau would counter that Locke's attitude only continued to show why Locke's individuals would have never been citizens; they would have remained only property holders who make the protection of their own property the only issue in politics. A society such as Locke's, where people lived by rules that permitted them to gain as much wealth as possible, could have never been a society free from political inequality. Locke's civil society, as a result, would have consisted of people trying to obtain wealth to gain as much political influence as they could. This kind of society, however, would have caused the erosion of the natural moral sensibilities, thus bringing to existence for Rousseau the individual as the beast that Rousseau loathes.

The differences between Locke and Rousseau recall the current debate between those advocating a strong conception of democracy, such as Rousseau's, and those advocating a doctrine of liberal civil society, with a strong commitment to individual rights, such as Locke's. For Locke, Rousseau's position suggested a view of democratic participation that represents a continuing threat to protecting individual rights. Rights, as Locke saw them, enabled people to pursue ways of life that individuals chose for themselves. But these ways of life were always pursued within a setting of a common commitment to basic rules and laws that limit conduct so that the rights of all people could be protected. But where the democratically determined common good is made the predominant objective in society, as in the argument of Rousseau, anyone who stands in the way of its realization must for the sake of common good be banished. Obviously, in this situation, individual rights, such as freedom of conscience and thought, might be placed in jeopardy, all in the name of a very strong commitment to a far-reaching view of democracy.

Now, Spinoza did not see this consequence arising from democracy at all. As long as there was a firm commitment to freedom of thought and speech on behalf of the overall commitment to advancing the full use of reason of the citizens, the citizens who made up the majority had ways to limit it and to prevent it from trampling basic liberties. Further, as long as there was in place a civil religion dedicated to the values of respect for freedom of speech and thought, there was a powerful force to ensure that the majority never acted against basic citizen rights but for them.

Hobbes might have sought the last word by contending that neither Locke nor Rousseau could secure citizens' happiness. And the reason would have been simple. Locke's government, which required a separation of powers format, was, no less than Spinoza's democracy, too weak and divided to protect people's basic rights. For Hobbes, Rousseau's government, which was based upon the deliberation of citizens, would be either too weak to protect people's rights or so strong and committed to the canons of the common good that it would threaten rights in general.

Rousseau would have rejected Hobbes's view with great force, pointing out that the best route to citizenship and to respect for civic virtue lies not with Hobbes's Leviathan but with the sense of responsibility gained from participating in making the laws by which one lives. Rousseau would argue that Hobbes, Locke, and probably Spinoza promote, in their individualism, the fragmentation of society by urging people to associate freedom with the right to deny the importance of those values that undergird a sense of belonging to a society that promotes the common good. For Rousseau, the tragedy of modern life, embellished by Hobbes, Locke, and Spinoza, is that our natural moral sentiments are silenced in favor of the values that urge us to deny any importance to community and to civic virtue, as we extol wealth and self-interest.

Notes

1. On this point, see George H. Sabine, *A History of Political Theory* (New York: Holt, Rinehart and Winston, 1961), 580.

2. Roger D. Masters, "Introduction," in Jean-Jacques Rousseau, "Discourse on the Question Proposed by the Academy of Dijon: Has the Restoration of the Sciences and Arts Tended to Purify Morals?" in *The First and Second Discourses,* ed. Roger D. Masters (New York: St. Martin's Press, 1964), 4–5, 9.

3. Rousseau, "Discourse on the Question Proposed by the Academy of Dijon," 51.

4. Ibid., 54.

5. Ibid., 56.

6. Jean-Jacques Rousseau, *Émile*, trans. Barbara Foxly (New York: Dutton, 1969), 174.

7. Jean-Jacques Rousseau, "Discourse on the Origin and Foundations of Inequality Among Men," in *On the Social Contract*, trans. Donald A. Cress (Indianapolis: Hackett Publishing Company, 1983), 147. All references to *On the Social Contract* and *Discourse on Political Economy* will be in this book, too.

8. Rousseau, *Émile*, 174. Elsewhere Rousseau says, "The first impulses of nature are always right; there is no original sin in the human heart . . . the only natural passion is self-love or selfishness taken in the wider sense," p. 56.

9. Ibid., 174–75.

10. Ibid., 181–82.

11. Rousseau, "Discourse on the Origin and Foundations of Inequality Among Men," 118.

12. Ibid.

13. Ibid., 115.

14. Ibid., 135.

15. Ibid., 137.

16. Ibid., 136.

17. Ibid., 126.

18. Ibid., 128–29.

19. Ibid., 141–42.

20. Ibid., 142.

21. Ibid.

22. Ibid., 142–43.

23. Ibid., 143.

24. Ibid.

25. Ibid., 143–44.

26. Ibid., 144–45.

27. Ibid., 145.

28. Ibid.

29. Ibid., 146.

30. Ibid., 146–47.

31. Ibid., 147.

32. Ibid.

33. Ibid.

34. Ibid., 148–49.

35. Ibid., 149–50.

36. Ibid., 150.

37. Jean-Jacques Rousseau, *The Government of Poland*, trans. Willmoore Kendall (New York: Bobbs-Merrill, 1972), 69.

38. Ibid., 67.

39. Rousseau, *Discourse on Political Economy*, 172.

40. Ibid., 173.

41. Ibid., 171.

42. Rousseau, *On the Social Contract*, 24, I:6.

43. Ibid.

44. Ibid.

45. Ibid., 31, II:3.

46. Ibid., 49, III:1.

47. Ibid., 49–50, III:1.

48. Ibid., 38, II:6.

49. Ibid., 26, I:8.

50. Ibid., 27, I:8.
51. Ibid., 74, III:15.
52. Ibid., 79, IV:1.
53. Ibid.
54. Charles Taylor, *Sources of the Self* (Cambridge: Harvard University Press, 1989), 360.
55. Ibid.
56. Rousseau, *On the Social Contract*, 45–46, II:10.
57. Ibid., 29, I:9.
58. Ibid., 30, II:1.
59. Ibid., 46, II:11.
60. Ibid., 31, II:3.
61. Ibid., 39, II:7, 40, II:7.
62. Ibid., 82, IV:2.
63. Ibid., 95, IV:7.
64. Ibid.
65. Ibid., 102, IV:8.
66. Ibid.
67. Ibid.

PART III

Late Modern and Contemporary Approaches to Civil Society

11

Immanuel Kant: Civil Society and International Order

I. Public Reason

Immanuel Kant (1724–1804) had, unlike Jean-Jacques Rousseau, great admiration for the Enlightenment. Why was this experience so important to Kant? An answer to this question can be gleaned from Kant's demand for protecting, as in Benedict Spinoza, intellectual freedom against those whose values threatened such freedom. Kant would complement the work of Spinoza, Thomas Hobbes, and John Locke, who each sought to predicate human life based on the truth made possible by reason. And the central truth upon which to base life for each of these writers was the need to secure freedom for each individual. Indeed, a civil society for Kant, as well as for Hobbes and Locke, was a rule of law setting designed to achieve equal freedom for each individual. Necessarily, for Kant, as for Hobbes, Spinoza, and Locke, then, traditions needed to be assessed in terms of how well they promoted the progress of reason, of truth, and of freedom.

For instance, Kant, like Spinoza, criticizes those members of the clergy who mandate religious doctrines to exercise "guardianship" over the minds of others. By doing so, the religious authorities restrict or deny the "public use of one's reason." By this phrase, Kant seeks the kind of public reasoning that can be used to discuss openly and critically policies and laws that affect many areas of social and political life. The public use of reason, or what is also called *public reason*, allows people to discuss important questions, and it is through this activity that people are able to expand their knowledge and "progress in general enlightenment."[1] In effect, then, Kant is making a plea for what we today refer to as critical thinking, or the need to learn how to use one's reasoning skills to examine propositions and evidence, with the overall intention of expanding the knowledge base of society.

So, given the interest in public reasoning, what is involved for people engaged in the activities associated with the public use of reason? For Kant, public reasoning is bound by certain rules of communication. What is the nature of these rules? Or, in other terms, what rules or authoritative standards should we follow as we engage in public reasoning and communicate with each other and think critically about public matters? It is necessary to make these rules of communication clear so that the Enlightenment Kant lauds can be clarified.

In the first place, to engage in public reason, a person must liberate oneself from "self-incurred tutelage," or his or her reliance upon others who are allowed to shape their own views.[2] The first rule one should follow, then, is that each person should "think for oneself," and this rule, or what Kant calls "enlightenment," suggests the need for an individual's "deliverance from superstition." The latter only places us under the control of others, who impose their thoughts on us and force us to accept their beliefs without question. The importance of this rule is that it establishes the legitimacy of comparative thinking. In particular, for persons to formulate their views, they must test them against, and compare them with, the views of others. But where all views are the same, as is the case when people do not think for themselves and accept whatever way of thinking is imposed upon them, this objective cannot be met.[3]

The second important rule of public reason is what Kant refers to as the maxim of "enlarged thought." This rule is the basis for establishing with others a common and universal viewpoint that one may use for assessing one's own opinions and judgments and for searching with others for public approaches to shared concerns. What is the universal standpoint and how is it attained? Take the last question first. The basis for such a standpoint is not a point of view that transcends human discourse, say, in some imagined and unreal perspective found outside the experience of society, but, instead, a common standpoint arises as people try to understand each other's views in as full a way as possible. As we communicate with others with this intention, we expand our range of understanding so that we can gain a comprehensive perspective on the matters under discussion.[4] Thus, the common standpoint is as full and as educated an understanding as is possible of an issue or question at hand, and obviously this standpoint transcends the boundaries of ordinary prejudice. All people need to do to achieve this expanded, or what Kant calls "enlarged," understanding is to open themselves to the views of others. People accomplish this objective by not allowing their own "subjective private conditions" to dictate their own thoughts. The result of this enterprise is that individuals can place themselves "at the standpoint of others."[5]

The third rule to follow in making possible the public use of reason is to "think consistently."[6] Here, individuals must constantly be governed, as a matter of habit, by the first two rules. In particular, individuals must not allow prejudice to determine their thinking, and individuals must constantly seek to understand the views of others while achieving a common standpoint from which to make judgments about issues. Presumably, when people follow these rules and deliberate with others in a way that maintains them, it is possible to uphold the *civic virtue of mutual respect*, discussed in Chapter 1.

But why should people adopt these rules and make them a primary basis for their communication with each other and thus for securing the public use of reason? Kant's moral philosophy is designed to address this question. Kant's moral philosophy argues that each of us should live by a *categorical imperative*, which requires that each person in society be treated as an end and not solely as a means. In treating people as ends, we are to respect their freedom, and we are not to make people serve as a means to the various projects of others or of ourselves. By communicating with others in the way required by the rules just elaborated, we thus accommodate ourselves to the imperative to treat others as ends during the course of public reasoning. Indeed, it would appear that the categorical imperative, in obligating us to treat others as ends and not as means, would require us to conduct our interactions with others in such a way as to uphold the standards of communication that Kant defines for securing the public use of reason.[7]

Now, to make possible the kind of communication among people that allows them to treat others as ends and to consider fully their views, there are certain institutions and ways of life that must be established. The most obvious public institution in this regard is a commitment to permit people an "unlimited freedom to use [their] own reason to speak in [their] own person."[8] A truly free person seeks full liberation from all elements that blunt or destroy his or her ability to cast off the hindrances to thinking, in order to define with others those common, reasonable standards that all can respect. Clearly, given the need for freedom, it would follow that the public use of reason can take place only in a society that guarantees this freedom. And the only kind of society that does is a civil society because only a civil society assures each person the basic rights needed to engage in an enlightened discourse.

In the next several sections, our discussion of Kant's political theory is designed to demonstrate how the principle of the need to treat others as ends can be given concrete expression. Here, we demonstrate the way the expression of this principle is manifested in both the domestic institutions of a civil society and in international relations among states that maintain the atmosphere of peace necessary to secure a civil society. In doing so, we demonstrate the institutions that support a society committed to maintaining the public use of reason. The first step in addressing this objective is to discuss further Kant's notion of the categorical imperative by demonstrating how Kant derives this basic moral duty from reason and makes this principle primary to his own system of politics. To this end, it is necessary to describe Kant's understanding of *practical reason*.

II. The Process of Practical Reason

For Kant, the term *practical reason* is used to signify the employment of reason to determine the moral concepts and principles by which individuals should conduct their affairs in public, including political and social settings. Thinking or reasoning in keeping with this commitment really is designed to address a particular question. What is that question? Kant says:

> *Ask yourself whether, if the action which you propose should take place by a law of nature of which you yourself were a part, you could regard it as possible through your will. Everyone does, in fact, decide by this rule whether actions are morally good or bad. Thus people ask: if one belonged to such an order of things that anyone would allow himself to deceive when he thought it to his advantage, or felt justified in shortening his life as soon as he were thoroughly weary of it, or looked with complete indifference on the needs of others, would he assent of his own will to be a member of such an order of things?*[9]

Kant believed that the way to determine universally valid moral concepts was to ask which norms all rational individuals would consider to be universally binding. Here, in determining the moral bases for conduct, one is to ask oneself: what is the moral course not only for oneself but also for all rational people? When one takes this approach to determining the basis for action, one can determine moral norms that all rational persons would agree should ground actions. Thus, for Kant, no one who is rational would accept deception as a proper course in life, nor would such a person opt for suicide when times are difficult. Further, a rational individual would not accept that one should allow one's talents and abilities to go undeveloped, nor would such an individual manifest a complete absence of concern for the needs of others.[10]

These examples of moral duties derived from practical reason suggest a larger, more encompassing truth; in particular, for Kant, there is a universal duty to uphold a fundamental moral principle, called the *categorical imperative*. The categorical imperative says that we are to act "*only on that maxim through which you can at the same time will that it should become a universal law.*"[11]

Kant thinks his conception of the categorical imperative provides a precise statement pertaining to the way individuals should conduct themselves as they interact with each other. How is this possible? Principally, the categorical imperative is based on the principle of noncontradiction. This means that a moral norm specifies a way of life that never advocates dueling, contradictory tendencies. For instance, the norm of promising to repay money says that when faced with upholding the promise and not upholding the promise to repay, one must always do as one promised and repay the money. If the notion of promising permitted me to not repay money that I promised to another, then "no one would believe that anything was promised him, but would ridicule all such statements as vain pretenses."[12]

Further, the categorical imperative, in requiring that we live by norms that are not contradictory, provides a basis for defining the specific, concrete duties to which we each should adhere. And these duties indicate a clear outline of the kinds of conduct with which we are to treat each other. Thus, Kant says the universal moral law requires that any moral norm we adopt as the basis for our action be designed so as to *treat others as ends in themselves, and not as a means to the ends of others.*[13]

In specifying the need to treat others as ends as a universal duty, Kant's intention is to define a principle that everyone is to follow throughout the course of his or her life. To do so, the various ways by which this principle is to be manifested must be clearly outlined. Kant hopes to give this principle concrete expression not only in the definition of our duties, but in the various social and political institutions that enable each of us as well as the society as a whole to treat people as ends and not as means.

In the first place, then, Kant seeks to demonstrate the actual duties individuals must uphold to accord others the dignity they deserve. To this end, he distinguishes ethical from juridical duties. Ethical duties, which embody the requirement to treat others as ends, include duties such as developing our capacities to the fullest extent, showing benevolence to others as we relate to them, and not lying. In our day-to-day conduct, we are to demonstrate "dispositions" that include "self-constraint" or "virtue" by making these duties the basis of our actions. The rules for communicating with others, which we elaborated upon earlier, would seem to fall under the category of ethical duties since they describe how we should communicate with each other while attempting to make possible the public use of our reason. Juridical duties, on the other hand, are legally binding rules imposed from the outside by legitimate political authority.[14] These duties, too, embody the commitment to treat others as ends, and, as we see in the discussion of civil society, juridical duties are adhered to through externally imposed constraints, as opposed to, in the case of ethical duties, moral dispositions that are self-maintained and self-enforced restraints. In particular, juridical duties refer to those rules that must be followed to protect the same rights and freedom for each person.

We more fully demonstrate Kant's effort to embody his key moral principle of treating people as ends into the main institutions of civil society in the next section. Before proceeding, it is well to point out, as a way to anticipate our discussion of G.W.F. Hegel in the next chapter, that Hegel did not think Kant had done an adequate job demonstrating the nature of actual institutions and practices that embodied Kant's central, governing moral principle. Indeed, Hegel's hope was to achieve what he thought Kant failed to attain: namely, a description of the institutions and practices that properly carry into practice Kant's hope to make genuine freedom possible.

III. Kant's Civil Society

Kant's civil society is designed to achieve freedom for each person through the rule of law. A civil society is based upon the existence of laws, established and maintained by a constitution, to secure the rights of all citizens. The state in a civil society is to uphold the laws that protect the rights of people.[15] In accepting the authority of the state, then, individuals maintain a basis for securing their rights, and it is principally for this reason that they enter civil society. Affording people basic rights is in keeping with the key Kantian principle that states that individuals are to treat each other as ends. This is the case because Kant believes that, in a civil society, individuals are treated as ends only when they have equal liberty, but clearly the latter is not possible if individuals do not have equal basic rights. Thus, for Kant, the "universal principle of right" is that "every action which by itself or by its maxim enables the freedom of each individual's will to coexist with the freedom of everyone else in accordance with a universal law is *right.*"[16]

Moreover, in a civil society, the principle of equal liberty is achieved with the proper use of coercion. This means that individuals have equal liberty to others only when there are juridical constraints in place, that is, legally binding laws that use coercion to ensure people do not act as a "hindrance to freedom" or as an obstacle to others having the rights they deserve.[17] The laws must be designed to maintain a form of "reciprocal coercion," by which Kant means that each person is to be equally governed by rules and made subject to constraints, whose only purpose is to protect the freedom of all persons equally. Of course, some people might do as the law requires because of an awareness of obligations they owe to others under the law, or what might be referred to as a sense of duty. Still, Kant does not want to predicate the protection of equal liberty upon a sense of duty but only upon the possibility of external coercion, which ensures that all uphold the laws that extend rights to all people.[18]

But why is coercion necessary at all? Why would not rational people accept that they have ethical duties and adapt themselves, voluntarily, to the norms that uphold the rights of others? Kant believes that, even though a civil society is founded on the central idea to protect the liberty of each person in an equal way, still, it is likely that individuals will be motivated in their day-to-day activities by nonmoral factors, such as the pushes and pulls of interest and desire. Kant is more like Hobbes than Locke on this point. Locke's state of nature demonstrated that individuals were rational, and they accepted constraints needed to secure rights. But Hobbes did not harbor a similar optimism, and *his* state of nature was a state of *war.* For Kant, then, like Hobbes, the actual motive for acting as one should is fear of punishment. People do as morality requires, then, but not always from moral motives. Thus, a civil society is an important device that furthers the purposes of practical reason or morality, even among individuals who, for the most part, may not themselves be motivated to act as reason demands. In this context, Kant says:

Each individual can be free so long as I do not interfere with his freedom by my external actions, even although his freedom may be a matter of total indifference to me or although I may wish in my heart to deprive him of it.[19]

Moreover, coercion is not the only way by which to ensure compliance with the norms of moral law, in particular, respect for the rights of others. In addition, Kant suggests that in a "civic society," the various interests come to be arranged in such a way that each interest can check and limit the influence of others. In this way, a context arises in which no single individual or group of individuals has so much power that the rights of others might be threatened. This situation is "one in which there is mutual opposition among the members, together with the most exact definition of freedom and fixing of its limits so that it may be consistent with the freedom of others."[20] In this arrangement, individuals are able to preserve a "civic union" in which each realizes the importance of others in making possible a society in which all benefit.[21] Kant says that even a race of "intelligent devils" should be able to achieve this social organization.

Given a multitude of rational beings requiring universal laws for their preservation, but each of whom is secretly inclined to exempt himself from them, [the hope is] to establish a constitution in such a way that although their private intentions conflict, they check each other, with the result that their public conduct is the same as if they had no such intentions.[22]

Despite Kant's rather Hobbesian view of human nature, it is important to note that Kant does not accept Hobbes's unitary form of state in which the major powers are located together in one branch of government. Instead, Kant accepts a state that includes Locke's separation-of-powers view.[23] By dividing up the tasks of a government in a civil society into separate branches – the executive, the legislative, and the judicial – no single element of government can become so powerful that it is able to threaten the liberty of any single citizen. As for Locke, the legislative power would be the supreme power, for it is referred to as the *ruling power*, whereas the executive is the individual who is to govern in keeping with the law. The legislative power is to make laws that are just for all people, and thus the legislature would no doubt have the responsibility for protecting the basic rights of all citizens.[24] Indeed, Kant says, that in any true republic, it is the *"representative system* of the people whereby the people's rights are looked after on their behalf by deputies who represent the united will of the citizens."[25] Here, it would seem that, like Locke, Kant does not want a state whose powers would be as potentially unchecked as was the case in Hobbes's view of the state in civil society.

For Kant, then, mechanisms are in place in a civil society that enable individuals to subordinate their interests to the larger requirement to protect the same rights for all people. Individuals are willing to support the practices and institutions of a state that maintains this objective, even as they are more personally committed to make certain that their own interests are given priority. Why and on what basis would individuals, who are so motivated to realize their material interests, embrace this idea of civil society?

IV. Nature's Secret Plan

Kant's answer to the previous question arises from his approach to interpreting the meaning of history. History, when viewed only from the standpoint of individuals (each of whom lives according to his or her own inclinations), would suggest a world that is incapable of achieving a civil society. Each person would be content only with pursuing his or her own interests, without concern for establishing a society committed to the provision of equal freedom. But Kant believes that moral progress is inescapable and that, on this view, each human life contributes to the rational end of equal freedom. Given this perspective on society, then, even the experience of self-interest is somehow a contributing part to the larger progress that makes possible the equal freedom and rights that a civil society secures. The natural course of human development does not unfold by mere chance, for Kant, but by the "guiding thread" of reason, and consequently, all individuals work to help realize the larger goals of reason, even if they are unaware that they are doing so. Thus, when we view history from Kant's progressive perspective, it is possible to write a scenario that demonstrates the likely development of humankind from the earliest beginnings in a state of nature in which humankind is dependent upon pure instinct and desire, to the later development of culture, where rational laws and civil society frame human encounters.[26]

Kant's interpretation of the course of history resembles Hobbes's view of the evolution of civil society from the state of nature. Kant assumes that human beings in the state of nature manifest toward each other a kind of mutual antagonism that threatens to destroy society. Kant calls this experience the condition of "unsocial sociability." The natural desire of humankind is for each person to "have everything go according to his own wish."[27] Instead of threatening life, however, this natural yearning helps to make people more resilient and creative. The experience of others posing a danger to one's existence awakens in persons all the basic powers that might otherwise have lain hidden. Here, individuals, in the face of the many dangers confronting them, learn to harness all the energies needed to ensure their survival.[28]

With this new-found awareness, individuals gradually become enlightened enough to begin to appreciate the importance of creating a society that is a "moral whole" or a society in which each is no longer threatened by others.[29] People then move from a condition in which they live at the mercy of one another, to a situation in which they live in social settings that facilitate the attainment of higher purposes. The "higher purposes" of life are in keeping with the dictates of morality, or respect for the constraints that protect other people's freedom. In this new situation, individuals discover that "civic freedom can hardly be infringed without evil consequences being felt in all walks of life."[30] The condition of "unsocial sociability" is really, then, a gift of nature, for, in reacting to the negative features of this condition to survive, people create higher forms of life that not only provide security, but civility as well. Kant says, "Thanks be to Nature, then, for the incompatibility, for heartless competitive vanity, for the insatiable desire to possess and to rule! Without them, all the excellent natural capacities of humanity would forever sleep, undeveloped."[31]

On this reading of history, however, people never completely overcome their selfishness. Thus, it is the case that people discover the need to be under a "master," because even though people realize the need for laws that limit freedom as a way to protect it, it is the case that selfishness tempts people to find ways to "exempt" themselves from such laws. To counter this tendency, people need laws that will "force" them to uphold a commitment to protect the rights of all people. Thus, for Kant, each person will "always abuse his freedom if he has none above him to exercise force in accord with the laws."[32] A civil society is needed, then, to provide the laws that regulate the lives of each person in such a way that one's selfish nature does not interfere with the requirements of maintaining a civil order, a way of life based on the need to respect the freedom of others. Respecting others' freedom, a major and great *civic virtue*, becomes embodied in society when there is a "correct constitution," which supports a civil society, as well as a "good will ready to accept such a constitution."[33]

Presumably, then, history unfolds in a way that allows individuals to recognize the fundamental importance of a need to live under the constitution of a civil society. Given this evolution of culture, people who are "crooked wood" from which "nothing perfectly straight can be built,"[34] realize that, all along, nature is seeking to realize its "secret plan," that of making people subordinate to the truths of morality and reason.[35] Here, individuals become enlightened enough to understand the importance to their lives of a civil society, and in consequence are quite willing to give their allegiance to institutions that protect the rights of all persons equally. A civil society is seen as an environment in which individuals, who are prone to act from self-interest, will, owing to the coercive force of public laws that protect the rights of all, act toward each other in ways *as if* they were committed to maintaining throughout their lives the moral law.

There is another realization that accompanies the idea of civil society as well. Civil societies represent a moral order that cannot be sustained as long as nations are continually committed to preparing for or engaging in war. States that seek to expand their power through war divert resources from the kind of education that improves the minds of citizens and that makes possible respect for morality.[36] As a result of war's actual or potential devastation, then, individuals conclude that it is best to enter a "league of nations," committed to peace and to an international environment that ends war.[37]

V. The New World Order: A Federation of Civil Societies

Kant's intention, then, is to help advance the cause of civil societies by demonstrating a way to make peaceful relationships possible among states. There are two steps in the process. The first step is to accept certain basic or what he calls "pre-liminary articles for perpetual peace among states." They include the following:

> *No treaty of peace shall be held valid in which there is tacitly reserved matter for a future war, . . . no independent states, large or small, shall come under the dominion of another state by inheritance, exchange, purchase, or donation, . . . standing armies . . . shall in time be totally abolished, . . . national debts shall not be contracted with a view to the external friction of states, . . . no state shall by force interfere with the constitution or government of another state, . . . [and] no state shall, during war, permit such acts of hostility which would make mutual confidence in the subsequent peace impossible.*[38]

These basic articles are not in themselves sufficient to secure a lasting and enduring peace among nations. In addition, there are the "definitive articles for perpetual peace among states." Taken together, both the preliminary and definitive articles of peace suggest that even if the natural condition among states is war, this condition can be defeated if an environment is created that encourages civil societies to flourish on a worldwide basis.[39] We turn now to the definitive articles of peace.

The first definitive article is that the "civil constitution of every state should be republican."[40] As seen earlier, the legislative branch is the most important branch of government. Kant believes that, in a republican regime, citizens make the laws through their representatives, and, since citizens are desirous of securing their rights, they instruct their representatives to make laws that protect their rights. Moreover, because citizens have such an important place in the law-making process, no republican regime can engage in war without the consent of the citizens. And, since average citizens are most affected by war, and it is they who have to pay for it or fight in it, it will be less likely that in a republican regime there will be a war tendency. Kant says:

> *If the consent of the citizens is required in order to decide that war should be declared . . . nothing is more natural than that they would be very cautious in commencing such a poor game, decreeing for themselves all the calamities of war.*[41]

The second definitive article for perpetual peace is that "the law of nations shall be founded on a federation of free states."[42] Of critical importance to making this framework of peace possible is the absolute commitment on the part of nations to end war. In effect, nations must take an oath that says that "there ought to be no war among us. . . [and instead of war] we want to establish a supreme legislative, executive, and judiciary power which will reconcile our differences peaceably."[43] Why would a state join such a federation? Kant believes that, as societies become republics, there will be an inherent interest in avoiding war, and this interest will help to propel such states into alliance with other states who similarly want to avoid war. Kant says:

> *For if fortune directs that a powerful and enlightened people can make itself a republic, which by its nature must be inclined to perpetual peace, this gives a fulcrum to the federation with other states so that they may adhere to it and thus secure freedom under the idea of the law of nations. By more and more such associations, the federation may be gradually extended.*[44]

The federation or "league of peace" will end all wars among member states. Moreover, member states will achieve this objective without threatening their sovereignty. And thus, Kant says:

> *This league does not tend to any domination over the power of the state but only to the maintenance and security of the freedom of the state itself and of other states in league with it, without there being any need for them to submit to civil laws and their compulsion, as men in a state of nature must submit.*[45]

The third definitive article states, "The law of world citizens shall be limited to conditions of universal hospitality."[46] Citizens from one state will be able to move freely into other states and exchange ideas and engage in business opportunities. Whereas states will not extend citizenship status to visitors from other states, each state will extend full respect and dignity to foreign visitors. For Kant, hospitality would no doubt cultivate a "spirit of commerce" that is "incompatible with war," and that "sooner or later gains the upper hand in every state."[47]

These articles of peace suggest that individuals look at the world from two standpoints: namely, as members of their particular home state, possessing legal citizenship status, and as citizens of the world, possessing a moral responsibility to maintain an international order that can sustain civil societies everywhere. As citizens of particular states, they are to uphold the laws and interests of their own nations. But, at the same time, these individuals are also citizens of the world, and, as such, they must see to it that their own state maintains its commitment to the principles of a peaceful international order, lest it find itself outside the family of nations, subject to censure. It is this sense of being part of the audience of world citizens that provides the basis for a sustaining pressure, emanating from an international culture, to enable different parts of the world to be at peace with each other. Kant hopes that "the human race can gradually be brought closer and closer to a constitution establishing world citizenship."[48]

VI. Public Reason and Civil Society

As we said at the beginning of this chapter, practical reason established the basis for a civil society by justifying the key moral principle to treat others as ends. Further, Kant's view of civil society, including its domestic institutions and its need for a federation of peaceful nations, helps to explain the way this principle is given a concrete form of embodiment. In this setting, there is a chance for the public use of reason to become an integral part of the lives of citizens. Here, individuals, despite the presence of self-interest concerns in their lives, can still learn to conform their public deliberations to the rules, described at the beginning of this chapter, that allow people of different views and understandings to search with each other for acceptable and reasonable solutions to shared public problems.

Now, it might be the case that individuals, who engage in a deliberation on the basis of Kant's conception of the public reason, may end up disagreeing with the results. For instance, people who debate the best policy with respect to school prayer may, as a result of following Kant's rules for public reasoning, each be able to understand fully the points of views of all others in the debate. Thus, each will be in a position to think about the question from a broad and encompassing, or common, perspective that includes respect for all points of view. Here, those who want prayer understand the reasons behind the view of those who do not, and vice versa. Still, after the deliberation has concluded and a result has been reached, as, for instance, by a vote of the chief legislative institution of the society, it still may be the case that, because people feel so strongly about their respective, differing views, there is no basis for reaching an agreement on a policy all can fully support.

But even in this situation, people may find themselves able to tolerate the policy outcomes they do not accept personally. Why is this? The public use of reason suggests an ability on the part of each person to carefully consider the views of others that one does not agree with. In doing so, space would be created in society that would include a wide variety and diversity of people. As a result of the public use of reason, individuals manifest to each other the civic virtue of mutual respect. And, because they do, people who disagree with the outcome of a deliberation could still tolerate the results because they each realize that every effort has been made, and will continue to be made, to preserve the basic freedom and rights of each person.

From this account, Kant's conception of society could accommodate a civil society understood as a separate sphere of associations, standing independently of the state. Indeed, as we have seen, Kant envisions a society with a diversity of interests, each of which is checked and limited by the others, thus creating an environment that works to prevent any single group or interest from becoming dominant over the rest. Clearly, this environment of diverse interests would not only permit individuals opportunities to pursue self-defined life choices but would also provide a setting suitable to a government based on the idea of the separation of powers.

Finally, in Kant's view of civil society, a principal concern of those using public reason would be to find ways to create approaches to rights that made them secure and available to all throughout the society. In doing so, the key principle of Kant's moral philosophy, the need to treat others as ends and not as means, would be given concrete expression. What kinds of questions would be addressed? Using today's experience as examples, let us provide some illustrations. For instance, in discussing the principle of the right to speak one's views, there would be questions pertaining to what kinds of limits are acceptable on speech and what kinds are not. Or, in discussing the right of persons to determine their religious preferences, there would be much debate and disagreement pertaining to how far the state may go in limiting religious organizations' access to public schools. During the process of public reason, individuals in the society would have to make such determinations. A civil society should be hospitable to encouraging public deliberations on matters of this sort, deliberations that involve the widest possible range of views in the society and that aim to make clear the meaning and application of basic rights that all are to enjoy in society.

Whereas this kind of political agenda follows from Kant's view of the public use of reason, it is not at all clear that Kant would take a democratic approach to who is and who is not to be included in the deliberative processes that are grounded in the public use of reason. We hold this view of Kant because he excludes a long list of people from citizenship based on the criterion that for a person "to be fit to vote, a person must have an independent position among the people."[49] Here, Kant's view on exclusion is based on his position that some people in society will not have sufficient independence to engage in the public use of reason with others. Excluded from participation and voting are people engaged in apprenticeships, domestic servants, minors, and women in general because they must depend for livelihood on others. Even though these people can and should be accorded the same basic rights provided all other citizens, these people "do not have a right to influence or organise the state itself as *active* members, or to co-operate in introducing particular laws."[50] Kant argues that the public use of reason is the preserve of those who approach matters from the standpoint of the scholar, or those people who are willing and able to "submit for public testing their judgments and views which here and there diverge from the established symbol [or sets of opinions]."[51] Presumably, these people have sufficient independence, so they are able to approach questions from the standpoint of enlightened public reason.

Now, to be sure, Kant's conception of civil society, as we know, is later used by proponents of a liberal civil society to justify access to the public realm to previously excluded groups. Indeed, it is possible that Kant leaves open the door to this possibility by suggesting that the basis for exclusion is social position, or the idea of being dependent upon another for one's livelihood. As individuals are provided social independence over time, more people would be included in the citizen category. That Kant does not advocate such a policy himself should not deflect attention from the fact that, in promoting the idea of the public use of reason, he seeks to maintain civil society upon the great civic virtue of mutual respect. It would seem, then, that, given his commitment to this civic virtue,

Kant's civil society would grow to the point that all of those previously excluded would, over time, become a main part of society.

A theme that is apparent in the chapters on Hegel, John Stuart Mill, and John Rawls that follow is that each of these writers, in developing further the idea of public reason, attempted to provide a more democratic approach to the practice of public reason. In taking this view, Hegel, Mill, and Rawls sought to expand both the number of rights as well as the number of people covered by them in a given society. The person providing the most comprehensive account of this activity, an account that embellished Kant's view of public reason while accepting most facets of it, is Rawls, whom we discuss in Chapter 15.

VII. Response and Rejoinder

There are several problems that Locke and Rousseau would find with Kant's arguments. First, we comment on Locke. As we saw, Locke tied the existence of rights to his concept of private property. Locke said that individuals who work and who add value to the world through their labor have a right to enjoy the benefits of their endeavors. Indeed, for Locke, God has given us property for the sake of our enjoyment. It is in relation to the right of private property that individuals must accept restraints on their conduct with respect to accumulating wealth, including, for instance, that it is acceptable to accumulate wealth on the condition that one's activities in this regard benefit society as a whole.

But Kant would question this approach to ensuring support for rights because it would predicate such activity on a commitment to securing material happiness and thus not predicate rights on an authentic dimension. What is the authentic dimension of rights? If we return to Kant's approach to defining the moral foundations of life, then the basis for guiding concepts, such as rights, should be moral reasons, as mandated in his view of the categorical imperative. But when rights are based on the material pleasures associated with them, then rights are used to support almost any kind of behavior, including behaviors that are a threat to Kant's key moral principle, that is, the need to treat individuals as ends and not as means.

Indeed, a case could be made to support Kant's position. Originally, we associated in our culture the doctrine of rights with political liberties, with due process of law and private freedom of choice. These rights are justified by the argument that it is morally acceptable to grant rights if the latter permits citizens sufficient independence in thinking and action so that they can make judgments free from the arbitrary control of others. But today, we hear people talking about a right to see pornography, even though it depicts women made subject to death and rape. We hear people demanding a right to own a machine gun, even though these guns have no other use but to kill people. Over time, where rights are linked merely to what brings pleasure to individuals, rights become nothing more than licenses to promote individual interests at the expense of many others. And in the process, the notion that having rights includes respect for those limits and constraints that secure each person's liberty is lost.

What would Locke have said in response? Locke would have argued that, in the end, governments should be predicated upon the consent of the great majority of citizens. And the majority would, after all, have some political wisdom. Because, for Locke, majorities were constrained by the need to protect the general rights of all citizens, they would discover that, at times, they may have permitted too much freedom in certain areas. When the majority recognized this reality, they would realize the need to limit and narrow the content of rights, as reason and experience dictate. Here, the majority would recognize that, in extending rights to own machine guns and to see violent pornography, the majority would actually invade the rights of those who were harmed by these experiences. Given that the majority must provide rights to all in an equal manner, it would realize the need to pull back and to place some limits and constraints on people so that the rights of all could be protected.

But Kant would have questioned Locke's majority, wondering whether, in its quest to achieve material satisfaction, it could exercise the public use of reason. If it could not, then it would not be in a position to establish a common, universal point of view from which to overcome the impact of prejudice and self-interest on thought. But Locke would wonder how the public use of reason could be sustained if people in their ordinary lives were motivated by self-interest. Kant's answer would be that the public use of reason would be a natural by-product of civil society and the Enlightenment. Because of these cultural realities, individuals would be more and more likely, as the Enlightenment continues, to make public reasoning a part of their outlooks, even if their private lives remain, as always, dedicated to self-interest. To Locke's critique, Kant would argue that, in an enlightened age, it would not be uncommon for individuals with various prejudices of one sort or another to avoid relying upon them when discussing public issues.

Who is right here, Kant or Locke? Ordinary experience indicates elements of truth in both views. For instance, in defense of Kant, in our society today, no one publicly utters racist or anti-Semitic views on behalf of supporting one's positions without being classed as a person whose arguments lack worth. If people want to be heard and to be seriously considered by others, they will avoid certain kinds of utterances, even though they might maintain them in their private lives. Thus, on college campuses today, many administrations discourage racist speech, so students and faculty avoid it to appear enlightened. However, when alone with friends and close associates, the language of the gutter may well reappear.

On the other hand, Locke might point out that the public and private worlds easily become entangled, and the result is a situation in which individuals really have no desire to defend the rights of those whom they think are inferior because of race, religion, and so on. That is why Locke suggested the live-and-let-live option of his doctrine of toleration. Knowing that people would not be able to remove bigotry from their understanding, it is best to expect only that people will learn to tolerate those who are different from them. Hopefully, then, the rights of all will be protected, even if individuals have no respect for each other.

Now, Kant would have accepted Locke's notion of toleration, but he would have argued that toleration must be predicated on a firmer ground than just a live-and-let-live attitude. In particular, toleration could survive as a principle of conduct only when individuals were competent in the art of the public use of reason. For, in this case, individuals would learn to understand the views of others, and in the process of doing so, people would make room for them, thus displaying the civic virtue of mutual respect. Clearly, this view is in line with Spinoza's expectation, that in a democracy premised on freedom of thought, people would learn to live together on terms that sought mutual accommodations.

Rousseau, like Locke, would criticize Kant for inconsistency. Kant, like Rousseau, started off hoping for a general moral will. Indeed, all Kant was really doing in arguing that individuals should live by a law that all rational persons would accept, was giving greater specificity to Rousseau's notion of the general will. Here, in treating others as ends, we live, as for Rousseau, by a general moral will that all rational human beings would support. But owing to the inability of people to adhere to it, Kant constructed a system that allowed people to live by nonmoral motives and still achieve moral ends. Rousseau would find this approach destructive to the general will. He hoped that individuals would learn to put to the side the impact of self-interested concerns in their lives and instead promote the interests of the community as the primary objective in their lives. To this end, his social contract sought to transform people from self-seekers into citizens who make the commitment to the common good the most prominent dimension of their lives.

Kant and Rousseau would probably disagree on the possibilities of public reasoning as well. Indeed, Kant and Rousseau would likely hold different expectations as to what could be achieved by public reason. For Rousseau, public reason could not always resolve wide differences between people over major issues. As we saw in Rousseau, the kind of public reasoning that makes possible a definition of the common good could materialize only when people hold views on major issues that were, for the most part, already close to each other in substance.

Now, based upon our interpretation discussed in the last section of the implications of public reason for Kant, Kant would not want to restrict public reason as much as Rousseau did. Our view of Kant's conception of public reason suggests that his position would require him to accept that public reason might not lead to agreement on every issue. However, a virtue (which Rousseau did not see) could be gleaned from public reason for society, even in this circumstance. Kant might argue that, when public reason did not resolve differences among people, still, because people respected the process of public reason and because public reason allowed people to understand fully the views of others, people were able to live together in peace, in a setting of mutual respect.

Rousseau would question this presumption and likely say that, were Kant to hold this view, it would be acceptable to charge Kant with being overly naïve.

Rousseau would argue, in support of this position, that, where wide differences exist over major issues, there would likely be internal hostility in society and an absence of a shared commitment to uphold the common good. Rousseau hoped to avoid this outcome by advocating a situation in which differences in views and opinions, as to both quantity and intensity, could be reduced as a result of people's sharing common perspectives and values. Remember that Rousseau had hoped that peasants, a metaphor for ordinary people, would make the law, unencumbered by complex and competing ideas and ideologies.

But Kant, much like Spinoza, would certainly claim in response that this picture of life did not describe modern society well, where people would no doubt come into contact with many diverse views on many different issues. To impose a Rousseau-inspired homogeneity of outlook on this kind of pluralism, for the sake of eliminating many contesting views, would be destructive of freedom in a civil society, and this approach would deny any need for the public use of reason, promised in the new enlightened world.

Notes

1. Immanuel Kant, "What Is Enlightenment?" in *On History*, ed. Lewis White Beck (Indianapolis: Bobbs-Merrill, 1957), 6–8. Also see, Onora O'Neill, "The Public Use of Reason," *Political Theory* 14, no. 4 (November 1986): 533–34.

2. Kant, "What Is Enlightenment?" 3.

3. Immanuel Kant, *Critique of Judgment*, trans. J. H. Bernard (New York: Hafner, 1951), 136–37. See also O'Neill, "The Public Use of Reason," 543–44.

4. Kant, *Critique of Judgment*, 136.

5. Ibid., 137. Also, O'Neill, "The Public Use of Reason," 544.

6. Kant, *Critique of Judgment*, 136–37. Also, O'Neill, "The Public Use of Reason," 544–45.

7. O'Neill, "The Public Use of Reason," 541.

8. Kant, "What Is Enlightenment?" 6.

9. Immanuel Kant, *Critique of Practical Reason*, trans. Lewis White Beck (Indianapolis: Bobbs-Merrill, 1956), 72.

10. Immanuel Kant, *Groundwork of the Metaphysic of Morals*, trans. H. J. Paton (New York: Harper Torchbook, 1956), 89–91.

11. Ibid., 88. Italics are in the text.

12. Immanuel Kant, "Metaphysical Foundations of Morals," in *The Philosophy of Kant*, ed. Carl Friedrich (New York: Modern Library, 1949), 171.

13. Kant, *Groundwork of the Metaphysic of Morals*, 95. Also, Kant, "Metaphysical Foundations of Morals," 178. Here, Kant says that the main practical imperative is: "*Act so as to treat man, in your own person as well as in that of anyone else, always as an end, never merely as a means.*" Italics are in the text.

14. Immanuel Kant, *Ethical Philosophy, Part II: Metaphysical Principles of Virtue*, trans. James W. Ellington (Indianapolis: Hackett Publishing Company, 1983), 53, 82–141.

15. Immanuel Kant, "The Metaphysical Elements of the Theory of Right," in *Kant's Political Writings*, ed. Hans Reiss (Cambridge: Cambridge University Press, 1970), 136.

16. Ibid., 133. Italics are in the text.

17. Ibid., 134.

18. Ibid., 134–35.

19. Ibid., 133. Italics in text. See on this point, Patrick Riley, *Kant's Political Philosophy* (Totowa, NJ: Rowman and Littlefield, 1983), 9–17.

20. Immanuel Kant, "Idea for Universal History," in Beck, *On History*, 16.
21. Ibid., 16–17; Immanuel Kant, "Perpetual Peace," in Beck, *On History*, 113.
22. Kant, "Perpetual Peace," 112.
23. Kant, "The Metaphysical Elements of the Theory of Right," 139.
24. Ibid., 138–39. Italics are in the text.
25. Ibid., 163. Italics are in the text.
26. Kant, "Idea for a Universal History," 11–13.
27. Ibid., 15.
28. Ibid.
29. Ibid.
30. Ibid., 22.
31. Ibid., 16.
32. Ibid., 17.
33. Ibid., 18.
34. Ibid., 17–18, 21.
35. Ibid., 21–22.
36. Ibid., 21.
37. Ibid., 18–19.
38. Kant, "Perpetual Peace," 85–89.
39. Ibid., 92.
40. Ibid., 93.
41. Ibid., 94–95.
42. Ibid., 98.
43. Ibid., 101.
44. Ibid., 100–1.
45. Ibid., 100.
46. Ibid., 102.
47. Ibid., 103, 114.
48. Ibid., 103.
49. Kant, "The Metaphysical Elements of the Theory of Right," 139.
50. Ibid., 139–40. Italics are in the text.
51. Kant, "What Is Enlightenment?" 5–7, 9. Here, Kant had in mind "venerable ecclesiastics," who would submit their opinions to public testing, but his view of public reason would suggest that others engaged in public offices, as well as active citizens, should also adhere to the standards of public reason.

12

G.W.F. Hegel: Civil Society and the State

I. Introduction

In this chapter we discuss G.W.F. Hegel (1770–1831), whose *Philosophy of Right* presents an important statement on civil society. The starting point for this discussion is Hegel's critique of Immanuel Kant. Hegel believes that Kant's approach to morality represented a kind of "empty formalism." What this claim means is that Kant's depiction of his basic moral principles merely said that individuals were to act in keeping with what constitutes necessary moral duties, but, at the same time, Kant's approach to defining these duties did not clearly specify their actual content.[1] Kant's moral philosophy was an empty formalism for Hegel, then, because although Kant said that individuals were always obligated to do their duties, they were never told what precisely those duties were. Kant, of course, would have objected to Hegel's characterization of his views, and Kant would have argued that he did in fact demonstrate the concrete character of people's duties when he developed his views of civil society. The latter represents those institutions that can best realize equal liberty and by doing so carry into practice the requirement to treat each other as ends and not as means. In our view, Kant would seem to have had a good case against Hegel. However, Hegel thinks otherwise.

Thus, Hegel, in his discussion of what he calls the *ethical life*, seeks to demonstrate the precise content of the modes of conduct and required obligations that individuals are to uphold. His chief concern is to argue not only that individuals have an obligation to respect the rights of others but that, in addition, there must be institutions in place that describe the nature of the conduct that individuals must uphold to meet this objective. For Hegel, then, each person possesses a "capacity for rights," and it is the obligation of each person to respect these rights and thus to live by the imperative that says we are to "be a person and respect others as persons."[2]

II. *Phenomenology of Spirit*

The institutions for realizing this purpose are discussed in Hegel's views of both the state and civil society. Before proceeding to discuss Hegel's view of civil society, however, we stress Hegel's view that the state and society of his time represent a triumph of the highest forms of these institutions over less desirable ones. He approaches an argument to this effect initially in his *Phenomenology of Spirit*, published in 1807. This work provides a basic justification for the concepts of both civil society and the state, which we discuss in subsequent sections of this chapter.[3] His general argument is designed to demonstrate that history has followed a course that clearly shows that the highest and best form of society and state is one that upholds the rights of each citizen in a regime characterized by a representative government with strong leadership in the executive branch.

In the *Phenomenology of Spirit*, Hegel illustrates the different levels of human understanding, starting at the level of experience, as nothing more than raw sense perceptions and moving from there to attain full knowledge of the rational and moral content of human experience. Moreover, for Hegel, moral awareness evolves across history, starting with notions of society that lack moral completeness and concluding, at the "end of history," with a comprehensive understanding both of the nature of morality and of the material structures necessary to realize it. For Hegel, history ended in 1806, when humankind reached a point beyond which further moral progress was not possible. At the end of history, the ideals of liberty and equality were spread throughout the world, and these ideas were embodied in the modern state and, in particular, the modern civil society that Hegel describes.[4]

Space permits only a brief summary of Hegel's pathway to knowledge of Spirit (or the attainment of complete moral awareness) in the *Phenomenology of Spirit*. In the first stages of awareness, called *sense-certainty*, a person's self-understanding is merely that of raw sense perception of the world, or a "knowledge of the immediate or of what simply *is*."[5] In this phase, one points out the characteristics of objects of perception, as a "this Now" or a "this Here." But one is unable to integrate the perceived features into a unified form and thus constitute the whole object of which each of the perceived features is an essential part. I may see "this branch" and "this leaf," but I lack the conceptual ability, at this point, to derive from these experiences the statement that says, "this tree."[6]

The next level of awareness is that of self-consciousness. Here, we understand ourselves to be independent, particular persons, possessing an identity that makes ourselves distinguishable from other people. At the earliest phases of self-consciousness, we do not possess a full knowledge of Spirit or of the moral concepts that should govern life, but still the existence of self-awareness signals that such knowledge "lies ahead."[7] In this stage, then, we leave behind a life defined in terms of an experience charted as the here and now, and we begin to move to the higher level of self-conscious moral understanding. "It is in self-consciousness, in the Notion of Spirit, that consciousness first finds its turning point, where it leaves behind it the colourful show of the sensuous here-and-now . . . and steps out into the spiritual daylight of the present."[8]

Self-consciousness begins to manifest its full moral character in what Hegel depicts as the "first man." The discussion of the latter is akin to the description of the state of nature, as provided earlier in chapters on Thomas Hobbes, John Locke, and Jean-Jacques Rousseau. As we pointed out in previous chapters, the state of nature is a description of what is presumed to be the condition of people prior to formal society, and thus the conception of the "first man" provides a picture of human character in its earliest phases. For Hegel, individuals in this category need to be "recognized" by others and to receive from others acceptance of themselves as human beings.[9] In seeking recognition from others, people are shown to want more than just satisfaction of essential desires, such as the need for food, shelter, or sustained life. In addition, for Hegel, people want others to accord worth and significance to their lives, what Hegel refers to as recognition. Individuals could not become aware of themselves as particular persons, unless others accord them recognition or worth as particular people.[10] But at this point in history, when the main experience is that of the "first man," destructive relationships ensue. Why is this? For Hegel, whereas each person seeks recognition from others, it is natural for a person to try to get recognition from others without returning it to others. This situation culminates in strife, reminiscent of Hobbes's state of nature, in which individuals seek to force others to accord themselves the worth they seek from others, while not according similar respect for the worth of others.[11]

Hegel's account of this experience embodies his view of his often-cited conflict between master and slave. For Hegel, in a setting such as a Hobbesian state of nature in which each person seeks to gain from others recognition without returning it, those who are the victors, the masters, subordinate the others and make them into slaves. Here, the masters permit the slaves to live, but only to serve the masters as slaves. Indeed, this situation creates the relationship of master and slave, where the slave is reduced to a frightened animal, without dignity or humanity. But this experience is self-defeating, and it leaves both the master and the slave unhappy.[12] For the master finds himself receiving recognition from a slave for whom the master has no respect. Consequently, the master is recognized by someone that cannot really accord him the regard he demands. Similarly, in this relationship, the slave cannot be happy either, for he is never recognized as a real human being but only as a device the master uses for his own ends.[13]

The slave's experience ultimately becomes the basis for his freedom and for the creation of a civil society based on the commitment to full rights for all. How does this event take place? Initially, the slave finds himself working for the master and, through this work, providing for the master's satisfaction. Here, the slave's motive for working is fear of the master. Later in history, however, the slave develops a capacity to perform work from motives that give work value, motives such as a sense of responsibility. In developing these motives, the slave realizes that he is not just a tool of the master but a real human being. His evolution as a human proceeds further when he realizes that he is capable of creative work, which leads to his inventing technologies that allow him to alter the external world. This experience enables him to envision a society in which he overcomes his fear of the master and claims his freedom. Still, since the slave is bound to his master, he is not yet free. The slave is at a stage at which he can only yearn for freedom and envision what life would be like were he to have it.[14]

The slave develops a philosophy that speaks to his desire for freedom, and the most important of these is Christianity. For Hegel, the latter is a way of thinking that ultimately leads to building a civil society based on the idea of providing liberty to all. How does this event take place? Christianity is based on the view that all people have a capacity to make moral choices. Thus, to be free is to be in a position to choose morality over evil. With their freedom, then, individuals can make morality the basis for their lives. However, this objective for the Christian cannot be realized fully in life on earth but only in the life beyond this world, or in God's Paradise. Thus, whereas Christianity has the correct understanding of freedom, it tells people not to expect it in this life. For Hegel, with the progress of humankind in history, a civil society emerges that permits people to realize the Christian moral vision in *this* life. Civil society is a setting in which the quest for freedom materializes in the possibility of *mutual recognition*, or shared respect for the rights of all people.[15] This experience is discussed in the *Philosophy of Right*, in which Hegel describes the relationship of the state to civil society.

III. Civil Society

But what is a civil society, and how does it achieve mutual recognition? For Hegel, a civil society is viewed as a separate sphere of interests existing outside the state, and thus a civil society is conceived as a "battlefield where everyone's individual private interest meets everyone else's." Owing to this viewpoint, a civil society represents a sphere of life that is hostile to the state and its commitment to promote a "higher outlook," or conception of the common good.[16] In this view, the civil society experience suggests a setting in which individuals pursue their self-interests, often without regard for obligations and duties that are considered essential for protecting the rights that all members are to be accorded. The state must work to overcome the destructive features of these tendencies toward self-interest to make possible an atmosphere of civic virtue and a concomitant support for the common good, including respect for the rights of others.

What are the features of modern life that make civil society into a "battle-field" of competing interests, and how is civil society to rise above this situation to create a community in which mutual respect for rights is possible?

We discuss the first part of this question in the next several paragraphs, and the discussion of both the roles of corporations and the state addresses the second part of this question.

In the first place, people are both workers and consumers of the products of others' work. Take the latter dimension first. For Hegel, unlike for Marx, as we will see later, the main characteristic of individuals in civil society is not that they are commodities. As commodities, people are bought and sold by more powerful people who seek to exploit the labor power of the less powerful. But for Hegel, individuals are driven by desires to create a variety of new needs, each of which they hope to satisfy in the marketplace through the purchase of goods.

Why do needs proliferate? People, says Hegel, hold to a "demand for equality of satisfaction with others." In emulating each other as consumers, individuals create a sense of equality among themselves. Furthermore, in this context, where everyone manifests similar desires to consume goods, there is always a need to be different from the rest, and this need to be distinctive is expressed when individuals demand to own distinctive goods. Thus, in this setting, there is an ongoing and continual expansion of needs, as individuals develop appetites that must be satisfied with the development of new products.[17] Hegel, in discussing the proliferation of needs, certainly has in mind the modern market setting, where people hope to make enough money to satisfy their desires, and where people hope to find ways to satisfy the many desires others may be engendered to have, as a means of making money. The American shopping center, filled with diverse brand names and styles, is emblematic of what Hegel means.

We provide for our needs through *work*. It is work that produces the goods that people consume and, in the process, use to satisfy basic needs.[18] The work each person performs is part of a larger work process or division of labor. This system allows the work of each worker to be made "less complex," and thus each worker's tasks are easier to perform. By virtue of this fact, each worker's overall output is increased. Here, individuals find themselves in mutually dependent relationships, contributing to the larger task of producing as efficiently as possible the various goods that will satisfy the various needs that members of the society have. For Hegel, the division of labor symbolizes "everywhere the dependence of men on one another and their reciprocal relation in the satisfaction of their other needs."[19] Moreover, as time goes on and as work becomes more and more defined in terms of a division of labor, the work becomes so mechanical and routine that machines can replace individuals.[20]

Undergirding the entire market environment of consumption and work is a civil society built upon class divisions. There is an agricultural class, a business class, and a class of civil servants. The agricultural class consists of the landowners whose income derives from farming activities. Their cohesion as a class is located in that which secures their independence in society, in particular, the social importance and prominence society accords certain families and their property holdings. The business class constructs the system of work that produces the goods that make the attainment of needs possible. Included in this group are the mass production workers and the craftsmen, who work in the system set up by the businessmen to produce goods, and those types of businessmen who are engaged in the art of exchange and trade of manufactured goods. Naturally, this group is interested in finding ways to make financial gains or profits a primary objective of their endeavors. The class of educated, middle-class civil servants makes up the executive bureaucracy, whose main task is to implement the law in a fair and objective way, and thus these individuals are called the "universal class" because they are presumed capable of rising above self-interest.[21]

Civil society in this setting is characterized by many factors. Included among them is the need of individuals to make a living, the hope of gaining ownership of the resources with which to fulfill desires, the efficient organization of work, and the class structure of society. These factors, when taken together, turn civil society into a setting characterized by competing interests, without regard for the common good. How are these competing interests to be transcended so that the interests of one class alone, say, the business class, is not made predominant, thus denying any importance to the needs of other groups in society? To achieve this end, Hegel turns to a discussion of *corporations*.[22]

Corporations are associations of workers and businessmen, and they are designed to achieve some productive end in society. In this regard, then, each corporation performs an important type of work, which is necessary to the well-being of society. Moreover, each corporation would, as Hegel says, "look after its own interests within its own sphere."[23] Thus, there could be corporations for various types of manufacturing activities, say (to use modern examples), making steel or electrical equipment, and each of these corporations would have a monopoly of control over the production of the products associated with its own sphere of activity. Further, these corporations, as they operate in their own spheres, might become competitors with each other. For instance, the interests of the electrical corporation might conflict with those of steel, as the former hoped for a reduced steel price so that electrical equipment would become less costly. But because Hegel says the corporations are subject to the "surveillance of the public authority," it is the case that their activities would be regulated by the state.[24] Conflicts could be mediated in the name of the general welfare of the whole society. Given this possibility, the state would have as one of its main tasks that of coordinating the activities of the corporations, so that each could, as it contributed to its own good, contribute to the common good as well.

Part of that larger good would be to provide individuals with useful and productive employment. In the corporation, which becomes a "second family" to individuals, they are given the training needed to learn the skill they are to perform, and, in addition, they are monitored so that they continue to maintain a high level of competence. Moreover, in exchange for their work, individuals are guaranteed a suitable livelihood. Also, as members of a corporation, in good standing, individuals are provided in the eyes of the world with public recognition, or, as Hegel says, with the evidence that they are "somebody," and that they belong "to a whole which is itself an organ of the entire society."[25]

Further, the pursuit of recognition seems to indicate that unless one can perform work well and thus be a member in good standing of a corporation, one might not even be permitted to enjoy, to his or her fullness, the same rights guaranteed to all persons. "Unless he is a member of an authorized Corporation, . . . an individual is without rank or dignity, his isolation reduces his business to mere self-seeking, and his livelihood and satisfaction become insecure."[26] Although not arguing here that people without membership in a corporation should have their rights taken from them, Hegel seems to indicate that whatever rights such people might have would have much less value than the rights of people enjoying full membership in a corporation.

Given this view, then, people in professions that are highly esteemed would certainly have more respectability than would people without jobs or what we and Hegel would call a "day laborers" people who engage in casual as opposed to long-term career employment.[27] Day laborers would have the same rights as others, but owing to their lowly position in society, these rights would give them much less leverage in society to get for themselves what those rights are said to guarantee. Thus, day laborers might be able to exercise the right of free speech, but who would listen to them? They might have access to health care, but would it be as good as that provided the more respectable members of society?

The likely failure to provide full worth to the rights of all those who fall outside the sphere of the corporations appears as well in Hegel's treatment of the poor. For Hegel, a prosperous economy emphasizes jobs for those with the skills that a society most needs. But, at the same time, there will not be jobs for those who do not have the requisite skills.[28] Consequently, there is a "large mass of people [who] falls below a certain subsistence level." What should be done for them? Hegel does not advocate that the wealthy or charities should provide the poor with direct cash payments. He takes this position because he believes that if the poor are given direct welfare assistance they would not be encouraged to work. And in the absence of work, they could not gain for themselves what, for Hegel, is a main principle of a civil society: namely, a sense of self-respect and independence.[29]

Finally, Hegel does not think the state should create work for the unemployed because this action would inflate the "volume of production," producing more goods than society can afford. And this situation would only cause growing unemployment, as many would be laid off in the face of a weakening demand for goods. It follows for Hegel that a free market–oriented civil society is often not able to keep people from falling into poverty and becoming part of the "rabble," or those individuals who, owing to their poverty, have no regard for basic moral values such as right, wrong, and self-respect.[30] Hegel's state is to enter civil society and regulate conflicts regarding work, class, production, and consumption. But it is never clear that the state should be concerned to protect the interests and needs of the poor.

IV. The State and Civic Virtue

For Hegel, the state thus stands above the particular interests that make up a civil society and provides a basis for moving society toward a concept of the common welfare. Once again, it is worth restating that, for Hegel, the state must not be confused with "civil society." In the latter, individuals manifest particular interests, each of which expresses a person's conception of personal freedom. Were individuals to identify themselves exclusively with the interests they hold as members of civil society, they would think their membership in the state was "optional" and largely predicated upon whether the state would support their particular interests. But for Hegel, each person, as part of what it means to live a fully civilized life, is destined to live his or her life in keeping with universally valid and binding notions of obligation. The state that embodies these obligations is thus not optional, but a necessary fact of any fully flourishing human life.[31]

Thus, Hegel does not predicate the authority of the state upon a notion of the consent of various interests in society to accept the state's authority. The state's authority rests upon the understanding that there is a rational truth that exists independently of the various interests in society and that the state exists as an autonomous agency in relation to these interests, with the sole purpose of promoting this truth.[32]

Hegel's view of the state differs significantly from those we have studied thus far. Locke's state, because it emanates from the consent of the citizens, is conceived as representing the different interests in society. For Locke, in ways not dissimilar from Benedict Spinoza, it would not be possible to create a state separate and distinct from the society, since the state, as a representative of the majority, is an embodiment of the various interests that constitute society. Kant's state is closer to Locke's state, thus it is predicated upon the need to support the basic interests of society as well, even as it expects these interests to approach issues from the standpoint of public reason.

Hobbes would seem to define a state as that which contained both Lockean and Hegelian aspects. Like Locke, Hobbes's state evolved from consent, and thus it too had to advance the common good of society. But for Hobbes, one of the expectations that people in society wanted to advance through their consent was the need for a strong unitary or non-separation-of-powers state. Such a state was needed to stand above competing interests to resolve conflicts and to uphold rights. As a result, Hobbes described a state that could stand outside and be independent of competing interests for the purpose of achieving stability. Hobbes's state, then, would take on a Hegelian character. In consequence, Hobbes would be more likely than Locke and Kant to accept Hegel's separation of the state from "civil society."

Finally, Rousseau probably would not accept Hegel's separation of the state and society. The state, its purposes and goals, were always associated with the citizen's conception of the general good. On the other hand, Rousseau was with Hegel in not wanting society filled merely with a variety of self-interest-oriented groups who had little or no concern for the common good. Were it not possible to achieve a general will in society among the different interests, Rousseau might have found Hegel's separation of the state and civil society appealing, as a way to define and then impose the general will onto an otherwise unruly and interest-contentious society.

Who is right in these matters, Hegel or the others? In general, it would seem that a state in a civil society contains elements of both views, each of which coexists with the other. In this case, the state in a civil society is defined neither in exclusively Hegelian terms, nor in exclusively Lockean terms. For, in the first place, there is no question that the state is, in some sense, a product of the different interests that constitute the society over which it has authority. Thus, it is not possible to separate the state completely from the sphere of civil society as Hegel tried to do. But on the other hand, the state must exercise independent powers of judgment on behalf of those critical and fundamentally important principles that rational people uphold. In this role, the state must, at times, stand apart from society, as depicted by Hobbes and Hegel. Even for Locke the state was to be a neutral umpire between competing interests, all in the name of protecting the rights of each citizen.

Returning to Hegel's view of the state, when the state can provide the concept of the common welfare, then civil society becomes transformed from a milieu of conflicting interests into a setting in which the diverse groups are able to cooperate for the achievement of long-term, shared interests. In this context, Hegel expects that all members of society would contribute to the common welfare, and, if they would, then instead of remaining as competing interests, they would become integrated into a community, working toward the same goals. For Hegel, even as individuals have private interests, they are still able to consider themselves as contributing members of a community.

How is Hegel's state arranged to achieve this objective? The modern state is predicated upon its *constitution*, which consists of both the basic, universally rational principles that define the state's nature and the institutions that carry these principles into practice.[33] This means that the principles that guide the state are not so much the product of social consensus among different groups but rather manifest the universal truths of reason, which should always be followed. First, we discuss the main principles upon which the state rests.

In general, the modern state is committed to securing the basic rights of each individual. A right helps to secure a person's freedom to make fundamental choices about the way he or she wishes to live. But at the same time, rights are seen as existing in a context in which individuals also must recognize basic duties. These duties must be upheld by all as a condition for securing the rights of all citizens. Duties and rights are bound together, and both are "united in one and the same relation."[34] Individuals have particular interests, and they use their rights to pursue them, but in doing so, they should uphold all the norms associated with the duties considered to be universally binding on all citizens. Indeed, an individual realizes that it is in upholding his duties while pursuing his interests that he becomes a member in good standing of community with his rights fully protected. Hegel says:

> *the isolated individual, so far as his duties are concerned, is in subjection; but as a member of civil society he finds in fulfilling his duties to it*

protection of his person and property, regard for his private welfare, the satisfaction of the depths of his being, the consciousness and feeling of himself as a member of the whole; and, in so far as he completely fulfills his duties by performing tasks and services for the state, he is upheld and preserved.[35]

The institutions of the state that carry into practice the protection of both rights and duties are organized into three divisions: the crown, the executive, and the legislature.[36] At the apex of Hegel's state is the *monarch*. Hegel believes that constitutional monarchy is "the achievement of the modern world."[37] The monarch symbolizes the state's commitment both to its general principles and to the institutions that can best put them into practice. Now, the idea of monarchy as developed here is not an absolutist one, and, indeed, it is clear that the monarch is viewed as sharing responsibility for ruling with others. Hegel's discussion of the relationship between the monarch and the other elements of government helps show how the sharing of responsibility takes place. How Hegel avoids falling into monarchical absolutism is an important topic for a state committed, as Hegel's state is, to securing basic rights for all. This topic is doubly significant given that the monarch is not an elective office but a hereditary one.[38]

The monarch, for Hegel, is responsible for initiating a political deliberation, or what we have already referred to in discussing Kant as a form of *public reason*. What is the objective of public reason for Hegel? Public reason includes consideration of all points of view with respect to various issues. The hope in taking this approach is to achieve an agreement on those issues that preserves a societal commitment to the universal principles of the constitution, in particular, the need to protect the rights of all, while making clear the duties associated with this endeavor.

Thus, the monarch as the person to whom "ultimate decisions belong"[39] demands that any particular policy be one that carries forward and in no way violates the basic principles of the constitution. Here, the crown determines that the particular policies always be subsumed under the "universal." This means that the monarch and his council can initiate discussions about policy, making suggestions about "the current affairs of state or the legal provisions required to meet existing needs."[40] The monarch will consider the needs of the society, the state of existing law as it pertains to these needs, and suggest certain policy initiatives that the society should consider. Throughout, the monarch's intention is to remind members of society to guide their thoughts about an issue so that particular conceptions of interest do not supersede the importance of solutions that carry forth and embody the universal principles of the constitution.

Further, the monarch's decisions are carried out by the executive agency of government, which includes the judiciary and the police, as well as the civil servant class. The latter, as members of the middle class, as we see next, oversee the activities of the corporations to ensure that the latter carry out their objectives in keeping with the general principles that the constitution establishes and the monarch maintains. The function of the executive is to "make the universal interest [the notion of the common good] authoritative over its [civil society's] particular aims."[41] The executive always has the task of ensuring that the main purpose of the monarch, the commitment to promoting the same basic rights and duties, is always upheld. The way Hegel describes the executive agency of government suggests that it is a wing or branch of the crown, always obligated to uphold in its activities the basic principles that the crown embodies and symbolizes to the nation. Indeed, Hegel says that key elements of the executive branch report to top executive officials who are in "direct contact with the monarch."[42] These "key elements" are the civil servants who oversee the corporations and the advisory officials who give advice to the executive on how to implement or interpret policies so that they embody the commitment to securing basic rights and duties.

In the remaining part of this section, we discuss Hegel's view of public reason, which largely occurs between the monarch and the legislature. As an illustration of how public reasoning to achieve a rational consensus takes place, we use the example of health care. The monarch might suggest, after reviewing with his council the needs of the society and its existing laws with respect to them, that the country needs a policy on health care. In discussing health care, the monarch would provide a version of the commitment to equal rights for all that would be relevant to the health care arena. He might, for instance, suggest that whatever policy is adopted, it should be one that makes possible universal coverage for all citizens. Then, the monarch would, upon reviewing existing laws and traditions on the subject, suggest certain limits that should not be abridged. For instance, if protecting the private choice of doctors seems to be essential, he would point out the need for doing so in any plan that was finally accepted. The monarch might even suggest possible plans that would work to achieve universal coverage.

The actual decision, however, about how best to attain the principle of universal coverage would rest with the legislature. In doing so, the legislature would seek to realize the basic "well-being and happiness" of the citizens by defining the specific rights each is to have with respect to the policies in question, as in this case with health care. At the same time, the legislature would define for citizens the basic duties they must uphold as a condition of achieving these rights. Hegel refers to these duties as the "services to be extracted from people," or, using other terms, he refers to what people must contribute financially to receive the rights accorded them. Thus, in our example, included in the list of citizen duties is a requirement to pay the necessary costs of the health care rights that are provided to people.[43] The legislature would pursue the cost issue by allowing the different views of the society on the matter to be articulated, and the hope would be that a consensus would be reached on what tax policy would best be able to realize the principle of universal coverage.

To accomplish this task, the legislature, also called the *Estates*, has two houses, each representing a different class found in civil society.[44] The upper house consists of the agricultural class, and the lower, the corporations. Hegel believes that the "Estates are a guarantee of the general welfare and public freedom."[45] The classes in the legislature, over time, gain experience in government, and they understand the needs of the ordinary people and the problems of the executive in governing corporations. Indeed, the classes in the legislature are most likely to anticipate "public criticism," from the "Many" before it occurs, and thus they are able to suggest policies that avert unnecessary conflict.[46]

The upper house contains members of agriculture who are able to maintain their detachment and independence because their wealth is not affected by the ups and downs of the business cycle or by the "quest for profit" so near and dear to the businessman. Another reason for this class's independence is that it is not tied to the state's financial base. Indeed, its inheritance rights guarantee the agricultural class's place in society, and thus they do not have to predicate their political views on the need to seek favor either from the public or from the executive class.[47] Further, Hegel envisioned members of this class being able to represent themselves in person in the legislature.[48] Since this class never has to run for office, they will be free from having to engage in political gamesmanship. Owing to their detachment, then, they would be able to carry out one of the chief functions of the legislature by acting as mediators between the monarch and the other interests of civil society.[49] With respect to health care, then, this class might be able to work out compromises between the crown, for instance, who wished to move toward a form of state-sponsored medical care and those interested in civil society, who wanted to establish a system of private care. As a result of the agricultural class's effort, there would be "less chance" that the other classes of civil society would be in "direct opposition" to the monarch or to the executive, thus avoiding government stalemate or societal warfare.[50]

The lower house is composed of deputies, or representatives, from the various communities, in particular, the corporations. Hegel sees this part of the government as the "fluctuating" element because corporations are more affected by changes in the external or economic circumstances than are people engaged in agriculture. The deputies in the lower house, then, are to represent "the special needs, difficulties, and particular interests" of the corporations.[51] The members of this branch would be more in tune with the day-to-day problems corporations face as they perform their functions in society. In fashioning legislation, in this case a health care plan, the lower house would hope to make certain that the general principle, universal coverage, could be construed in such a way as to respect the needs of corporations. Indeed, this understanding might lead to the creation of a plan neither proposed by the monarch nor initially acceptable to the other house. But owing to the discussion that would occur about the proposed plan, over time, both the other house and the monarch might, in the end, make needed concessions.

The crown can "summon" a corporation to send a representative to the lower house, and when this happens the corporation in question elects a deputy for this purpose.[52] Each corporation, then, elects its own members to represent it. Hegel emphasizes that each of the "essential spheres" in a civil society should have a representative to represent its respective interests. Hegel presumes that each person's political commitments and concerns would be tied directly to the particular communities in which he works. To think of himself as isolated from those communities during political deliberation would be to deny a reality central to his identity.[53]

Hegel hopes that permitting the different spheres of civil society to be represented in this way would not lead to social fragmentation, however. How is this possible? As we saw, the corporations manage the day-to-day work needs of the society and operate within the context of the "higher outlook" that the state defines. This objective is achieved because the heads of the corporations are chosen by a combination of popular elections and certification by those in executive authority. Moreover, those who run the corporations do so under the guidance of the civil servants in the executive branch. Presumably, then, the civil servants, who make up the executive branch as educated, professional bureaucrats, would oversee the corporations and make certain that, during the course of achieving particular commercial and business objectives, the corporations adhered to the policies that the state establishes.[54] In consequence, the officials and members of corporations, aware of the presence and watchful eye of the state officials, become oriented to uphold the policies of the state as they carried out the work of the corporation. Any tendency, then, for the corporation to move off in its own direction, defying public directives, is thus severely limited. Indeed, Hegel says that "the corporation mind . . . is . . . inwardly converted into the mind of the state," and this experience is the "secret of patriotism."[55]

Thus, when corporations enter the legislature, they do so not just to promote a narrow conception of the public good but to promote a conception of the public good that embodies the full commitment to realize the policies and initiatives of the monarch. Here, even if the experience of corporate life is more directed to particular interests because the corporation is part of the larger community that the policies of the state governs, individuals in espousing corporate interests are more likely to be cognizant of the need to define them in ways that promote the interests of the community, also. Clearly, corporations would then practice as well as teach civic virtue or the need to promote the common welfare.

In this context, each class in the legislature must contribute "something peculiarly its own to the work of deliberation,"[56] and the hope of this enterprise is the creation of a consensus that embodies the state's main principle to secure the rights for all, within a setting of respect for the associated duties. Here, the policy that is developed on health care would carry into practice the main rational principle, the need for universal coverage, which the monarch would articulate at the beginning of the policy discussion.

The great tragedy of modern politics for Hegel is that it often takes place outside the type of public reasoning just described. Public opinion, for Hegel, suggests a tendency of people too often to promote their own private and personal views, devoid of a concern for the rational principles that should ground public decisions about public matters. Hegel says that "to be independent of public opinion is the first formal condition of achieving anything great or rational whether in life or in science."[57]

Hegel's view of public opinion brings to the forefront his commitment to secure the civic virtue of mutual respect in a civil society by making possible the prospect of mutual recognition. Mutual recognition could be achieved in a variety of ways. In the first place, recognition arises from an effort to protect the rights of each person. Also, recognition arises from a public deliberation in which major public issues would be decided in a setting committed both to shared rational principles and to a willingness to listen to diverse views in determining how best to put these principles into practice.

V. Response and Rejoinder

Hobbes, Spinoza, and Locke would probably claim that Hegel's approach to protecting individual freedom fails because Hegel's view of corporations places individuals into groups that shape and define the identity of each individual. To the extent that individuals become dependent upon corporations, they would lose the independence they must have if they are to define a way of life separate from the path prescribed by the norms of group life. Hegel would no doubt answer that his view of the state and corporations, designed as it is to limit and to constrain the private interest orientation of civil society, intends to restore civic virtue to civil society. Without compliance with the norms of civic virtue that the corporations and the state teach, civil society would be overrun by the self-serving, selfish conduct of those who seek, within the market setting of civil society, their own private interests. A civil society, for Hegel, is not just a setting for individuals to accumulate as much as they can, but it is a context that locates each individual in a community that is grounded in the norms of civic virtue.

Moreover, Hegel could maintain that, in this setting, the great civic virtue of mutual respect, or what Hegel calls *mutual recognition*, would become a mainstay of life. Indeed, in the context of public reason that Hegel devises, individuals of different viewpoints would come to understand and to make room for one another. Self-interest considerations would not become an obstacle to achieving respect for diversity. If this is the case, then, Hegel could argue that, by promoting the civic virtue of mutual respect, his view of civil society avoids the tyrannous implications that others might associate with it.

Rousseau would have accepted the importance of civic virtue to achieving freedom, but he would have questioned Hegel's approach to achieving civic virtue. For Rousseau, Hegel would have failed to define civic virtue in terms of a general will that all members of the society would be able to uphold. And the reason that this was the case for Rousseau was that Hegel did not have a view of citizenship that would ensure full participation to all members in determining the common good. Hegel's system of representation from the various classes would have for Rousseau permitted only a few to make the decisions for all, and instead of a general will emerging from this activity, only a particular will would emerge, and this will would be imposed on the rest. Hegel would respond to this criticism by arguing that the general will and Rousseau's concept of participation were abstractions. To give real substance to either of these terms, it is necessary to define the institutional setting in which both emerge. And that is what he, Hegel, tried to do.

It must be remembered, as pointed out at the beginning of this chapter, that Hegel is convinced that, over time and across history, human progress followed a path that made possible a rational social and political order. This order embodied in the concrete institutions and practices the key moral and ethical norms that secured the conditions of real freedom. As he states in the *Philosophy of Right*, "What is rational is actual and what is actual is rational."[58] This means that, at the advanced stages of history, and, in particular, during the period that encompassed Hegel's life, the material circumstances of day-to-day life embody the concepts and practices necessary for a rational social order that secures the rights of each individual.

Now, there are those who, like Alexandre Kojève, claim that Hegel is, in the main, correct when he argues that, in 1806, history had come to an end, with the emergence of the modern state and civil society. This setting makes possible mutual recognition, or the shared and reciprocal provision of basic rights. A person becomes, for Kojève, "truly human – that is, [an] individual" only to the extent that he or she is "recognized" as a citizen of a modern state dedicated to securing the liberty of each person. For Kojève, then, the reason history is completed at this point is that the fully developed state, which makes possible full liberty and equality for all, presents a condition that all humankind would accept. Indeed, no reasonable individual would "be tempted to negate" this condition and thus attempt "to create something new in its place."[59]

But others would question Kojève's view. In the first place, Kant would wonder whether Hegel had properly conceptualized the end of history because Hegel did not embrace Kant's view of a peaceful federation of civil societies. Hegel, ever the realist in international matters, scoffs at this idea because he believes Kant's idea presupposed an underlying basis for accord among states. But attaining such accord is fraught with many difficulties for Hegel. Indeed, nations follow their own interests, and they are often prone to settle their differences by war and not by resorting to Kant's league of nations.[60] Kant would respond by saying that Hegel's view of history, in that it makes continued war necessary and likely among civil societies, demonstrated an underdeveloped view of what a civil society is. For Kant, a civil society could not achieve freedom and rights in a setting characterized by a constant commitment to war-related activities. In this contest, there would be insufficient attention to education, and the state would become so committed to war that it would lose interest in securing the rights citizens demand.

Francis Fukuyama also takes issue with Kojève's support for Hegel's end-of-history view. For, in the first place, inequality remains in today's civil society. A major source of continuing inequality today arises from differences in cultural circumstances. Those who are part of an underclass culture, which includes the absence of suitable home environments to prepare people to perform well in society, must inevitably suffer from having to live in social conditions that make them unable to take advantage of educational opportunities. And in a society in which status depends largely upon educational attainment, an underclass culture works only to continue to maintain the underclass in a situation of perpetual inequality. In consequence, achieving the end of history and, by doing so, providing full legal equality as well as economic opportunity to the underclass will make little difference in the lives of underclass people if they cannot overcome the cultural obstacles that prevent them from using these opportunities fully. But for Fukuyama, "no one has solved the problem of 'creating culture' – that is, of regenerating internalized moral values, as a matter of public policy." Thus, while the principle of equality of opportunity has been established in the United States, it has yet to be fully implemented throughout the society, and the prospect of its happening remains problematic.[61]

Whereas those who argue for mutual recognition of each other's rights are disappointed by its lack of attainment and thus use this fact to demonstrate that we have not reached the end of history, others will question whether mutual recognition is a good thing to have in the first place. For instance, Fukuyama argues, following Friedrich Nietzsche (whom we discuss in Chapter 17), that the ethos of mutual recognition ends in making everyone content with equality of conditions. But what of those who do not see themselves as equal to others and who, in consequence, demand special privileges from the rest of society? Here, there are always some people who strive to be superior to others and who create things of lasting value and importance to society, things such as "great symphonies, paintings, novels, ethical codes, or political systems."[62]

But in a democratic civil society, where equality is the norm, the actions of the few who seek to leave a lasting impact on society are always stifled. Why is this? A main value of a democratic civil society is toleration, which suggests that we should learn to live and let live and to see all ways of life as basically equal in worth, with no way of life better than any other. The best way to achieve this objective is to diminish the importance of those with superior talent, ability, or vision and to concentrate only upon common, everyday needs, such as those having to do with ensuring our material and physical comforts. Here, the focus is to make everyone as materially satisfied as possible and eliminate as much physical suffering as is feasible. This attitude means that there is a preoccupation in civil societies with achieving material happiness and with allowing people to be successful in the market setting, where they compete for the variety of goods provided there. Such an environment leaves little room for the individual who is unique and different and through whose efforts important contributions to culture are made.[63]

Thus, in this environment, how can there be the contributions of greatness, such as are found in new philosophies, new forms of politics, or new styles of art?[64] For writers such as Nietzsche, Hegel's "end of history" is associated, then, not with a great roar of approval but with a yawn, as many find themselves bored by the absence of anything majestic and enduring.

Notes

1. G. W. F. Hegel, *Hegel's Philosophy of Right*, trans. T. M. Knox (Oxford: Oxford University Press, 1952), 89–90, Para. 135. Also see Peter J. Steinberger, *Logic and Politics: Hegel's Philosophy of Right* (New Haven: Yale University Press, 1988), 149–50.
2. Hegel, *Hegel's Philosophy of Right*, 37, Para. 36.
3. G. W. F. Hegel, *Phenomenology of Spirit*, trans. A. V. Miller with analysis of text by J. N. Findlay (Oxford: Clarendon Press, 1977). Our discussion follows, in part, the excellent synopsis of Findlay's argument, "Foreword," v–xxx.
4. In discussing this aspect of Hegel, we rely upon Francis Fukuyama's discussion of Alexandre Kojève's view of Hegel in Fukuyama's *The End of History and the Last Man* (New York: The Free Press, 1992), 66–67.
5. Hegel, *Phenomenology of Spirit*, 58, Para. 90. Italics in text.
6. J. N. Findlay, "Foreword," in Hegel, *Phenomenology of Spirit*, xvi.
7. Hegel, *Phenomenology of Spirit*, 110, Para. 177.
8. Ibid., 110–11, Para. 177.
9. Fukuyama, *The End of History and the Last Man*, 146. The latter uses the term "first man." See also Charles Taylor, *Hegel* (Cambridge: Cambridge University Press, 1975), 152–53.
10. Fukuyama, *The End of History and the Last Man*, 146–47.
11. Ibid., 147; Taylor, *Hegel*, 153.
12. Fukuyama, *The End of History and the Last Man*, 192–93; Taylor, *Hegel*, 154.
13. Ibid.
14. Fukuyama, *The End of History and the Last Man*, 194–95.
15. Ibid., 196–98.
16. Hegel, *Hegel's Philosophy of Right*, 189, Para. 289.
17. Ibid., 127–28, Para. 193.
18. Ibid., 128–29, Para. 196.
19. Ibid., 129, Para. 198.
20. Ibid.
21. Ibid., 131–32, Para. 203–5.
22. Ibid., 152–55, Para. 250–56.
23. Ibid., 152, Para. 252, 152, Para. 250–51.
24. Ibid.
25. Ibid., 153, Para. 253, 252.
26. Ibid.
27. Ibid., Para. 252.
28. Ibid., 149–50, Para. 243, 153, Para. 253, 153, Para. 252.
29. Ibid., 150, Para. 244–45.
30. Ibid.
31. Ibid., 156, Para. 258.
32. Ibid., 157, Para. 258.
33. Ibid., 174, Para. 272.
34. Ibid., 161, Para. 261.
35. Ibid., 162, Para. 261. Italics are in the text.
36. Ibid., 176, Para. 273.
37. Ibid., 176, Para. 272.
38. Ibid., 185, Para. 281.
39. Ibid., 195, Para. 300.
40. Ibid., 187, Para. 283.
41. Ibid., 188–89, Para. 287, 189, Para. 289, 193, Para. 297.
42. Ibid., 189, Para. 289.
43. Ibid., 194, Para. 299.

44. Ibid., 203, Para. 312–13.
45. Ibid., 196, Para. 301, 198, Para. 303.
46. Ibid., 197, Para. 302.
47. Ibid., 199, Para. 306.
48. Ibid., 199, Para. 307, 200, Para. 308.
49. Ibid., 197, Para. 302. See also Knox's note, p. 373, Sect. 312.
50. Ibid., 203, Para. 312–13.
51. Ibid., 202, Para. 311, 200, Para. 308.
52. Ibid., 200, Para. 308, 201, Para. 309, 202, Para. 311.
53. Ibid., 202, Para. 311, 198, Para. 303.
54. Ibid., 189, Para. 288–89.
55. Ibid.
56. Ibid., 203, Para. 312, 201, Para. 309.
57. Ibid., 205, Para. 318, 204, Para. 316–17.
58. Ibid., preface, 10.
59. Alexandre Kojève, *Introduction to the Reading of Hegel* (New York: Basic Books, 1969), 236–37. Also see Fukuyama, *The End of History and the Last Man,* 66.
60. Hegel, *Philosophy of Right,* 213–14, Para. 333–34.
61. Fukuyama, *The End of History,* 291–92.
62. Ibid., 304.
63. Ibid., 304–5.
64. Ibid., 305–6.

13

Karl Marx and the Economic Argument About Civil Society

I. Marx's Reaction to Hegel

To understand Karl Marx's (1818–1883) political theory, it is necessary to discuss, briefly, his reaction to G.W.F. Hegel.[1] As we demonstrated in the previous chapter, Hegel, in his *Phenomenology of Spirit*, argued that history could be understood as driven by a central idea Hegel called *Spirit*. The latter signifies the moral directions that should be embodied into the social, political, and economic institutions that govern human life. This knowledge evolves incrementally over time, and as our understanding of Spirit, or our moral possibilities, emerges, individuals gain a more precise picture of what morality consists of and how it is made manifest. Ultimately, at the "end of history," Spirit is fully revealed, and thus as full an understanding as possible both of the moral concepts that govern life and of their corresponding institutional forms is made known to humankind. The Hegelian state is the most essential embodiment of Spirit because it, the state, stands over civil society, which is a setting of competing interests, and gives to civil society necessary moral parameters. Thanks to the moral direction the state provides, there can be many diverse interests in civil society, but at the same time there will be no social fragmentation or destructive competition.

Hegel's vision suggested that Spirit constructs a way of life and an identity for humankind, in keeping with the objectives of Spirit. Marx, however, turns that argument around and argues that Spirit is a function of the projections and thoughts of human beings. Moreover, the thoughts and projections of human beings that create a concept of Spirit, and thus moral order, reflect the real course of events that occurs in history. This means that history is said to unfold according to a certain logic and pattern. The main feature of this pattern is that human beings initially find themselves in circumstances that deny their authentic possibilities, and this fact is overcome later when capitalism is replaced with socialism. Marx, then, in arguing that human self-understanding is a function of the evolving pattern of historical events, seeks to turn Hegel "right side up." Marx does so by demonstrating that Spirit is not an independent force existing outside the lives of people and having the power to determine how we come to see and to understand ourselves.

Rather, for Marx, what Hegel called Spirit is really our conscious understanding of our needs and how well our environment either serves our needs or hinders them. For Marx, people find themselves in circumstances that deny the full expression of their capacities. Marx is, as we discuss in the next chapter, starting from the same point of view as John Stuart Mill. Marx thus believes that real freedom involves the fullest development possible of our highest capacities. But Marx understands that the material settings in which we live often thwart that development. As we recognize this, we become alienated from our world, believing that it does not support our real interests and needs. In responding to this situation by demanding constructive changes, we hope to create a better world, one that will facilitate our potential to the fullest. So, when Marx seeks to revise Hegel, his intention is to demonstrate how the structures of material existence create estrangement for humankind by denying humankind fulfillment of people's real needs and potentials.[2] Only when these structures are both understood and then changed would humankind finally be capable of realizing its most authentic needs and desires.

In this vein, Marx argues in his critique of Hegel's *Philosophy of Right* that Hegel misunderstood the proper relationship between the state and society. Hegel's state, as a manifestation of the idea of Spirit, reversed the relationship between the state and society.[3] For Hegel, the highest hope was a state that embodied his ideal of moral life. This state then would create the conditions that defined the bases for human life. But for Marx, democracy is the highest ideal that a state can embody. In a democracy, the citizens acting together create their own constitution and determine the conditions under which they will live and at the same time prescribe the conditions under which the state will relate to its citizens. "Hegel starts from the state and makes man the subjectified state; democracy starts from man and makes the state objectified man."[4] In fact, Marx believes that democracy, as a form of government, is the only true expression of the universal interests of people. "Only democracy . . . is the true unity of the general and the particular."[5]

Further, Marx rejects categorically Hegel's suggestion that the bureaucracy stood for a class of high-minded and well-educated civil servants who carried forth the idea of Spirit and formed civil society in a manner that was able to attain this ideal in practice. Hegel, as will be remembered, saw civil society as a battleground of private interests, and he expected the state, working through its bureaucracy, to turn civil society into a community with shared interests. But for Marx, bureaucrats tend to represent a "crass materialism." The highest concern of each member of the bureaucracy is his own separate ambition and need for advancement within the organization. Further, bureaucrats are people who accept their subordination and obedience to the state as a condition for securing their future. Instead of being independent thinkers and actors, they do what is needed to maintain the state's power, all to promote their own material ambitions. In doing so, the bureaucracy sets itself up, under the guise of promoting the general interest, as a very powerful private interest that competes with other private interests.[6]

A theme that runs throughout Marx and that helps to explain the views just stated is Marx's critical view of Hegel's notion of civil society. For Hegel, as we have seen, a civil society is located in a market setting that permits individuals to pursue their own interests, subject to the rules and constraints that the state placed on the market. Indeed, Hegel's view of the state–civil society relationship suggested that the state could bring community and a sense of the common welfare to a market-oriented society. But Marx, as the views just described indicate, does not believe a civil society that is predicated on the free pursuit of self-interest, even if subject to a conception of the common good that the state ordains, could produce community and a sense of the shared welfare. All such a setting could produce is individuals, each of whom has his or her own self-interests to pursue and each of whom has little or no concern for a larger good.

Finally, Marx believes that Hegel's view of the state tended to mystify it or, in other terms, tried to convince people that the existing state actually manifested notions of freedom and rights for all when in fact it did not. To demystify the state and thus to expose the fact that Hegel's ideas have not been realized in the state Hegel described, it is necessary to cast off Hegelian misconceptions. To this end, Marx seeks to point out that Hegel's liberalism really places blinders on people. People who wear these blinders think society is becoming progressively freer over time, with more and more people enjoying the benefits of a rights-based state, including the opportunity to realize and to be recognized for the fulfillment of their highest capacities. This liberalist depiction of society prevents people from understanding the alienation and exploitation that capitalism produces. Liberalism works to shield capitalism from criticism by suggesting that the latter is the basis for the rights that the former provides. Marx hopes to strip away these misunderstandings, so he can expose the real tragedies of capitalism and what for him is the untruth of liberalism. Marx's early writings, including *Economic and Philosophical Manuscripts* and his essay "On the Jewish Question," were written with this objective in mind. We now turn to these essays.

II. Political Emancipation: Rights in Civil Society

Marx's discussion of modern civil society is multilayered. At the core of a civil society is a capitalist economic system. Wrapped around that core are various layers, or ways of life, each of which we discuss here and each of which contains a description of how life in a civil society denies priority to the full development of persons. In discussing the different layers of life, we start from the outside and work inward. Our first concern is Marx's discussion of a liberal civil society and what significance, in his view, the idea of equal rights has for people's lives. Once we have completed this discussion, we discuss the next layer of reality, alienation. After that, we address the sources of alienation and its corresponding experience, exploitation. In discussing these matters, we examine Marx's historical and economic critiques of capitalism. As we do, we return to the core problem, a discussion of the dynamics of a capitalist economy.

To begin, in "On the Jewish Question," which includes Marx's view of the significance of rights in a civil society, Marx says that the modern, secular state suggests a "double existence." On the one hand, individuals, as members of civil society, view themselves as private persons pursuing their own interests and seeking their own welfare. But, on the other hand, individuals see themselves as citizens committed to the common good. In discussing the individual element of civil society, Marx has in mind the view that life in a civil society takes place in a capitalist-dominated market setting. Here, the members of this environment compete with each other as individuals to gain as much for themselves as they can, subject, of course, to the rules that govern the competitive process. Each person thus "acts simply as a *private individual*, treats other men as means, degrades himself to the role of a mere means, and becomes the plaything of alien [market] powers."[7]

But regarding the communal element, individuals think of themselves as citizens in a *political community*, and in this role believe that the state is able to create a prospect for a universal, rational order binding on all.[8] Indeed, as we have seen, this was Hegel's view of the modern state/society relationship. For Hegel, the state that stood above civil society as well as the market setting would produce order and unity within both domains. Here, as a result of state actions, individuals in civil society would see themselves not as separate individuals competing with each other but as members of a community sharing a common sense of responsibility for the welfare of the society. This perspective, for Marx, substitutes for the Christian religion a new secular version of religion. Thus, Marx says that the political state "in relation to civil society, is just as spiritual as is heaven in relation to earth."[9]

For Marx, of the two faces of life in civil society, the private, individual dimension seems to dominate and dictate outcomes, making the creation of community impossible. Marx demonstrates this point by indicating that the main advance of civil society, the provision of basic rights for all people, leads to conditions antithetical to community. The "*rights of man,* "in the French *Declaration of the Rights of Man and of the Citizen* of 1793, signify for Marx "the rights of a *member of civil society,* that is, of egoistic man, of man separated from other men and from the community."[10] The rights that Marx refers to here are liberty, property, equality, and security. Liberty is the right to do whatever one wants as long as one does not harm others. The right of property is the right to "enjoy one's fortune and to dispose of it as one will; without regard for the other men and independently of society." This right signifies nothing more than a "right of self-interest."[11] Equality is equal liberty or the equal entitlement to do what one wants and on this view each person is a "self-sufficient monad." Security is the protection of all one's rights or, as Marx puts it, the "*assurance* of egoism."[12]

Having rights in a civil society, dominated by market relations, then, tends to turn individuals into people who think of themselves as separated from every other person while doing whatever they want, as long as they do not harm another. Here, each person knows others only as co-participants in a quest to realize his or her own self-interest, but, in this setting, individuals are unable to find a basis for a mutual commitment to a shared notion of the common good and to the conditions that make community possible. As a consequence, Marx says that, in a civil society, "liberty as a right of man is not founded upon the relations between man and man, but rather upon the separation of man from man. It is the right of separation. The right of the *circumscribed* individual, withdrawn into himself."[13]

The problem of living in an environment such as this, where people are so separated from each other and living in antagonistic relationships to each other, is that there is no basis for "human emancipation."[14] To attain this status, another set of rights must be considered as ultimately more important than the rights of man. Here, Marx has in mind the "*rights of the citizen.*"[15] The latter pertain to the right to take part in determining the common policies, the right to have open and free communication of views, and the right to demand that public officials justify their actions. Having political rights enables individuals to establish a basis for engaging in common action with each other.[16]

Indeed, Marx says that "human emancipation will only be complete when real, individual man has absorbed into himself the abstract citizen . . . and when he has recognized and organized his own powers . . . as *social* powers, so that he no longer separates this social power from himself as *political* power."[17] Marx means by this statement that individuals must have the capacity to forge a political community that represents the common interests and needs that all share. Moreover, such a political community must be arranged in a way that permits individuals to shape and organize the economic life of society so that the full development of people's potential is made possible. Thus, individuals must be a part of communities that are engaged in the production of goods, and, furthermore, these communities must be grounded in social relationships that the members themselves control and organize. In this setting, the workers use their rights as citizens to determine what will be produced and how the various skills and powers of people will be arranged to produce these goods.

For Marx, people obtain meaning in their lives when they are recognized for their contributions through the productive work they perform. But when others control people's work, in this case the capitalists, then individuals are never allowed to express their full capacities in their work, nor are workers allowed to be recognized by others for their contributions to society. Only when workers control the economic process will real emancipation – the kind that allows full recognition by others for the work people do – be possible. As Jeremy Waldron says, for Marx, "full-blooded emancipation, therefore, requires not just the existence of a political community, but the involvement of that community in the democratic organization and running of productive economic life."[18]

The problem, however, is that political rights, although an important progressive step, will not permit full emancipation as long as these rights take place in a capitalist society.[19] Liberalism's great failure is that it permits people to use their freedom to promote only the individualistic, egotistical existence that Marx says characterizes modern civil society. And as a result individuals will never become the citizens, taking part in shaping the economic life of society, that Marx hoped for. Continuing alienation, in a capitalist society, explains why this outcome is inevitable.

III. Modern Alienation

The fundamental fact of life for the ordinary worker in a capitalist-dominated civil society is that workers not only produce commodities, but they become a commodity as well.[20] The workers are a mere commodity because their only value comes from the fact that they have only their labor to sell to those who can use it to manufacture products. In a capitalist economy, workers are not recognized for their diverse and different skills or for their particular powers and capacities. Instead, workers are understood to be a package of energy that, when employed properly like any other machine, can produce certain desired results for the owner class. And yet, what Marx most wants is to engender the full development of people's potentials, just as Mill had desired. Marx says:

> *the real, active orientation of man to himself as a species being, or his manifestation as a real species being (i.e., as a human being), is only possible by his really bringing out of himself all the powers that are his as the species man.*[21]

In consequence of capitalism, however, workers know themselves only through what they become as individuals engaged in "estranged labor," or in activity that separates them from both recognizing and fulfilling their basic skills and powers. From the standpoint of this experience, *alienation* refers to a type of work that prohibits an individual from either knowing or developing one's talents and powers.

In the *Economic and Philosophic Manuscripts of 1844*, Marx discusses four different ways in which alienation manifests itself. First, there is the estrangement from *the product the laborer produces himself.*[22] In effect, as a result of the work in which workers engage, they become dependent on society needing the products that they produce because unless society needs these products, there is no work for the workers and thus no means for the workers to support themselves. But at the same time, the products that workers produce do not change in any way the social conditions under which production takes place. These conditions are radically alienating in the sense that they deny the worker a basis for engaging in the kind of work that would allow the worker to realize his or her potential.[23] The goods workers produce in a capitalist society symbolize, then, the continuation of economic conditions that create alienation for workers by making it impossible for them to control their own workplace for the purpose of creating goods and arranging productive relationships that make human emancipation possible.

There is also alienation from the "*act of production*" itself.[24] Here, individuals are forced to engage in work in which they have no interest in performing and that has no relationship to the evolution of their basic potential as human beings. "He is at home when he is not working, and when he is working he is not at home. His labour is therefore not voluntary, but coerced, it is *forced labour*."[25] The experience Marx has in mind is that of the production-line workers who labor long hours, repeating in endless fashion the same routine over and over.[26] This kind of work leads to the "emasculating" of workers' physical and mental powers.[27] Moreover, because work of this sort makes us live in a remote relationship to our basic powers and capacities, we live with a sense of permanent estrangement from ourselves. In effect, we can never know the nature of what we can be, nor how to go about a life that permits us to realize to the fullest extent all our basic capacities and powers. "Here, we have *self-estrangement*, as we had previously the estrangement of the *thing*."[28]

Moreover, in the third form of estrangement, *we lose an ability to understand our potential as a species*. This means not only that we cannot discern our particular capacities as unique persons but also that we cannot discern the whole panorama of capacities that human beings as a species have open to them. Here, Marx makes a distinction between the capacities associated with human work and those related to animals. Animals can produce goods only to satisfy immediate needs associated with their survival. Humankind knows how to produce goods that are in keeping with the standards of all types of species and not just the lives of human beings.[29] Further, as conscious beings who seek to produce the basis for all life, human beings, unlike animals, can make judgments "in accordance with the laws of beauty."[30] Of significance here is that human beings can know their capacities and choose to pursue those ways of life that ensure human flourishing. This possibility is denied in the work setting Marx critiques in large part because human beings are never freed from living like animals, concerned only to secure their immediate physical survival needs.

But in a culture that fails to protect this prospect, individuals naturally become, in the final form of alienation, *estranged from others*. For just as one cannot understand one's own essential nature, then it is also the case that no one can know the essential nature of another.[31] The sad aspect of this experience is that it dashes the Kantian hope of respecting others as ends and not solely as means. To treat others as ends in the Marxian context requires people's ability to recognize and to support in others the qualities of their wholeness, including acknowledgment of their full powers. But in a capitalist society, where each person is nothing but a commodity pursuing basic survival needs, this objective cannot be realized.

The Norms of Alienated Life

Perhaps the greatest tragedy of alienated existence is that the norms of alienated life produce in citizens, workers, and owners alike a loss of regard for the basic virtues that make possible a society dedicated to the fullest possible development of each person. The major values that replace virtues of this sort are those associated with avarice. Two key factors in this tragedy are the introduction of machines and the overwhelming urge for money.

As we have seen, the organization of work makes each worker a machine tender. The worker "becomes an appendage of the machine, and it is only the most simple, most monotonous, and most easily acquired knack, that is required of him."[32] By requiring each person to perform a simple task for a machine, each person is kept as an "immature human being" or as a "child."[33] Moreover, in order to serve machines, workers must adapt to the doctrines associated with wealth production. This means that workers must accept a subsistence-level existence so that the major portion of the earnings of their work will go to a fund, controlled by the owners, that can be used to purchase new machines. To accomplish this objective, workers are taught to lead a life of self-denial. Indeed, workers are changed into "insensible being[s] lacking all needs."[34] Here, workers are made into compliant people who have no needs beyond a subsistence-level life so that the owner can use the wealth the worker generates, not to enable workers to realize their full powers, but to acquire more machines or capital for the owner. Marx says, "The less [the workers] think, love, theorize, sing, paint, fence, etc., the more [the capitalists] *save*, the *greater* becomes [the capitalist's] treasure . . . your *capital*."[35]

Moreover, in this setting, there is one goal that motivates the owner class – the quest for money.[36] Indeed, money must be given pride of place. But at the same time, owing to the preoccupation with money, another value becomes fundamental, namely, avarice. "*Excess* and *intemperance* come to be. . . [the] true norm."[37] This tendency is associated with the effort to create within the minds of people a sense of the need for specific kinds of goods that people are told they should learn to desire. The goods in question are promoted by those who know that, if they can get enough people to buy them, then they, the sellers, will acquire wealth and social power over the consumers as well as over the workers who produce them. The objective of the seller, then, is to create in the mind of the consumer a "*new* need" for the things the seller is producing. Here, the seller must convince buyers to want something for which they presently have no need. When the seller is successful, the consumers now must make the necessary sacrifices to accumulate the money the seller demands for the good, and in making these sacrifices a new form of dependency is born, one that makes consumers subordinate to the producer class. In this way, the seller has "seduced" consumers into a "new mode of *gratification* and therefore economic ruin."[38]

Finally, money is the basis for determining what each person can be and who each person is. This means that a function of the money a person has as well as what a person must do to acquire money actually defines that person. If to obtain money it is necessary for individuals to forgo their native powers, then they will. Perhaps, owing to their native powers, they could be a great doctor, but because their families have no money to help them become one, individuals cannot pursue that career. Instead, they turn themselves into businessmen whose sole interest in life is to acquire money. But on the other hand, let us say that some individuals have no acumen to be a doctor, but nonetheless they have the desire and the money to become one. In this case, they will become a doctor despite the fact that they should not be one. Marx says, "That which I am unable to do as a *man*, and of which therefore all my individual essential powers are incapable, I am able to do by means of *money*."[39] It is easy to understand how in this setting many traditional virtues lose their place of importance. People still talk about virtues such as fidelity and love, but these virtues are easily displaced with their opposites, vices such as hatred and infidelity, when for the sake of making money it is necessary to do so.[40] Thus, if to be successful in achieving wealth today individuals must be loving, then they will be, but, if tomorrow they must be nasty and mean-spirited for the sake of getting ahead and making money, then individuals will be as nasty as they have to be. Here, no permanent, fixed, and traditional virtues can ever become the mainstays of life. Instead, individuals' values will be modified with the changes in their circumstances.

How, in this setting, can people have relationships based upon mutual regard for the development in each person of his or her best, most important powers? For Marx, the exchanges we have with each other should be designed not so much to make people materially wealthy, but these exchanges should make possible a community based upon virtues that help sustain mutual respect and love for the basic powers and abilities of human life. In particular, our relationships should be designed to be honest efforts to enable others to share their hopes and powers with us and to enable us to share our hopes and powers with others.[41]

Historical Context of Alienation

Understanding the source of alienation is critical to ridding ourselves of it. The purpose of Marx's philosophy is, after all, not just to understand existing reality but to change it. "The philosophers have only *interpreted* the world, in various ways; the point, however, is to *change* it."[42] Marx believes that history must be used to change the circumstances of human beings for the better. In effect, it is possible to learn from history and, in doing so, use the lessons of the past to change the course of the future. History demonstrates the way in which individuals are part of processes designed to produce for human needs.[43] These forces often shape human lives in ways that are against their best interests, as in a capitalist society, but at the same time, individuals can and do react to the forces shaping them, with the intention of creating productive relations that are no longer alienating. Marx says that "circumstances make men just as much as men make circumstances."[44] In this section, we set forth a reading of history from Marx's standpoint to demonstrate the opening history provides to change human circumstances and free humankind from alienation.

For Marx, after the medieval society had already passed from the scene, civil society emerged in the eighteenth century, with a system of production and commerce dominated by the bourgeoisie. Further, it is this class that is associated with the "superstructure" or social and political values that grounded the idea of civil society and that provided cultural support for maintaining the system of production found in a capitalist society.[45] But at the same time, the new system of production created tensions between itself and the workers, and ultimately these tensions would be resolved in a revolution that brings about communism. Before discussing the economic argument that explains this contention, a few paragraphs are in order that describe the character of the society that the bourgeoisie built and that explain why a civil society for Marx will have to be transformed into a communist one.

Civil society emerged from the transition from a productive process based on guilds in the Middle Ages to large-scale factory manufacturing. This change brought about a new relationship between worker and owner. In the guilds, which were home for many craftsmen producing needed goods, a "patriarchal relationship" characterized the association between the "master" and the skilled, so-called journeyman worker.[46] The patriarchal relationship gave the master power over the worker, but the master's power did not lead to intense worker-versus-owner antagonism. The reason was that the worker himself wanted to become a master, and he hoped that by working in a guild he could gain the experience and means to become one. Given this desire, the worker had no interest in overthrowing the guild system, even if the master had complete power over him.[47]

But with the emergence of the "big bourgeoisie," or new owner class, who promoted factory manufacturing, the seeds were planted to create worker-versus-owner conflict, and this conflict ultimately for Marx would lead to the workers overthrowing the owners. Why is this? The new owner class, unlike the guilds, wanted to be part of a trading system that included not just the local economies but the world economy as well. To compete on this basis, it was necessary to accumulate large amounts of "movable" capital, or resources that could be shifted from region to region as business and production needs might dictate. The guilds were always locally based, and the guild owners, the "petty bourgeoisie," did not envision investing their resources in a distant endeavor. But the new "big bourgeoisie" seized on the opportunity to invest resources wherever they thought it would be helpful in augmenting their share of the world market.[48]

Naturally wanting to provide security for their investments, the "big bourgeoisie" sought ways to secure their positions against any would-be competitors.

To this end, for instance, they received from home governments protective tariffs and customs legislation.[49] Still, despite these protective policies, competition among large industries in the seventeenth and eighteenth centuries became the main mode of interaction among producers. The competition compelled individuals to channel their energies to achieve success in the market, and in doing so the only objective that mattered was to increase industrial growth. In this context, all investment money was used to support the development of industry and of what supports industry, such as modern means of communication and the development of a supporting financial system. Moreover, the ownership of industrial capital became concentrated into the hands of a few. Large industrial cities emerged, and, as they did, all traditional crafts found in guild life were destroyed, and the countryside lost importance in the political and social affairs of capitalist countries. In the face of these changes, "ideology, religion, and morality," all factors that might threaten the new way of life, were diminished as important sources of public belief. Moreover, while the "big bourgeoisie" in each country saw themselves as each holding separate national interests, this class had the same interest, and, because of this fact, all the nations they dominated made that interest primary, even to the point of denying any place to nationality. In each case, each industrial nation made the promotion of the needs of "big industry" its main goal, with the result that the life of the working class was made "unbearable."[50]

In this context, the state itself, then, could only become a protector of the interests of the bourgeoisie. Now, as we saw, for Hegel, the state was conceptualized as a separate, independent force, standing above particular interests engaged in competition and defining the common good that each separate interest in the civil society was to uphold. But for Marx, this conception of the state is a fiction. The state is "nothing more than the form of organization which the bourgeois necessarily adopt both for internal and external purposes, for the mutual guarantee of property and interests."[51] Indeed, the state is the vehicle by which the "ruling class" promotes its interests by forming and shaping other institutions, in particular the law, to meet the needs of manufacturing.

In this environment, a system of production is established that maintains a division of labor among the various parties who are part of the process of production. The owners provide the tools and organize the work, and the workers, who have no other means by which to make a living, must enter the workplace on terms that the owners have assigned them. The owners demand control of the process of production because without it they cannot continue to accumulate the capital they must have to retain competitive advantage over other manufacturers. Private property comes to symbolize for the worker a division of labor that gives the capitalist complete control over the nature of work. In this setting, the worker has no hope that he at some point will, as the journeymen in the guilds had expected, acquire some control of the process of the work himself.[52]

The spiraling demands for greater profit lead to the owners seeking to acquire more and more power over the workers, but this situation culminates in the evolution among the workers of the need to overthrow the domination of the owner class. The workers have no choice because they are who continue to bear more and more burdens without gaining any advantages, even as they are the majority of the society. The workers cannot appeal to the state for reforms because the bourgeoisie controls the state. Thus, the objective of the workers is to overthrow the bourgeoisie and the capitalist system that protects their interests. The hope is to create a society in which, for the first time, class rule is completely abolished.[53] For this kind of action to take place, "the alteration of men on a mass scale is necessary, an alteration which can only take place in a practical movement, a *revolution*."[54] The result of this revolution will be as Marx describes the outcome in the *Communist Manifesto*: "In place of the old bourgeoisie society, with its classes and class antagonisms, we shall have an association, in which the free development of each is the condition of the free development of all."[55]

IV. The Economic Argument: The Sources of Exploitation

Coinciding with this historical analysis is an economic critique of capitalism that explains the inevitability of the downfall of the capitalist class and the transition to communism. In this section, our intention is to explain the rudiments of Marx's analysis of the emergence of exploitation as well as to show how the tendencies that produce exploitation also contribute, in the end, to the overthrow of capitalism.

In a capitalist society, workers become wage laborers when they are forced to exchange their labor for the means of survival. Workers, then, are not in a position to demand parity with capitalists, suggesting, for instance, that both should share in the profits of work.[56] The capitalists' power over the workers stems from the fact that the capitalists own the conditions of work or *capital*. The latter includes (but is not limited to) the raw materials and the tools and machines used to produce "new raw materials, new instruments of labour [such as machines], and new means of subsistence [that are used to make possible the workers' survival]."[57] Further, the capitalists are in a position to control all the social relationships that surround production.[58] This means that the capitalists control the conditions that advantage them against the workers, and the capitalists promote norms that benefit them by diminishing workers' status. Moreover, the capitalists have the power to introduce new technologies or machines into the workplace in the hopes of reducing the cost of production.[59] When the capitalists do this, they create more capital, which enables the capitalists to strengthen their power over workers.

Maintaining this favorable (to the capitalists) relationship is crucial to their ability to accumulate capital or the resources, including machines and raw materials, that are the bases of the capitalists' control of the economic system and ultimately of the capitalists' *exploitation* of the workers.[60] To understand what exploitation is and how it arises, it is necessary to comprehend the relationship between "constant capital," "variable capital," and "surplus value." The constant capital, which includes machinery and raw materials, is tied to the value of the labor power or what Marx refers to as the "sum total of wages," or variable capital. The workforce, of course, is used to run the machines that turn raw materials into finished products sold for a profit in the marketplace. Now, the owners seek to make the labor process as efficient and inexpensive as possible. It is only in this way that the owners can increase their profits. To this end, the owners have every interest in taking as much value as they can from the worker and using it to purchase machines to make the work process more profitable. And this owner interest takes us to a consideration of surplus value.

Surplus value originates from a situation in which workers produce enough wealth to support themselves as well as additional amounts of wealth, or a surplus, which the capitalists control.[61] Here, it must be clear that surplus value for Marx derives only from the labor of workers, who produce the basis for their survival in many fewer hours than they actually work.[62] This fact, and this fact alone, is what makes capitalism for Marx an enterprise of exploitation. The workers always end up, as one commentator says, performing "more labor than is necessary to produce the goods he consumes."[63] And the surplus value of their labor, or that amount above what is necessary to maintain them in the workplace, is returned not to the workers but to the owners. The latter use this added value to purchase more machines to make the work process more profitable.

The evils of capitalism and of exploitation are associated with the capitalists' drive for higher rates of surplus value, a drive that initially requires capitalists to increase the length of the workday. How does this situation come about? As just indicated, the capitalists are constantly seeking to take the surplus value from the workers and, with this wealth, purchase more machines with which to replace the workers. But as the workers are replaced with machines, there will be fewer workers and since surplus value comes from making the workers produce more than is needed to maintain themselves, there will be less surplus value for the capitalists to control. So, to overcome this problem, it is necessary to lengthen the workday of those workers who remain. Marx uses the example of a workforce shrinking from 24 to 2 workers, where, before the contraction of the workforce, each person contributed one hour of surplus value in a 12-hour day, or a total of 24 hours for the whole workforce. With two workers, the owner wants to have just as much surplus value, if not more, than in the past. So, two workers will have to produce 24 hours of surplus value, or 12 hours each. It is unlikely that the two workers can provide such a large output of surplus value, even if they work longer hours. Still, the capitalists will try anyway, for their quest is to increase the amount of surplus value they control. The capitalist, Marx says, without even being "conscious of the fact" must move to "excessive lengthening of the working day in order that he may compensate [for] the decrease in the relative number of labourers exploited."[64] In other terms, capitalism requires that the capitalists must constantly exploit the workers, making their lives more and more miserable.

In addition to lengthening the workday, other methods of exploitation are used. First, because machinery requires workers who need not be overly strong, women and children can be employed in the productive process. Indeed, "machinery by throwing every member of that family on to the labour-market, spreads the value of the man's labour-power over his whole family. It thus depreciates his labour-power."[65] Further, work becomes more and more regimented and beyond the control of the workers. The workplace is organized like an army unit, with officers and overseers constantly making sure that workers walk in lockstep compliance with the productive order the owners lay down.[66] Here, the work itself becomes overly simplified so that the "special skill of the worker becomes worthless."[67] As a consequence, in the factory, the workers' minds and bodies are crippled.[68] Moreover, by making work as simplified as possible, the pool of workers is dramatically increased. In the guild system, the journeyman was a skilled worker who could not be easily replaced. Now, there is no obstacle to replacing any worker with any other worker, and this explains the existence of a large pool of workers competing for work, thus driving down the cost of wages. An "industrial reserve army" of unemployed workers is inevitable, and the owners keep these individuals, ever ready to step in and take the job of any worker who will not accept the discipline of the workplace, in misery.[69]

Crisis of Capitalism: Declining Profits

The most serious crisis for capitalism is explained in Marx's falling-rate-of-profits theory. As we explained, capitalists are seeking constantly to replace workers with machines. When capitalists replace workers with machines, capitalists act in a manner that is contrary to their own interests. Because the main source of all value is the surplus value that the workers produce, the rate of the capitalists' profit declines as the workforce engaged in production declines. Thus, says Marx, as the production process is characterized by ever-larger amounts of constant capital and ever-smaller amounts of labor time, or variable capital, the "rate of profit" for capitalists falls.[70]

Capitalists respond to this problem by repeating the process of replacing workers with machines in the hope of introducing efficiencies that can enhance the capitalists' profit picture. To this end, capitalists will further reduce as much as possible the number of workers engaged in production by introducing new machines to take the workers' places. This strategy increases the amount of surplus labor or, in other terms, drives many workers into the unemployment line.[71] But this strategy cannot be repeated forever before the whole system breaks down. Marx says:

> *The highest development of productive power together with the greatest expansion of existing wealth will coincide with depreciation of capital, degradation of the laborer, and a most straitened exhaustion of his vital powers.*[72]

This situation will only result in "recurring catastrophes," repeated on higher scales and "finally to violent overthrow."[73]

As many would argue today, however, worker rebellion actually leads, in the end, not to a Marxist revolution in which the workers own the capital and shape the work setting, but to a society in which there is a balance between the power of both groups. That balance of power is manifested in liberal forms of government, which seek to secure the rights of each individual. As we will see in Chapter 14, Mill's approach to achieving the full development of persons was to equalize the power of both classes in a liberal democratic form of government. He would have seen Marx's route as futile just as Marx would have seen Mill's approach as nothing more than an attempt to mask of the evils of capitalism through resort to liberal democratic institutions.

The New Order

What is the ethos of the communist society that will follow the capitalist society? It is easier to understand Marx's views on this issue by first being clear about what he does *not* support. Marx rejects "the application of an equal standard" as the basis for distributing basic goods in society. Here, people are considered to be workers only, and, as such, workers are paid for the work they perform in accordance with a common standard. Thus, if the common standard requires that each person be paid $10 an hour, then each person is to be paid that much, as long as each person meets the obligations associated with this standard. Marx refers to this view of the treatment of people as an "equal rights" approach. But this approach does not take into consideration that each person is more than just a worker. Each person has different needs. One worker "is married, another not; one has more children than another, and so on and so forth."[74]

Now, Marx believes that, in a "higher phase" of communism, the forces of production in society would evolve to enable "the all-around development of the individual." In this new setting, workers will no longer be commodities that the capitalists own, but they will be regarded as full human beings with diverse powers in need of development. Here, workers will not be regarded as just machines that tend machines, but as people who, in addition to having basic physical needs, have intellectual and moral ones, too. In consequence, the focus of society will be how to secure the fullest possible development of each person. Some people, because they have larger families, will need more income. Others, because their musical talents require special training, will require help from society to make possible the development of their musical skills. In advanced communism, the ethos is: "From each according to his ability, to each according to his needs!"[75]

Thus, Marx hopes to make possible a community in which individuals could develop as fully as possible all their many and varied skills and capacities. Marx says that in a capitalist society, a man is confined to a single sphere of activity and "is a hunter, a fisherman, a shepherd, or a critical critic and must remain so if he does not want to lose his means of livelihood."[76] But in a communist society, Marx says:

> *Where nobody has one exclusive sphere of activity but each can become accomplished in any branch he wishes, society regulates the general production and thus makes it possible for me to do one thing today and another tomorrow, to hunt in the morning, fish in the afternoon, rear cattle in the evening, criticise [sic] after dinner, just as I have a mind, without ever becoming hunter, fisherman, shepherd or critic.*[77]

V. Response and Rejoinder, Especially Adam Smith

The proponent of civil society might respond to Marx by pointing out that the commitment to political rights makes possible the creation of many groups and associations, each of which can enter the public sphere with the intention of making changes and modifications in the public policy of society. Indeed, the civil society proponent would argue that a civil society secures a separate sphere, where worker groups (or labor unions) can develop themselves as independent forces that challenge government and large economic actors, such as capitalists. It is this kind of activity that in fact has led to major reforms of the capitalist system in the United States. Worker movements throughout this century have had impact not only at the collective bargaining table, but in the legislative arena of Congress as well.

Marx would not so much reject this possibility as reject its importance. After all, if the main variable that affects the way we live is the dominant economic class, then voluntary associations that seek redress will never be in a position to do anything more than to make cosmetic changes. Thus, the separate sphere of a civil society will always be overridden by the power of the dominant class, and the larger environment of rights that is to protect this separate sphere will never be strong enough to resist the power of the dominant economic class. In this case, a civil society is largely irrelevant in providing a basis for worker liberation from capitalist structures. Marx would insist that the latter must be removed before workers regain any dimension of freedom.

The proponent of civil society might see some truth in this response. After all, there is no reason why civil society advocates would not recognize some of the dangers of capitalism. Certainly, the society Marx describes represents tendencies that, if left unchecked, can seriously damage a civil society by making large numbers of individuals feel that civil society does not treat them fairly and therefore does not deserve their support. Any society, for instance, that is predicated on maintaining an exploitative relationship between the worker and owner classes would create a sentiment of unfairness among many people. If most of what we work for is taken from us and used by others for their benefit, leaving us with nothing, then why should we feel good about a civil society that protects this kind of undertaking? The question is whether a civil society is a vehicle to reversing this situation. Proponents of civil society think that it is.

What about Marx's response to Adam Smith, a major founder of capitalism, who was discussed in Chapter 1? For Smith, although it is true that capitalist society ends up with differentials in wealth, the overall impact of capitalism is to create far more wealth than other systems could possibly provide.[78] For Smith, working people, although not as well off as the rich in their own country, will, as we pointed out in Chapter 1, be far better off than the wealthiest people in the poorest countries during Smith's time. Capitalism is a great engine of wealth, much of which is shared throughout society.

Now, Smith recognizes, as did Marx, that a major problem of capitalism is that it makes money the main value. And Smith knew that where money is the only thing of great value, then all human activity is measured by money alone. But there are other values, too. And Smith recognizes this fact. Thus, as we saw in the Chapter 1 discussion of *The Theory of Moral Sentiments*, he makes clear that we must learn to temper our quest for money and our tendencies to selfishness so that we can serve larger, more ennobling goals. Part of what makes this possible is acknowledging the perspective of Smith's "impartial spectator." If we look at the world from the perspective of a person who is not partial to any particular way of life but wants only flourishing for us all, then we have to ask if we want to live in a society where money is the only thing of value. And Smith says that we do not. From the vantage point of the impartial spectator, we want to live in a society where we are directed by our natural moral sensibilities – in particular, our natural sympathy[79] – to put ourselves in the shoes of others, especially others in need, and to help them thrive. Smith says "generosity, humanity, kindness, compassion, mutual friendship and esteem, all the social and benevolent affections, when expressed in the countenance or behaviour, even towards those who are not peculiarly connected with ourselves, please the indifferent spectator upon almost every occasion."[80]

But how do we bring this way of life about? The state must have a major role in ensuring justice to all. At times, this means that, regardless of his respect for free markets, Smith puts a priority on the protection of citizen rights, which means not only protecting private property, but protecting what each has a right to and, in consequence, others have an obligation to respect.[81] At other times, despite his concern with state interference in markets, it may be necessary for the state to protect markets from monopolies.[82]

So, Smith would say to Marx that capitalism, when governed by a state dedicated to justice, which is to say to the assurance of the full rights for all, is a system that can produce wealth without destroying civil society or turning people into greedy maniacs who care only for money. The values of his impartial spectator will thrive in this case, ensuring in the process that money is just one value, and the good steward of that money must find a way to ensure high values, like justice and morality, even as he pursues greater material rewards.

Marx, in response, would say that Smith, like Hegel, mystified the capitalist state as the path to freedom and economic abundance, when in fact the capitalist state is merely the advocate of worker exploitation, and civil society is nothing more than a way to mask the resultant injustice.

Regarding Hegel, Marx's democratic approach to the economy would surely be seen as a way to overcome the bureaucratic state that Hegel had argued for. For Hegel, as will be remembered, the state stood above civil society, in charge of managing the economy for the common good. But this objective could not be met unless there was a class of experts in charge of carrying out the state's directives, especially in the settings of the various corporations. Here, a powerful bureaucratic caste, composed of experts in policy management, would manage the economic life of society. But in doing so, average individuals would be told that they were to do whatever their function in the work environment might be and not to expect to participate in the decision-making process that determined the overall objectives of the economy. Clearly, Hegel would have had no sympathy for a democratization of the economy, in contrast, of course, to Marx, who would.

In keeping with this commitment to democratization or to putting the wealth produced by workers under their own control, the Marx of the *Communist Manifesto* advocated reforms such as free education for all, a progressive system of taxation, a central bank not unlike our Federal Reserve system, a work requirement for all, and public ownership of factories (which modern society has adopted in some areas of the economy, such as those having to do with power generation).[83] All these advances were possible and continue to be possible in a rights-based civil society with a state that stands above markets in the manner of Smith and Hegel to ensure justice. Indeed, can these goals be found in anything but a rights-based civil society? Marx, of course, would say no and point the way to communism as the only place for achieving goals like the ones just described.

Notwithstanding this contention, however, Marx would have difficulty demonstrating the success of his theory, and it is on this basis that Marx's critics might rest their case. Of principal concern here is that the communist revolution Marx prophesied and the demise of capitalism it was supposed to bring about have not occurred. Indeed, in the wake of the efforts of the countries of the former Soviet Union and of Communist China to install capitalism, it would appear that capitalism remains a strong force in the world. Moreover, in Russia and China, where capitalism has gained ground, the space for civil society has contracted.

But if civil society helps to incubate the values that Smith described in his discussion of sympathy and the natural moral sentiments, then civil society can have, potentially, a positive effect on the state, moving it to the protection of individual freedom and rights that is characteristic of a liberal democracy.

All of this leads to a closing question: don't we need civil society to balance the tendencies toward a money-only way of life of capitalism – as described by Smith and Marx – and thereby achieve the kind of goals for a humane society Marx advocated? How might Marx have responded to this question? And how might you respond to Marx's answer?

Notes

1. Robert C. Tucker, ed., *The Marx-Engels Reader*, intro. Robert C. Tucker, 2nd ed. (New York: Norton and Company, 1978).

2. Ibid., xxiii.

3. Karl Marx, "Contribution to the Critique of Hegel's Philosophy of Right," in *The Marx-Engels Reader*, 2nd ed., ed. Robert C. Tucker (New York: Norton and Company, 1978), 18.

4. Ibid., 20.

5. Ibid., 21.

6. Ibid., 24–25.

7. Karl Marx, "On the Jewish Question," in Robert Tucker, *The Marx-Engels Reader*, 34. Italics are in the text.

8. Ibid. Italics are in the text.

9. Ibid.

10. Ibid., 42. Italics are in the text.

11. Ibid.

12. Ibid., 42–43. Italics are in the text.

13. Ibid.

14. Ibid., 35.

15. Ibid., 42–43.

16. Ibid., 41; Jeremy Waldron, ed., *Nonsense Upon Stilts: Bentham, Burke and Marx on the Rights of Man*, introductory and concluding essays by Jeremy Waldron (New York: Methuen, 1987), 129–30.

17. Marx, "On the Jewish Question," 46. Italics are in the text.

18. Waldron, *Nonsense Upon Stilts*, 131.

19. Marx, "On the Jewish Question," 35, 41, 43.

20. Karl Marx, "Economic and Philosophic Manuscripts of 1844," in Robert Tucker, *The Marx-Engels Reader*, 71.

21. Ibid., 112. Italics are in the text. On the nature of species life, see Jon Elster, *An Introduction to Karl Marx* (Cambridge: Cambridge University Press, 1986), 43–44.

22. Marx, "Economic and Philosophic Manuscripts of 1844, 72. Italics are in the text.

23. Ibid., 72–73.

24. Ibid., 73.

25. Ibid., 74. Italics are in the text.

26. See Karl Marx, "Capital, Volume One," in Robert Tucker, *The Marx-Engels Reader*, 399–403.

27. Marx, "Economic and Philosophic Manuscripts of 1844," 75.

28. Ibid. Italics are in the text.

29. Ibid., 76.

30. Ibid.

31. Ibid., 77.

32. Karl Marx, "Manifesto of the Communist Party," in *The Marx Engels Reader*, ed. and intro. Robert C. Tucker, 2nd ed. (New York: Norton and Company, 1978), 479.

33. Marx, "Economic and Philosophic Manuscripts of 1844," 95.

34. Ibid.

35. Ibid., 95–96. Italics are in the text.

36. Ibid., 96.

37. Ibid., 93. Italics are in the text.

38. Ibid.

39. Ibid., 104. Italics are in the text.

40. Ibid., 105.

41. Ibid.
42. Karl Marx, "Theses on Feuerbach," in Robert Tucker, *The Marx-Engels Reader*, 145. Italics are in the text.
43. Karl Marx, "The German Ideology," in Robert Tucker, *The Marx-Engels Reader*, 164.
44. Ibid., 165.
45. Ibid., 163.
46. Ibid., 182.
47. Ibid., 177.
48. Ibid., 182.
49. Ibid., 183–85.
50. Ibid., 185–86.
51. Ibid., 187.
52. Ibid., 189–90.
53. Ibid., 192–93.
54. Ibid., 193. Italics are in the text.
55. Marx, "Manifesto of the Communist Party," in Robert Tucker, *The Marx-Engels Reader*, 491.
56. Karl Marx, "Wage Labour and Capital," in Robert Tucker, *The Marx-Engels Reader*, 204–5.
57. Ibid., 207.
58. Ibid.
59. Ibid., 210.
60. Marx, "Capital, Volume One,"419–21.
61. On this point, Elster, *An Introduction to Karl Marx*, 67.
62. Marx, "Capital, Volume One," 405.
63. Elster, *An Introduction to Karl Marx*, 80.
64. Marx, *Capital, Volume One*, 406.
65. Ibid., 404.
66. Ibid., 386.
67. Marx, "Wage Labour and Capital," 214; Marx, "Capital, Volume One," 409.
68. Marx, "Capital, Volume One," 399, 408–9.
69. Ibid., 413.
70. Karl Marx, *Grundrisse*, trans. Martin Nicolaus (New York: Vintage Books, 1973), 747.
71. Ibid., 750.
72. Ibid.
73. Ibid.
74. Marx, "Critique of the Gotha Program," in Robert Tucker, *The Marx-Engels Reader*, 530–31.
75. Ibid., 531.
76. Marx, "The German Ideology," in Robert Tucker, *The Marx-Engels Reader*, 160.
77. Ibid.
78. Adam Smith, "Early Draft of Wealth of Nations," in *Lectures on Jurisprudence*, ed. R. I. Meek, D. D. Raphael and P. G. Stern (Indianapolis: Liberty Classics, 1978), 563.
79. Adam Smith, *The Theory of Moral Sentiments*, intro. E. G. West (Indianapolis: Liberty Classics, 1976), 31.
80. Ibid., 94, Section II, Ch. 4.
81. Smith, "Early Draft of Wealth of Nations," 7.
82. Ibid., 363–64, 496–97.
83. Marx, "Manifesto of the Communist Party," 490.

14

John Stuart Mill: Civil Society as a Higher Calling

I. Mill's Perfected Civil Society

John Stuart Mill (1806–1873) was a strong proponent of a liberal civil society whose rule of law commitment was dedicated to securing as broad a liberty as possible for people. In taking this view, he not only supported equal liberty in the tradition of Immanuel Kant, but he also sought a liberty that was as inclusive as possible of all the choices individuals may wish to make in life. But Mill was interested not just in expanding the choices individuals had but he wished to make it possible for people to use their freedom to enhance what was best in human-kind, in particular, their intellectual and moral qualities. In promoting this view, Mill was equally a stern critic of civil society, suggesting that civil society may be a way of life that, in the end, destroyed what was best in people. For this reason, it might be possible to place Mill into the last section of the book, as one of civil society's major critics. But we have resisted the temptation to do so because, in the long run, we believe that Mill believed that civil society was the best approach to achieving a humane existence.

In this chapter, starting with Mill's revision of Jeremy Bentham's utility prin-ciple, we explain how Mill's view of civil society is designed to facilitate what Mill most treasured, the development of the higher mental and moral capacities. Here, Mill argues for a conception of civil society that lessens the impact of the worst features of the market economy on the lives of individuals. As players in the market setting, individuals frequently engage in destructive relationships. Often, in the market setting, individuals, as they pursue their self-interest, only seek to enhance their power and position against others. Indeed, Mill says that economic life is "the parent of envy, hatred, and all uncharitableness; it makes everyone the natural enemy of all others who cross his path, and every one's path is constantly liable to be crossed."[1] Mill's discussion of the utility principle points the way to the cultural context that can promote, despite the experience of economic life, the higher capacities of persons. In this reformed and revamped culture, which a civil society is to embody, restraints can be placed on the economic arrangements, posed by the market setting, to avoid the threats to Mill's fuller freedom.

II. Mill and Jeremy Bentham and the Principle of Utility

Mill's starting point was Jeremy Bentham's principle of utility, which Mill both adopts and revises in his essay "Utilitarianism."[2] The utility principle, also called the greatest happiness principle, as found in Bentham, says that "actions are right in proportion as they tend to promote happiness, wrong as they tend to produce the reverse of happiness. By happiness is intended pleasure and the absence of pain; by unhappiness, pain and the privation of pleasure."[3] Mill argues that this principle is the "ultimate appeal on all ethical questions, grounded on the permanent interests of man as a progressive being."[4] Bentham's main concern in discussing utility is to demonstrate how it would be useful in making judgments pertaining to the development of laws and public policy.[5]

Bentham's Pleasure Calculus

In Bentham's view of the utility principle, before putting into law a proposed measure, a legislator must determine the sum total of pain or pleasure that the proposed measure suggests. He says:

> *pleasures then, and the avoidance of pains, are the ends which the legislator has in view: it behoves him therefore to understand their value. Pleasures and pains are the instruments he has to work with; it behoves therefore to understand their force, which is again, in other words, their value.*[6]

The objective of this enterprise is to compare the total quantity of pleasure of a proposed action to the total quantity of pain. Those policies that, on balance, provide greater pleasure describe a *"good* tendency" for the community, and those policies that, on balance, suggest more pain than pleasure suggest an *"evil* tendency."[7] To make this calculation, it is presumed that all pleasures are quantifiable in terms of the following indicators of pleasure or pain: the amount or degree of a pleasure's or pain's intensity, duration, certainty, remoteness, fecundity, purity, or extent (the number of people it affects).[8] Bentham's calculus is followed by a long list of possible pleasures, including things such as making money, achieving good reputation, gaining power, realizing goodwill, having hope for the future, and being a part of associations with others.[9]

Clearly, the pleasures Bentham lists represent the objectives that individuals, as competitive businesspeople in a market setting, always have. Thus, Bentham's political program embraces an ethics that derives directly from the market experience in a commercially based capitalist society. And Mill, by seeking to revise Bentham's philosophy, does not reject the modern market context so much as he seeks to reform it, making it capable of embracing the possibilities of enhanced intellectual and moral life. How does Mill go about achieving this objective?

Mill rejects Bentham's approach to measuring the value of a given pleasure, and, in doing so, Mill provides an alternative basis for grounding his ethics and his politics. Mill believes that measuring a particular way of life's worth should not depend solely upon the quantity of pleasure associated with that way of life but should include an assessment of the quality of pleasure connected to the way of life in question, also.[10] Thus, let's say someone enjoys reading philosophy as well as watching television. Still, when faced with the choice of being able to read more or watch television more, let's assume the person chooses reading philosophy, even though reading is associated with a greater amount of work and concentration than watching television. On what basis would the person make this choice? The reason for the choice would be that reading represents a higher-quality pleasure, and, consequently, no additional amount of television watching would be sufficient to warrant choosing television over reading.

For Mill, pleasures that are qualitatively rich are those associated with the use of the "higher faculties" of the mind. Now, it is true that those people who set their sights very low in life will have a greater likelihood of realizing their objectives than those people whose objectives aim to realize the fullness of the "higher faculties." After all, a life dedicated to achieving the "higher faculties" may always be associated with various forms of unpleasantness, such as hard work and a risk of failure. But still, despite these difficulties, people, who understand both the "higher faculties" of the mind as well as those pleasures that Mill refers to as those of "lower animals," will pursue the life of the "higher faculties" of mind over all animal pleasures. People who appreciate the "higher faculties" will take this course despite the fact that they may be convinced that the lower pleasures bring more satisfaction and less discomfort. Mill says that it is better to be a dissatisfied Socrates than a satisfied fool.[11]

Why are the higher faculties of mind so important? Mill says:

[A] cultivated mind – I do not mean that of a philosopher, but any mind to which the fountains of knowledge have been opened, and which has been taught, in any tolerable degree, to exercise its faculties – finds sources of

inexhaustible interest in all that surrounds it; in the objects of nature, the achievements of art, the imaginations of poetry, the incidents of history, the ways of mankind past and present, and their prospects in the future. It is possible, indeed, to become indifferent to all this, and that, too, without having exhausted a thousandth part of it; but only when one has had from the beginning no moral or human interest in these things, and has sought in them only the gratification of curiosity.[12]

Several important points seem to follow from this view of intellectual life. Mill contends that only when we make satisfactory use of the higher faculties of mind do we find unlimited interest in life. Through experience we can know that there is a vast world out there, of course, but unless we really engage that world with our mental faculties, we can never know the joy and happiness of learning about, as well as confronting, the world's mystery and allure. As a consequence of this engagement, the world is always a place that fascinates and that presents new avenues of discovery and delight.

In this view, then, what would seem to disturb Mill so much about the ways of life that have quantifiable pleasures as their objectives is that, in pursuing those pleasures exclusively, individuals make only a limited and incomplete use of their mental faculties. Thus, if the one thing individuals most want to do is to make money, they can go into business and use only that part of their mental abilities that is useful in the business world. If they want to lead lives dedicated to acquiring power, then they must engage only that capacity of mind concerned with this objective. In all these cases, according to Mills, real and enduring happiness cannot be attained because the higher faculties of mind are not properly employed. On the other hand, a businessperson might have a fully cultivated mind, too, thus enabling him or her to engage and to find wonderment and interest in all aspects of life, especially those beyond the business world. The same could be true for those involved in the pursuit of power.

A truly satisfactory life, or a life dedicated to the pleasures that are high quality in nature, is also associated with an ability on the part of individuals to be concerned for others. Mill argues that people who think only of their own needs become disconnected from "the collective interests of mankind." It is only when we retain an intimate association and concern for the needs of others that we are more likely to have "as lively an interest in life on the eve of death as in the vigor of youth and health."[13]

Some might argue that Mill's view is elitist, since not all people have the *capacity* for engaging in the cultivation of the higher-quality pleasures just mentioned. But Mill would deny this claim. "There is absolutely no reason in the nature of things why an amount of mental culture sufficient to give an intelligent interest in these objects of contemplation [such as history, poetry, etc.] should not be the inheritance of every one born in a civilized country."[14] As a matter of fact, the utilitarian project suggests the need to eradicate whatever stands in the way of all people's enjoying what is their birthright, namely, their full mental and moral life. Poverty and disease as well as other factors that are obstacles to the full enjoyment of the mental life can be eliminated. "All the grand sources, in short, of human suffering, are in great degree, many of them almost entirely, conquerable by human care and effort," and people who enter the field to fight for the full development of persons in this way "will draw a noble enjoyment from the contest itself."[15]

Utility, Justice, and Rights

The utility principle, defined broadly to include not only the provision of quantitative pleasures but qualitative ones as well, Mill conceives as contributing to and supported by what he understood to be a "natural sentiment" or desire to "be in unity with our fellow creatures."[16] For Mill, as for Aristotle, we are social animals by nature, and because we are, we seek ways to create cooperative settings that facilitate the happiness of each individual. But for Mill, unlike for Aristotle, this project cannot be achieved unless we all regard each other as equals. In Mill's view, a "society between equals can only exist on the understanding that the interests of all are to be regarded equally."[17] And this means that, in pondering actions, individuals must always consider the interests of others, and, in particular, individuals must see themselves as part of an association in which each of the members accepts the obligation to be a cooperative citizen promoting a collective objective.[18] Indeed, the utility principle requires that each person be concerned with his or her own happiness as well as with the happiness of others. Here, the Golden Rule propounded in the spirit of Jesus is "the ideal perfection of utilitarian morality." The utilitarian is committed, then, to "laws and social arrangements," as well as to a system of education that enables each person to live in harmony with the whole of the society, while advancing the quest for freedom defined in both quantitative and qualitative terms.[19]

As an embodiment of the Golden Rule, the utilitarian ethic presumes a "sentiment of justice" or the feeling of a need to be rightly outraged and to seek punishment for those who harm us or those with whom we sympathize. This "sentiment of justice" is widened to include all persons in society by virtue of "the human capacity of enlarged sympathy" and "intelligent self-interest." As a result, we find ourselves experiencing the harm caused to others as though it were caused to us, and, in light of this experience, we are driven to demand protection by society for the rights of all people.[20] Here, to have a right is to have something that, for Mill, society must defend "either by the force of law, or by that of education and opinion."[21] Only then can individuals have *security*, for Mill, "the most vital of all interests."[22]

From this account, it is clear that Mill wants a broader and richer happiness than Bentham had ever contemplated. Moreover, Mill predicates this broader happiness on the civic virtue commitment to mutual respect, which he sees as central to the utilitarian ethic. But what kind of culture, political and social, is needed to secure the setting that makes possible the happiness that Mill's utilitarianism seeks? This question is addressed in the rest of this chapter, first with a discussion of Mill's *On Liberty* and then later with discussions of Mill's views of political economy and government.

III. *On Liberty*: The Culture of Civil Society

Well-Developed Persons

On Liberty was written to suggest the kind of culture a civil society must have if individuals are to become "well-developed human beings."[23] What is sought is a social and political environment that enables individuals to develop to the fullest extent possible their mental faculties. Key to their doing so is that individuals be permitted every opportunity to make their own choices as to which paths in life to take. Mill argues that the basic faculties, those "of perception, judgment, discriminative feeling, mental activity, and even moral preference, are exercised only in making a choice."[24] In making choices, people learn to rely on their own faculties of mind as they evaluate the various options before them. As they do so, they further develop these mental capacities, leading, then, to a fuller, happier life. "The mental and moral, like the muscular powers, are improved only by being used."[25]

Thus, human capacities are stunted to the extent that a person allows customs and traditions to dictate his or her way of life. Mill's point is not that customs are always necessarily wrong, but that, in living as they require us to, without questioning them, we desist from making choices about what is best for ourselves. And when we follow this course, we do not develop the kinds of qualities that enable us to reach our higher capacities. "He who lets the world, or his own portion of it, choose his plan of life for him, has no need of any other faculty than the apelike one of imitation."[26] Blind following of custom makes all people uniform and thus incapable of becoming what, for Mill, are the "noble and beautiful objects of contemplation."[27]

Human liberty, and the self-development that evolves from it, is best nurtured when society permits individuals to be free to pursue their own choices, within settings they design either by themselves or with others.[28] In these contexts, individuals are not to be interfered with by the state or by other individuals. What secures this prospect is the assurance of certain basic liberties, including, for instance, the liberty of conscience, of expression, of determining one's own life plans, and of being able to join together in groups and associations.[29] Here, a civil society is not just a place for people to act upon market imperatives and seek to own property, gain riches, or perform necessary work, but, in addition, a civil society is a place in which people further enhance their higher qualities.

Mill's view of civil society suggests a recurrent danger for Mill's approach to individual development. Society, with its basic social and political institutions, cannot provide the rights or the protective space Mill hopes for without exercising power over individuals. But the power society possesses might itself make impossible the kind of liberty Mill expects. Therefore, the quest for individual development always in the end becomes a question of how to define "civil liberty," or "the nature and limits of power which can be legitimately exercised by society over the individual."[30]

In addressing this question, Mill starts from what he considers a basic truth about government in modern society. Governments are no longer conceived of as entities with interests separate from the people but as institutions that are responsible to the interests of the citizens.[31] Still, a new threat to freedom emanates from the idea that governments, as democratic republics, should be ruled by the "will of the people." Instead of signifying a form of government in which citizens governs themselves, the idea of the "will of the people" has come to mean

the will of the most numerous or the most active part of the people; the majority, or those who succeed in making themselves accepted as the majority; the people, consequently, may desire to oppress a part of their number: and precautions are as much needed against this, as against any other abuse of power.[32]

A politically active class may consist of a small number of people, but owing to its skills and its endurance, it may be able to dominate the policymaking process. These groups achieve their objectives by having great influence on government, as well as by imposing their orthodoxy onto all members of the society. The result of this strategy is "to fetter the development, and, if possible, prevent the formation, of any individuality not in harmony with its [prevailing opinion] ways, and compel all characters to fashion themselves upon the model of its own."[33]

Mill's political solution to this problem involves his drawing a distinction between opinions and the actions that might follow from opinions. Whereas people should not be hindered in their expression of opinions, it may be necessary, at times, to place limits on the actions that various opinions suggest. For instance, Mill says that the view that corn dealers are corrupt and negligent ought to be able to be communicated in the press without restraint. The same idea, issued before a mob standing in front of the house of a corn dealer, may have to be limited, owing to the potential harm that might result from an emotionalized group.[34] Mill suggests that freedom of speech is not unlimited. We cannot use speech to cause a riot that results in injuries, just as we cannot give state secrets to another nation.

The freedom of speech of those seeking through their speech to dominate others represents a special problem for Mill. Mill knows that in a society dedicated to open speech, those seeking to dominate the political process through public position-taking cannot have their right to speech or association limited. This situation, for many, describes the current problem with the demand for more thorough campaign finance reform. For some, extensive reforms of campaign funding might deny full freedom of political speech to those who are placed under these limitations. Yet, with the freedom candidates have to garner large amounts of money, it is possible for special interests to dominate vital policy areas in society. So, what is the solution in a situation where outright bans on speech are not possible?

Mill insists, as we demonstrate throughout the rest of this chapter, that a civil society be a place where public policy decisions are made in the context of a full, open, and rational public discourse, as opposed to the shoving-match tactics of powerful interest groups. No doubt, Mill would have rejected the appeals to emotion found in many political advertisements today because these techniques deny the proper place to reason in political discourse. By emphasizing in public culture the role of fair, rational, and open public deliberation, the hope is that the tactics of oppressive, single-issue groups are avoided.

Opinion Advocacy and Civic Virtue

Mill, like all civil society thinkers discussed to this point, including Thomas Hobbes, John Locke, and Immanuel Kant, argues that a civil society must secure liberty. Further, Mill follows other civil society thinkers in arguing that people who receive benefits from society are obligated to "observe a certain line of conduct toward the rest."[35] Thus, with freedom goes the need to observe certain basic social obligations, or what we have referred to as civic virtues. In particular, we are not to harm the interests of others by denying others their legally provided or tacitly-understood-to-exist rights, and, further, each person is to share the burdens of defending the society "or its members from injury or molestation."[36]

Mill's *On Liberty* would seem to provide two approaches to defining the precise limits or the particular content of the civic virtues that individuals must observe if the harms just described are to be avoided. The first approach, discussed in this subsection, pertains to Mill's view of the culture of open discourse and the discovery of truth. The second approach, discussed in the next subsection, has to do with what can be referred to as self-regarding conduct, or the denial to the society or to individuals the authority to interfere with those individually chosen ways of life that do not cause harm to others or to society. The institutional settings that seem most able to promote a respect for the limits that maintain Mill's civil society are embodied in Mill's views of a stationary economy and representative government, both of which are discussed in subsequent sections of this chapter.

First, we need to discuss Mill's view of open discourse. For Mill, the basis for discovering truth in a society with diverse opinions on the many issues before society is that we must not deny a hearing to any opinion, lest, in doing so, the truth may be suppressed. Where opinions are suppressed, there is in place a presumption of infallibility on the part of those who are able to avert discussion.[37] Mill's view is that we do not learn what is best for us simply from experience alone, but also, in addition, "there must be discussion, to show how experience is to be interpreted." In this context, "wrong opinions and practices gradually yield to fact and argument."[38] No one can marshal by him or herself all the facts pertaining to a question or generate all possible arguments against which to test his or her view. We have an obligation, therefore, to listen to all the views that can be given against our positions and to consider them carefully while deriving our positions. Mill advocates the benefits of an enlarged discourse, or what has been called *public reason*, when he says:

> *The steady habit of correcting and completing his own opinion by col-*
> *lating it with those of others, so far from causing doubt and hesitation in*
> *carrying it into practice, is the only stable foundation for a just reliance*
> *on it: for, being cognizant of all that can, at least obviously, be said*
> *against him, and having taken up his position against all gainsayers –*
> *knowing that he has sought for objections and difficulties, instead of*
> *avoiding them, and has shut out no light which can be thrown upon the*
> *subject from any quarter – he has a right to think his judgment better*
> *than that of any person, or any multitude, who has not gone through a*
> *similar process.*[39]

In promoting this view of opinion advocacy, Plato's Socrates lurks in many passages of *On Liberty*.[40] Like Socrates, Mill exhorts holders of any opinion to provide the grounds for their judgments. Mill rejects the kind of argument for an opinion that starts out with the statement: "The reason I believe in X is that I feel that X is correct." What are the reasons, Mill would ask, for this person holding to X? And can this person defend those reasons in the face of the following counter-arguments that Mill would give to them? This approach is not only the source of truth, but it is the basis for a culture in which individuals maximize the development of their highest-order mental capacities. In contrast

> *where there is a tacit convention that principles are not to be disputed,*
> *where the discussion of the greatest questions which can occupy human-*
> *ity is considered to be closed, we cannot hope to find that generally*
> *high scale of mental activity which has made some periods of history so*
> *remarkable.*[41]

Further, when we must justify our positions with good arguments, we not only develop our mental capacities, but, in addition, we demonstrate both to others and to ourselves why we feel justified in believing as we do. In effect, we acquire throughout this process a publicly defensible ground for our opinions, and, consequently, we are less likely to be timid or hesitant to act on their behalf.[42] There is, in the modern world, a tendency to associate firm commitments with dangerous fanaticism. But Mill would no doubt argue that fanaticism arises from a need to flee from subjecting beliefs to the give-and-take of argument and debate. The latter relies upon the participation of others, particularly those holding views different from our own. Fanaticism would close us off from a discourse of this type. For this reason, unreflective acceptance of beliefs, a mental state associated with fanaticism, would have no place in Mill's discourse setting.

Self-Regarding Conduct

Mill distinguishes self-regarding conduct, or individual actions that do not harm others by denying them their rights, from other-regarding conduct that harms others by taking their rights from them. In general, Mill thinks society should permit each person to live his or her own life as that person chooses. Thus, even though it is best for individuals to pursue ways of life that enhance their "higher faculties," still, all individuals, in their "ripe years" or as mature, experienced adults, should have the freedom to determine that way of life that they consider best for themselves. When society interferes with a person's choices, perhaps to promote what it considers to be the best interest of a person, it unnecessarily limits that person's freedom and quite often makes mistakes about what is best for another.[43] Moreover, actions that demonstrate deficiencies in our character and that are harmful to us, such as a tendency to deny importance to the higher faculties, what Mill refers to as "self-regarding faults," should not be made subject to legal sanction. Mill argues that behaviors that cause harm only to the individual engaging in them are "inconveniences" that society "can afford to bear, for the sake of the greater good of human freedom."[44] However, this view does not mean that we are obligated to show respect for people who commit self-regarding faults. Such individuals will necessarily be viewed with less favorable opinion by most people.[45] Still, only acts that injure others, such as those that violate another's rights, are acts that can be punished legally. To use Mill's example, although it is permissible for a person to become drunk, it is not permissible for a policeman or soldier to become drunk on duty.[46]

For Mill, then, the state may regulate the lives of people only to prevent serious harm to others or to society. An example of particular importance to justify state interference into others' lives is when one person's conduct denies rights to others. Men often act toward women with precisely this intention and effect, and Mill condemns this kind of other-regarding conduct. Mill is adamant that men should not be able to control the lives of their wives, with the result that women suffer loss of opportunities, and to remedy this situation, he believes it necessary to give to women the same rights that men have.[47]

Furthermore, Mill argues that there is a duty incumbent upon parents to educate their children. And those parents who do not perform this duty have, for Mill, committed a "moral crime." To prevent such crimes, against both children and society, the state has the right to force parents to educate their children. Still, Mill fears placing the task of educating people exclusively into the hands of the state because he believes that a state education would end up molding people to be copies of each other. Thus, he argues that, if the state must sponsor schools, these schools should be designed to provide a standard that other systems of education in society, including presumably private ones, should try to match or to exceed. State-sponsored schools should try "to keep the others up to a certain standard of excellence."[48] Ultimately, however, the state's right to ensure an education for everyone is justified by the fact that education is the best way to teach people to avoid actions that exceed the proper limits of conduct. For Mill, "if society lets any considerable number of its members grow up mere children, incapable of being acted on by rational consideration of distant motives, society has itself to blame for the consequences."[49]

In conclusion, it is well to make clear the nature of the civic virtues that the notions of open discourse and the need to avoid interfering with the lives of others both suggest. By not interfering in the lives of those who harm only themselves, individuals manifest the virtue of toleration found in Locke. By manifesting understanding of views different from one's own, as is required in Mill's form of enlarged discourse, individuals manifest the civic virtue of mutual respect. Each of these ideas, as argued in Chapter 1, can mutually support the other, and taken together they are fundamental to securing rights for all in a civil society.

IV. The Stationary Economy and Private Property

From the preceding account of self-regarding freedom, it is clear that Mill believes civil society must be designed to protect people from intrusions that threaten their personal liberty. Mill argues that, whereas civil societies understand this need, they are often blind to the factors that threaten it. Indeed, civil societies, ironically, end up promoting certain ways of life that actually make the protection of the full development of persons extremely difficult. Here, Mill has in mind the concept of a free-market economy that is associated in Mill's time with furthering industrial growth and individual freedom but that, in fact, often jeopardizes the general happiness. In this section, we explain Mill's position by discussing his advocacy both of a stationary economy and of the concept of private property.

The conventional wisdom held by many people even today and the view that Mill attacks is the idea set forth by Adam Smith, discussed in Chapter 1, that says the total amount of wealth and capital in society must always be expanding and growing. But Mill believes that a fixation on growing "as rich as possible," what Mill also refers to as "one of the phases of industrial progress," makes the "normal [or Smithian growth] state" a competitive jungle filled with "trampling, crushing, elbowing, and treading on each other's heals [*sic*]."[50] Although the quest for economic growth may be a "necessary stage in the progress of civilization," it is not, for Mill, the kind of social setting he would want to encourage. A better condition is one in which there is a "stationary state of capital and wealth," a situation in which "no one is poor, [and] no one desires to be richer."[51] Mill's position is clearly offered as a challenge to Smith's views.[52]

Now, in supporting the idea of a stationary economy, it should be clear that Mill does not deny the principle of private property. For Mill, private property suggests that individuals should be permitted to keep the fruits both of their own labor and of the various sacrifices they accept as a consequence of their work.[53] However, this principle is violated in a society in which the actual distribution of property, as embodied in the law, has worked to heap "impediments upon some, to give advantage to others."[54] Still, Mill believes that the principle of private property is not the cause of this imbalance, as socialists in Mill's time claimed. The source of this imbalance is the government's failure to diffuse wealth, and, by failing to do so, to permit large concentrations of wealth to remain in the hands of a few.[55] Indeed, Mill believes that "the principle of private property [which has been attacked as the source of imbalances in wealth] has never yet had a fair trial in any country."[56] Thus, Mill hopes for legislation that, while "favoring equality of fortunes," does so in a way consistent with respect for "the just claim of the individuals to the fruits, whether great or small, of his or her own industry."[57]

The idea of a stationary economy is associated with several important ideas. For Mill, there should be efforts to limit the growth of the population so that the quest for ever-larger amounts of wealth is not necessary to feed ever-larger numbers of people. Indeed, Mill's support of equal rights for women evolves not just from his commitment to equal rights for all. His commitment to equal rights for women arises from his view that when women are kept in the household and denied the same opportunity for employment as men, it is likely that women will produce larger numbers of children than the world needs, thus contributing to overpopulation.[58]

Moreover, in a stationary economy, there would be an ethos of ecology and conservation, both of which would humanize society and make it into a place more hospitable to the full development of people's "higher faculties." In contrast, an ever-expanding economy is bent upon turning every scrap of land into an instrument to aid further production. Forests and beautiful fields filled with flowers and clean rivers are turned into trash dumps for factories. In laying waste to the environment in this way, there are fewer places on the earth left where a person can stand apart from others, in "solitude," and reflect on the course and direction of his or her life. "Solitude in the presence of natural beauty and grandeur is the cradle of thoughts and aspirations which are not only good for the individual, but which society could ill do without."[59]

Finally, within the stationary economy, it would be possible to advance methods of manufacturing that reduce the total amount of time spent in laboring, so that individuals would have the free time needed to develop their "higher faculties." Mill wants a work setting in which the workers would be able to pursue the "art of living," or a life in which the enhancement of "mental culture" and "moral and social progress" is made possible. But he laments that, in the circumstances of his day, the laboring class grew without any decrease in the drudgery associated with work. In contrast, the expanding economy was a great boon to the manufacturers or the owner classes that made great amounts of money. The comforts of the middle class were greatly increased, too. For Mill, this circumstance is a great injustice that needs to be corrected, and it could be if the economy were put on a stationary as opposed to an ever-expanding basis.[60]

Correcting the imbalances between workers and owners is a primary consideration of his argument, then. To this end, Mill also hopes for a fairer distribution of influence in the workplace. But this goal is hindered by the demand for an expanding economy. Indeed, in a setting in which growth is constantly demanded, the owner stands toward the workers as a superior, demanding more and more sacrifice, and turning worker sacrifices into profits to fund more growth. But this kind of relationship creates hostility between owners and workers, and it freezes the worker out of important decisions affecting what is produced and how production occurs. When the worker has no chance to participate in major decisions in the workplace, the worker does not develop the "higher faculties" of mind that allow him or her to contribute to critically important decisions affecting society. Mill wants to correct the imbalance between the owners and workers by giving the workers a larger stake in the production process. Thus, Mill hopes the relationship between workers and owners will be transformed to permit partnerships either between owners and workers or among the workers themselves.[61] In the first instance, workers would share profits with the owners, and, in the second instance, workers would own the entire production setting and help choose their own managers.[62] These new economic arrangements would permit the workers to take part in the decisions concerning the productive process, and, consequently, workers' intellectual and moral capacities, as well as their sense of responsibility to society, would be enhanced.

It would appear that Mill's commitment to a stationary economy, as well as to cooperative work arrangements, is designed to reform, but not to eliminate, a private property–based market economy. Socialism, the collective ownership of property, remains an alternative if it becomes the case that the reforms Mill advocated did not come to pass. At the time he wrote, however, Mill believed the most desirable form of economy was yet to be decided. Indeed, the form of economy considered best for society still remains to be determined by the future course of events. "We are too ignorant either of what individual agency [private-property forms of society] in its best form, or Socialism in its best form, can accomplish, to be qualified to decide which of the two will be the ultimate form of human society."[63]

V. On Representative Government

The kind of civil society most likely to produce the reforms just discussed is one that engenders in citizens an active participatory role in politics and society. Citizens would develop the capacity to consult the views of others as well as the guiding principles that secure the greater good while devising their own opinions. Mill believes this experience is already a part of contemporary English lower-middle-class life. Mill says the English citizen who sits on juries, who participates in parish offices, and who participates in public functions

> *is called upon, . . . to weigh interests not his own, to be guided, in case of conflicting claims, by another rule than his private partialities, to apply, at every turn, principles and maxims which have for their reason of existence the general good: and he usually finds associated with him in the same work minds more familiarized than his own with these ideas and operations, whose study it will be to supply reasons to his understanding, and simulation to his feeling for the general good.[64]*

Furthermore, Mill, in keeping with his commitment to active citizen participation in the affairs of society, believes, for several reasons, that many social functions should be performed by citizens themselves rather than by the government. In the first place, citizens are likely to do a better job than government in performing such functions. And in the second place, even in those situations in which citizens may not perform certain functions as well as the officers of government, society is better off overall when citizens take an active role in their society. Here, Mill believes that citizen participation in government and society is a means to people's "mental education – a mode of strengthening their active faculties, exercising their judgment, and giving them familiar knowledge of the subjects with which they are thus left to deal."[65] Mill fears government by bureaucracy because these agencies, in putting the most capable men into government positions, as Hegel had wanted to do, would ensure that "all the enlarged culture and practised intelligence in the country . . . would be concentrated in a numerous bureaucracy."[66] This situation would exclude the rest of the citizenry from taking part in broad discussions of key public issues. Consequently, the public would not be encouraged to participate in the shaping of policy themselves.

Mill thus advocates a view of civil society that, in addition to having a culture that emphasizes the importance of protecting rights and enhancing the intellectual faculties of citizens, also emphasizes, as part of this culture, the importance of direct citizen involvement in government functions. Citizens would engage in these functions either in the context of local governments and juries, or through a separate sphere of voluntary groups, which undertook, for instance, philanthropic activities.[67] Clearly, Mill supported and indeed makes room for what we have called the separate sphere of a civil society in which individuals can participate in a variety of groups and associations, learn the skills of citizenship and deliberation, and build a strong buffer to central government power.

Moreover, as an additional way to promote broad public participation in the governmental processes, Mill supports representative forms of government because he believes these forms of government encourage a wide-scale public discourse of public policy. He takes this position in spite of the fact that he does not envision the representative body itself as the sole arena for making laws. Mill says the representative assembly is too unwieldy and cumbersome to be in a position to make good laws through its own deliberations. Thus, Mill advocates a "Commission of Legislation" whose task would be to craft laws. The crown would appoint the Commissioners for a fixed term, unless removed by the Houses of the Parliament. The Commissioners would be above politics, acting with expertise as they addressed the issues before them and acting with a full understanding of the whole structure of law. The proposals of the Commission would be presented to the representative bodies, who would ultimately have to approve them.[68]

The representative branch, while the "ultimate controlling power" in government,[69] must not take upon itself administrative duties.[70] The representative branch cannot administer the laws and lead the nation, but it can perform a useful watchdog role. Thus, the representative agency should always be in a position to "throw the light of publicity" on the actions of the administration, demanding explanations of the administration for any acts considered questionable.[71]

But how, in this case, does a representative government contribute to a participatory, self-educating form of politics? A great danger of representative government is that it could make individuals passive citizens, willing to turn over the affairs of state to others. Mill says that the main function of the representative body is to provide a forum for public discussion of the issues before society. Mill says:

I know not how a representative assembly can more usefully employ itself than in talk, when the subject of talk is the great public interests of the country, and every sentence of it represents the opinion either of some important body of persons in the nation, or of an individual in whom some such body have reposed their confidence.[72]

The representative body must be a place where all the diverse opinions can be shared and debated. Each representative must form his or her own opinion by first consulting the opinions of all the others. Mill believes, apparently, that representatives engage in deliberation in a fishbowl setting, with the great bulk of the society watching. Indeed, citizens themselves, as they watch and listen to the debates taking place in front of them, necessarily form their own opinions by carefully and fully considering the positions of others. And in this atmosphere, individuals are able to enlarge their own understandings of issues and predicate their judgments on a careful consideration of others' views. Clearly, this experience would support a form of public reason in which people formed their opinions by carefully considering and testing the views of others in as broad-based and society-wide a discussion of the issues as is possible.

Representative government is threatened by two major dangers: class conflict and ignorance. Regarding the former, it is always desirable that no single class is allowed to be in a position to dominate the politics of society. This situation would divide society into hostile camps and destroy the chances for open deliberation based on mutual respect for political differences. Mill has in mind, when he talks about the dominant interests, the "employers of labour," those who control industry, and the laboring class. To prevent one class from dominating the other, Mill argues for balancing these giant interests against each other in the legislative setting by allowing each to have the same number of votes in the representative body.[73] Presumably, this approach would require that the two classes learn to compromise with each other as a precondition for achieving public-policy objectives.

The second problem, ignorance, can best be addressed by limiting, not eliminating, public participation. Mill argues that those less capable in the society develop enhanced capacities, including a respect for the needs of the community, a respect that helps to overcome the forces of divisiveness by engaging in public discussion about the issues of the day with their fellow citizens.

It is from political discussion, and collective political action, that one whose daily occupations concentrate his interest in a small circle round himself, learns to feel for and with his fellow citizens, and becomes consciously a member of the great community.[74]

But when people are denied the franchise, they are precluded from taking part in the public deliberation. They are forced into isolation from the rest of the society; they engender feelings of resentment on the one hand or, on the other hand, they may just become indifferent to public concerns. The best remedy to defeat ignorance then, and at the same time to promote political community, is participation.[75]

But Mill argues that, although all should participate, not all should be allowed to do so equally. In this regard, everyone who pays taxes and who can "read, write and do arithmetic" should have a voice. This includes women, who should have political rights equal to men.[76] But not everyone should have an equal voice.[77] Mill advocates a system of weighted voting by which those individuals with greater ability than others would be provided with more votes. The actual procedure used in determining who gets more or fewer votes is not extensively developed. Mill provides some examples of his position, however. For instance, an employer of labor, because he uses his mind, is more competent than a common laborer, whereas a foreman is more qualified than an ordinary worker, and a banker or merchant more qualified than a tradesman, and so on.[78] Furthermore, Mill does not support the idea of the secret ballot. If the vote is a public trust, why should not others know how we vote? Part of voting entails responsibility to the public interest. Should we be able to say one thing in public but vote the opposite way in the privacy of the voting booth?[79] Mill thinks not.

Even though these remedies may seem a bit farfetched to some, it is important to keep in mind Mill's central objective. Mill feels that civil society, one that protects the liberty of each person under the rule of law, could survive only in a setting that encouraged wide-scale public discussion of the major issues before the society. Such discussion would prevent the likelihood of powerful classes or groups from dominating politics and acting against the interests of the whole society. Moreover, this discussion would help ground civil society in a context that protected the full development of each individual as well as respect for protecting political community.

VI. Response and Rejoinder

Mill's commitment to the full development of the "higher faculties" for all citizens gives civil society a mission that previous writers on civil society might seriously question. It is not that previous writers would refuse Mill's objectives. The other thinkers we have studied might question Mill's strong emphasis on them. For instance, individuals in Mill's views are to be free to make choices, as we saw in Hobbes and Locke, about which ways of life people think best for themselves. If individuals want to be exclusively businesspeople, fine. If they want to be farmers, fine. If they want to make money the main interest of their lives, fine. Just as long as people, as for Kant, uphold for others the same freedom they each want for themselves, the choices people make should not be questioned. But, in addition, Mill, as in Benedict Spinoza, would urge that each person must assess the likelihood that a given way of life would open the doors to the full development of his or her higher mental faculties. If the ordinary day-to-day opportunities for people do not facilitate such development, Mill, like Spinoza, could not say that people in this situation would be truly free. However, from the standpoint of Hobbes and Locke, Mill places too high an expectation for most individuals to achieve; indeed, most individuals are happy with ordinary endeavors, and thus most do not wish to pursue Mill's concept of self-development. To press them in this direction in spite of themselves would be a great threat to their freedom.

Mill would respond by saying that the views of his critics manifest too low an expectation of people, and it is because of this fact that people are assumed unable to carry important burdens for the sake of a higher freedom. But if it is important for individuals to experience the richness associated with the "higher faculties," then individuals will have to accept the various burdens associated with these experiences. After all, developing one's higher capacities is not always easy. This kind of conduct takes hard work, persistence, and sacrifice. It is for this reason alone that society must encourage people in this activity.

Jean-Jacques Rousseau would argue that Mill was reaching for a level of life that would be well beyond the general will. People form into associations to provide those things that all acknowledge are of common benefit. The things in question here are the goods that most understand will contribute to an ordinary life. Once again, it is necessary to remember that the people who make Rousseau's laws are the peasants who sing and dance under a tree. This view of political participation is a metaphor for Rousseau to describe a society in which the differences in viewpoint among people are not very great or intense. For Rousseau, without this possibility, there would be no basis upon which to build a community founded upon a commitment to the common good. But in emphasizing the "higher faculties," Rousseau would say that Mill has made the same mistake that the philosophers of Rousseau's age had made. For Rousseau, Mill would teach people to criticize existing ways of life and traditions. And, in the process of doing so, Mill, in Rousseau's view, would engender in people a general disrespect for the traditions of civic virtue that help to create consensus among the people of the society and that help to make possible respect for the common good.

Mill would have countered this view, pointing out that his conception of deliberation in a representative democracy, or of what we have called *public reason*, is designed to include as wide a participation as possible by all. Indeed, participation for Mill, just as for Rousseau, enhances a sense of the importance of civic life, and it builds the ties of community. No doubt Kant and Spinoza would have embraced Mill's commitment to a type of public reason that encompasses as broad a spectrum of views as is possible. Like Mill, Kant and Spinoza would have supported the freedom of intellectual opinion and speech that supported this process. But unlike Mill and Spinoza, Kant did not strive to make his discourse of public reason as inclusive of everyone as did. Kant would not have accepted Mill's compromise position, which, in allowing all to participate, sought to limit the participation of those whose capacities made them less capable than others.

Hegel would have argued that a commitment to uphold the public good, within a setting that secures basic individual rights, cannot be attained by Mill because Mill does not establish a proper relationship between the state and the civil society, defined as a separate sphere from the state. The state must stand above civil society, ready to control and regulate it as necessary. Hegel saw civil society as filled with competing groups and interests, which, taken together, might not promote the common good. To overcome this problem, Hegel would allow the state the power to intervene in civil society and institute the common good.

Mill would no doubt argue that Hegel's view of civil society is harmed by Hegel's emphasis on those institutions that carry out his plan, in particular, corporations. These entities would constantly intrude into people's lives and dictate to them the terms of their existence. Mill would ask: How could real freedom ever be achieved in this setting? Moreover, the corporations provide a basis for a bureaucratic life that, over time, places a group of experts in charge of society. And these people would monopolize information and decision-making to such large degrees that the rest of society would no longer have an interest in participating in making decisions. When this event occurs, people's ability to fully take part in government would be diminished, along with the mental faculties needed for this enterprise. In consequence, Mill advocated, as part of his conception of civil society, the notion of a separate sphere of groups that would be able to perform, without the interference of government or of bureaucracy, many of the functions of both. This setting would encourage the development of public reason among all members of the society, in contrast to Hegel, whose corporations, from Mill's point of view, would severely limit the extension of public reason to all citizens.

Notes

1. John Stuart Mill, "Chapters on Socialism," in *Collected Works 5* (Toronto and Buffalo: University of Toronto Press, 1967), 715, quoted in Richard J. Arneson, "Prospects for Community in a Market Economy," *Political Theory* 9, no. 2 (May 1981): 207.

2. John Stuart Mill, "Utilitarianism," in *The Philosophy of John Stuart Mill*, ed. Marshall Cohen (New York: The Modern Library, 1961). *On Liberty*, which we refer to, is in this volume, too.

3. Ibid., 330. Also see, Jeremy Bentham, "Introduction to the Principles of Morals and Legislation," in *John Stuart Mill and Jeremy Bentham: Utilitarianism and Other Essays*, ed. Alan Ryan (London: Penguin Books, 1987), 65–66.

4. Mill, *On Liberty*, 198.

5. Bentham, "Introduction to the Principles of Morals and Legislation," 86, 97–111.

6. Ibid., 86. Italics are in the text.

7. Ibid., 88. Italics are in the text.

8. Ibid., 87.

9. Ibid., 89–97.

10. Mill, *On Liberty*, 331–32, 336–37.

11. Ibid., 332–33.

12. Ibid., 338–39.

13. Ibid., 338.

14. Ibid., 339.

15. Ibid., 340.

16. Ibid., 358.

17. Ibid., 359.

18. Ibid.

19. Ibid., 342.

20. Ibid., 384.

21. Ibid.

22. Ibid., 385.

23. Ibid., 258.

24. Ibid., 252.

25. Ibid.

26. Ibid.

27. Ibid., 257.

28. Ibid., 199.

29. Ibid., 200.

30. Ibid., 187.

31. Ibid., 189.

32. Ibid., 190–91. Italics are in the text.

33. Ibid., 191.

34. Ibid., 249.

35. Ibid., 271, 275.

36. Ibid., 271.

37. Ibid., 205.

38. Ibid., 208.

39. Ibid., 209.

40. Ibid., 213.

41. Ibid., 224.

42. Ibid., 231.

43. Ibid., 273, 282.

44. Ibid., 280, 274–76.

45. Ibid., 274–75, 279.
46. Ibid.
47. Ibid., 306–7. Additional discussion of this position is provided in Chapter 16, where we discuss his essay "The Subjection of Women."
48. Mill, *On Liberty*, 308, also pp. 306–7.
49. Ibid., 280.
50. John Stuart Mill, *Principles of Political Economy*, ed. W. S. Ashley (New York: Longmans, Green, and Co., 1929), 748.
51. Ibid., 748–49.
52. Ibid., 747–48. Here, Mill says that Smith believed a stationary economy "pinched and stinted people," unlike a growth economy. But Mill says he cannot accept the "political economists of the old school," such as Smith, who hold this view.
53. Ibid., 208–9, 749.
54. Ibid., 209.
55. Ibid.
56. Ibid., 208.
57. Ibid., 209, 749.
58. Ibid., 759–60.
59. Ibid., 750.
60. Ibid., 751.
61. Ibid., 763–64.
62. Ibid., 768, 773.
63. Ibid., 209.
64. John Stuart Mill, *Considerations on Representative Government*, intro. F. A. Hayek (Chicago: Henry Regnery Co., 1962), 72–73.
65. Mill, *On Liberty*, 312.
66. Ibid., 314.
67. Ibid., 312.
68. Mill, *Consideration on Representative Government*, 104–9.
69. Ibid., 92.
70. Ibid., 98.
71. Ibid., 111.
72. Ibid., 112.
73. Ibid., 136–37.
74. Ibid., 168.
75. Ibid., 169.
76. Ibid., 170, 172, 187–89.
77. Ibid., 178–79.
78. Ibid., 178–81.
79. Ibid., 204, 206–7.

15

John Rawls: The Just and Fair Civil Society

I. Introduction

Many view John Rawls (1921–2002) as the most important political theorist in the twentieth century, and his concept of justice as fairness is of central importance to contemporary discussions of civil society. Rawls's conception of justice responds, in part, to two different political concerns. In the 1960s, the problem of American society was how to make a part of the mainstream life of society those people, in particular African Americans, who for so long had been excluded by both custom and law from jobs, rights, and political participation. Today, in addition to continuing the quest for equality of opportunity for minorities and women, we confront the problem of how to maintain the stability of a democratic regime in the face of competing views of religion, of gender, of sexuality, and of culture. Rawls's work tracks both concerns. In *A Theory of Justice*, published in 1971,[1] Rawls's concept of justice as fairness is designed to secure basic liberties and opportunities for all citizens, including those who have been subject to forms of iniquitous discrimination. His book *Political Liberalism*,[2] published in 1993, revamps his concept of justice in a way that makes it possible for diverse and often contradictory ways of life to flourish within the context of a stable civil society. In both works, Rawls wants to show how his theory of justice defends continued and long-term support for the basic institutions and principles of a constitutional liberal democracy.

As we examine Rawls's doctrines, we not only hope to provide a lucid picture of modern liberal civil society, but we also hope to provide a discussion of some of the problems that this kind of society must address.

II. Rawls's Principles of Justice in *A Theory of Justice*

To begin, it must be made clear why it is vital to determine the principles of justice upon which a liberal civil society rests. Justice is a value of central importance to a civil society because the concept of justice is the basis for determining how basic goods, including rights and opportunities, should be distributed among citizens. Now, a civil society is composed of individuals, each of whom has his or her interests to pursue, and often enough, there will be conflicts over how these goods should be distributed. For instance, every civil society guarantees individuals equal access to basic rights, but at the same time, there always emerges differences in wealth and social and political influence. Reconciling the provision of equal rights with differences in wealth and social power becomes an important issue in a civil society. Central to resolving this conflict are clearly established and generally accepted principles of justice. Once these principles are determined, then all public institutions, such as the government and the economy, must distribute basic goods in accordance with them. Rawls's concept of justice as fairness regulates the institutions of a just civil society in keeping with a clear statement as to how rights and basic goods must be distributed to ensure equal freedom in a setting characterized by differences in wealth and status.[3]

The major question for a civil society to address pertains to which principles of distribution are most fair. There are many possible conceptions of justice from which to choose. For instance, one might argue that goods should be distributed in such a way as to ensure the greatest benefit for the greatest number of people, even if this means accepting certain injustices for the rest. Still others, as John Locke had argued, might claim that each person should be allowed to pursue his or her own interests in keeping with rules that encourage those with the most talent and ability to keep the gains of their work. The only restriction on this principle is that the work individuals perform must contribute to the general welfare of society. Or some might argue for a purely egalitarian form of distribution in which each person is entitled to the same amount of basic goods.

Rawls realizes that there are many possible principles that persons could choose to make the basis for distributing basic goods such as rights and opportunities. Given the diversity of possibilities, how does a society determine the set of principles that all would consider fair? Owing to Rawls's intention to find a single set of principles that all members of the society would accept as fair, it is necessary to start from a perspective that is common to all rational persons. This approach would exclude from the deliberation about justice all forms of bias. For if people were to discuss the question of justice from the standpoint of their particular interests, each person would define a conception of justice that best suits his or her own needs, and consequently, no common, shared view of justice would emerge.

To find a common standard, Rawls starts from what he considers an imaginary, but nonetheless universal, standpoint. His viewpoint, called the "original position," is presumed to be a point of view that all rational persons would find as an acceptable starting point for deliberating about justice. The original position is built upon what Rawls calls the "veil of ignorance." Each individual in the original position wears this veil when considering which principles of justice to choose. This veil would prevent him or her from knowing anything about his or her particular life circumstances, including his or her place in society, his or her abilities, his or her fortunes, and so on.[4] What kinds of knowledge would people have behind the veil? All persons in this situation would have general knowledge about the way society is structured and how it works in carrying out its basic functions. Rawls says that people in the original position "understand political affairs and the principles of economic theory; they know the basis of social organization and the laws of human psychology."[5] Of particular importance is that individuals will know that society has a top and bottom rung, as well as stages in between. Some people, owing to greater abilities than others, will occupy more important positions than will others. Moreover, each individual realizes that every person in society will want as many as possible of the goods that facilitate the enjoyment of life.[6] Thus, all people would like to end up in the most important positions, but at the same time, each knows that there are not enough of these "top" positions to go around.

But, and this is the most critical point, no one from behind the veil of ignorance knows for certain in which level of society he or she will end up. In the original position, then, uncertainty pervades people's minds. Responding to the uncertainty is a major factor determining one's choice of principles. Indeed, given the uncertainty, each person is prone to pursue a strategy that makes it possible for him or her to have a reasonable life, should he or she end up at the bottom. Each person does so by choosing a view of justice that guarantees those in the worst-off position a decent life, thus assuring their self-respect. In taking this view, each person assumes that the worst outcome could befall him or her, and, given that this outcome is possible, he or she hopes to make the worst situation as much a harbinger of a decent life as is feasible. Here, persons are not prone to gamble on the hope that, when they leave the veil of ignorance behind and enter society, they will be in the best position. Were they to take this gamble, they, of course, would want to fill the best situation with as many benefits as possible, and they would care little about securing the fortunes of the worst situation. However, Rawls's original position is predicated upon the premise that people would be far more cautious and "conservative" and much less prone to taking a risk of this sort.[7]

So, what are the principles of justice that individuals would derive in the original position? That is, which principles will be the basis for distributing what Rawls calls fundamental "social primary goods,"[8] such as rights, liberties, opportunities, income, wealth, and self-respect? His principles are:

First: each person is to have an equal right to the most extensive total system of equal basic liberties compatible with a similar system of liberty for all. Second: social and economic inequalities are to be arranged so that they are both: (a) to the greatest benefit of the least advantaged . . . and (b) attached to offices and positions open to all under conditions of fair equality of opportunity.[9]

Rawls's principles of justice distinguish between two parts of the social system, with the first principle applying to the first part and the second principle applying to the second part. The first of his principles of justice protects equal basic liberties, and the second of his principles is concerned with the social and economic inequalities that arise even in just societies. Included under the first principle, the principle of equal liberty, is the need to provide to each person, regardless of his or her social position, basic political liberties, such as the right to vote and hold public office, as well as the freedoms of speech, conscience, thought, and association. The list of basic liberties also includes what Rawls calls "freedom of the person." The latter protects people from physical assault as well as "psychological oppression." Also, there is a right to own personal property. Finally, Rawls's list of basic liberties includes "freedom from arbitrary arrest and seizure as defined by the concept of the rule of law."[10] The second principle, which addresses social and economic inequalities arising from the distribution of wealth, in particular the second part of the second principle, what Rawls calls the "liberal principle of fair equality of opportunity," requires that all people should be accorded equal opportunity to compete for all positions.[11]

Now, Rawls realizes that as a result of open and fully fair competition, some people will end up with more important positions as well as more wealth and status than others. Inevitably, then, there will be inequalities emerging from a situation in which a firm commitment to equal opportunity exists. The question for Rawls is how to permit inequalities without at the same time creating a society that denies full rights and basic opportunities for all. To achieve this objective, Rawls approaches the concept of justice from the standpoint of what he calls "democratic equality." Here, by adding to the fair equality of opportunity principle the *difference principle*, which is part *A* of the second principle, he argues that "the social order is not to establish and secure the more attractive prospects of those better off unless doing so is to the advantage of those less fortunate."[12]

Two important commitments are embodied in the principles of justice. First, the basic structure of the society's political institutions must be designed to protect the same basic rights for all persons. To this end, the equal liberty principle is given priority. This means that to secure wider economic and social opportunities for people, it is not acceptable to deny to others their basic liberties. Still, at times, liberty can be limited for the sake of securing a greater overall liberty for each person in society. For instance, liberties can be limited when they conflict with each other. In this circumstance, what is sought is an overall system of liberty in which competing liberties, such as speech and freedom from personal harassment, are placed in a reasonable, balanced relationship so as to better approximate the ideal of equal freedom for each person.[13] Second, Rawls recognizes that owing to the differentials in status and wealth, it is possible for a deep sense of unfairness to emerge in society. People who lack similar status or whose status provides them with little or no opportunity whatsoever will be deprived of what Rawls calls the most important primary good of self-respect, without which "nothing may seem worth doing."[14] To avert the loss of self-respect and the social instability such a situation causes, it is necessary, according to the difference principle, that the better-off classes transfer some of their gains to the least well-off members. This transfer is undertaken in the hope of ensuring for these individuals not just a basic minimum, what we call a safety net today, but a fair chance to achieve success at a variety of opportunities pertinent to their needs and specific abilities. For Stephen Holmes, it is the quest for equality of opportunity for everyone that makes Rawls a "radical among liberals." Rawls does not just settle for the safety net or a basic social minimum, he wants, in addition, the better off to help make possible full equality of opportunity for all people.[15] Inequalities are seen as acceptable by all, including, of course, the worst-off members, because these inequalities are shown to be to the advantage of everyone. This situation manifests the intention of what Rawls calls the "general conception of justice": "All social values – liberty and opportunity, income and wealth, and the bases of self-respect – are to be distributed equally unless an unequal distribution of any, or all, of these values is to everyone's advantage."[16]

Why would people choose Rawls's principles of justice over others? In the first place, his concept of justice ensures all people that, if misfortune should befall them and they end up in the lowest position in society, their lives will be decent, and they will be afforded an opportunity for self-respect. Here, whatever else happens, individuals will have their basic rights secured, and, in addition, all people will have a full plate of opportunities. In addition, Rawls's concept of justice incorporates merit as opposed to inherited social position as the basis for distributing opportunities. Yet, society must benefit from meritorious acts. Certainly, individuals who are meritorious would benefit personally, but their actions are to contribute to the welfare of society, too. Finally, Rawls argues that individuals realize there is more to gain from cooperation than from conflict. Indeed, cooperation is the basis for achieving the highly prized primary good of self-respect, which has a "central place" in his scheme.[17] As a first step toward realizing a cooperative society, it is necessary to remove the potentially destabilizing consequences arising from differences in power and ability by allowing them only on the condition that these differences benefit everyone. Only in this kind of social setting, governed by Rawls's view of justice, will there be sufficient peace and stability to ensure the basic rights and opportunities that make possible the attainment of self-respect for all people.

The Well-Ordered Society

Given this view of justice, Rawls believes, in *A Theory of Justice*, that it would be possible to construct what he refers to as a *well-ordered society*. A well-ordered society is one in which all citizens accept the principles of justice and each person in the society has a "strong and normally effective desire to act as the principles of justice require."[18] What kind of social experience emerges for people in this setting? Rawls describes a society in which purely private interests do not motivate individuals. In a "private society" people have their own ends, each has little or no concern for the "good of others," and each "prefers the most efficient scheme that gives him the largest share of assets."[19] A private society is a place in which each person acts by his or her own calculations to both define and pursue his or her personal ends without regard for a larger conception of justice that should regulate everyone's life. Presumably, in a private society, or what we have also at times referred to as the market setting, individuals remain in an antagonistic and competitive relationship with others, and each is concerned with finding ways to accumulate and acquire as much for him- or herself as possible. But in a well-ordered society, where each person shares the conception of justice just described, people understand that they need each other as "partners," each realizing that "the successes and enjoyments of others are necessary for and complementary to our own good."[20]

Here, each understands that people have various capacities and that the latter are best realized in a cooperative society in which different people help each other to realize their potential. Moreover, because people are seen as cooperating with each other to realize diverse capacities, there is no destructive competition, and thus individuals "appreciate the perfections of others."[21] The result of this experience is a social cohesiveness in which "we are led to the notion of a community of humankind the members of which enjoy one another's excellences and individuality elicited by free institutions, and they recognize the good of each as an element in the complete activity the whole scheme of which is consented to and gives pleasure to all."[22]

III. Political Liberalism and Value Pluralism

Rawls's depiction of a well-ordered society illustrates a fear common to some civil society theorists such as John Stuart Mill and G.W.F. Hegel. The fear is that the market orientation and the private freedom it encourages could create a society filled with self-serving individuals, no longer committed to maintaining mutual respect or regard for the needs and rights of others. But a well-ordered society would not suffer this fate. Instead, a well-ordered society offers a picture of cohesiveness based on the fact that individuals, of whatever type, can all agree to maintain a commitment to the same principles of justice and see to it that these principles are embodied into the main institutions of the society.[23]

Rawls's view of a well-ordered society suggests, then, that individuals are to make his principles of justice the basis for all relationships. Here, a single doctrine of justice would govern all phases of life for all people. This doctrine, for instance, would ensure each person equal political liberty throughout their lives, either as members of any particular group or as members of society in general. For instance, as members of a labor union, we must agree to accord others who are not members of our union the same basic rights that the first principle of justice guarantees. In this case, then, during a strike, we would grant those people who do not want to abide by the picket line a chance to cross it, enter the company against which we are striking, and, if need be, even take the jobs we now hold. The same right to freedom of expression that guarantees us the right to strike also guarantees opponents the right to cross the picket line. Moreover, internally within the union, we would have to abide by the principle of equal political liberty for how decisions within the group should be made. For instance, each member should have the same right to run for positions of union leadership. Thus, where there has been a tradition of preventing certain members, say, minorities or women, from holding union office, this tradition must be changed and union life made to be in accord with the principle of equal freedom.

Rawls even provides a view of moral development that indicates how people are socialized to make the principles of justice the main dimensions of their lives.[24] For instance, children must experience a family setting that nurtures a sense of self-respect by providing them with unconditional love. Once one leaves the family, respect for the principles of justice is further enhanced, as individuals become part of cooperative associations with others. In these settings, individuals must learn to understand the way people contribute differently to achieve the common ends of an association, and, further, they must develop a basis for cooperation through building ties of friendship and maintaining virtues such as fidelity and trust.

These views suggest that, in a well-ordered society, individuals accept that the principles of justice should be the key governing factors throughout all major phases of their lives, including their associations in groups, or with families, or with friends. In this case, there is a single, comprehensive political doctrine that should be the basis for regulating all relationships and for thus achieving a just and stable society. Rawls, now, in *Political Liberalism*, finds this depiction of the route to a just society "unrealistic."[25] What is unrealistic about suggesting that one comprehensive political doctrine for all of life should be made the basis for society?

Rawls realizes that his argument for a single comprehensive political doctrine to guide all the affairs of life will not be practical where there are, as in today's society, so many people holding different moral, religious, and philosophical doctrines. For instance, a deeply religious person may argue for a way of life encompassing prayer throughout the day, and a less religious person will find such a life onerous in the extreme. Some people may demand a chance to promote certain moral doctrines that conflict with the moral views of others, on such matters as abortion, prayer in schools, and so on. Further, Rawls realizes that many of these doctrines are reasonable, even if they conflict with each other. Consequently, there is no single doctrine – including his doctrine of a well-ordered society – that can be given a priority without denying some space to the different moral doctrines in society. For Rawls, a modern democratic society "is characterized not simply by a pluralism of comprehensive religious, philosophical, and moral doctrines but by a pluralism of incompatible yet reasonable comprehensive doctrines."[26] The new problem Rawls addresses in his discussion of political liberalism, then, is how it is possible to have a *"stable and just society"* or a society in which citizens "live together and . . . affirm" the principles of a constitutional democracy, even when it is the case that citizens are "divided by reasonable though incompatible religious, philosophical, and moral doctrines."[27]

Given this new problem Rawls identifies, the approach to achieving stability must be "recast" from the strategy developed in his view of a well-ordered society.[28] Because there are so many different ways of life, no single political doctrine, as was the case with his conception of the well-ordered society, can be made primary. This means that Rawls's principles of justice cannot be pushed down to cover all phases of life of each person in each domain of society. The principles of justice should extend to the relationships individuals have with each other as citizens but not to relationships they have with each other in the family or in private clubs. As citizens, individuals are to have to equal rights, but in the setting of family, the parents do not accord to children equal say. And in many private organizations, such as religious ones, the congregation members do not have the same input as do those who are in authority, such as elders or priests.

In place of an approach to achieving justice that would extend his principles of justice deeply into all phases of life in society, in his book *Political Liberalism*, Rawls now argues for a *political conception of justice* as the basis for society. In this view, there are certain fundamental political ideas that are said to be "implicit" in a democratic society, and, furthermore, these ideas would permit a wide range of diverse moral doctrines to flourish.[29] As we now explain, Rawls's concept of *political liberalism* embodies and defines the nature of these understandings.

In developing his doctrine of political liberalism, Rawls first refers to what he calls the "basic structure" of modern constitutional democracy. This structure pertains to the basic political, social, and economic institutions, which, together, constitute a system that makes possible social unity and continuing cooperation among citizens with diverse beliefs and views, from "one generation to the next."[30] For instance, Rawls has in mind the various government institutions on which a society depends, the type of economic life that a society upholds, and the general and basic institutions that a society seeks to maintain, such as a system of education, forms of socialization, and so on.

Now, these institutions, or the basic structure of a constitutional democracy, are directed by certain shared public values, defined in what Rawls calls a political conception of justice. These values orient society and arrange the basic institutions to achieve certain shared purposes, or what Rawls calls the "public political culture of a democratic society." If this is the case, to what ends and purposes would the major institutions of the basic structure be arranged?[31] In general, the main public political principles that a constitutional democracy is designed to achieve are a commitment to secure basic rights to all citizens and to ensure that these rights are given priority.[32] To this end, Rawls will discuss, as we describe next, elements of the political culture, such as an overlapping consensus and public reason, both of which are designed to make certain that the chief objective of the public, political culture – to protect the basic rights of all citizens – is secured. On this view, then, the main institutions that make up the basic structure of a society are to be arranged in keeping with a commitment to the major values of the public political culture, thus securing basic rights for all citizens.[33]

Outside the public political culture is a social, or what Rawls also calls the nonpublic, domain, or "the culture of daily life." Rawls refers to this realm as the "background culture of a civil society," or a setting in which exist the diverse associations of daily life, including "churches and universities, learned and scientific societies, and clubs and teams."[34] Here, individuals are to guide their lives by the particular values found in the group setting of which they elect to be a part.

Rawls, in referring to the nonpublic dimensions, is careful to point out that he is talking about a social sphere in which individuals guide their lives by certain moral conceptions, pertinent to the associations of which they are members.[35] Moreover, in the nonpublic setting, there will be many different values, and these values will be attached to the different nonpublic associations. Further, these values are freely accepted by people, whose choices are based on their experiences with a host of commitments and attachments to nonpublic groups that they develop over a lifetime.[36]

Each of the nonpublic groups or associations has what Rawls refers to as a *comprehensive doctrine*. A doctrine is comprehensive "when it includes conceptions of what is of value in human life, as well as ideals of personal virtue and character that are to inform much of our nonpolitical conduct." Thus, a comprehensive doctrine defines the general values and virtues that are found in various associations in the nonpublic settings and that govern the outlooks of people who choose to live in those settings.[37] Moreover, there are many conflicting and competing moral and religious doctrines. Some groups will advocate strong religious upbringings; others will advocate atheism; some groups who are religious advocate this religion and not that one; others who reject religion may make a particular philosophical view of life a dominant element, and so on.

Given the presence of many diverse comprehensive doctrines, it is clear now how Rawls's doctrine of political liberalism differs from the concept of a well-ordered society found in *A Theory of Justice*. Rawls's political liberalism suggests a political conception of justice that refers only to the "main institutions of political and social life, not for the whole of life."[38] Rawls no longer sees his conception of justice as designed to present a single set of principles that would be applicable to all dimensions of life, from activities related to interacting with government, to associations with friends and family. Our lives take place in two cultures, and, when we enter the public political culture, we live by values that are not necessarily operative for us in the nonpublic setting. Still, the values of the public culture are considered reasonable and thus worthy of our support because they contribute to the maintenance of a constitutional order that people in a democratic culture generally support. Indeed, these values are taken for granted and are considered "latent in the public political culture of a democratic society."[39]

In developing the distinction between nonpublic and public cultures, Rawls has conceived of a civil society in the two senses that have permeated this book. First, a civil society consists of public principles and laws that sustain a commitment to basic rights and a constitutional democracy. Second, a civil society also includes a separate sphere of groups, independent from the state or large economic organizations, whose particular moral conceptions guide association life. Indeed, the political conception of a constitutional democracy is defined in such a way as not to interfere with the ways of life of the various nonpublic settings, each of which is driven by different moral, religious, or philosophical conceptions. But at the same time, the political conception of society also suggests that no single comprehensive doctrine, which might emanate from a nonpublic setting, is to become the preeminent basis for determining the nature of justice in society. Were this to happen, the state would be turned into an oppressive regime, losing, thereby, its constitutional democratic character.[40]

The Overlapping Consensus and Civic Virtue

In line with the preceding point, then, for Rawls, the values of the political conception of a constitutional democracy are fundamental ones. Thus, when other values come into conflict with the main values of the political conception of a constitutional democracy, in particular the importance and priority of basic rights, the latter always must "outweigh" in importance other values.[41] Unless this commitment is possible, society would not retain its character as a constitutional democracy.

Rawls's willingness to make the values of a constitutional democracy have priority evolves from his concern to find a basis for maintaining the unity and stability of this kind of society. It is in keeping with this view that Rawls emphasizes the importance of an overlapping consensus. What is an overlapping consensus, and why is it important?

In his discussion of political liberalism, Rawls argues that a constitutional democracy can only survive when support for its basic institutions is shared universally by all citizens. This means that all citizens, regardless of the particular comprehensive doctrines they adhere to, must make as the primary basis for their citizen role a commitment to an overlapping consensus that enshrines support for constitutional democracy throughout society. The central idea of an overlapping consensus is that supporters of different but reasonable comprehensive doctrines find it possible to "endorse the political conception [of a democracy], each from its own point of view."[42] For Rawls, support for the overlapping consensus involves people being able to uphold, regardless of their nonpublic commitments and values, a general commitment to the "liberty of conscience and freedom of thought, as well as fair equal opportunity and principles covering certain essential needs."[43]

In addition to a commitment to these principles, the overlapping consensus includes support for three important dimensions. The first is to clearly fix "once and for all" the nature of the basic rights and liberties that all citizens are to secure as a "special priority." This principle removes the definition of basic rights from the "calculus of social interests, thereby establishing clearly and firmly the rules of political contest." The second idea is that, in discussing public matters, citizens must rely upon the processes of what Rawls calls *public reason.*[44] We will discuss the nature of public reason later in the chapter. For now, suffice it to say that public reason represents a shared approach to deliberating and developing judgments about public matters, an approach that will be helpful in achieving a principled consensus or a consensus that protects basic liberties for all. The final element of the overlapping consensus is a willingness of people to meet each other "half-way," and to "cooperate with others on political terms that everyone can publicly accept."[45]

Before proceeding further, it is well to enumerate the important implications for civic virtue of the notion of an overlapping consensus. In particular, the over-lapping consensus embodies the civic virtue dimensions of Lockean toleration and of a Kantian view of mutual respect. Rawls's overlapping consensus includes Lockean toleration when he says we should learn to meet others halfway. By doing so, we practice the art of learning how to live and let live. The first two dimensions of the overlapping consensus, on the other hand, are versions of the mutual respect principle. In according to others the same rights we expect for our close associates and ourselves, we ensure that each person is treated with dignity and is accorded self-respect. Moreover, the doctrine of public reason, like Kant's view of the public use of reason discussed earlier, asks individuals to engage one another in a deliberation about common issues. And this enterprise requires us, as we see next, to consider the points of view of others with whom we disagree. In doing so, we manifest toward others respect once again, but this time, respect is associated with the effort of each of us to include others in forging agreements on important public issues.

Further, it should be clear that Rawls incorporates Locke's notion of toler-ation, but in a manner that recasts the idea considerably. As we saw, Locke did not include toleration for Catholics, agnostics, and atheists, in large part because his view of toleration suggested that, even when people of differing views agree to live and let live, a deep sense of difference might remain between people. And this sense of difference might contribute to a tendency to deny to those who dif-fer widely from accepted social norms the same rights guaranteed to all. Thus, Locke's notion of toleration would be used to impose certain comprehensive con-ceptions of justice, appropriate for the nonpublic setting only, onto all people.

Rawls avoids this problem for himself by grafting the practice of mutual respect onto toleration.

Public Reason and Democratic Citizenship

In a constitutional democracy, citizens should discuss and reach agreements about issues of great importance – such as abortion, gay rights, family policy, health care, the place of religion in public policy debates, matters touching on war and peace, the distribution of basic resources, and so on – by employing what Rawls refers to as "public reason." Issues like these are important because they require citizens to address concerns pertaining to the "basic justice" of the society – those matters that have to do with maintaining a constitutional democracy – not from the standpoint of particular comprehensive doctrines, such as those emanating from religious or ethical perspectives, but from the common standpoint of the shared values embedded in the overlapping political consensus.[46] Given this commitment, public reason requires that citizens "conduct their fundamental discussions within the framework of what each regards as a political conception of justice based on the values that the others can reasonably be expected to endorse."[47]

The common standpoint that public reason embraces is liberal in character since it contains a "political conception of justice" that "specifies" certain basic rights, liberties, and opportunities, that "assigns a special priority to these rights, liberties, and opportunities," and that provides individuals with the "adequate all-purpose" means to make use of their basic rights, liberties, and opportunities.[48] Generally, Rawls's basic rights include the right to vote, the right of participation in politics, freedom of conscience, thought, and association, and coverage by the rule of law.[49] These basic rights and the principles that define the structure of the government that provides them – such as the enumerated powers of various branches of government – are what Rawls refers to as "constitutional essentials."[50]

Discussions of public issues, when undertaken from the perspective of public reason, seek an application of the main values of the political conception of justice, as cited in the previous paragraph, to resolve the matter at hand. This means that particular comprehensive doctrines can never be used to resolve issues, but instead only the main principles of the political conception of justice can be used. For instance, in discussing abortion, people agree to set to the side particular religious views and instead only discuss abortion from the standpoint of shared, common principles, which include an understanding of the rights that are at stake. Thus, citizens would ask how the rights relevant to the discussions, such as to privacy, for instance, should be interpreted to reach a resolution of the abortion issue. In addition to not relying upon particular comprehensive doctrines as the basis for this discussion, there are certain "guidelines" that people should follow. These include efforts to ensure the integrity of the information used in the discussion by employing commonsense understandings and the methods of science.[51] Also, the inquiry should be open to all and civic virtues such as "civility" and "reasonableness" should guide citizens to "make possible reasoned public discussion of political questions."[52]

For the sake of maintaining a constitutional democracy, public officials and citizens are to act in keeping with the canons of public reason as just described. Public officials, such as judges and legislators, do so when they

> *explain to other citizens their reasons for supporting fundamental political positions in terms of the political conception of justice they regard as the most reasonable. In this way they fulfill what I shall call their duty of civility to another and to other citizens.*[53]

Ordinary citizens act in accordance with the norms of public reason when they think about critical public matters "*as if* they were legislators" and formulate judgments about them from the standpoint of the central values of the overlapping political conception of justice in a constitutional democracy.[54] Moreover, citizens have an obligation to hold public officials accountable to the standards of public reason and thus citizens should "repudiate [through the ballot box] government officials and candidates for public office who violate public reason." Indeed, this practice is vital to the "enduring strength" of a constitutional democracy.[55]

For some people, this view of public reason is unnecessarily limiting.[56] And this is because people are asked during the discussion of substantial public issues to diminish the importance of particular comprehensive doctrines, in deference to the values of the overlapping political conception of justice. For example, some proponents of a greater role for religion in society complain that in discussions of the place of religion in the public realm, including matters pertaining to public prayer, the only values upon which the discussion can center are those that pertain to freedom of conscience and to the separation of church and state principle. In consequence, religious values – such as those proclaiming religion's importance to the moral and spiritual development of people – are given short shrift and are thus denied a prominent place in the discussion of religion and society. To be sure, as the proponents of public reason would counter, people may practice religious values in the nonpublic realm, and they may articulate them in the public realm discourse, too – freedom of speech always protects this option. But the practice of public reason upholds the expectation that during the discussion of public issues people will bracket out of their arguments – that is, not rely upon – values emanating from their religious or other comprehensive views. How else, advocates of public reason claim, can a constitutional democracy, based on the separation of church and state and freedom of conscience, be preserved? Those opposed to this approach will nonetheless register the complaint that their moral or religious views have been treated unfairly either by being excluded from consideration or, if considered, by being denied as prominent a place in law and public policy as is given to others.

Now, Rawls, who sees public reason as a basis for agreement among people with diverse religious and moral comprehensive doctrines, nonetheless does not view public reason as a panacea that will always engineer agreement among these people. Rawls says that the practice of public reason does not "always lead to a general agreement of views [on the resolution of particular issues], nor is it a fault that it does not."[57] There are a variety of reasons to explain this situation, each of which is discussed in what Rawls refers to as the "burdens of judgment." For instance, the evidence used by people to support their positions on the issue in question may be conflicting and complex, making it difficult to achieve a basis for agreement. Or, there are competing normative perspectives at play on each side of an issue, and this affects the way people interpret the information at hand as well as the way a public principle should be interpreted in a given case.[58] Owing to these aspects and others, many political discussions of important issues, based on the salient values of the political conception of justice discussed here, may end in a "stand-off," that is, without agreement. As Rawls says, "Reasonable political conceptions of justice do not always lead to the same conclusion."[59] In these circumstances, where issues are hotly contested, the best way to decide them is through a vote, the outcome of which is "seen as legitimate," so long as those government officials who vote do so in "accordance with the idea of public reason."[60]

This circumstance, which features consideration of diverse views by many people, need not be a sign of the inability of public reason to contribute to a stable constitutional democracy in a society filled with competing comprehensive doctrines but, to the contrary, as evidence of its likelihood of doing precisely that. Being able to engage in debate, which culminates in citizens understanding and making room for diverse views that they had not, perhaps, carefully considered before and recognizing the importance that the principles of the political conception play in making this possible, only secures an ever-deeper respect among citizens for these principles and for the constitutional democracy they establish. Rawls says that "citizens learn and profit from debate and argument, and when their arguments follow public reason, they instruct society's political culture and deepen their understanding of one another even when agreement cannot be reached."[61]

Civil Society and Political Liberalism

In general, Rawls's approach to public reason, especially in the context of its failure, at times, to reach consensus as well as the criticisms by those who believe their comprehensive doctrines are not adequately considered, can survive only if people uphold the values of the overlapping political conception of justice. What are the ways to maintain support among people for the overlapping political values of a constitutional democracy? Four of them follow.

First, Rawls argues for minimum forms of civic education for all. For instance, children who are members of different religious sects, including those who want to have their members live apart from the influences of the modern world, should be taught the constitutional essentials of a liberal regime. Teaching children about their basic rights is necessary so that, according to Rawls:

> *They know that liberty of conscience exists in their society and that apostasy is not a legal crime, all this to ensure that their continued religious membership when they come of age is not based simply on ignorance of their basic rights or fear of punishment for offenses that are only considered offenses within their religious sect.*[62]

Indeed, children's education must enable them to understand the basic values and norms of civil society so, they "honor the fair terms of social cooperation in their relations with the rest of society."[63]

Second, Rawls is aware that people who support the values of the overlapping political conception do so because they expect the state not to interfere in the lives of the diverse civil society groups, which hold different, even if reasonable, moral doctrines in the nonpublic sphere. To this end, the state must be neutral to the various values and ways of life apparent in society, subject to the provision that the values in question fall within the public political conception of justice. Thus, it is clearly the case that Rawls's view of neutrality, or the idea that the state should provide room for a diversity of competing values without giving favor to any one of them, does not mean that people have a right to pursue a way of life that threatens the basic rights of other citizens. Indeed, Rawls says his view of neutrality, what he refers to as the "priority of right," or the idea of securing basic rights for all, "allows [that] only permissible conceptions (those that respect the principles of justice) can be pursued."[64]

Third, because of the predominance of a basic structure that is grounded in a commitment to the principles of a just constitutional regime, it is the case that, over time, nonpublic associations, which have values that violate these principles, would, in all likelihood, end up discarding them, a phenomenon Rawls refers to as the "facts of commonsense political sociology."[65] Rawls believes the basic structure of a constitutional democracy and the values upon which it is based would influence which comprehensive doctrines various groups in civil society would end up holding. For instance, religious groups that require government-sponsored religious intolerance would "cease to exist."[66] Moreover, as a result of adaptation by nonpublic groups to the values of public reason, over time, certain issues would never even be considered in the society Rawls describes. Thus, any effort to legislate serfdom and slavery would be considered a violation of basic principles of justice and so would be "off the [political] agenda."[67]

Fourth, people will support the overlapping consensus when, as citizens, they are permitted to promote their particular comprehensive moral doctrines during the process of public reasoning about public issues. Rawls would thus agree that it is acceptable for individuals to enter the public realm and present particular reasons derived from their religious experience as the basis for their position on a public issue. They may do so, that is, subject to one important limitation. In particular, as they present their comprehensive moral values, they must act "to strengthen the ideal of public reason itself."[68] Here, one could argue that the society needs to be made more respectful of religious values for a whole host of reasons, including that religious beliefs contribute to moral stability or that they help people find contentment and happiness not otherwise available in the highly competitive setting of modern society. These values in the public realm could be presented in a way that demonstrates how religious traditions strengthen the values of public reason. For instance, during the process of discussing how to handle out-of-control children, X, who is not wedded to promoting religious ideas for this purpose, may be shown the virtue of such a practice. In this case, X would have to be shown that religious practices help sustain an environment that secures what is a major value of public reason, the basic rights for all people. Thus, for Rawls:

> *Reasonable comprehensive doctrines [those that support a democratic society], religious or nonreligious, may be introduced in public political discussion at any time, provided that in due course, proper political reasons – and not reasons given solely by comprehensive doctrines – are presented that are sufficient to support whatever the comprehensive doctrines are said to support.*[69]

For Rawls, this experience enables people to understand how citizens' respect for the values of a constitutional regime is closely aligned to their commitment to particular comprehensive moral and religious values.[70] What strengthens the connection between everyday moral and religious beliefs and basic constitutional values intensifies respect for the overlapping consensus that sustains public reason. Rawls believes that judges contribute to the strengthening of public reason when they decide cases, and thus it is appropriate for citizens to pay heed to the way the judicial system interprets and applies "basic constitutional values" in rendering the judges' decisions.[71] Even when citizens disagree with these decisions, and are thus driven to take part in discussions to defend their views, they are likely to gain a greater grasp of the constitutional principles at stake.[72] In either case, an education in civic understanding of public reason becomes more likely through the important influence of the judicial system.

Clearly, the effect of Rawls's political liberalism on the members of a society would be to demand that, throughout the variety of nonpublic associations, such as the church and family, as well as all the other groups of civil society, it would be necessary to teach the values of the overlapping consensus and to expect that nonpublic groups conform to them. There is no question, then, that Rawls's view of political liberalism promotes a single comprehensive moral doctrine not unlike the concept of a well-ordered society in *A Theory of Justice*. And his political conception does reach deeply into many phases of life in society. This means that Rawls's views require that individuals throughout their engagements in the nonpublic spaces of civil society – including families and religious institutions – should make certain that the major doctrines of Rawls's political conception of justice, in particular respect for basic rights and for public reason, should always be maintained. As Susan Okin indicates, Rawls seems, with his concept of political liberalism, to be arguing that "persons in the just society should order their whole lives – not just the political aspects of them – in accordance with justice."[73]

It is the comprehensive nature of Rawls's political liberalism, however, that makes it very appealing to some advocates of a liberal civil society. In the first place, Rawls's political liberalism would make possible the separate sphere of various nonpublic groups, and these groups would certainly permit not only diverse life possibilities, but they would act as buffers against the power of government. Further, Rawls's separate sphere exists within and upholds a larger moral environment that includes respect for the civic virtues of toleration and mutual respect. The former virtue asks that we live and let live with people holding values different from our own, and the virtue of mutual respect requires us to carefully consider the views of others in public realm discussions of issues but always in ways that advance the commitment to secure for each person their basic rights.

IV. Response and Rejoinder

Locke, like Rawls, wanted to remove issues of religious controversy from the political arena. Locke, thus, was concerned that the state only be involved with civil interests, such as life, liberty, and health, but the state should not get into the position of advocating a commitment to religious doctrines or organizations. Of course, as we saw in Chapter 9, Locke did not carry this view out fully since he talked about potential restrictions by the state for agnostics, atheists, and Catholics. Rawls would have criticized this absence of consistency in Locke by saying that he, Rawls, hopes to carry out Locke's project in a complete way. The state should only advance truly public principles, which means freedom of religious belief, as opposed to promoting a particular sectarian religious perspective as Locke seemed to do. Locke might have agreed with this view except for the fact that he might have argued back to Rawls that the beliefs people hold in what Rawls calls the nonpublic sphere will be too strong to completely eliminate them from the public realm. This objective could only be achieved if individuals could approach nonpublic values with a certain degree of skepticism. But is this outlook likely, especially in a society in which so much of one's sense of identity is associated with a belief in the truth of one's nonpublic values? Locke would think not.

Rawls would argue in response that skepticism is not the issue here. More important is the presence among people of an overlapping standpoint, committed to uphold the public principles of a constitutional democracy. In this context, people could enter the public realm advocating particular religious views, but they would have to do so in ways that gave priority to the public values of the society.

Locke would no doubt have said that this position salvaged his point. For people to do what Rawls wants of them requires that they dilute their religious beliefs, which is to say, become somewhat skeptical of their importance. And Locke did not see this happening, and he would probably say that people would see this practice as too high a price to pay for achieving a civil society. But Rawls would say that people's intensity of belief could be reduced in deference to the norms of public reason, and their doing so is not a function of skepticism but of the very same toleration that Locke advocated. Indeed, one way to read Locke is to suggest that this possibility emanates from his doctrine of toleration.

To Jean-Jacques Rousseau, Rawls would say that Rousseau had hoped to make possible a general will that, to be sure, would not eliminate the nonpublic realm, but would, in all likelihood, reduce its significance. Rousseau had no choice but to diminish the nonpublic realm, given his commitment to the norms of the public realm. Now, Rawls would argue that modern civil society would reject Rousseau for devaluing the nonpublic setting. Most people in the contemporary world want to make the nonpublic realm ever larger and more prominent, and they resist public encroachment into the private life by a democratic experience. Further, for Rawls, Rousseau's view of public participation, while laudable to some extent, lacks the kind of structure provided by Rawls's view of public reason. Rawls would argue that the great virtue of public reason is that it permits individuals to achieve a form of principled consensus, in this case, a majority view that does not deny equal protection of rights to all. But Rousseau's general will, for Rawls, might encourage people to meet to decide issues without regard for the rights of individuals who do not agree with the concept of the general good defined by the collective will of the people. Although Rousseau would hope this would not happen, what is to prevent this situation from occurring? Rawls's public reason would ensure, as Hegel had hoped to do, that the consensus that emerges is a principled one that carries forward the commitment to shared rational principles.

No doubt Rousseau would respond to Rawls by declaring that Rawls no less than himself has diminished the nonpublic realm by making it subservient to the norms of public reason. After all, if these norms are so prominent, what is to keep them from being pushed so far down into the nonpublic realm that the traditional beliefs found there lose their significance for people? Further, Rousseau would say that Rawls has not fully developed a basis for public reason and deliberation among the citizens because Rawls permits many diverse and often contradictory views of life to remain a part of the common life of the members of civil society. After all, Rawls argues that there is a multitude of reasonable, if not contradictory, moral doctrines existing in the nonpublic sphere of civil society. Rousseau would argue that, if this be the case, then deliberation on issues would always be suffused with diverse and contradictory moral viewpoints, making agreement on the nature of the common good difficult, if not impossible, to realize. Rousseau would argue, then, for the need for a civil religion that would reduce the presence and impact of such doctrines on public debate, so that a conception of the common good could be reached. Rawls would view this move as a threat to basic rights.

Mill's liberalism, for Rawls, would seek to impose a single comprehensive moral doctrine onto the whole of society.[74] As we saw, Mill emphasized the importance of the higher faculties of mind and associated them with a fuller and more wholesome freedom. Rawls would argue that for some, indeed for many, there are more important values, such as living within religious traditions, building friendships, or enjoying leisure. None of these values can be denied without undermining the full freedom of each individual. Mill would respond to Rawls by claiming that Rawls, in promoting the prominence of public reason, is in fact fostering if not Mill's person of higher faculties, at least something akin to it in the form of the ideal democratic citizen who practices public reason in discussions of important issues. Indeed, Mill might say about Rawls's doctrine that if democratic citizens are to make public reason the basis for decisions about public issues, they must highlight the importance of Mill's higher faculties, for it is the latter that makes possible the full attainment of public reason. Rawls would, of course, not accept this critique of his view of public reason. But Mill would argue that Rawls could not have it both ways. He could not promote a conception of public reason that requires giving priority to something like the higher faculties, while, at the same time, denying that these faculties should have priority.

Kant would argue that, to ensure that just institutions were protected, it would be necessary to establish a system in which the various interests in society were arrayed in such a way as to limit and check each other. Unless this approach was taken, even just institutions, or those intending to uphold fair principles, would be overrun by whatever interest or coalition of interests dominated society. But Rawls would reject what he refers to as a "modus vivendi" basis for supporting just institutions. He alludes to the example of religious toleration to make his point. In this situation, various groups learn to put up with each other. But their doing so depends upon a power equivalence between them. When that equivalence no longer exists, as, for instance, happens when one group gains superior power to others, then the *modus vivendi* breaks down and the inferior group, power-wise, is no longer tolerated.[75] For Rawls, there needs, then, to be a stronger basis for securing just institutions. So, he argues that, to maintain a civil society dedicated to securing the rights of all, the citizens must have a strong commitment to the values associated with his view of political liberalism, including support for what he calls the overlapping consensus.

Hegel would respond to Rawls by arguing that the latter's view of the relationship between the state and society is not well conceived. Hegel, as addressed previously, described civil society as composed of competing interests, none of which by themselves would maintain respect for the needs of the larger society. To achieve the prospect of the common good, the state entered civil society and defined the norms to which the various social interests should adapt themselves. The state achieved this objective through the maintenance of what Hegel called corporations. Now, Rawls would respond to this view of the state's relationship to society with a great degree of skepticism. Of fundamental importance to Rawls is that the various groups that make up the separate sphere of a civil society are free to pursue their own self-determined moral doctrines and ways of life. Were the state to enter the activities of these groups and determine their outlooks, then the state would be imposing on these groups a particular comprehensive moral doctrine, and, by this act, the state would be undermining the autonomy these groups deserve. This approach might threaten the rights that Rawls's political liberalism guarantees.

On the question of the common good, Michael Sandel points out that Aristotle would say that conceptualizing issues in terms of Rawls's public reasons wrongly forces people to frame issues in ways independent of a conception of the "good life."[76] Those who take this view in today's society would say that in discussing any issue we should start by depicting the values all people must embrace for the sake of achieving the "good life" for all of us. Then we should decide issues in ways that achieve these values. For Rawls, Aristotle's approach imposes on all people a single conception of the best way to live, and doing so is inconsistent with protecting the same liberties and rights for all.[77] Where do you stand?

Notes

1. John Rawls, *A Theory of Justice* (Cambridge: Harvard University Press, 1999). The first edition was written in 1971, but we have used the new edition here.
2. John Rawls, *Political Liberalism* (New York: Columbia University Press, 1993).
3. Rawls, *A Theory of Justice*, 10–15.
4. Ibid., 118–19.
5. Ibid., 119.
6. Ibid., 123.
7. Ibid., 132–33.
8. Ibid., 54.
9. Ibid., 266, also p. 53.
10. Ibid., 53.
11. Ibid., 73, 53.
12. Ibid., 65.
13. Ibid., 53–54, 266.
14. Ibid., 54. Also, Rawls, *Political Liberalism*, 318.
15. A review of Rawls's *Political Liberalism:* Stephen Holmes, "The Gatekeeper," *The New Republic*, October 11, 1993, 42.
16. Rawls, *A Theory of Justice*, 54.
17. Rawls, *Political Liberalism*, 318; Rawls, *A Theory of Justice*, 54.
18. Rawls, *A Theory of Justice*, 398.
19. Ibid., 457.
20. Ibid., 458.
21. Ibid., 459.
22. Ibid.
23. Ibid., 400–1.
24. Ibid., 403–4, 406–13, 414–19.
25. Rawls, *Political Liberalism*, xvii. Also see Susan Moller Okin's, "Review of Rawls's *Political Liberalism*," *American Political Science Review* 87, no. 4 (December 1993): 1010.
26. Rawls, *Political Liberalism*, xvi.
27. Ibid., xviii. Emphasis added.

28. Ibid., xvii.
29. Ibid., 13.
30. Ibid., 11–13.
31. Ibid., 13–14.
32. Ibid., 175, 156–57.
33. Ibid., 175.
34. Ibid., 14; also, p. 220.
35. Ibid., 220.
36. Ibid., 221–22.
37. Ibid., 175, 14.
38. Ibid., 175.
39. Ibid.
40. Ibid., 37; also, 175.
41. Ibid., 156–57.
42. Ibid., 134, 224.
43. Ibid., 164.
44. Ibid., 161–62.
45. Rawls refers to these three dimensions as central to describing the basis of a "stable constitutional consensus," but in his account, these dimensions are also integral to and incorporated into the idea of an overlapping consensus. See Rawls, *Political Liberalism*, 144, 156–57, 161, 164–65.
46. Ibid., 224–25.
47. Ibid., 226.
48. Ibid., 223.
49. Ibid., 227.
50. Ibid., 227–32.
51. Ibid., 224.
52. Ibid.
53. John Rawls, *The Law of Peoples* (Cambridge: Harvard University Press, 1999), 135.
54. Ibid. Italics are in the text.
55. Ibid., 135–36.
56. William A. Galston, *Liberal Pluralism: The Implications of Value Pluralism for Political Theory and Practice* (Cambridge: Cambridge University Press, 2002), 116–17, 121; Fred M. Frohock, "The Boundaries of Public Reason," *American Political Science Review* 91, no. 4 (December 1997): 841–42.
57. John Rawls, "The Idea of Public Reason Revisited," in *The Law of Peoples* (Cambridge: Harvard University Press, 1999), 170.
58. Rawls, *Political Liberalism*, 54–58.
59. Rawls, "The Idea of Public Reason Revisited," 168–69.
60. Ibid., 169.
61. Ibid., 170–171.
62. John Rawls, *Justice as Fairness: A Restatement* (Cambridge: Harvard University Press, 2001), 156.
63. Ibid.
64. Rawls, *Political Liberalism*, 192–93.
65. Ibid., 193.
66. Ibid., 196–97.
67. Ibid., 151.
68. Ibid., 247.
69. Rawls, "The Idea of Public Reason Revisited," 152.
70. Ibid., 153.
71. Rawls, *Justice as Fairness*, 146.

72. Ibid.

73. Okin, "Review of *Political Liberalism*," 1011.

74. Rawls, *Political Liberalism*, 199.

75. Ibid., 147–49.

76. Michael Sandel, *Justice: What's the Right Thing to Do?* (New York: Farrar, Straus, and Giroux, 2009), 217.

77. Ibid., 212–23.

16

The Conservative View: Edmund Burke, Alexis de Tocqueville, and Michael Oakeshott

I. Introduction

In this chapter, we examine the ideas of Edmund Burke (1729–1797), Alexis de Tocqueville (1805–1859), and Michael Oakeshott (1901–1990). For these writers, society is a repository of the wisdom contained in cumulative experience. Each writer discussed society in terms of those values, traditions, and institutions that have stood the test of time while confronting recurring and enduring challenges and problems. The conservative tends to view these traditional dimensions of society as the critical bases for establishing a civil society, which can provide rights and liberties as well as an atmosphere of civic virtue.

There are several reasons for this approach. First, conservatives seek to learn from these traditions the practical and enduring truths that, when properly upheld, help to maintain long-term commitment to a civil society. Moreover, these traditions are the ground for each person's identity. For conservatives, no matter how free we are, without the presence of shared traditions, our lives would lack meaning. And the reason for this is that, while freedom permits us to have many choices, it does not provide, by itself, those core values as, for instance, are found in religious or particular cultural settings, that enable our lives to have enduring meaning.

In the cases of the three conservative writers discussed in this chapter, existing traditions and customs are seen as major contributing sources for securing among citizens a sense of personal identity, the protection of basic rights, and a commitment to civic virtue.[1] Each of the writers discussed in this chapter advocates different kinds of social values that are considered responsible for both social cohesion and individual identity, and thus there are different conceptions of society and of the role civic virtue plays in it.

For Burke, in addition to religion and regard for the traditions associated with both a natural aristocracy and a natural order to society, society is characterized by respect for the importance of local affiliations and of moderation. For Tocqueville, who, like Burke, also demonstrates the importance of religion and moderation, there is a supreme importance placed upon the separate sphere of voluntary associations as well as a form of individualism that is receptive to and is formed by the democratic experience. Also, for Tocqueville, a spirit of equality replaces Burke's natural aristocracy. Oakeshott seeks to define those traditions that make possible a wide array of life possibilities while freeing people from the tyranny and the regimen of large organizations that impose their will on people, thus denying their freedom. In choosing these three representative thinkers, then, our intention is to demonstrate that conservatism, no less than the different liberal views of civil society, has diverse voices, too.

II. Burke: The Purpose of Civil Society

Edmund Burke had a long political career as a member of the British parliament during the eighteenth century, and he was among those who attacked the French Revolution.[2] It should be clear, however, that Burke was not unalterably opposed to revolution, because he supported the American Revolution. Why support one revolution and not the other? He supported the American cause because he disagreed with British policies that threatened prosperous commercial enterprises in America. Burke believed the American commercial setting followed a free-market approach that was associated with a form of self-regulating economic life that both acted as a restraint upon government interference in people's lives and contributed to societal stability by securing property rights. But in France, the revolutionaries sought to tear asunder the guiding traditions of society, including those having to do with property and commerce, and the only institution that was attempting to preserve them was the monarchy that Burke supported.[3] So, in the American case, the revolutionaries protected useful social traditions, but in France, they threatened them. Burke consequently supported the former and not the latter.

Most of Burke's political writings appeared as speeches or arguments provided in response to particular political issues. His reaction to the French Revolution was an occasion for writing a statement of the political principles upon which he acted.[4] In discussing his *Reflections on the Revolution in France*, we develop some of these principles and provide a review of Burke's account of civil society. In this section, we discuss Burke's views of the bases of civil society, including the importance of rights, as well as the role of government in a civil society.

So, what is Burke's view of civil society? A civil society must protect the rights of individuals. In emphasizing rights, for Burke, there is no question that a civil society is prized because it is a way of life that is best able to meet basic human needs. Burke says that "if civil society be made for the advantage of man, all the advantages for which it is made become his right. It is an institution of beneficence; and law itself is only beneficence acting by a rule."[5] Thus, by virtue of having basic needs, individuals have a right to a variety of goods, including, for instance, a right to justice both with respect to the way the state treats them and with respect to their relationships with other people, a right to benefit from their own labor and to be able to make a decent living, a right to have their children educated, a right to inherit the property of one's parents, and a right to obtain "consolation in death," or, in other terms, people have a right to partake in religion.

Moreover, a civil society is to allow citizens to "have a right to a fair portion of all which society, with all its combinations of skill and force, can do in his favor."[6] On this view, however, even though all have the same right to be treated justly, it is not the case that each will end up with the same advantages and material benefits. For Burke, "men have equal rights; but not to equal things."[7] Burke's view of civil society would permit those with greater ability to gain larger shares of the society's wealth, when their efforts are productive and useful to society. This characteristic of civil society signals Burke's intention to place heavy emphasis on protecting a natural aristocracy, a feature of Burke's thought that we discuss next.

Burke's account of civil society helps to explain why he did not ground government in a natural rights argument. A natural rights doctrine, such as John Locke had used to justify the obligations of government to protect property rights, for instance, suggests that individuals have certain freedoms by virtue of being human beings. No government can abridge natural rights. Although not denying that there are certain basic natural rights for all, Burke argues that natural rights doctrines can be used as the basis for establishing a government.[8] Burke rejects this approach because, as pointed out, Burke believes rights arise from a society's commitment to secure human needs. Burke says that "government is a contrivance of human wisdom to provide for human *wants*. Men have a right that these wants should be provided for by this wisdom."[9]

In refusing to accept a natural rights foundation for government, Burke rejects the view that a government exists to promote an abstract and perfected view of society. A perfected view of society suggests a vision of a future society that would replace the existing order in a complete way. Why is this approach such a problem for Burke? There are several reasons. First, when individuals are told they can live in keeping with an abstract idea of the perfect society, they necessarily take the view that anything they have a desire for they can have. And the justification for this view is that they have a natural right to all things made possible in the perfected vision of society. Thus, "by having a right to every thing they want every thing."[10] Were this attitude to prevail, there would be anarchy, and society would not be governable. Burke rejects this position because he believes that "society requires not only that the passions of individuals should be subjected, but that even in the mass and body as well as in the individuals, the inclinations of men should be frequently thwarted."[11]

Citizens need to recognize their obligation to uphold the norms of civic virtue because these norms check and restrain unruly passions. Possessing rights, then, means more than just having a license to act in ways that attain basic needs. In addition, rights signify the constraints on life that we are to abide by. "In this sense the restraints on men, as well as their liberties, are to be reckoned among their rights."[12] A central doctrine of civil society that Burke shares with other civil society thinkers is that rights can be sustained only in a setting where there is a commitment to those civic virtues that define the restraints that all must obey.

The second problem for Burke with a natural rights argument and with the abstract conception of a perfected society that the natural rights argument symbolized is that this approach fails to recognize that rights are not written in stone but that they may change as the circumstances of society change. Burke says that the nature of liberties as well as restraints varies with circumstances, and "they cannot be settled upon any abstract rule; and nothing is so foolish as to discuss them upon that principle."[13] As circumstances change, controversies develop pertaining to what should count as a right or a proper limitation on human conduct. For instance, today there is great controversy around the issue of what should constitute appropriate ways to manifest religious expression in the public sphere. Can such expression be denied completely, or should some dimension of it be permitted in ways consistent with respect for diverse religious views? Where controversies exist with respect to what is best in matters of this sort, we cannot rely upon an abstract principle to determine the best course. This means, for instance, that, instead of making an abstract principle – such as the notion of the separation of church and state – the basis for judgment, we should ask ourselves in determining the place of religious expression in public settings, what the overall effects of changes in existing practices will be. If we determine that the consequence of allowing greater religious expression in government settings, such as posting the Ten Commandments in all government buildings, is to protect against corruption by enabling citizens to bind their leaders to important norms, then the society may support this practice, even if it means that the separation-of-church-and-state principle is, in some sense, violated. The benefit of creating a culture that places constraints on the corruption of public officials might be seen as a benefit that trumps all other objections.

Burke's approach is conservative because his starting point for thinking about issues such as religious practices is to ask what the effect will be to society of changing an existing practice. If we deem that effect to be in the interest of people, then the existing practice can be changed. But, in discussing changes to society, if we start from an abstract picture of an ideal society, we seek a society that can embody an ideal. In this case, we do not ask nor do we care whether the proposed changes to existing ways of life cause serious harms to the people in the society.

Burke would thus reject the rationalist view of civil society, a view typical in the thinking of many of the liberals discussed earlier. In general, liberal views often start with basic assumptions about political life, such as those found in Locke's or Thomas Hobbes's view of the state of nature, G.W.F. Hegel's expectations for and understandings of a civil society, or John Rawls's conception of the original position. From these assumptions, a perfected vision of politics and society are sketched. But this approach misses the mark entirely, for it fails to take into consideration how the disruption of existing practices might harm a civil society's ability to secure basic needs. It is necessary always to understand clearly what Jeremy Waldron, quoting Burke, refers to as the "mysterious wisdom" that undergirded and explained society.[14] It is this wisdom that rationalist approaches disregard but that individuals must understand and work with if a society that can preserve human freedom is to be maintained.

Given Burke's views of the bases for civil society, including the place of rights, the final question to ask is what role government has in Burke's civil society. For Burke, government, as Bruce Frohnen says, "does very little and . . . acts according to rather utilitarian rules."[15] Governments must promote equity and utility. Equity means that the government is to treat individuals equally in conjunction with the law, and, in promoting utility, the government must ensure that the laws are in the interest of all citizens and thus secure basic needs.[16] But governments, in undertaking these activities, must move carefully and cautiously, refusing to make as the basis for its conduct an abstract, perfected vision of society. Further, the government is not to be the main social force for instilling virtue. The real instructors of virtue are the traditions and customs of society that the government should protect from those who would undermine these traditions, such as atheists, and, as Frohnen says, "those men who do not recognize the need for the maintenance, and supremacy, of existing traditions, manners, and prejudices."[17]

The Natural Aristocracy

As we have indicated, a society based on tradition is a society that has worked out, over a long period of time, the best way to achieve and to maintain basic needs. Individuals must respect the resulting arrangements. Thus, citizens have distinct obligations that are given in their traditions and customs. What is the nature of these obligations? It is essential that individuals accept the fact that society is divided into various, hierarchically organized roles, and those individuals serve society through the roles in which they find themselves. Frohnen argues that for Burke there is a "Great Chain of Being" in which each person has a particular place in the overall organization of society. Some, owing to their superior talent and virtue, can make a larger contribution to public life, including the political, social, and economic structures, than others.[18] In this regard, Burke accepts the existence of a hereditary aristocracy. He said, "Some decent regulated preeminence, some preference . . . given to birth, is neither unnatural, nor unjust, nor impolitic."[19]

But at the same time, he also accepts a "natural aristocracy." Burke says, "Woe to the country which would madly and impiously reject the service of the talents and virtues, civil, military, or religious, that are given to grace and to serve it [society]."[20] Burke expects that positions should be filled based on talent. The different needs of society can best be met when those most capable of performing them are given the opportunity to do so. Hereditary class background in this case must not stand in the way of the evolution of a natural aristocracy. In his *Reflections on the Revolution in France*, Burke says in response to a critic:

> *You do not imagine, that I wish to confine power, authority, and distinction to blood, names, and titles? No, sir. There is no qualification for government, but virtue and wisdom, actual or presumptive. Wherever they are actually found, they have, in whatever state, condition, profession or trade, the passport of Heaven to human place and honour.*[21]

In supporting a natural aristocracy, then, Burke defends a society predicated upon a qualified elite as the best way to maintain stability and the overall justice of society. How would a natural elite be selected for purposes of managing government? Elections would be an acceptable basis for determining the natural aristocracy.[22] As Hanna Pitkin says, Burke's concept of representation presumed an elected "aristocracy of virtue and wisdom governing for the good of the entire nation."[23]

The Role of Virtue: The Importance of Moderation

Regarding who is qualified to be part of the political elite, at least with respect to Parliament, it is clear that owning property was the key consideration. Indeed, Burke attacks the French National Assembly because it is virtually without men of property.[24] Singled out for criticism are lawyers whose litigiousness encourages disregard for the traditions that accorded protection to private property. Referring to lawyers, Burke asks, "Was it to be expected that they would attend to the stability of property, [when their] existence had always depended upon whatever rendered property questionable, ambiguous, and insecure?"[25]

No doubt a major reason for Burke's support of men of property is that he views them as being capable of practicing the virtue of moderation. Learning to avoid extremes in outlook and deeds while pursuing life goals or considering public issues is a civic virtue of utmost importance. When extreme positions are the order of the day, the social fabric is severely strained, threatening the sustaining traditions and customs. Thus, the legislative assembly must be a place where individuals are able to manifest what Burke calls "steady and moderate conduct." And the best way to achieve this condition is when the legislative body of society is composed of people who have the following traits: property, a good education, and "such habits as enlarge and liberalize the understanding."[26] Burke has in mind, then, individuals who, as property owners, are still subject to the constraints that a good education and an enlarged view of events help to secure. People so educated have been schooled in the main qualities of good conduct. In particular, they have been exposed to science and the arts, they are able to have a broad view of a large range of issues that society addresses, they have been trained to be diligent and respectful of the standards of justice, and they have learned how to reconcile the ways of man to that of God.[27]

Moreover, to maintain the civic virtue of moderation, Burke advocates a political environment composed of different interests, each of which can check and balance the others. In a society where no one group has all the power, but where each realizes the necessity of sharing power, people are more able to compromise, thus avoiding extremist forms of thinking. This setting is the basis, then, for rendering "deliberation a matter not of choice, but of necessity." And the benefit of this approach is that decisions made by deliberation and principled compromise ensure moderate policies and politics. This view of politics prevents "the sore evil of harsh, crude, unqualified reformation; and rendering all the headlong exertions of arbitrary power, in the few or in the many."[28]

Local Affiliations and Religion

The natural aristocrat must perform well the tasks allied with public service, just as the person with other talents must perform well the various duties connected with his or her role in life. In doing so, people manifest a commitment to a life of civic virtue. Maintaining this orientation is fundamental to the good order of society. Burke supports this objective by arguing that a love for virtue grows from the local affinities associated with family, neighborhood, and shared beliefs, including religion. For Burke, the affections that people develop for those people and those ways of life closest to them become the basis for a sustained and continuing commitment to uphold the norms of civic life.[29] How is this possible?

When we view society from the perspective of our local affinities, such as family, society becomes for us not a large and impersonal world, a world toward which each member feels a sense of estrangement and distance. Rather, society is a friendly and pleasing setting; it is the neighborhood we grow up in, the friends we have for a lifetime, the religious institutions that provide solace, and the local government with which we interact on a day-to-day basis. In viewing society this way, people develop strong affections for those civic responsibilities that preserve the way of life in society and the traditions of the common life that all love. Instead of a society consisting of competing interests always at war, it is a unity based on shared affinities.

Of special importance to maintaining respect for civic virtue and for society is religion. Each person is by nature a "religious animal." In consequence, atheism is against not only reason, but people's basic instincts, and thus "it cannot prevail long."[30] Indeed, religion is the "basis of civil society, and the source of all good and all comfort."[31] Burke has nothing but distaste for the French revolutionaries who would sabotage religious life by attacking the Catholic Church and threatening its property holdings. Individuals need to understand their relationship to the divine, and thus all social institutions must aid "the rational and natural ties that connect the human understanding and affections to the divine."[32] Religion is the foundation of a civil society because it teaches that all that is good comes from God, including virtue, good manners, and of course the state itself. Burke says that people "conceive that He who gave our nature to be perfected by our virtue, willed also the necessary means of its perfection – He willed therefore the state."[33]

The enemies of civil society for Burke, then, are those who would destroy the great traditions of civility and religion in the name of equality, which is what Burke believes the advocates of the French Revolution were doing. And in sweeping away the traditions of good order, what is lost in the process are the conditions to secure the rights upon which a good civil society is built. Tocqueville, as we will see, demonstrates a way to maintain Burke's commitment to civic virtue while embracing equality, as well. Before turning to Tocqueville, it is necessary to make a few additional comments on Burke.

Identity and Civic Virtue in Burke

How would individual identity be constituted in Burke's society? For Burke, one's basic needs can be secured only by a society that protects the rights of each and that expects each individual to maintain those civic virtues associated with having rights. Part of what is included in this understanding is that society is predicated upon a natural order of abilities in which each person has a role to play. What helps to maintain a commitment to fulfill these roles is that individuals view themselves as linked in close and intimate ways to others who are friends and neighbors. Moreover, a strong sense of religious commitment further cements one's sense of community with the others who form an integral part of one's life. In this setting, people would feel themselves a part of society's natural order, and they would thus not be prone to question it.

Now, people's identities would reflect these values, and, in the civil society Burke describes, it is not likely that individuals would question the moral order that all are expected to accept. There would not be competing conceptions of society, as is the case in our own society, in which some argue for a natural order and others argue against it, or in which some support religious practices and others condemn them. It is the contemporary diversity of moral views that caused Rawls to argue that there are many different moral conceptions, and each of them pertains to the particular self-identity that individuals carve out for themselves. Rawls sought to provide a way to ensure that people who hold different moral conceptions have a way to live in peace with mutual respect for one another's rights. The moral complexity of life that Rawls addressed would not be a major item of concern on Burke's agenda. Indeed, had Burke had to confront the issue of moral pluralism, he might have argued that the fact that it exists at all represents the triumph of destructive individualism urged on by a perfectionist view of government and society.

III. Tocqueville and the Commitment to Equality

Alexis de Tocqueville published the first two volumes of *Democracy in America* in 1835 and the last two volumes in 1840.[34] He was a sociologist as well as an active politician in France.[35] Tocqueville provides an analysis of American mores, based on his visit to America – what he calls the "habits of the heart" or the basic ideas and opinions of Americans as well as an understanding of the ideas that shape the general outlook and "mental habits" of Americans.[36] Like Burke, for Tocqueville, liberty is not a license to do whatever one wants but is the right to engage in those activities that the existing beliefs and traditions permit and encourage. In abiding by the norms of that order, one manifests virtue while promoting one's liberty.

But each had a very different concept of the existing order that gave shape and pattern to liberty. For Burke, an aristocratic order, either natural or hereditary, is the predominant shaping force in society, but, for Tocqueville, American life replaced the aristocratic order with a new commitment to individualism and equality. Tocqueville seeks to demonstrate the nature of liberty within a society committed to these new values. There is no question that in doing so he believes that a society promoting individualism could at the same time maintain a civil order. This means that, in an individualist-oriented society, there can still be a commitment to virtue, if self-interest, as he puts it, were "properly understood." Self-interest, properly understood, is a condition in which individuals, in pursuing their own particular needs, do so in ways that at the same time promote a larger good than just their own interest. Tocqueville says that "Americans . . . enjoy explaining almost every act of their lives on the principle of self-interest properly understood."[37]

Tocqueville thought that in America there was a good chance for self-interest to be understood in precisely these terms, but there was also a chance that it would not be. In the event of the latter, civil society would give way to despotism. So, what is a civil society when self-interest is properly understood? And what are the threats that American society must confront to secure a civil society and avoid despotism?

The Passion for Equality

There is a passion for equality in America, and this passion, common to democracy, is so strong that it "seeps into every corner of the human heart, expands, and fills the whole."[38] Individualism is the way of life that democracy and its commitment to equality bring into existence, and individualism will grow "as conditions become more equal."[39] Individualism suggests a way of life in which people think it best to "isolate" themselves from the great multitude of society by placing themselves into small groups of people, such as families or friends. In this setting, an individual "gladly leaves the greater society to look after itself."[40] Individualism is an attitude that, for Tocqueville, "dams the spring of public virtues," and in the end may destroy regard for all other virtues, too, as it becomes the basis for a form of highly self-centered egoism. Individualism, then, is viewed as a threat to a form of self-interest properly understood, or a life that embraces regard for civic virtue.

Tocqueville, nonetheless, saw the possibility that this unfortunate situation could be avoided and that individualism could be constrained and made to conform to the norms of good citizenship. At the heart of his argument is the view that American society provides an experience, located in a society based on equality that teaches to all people the traditions of civic virtue. Central to this experience is the place in society of voluntary associations and local government.

Voluntary Associations and Local Government

The irony of democracy and the individualism it helps to spawn is that it makes people both "independent and weak." "[People] can hardly do anything for themselves, and none of them is in a position to force his fellows to help him."[41] In contrast to an aristocratic society in which the privileged join together around the common class objective of protecting their place, in American society, people are weak because, as equals to everyone else, each stands alone and no one is obligated to help another. The only way individuals can muster the strength to achieve particular self-defined ends is to form themselves into groups. "As soon as several Americans have conceived a sentiment or an idea that they want to produce before the world, they seek each other out, and when found, they unite."[42] Participation with others is designed to achieve a variety of purposes. Indeed, for Tocqueville, there are associations for all activities and occasions, "to give fetes, found seminaries, build churches, distribute books," and so on.[43] By grouping together, people gain the collective power to achieve their objectives. In a democratic society, "associations must take the place of powerful private persons [typical of aristocracies] whom equality of condition has eliminated."[44]

The purposes pursued inside groups affect fewer people in comparison with society-wide activities that might affect everyone in society. But the experience of participation in smaller groups, such as those involving business endeavors, can teach people the required virtue needed to pursue interests that encompass not just the members of one's own group, but the interests of many others in society, including people beyond one's own group. "The more there are of these little business concerns in common, the more do men, without conscious effort, acquire a capacity to pursue great aims in common. Thus civil associations pave the way for political ones."[45]

Civil society groups consist of people from different social outlooks and with diverse values. In civil society groups, then, individuals learn to work with people from diverse walks of life to achieve shared ends and purposes. To do so, individuals must learn the art of communicating across the many differences that make up society. As people engage in this activity, each learns about the needs of others, and each becomes more capable of making space for those who are different. People, in this context, practice the art of give and take with each other and from this experience realize that, to achieve common objectives, individuals must subordinate at times their interests to the needs of the whole. As a result, individuals learn the importance of thinking in terms of the many interests that make up society and that must be accommodated to achieve a definition of the common good. This is the essence of civic virtue, or self-interest properly understood.

Individuals who gain these skills in civil society are prepared to make good use of them in their participation in government. Individuals participate in government at many levels. People may have direct input into matters involving local concerns at the village or state government levels. As the governing unit becomes larger in scope and power, individuals have less access and less chance to have direct influence on government policies. At the federal level, individuals may have impact indirectly through the election of legislators or the executive. But because of their ability to understand diverse interests, individuals can conceptualize politics as containing a broad arena of needs, each of which must be considered when determining the common good. And, in this way, individuals advance to thinking in public terms, and not solely private ones; this public point of view, once again, is another manifestation of self-interest rightly understood.

Thus, the lessons of civil society help to create active, educated citizens whose impact is conducive to democracy. These lessons, owing to the reality of political liberty, can be used by all and not just, as for Burke, the aristocratic few. Indeed, when people enter the political arena, they can converse with many different people who otherwise might have remained strangers.[46] Moreover, during this experience, people redefine their own interests to include the needs of others, for, unless they do, people realize they will get nothing for themselves. Here, one defines as one's self-interest "forgetting about" oneself so that one can think about others.[47] For Tocqueville, Americans have used political liberty "to combat the individualism born of equality, and they have won"[48] because they have forged linkages to achieve shared ends.[49] The experience of civil society prepares individuals to pursue their own interests, but in ways that are always cognizant of the needs of others. Consequently, politics remains democratic, and political liberty is protected for all citizens.

As just indicated, an important political setting in which this experience is nurtured is the environment of local government. Because of the absence of a centralized administrative authority over all society, local governments must manage the towns and counties. Through them, people manifest a robustness of initiative as they build schools, churches, and roads, each of which reflects the needs of the local areas. In this context, people maintain a firm commitment to the idea that they should not rely upon the national government to take care of them, and by virtue of this attitude, they protect their freedom.[50] Moreover, the experience of citizen involvement in local government helps to sustain a citizen's respect for the nation as a whole. Indeed, for Tocqueville, an understanding of the needs of the whole society is woven into the fabric of local government life. One cares for one's country in much the same way that one would care for one's family.[51]

Experiences such as those mentioned in this section would help make possible Tocqueville's doctrine of "self-interest properly understood." Now, it must be clear that this doctrine "does not inspire great sacrifices, but every day it prompts some small ones."[52] Thus, self-interest, when properly understood, is associated with "orderly, temperate, moderate, careful, and self-controlled citizens."[53] These habits of civic virtue contribute to people's being able to be good citizens who make the needs of the larger community important reference points in their daily lives. For with these habits, people can be citizens who approach large public concerns not simply from a one-dimensional desire to achieve their own ends, but from a willingness to consider other needs, including those of the society in general.

Materialism and Religion

The religious life buttresses the idea of self-interest properly understood. To see how religion is important in this regard, it is first necessary to discuss a major consequence of equality for Tocqueville, namely, materialism. Equality reduces all people to a common denominator of belief, just as it reduces all to the same social status. In democracies, "all men are alike and do roughly the same things."[54] To say that all are equal is to say that all, for the most part, hold the same beliefs about what is important in life and that all are committed to pursue whatever everyone considers important. What is the one thing all wish to pursue? In America, what is good is the acquisition of material things, the goods that bring immediate pleasure and happiness to the person who possesses them.

> *Americans cleave to the things of this world as if assured that they will never die, and yet are in such a rush to snatch any that come within their reach, as if expecting to stop living before they have relished them.*[55]

Here, the experience of market life, where each seeks to realize his or her material desires, becomes a major focus of concern for Tocqueville, as it did for others we have studied, such as John Stuart Mill. As Tocqueville says, people in democratic settings, governed by the ethos of equality and market life, have many different passions, but each of them redounds to the same thing: a quest for wealth.

But at the same time each realizes that, owing to differences in intelligence, some will end up with greater advantage in the market setting. This fact creates an understanding among individuals that society will never achieve the "equality they long for," an equality in which each is content with what he or she has and where no one has an unfair advantage over others. Given this understanding, each looks warily at the other, worried that the other may have an unfair advantage in the pursuit of wealth. After all, in the age of equality, no one should have more advantage than another, but equality of conditions, including intelligence, is not perfectly realized, and all individuals, knowing this, live with the constant anxiety that another will succeed where they have failed. This is the reason for "strange melancholy" in democracies, including, of course, America.[56]

But the requirements of group life are such that individuals must learn to temper their quests for immediate material pleasure. Indeed, individuals must practice a degree of self-discipline so that they are able to postpone immediate pleasure and satisfaction for the sake of achieving long-term goals. A person must be able to avoid yielding to the "first onrush of his passions" so that he or she is able to "effortlessly sacrifice the pleasure of the moment for the lasting interests of his whole life."[57] But where material prosperity has such a prominent place, achieving self-discipline is difficult. Religion helps to counter the negative effects of materialism by giving us a wider and broader vision of life. The religious experience encourages people to focus upon a life beyond this one. And in the context of the life beyond this world, the quest for material things becomes much less important and pressing.[58] Thus, when individuals have no concept of a future broader than the present moment, they easily fall into a pattern of behavior in which their main objective is to "satisfy their least desires at once; and it would seem that as soon as they despair of living forever, they are inclined to act as if they could not live for more than a day."[59]

Given the quest for equality and material self-enhancement, the pressure to live for today is strong. Indeed, this outlook may even diminish the ability of religion to install a sense of the future in the minds of people. Tocqueville says that the interest in the future is something "which neither religion nor social conditions any longer inspire[s]."[60] Tocqueville hopes that government might re-instill a concern for the future in people so that, with a broader horizon, they will not be so wedded to material self-enhancement. He believes that, if governments succeeded in this regard, people would be brought back to religious belief. And this moment will help restore the importance of moral values and civic concern.[61]

Threats to Civil Society

Still, in Tocqueville's day, there were forces afoot in American society that threatened to destroy the sense of a civic virtue commitment to uphold the common good. In this case, neither the experience of voluntary associations nor religion could secure a society with civic virtue. What reasons did Tocqueville provide to justify his fears? There are two main ones. The first has to do with the possibility that citizens would forfeit their political liberty, and the second has to do with the failure of America to realize its commitment to equality for *all* citizens. In the next two paragraphs, we discuss the threats to equality, and in the subsequent paragraphs, we discuss Tocqueville's reason for suggesting that individuals would be willing to give up their political liberty.

African Americans, at that time, owing to the experience of slavery, were not permitted to become a part of normal community life that white people dominated. An African American did not even own his or her own body and could not sell his or her own labor without committing what for society was a crime.[62] These practices were in direct contradiction to the tradition in society that emphasized equality. For Tocqueville, the treatment of African Americans is cause for a "great revolution."[63] Here, in a society in which equality is the norm, inequality is certain to create the conditions that would lead African Americans to engage in an upheaval that would win for themselves what the whites already had.

Another harmful way of life, again one that ran contrary to equality, is the experience of industrialization.[64] The workplace Tocqueville describes pitted the owner class against the working class and, in doing so, created a "new aristocracy" whose main concern was to organize the work of others for the sake of enhancing the wealth of the owner class. Opportunities for success in the manufacturing arena abounded, Tocqueville argues, because as the conditions in society become more and more equal, the need for acquiring manufactured products becomes more widespread. Everyone who is an equal to everyone else has a right to own what every other person owns. To make this possible, goods must be produced more cheaply so that everyone can have them. But efficiency in production could not be attained unless the new manufacturing aristocracy could find ways to harness properly the labor of the workforce. To this end, the owner classes introduced a division of labor into society, and workers who wanted to make a living had to enter the factory and produce goods in keeping with the labor patterns that the new, more efficient process mandated. In consequence, the worker, who might have been a skilled craftsman before the industrial system was established, now had to give up his craft to become a factory worker. The worker has no choice but to sell his labor, as Karl Marx pointed out, to the owner class, and this class used the worker's labor to enhance the owner's position and wealth at great cost to the working class. The worker was no longer able to nurture his skills as an individual craftsman, and he belonged entirely to the industrial production process that the new aristocracy owned. Inequality between the two, owners and workers, grew. In this context, as in the slavery problem, it is difficult to understand how, given the animosity likely to be generated, a civic virtue commitment to the common good could have been sustained.

A final threat to civic virtue was the loss of political liberty. As already indicated, Tocqueville feared that, over time, it might be the case that the quest for material goods, so central to the new life of an industrial nation, might overwhelm religion and its positive effect on accommodating individuals to virtue. Tocqueville worried about American society's turning itself into a milieu of "men, alike and equal, constantly circling around in pursuit of the petty and banal pleasures with which they glut their souls."[65] These types of people exist only for themselves, and they have no concern for others, including their country. Having no interest in public affairs, and no time for it either, they look to someone else to take care of their interests. Here, individuals forfeit entirely their political liberty, turn the state into a father figure, and ask it to take care of them. Tocqueville said:

> *[The state] gladly works for their happiness but wants to be the sole agent and judge thereof. It provides for their security, foresees and supplies their necessities, facilitates their pleasure, manages their principal concerns, directs their industry, makes rules for their testaments and divides their inheritances.*[66]

In this context, "the exercise of free choice" becomes "less useful and rarer." Indeed, to maintain this "fatherlike" form of government, individuals must be made subject to more and more control by those in authority, and ultimately each citizen, over time, is robbed of the "proper use of his own faculties."[67]

Tocqueville might have been describing the plight of many people today under what many conservatives attack as the welfare state. In this view, people become dependent upon a state who rules as a benevolent dictatorship. The old ways of tyranny, in particular, resort to torture and brutality, are no longer needed to maintain control in the modern world. In the new form of despotism, a state resorts to gentler means of subduing citizens. The despot Tocqueville worried about who would use more "mild" forms of control than those used by the old-fashioned tyrannies. The new despotism "would degrade men rather than torment them."[68]

Tocqueville, Identity, and Civic Virtue

The individual in Tocqueville's society locates him- or herself in traditions or habits that sustain equality, the equality that is necessary to maintain for people their personal freedom and rights. Unlike Burke, the Tocquevillean individual would be suspicious of natural forms of social order that place people into various roles and that permit an elite to rule, owing to their enhanced place in the social hierarchy. But for Tocqueville, equality is best manifested in settings that permit individuals to take part in the ongoing activities of group and local government life and in the forming of group and local government objectives and goals. Moreover, individuals in Tocqueville's society must manifest those civic virtues, such as self-control and moderation, as a basis for maintaining an atmosphere suitable for democratic participation. But just as important, these individuals, by virtue of being able to help formulate solutions to common problems in local government settings, would be fiercely independent people, who do not look for government to take care of them. Further, Tocquevillean individuals would be people who would try to avoid becoming seduced by the lure of materialism. To this end, individuals, while seeking the goods associated with a life of material self-aggrandizement, would be suspicious of allowing the latter to dominate society. For, in this case, some would end up far better off than others, and the state would reduce the rest to a status of social dependency.

IV. Introduction: Oakeshott and Civil Society[69]

Michael Oakeshott, a twentieth-century British conservative philosopher, attacks the rationalist perspective in politics. He does so because, for him, a rationalist outlook reduces knowledge about the world to a system of principles and maxims or to a perfectionist vision that denies regard for variety and that has no appreciation for the "cumulative effect" of experience.[70] For the rationalist, experience is counted as important only as it fits into a systematic scheme, such as the one provided by Hegel, to demonstrate that scheme's overall intent and purpose, which for Hegel was the revealing, over time, of the moral and ethical purposes in history. But to understand the actual context of our lives, we must for Oakeshott, like Burke and Tocqueville, set aside rationalist schemes of a perfected form of social order and instead concentrate upon the "customary or traditional ways of doing things."[71] In other terms, we must understand the day-to-day context of life in which people make decisions and undertake actions. In taking this approach, we can best understand how our lives are "qualified by a genuine, concrete knowledge of the permanent interest and direction of movement of a society."[72] Providing an understanding of the actual context of life, as well as discussing the view of politics that emerges in this setting, is the objective of his *On Human Conduct*.

Oakeshott's Free Agent

Oakeshott's understanding of European civilization is predicated upon a conception of the individual as a "free agent." Oakeshott's free agent is a person with "intelligence." And the latter permits one to recognize the nature of the situation in which one lives. What does Oakeshott mean by one's "situation"? He suggests that each of us shares a setting governed by various "moral and prudential procedures and practices."[73] Now, a practice refers to a particular "way of life" that individuals can engage in while pursuing their objectives. As such, practices denote basic rules, customs, standards, or canons that people engaged in a particular practice are to follow. And there are many different types of practices and thus many different rules by which to be governed. For example, to name only a few practices, there is the practice of teaching, of doctoring, of lawyering, of parenting, and so on.[74] An intelligent person understands the nature of the rules that govern a practice and adapts to them. To fail to recognize the common rules of conduct that are used to regulate, limit, and constrain interactions is to condemn one's self to failure. For instance, were X to try to practice the craft of teaching outside the norms of the teaching profession, X would be a failure as a teacher. These norms require that X prepare lectures carefully, that X respect the views of students, and so on. Were X to teach a class without preparation and without respect for students, he or she would not be able to pursue his or her career choice, nor would he or she be able to engage in the common activities referred to as teaching and learning.

A person is a free agent when one is not driven solely by "biological or other urges." In this mode, one is unable to understand the basic practices to which one is to adapt oneself when engaging in activities of one's choice, such as teaching or parenting.[75] Here, it would seem that an unfree person, owing to the presence of uncontrolled passions, would be unable to understand the practices one must learn to engage in self-chosen activities in society. People are free because they are intelligent individuals who are capable of understanding the different practices of society, and such individuals are able to use them to participate in the activities that are most important to them. What kind of social setting best secures the life of the free agent? And what kind of social setting most upsets it?

Civitas Versus Universitas

Oakeshott compares the *civitas* or civil society to the *universitas*. Each of these forms of life exists in modern Europe in tension with the other. Now, to be sure, the *civitas* represents an ideal character of society, which in no sense can be found in completed form. Nonetheless, the possibility of a *civitas* is suggested by the patterns of ongoing ways of life or practices.[76] As just indicated, there are many different practices pertaining to a variety of different activities that individuals may choose, from doctoring to parenting, to buying and selling, and so on. In a *civitas* these practices are defined in terms of "rules of conduct" that people who take part in the practice together must follow. By following the rules of the practice, each party in a relationship, governed by a particular practice, understands what to expect from the other and how to interpret the other's actions.[77] Here, we "acknowledge the authority of certain conditions in acting."[78] For instance, owing to the practice of buying and selling, as a buyer, we understand what to expect from the seller when we relate to him or her, and, in a similar fashion, the seller understands the buyer's behaviors in terms of the practice of buying and selling. In contrast, a *universitas* is a form of society in which all members acknowledge shared objectives, and each member of society accommodates to them. This kind of association suggests "some identified common purpose, in the pursuit of some acknowledged substantive end."[79] In abiding by the norms associated with achieving the common purpose, our ability to engage in the wide variety of activities linked to free agency is very much limited for the sake of achieving the common purpose or substantive end.

Now, had the *civitas* become the main mode of life in modern Europe, then "the disposition to cultivate the 'freedom' inherent in agency" would have become the principal undertaking of society. Here, the main virtue of society would be personal autonomy, gained through the fullest possible understanding of the rules that govern the activities in which a person wants to engage. While the idea of the *civitas* remains strong in Europe, it has not been fully realized, nor has it been made the main mode of life. Instead, the *universitas*, or what Oakeshott also calls a "compulsory enterprise association," emerged as the dominant mode of life.[80] The latter, when it defines the "character of a state," in addition to mandating a common, substantive good, establishes the reign of a managerial class or a government that imposes an order on all in the hope of achieving the postulated ends. In this context, individuals must tailor their lives to include only those activities that the dominant purpose and the managerial class implementing that purpose sanction. Indeed, the government, as a compulsory enterprise association, makes "substantive choices" for people about how they should live, and often these people are unable or unwilling to make such choices for themselves.[81]

Civitas, Politics, and Government

Political life in a *civitas* suggests the right of citizens to inspect and to assess the rules that govern various kinds of practices and determine whether these rules should be changed and modified. In a *civitas*, there are "known procedures" by which this conversation and inquiry take place, and here Oakeshott has in mind the rules of the political process that govern rule-making and rule modification.[82] In our political system, discussions and decisions pertaining to the rules governing various domains of activity must be made in keeping with the law-making process that the Constitution of the United States established. For instance, let us say that we accept, after a deliberation in the US Congress, a need for changing the rules pertaining to the way public parks are used for recreational purposes. At present, the rules do not permit as wide a variety of activities as people are calling for. The parks permit hiking and fishing, but they do not allow dirt biking. The problem that may emerge is that hikers do not want to extend much additional space to bikers, because in doing so the bikers may enter areas normally reserved for hikers. And when bikers ride their bikes on the hiking trails, hikers may believe both that they will be subject to possible injury should bikers run over them and that the trails will be eroded. The challenge of the political discussion is to determine rules that permit all the various activities that different individuals may choose to engage in while they are in the wilderness.

The role of government in the setting of the politics of the *civitas* is to find ways to reduce the "collisions" between competing views so that rules of conduct can be defined that allow individuals to take part in those activities that they themselves choose. Here, government does not insist that all citizens, in the manner of a *universitas*, accept the way of life posed by a grand vision of a better society to come. But government provides a way to reconcile divergent needs so that, to refer to our previous example, hikers and bikers can utilize, without conflict, the great forests of a society.[83] In this setting, governments provide rules of conduct not to impose collective goals onto people but to enable people "to pursue the activities of their own choice with the minimum [of] frustration."[84]

What the politics of a *civitas* is not about, however, is equally clear. Oakeshott would not use the word *politics* to refer to the exclusive pursuit of the things that facilitate want satisfaction alone. "We do not need the word 'politics' to distinguish the engagement of satisfying wants whatever they may be."[85] For in a politics of want satisfaction, all that matters is to design a system for distributing those goods that satisfy basic wants. Rawls, as we saw, discussed principles of justice to distribute basic goods that all people need, and Rawls's expectation was that the political and economic system would distribute goods in keeping with these principles. Indeed, people in his original position defined these goods as necessary to secure basic wants.

But in emphasizing want satisfaction, for Oakeshott, we de-emphasize something that is just as important, if not more so. In particular, Oakeshott sees the *civitas* as making possible a variety of practices in which individuals can choose to participate. And the purpose people have in utilizing these practices is to provide a context in which individuals can engage in activities, the performance of which by themselves brings enjoyment. This viewpoint is the essence of what Oakeshott calls "conservatism." For Oakeshott, "there are relationships . . . in which no result is sought and which are engaged in for their own sake and enjoyed for what they are and not for what they provide."[86]

For instance, the enjoyment a baseball player should receive from the game of baseball derives from the activity of the game itself. Thus, for baseball players, what should be enjoyable about baseball are the activities associated with playing the game: hitting, fielding, running the bases, and so on. The player should love the game itself, including all elements associated with it, such as the grass, the fans, and the excitement. These things symbolize a place where the player can engage in activities that, by themselves, are enjoyable. In addition to sports, there are many activities Oakeshott might accept as enjoyable for their own sakes. He might point to friendship,[87] to intellectual undertakings, to listening to music or seeing fine art, to aiding others in need, to loving another, and so on. For Oakeshott, a conservative disposition includes "all activities . . . where what is sought is enjoyment springing, not from the success of an enterprise but from the familiarity of the engagement."[88]

Now, to be sure, not all relationships can be the type that Oakeshott's conservatism celebrates. Clearly, some relationships in a *civitas* are entered into not simply because of the pleasures associated with the activities themselves but because these activities provide something we want. For instance, a consumer seeks from the seller a product, a worker seeks from his or her employer a wage, and so on. It would be a mistake to argue that what makes these kinds of relationships pleasurable is solely the performance of the activities associated with them. People enjoy the activity of work for the most part when they receive adequate pay; they enjoy consuming when they can purchase the products they seek at prices they think are favorable; they enjoy selling when they receive an adequate profit, and so on. But few enjoy these activities simply for the fact that they perform them.[89]

Given the foregoing, it is clear that sometimes relationships pertain to activities that are pursued for their own sakes, and at other times activities are pursued on behalf of the ends associated with them. What fascinates Oakeshott are the rules that must be followed in either case. This concern with understanding the rules for relationships and practices of all kinds carries over into politics. Oakeshott thinks that discussions of basic relationships between actors in the public realm should be concerned with describing rules that enable actors in a relationship to work through their differences. The politics of *civitas* does not prescribe outcomes, but it creates rules that allow the actors to determine outcomes based on judgments emerging from the adjustments each makes to accommodate the other.

For instance, in discussing the relationship between owners and workers, the concern should be to define the rules that govern the activities of each party in their relationship to each other. The state is not to determine both the amount and the types of specific benefits that should be provided to each party, such as certain profit levels for owners or certain wages and benefits for workers. Within the context of the rules that govern the relationship of owner and worker, each party is free to pursue ends such as wages or profits with each other, with the agreement reached between the parties being determinative. Here, each side must find ways to accommodate the wishes of the other, and the rules that govern their relationship ensure this possibility. Or in the health care debate, the state should create a rule-governed environment that permits the relevant actors to determine what is best on this issue. To do otherwise is to put the state into the position of a commander, making decisions for each of the actors.

Modern political economy and modern politics are designed to make the state the commander, however. The reason for this situation is the powerful influence of an economy that emphasizes satisfying the many desires people have, along with a state that is committed to sustaining this kind of economic enterprise. In this context, people are to be permitted to purchase whatever they may desire to have in life. Here, each seeks to acquire as many goods as possible. But a market setting of this type is subject to various problems, including, says Oakeshott, "external enemies and internal corruptions." The state is asked to intervene and to protect the market setting from its enemies, and the state achieves this objective only when it can establish itself as a powerful, compulsory enterprise association. In this role, the state manages the economy by instituting bureaucratic organizations that organize the work of the society. Here, work is organized in as efficient a way as possible, and the benefits from that work are distributed to the members of the society. The cost to people of this approach to government is clear, however.

Individuals are given a role in society that defines their tasks, even as it ensures them basic benefits. From this point on, individuals accept a life that is orchestrated by powerful actors who control the bureaucratic organizations in which all people find themselves. In effect, individuals are no longer capable of making their own choices, and, instead, the organization they are part of determines the entire course of their lives.[90]

Why do people forfeit their freedom in this way? Sometimes, in searching for activities in which we can place our mark on the world, we find ourselves in domains that do not work well for us. We may try the intellectual life, but we may find this activity just too onerous. Or, we may embark upon a life of helping others and discover we are not happy in it. Not wanting to face defeat, many people opt for a safer route. In doing so, they enter those domains where they can attain the goods that secure them a niche in life, a life in which the price of success is forfeiture of one's judgment to others who make decisions for them.[91] Of course, people who put themselves in this situation both deny their autonomy and jettison having responsibility for their own lives. This situation, while demeaning to many, is offset by the many goods they receive in return. Here, the enterprise association triumphs, but people lose a prime basis for meaning when they shed autonomy and responsibility in exchange for material benefits that provide both security and comfort.

When we fully embrace the life of want satisfaction, we pave the way for the *universitas*, which seeks to provide for our wants, but this way of life causes the destruction of the *civitas* that is the ground for freedom and agency.[92] Here, Oakeshott may have in mind the modern welfare state, which some think caters to those who want to be taken care of by the state. The rest of society, who wants to take responsibility for their own lives and embark on individually defined missions in life, find their efforts interrupted constantly by the need to serve the state's larger goals of providing basic goods that satisfy the different material wants of citizens.

Civitas is always threatened, then, by the abandonment of freedom. The fear of the voluntary dismissal of freedom remains as strong in Oakeshott as in Tocqueville. As Hanna Pitkin says, Oakeshott, like Tocqueville, fears in politics the "short-sightedly utilitarian, narrowly selfish, crassly competitive orientation"[93] that the modern market setting helped to spawn. Individuals would not have civic virtue in Oakeshott's society unless they manifest the capacity for self-direction and respect for those rules that facilitate individually defined life objectives.

Oakeshott's view of politics has many troubling aspects, however. In emphasizing the priority of rules that define the practices that regulate conduct, Oakeshott denies a place in politics for the pursuit of ends. But Oakeshott, as Benjamin Barber has argued, by "proscribing ends" in favor of the rules that are to govern conduct, excludes from politics concerns for matters such as "distribution [of basic goods, such as rights], allocation, equality, and justice."[94] How, one can ask, can the rules that regulate conduct ever be fair if concerns about the distribution of basic rights, a central objective in modern life, cannot be considered a necessary dimension of political life? Oakeshott's conservative account of politics sweeps these concerns aside because he is worried that any distribution system, even one that is designed to achieve good ends, will only undermine the chances for autonomy and freedom that a politics dedicated to defining the procedures and rules of a *civitas* can provide.

V. Response and Rejoinder

How does Oakeshott's view of identity differ from the other conservatives? In the cases of Burke and Tocqueville, the bases for identity are substantive values. And these values suggest a way of life to which people are to accommodate their lives. For Burke, one is to orient one's life to "fit" the natural order of occupations and status in society, and, for Tocqueville, identity is shaped by equality and its concomitant values, in particular, the importance of individuals helping to forge common purposes with others. When confronted with choosing between group participation or totally private pursuits, the norms of Tocqueville's society push one to the former over the latter. Similarly, Burke gives a priority to people following ways of life associated with a natural order.

But for Oakeshott, substantive values that define a general way of life for each person are a danger to personal freedom in a civil society. Oakeshott sees the community as grounded in practices and rules that, while not dictating to each individual what each one should do with his or her life, nonetheless give to each person the opportunity to determine that life. The role of government is merely to help these practices along and to prevent their diminishment by a welfare state that, if it were to exist, would assign people their identity, taking from them the freedom to determine their own ways of life. In this way, the Oakeshottian individual understands civic virtue to mean having respect for the collective processes of the society, including an understanding of the need to abide by fair rules. Further, in a way similar to Tocqueville, the Oakshottian individual would understand civic virtue to suggest a desire to not become dependent upon government. But the difference for Oakeshott is that a person's sense of responsibility would be nurtured not by communities that focus an individual's attention on the democratic obligation of helping to shape the common ends, but by rules that put into place practices that permit a wide range of individual choices. Of the three people discussed in this chapter, Oakeshott comes closest to moving into the liberal column.

Putting aside the differences among the conservatives, what, in general, would each share with respect to a possible critique of liberal views, discussed earlier, including those of Spinoza, Kant, Hobbes, Locke, Mill, Hegel, and Rawls? The likely critique of liberal views of civil society that conservatives would provide is the fear that liberal individualism would orient people away from regard for traditional civic virtue. For Burke, this outcome would mean a diminished concern for the traditions associated with each person's contributing to the well-being of society as his abilities allowed him to do. For Tocqueville, liberal individualism means that equality would become the basis for a form of egoism wherein people have no regard for the needs of the larger community. For Oakeshott, liberal individualism means that individuals, because they have turned over the authority for their lives to a state that provides basic benefits, have no capacity for individual agency.

Liberal proponents of civil society would all agree that individualism can erode a sense of civic virtue and undermine the overall commitment to secure basic freedoms for each person. To offset this outcome, each of these writers hoped to maintain a kind of civic virtue that could constrain individualism in ways that avoided the unleashing of its harmful effects. For instance, Locke spoke of the virtues of toleration and the live-and-let-live mentality that toleration suggested. Spinoza emphasized the free use of reason in a setting that honored values like friendship and community. Similarly, Mill maintained the importance of individuals according to each other the respect that permits each person to develop his or her higher faculties. Rawls's commitment to public reason sought to create a deliberation in which each person not only recognized the rights of others but listened to and took into consideration the views of others while making public judgments. Hegel hoped to place individuals into corporations overseen by an ethical state, and he expected this institutional setting to accord each person not only his or her basic rights but a respect for the larger good of the community as well.

Liberals, in trying to avoid the negative ramifications of their own forms of individualism, also suggested the need for establishing governmental structures that protect the rights of citizens against intrusions by others. Thus, Hobbes's unitary state is provided with all the power it must have to protect the rights guaranteed to individuals. Spinoza, Locke, Kant, Mill, and Rawls hoped to avert the absolutism suggested by Hobbes's unitary state by accepting the need for constraints on government power through the various means each suggests.

Still, the conservative fear is always that the liberal state may, in the name of meeting its objectives, grow in power to such an extent that the state ends up ultimately opposed to its commitment to secure the rights of each person. We saw the tendency to manifest a concern of this type in Burke's rejections of a French revolutionary government that would destroy all pre-existing traditions involving religion and private-property rights. Similarly, suspicion of the liberal state was manifested in Tocqueville's concern that the central government would become a father figure that controls the lives of each citizen. And Oakeshott's paean to individual agency and his condemnation of the state as a compulsory enterprise association would fit well with those who advocate a minimalist state. The argument concerning how powerful government must be to protect our rights rages today between conservatives and liberals, along similar lines.

But with respect to this question, liberals and conservatives do share a common concern. Both advocate sources of power outside of government to balance government and to prevent it from becoming too powerful. Tocqueville's voluntary associations, Burke's local affinities to neighborhood, and Oakeshott's shared practices would achieve this end. Liberals take the same course when they advocate institutions such as Locke's constrained majority, Spinoza's democratic and watchful majority, Kant's competing-interest view of society, Mill's commitment to workplace participation in determining job requirements, and Rawls's respect for and protection of groups in the nonpublic realm. In both instances, then, conservatives and liberals see a civil society as a place with a separate sphere in which people can join in associations that act as buffers and restraints on the state's authority.

For the conservatives, the separate sphere is buttressed by traditions found to exist in various forms of associations, which the members of the society consider to be essential to the development of their own identities. Thus, there are strong commitments to uphold a separate sphere owing to the long-standing respect for a host of traditions found in religious organizations, families, neighborhoods, or other voluntary associations. For liberals, these traditions are acceptable only insofar as they maintain the norms found in the moral environment of a civil society, in particular, the commitment to secure basic rights, within a setting where there is a strong commitment to both the civic virtues of toleration and mutual respect. Where the traditions supporting a separate sphere threaten these civic virtues by teaching people to act intolerantly to those who are different from them or where these traditions deny any importance to mutual respect, then the traditions the conservatives extol actually harm, rather than aid, a civil society. The question liberals always pose to conservatives, then, is whether the latter are willing to take a similar questioning stance toward traditions that are considered harmful to the moral environment of a civil society.

Liberals might argue that they are just as much concerned to maintain healthy traditions as conservatives are. Indeed, each of the liberals might argue that he hoped for traditions that would sustain the central features of the society he proposed. Spinoza expected traditions that secured democratic, enlightened majority rule–based decisions; Locke would hope for traditions that secured toleration; Hegel, for traditions that maintained corporation life; Mill, for traditions that secured open inquiry and toleration; and Rawls, for traditions that embodied in more complete forms the overlapping consensus. The traditions liberals support in each case make rights and liberties a primary objective. Here, for liberals, to use an example, whereas religious traditions are important, they are acceptable only when associated with toleration and, hopefully, mutual respect.

Conservatives, without denying the importance of toleration and mutual respect, might wonder, however, whether liberals miss the fact that many core values people need for giving their lives worth and meaning are contained in traditions. Not only is freedom associated with certain traditions but so too is religious life, as well as many other significant values found in society. And for conservatives, the mark of traditions is their contribution to helping people experience life's significance. Here, we have in mind the happiness associated with participating in voluntary groups (as in Tocqueville), the life setting conditioned by religion and a natural order (as in Burke), or the happiness found in engaging in activities that are enjoyable for their own sakes (as in Oakeshott). It is important not to neglect these (other than freedom) dimensions of tradition. What good is freedom, a conservative might ask, if, in the process of gaining freedom, all other important and critical ideas – ideas that give value and meaning to life – are lost sight of or destroyed? This issue raises important questions that are addressed more thoroughly in our chapter on Friedrich Nietzsche.

Notes

1. In developing our view of Burke, we rely upon Bruce Frohnen, *Virtue and the Promise of Conservatism: The Legacy of Burke and Tocqueville* (Lawrence: University Press of Kansas, 1993); Jeremy Waldron, ed., *Nonsense Upon Stilts*, ed., introductory and concluding essays by Jeremy Waldron (New York: Methuen, 1987), 77–96.

2. Mulfrod Quickert Sibley, *Political Ideas and Political Ideologies* (New York: Harper and Row, 1970), 503–4.

3. Waldron, *Nonsense Upon Stilts*, 79–80.

4. George Sabine, *A History of Political Theory* (New York: Holt, Rinehart and Winston, 1963), 611. For good background sources, see as well Frohnen (*Virtue and the Promise of Conservatism*, cited in note 1); Frank O'Gorman, *Edmund Burke: His Political Philosophy* (London: George Allen and Unwin, 1973). Finally, the main source on Burke is his *Reflections on the Revolution in France*, ed. Conor Cruise O'Brien (London: Penguin Books, 1982).

5. Burke, *Reflections on the Revolution in France*, 149.

6. Ibid., 149.

7. Ibid., 149–50.

8. Ibid., 150.

9. Ibid., 151. Italics are in the text.

10. Ibid.

11. Ibid.

12. Ibid.

13. Ibid.

14. Waldron, *Nonsense Upon Stilts*, 91.

15. Frohnen, *Virtue and the Promise of Conservatism*, 60.

16. Ibid.

17. Ibid., 60–61.

18. Ibid., 71, 73.

19. Burke, *Reflections on the Revolution in France*, 141.

20. Ibid., 139.

21. Ibid.

22. Hanna Fenichel Pitkin, *The Concept of Representation* (Berkeley: University of California Press, 1967), 171.

23. Ibid., 172.

24. Waldron, *Nonsense Upon Stilts*, 88–89.

25. Burke, *Reflections on the Revolution in France*, 131; also p. 130. Also see Waldron, *Nonsense Upon Stilts*, 89.

26. Burke, *Reflections on the Revolution in France*, 129.

27. Burke cited in O'Gorman, *Edmund Burke*, 121.

28. Burke, *Reflections on the Revolution in France*, 122.

29. Frohnen, *Virtue and the Promise of Conservatism*, 84–85.

30. Burke, *Reflections on the Revolution in France*, 187.

31. Ibid., 186.

32. Ibid., 189.

33. Ibid., 196.

34. Alexis de Tocqueville, *Democracy in America,* ed. J. P. Mayer and Max Lerner (New York: Harper and Row, 1966). Also see J.P. Mayer's essay in this volume, "Tocqueville's *Democracy in America*," xi–xii.

35. Ibid., xiii–vii.

36. Tocqueville, *Democracy in America*, 264.

37. Ibid., 498.

38. Ibid., 475.

39. Ibid., 477.

40. Ibid.

41. Ibid., 486; also, p. 648.

42. Ibid., 488.

43. Ibid., 485.

44. Ibid., 488.

45. Ibid., 492.

46. Ibid., 482.

47. Ibid.

48. Ibid.

49. Ibid.

50. Ibid., 83–85.

51. Ibid., 85.

52. Ibid., 499.

53. Ibid.

54. Ibid., 590.

55. Ibid., 508.

56. Ibid., 510, 590.

57. Ibid., 501.

58. Ibid., 519.

59. Ibid.

60. Ibid., 521.

61. Ibid.

62. Ibid., 292–94.

63. Ibid., 614.

64. Ibid., 528–29.

65. Ibid., 666.

66. Ibid., 667.

67. Ibid.

68. Ibid., 666.

69. We refer to Michael Oakeshott in two major works, *Rationalism in Politics and Other Essays* (London: Methuen, 1962) and *On Human Conduct* (Oxford: Clarendon Press, 1975).

70. Oakeshott, *Rationalism in Politics and Other Essays*, 1–2, 5–7, 10–11.

71. Ibid., 10.

72. Ibid., 22.

73. Oakeshott, *On Human Conduct*, 234–35.

74. Ibid., 55–57.

75. Ibid., 234–35.

76. Ibid., 108, 180–81, 203.

77. Ibid., 112–13.

78. Ibid., 201.

79. Ibid., 203.

80. Ibid., 274.

81. Ibid., 157–58, 205–6, 264, 274.

82. Ibid., 161.
83. Oakeshott, "On Being Conservative," in *Rationalism in Politics*, 188–92.
84. Ibid., 184.
85. Oakeshott, *On Human Conduct*, 162.
86. Oakeshott, "On Being Conservative," 176–77.
87. Ibid., 177.
88. Ibid., 178.
89. Ibid., 176.
90. Oakeshott, *On Human Conduct*, 294–95.
91. Ibid., 277–78. See his discussion of the "individual *manqué*," who is unable to accept the responsibility that accompanies freedom.
92. Ibid., 294–95.
93. Hanna Fenichel Pitkin, "The Roots of Conservatism, Michael Oakeshott and the Denial of Politics," *Dissent* (Fall 1973): 513.
94. Benjamin R. Barber, "Conserving Politics," *Government and Opposition* 10, no. 3 (October 1977): 459.

PART IV

Critiques of Civil Society

17

The Critique of Power in Civil Society: Friedrich Nietzsche and Michel Foucault

I. Introduction

What if civil society was the source of restrictions to human freedom and creativity, rather than the arena in which freedom and creativity were exercised? Political philosophers who raise this concern are important to include in the dialogue about civil society. To this end, we start with Friedrich Nietzsche (1844–1900), move to Michel Foucault (1926–1984), and conclude with Alasdair MacIntyre's important critique, from an Aristotelian perspective, of Nietzsche's argument. Throughout this chapter, a major concern of modern life that continually resonates is the idea that the European Enlightenment that dominates our lives today, and that makes reason the main source of truth seeking, is hostile to the attainment of meaningful lives.

II. Nietzsche and the Will to Power

Nietzsche is perhaps best known for his view that Christianity, once the dominant value system of the Western world, had lost its force in modern society. This event is of singular importance, for, with the demise of Christianity, human experience has suffered what E.E. Sleinis calls, in referring to Nietzsche's views, "a belittlement, a vilification, a devaluation of this world." The present setting suggests that there is not a sufficient basis to justify human existence. To those who ask why life is worth living, then, the circumstances of the times do not suggest a good answer, and new, substantive values must be found to replace the Christian ones to demonstrate why life has significance and *is*, thus, worth living. The problem, however, is that, to create new values, individuals must have what Nietzsche often refers to as a "will to power." Such individuals marshal the power, as a result of making proper use of their abilities and energy, to embed new substantive values into the day-to-day reality of society. These values are the basis for instituting new ways of understanding and seeing that enhance life and that create the conditions, as Sleinis says, for "the thriving and flourishing of life." In augmenting life-enhancing values, a person with a will to power would embark upon actions that lead to the many products of human flourishing, such as those found in art or in new forms of social organization.[1]

For Nietzsche, however, a civil society possesses an atmosphere that can often frustrate and discourage the willfulness that Nietzsche demands. In a civil society, we find ourselves unable to call forth our full powers, and we lack, in short, the focused intensity we need to create new values. Nietzsche's arguments in this regard would agree with some of the views about modern civil society found in writers like the German sociologist Max Weber, who demonstrated that modern, rationally organized, technocratic life denies to individuals a chance to maintain substantive values that secure significance to life. For Nietzsche, a civil society, then, suggests a kind of pervasive sickness of the spirit. And it is this sickness for which Nietzsche hopes to provide a remedy in his discussion of an aristocratic culture of creative people, those who do have the will to power that makes possible the full freedom that civil society extols but that it seems unable to deliver.

III. Dionysus Versus Apollo and the Quest for a New Culture

The first question we must ask pertains to where we should turn to find a justification for life, a justification that is "life-preserving, species-preserving, perhaps even species-breeding."[2] Nietzsche argues that we cannot rely upon modern Enlightenment philosophers of reason, especially Immanuel Kant and G.W.F. Hegel (and no doubt Benedict Spinoza). These thinkers use reason, or a "cold, pure, divinely unperturbed dialectic," to determine those objective truths that can be made the basis for justifying life. But a major theme in Nietzsche's thinking is that what modern philosophers label as *truth* merely represents the philosophers' particular values or prejudices that they "baptize as truth." Nietzsche believes this is certainly the case with Kant's categorical imperative, the idea that there exist universally valid moral propositions. Nietzsche characterizes Kant's efforts to make us believe in universal moral truths as nothing more than the "subtle tricks of old moralists and moral-preachers."[3] This makes Nietzsche one of the first philosophers whom we might identify as "postmodern," a term used to describe thinkers or thinking that challenge the rational and universal notion of truth that emerges in the Enlightenment from writers such as Kant and Spinoza.

On what basis did Nietzsche assert this critique? He argues that prevalent internal impulses or drives dominate philosophers, like anyone else. In the case of philosophers, the "ultimate goal of existence" and "the legitimate *master* of all other drives" is not, for Nietzsche, a "drive to knowledge," but another impulse that may take hold of the philosopher and use knowledge as a means to achieve the impulse driving him or her.[4] To understand a philosopher, we need to comprehend the nature of his or her various "innermost drives," and in addition, we need to know how they have been ordered and which one has been made dominant. Ultimately, then, one impulse captures a philosopher's attention and focus, and it becomes the basis for his or her point of view and approach to understanding. When we understand this dimension, we can know the nature of the philosopher's values and perspective. Thus, the philosopher's "morality bears decided and decisive testimony to *who he is* – that is to say, to the order of rank the innermost drives of his nature stand in relation to one another."[5]

What a philosopher says about the world is highly dependent upon the philosopher's own values and perspective. To clarify this point, we need to provide more details that pertain to the way values and perspectives are shaped. Human values are developed from a combination of realities, including our instincts and passions as well as by customs and traditions that are part of our lives. Thus, in the first place, as we just saw, there are the impulses that lie at the core of one's life. Nietzsche, following the ancient Greeks, refers to this dimension as Dionysian, after the Greek god, Dionysus. For Nietzsche, human beings are a combination, as Bruce Detwiler puts it, of "conflicting tendencies and impulses."[6] There is no inherent, natural order among our passions and feelings, as there was for Plato and Aristotle. For them, even the appetite was susceptible to rational constraint. But as Detwiler says, for Nietzsche, the Dionysian element suggests that a person "is at bottom a chaos, he needs guiding principles in which he can believe to order his life so that he can function in the world."[7]

Civilization and culture are invented to provide life with structure and continuity. Again, following the ancient Greeks, Nietzsche calls this need for order Apollonian, after the Greek god, Apollo. Here, our identities and thus our values are also fashioned by the existing cultural realities, such as customs and traditions. Often, however, over time these norms come to emphasize order above all else, and, in doing so, throw up roadblocks to people as they develop their lives according to their deeply rooted passions. The Apollonian dimension seeks to squelch the inner passions of the Dionysian dimension. But for Nietzsche, Dionysus often comes to the rescue with, to use Detwiler's words, "orgies of creative annihilation and awakened passions that had fallen asleep under the orderly governance of his [Dionysus's] counterpart, Apollo."[8] Thus, the source of willfulness is clearly the Dionysian element, which defies Apollo's quest for order and which, for Nietzsche, in the modern world is largely denied its proper voice.[9] The Dionysian dimension is the basis for resisting a life setting that is overly constraining and confining, if not numbing. Indeed, the Dionysian dimension seems to save us from a world in which the traditions and customs, rules and methods for securing order, deny any chance for forms of creative expression that can transform the structure of human living.

Nietzsche places great emphasis, then, upon our Dionysian-based drives, for it is Nietzsche's view that, in the modern world, this dimension is not given its full due. But in taking this position, it is not correct to conclude that Nietzsche advocates only the Dionysian dimension. Indeed, he wants a culture in which Apollo's dictates for order could facilitate the richness of Dionysus, and thus he calls for a society that is not dominated by either tendency.[10] The Apollonian quest for order should be redesigned to house properly and to permit the fullest possible expression of Dionysian demands to manifest one's drives, passions, and creative powers.

As we demonstrate in the next section, there is a place for morality in Nietzsche's scheme, as long as the order it provides makes possible a setting that allows for the creative expression of Dionysus. In this regard, politics is not so much concerned with achieving a liberal civil society, one that emphasizes equal rights, as it is with establishing those forms of order that permit the flourishing of our creative instincts. Nietzsche's politics would encourage an aristocratic class of willful persons, or what he would call "free spirits," to create new values that replace the discredited Christian ones.[11]

IV. The Place of Morality

From Nietzsche's position that the morality espoused by philosophers manifests more than anything else the particular values of the philosophers in question, it is clear that Nietzsche embraces the view that moral notions emanate from many important factors, including culture, tradition, drives, and impulses. Nietzsche's view of morality indicates that what we understand as truth, in this case moral truth, is a function of the particular perspective we hold, and thus we are not capable, intellectually, of establishing moral absolutes.[12]

This view does not mean that, for Nietzsche, it is impossible to demonstrate that some perspectives have more value than others. After all, Nietzsche has spent much time attempting to diminish the importance of Christian arguments and Western philosophy since Socrates.[13] Further, Nietzsche suggests that there is much to praise in those perspectives that make morality a preeminent part of existence. Such contexts can provide a kind of Apollonian order that makes room for Dionysian creativity. Moral systems suggest constraints that are used to create substantive values.

In discussing morality in the first place, then, for Nietzsche, "the essential and invaluable element in every morality is that it is a protracted constraint."[14] This view suggests the possibility of a focused intensity when pursuing one's basic insights or impulses, and this capacity is critical to creating substantive values that enhance life. Whatever a person's dominant drives or passions, a person must focus on them and overlook those distractions that might deny one's ability to pursue them. Here, acts of creation, which take place when one pursues an insight, such as an artist might experience when attempting to render a particular feeling for nature in a painting, can be carried to fruition only when the artist maintains a disciplined commitment to see his or her project to completion.

Indeed, Nietzsche says that individuals are often moved to act in keeping with a flash of inspiration. "Anyone who looks at the basic drives of mankind [realizes that they] . . . come into play as *inspirational* spirits."[15] That inspiration prescribes the path one is to follow, and that path is raised almost to the level of a moral law that one is commanded to obey. Nietzsche says:

> *Every artist knows how far from the feeling of letting himself go his "nat-ural" condition is, the free ordering, placing, disposing, forming in the moment of "inspiration" – and how strictly and subtly he then obeys thousandfold laws which precisely on accord of their severity and defin-itiveness mock all formulation of concepts.*[16]

From this experience of "protracted *obedience* in *one* direction," we derive everything that makes life "worthwhile to live on earth," including "virtue, art, music, dance, reason, spirituality," and these experiences are "transfiguring, refined, mad and divine."[17]

All the great value systems, including Aristotelian and Christian perspectives, symbolize a disciplined commitment to embody into an age particular values arising from strongly held passions. Indeed, as Nietzsche states:

> *All these violent, arbitrary, severe, gruesome and antirational things [or passions] have shown themselves to be the means by which the Euro-pean spirit was disciplined in its strength, ruthless curiosity, and subtle flexibility.*[18]

Because disciplined actions create values that enrich life, it is clear that another important element of morality is that it is the basis for changing the world, and not merely for maintaining the world as it is.[19] Thus, in discussing morality,

Nietzsche is not interested in using morality as the basis for explaining and for maintaining the current order of society. That is what Hegel did when he said philosophers can only explain the "truths" embodied in the existing ways of life, which, in Hegel's case, meant his view of what he said was the arrival, at the end of history, of the ethical state. Nietzsche rejects those "philosophical laborers" who follow Hegel and who have taken "everything that has hitherto happened and been valued, and make it clear, distinct, intelligible and manageable."[20] The new "philosophers of the future," Nietzsche's *true free spirits*, will seek to embody the values that are uniquely theirs into the world.[21] Indeed, Nietzsche's new philosophers will become commanders and leaders. "*Actual philosophers . . . are commanders and lawgivers.*" The new philosopher's willfulness manifests a "*will to power.*" And Nietzsche asks, "Are there such philosophers today? Have there been such philosophers? *Must* there not be such philosophers?"[22] For Nietzsche, the answer to this question must be yes because the new philosophers or free spirits will lead the way in demonstrating the need to transform culture so that it is once again hospitable to the Dionysian dimension and thus to a new manifestation of a will to power.

The Master and Slave Moralities

Nietzsche's discussion of civil society is designed to demonstrate the differences between the values of the free spirits, who are his practitioners of the new philosophy and who are Nietzsche's new aristocratic class, and the slave mind. In pointing out these differences, Nietzsche demonstrates the wide gulf between two different systems of morality. Nietzsche gives greater importance to the master morality because it is the basis for creating values that enhance life and give it meaning, in contrast to the slave morality that is seen as central to modern civil society.

The noble type of man, also referred to as the "free spirit,"

> *feels himself to be the determiner of values, he does not need to be approved of, he judges "what harms me is harmful in itself," he knows himself to be that which in general first accords honour to things, he creates values.*[23]

This man embodies the master or aristocratic morality, and he has an iron will that makes it impossible for anyone to make him doubt either himself or his values. Nietzsche says of this individual that

> *he shall be the greatest who can be the most solitary, the most concealed, the most divergent, the man beyond good and evil, the master of his virtues, the superabundant of will; this shall be called greatness: the ability to be as manifold as whole, as vast as full.*[24]

Nietzsche tells these people to "remain *hard*, we last of the Stoics!"[25] And thus the noble type will persist toward his goals despite the presence of the many obstacles, including the temptation to just give up the fight and return to a less difficult life. But this persistence hardens him and makes him capable of waging the continuing struggle. Nietzsche says that "continual struggle against ever-constant *unfavourable* conditions is . . . that which fixes and hardens a type."[26]

Moreover, this individual "counts intolerance itself among the virtues under the name justice."[27] For the master class mainly seeks to create conditions that are favorable to himself and that enhance the lives of the noble type only.[28] He cannot afford to tolerate anything that might impede his efforts. In this regard, unlike the slave class who, as we see next, establishes universal values designed to stop suffering, the master class is mostly concerned to embellish his own life through the values he creates. Still, Nietzsche argues that what the noble type creates is valuable in general, because the noble type's willfulness is the basis for life-enhancing, substantive values, such as are found in art, philosophy, and in many other areas of life. Indeed, through his activity, the aristocratic personality seeks to make his own values the dominant ones in a culture.

In contrast to the master morality, there is the slave point of view, which is the moral orientation of modern society. The slave point of view represents the understandings of the "abused, oppressed, suffering, unfree, [and] those uncertain of themselves." Nietzsche asks if these people were to create a moral system, what would it contain?[29]

The slave mentality distrusts the values and way of life of the aristocratic class, and consequently, sees little in it that is good. After all, the slave sees the master class as the oppressor class, and given this fact, it is likely that the slave would always count the master class's values as contrary to the needs and interests of the slave. Perhaps the latter's attitude can be better understood if we associate the word *slave* with ordinary persons. Ordinary people distrust the values of a self-appointed cultural elite that attempts through their art or philosophy to shape the way a whole society should interpret experience.

The slave typifies in modern society the individual who lacks the self-confidence to free him or herself from the misery of uncertainty, emanating perhaps from a need to find the significance to existence. The slave seeks to overcome the unhappiness that emerges from his or her uncertainty by promoting universal values that would end the suffering of all people. Thus, unlike the master class, the slave class supports values such as pity, charity, patience, industriousness, humility, and friendliness. The slave emphasizes these values because they are "useful" and because they are the only "means of enduring the burden of existence."[30]

In saying the values just mentioned are useful, Nietzsche suggests that, for the slave, the best way to give meaning and purpose to life is to pursue a course that embodies the value of utility. In doing so, each person finds a way to make contributions that are considered necessary to maintaining an ordinary life in society. One does not aspire to the values of the master class in this case, but one seeks to absorb oneself in activities that, if performed well, will, it is hoped, give significance and importance to life. For Nietzsche, then, utility "is the source of the famous antithesis [between] 'good' and '*evil.*'"[31] One does "good" by giving oneself over to the norms of good order or by finding a niche in society where one can perform an acceptable function.

But in keeping with the norms of good order, and thus in doing what is good or useful in life, the slave is likely to prompt a kind of nagging doubt about slave values. For in adhering to the requirements of a useful life, one does not necessarily make primary to one's life those substantive values that give one's life a sense of significance. Instead, one may just become a cog in a routine and mechanical work environment, or one may become oriented to attaining material and financial improvement. But these experiences, which tell one how to get along on a day-to-day basis, do not necessarily speak to the nature of those enduring values that give overall importance and significance to life.

In fact, after a fashion, it is likely that many in society will question the slave's way of life. Nietzsche says that there comes a time when a kind of "benevolent disdain" is attached to the slave morality, and those holding this mentality are viewed as basically "good-natured" and "*harmless*" people, who are "easy to deceive, perhaps a bit stupid." This view of the slave suggests that the slave mind, in order to gain happiness and his or her undying hope for freedom, buys into a way of life that is far short of what he or she needs to live a substantive and meaningful life.[32]

Nonetheless, one might contend that the slave's values at least bring into existence a humanistic orientation that suggests that society should be designed to secure the same rights for all. Thus, despite their shortcomings, slave values might be considered important additions to society. Indeed, it is the case that, because the ordinary person of civil society, or Nietzsche's slave, hopes to refrain from "mutual injury, mutual violence, mutual exploitation, [and instead] to equate one's own will with that of another,"[33] the slave would extol the Kantian ethic of treating others as ends. Now, Nietzsche says the slave's commitment to these principles is acceptable only when understood as the basis for "good manners" between individuals. But when these principles are made the fundamental basis for society, there emerges a "will to the *denial* of life," and the principle of good manners is then turned into the basis for "dissolution and decay."[34]

For Nietzsche, the Kantian ethic is unrealistic, especially from the standpoint of the master class who creates values. Nietzsche says that "life itself is *essentially* appropriation, injury, overpowering of the strange and weaker, suppression, severity . . . exploitation."[35] The concept of the will to power suggests that Nietzsche's noble man can survive only by conquering. Exploitation is at the center of the noble individual's experience. Exploitation "pertains to the *essence* of the living thing as a fundamental organic function, it is a consequence of the intrinsic will to power which is precisely the will of life."[36]

It is only through this activity that the foundation of a "higher culture" is made possible, a culture that includes morality, religion, art, and philosophy. But these achievements cannot take place without the strong, in this case, the free spirit, dominating the weak. Nietzsche says:

> *Let us admit to ourselves unflinchingly how every higher culture on earth has hitherto begun! Men of a still natural nature, barbarians in every fearful sense of the word, men of prey still in possession of an unbroken strength of will and lust for power, threw themselves upon weaker, more civilized, more peaceful, perhaps trading or cattle raising races.*[37]

For a "healthy aristocracy," society is merely a "scaffolding upon which a select species of being is able to raise itself to its higher task and in general to a higher *existence*."[38] The master class, or free spirit, is a man who must order society to serve his need to create new values, and the weak must be made servants to this effort, totally subordinated to the demands of the strong. Obviously, then, a tendency toward equality of rights, which is a doctrine that would emerge from the Kantian dimension of slave thinking, is a proclivity to make slave values predominant, and, were this to happen, the way of life of the superior person would be diminished, if not denied entirely. It is this frame of mind that prepares the ground for the herd mentality we discuss in the next section.

Origin of Slave and Herd Moralities

For Nietzsche, there is a ranking of moralities. Clearly, the master morality is superior to the slave morality. In this section, we discuss the origin of the slave morality to demonstrate a basis for another inferior morality, the herd morality.

To begin, it must be clear that, in demonstrating the origin of the slave thinking, we can demonstrate the basis for the herd morality as well. Now, at first, it might appear that the two ways of thinking are quite different in nature. The slave seeks to change the world in keeping with universal values that end suffering and the domination of the master class. The herd mind hopes to keep things the way they are and to avoid change. So, how is it possible for the slave mentality to have an affinity with and even to contribute to the herd mentality?

As just indicated, the morality of the slave represents universal values whose ultimate purpose is to end suffering. But when people make these universal values their own, what is good is what is useful, and from this view there follows the commitment to conform one's conduct to the regimen of an ordinary life. The herd mind has a similar view. Thus, the herd mentality condemns anyone who challenges the ordinary in the name of pursuing strong Dionysian passions, such as the master class, of course, does. Such people are seen as evil and dangerous by the herd mentality. Indeed, the herd mentality preaches values such as obedience, modesty, fairness, and the lasting importance of a mediocre life in keeping with "mean and average" desires.[39] These values fit in with the need to lead an easy life, a life that is free from suffering. As in the case of the slave mind, then, there is a desire that all suffering be abolished, and, to this end, there must be equality of rights and sympathy for all who suffer.[40] However, the doctrine of equality of rights, played out in the midst of society dominated by the herd mind, is easily abused and transformed into a doctrine of the "equality of wrong doing," in which there is a "general war on everything rare, strange, privileged, the higher man, the higher soul, the higher duty . . . creative fullness of power and mastery."[41]

It would seem, then, that the slave mind, insofar as it is a basis for commonality of outlook and universality of values, creates the foundation for the herd mind. In discussing the origin of the former, we also discuss the basis for the latter. Thus, for Nietzsche, we live in an age in which the values of the slave class predominate, and, in consequence, have led to the herd mentality. But how and why has this occurred? Addressing this question, which we discuss in the rest of this chapter, requires an assessment, or reevaluation, of existing values, demonstrating where and how the values of the slave class have arisen, and why and on what basis these values may begin to lose prominence.

To provide a general overview of Nietzsche's argument before discussing its details, it must be clear that, for Nietzsche, moral categories arise from a struggle between competing social forces. In a battle, the side that wins determines the substance of morality, including the ethos that the losers must accept. The earliest struggle of this kind took place, beginning in pre-Christian days, between an aristocratic class and the rest of society. In effect, the struggle between Apollo and Dionysus is mirrored in society as the conflict between a powerful aristocratic class attempting to impose its values onto all, and a weak, enslaved class. The slave class's rebellion against the powerful culminates in Christianity and the slave mind, which makes protection of the weak the main objective. Let us now turn to an examination of the details of this argument.

Modern morality has its roots in pre-Christian times because of the aristocratic class's desire to maintain in society an order that made it the predominant source of values. This view of morality diminished the place of the lower classes in society. The latter, however, could not accept their subordinate position. And in revolting against the master class, modern Christian morality was born. This revolt had already begun in Greece during the fifth century before Christ, but the main round of the revolt involved ancient Judea and Jewish resistance to Roman domination.[42] Here, the Jews, the weak and subordinate class, were determined to reorder the values of society, making their own values superior to those of the Romans. By doing so, the Jews sought to create a revolution in culture, one that would make themselves and what followed from their efforts – Christianity – predominant.

A brief description of this revolt is now in order. To begin, all of society was designed by the Roman aristocracy to manifest and to highlight *their* personality and values. To them, the low-born were to be used as means to serve the larger ends that the high-born determined were right for the society and, most important, themselves. This situation was the basis for a special kind of revolt by the Jews.

Nietzsche says that prior to the revolt, the Jews were powerless before the high-born types whom they had to serve. The Jews had no ability to resist the nobility physically because the master class simply had too much power. But the Jews did not accept a way of life that kept them in subordination. As a result, their resentment grew stronger and even turned to hatred.[43] Nietzsche says that the Jews' "hatred grows to monstrous and uncanny proportions, to the most spiritual and poisonous kind of hatred."[44] Jewish hatred fueled a drive for resistance. Nietzsche says that a slave morality cannot exist without "a hostile external world; it needs, physiologically speaking, external stimuli in order to act at all – its action is fundamentally reaction."[45]

In Nietzsche's account, the Jewish resistance was clever and successful. The Jews, unable to conquer the nobility in war, found a more resourceful way to bring down the high-born. They hoped to replace the values of the master class with new values. In effect, the Jews committed an act of *"spiritual revenge"*[46] in which they redefined and reshaped culture so that, in the new culture, they and all ordinary people were viewed as the protectors of sacred values. Here, the Jews "inverted" the values of the aristocratic class by saying that everything that was good, noble, beautiful, and the source of happiness derived not from the aristocratic class but from a "love of God." A reversal of rank followed from this reevaluation of values. Now it is said that those who love God, the low-born types, were of a higher importance than the aristocracy, who, because they were godless, were condemned to eternal damnation. The Jews proclaimed:

The wretched alone are the good; the poor, impotent, lowly alone are the good; the suffering, deprived, sick, ugly alone are pious, alone are blessed by God, blessedness is for them alone – and you, the powerful and noble, are the contrary, the evil, the cruel, the lustful, the insatiable, the godless to all eternity; and you shall be in all eternity the unblessed, accursed and damned![47]

The words used by the Jews to conduct their campaign were splendid for the purposes the Jews had in mind, according to Nietzsche. These words did not exhort victory on a battlefield where the Jews were outnumbered and militarily weak, but it urged the masses to triumph by being better, spiritually, than the hated aristocratic class. The masses were told: "Let us be different from the evil, namely good! And he is good who does not outrage, who harms nobody, who does not attack, who does not requite, who leaves revenge to God."[48] But this message really is another way of saying "we weak ones are, after all, weak, it would be good if we did nothing *for which we are not strong enough.*"[49] As Detwiler says, this account demonstrates how it came to be that "the downtrodden and oppressed, who had no hope of attaining physical superiority over the nobler type, proclaimed their moral superiority and proceeded to conquer the world with their gospel of meekness and love."[50]

V. Democracy and Civil Society

The Jewish revolt for Nietzsche was "remarkable"; it defeated Roman rule, and it became the basis for Christianity. But, for Nietzsche, this revolt, remarkable as it was, created a value system that has now, even though still in force, outlived its usefulness. Nietzsche indicates this latter view when he says that Christian images, in the form of such individuals as Jesus and Mary, continue to exist, "as if" Christianity "were the epitome of all the highest values – and not only in Rome but over almost half the earth."[51] This statement suggests that Christianity is, for Nietzsche, no longer the major source of substantive values, even as Christian culture continues to have prominence.

Christianity, although no longer a value system that can give life significance, continues to be an important factor in the modern world for Nietzsche. Its importance is manifested in the modern effort to end suffering through democracy. In effect, the Christian idea has been given a secular form of expression. "It has got to the point where we discover even in political and social institutions an increasingly evident expression of this morality: the *democratic* movement inherits the Christian."[52] But these values merely mirror the values of ordinary slave life, values that pose a threat to the creation of a higher culture. Nietzsche says that throughout Europe are people, whom he refers to as "anarchist dogs," whose main objective is to promote the philosophy of the herd life, using, in the process,

> *the religion of pity, in sympathy with whatever feels, lives, suffers; (down as far as the animals, up as far as "God" – the extravagance of "pity for God" belongs in a democratic era); at one and all, in the cry and impatience of pity, in mortal hatred for suffering in general.*[53]

This secularized form of Christianity has no sympathy for the special man, the free spirit, and instead argues that all are to be reduced to the same common level. Everyone is to be equal, and there are not to be any "special rights and privileges" for those who are truly superior, the free spirit.[54] Unlike Hegel, who saw the master–slave conflict as a basis for a civil society that Hegel celebrated because it secured basic rights for all, Nietzsche sees the outcome of the master–slave conflict as supporting conditions of oppression for society's most honored class, his free spirit.

Like Burke, there is a tendency in Nietzsche to yearn for a society that would create a special place for a natural aristocracy. For Nietzsche, as we have seen, it is clear that the values of the slave mind, a concern to provide respect for all, leads only to a leveling of all to the same mediocre standard. The result is that there is no effort to provide a special place for the free spirit, but instead all people are made into passive and unwillful individuals of the herd. Nietzsche condemns this condition, and he hopes that this situation leads to its own undoing. For as people become more and more oriented to a civil society, they become very passive and soft. Indeed, Nietzsche says that Europe is marked by a "paralysis of the will," a situation in which people "no longer have any conception of independence of decision, of the valiant feeling of pleasure in willing."[55]

When individuals and society lack a sense of energy, arising from a belief in values that give significance to life, society, as well as individuals, begin to feel vulnerable and weak before anything and anyone who challenges society. Indeed, the herd mind readily succumbs to those with the stronger will. Ironically, this circumstance may create an opening for the master class. For as the weak become less capable of taking care of themselves, others who are stronger, in this case those of the master morality, may then ascend to a position of authority in society.[56]

In asserting this position, Nietzsche sees in the imminent collapse of democracy the basis for a new and positive form of tyranny. He says:

> *The democratization of Europe will lead to the production of a type prepared for slavery in the subtlest sense: in individual and exceptional cases the strong man will be found to turn out stronger and richer than has perhaps ever happened before. . . . What I mean to say is that the democratization of Europe is at the same time an involuntary arrangement for the breeding of tyrants – in every sense of that word, including the most spiritual.*[57]

The new, "spiritual tyrant" will not engage in the "petty" politics of our times. Nietzsche does not accept politics as an activity reduced to determining what rights people should have and how they are to be distributed. Instead, he hopes for the emergence of a strong class of people who have the will to end the morass of civil society and who, in doing so, make themselves the pinnacle of the new culture. The new politics would be what Nietzsche refers to as "grand politics." Nietzsche says, "The time for petty politics is past: the very next century will bring with it the struggle for mastery over the whole earth – the *compulsion* to grand politics."[58]

Who is this tyrant Nietzsche has in mind? He is the artist. For Nietzsche, as Sleinis says, "the potential of art to enhance life is ranked above that of morality and religion."[59] Thus, Nietzsche believes the artist is the source of the values that would enhance life. And for Nietzsche, a politics fueled by the artistic imagination would seek to define a basis for celebrating the joyfulness of life in a way that, as Sleinis says, makes possible "the thriving of the human spirit" and a "love of life."[60] This way of life suggests a new, yet-to-be-fully-experienced freedom, within a new, yet-to-be-fully-created social and political world. But the aesthetic vision such individuals create can nonetheless give us a good taste of what an affirming and enriching way of life would provide us. That taste would be the basis for building a politics that could make possible a significant and meaningful life, one that would restore to people a sense of self-importance and purpose.

VI. Politics of Bad Conscience

While creating the new society, what enemies would Nietzsche's new aristocracy hope to slay? It would seem that Nietzsche's politics would be dedicated to resisting the oppressive reality associated with attitudes of guilt and bad conscience, for these attitudes are at the heart of what helps to conquer and deny a reality to willful conduct. To understand the enemy that Nietzsche's politics has in mind, it is necessary to explain the nature and impact of bad conscience on society. And this can best be accomplished by comparing good conscience with bad.

Good conscience is associated with the fact that the individual defines himself as a *"sovereign individual,"* the man "who has his own independent, protracted will and the *right to make promises* – and in him a proud consciousness, . . . a consciousness of his own power and freedom, a sensation of mankind come to completion."[61] This individual experiences the "privilege of *responsibility*." Now, the sense of responsibility that good conscience communicates suggests that an individual has "power over oneself and over fate."[62] Here, a person realizes that he or she is accountable for the consequences of his or her actions and choices, and thus he or she must accept the need to restrain his or her passions when restraints become the best way to organize one's life to create values. The experience of good conscience, typical of the master morality, demonstrates real mastery over oneself and, insofar as a person possesses this quality, one can have both an intense sense of self-affirmation as well as a sense, as Detwiler says, of "mastery over others."[63]

But it must be clear, given the model of good conscience, that in restraining one's impulses, one should not relinquish or terminate them, for to do that would be to cut oneself off from the real energy that motivates life and that is the foundation of one's willfulness. It is here where the difference between good and bad conscience becomes apparent. The difference between the two states of mind arises from the fact that society does not want individuals thinking that their instincts are a proper basis for conduct, lest individuals lose respect for society's norms and rules. Once again, then, Dionysus's demand for spontaneity in keeping with one's passions and drives confronts Apollo's hope to maintain order. How does society historically approach the concern to maintain order? In addressing this question, we can see the importance society places on bad conscience.

Initially, society established respect for its rules through severe punishment. Here, society's approach to morality was to associate a failure to observe rules with excruciating pain. This experience taught people not to allow their instincts full play, and instead people were to learn to repress them. In discussing the ways society used to achieve conformity to rules, Nietzsche points out that, at first, methods of torture were used to burn forever into our collective memory a fear of doing wrong. Indeed, the first techniques of punishment were extraordinarily severe, including stoning, piercing people with stakes, tearing flesh off the body, and "smearing the wrongdoer with honey and leaving him in the blazing sun for the flies."[64] These harsh forms of punishment became a public spectacle or a kind of shared entertainment. People were drawn to watch others suffer, and the occasion was cause for celebration, even. Here, all watched what might happen to them, happy that it was happening to another, so joyful in fact that all were willing to celebrate the other's pain. Indeed, cruelty, as a way to mold people to uphold their obligations under custom and law, was even spiritualized and deified.[65] In this setting, "to see others suffer does one good, to make others suffer even more [good]."[66] The lesson, however, was not lost on anyone. Do what the norms require or risk being made the object of public celebration yourself!

This experience, no doubt, began to create the outlook of the herd mentality by teaching people to suppress their instincts because the latter could get them into trouble and make them liable for punishment. Moreover, the herd mind's aversion to instinct was further shaped by cruelty when society linked instinct life with all that brings shame.[67] Here, Nietzsche discusses the efforts of society to make man become "ashamed of all his instincts."[68] Christianity is a primary source of this lesson. Nietzsche quotes with sarcasm how the medieval Pope Innocent III carried out this project by listing as "repellant" many of our basic instinctual functions, such as gestation, procreation, salivation, and excretion of our natural wastes.[69]

In modern civil society, a new way is invented to teach people the rules of society and to carry on the Christian tradition of maintaining a basic distrust for one's instincts. The principal difference between the premodern and the modern approach is that in the latter setting, conformity is taught not through torture but by forging within the consciousness of individuals a sense of guilt for contemplating or for engaging in actions that violate the norms of society. People must learn to control their "unconscious and infallible drives." Society attempts to "tame" individuals by substituting for their native drives and instincts, a life dictated by "the oppressive narrowness . . . of custom."[70] In society, individuals are turned into people who fashion their lives so that they are in keeping with what society says is best for them and not with what they know is best for them, given the deepseated drives and impulses they feel.

But when people are forced to suppress their inner Dionysian drives in the name of social order, they end up at war with themselves. Here, because people are in a society that requires them to hold back and to not let their instincts have full play, they must learn to contain and to keep within themselves some of their sharpest feelings. And when instincts are suppressed, they acquire "depth, breadth, and height," and as they do they become aggressive emotions "of wild, free, prowling man turned backward *against man himself.*"[71] Indeed, Nietzsche describes these emotions as "cruelty, joy in persecuting, in attacking, in change, in destruction," and these emotions have as their target those who hold them, and thus they are "turned against the possessors of such instincts." Owing to the need to control the Dionysian side of our personality, we develop hostile emotions toward ourselves. Another way to refer to the hostility people have toward themselves is to say that people with such self-loathing manifest a sense of guilt and a *bad conscience.* Both states of mind symbolize the modern tendency to teach people to control their instincts by thinking of themselves as unworthy whenever they experience them.[72] And people are taught to experience guilt and bad conscience whenever they violate social norms.

Bad conscience is a "serious illness" because, while it teaches people to suppress the Dionysian side of their personalities, it necessarily creates for people a sense that they are prisoners within their own minds, without any hope of achieving freedom.[73] It is no wonder, then, that in a society that generates bad conscience each person is a "desperate prisoner," "rubbing himself raw against the bars of his cage." It is understandable as well that for such individuals, their willfulness is completely vanquished. For Nietzsche, this condition is the "gravest and uncanniest illness, from which humanity has not yet recovered."[74]

Clearly, the master class is the group in possession of good conscience, and the herd man is the group in thrall to bad conscience. The former is able to "stand security for [it]self and to do so with pride, thus to possess also the right *to affirm self.*"[75] Noble individuals are not afraid of their passions and basic drives. They have sufficient self-constraint to pursue a life that embodies these passions and drives in ways that manifest individuals' full powers, and thus they are in complete control of their lives, taking complete responsibility for their lives. Such individuals would not be tricked by society into repressing their emotions and restraining the aggression that results from this repression by embracing the mentality of bad conscience. But the herd man who must suppress all impulses experiences only unrelenting self-contempt and the continuing presence of bad conscience.

The politics of the new aristocracy would be a form of resistance against all the social and cultural institutions that are used to maintain the hegemony of bad conscience and guilt. Nietzsche's politics would suggest that we can imagine a life in which the forces of Dionysus fully triumph, in a setting that at the same time maintains some dimensions of Apollo intact so that there remains a necessary degree of order and self-restraint for the flourishing of Dionysus. The person who recently reflects this approach to politics is Foucault.

VII. Foucault's Nietzschean Critique

Michel Foucault attempts to develop a political and social vision for the present times based upon some of Nietzsche's insights. In following Nietzsche, a major theme of Foucault's critique of modern society is the conflict between the Apollonian and the Dionysian elements of personality. Individuals experience dual pressures. On the one hand, there is the pressure of culture, which imposes order-creating norms. On the other hand are internally located instincts, which seek a more spontaneous life apart from the patterning force of everyday life. Often, Apollo gets the best of Dionysus, and those who resist being made into cogs in a larger machine of social order are perceived by society as dangers to good order.[76]

Foucault thus focused upon the way society often responds to marginalized individuals, people whose lives are unconventional from the standpoint of society's norms, such as the insane or those in prison. In undertaking to describe the way society responds to such unconventional individuals, Foucault's interest is the implication of the Enlightenment to society. The Enlightenment, as we saw in Spinoza and Kant, promoted the kind of inquiry that sought to replace superstition as the basis for discussions of public matters with doctrines, supported by reason, which could secure the widest possible human freedom. Foucault's concern, however, is that, to a large extent, the Enlightenment fashioned existing social and political attitudes in the modern world. In accepting these attitudes without analyzing them, we may also accept political, economic, social, institutional, and cultural contexts that shape our experience, often to the detriment of the freedom that the Enlightenment – associated with writers like Spinoza and Kant – promises. Thus, Foucault argues that we should be neither "for" nor "against" the Enlightenment, but, instead, we should try to keep an open mind about its contributions so that we are able to distinguish between its useful and its detrimental legacies.[77]

Foucault points out both dimensions. In his early work, he describes some of its harmful effects, and we discuss these elements as a prelude to discussing its more lasting and important contributions. Here, we need to be clear that reason, which the Enlightenment praised, is not necessarily always our enemy, but it is not always our friend, either. Consequently, we should not fear that critiquing the contributions of reason "risks sending us into irrationality."[78]

Of great concern to Foucault's critique of the Enlightenment is that, he believes, the Enlightenment helped to institute and validate structures of power that are actually hostile to freedom. To understand how this development arose, it is necessary to understand the way power is used in the modern world.

Those who dominate others in society achieve conformity to norms by the use of power. What is Foucault's view of power? For Foucault, person A has power over B when A can "determine" B's conduct, without the use of brute force. In the modern age, an age that celebrates human freedom, brute force as a device for achieving conformity to patterning norms would be a violation of the commitment to freedom. Instead, power is exercised when individuals become "induced" by various behavior-managing techniques to do as patterning norms require. In this case, a person presumably always retains the possibility of doing other than what is being impressed upon him or her. Thus, A's power over B, where A gets B to do as A wants, is always accompanied by the notion that B's behavior is not coerced. Foucault says that there is no exercise of power "without potential refusal or revolt."[79]

The main approach, then, to achieving power over others is through means that induce people to do as those in power want, without resorting to brute force. In *Discipline and Punish*, following the path of Nietzsche in *The Genealogy of Morals*,[80] Foucault, through the analysis of punishment, hopes to demonstrate the techniques that have replaced brute force as the basis for domination, not only in penal institutions but in many domains of day-to-day life. In this case, then, punishment is not only a way to deter crime but to shape the way people act and think.[81]

Following Nietzsche, Foucault points out that, in the premodern setting, punishment involved terrible forms of torture inflicted upon the wrongdoer in a public ceremony. People's limbs were pulled out, and their skin was burned with hot lead and boiling oil. The purpose of this enterprise was to make an example of the individual in the presence of the public that was brought to watch, in the hopes that others, after seeing the agony of the prisoner, would become frightened of committing a similar crime. Others must see the punishment because "they must be made to be afraid."[82]

But in the enlightened world, this kind of punishment is rejected because it denies respect for a person's humanity and for the legal limits that must be observed if a person's humanity is to be left intact. In consequence, different forms of punishment, which no longer include infliction of pain upon the body, are used.[83] The new form of punishment did not need to resort to physical torture to control people. How was this objective achieved?

Foucault discusses Jeremy Bentham's model prison, the Panopticon, to address this question. The Panopticon was arranged as a circle of prison cells. The lighting allowed an observer to see into the cell from the outside to watch each prisoner. In the middle of the circle was a watchtower where the guards could observe each person in his cell. At all times, then, the prisoners could know that the guards watched them. However, each individual was in a cell that did not open to any other cells, thus denying each prisoner all contact with other prisoners. In this context, the guards could view each prisoner, but the prisoner was never in a position to communicate with anyone else. As Foucault says, the prisoner is "the object of information, never the subject of communication."[84]

The guard's gaze communicated to the prisoner that the prisoner was always being watched, monitored, and supervised. This setting was the basis for the guard's power over the inmate to make the latter conform to the regimen of prison life. But how did the guard communicate this message through a gaze alone? Remember, the prisoner had no human contact with any other person. In the absence of such contact, the sole source of external "support" for a prisoner was the guard in the watchtower who was always staring and monitoring the prisoner's behavior. In this setting, so transfixed did the prisoner become with the guard's gaze that it was as if the guard was always watching him, even when the guard was not physically present. In effect, the guard was always there, in the prisoner's imagination, acting as a control on the prisoner's thoughts, and the prisoner could never escape the guard's presence. It was in this way that power was exercised over the prisoner's life, and the latter did as he was told, as if voluntarily, without the use of brute force to ensure compliance.

Furthermore, for Foucault, the Panopticon is not to be "understood as a dream building; it is the diagram of a mechanism of power reduced to its ideal form."[85] Moreover, this new "political technology" is used throughout modern society to impose discipline and order onto people in all walks of life. Foucault says:

> *It [the political technology] serves to reform prisoners, but also to treat patients, to instruct school children, to confine the insane, to supervise*

workers, to put beggars and idlers to work. . . . Whenever one is dealing
with a multiplicity of individuals on whom a task or a particular form of
behavior must be imposed, the panopticon schema may be used.[86]

Indeed, this approach to power is a form of "subtle coercion" that governs modern social relationships.[87] The gaze of others, in this case those in positions of supervisory power over people in the institutions of society where people work, attend religious services, or go to school, defines the norms all are to uphold. And this gaze, which represents a continual effort to manage and to supervise people, exercises power over people as it is internalized and made a part of each person's consciousness. Thus, whereas a person knows that he or she could violate the norms of society, he or she will not do so because he or she does not want to live with a sense of condemnation. Foucault, in referring to this experience, says, "What developed, then, was a whole technique of human dressage by location, confinement, surveillance, the perpetual supervision of behavior and task, in short, a whole technique of management of which the prison was merely one manifestation."[88]

Foucault's discussion of prisons embodies the view that societies are governed by various techniques, each of which is designed to achieve particular ends. There are techniques that allow people to produce goods, those that define how to use language, and, finally, those that enable some to determine the way others should live. The latter type of techniques, which Foucault refers to as the *techniques of domination*, speak not just to the experience of prison but to the way in which that experience is exported to many domains of society beyond the prison. And the purpose is the same: to maintain the control needed to mold the lives of people.[89]

The picture Foucault draws of modern civil society, while critical of the circumstances that threaten freedom, does not rule out another more salutary approach to identity formation. In this alternative view, individuals may indeed carve out for themselves an identity that manifests a self that is different from and in contrast to the one society requires. Foucault believes that such an endeavor could be achieved by a technology "oriented toward the discovery and the formulation of the truth concerning oneself."[90] To suggest such a possibility indicates that Foucault was able to demonstrate the positive contributions of the Enlightenment, especially in his later work. In this work, as Alexander Nehamas says, Foucault provided the Enlightenment with a kind of "serious, if qualified, respect," arguing that the whole quest of the Enlightenment, as Kant celebrated, to realize the full liberation of human beings was still in process.[91] Indeed, Foucault says:

I do not know whether it must be said today that the critical task still
entails faith in Enlightenment; I continue to think that this task requires
work on our limits, that is, a patient labor giving form to our impatience
for liberty.[92]

What are the implications for politics of Foucault's technology for self-development? To address this question, we first must define clearly what he means by the technology that enables us to capture the truth about ourselves.

To provide an example of what Foucault intends in his discussion of the techniques of self-development, it is necessary to turn to his *The Care of the Self.* In this work, Foucault uses the example of the Stoic philosopher Seneca, who recounts the style of self-reflection that was the hallmark of his life.[93] In the morning, he prepared himself for the tasks of the day by examining these tasks and asking himself what was necessary for him to achieve them. In the evening, he reviewed the events of the day. He asked himself about the bad habits that he had faced that day, of the personal weaknesses he had resisted, and how, as a result of this reflection, he was or was not a better person.

As he reflected upon himself, he was desirous of finding not only the legitimate purposes of his life, but the "rules of conduct" that would enable him to achieve his ends. But a life of reflection does more for us than just provide us with rules of conduct that enable us to achieve particular ends. Presumably, reflections on the self are concerned as well with enabling us to preserve our freedom.[94]

How is this possible? As we reflect upon our lives and consider the various possible courses of life, including the different desires and passions that move us, we should accept only those over which we have control. Astute reflection makes a clear distinction, then, between passions and desires over which we have control and those over which we do not. For instance, suppose we know that to be successful in a particular type of work, we will have to work very hard. Let us also suppose that we know we want to retain time for the development of other aspects of our life, such as friends and family provide. But as we reflect on our lives, we realize that in allowing work to dominate our lives it is possible we will become so obsessed with work that we will not be able to feel good about time spent with friends or family. In this case, we would begin to resist time with friends and family, even though we longed for that experience. As a result of this reaction, we would lose our freedom to do what provides us with enjoyment.

To secure our freedom, we must plan ahead as we develop our preparation for the work we want to do by building into our lives habits that ensure we will never feel bad about making time for friends and family. Moreover, we must constantly monitor our lives to make certain we have not allowed ourselves to depart from a course that continues to be open to all our legitimate desires. Foucault refers to the activity of self-reflection as a kind of "administrative review" by which we continually evaluate our conduct with the intention of making certain that we do not lose the essential control necessary to maintain a course that keeps alive the possibilities we so want to pursue.[95] By carefully inspecting ourselves and admitting in an honest way the negative consequences to our freedom of taking certain approaches to life or of not pursuing others, we make certain we do not fall into situations in which we lose our freedom to direct our lives. Foucault says that "this inspection is a test of power and a guarantee of freedom: a way of always making sure that one will not become attached to that which does not come under our control." We are to accept as motivations in life only "that which can depend on the subject's free and rational choice."[96] Or, in another place, in speaking of the lessons of the Stoics with respect to the self, Foucault says that, for the Stoics, "the experience of the self is not a discovering of a truth hidden inside the self, but an attempt to determine what one can and cannot do with one's available freedom."[97]

It would seem, moreover, that an essential element of following this course of conduct is that we would be concerned constantly to distinguish situations in which circumstances prevent the pursuit of certain possibilities from those situations in which circumstances merely offer roadblocks to possibilities of our liking. In taking care of ourselves, we would preserve our freedom by not seeking to overturn those circumstances that we could not affect. Resisting circumstances that permit no chance for success draws all our energy and attention, and, in consequence, we would lose the freedom to pursue other elements of life that we want just as much. Alternatively, settings that offer us merely roadblocks, we would try to surmount creatively.

For Foucault, as for Nietzsche, to care for the self is to follow the model of the artist. For the artist, creative projects take place in time and history. In consequence, the artist's reach is limited by circumstances, and not everything the artist imagines or wants to realize will be possible, given the reality that constrains the artist's life.[98] But the artist, in framing projects, pushes his or her circumstances to his or her outermost limit by pointing to those possibilities that current circumstances do not seemingly permit and by showing the way these possibilities could be realized, even within these circumstances. That is what makes the artist's painting or music so unique and liberating. Similarly, a person committed to the ethos associated with the care of the self would be an individual who recognizes how arrangements in society might deny one certain hoped-for opportunity. But in reflecting on oneself and rearranging the relationships among the various dimensions of one's life, one may find a way to achieve these possibilities anyway, thus liberating oneself from the conditions that otherwise oppress one's life.

Foucault argues in *The Care of the Self* that his approach permits individuals to locate a basis for the "art of existence" in an ethos of "self-control."[99] To think in these terms is to be cognizant that in defining strategies for achieving goals, more than just the goals in question are involved. In addition, we are to find ways, as we pursue our goals, to preserve our freedom to make our lives encompass many possibilities of our choice, by not falling into a situation in which our circumstances or feelings over which we have no control determine our conduct. Here, the "art of existence" "revolves around the question of the self, of its dependence and independence, of its universal form and of the connection it can and should establish with others, of the procedures by which it exerts its control over itself, and of the way it can establish complete supremacy over itself."[100] When an individual masters the technology of the care of the self, one is no longer dependent but is completely free to depict one's life in ways that enable a person to have a rich and dignified existence, a life that includes many of the possibilities one hopes to realize.

The kind of self-mastery Foucault suggests is essential and that he associates it with Stoic practices can be viewed as having been made a part of sixteenth- and seventeenth-century Christian moral life. Here, Christianity, in embracing Stoic approaches, advocates that people engage in self-reflection or "administrative reviews," with the intention of discovering the limits of their freedom. Foucault points out, however, that whereas seventeenth-century Christianity wants to use these practices to build an increasing sense of "dependence upon God," the Stoic and Foucault (who supports the Stoic view) want to use the tactics of self-mastery to achieve "sovereignty over himself" so that a person is "dependent upon nothing."[101]

The political ramifications for society of Foucault's Stoic personality are clear. Such a person stands above others, like Nietzsche's free spirit, making a statement to everyone of the need to forge one's own life, despite the iron cage that seeks to place us under the throes of domination. Further, on this view of the care of the self, the essential activity that politics must protect is the ability of individuals to speak and to manifest the truth about themselves. Would this view of politics be receptive to supporting a civil society, as Kant claimed was necessary to sustain his view of Enlightenment?

Foucault would question whether the notion of a civil society can contribute to the care of the self. Foucault points out that, starting in the late eighteenth century, a civil society was conceived as a separate sphere that opposed the power of the state and thereby permitted individuals, often in the name of economic freedom, a degree of independence from state intrusions in their lives. This view suggests that the separate sphere of civil society symbolizes freedom and initiative, whereas the state in a civil society symbolizes authoritarian control. Consequently, the separate sphere of a civil society is a force for good, and the state is a force for evil.[102]

But for Foucault, this depiction is too simplistic, and it may hide the fact that power pervades the separate sphere of a civil society in ways that might be detrimental to people. Foucault suggests that even a separate sphere in a civil society would establish a power relationship between individuals and itself. And the question one would have to ask pertains to how to limit the effects of power, because, for Foucault, "every power relation is not bad in itself, but it is a fact that always involves danger."[103] It is thus necessary to carefully examine the power relationships that might appear in the separate sphere of a civil society to determine whether in fact they are harmful and how they should be rearranged if they are. This is precisely what Foucault has sought to do throughout his work. For Foucault, power pervades society by imposing on individuals certain ways of seeing, acting, and living, as Foucault discusses in his references to Bentham's model prison. In doing so, society denies people their freedom by requiring them to experience constant or continual supervision, manifested in the gaze of a powerful few who stand over and manage their lives.

It would seem that, since liberty is essential to engaging in the techniques of the care of the self, a civil society, which preserves such liberty, is a necessary basis for Foucault's self. But it may well be the case that what is central to a civil society, the civic virtue necessary to maintain it, Foucault would find as one more expression of the kind of power that denies one a chance to manifest care for the self. The question, then, is whether Foucault would accord a place to the civic virtues of a civil society as a means for protecting the rights of all individuals. A civil society depends on this possibility. In effect, will there be a general commitment to toleration and mutual respect, for instance, or will these values be condemned as Nietzsche did when he associated them with slave values and thus with an order destructive of the will to power? Or, to put the question in another way, can Foucault tolerate civil society any more than Nietzsche, even though it is quite clear that, like Kant, Foucault would need a kind of civil society to ensure the care of the self?

VIII. MacIntyre's Response to the Nietzschean Critique

The proponents of civil society discussed in this book maintain, as a central theme, the importance of civil society for securing basic rights. To this end, our point has been not only that a civil society suggests a separate sphere that stands as a buffer against the state, but, just as important, a civil society is a moral environment that seeks to secure individual liberty while at the same time providing respect for the necessary constraints, or civic virtues, that make such liberty possible. Hence, there are several ways by which liberty must be promoted in a civil society. Not only is the state in a civil society required to protect the rights of individuals, but, in addition, there must also be respect for civic virtues, such as toleration and mutual respect, that help to carry on a commitment to liberty.

With the importance of civic virtues in mind, we now consider a critic of the Nietzschean condemnation of civil society who nevertheless acknowledges the accuracy of several elements of Nietzsche's critique. Alasdair MacIntyre is a contemporary political theorist who, with others, agrees with the critique of modern civil society but believes that the critique needs a substantial alternative. This alternative, according to MacIntyre, can be found only through a return to classical political theory. Like Nietzsche, MacIntyre finds problematic the appeals to rational objectivity often made in civil society, but he believes Nietzsche goes too far in rejecting virtue altogether. Additionally, MacIntyre suggests Foucault does not go far enough to account for the moral presuppositions that are necessary for civil society, especially in the civil society through which Foucault wants to find liberation. Recalling the political thinking of Aristotle, MacIntyre argues that the underlying premise of the postmodern critique of the Enlightenment that Nietzsche initiated and that Foucault advanced, however insightful, is insufficient because it is incapable of promoting and sustaining the most important virtues of community.

Some readers may find it surprising that a political thinker who advocates a conservative return to traditional values would embrace elements of this most radical critique of civil society. The premise of MacIntyre's political thought, however, is that important virtues have already been lost to a modern scientific approach to political community. In much of his writing, MacIntyre criticizes what is sometimes called the "behavioralist" approach to civil society, which describes it as the function and product of a scientifically calculable set of human behaviors. MacIntyre is opposed to this approach to civil society because he believes it undermines the moral virtues and traditions that supersede scientific thinking. As a continuation of our analysis, we might also observe that deterministic scientific thinking about civil society also undercuts the individual liberty and freedom of choice that gives moral content to our decisions in civil society.

Agreeing with some critics of the Enlightenment, MacIntyre argues that the sets of rules that guide civil society are not timeless or beyond contention but come about only in particular social circumstances.[104] We are at risk of losing sight of civic virtues, according to MacIntyre, if civil society is reduced to a science that presupposes a morally neutral and objective point of view from which to judge social behavior. The problem with claims of "moral neutrality" is that they advance the idea of an absolute fact free from political judgment.[105] This is problematic not only because it renders the freedom of choice and judgment in civil society meaningless, but for MacIntyre, it more importantly neglects the fact that rational investigation requires a presupposed set of virtues and social goods that can be given to us only through tradition in a political community.[106] Rather than answering the questions of morality, therefore, the tradition of strict scientific investigation, when applied to civil society, can only beg the ethical questions. Instead, MacIntyre argues for the rationality of tradition, which recognizes the historical character of morality without undermining its truth or forcefulness.

In making this argument, MacIntyre agrees with Nietzsche that appeals to objectivity are merely appeals to subjective will. It is, after all, this willfulness that allows us to make political judgments in the first place. This recognition, however, does not necessitate a glorification of Nietzsche's "absurd and dangerous fantasy" of the "overman" – the free-spirited individual idealized by Nietzsche who overcomes the burden of civil society through the power of will. Despite the fact that the "life of virtues is continuously fractured by choices,"[107] these choices are always guided by a direction that virtue gives us. We are individuals making choices, and we often disagree, but these choices are made in the context of overarching values and beliefs that we can never truly escape nor ought to imagine that we can.

Our subjective will, and the collection of wills that compose civil society, must have a conception of the "telos," or direction, of human life. It is not enough to simply pursue "freedom" because we need to be able to answer the question "freedom for what?" The answer to this question for MacIntyre, following Aristotle, is that we need a freedom to sustain a civil society in which political thinking can be nourished, human life can flourish, and the freedom of choice can continue to be respected. Specifically, the virtues that should guide civil society are those that are necessary for sustaining political communities in which we seek the good together.[108]

From this perspective, civil society can succeed only if we address the postmodern critique of the Enlightenment while giving attention to the insights of Aristotle. We must remain mindful that true justice must go beyond consideration of the individual. The individual – whether an "overman" or a "self" – is too thin of a premise upon which to predicate the purposes of civil society.[109] According to MacIntyre, selfhood is most appropriately understood in the context of interlocking selves in the context of civil society. Our moral identity is never something that belongs only to ourselves, but something shared with others in a civic community linked by common values and commitments.[110] MacIntyre thus evaluates the Nietzschean critique of civil society on the same terms that he criticizes modern liberal society – that individualism can easily distract us from the purposes of civil society. Lacking in Nietzsche's glorification of the willful individual, as well as in many modern notions of the rational and autonomous individual, is any notion of a shared common ground.[111] This is not to say that the notion of an autonomous individual must be discarded but only that we are careful that individualism not obscure the communal nature of civil society. MacIntyre's key point is that virtues are not sought in isolation from everyone else.

There are dangers in Enlightenment thinking, including isolation, the illusion of certainty, and virtue nihilism, but these dangers do not require the wholesale rejection of civil society. Like Foucault, MacIntyre believes that people should be neither for nor against the Enlightenment. People need to keep an open mind about its contributions, but they must remain able to distinguish between its useful and detrimental implications for political virtues – those virtues that help people pursue the good life in community with others. As people participate in civil society, they already find themselves living in a community with a tradition of values and virtues. Everything people do and say, even as they operate according to their free will, takes place in a context that came before them and that they live within.

People might, like MacIntyre, agree with Nietzsche and Foucault that civic virtues have a historical character.[112] People simply make a mistake if they assume that "historical" means "without truth." They also make a mistake if they assume that critiques of Enlightenment reason and scientific certainty require a wholesale rejection of the notion of civil society. The greatest contribution of modern political thought, providing the context for the free exchange of ideas, is what allows political thinking to flourish and allows us an open and democratic society. This is a conversation that must include a diversity of voices, perhaps some subversive, speaking to the way people think, act, and live in a community. In the following two chapters, we discuss two important contributions in contemporary political theory that challenge notions of civil society in the hope of making it more tolerant and more inclusive. In this way, it could be said that even some of the most radical critiques simply demand that civil society live up to the civic virtues upon which it is built.

Notes

1. E. E. Sleinis, *Nietzsche's Revaluation of Values: A Study in Strategies* (Urbana: University of Illinois Press, 1994), 152–54, 13, 17.

2. Friedrich Nietzsche, *Beyond Good and Evil* (New York: Penguin Books, 1973), 35, Sect. 4.

3. Ibid., 36, Sect. 5.

4. Ibid., 37, Sect. 6. Italics are in the text.

5. Ibid., 38, Sect. 6. Italics are in the text.

6. Bruce Detwiler, *Nietzsche and the Politics of Aristocratic Radicalism* (Chicago: University of Chicago Press, 1990), 64–65.

7. Ibid., 64.

8. Ibid., 65.

9. Ibid., 65–66.

10. Ibid., 66.

11. Ibid. Our use of the word *willful* in relation to Nietzsche is influenced by Richard Flathman, *Willful Liberalism: Voluntarism and Individuality in Political Theory and Practice* (Ithaca: Cornell University Press, 1991), 185. Flathman says that willful conduct "pre-supposes considerable command [by the agent] over the agent's deliberations, decisions and choices."

12. Sleinis, *Nietzsche's Revaluation of Values*, 30, 58. See also Detwiler, *Nietzsche and the Politics of Aristocratic Radicalism*, 21. He cites Nietzsche as saying, "There is *only* a perspective seeing, *only* a perspective knowing." Italics are in the text.

13. Detwiler, *Nietzsche and the Politics of Aristocratic Radicalism*, 25.

14. Nietzsche, *Beyond Good and Evil*, 110, Sect. 188.

15. Ibid., 37, Sect. 6. Italics are in the text.

16. Ibid., 111, Sect. 188.

17. Ibid. Italics in text.

18. Ibid., 111, Sect. 188.

19. Sleinis, *Nietzsche's Revaluation of Values*, 58.

20. Nietzsche, *Beyond Good and Evil*, 142, Sect. 211.

21. Ibid., 71, Sect. 44.

22. Ibid., 142–43, Sect. 211. Italics are in the text.

23. Ibid., 195, Sect. 260. Italics are in the text.

24. Ibid., 144, Sect. 212. Emphasis added.

25. Ibid., 156, Sect. 227. Italics are in the text.

26. Ibid., 200, Sect. 262. Italics are in the text.

27. Ibid., 200, Sect. 200.

28. Sleinis, *Nietzsche's Revaluation of Values*, 61.

29. Nietzsche, *Beyond Good and Evil*, 197, Sect. 260.

30. Ibid., 197, Sect. 260. Also on the issue of universal values, see Sleinis, *Nietzsche's Revaluation of Values*, 61–62.

31. Nietzsche, *Beyond Good and Evil*, 197, Sect. 260. Italics are in the text.

32. Ibid.

33. Ibid., 193, Sect. 259.

34. Ibid., 193–94, Sect. 259. Italics are in the text.

35. Ibid., 194, Sect. 259. Italics are in the text.

36. Ibid.

37. Ibid., 192, Sect. 257.

38. Ibid., 193, Sect. 258. Italics are in the text.

39. Ibid., 123, Sect. 201; Sleinis, *Nietzsche's Revaluation of Values*, 87.

40. Nietzsche, *Beyond Good and Evil*, 72, Sect. 43.

41. Ibid., 144, Sect. 212.

42. For a good account of Nietzsche's history of slave morality, see Detwiler, *Nietzsche and the Politics of Aristocratic Radicalism*, 119–25.

43. Friedrich Nietzsche, "On the Genealogy of Morals," in *The Classics of Moral and Political Theory*, ed. Michael L. Morgan (Indianapolis: Hackett Publishing Company, 1992), 1243, 1245.

44. Ibid., 1243.

45. Ibid., 1245.

46. Ibid., 1243. Italics are in the text.

47. Ibid.

48. Ibid., 1250.

49. Ibid. Italics are in the text.

50. Detwiler, *Nietzsche and the Politics of Aristocratic Radicalism*, 122.

51. Nietzsche, "On the Genealogy of Morals," 1254.

52. Nietzsche, *Beyond Good and Evil*, 125, Sect. 202. Italics are in the text.

53. Ibid., 125–26, Sect. 202.

54. Ibid., 125, Sect. 202.

55. Ibid., 137, Sect. 208.

56. Detwiler, *Nietzsche and the Politics of Aristocratic Radicalism*, 174–75.

57. Nietzsche, *Beyond Good and Evil*, 173, Sect. 242. Italics are in the text.

58. Ibid., 138, Sect. 208. Italics are in the text.

59. Sleinis, *Nietzsche's Revaluation of Values*, 123.

60. Ibid., 146–47; also, pp. 128–31.

61. Nietzsche, "On the Genealogy of Morals," 1257. Italics are in the text.

62. Ibid.

63. Detwiler, *Nietzsche and the Politics of Aristocratic Radicalism,* 124.

64. Nietzsche, "On the Genealogy of Morals," 1258.

65. Ibid., 1260–61.

66. Ibid., 1261.

67. Ibid.

68. Ibid.

69. Ibid.

70. Ibid., 1271–72.

71. Ibid., 1271. Italics are in the text.

72. Ibid.

73. Ibid.

74. Ibid., 1272.

75. Ibid., 1257. Italics are in the text. Also, see Detwiler, *Nietzsche and the Politics of Aristocratic Radicalism*, 124.

76. James Miller, *The Passion of Michel Foucault* (London: Simon & Schuster, 1993), 69–70.

77. Michel Foucault, "What Is Enlightenment?" in *Foucault Reader*, ed. Paul Rabinow (New York: Pantheon Books, 1984), 42–43, 50.

78. Michel Foucault, "Space, Knowledge, Power," in Rabinow, *Foucault Reader*, 249.

79. Michel Foucault, "Politics and Reason," in *Michel Foucault, Politics, Power, Culture*, ed. Lawrence D. Kritzman (New York: Routledge, 1988), 83–84.

80. Miller, *The Passion of Michel Foucault*, 219–23.

81. Michel Foucault, *Discipline and Punish*, trans. Alan Sheridan (New York: Pantheon Books, 1977), 23–24.

82. Ibid., 3, 58.

83. Ibid., 73–74.

84. Ibid., 200–1.

85. Ibid., 205.

86. Ibid.

87. Ibid., 209.

88. Michel Foucault, "On Power," in Kritzman, *Michel Foucault, Politics, Power, Culture*, 105.

89. Michel Foucault, "About the Beginning of the Hermeneutics of the Self," ed. Mark Blasius, *Political Theory* 21, no. 2 (May 1993): 203–4.

90. Ibid., 204.

91. Alexander Nehamas, "Subject and Abject," *New Republic*, February 15, 1993, 33.

92. Foucault, "What Is Enlightenment?" 50.

93. Michel Foucault, *The Care of the Self: The History of Sexuality*, vol. 3 (New York: Vintage Books, 1988), 60–62.

94. Ibid., 62–64.

95. Ibid., 61.

96. Ibid., 64.

97. Michel Foucault, "On Genealogy of Ethics," in Rabinow, *Foucault Reader*, 368.

98. Nehamas, "Subject and Abject," 34.

99. Foucault, *The Care of the Self*, 238.

100. Ibid., 238–39.

101. Foucault, "On Genealogy of Ethics," 368.

102. Michel Foucault, "Social Security," in Kritzman, *Michel Foucault, Politics, Power, Culture*, 67–68.

103. Ibid., 168.

104. Alasdair MacIntyre, *After Virtue* (Notre Dame, IN: University of Notre Dame Press, 1984), 67.

105. Ibid., 77.

106. See especially MacIntyre's arguments against modern scientific rationalism in *Whose Justice, Which Rationality?* (Notre Dame, IN: University of Notre Dame Press, 1988), 3–4, 348, 354.

107. MacIntyre, *After Virtue*, 201.

108. Ibid., 219.

109. One of MacIntyre's primary criticisms of Foucault is that his thinking is ultimately incapable of critiquing itself and is therefore merely parasitic on the values that it purports to expose and criticize. See Alasdair MacIntyre's *Three Rival Versions of Moral Enquiry* (Notre Dame, IN: University of Notre Dame Press, 1990), 215.

110. MacIntyre, *After Virtue*, 218.

111. MacIntyre, *Three Rival Versions of Moral Enquiry*, 209.

112. MacIntyre, *After Virtue*, 211.

18

Feminism, Gender Equality, and Civil Society

I. The History of Feminist Thought

One of the glaring characteristics of the history of political thought is the silence of women's voices within it. At this point in the text, the reader may have noticed that very few women have been included in the discussion so far. This is because the social and cultural contexts of the Western world in which our philosophical legacy is situated did not recognize the full equality of women. The respect for women's rights, both philosophically and in political practice, is a relatively recent historical development and is the result of important thinkers and activists who have moved this progress forward. In this chapter, we will approach the exclusion of women as a significant problem for the history of political thought, consider feminist critiques of some influential philosophers, and examine several of the contributions feminist philosophers have made to the ongoing struggle for gender equality in political thinking, political theory, and civil society.

Historically speaking, the struggle for gender equality has been situated in contexts that have required activists to focus on particular political problems. Because of this, the rise of feminist philosophy in the twentieth century can best be understood as a set of phases, or waves, that have each focused on a set of problems and their possible solutions. Early feminism, arising in the nineteenth and early twentieth centuries, was focused primarily on the right to vote as a significant hindrance to equality. The liberal ideal of individual rights and liberties to that point in history had essentially been limited to men, and the first-wave feminists fought to have political rights extended to women.

While legal recognition of women's rights (specifically, voting rights and property rights) was accomplished by first-wave feminism, social and economic inequality continued. This led to feminist theories that challenged structures of oppression that continued to exist despite the achievement of equality in some legal and political forms. Second-wave feminism in the middle and late twentieth century focused on economic and social structures that disadvantaged women, and feminist theory focused on issues such as workplace rights, reproductive rights, and family rights. A set of legal issues was also important for second-wave feminists, including laws about domestic violence, rape, and sexuality. Feminist theory expanded, proliferated, and diversified during this period, and many of the philosophers discussed in this chapter are engaged in debates about these issues.

Third-wave feminism emerged in the 1990s, and its arguments challenge the gender assumptions and class suppositions its advocates find in the theories of earlier feminists. Third-wave feminism is influenced by the postmodern ideas of thinkers like Nietzsche and Foucault and rejects many of the ideas of gender, the body, sexuality, and victimhood its advocates find in earlier feminist thought. Not satisfied with gender essentialism or gender binaries, third-wave feminists instead argue that "man" and "woman" are not natural categories and that the relationship between genders should not exist as a two-option choice.

Third-wave feminism also resists the idea that feminism needs to reject the notion of gender altogether. The recognition that gender is socially constructed can lead to the conclusion that gender should be embraced and celebrated. With the advent of online communities, some activists challenge the idea that feminism requires any particular unified response and instead embrace individual celebrations of gender identity. In this stage of feminism, some have even argued that the notion of "feminism" itself should be rethought or rejected, as should the generational idea of "waves" of feminism.[1]

Particularly troubling for some recent feminist theorists is that many of the social and political projects of earlier feminist movements have focused on the experience of middle-class white women, where voting and economic equality means freedom only for people who already experienced racial and economic privilege. In more recent feminist philosophy, the ideas presented by its advocates become even more differentiated and diverse, leading to the question of whether these philosophers are continuing the feminist tradition or are engaging in a critical set of arguments that propose something new.

Perhaps most remarkable for feminist theory is how impactful it has been in civil society at the start of the twenty-first century. If there is a fourth wave of feminism, it is occurring right now, with an increased awareness and influence of the ideas of feminist theory in the broader world of society and politics. In 2017, millions of people went online to share their experiences of sexual harassment and oppression with the tagline "#metoo." Referred to now as the #MeToo movement, exposing and punishing those guilty of gender discrimination, harassment, and violence has become more prevalent. In this movement, the ideas found in feminist theory are applied to call out the patterns and behavior that exist in a society that continues to be dominated by a gender hierarchy.

As feminist theory continues to evolve, and the arguments it makes increasingly influence civil society, it is important to understand the philosophical history and underpinnings of the feminist political project. In the discussion that follows, we aim to highlight significant voices and arguments in feminist thought as they are influenced by the political theories that preceded them. This overview is intended to provide a look at the variety and scope of the dialogue and an understanding of how this dialogue engages the history of political theory that has been presented thus far and continues to push political theorists to think differently about gender.

II. The Public and the Private

A primary reason that the struggle for gender equality has been a difficult one, in both theory and practice, is the way gender was assigned in the composition of society itself. Traditionally, the family was considered a building block of civil society, and women were primarily responsible for caretaking in this realm. What happened in the family was important, but the realm of politics was widely considered to be that which occurs outside the home, and men were traditionally responsible for conducting matters in this other sphere of life. In this way, gender differences were tied to an ongoing tension between the area of life protected from politics and the realm of life in which political thinking and political action was expected. In the modern world, this tension has led to the notion of two distinct realms in which individuals carry out their lives. First, there is the "public" realm: the common world in which individuals interact with each other to purchase or to sell goods, to make a living, or to help make public policy. The "private" realm is the setting of friends, family, religion, sexual relations, and voluntary associations.

Imagining these two realms has been particularly important for recognizing individual rights in modern civil society, because it is widely regarded that we ought to have freedom to make choices about our private lives away from the restrictions of government or other individuals. The distinction between the "private" and the "public" is not clear-cut, however. Even though we recognize that certain rights of the private realm must be protected in public, we also must acknowledge that many of the values that guide our public decisions are formed and cultivated in the private realm. Additionally, decisions about what belongs in the private realm, and those things that we ought to have a right to do even if others disagree, often are decided in the public realm. Questions about the proper role of government, the relationship between religion and politics, and the virtues that are necessary for a healthy society all address important areas of the tension between the private and public realms.

The public–private dichotomy is also problematic in a civil society if it perpetuates injustice and unfairness, such as when it is used to justify the exclusion of certain individuals from participating fully in society. Our discussion of feminism in this chapter, like our discussion of Marxism in Chapter 13, examines the claim many political theorists make that the private realm in a civil society can be used to exclude whole groups of people from the public realm. Whereas in the case of Marxism the people excluded are workers, and the reason for this exclusion is class, in the case of feminism, the people excluded are women, and the reason is gender.

Many political thinkers in recent years have exposed the way in which much of traditional political theory has denied women a chance for full participation in the public realm. One such thinker, Jean Bethke Elshtain, argues that, in large part, the history of political thinking demonstrates a commitment on the part of political thinkers to refuse to recognize that women have a legitimate place in the public realm.[2] Elshtain's analysis of the history of political theory exposes ways in which women are too easily associated with the private realm, where they are connected to "sexuality, natality, the human body (images of uncleanness and taboo, visions of dependency, helplessness, vulnerability)."[3] Within this way of thinking about women, they are not allowed into the public realm to participate fully as equals with men. Indeed, the public realm exhibits a tendency to define and to limit the private realm in such a way that women's voices go unheard in the political world. "Politics is in part an elaborate defense against the tug of the private, against the lure of the familial, against evocations of female power."[4]

The political implications for women are unmistakable. A civil society is supposed to be a contract that provides the same rights to all citizens. But on Carole Pateman's reading of the social contract, similar to Elshtain's diagnosis, civil society is designed as a contract among men, a fraternal contract, that excludes women from any significant role in the public realm and that defines their lives as occupying a subordinate relationship to men politically, socially, and economically.[5] The fraternal social contract, in essence, maintains a patriarchy, or a society ruled by and for the advantage of men. If people are truly committed to a free and equal civil society, the feminist critique argues, people must understand the ways in which the history of political thought, and the institutions of politics and civil society, have excluded women over time. People must also understand the details of the critique itself, and the controversies that exist even among feminist political thinkers. Once people do this, they will have a better sense of the ideal of civil society for which they aim and how they might better include all members of the society in its consideration and discussion.

The question we want to address for the rest of this chapter pertains to how civil society might need to be rethought so that the goals of a civil society can be met for all and, in particular, allow women to participate fully in public life. In the following sections, our intention is to demonstrate several different approaches of feminist thinkers to criticizing traditional modes of political thinking, reconceptualizing the public and the private, and rethinking civil society. It will become clear that feminism itself represents a diversity of voices. In our discussion, we can only hope to highlight several important contributors to this conversation. To this end, we will consider Carole Pateman's treatment of the social contract as a sexual contract; Susan Okin's and Martha Nussbaum's advocacy of a modified liberal conception of feminism; Catharine MacKinnon's arguments about the extent of social oppression and the sources of empowerment; Jean Bethke Elshtain's elaboration of a feminist discourse; Nancy Hartsock's Marxist feminist critique; and the Nietzschean perspective that Camille Paglia and Judith Butler advocate. We then conclude by discussing several writers for whom the quest for gender justice is linked politically, socially, and ethically to racial and economic justice.

III. Perspectives on the Feminist Political Project

Pateman on the Sexual Contract

According to Carole Pateman, a *sexual contract* is preventing us from coming to terms with the place of women in society. Utilizing the idea of a social contract at the heart of civil society as we have seen in other liberal political thinkers, Pateman finds that, in the sexual contract, women are deemed to lack the "attributes and capacities" possessed by men. Operating like the social contract described by Locke, men use the implicit agreement of this contract to establish a society that guarantees men freedom and basic rights. At the same time, women are made subject to men's patriarchal authority.[6] The result of this endeavor is that women are denied the same rights as men.

For Pateman, the sexual contract also creates a sexual division of labor in a civil society. In discussing the nature of work, for instance, Pateman argues that women, in the modern patriarchal system, become dependents of men. The first sign of this appears when women obtain their means of support from their husbands. "She is dependent on the benevolence of her husband and can only endeavour to obtain a 'good master.'"[7] This relationship is manifested throughout society. Indeed, in the modern setting of civil society, where women have a juridical standing that is equal to that of men, women, nonetheless, do not enjoy the same status or opportunity as male workers. Free workers (most men) can enter the labor market and sell their labor to the highest bidder. But the unfree worker, in this case the housewife, lacks "jurisdiction over the property in her person, which includes [her] labour power."[8] A wife cannot contract out her labor power to her husband and earn a wage from him, so the labor of the woman becomes a form of "domestic service."[9]

One reason given for providing males the status of free workers, who can sell their labor on the market, is to ensure that they will be able to make enough money to support their families. However, increasingly in the modern civil society, it is the case that men cannot support their families by themselves and, consequently, women must also enter the public world of work.[10] But when women enter the marketplace to work, what they discover is an "aristocracy" of male laborers. This fraternity not only determines when and whether a wife will work, but when wives work, the best and highest paying jobs are reserved for men. Moreover, the working wife finds herself in a position where, in addition to receiving lower wages than her male counterpart, when she returns home at the end of the day most of the household and child-rearing duties remain her responsibility.[11]

For Pateman, then, the sexual contract undermines any positive possibilities for contractual agreements in civil society. As long as the patriarchal contract continues to oppress women, there can be no social justice within civil society. What is needed is a new contract, one in which women will have an equal agreement and equal contribution. It is likely that a new contract would include a rethinking of the value of the work that is typically done by women, but also a reconfiguration and transformation of the labor market so that women's wages and women's status becomes completely equal. Those who advocate a fully free and equal civil society would find it difficult to deny the importance of these demands.

Liberalism as Feminism: Gender Neutrality and Individual Rights

As it is for Pateman, many feminists view patriarchy as a pervasive fact of modern civil society. Susan Moller Okin is another theorist with such an assessment, and she argues that this patriarchy violates not only women's equality of opportunity in the workplace but also women's right to a life free from violence. Male domination in society, according to Okin, manifests itself in open violence against women, primarily within the family. Even though civil society no longer legally tolerates violence against women (unlike in the past when husbands were permitted by law to "chastise" their wives), male violence against women continues unabated and at epidemic proportions.[12] One of the causes of this is a persistent notion that what happens in the private life of a family is of no business to the public.

Further perpetuating this violence, according to Okin, is a male-dominated public sphere, which affords greatly reduced life options (in comparison with men) for women. These limitations are reinforced through a socialization process that continually teaches young girls to identify with the nurturing role of the mother. In this context girls, unlike boys, are not taught to hold aspirations that orient them to demand full participation in the public realm. Finally, in the public sphere, women's claims are not given the same legitimacy accorded to the claims men make. One example of this reality is gender bias in the courts where women, particularly in matters involving their vital interests, such as in domestic violence, alimony, or child-support issues, are not always taken seriously.[13]

What is needed then, according to Okin, is an approach to reconceptualizing the public and the private realms that is removed somewhat but not completely from John Rawls's conception of the original position. As described in Chapter 15,

Rawls creates a hypothetical perspective, called the *original position*, from which to determine principles of justice that all members of the society would support. In the original position, the parties are rational, and although no one knows one's particular circumstances, including the nature of one's talents, skills, and potential in actual society, all know the general facts about the way society works and is structured. From this point of view, the members of the original position must determine the principles of justice that should guide how the basic goods of society, including rights and liberties, are to be distributed. Okin's problem with Rawls's view is that he does not include in his discussion of the general facts the issue of gender and how gender structures society in ways to constrict women's opportunities.[14] Thus, for Okin, the original position is a powerful tool that allows one to consider "traditions, customs and institutions from all points of view, and [that] ensures that the principles of justice will be acceptable to everyone."[15] The problem, however, is that Rawls does not use the original position to examine "the justice of the gender system," which has "its roots in the sex roles of the family and its branches extending into virtually every corner of our lives, [and which] is one of the fundamental structures of society."[16]

In formulating and applying principles of justice, the parties in the original position should have knowledge of the way in which the gender structure of society disadvantages women.[17] Okin calls this understanding the "standpoint of women." Okin's intention in including the standpoint of women is to ask that all parties fully consider in the original position, men and women alike. When deliberation takes place on these terms, a fair set of principles can then be derived. As Okin says,

> *The notion of the standpoint of women, while not without its problems, suggests that a fully human moral and political theory can be developed only with the full participation of both sexes. At the very least, this will require that women take their place with men in the dialogue in approximately equal numbers and in positions of comparable influence.*[18]

The revised original position that included consideration of the "standpoint of women" would make it clear that Rawls's principles of justice "are inconsistent with a gender-structured society and with traditional family roles."[19] This suggests that Rawls's principles of justice would stipulate that gender – which traditionally is associated with practices and norms that disadvantage women – could no longer be made the basis for apportioning positions and opportunities either inside the family or outside of it. Women should not have to bear the lion's share of the responsibility for household and childcare duties, but these responsibilities should be shared, permitting women to have as many unrestricted choices for public-sphere activity as men have. Included in this concern are not just fair opportunities for careers but opportunities for full political participation as well. Finally, the commitment to self-respect, so central to Rawls's conception of justice, is not made possible in a society where, owing to gender-caused social and economic inequalities, women are forced to play servile roles to males.[20]

Okin's position is typical of liberal conceptions of civil society. Every person must enjoy the same recognition of rights, regardless of gender or any other social form of differentiation.[21] This means, then, that Okin's addition of the female point of view leads her to promote a *gender-neutral* perspective. The central idea of this perspective is that individuals are not to be accorded rights by virtue of their gender status. Or, to use other terms, to say that individuals are to be accorded the same rights is to say that no rights should be accorded to any one individual that are not accorded to all individuals.

Along with Okin, Martha Nussbaum is another feminist theorist who advocates the advancement of women's rights through liberal political theory. In her book *Sex and Social Justice*, Nussbaum defends liberal principles as the best way to advance the feminist goals of a free and equal society regardless of gender. Nussbaum is particularly committed to the liberal political ideal of universal human rights and argues that it is only through a liberal approach to civil society and politics that we can criticize violations of women's rights both domestically and internationally.[22]

With arguments such as this, defenders of the classical liberal approach to feminist theory are making an argument on two fronts. On one hand, Nussbaum is arguing that a consistent defense of the liberal political principles of freedom and equality requires the recognition of the rights of women as equal to those of the rights of men. On the other hand, Nussbaum also argues against more radical feminist positions that advocate a more thorough critique of liberalism as a part of the patriarchal problem. As we will see in the sections to come, several feminist theorists are unhappy with liberal political values themselves and believe it is the individualism, capitalism, and rationalism of liberalism that undermines full equality for women. Nussbaum's argument on behalf of liberal political values is thus not only a defense of feminism but also a defense of liberalism against other feminist critics.

Nussbaum argues that for our commitment to equality and to feminism to be consistent and persuasive, it must have the force of argument that is available only if we accept a universal commitment to human rights and human equality. Despite its sometimes flawed application, Nussbaum argues that any application of feminist theory that does not advance universal liberal notions will ultimately fail to transform political life. This transformation is the ultimate goal for Nussbaum, and it needs to happen in our local neighborhoods and all over the world. But, like Okin, Nussbaum does not believe Rawls's liberalism is enough, with only its "small list of basic goods and resources."[23] For Nussbaum, a feminist liberalism needs to recognize that resources do not simply have a value unto themselves but have a value insofar as they enable people to function fully as equals by overcoming whatever impediments may arise to equality in particular situations. This rethinking of the resource allocation would allow us to account for oppression, deprivation, and suffering in a liberal democratic society and to provide important reforms to eliminate them.

How might civil society be different if we applied Okin's and Nussbaum's feminist liberalism to social practices? If we reconceived the boundaries between public and private, an entire set of assumptions about shared responsibility would likely change. The private realm would be reconstituted, for example, to include shared responsibility for childcare.[24] In this context, women as well as men would be able to enter the public realm of work without fearing that having children and a family would harm their chances for success at work. In particular, women's chances for advancement in a company or profession would not be impeded by their taking a childbirth leave. Moreover, women and men both should be given chances for parental leave during post-birth months.[25] This policy would permit men as well as women to take full part in child rearing without harm to their career development.[26]

Additionally, the educational system must be designed to teach children about the difficulties that present inequalities pose for women throughout the society. Unless children are educated to the problems women face, reforming the public and private realms so women and men will be treated equally in both will be difficult to achieve. Further, the problem of the missing father, now rampant throughout society, must be resolved so that all children have a fair chance in society. This means identifying missing fathers and ensuring they pay support, and when they are unable to pay support, the government must provide backup aid. After a divorce, the family standard of living of either spouse should not suffer serious loss. Only then will all children have a fair chance in life.[27]

Also, both Okin and Nussbaum want to ensure that equal legal protection is afforded to men and women in cases such as family law. To this end, Okin suggests that employers should divide paychecks so that half of the money goes to the wife (or husband if the husband is staying at home while the wife works) and the other half to the husband (or to the wife, if the wife is the main wage earner). This plan would provide money to women directly for their labor in the house, and thus women would no longer remain as unpaid laborers in a male-dominated household.[28] Furthermore, in line with her understanding of liberal ideals, Nussbaum agrees with Okin and argues that divorce laws should better recognize the value of unpaid work in the home. Nussbaum acknowledges that, even though the feminist movement in the United States has accomplished much in opening the workplace for women, the persisting cultural expectation that women perform a majority of the unpaid housework and childcare constrains their economic productivity. Thus, when marriages end, the law needs to do more to compensate women for the years of unpaid service that supported the household.[29]

Although many feminists would disagree with their advancement of a liberal individualist feminism, Okin and Nussbaum represent important voices in feminist political thought that call for a more faithful and thorough application of the political ideals of individual freedom and equality to the gender discrimination that exists at all levels of society. As we consider their argument, we should also consider the other changes that society and law might have to undergo if it truly became gender neutral and how society might have to change for the liberal commitment to equality and individual rights to be applied more expansively throughout society.

MacKinnon on Female Empowerment, Social Censorship, and the State

Catherine MacKinnon rejects the liberal approach that Okin and Nussbaum advocate and argues that it is necessary to correct those underlying power relationships in society that define women as subordinate to men before rights can be made equal for both sexes. Until this transformation can occur, merely providing equal rights to women will never work to overcome the subordination they experience on a daily basis.[30] She argues that "abstract equality of liberalism permits most women little more than does the substantive inequality of conservatism."[31] The solution, MacKinnon urges, is one that overcomes the reality of social and political relationships that deny women equal status to men. Then women will "participate in defining the terms that create the standards [and they will have a] voice in drawing the lines."[32]

For MacKinnon, then, a liberal conception of individual rights is blind to the fact that, to have the full legal rights the state grants, persons must be free socially from any kind of impediment that would make it impossible for them to make full use of these rights. For instance, what good are the rights of speech, opportunity, and private property, to say nothing of due process of law, if the person granted these rights lacks the characteristics that enable a person to make full use of them? Here, a familiar contrast can be made between the plight of poor and rich people who are accused of murder and who seek to clear themselves in a court of law. Many think that a poor person accused of murder cannot get just as good an opportunity to defend him- or herself in a court of law as a millionaire can. And the reason is lack of money. Money buys lawyers skilled in manipulating the judicial system in ways that give their clients an advantage. By analogy, this fact extends to women's rights. One can argue that even with laws that provide women equality of opportunity, how can women make good use of these laws when men are ever-present throughout a woman's career, finding ways to legally deny her what is due to her? To overcome these barriers, women need the kind of social and political power that enables them to remove men from their paths, so they can make full use of the opportunities to which they are entitled. MacKinnon says, "No one who does not already have [rights] socially is granted them legally."[33]

But as long as men can structure social relationships so that women are always subordinate – that is, have the worst jobs, have to perform the lion's share of the housework, and so on – the social reality women experience will be one that makes them unequal in power and stature to men. How, then, can women be liberated from this situation? This question is particularly difficult to answer because, for MacKinnon, the power relationships that suppress women in civil society are not only pervasive, but they are in fact "invisible." Here, social relationships, specifically designed to place women in bondage to men, are considered by most members of society to be "just the way things are."[34] Women's lives, as subordinate to men, are viewed as a reality that cannot be changed. In this case, women are bound by chains that, unlike the chains of traditional slaves, are invisible. If one cannot see the chains that must be broken to free the enslaved person, how can that person be freed? More to the point, if there are no visible chains holding one down, how can one even say one is unfree?

This terrible situation for women emerges from the way men have chosen to see and to experience women, and what best symbolizes men's oppressive view of women is pornography. MacKinnon says that "men's power over women means that the way men see women defines who women can be. Pornography is this way."[35] The most important objective on the male agenda as they go about defining women is to put women in a situation in which they are objects of male sexual satisfaction. Indeed, pornography carries out this objective when it "defines women by how we look according to how we can be sexually used. Pornography codes how to look at women, so you know what you can do with one when you see one."[36]

Here, a woman's identity stems from men's making women into an "underclass," who "become objects for male sexual use."[37] Gender, as it is defined for women by men, refers to men's need to control women's bodies for men's pleasures, and for this reason, men maintain a dominant position toward women.[38] In keeping with this view of gender, "pornography turns a woman into a thing to be acquired and used."[39] But ironically, the abuse of women in the setting of pornography does not suggest a state of affairs that women are said to reject. Indeed, women are depicted in hard-core pornographic situations as wanting to be bound and as enjoying being viciously assaulted and even murdered. Soft-core pornography depicts women as desirous of being made the objects of male sexual pleasure.[40] In either case, pornography depicts women as never having enough abuse thrown their way because they can never have enough of the sexual "pleasure" that comes from such an experience. Men, by sexualizing the subjugation of women, then, create the illusion that women enjoy their inferior status. In consequence, women are not like slaves in the old South, many of whom hoped to flee their masters; rather, women willingly accept their inequality without a hint of frustration with it. Not only are women kept in bondage to men through these means, but the fact that they are in bondage is no cause for concern for society; thus, there is no need to discuss how to create equality of power between men and women. Pornography suggests that women's natural role is bondage, a role that women accept, and thus the call for liberation makes no sense.

For MacKinnon, as for all reasonable people, this viewpoint represents an absolute outrage and a tragedy of great proportions. After all, we live in a society dedicated to the freedom for all, but even as we say this, we accept terrible forms of terror aimed at over half the people in society. To change this situation, it is necessary to expose the harm that pornography inflicts on women. MacKinnon thinks that any work of pornography is designed to define the way men see women as powerless individuals to be used for men's needs.[41] Thus, an analysis of the impact of pornography is important because it is a form of activity by which men legitimize real harm to women, harm that prevents women as a class from full participation in the public realm. Indeed, the list of the kinds of harm that pornography is associated with is exceptionally long. For instance, in MacKinnon's view, pornography harms women who make pornographic films. These women are nothing more than sexual slaves, often forced against their will to perform a variety of harmful and crude acts.[42] Pornography is associated with physical assaults on women, including rapes.[43] Pornography harms men's ability to relate to women as human beings with authentic needs and emotions. Instead, when women are looked at through the lens of pornography, they are merely playthings in vicious and barbaric male fantasies.[44]

Overall, for MacKinnon, pornography is a practice that maintains the continued subordination of women to men in the most brutal ways possible. We must liberate women from this terrible, oppressive institution. But how? This will be a difficult question to answer because, presently, pornography is not viewed as a civil rights violation in the same way racial discrimination is a violation of the rights of African Americans. Yet, for MacKinnon, for women to make political and human progress, it is necessary to "define pornography as a practice of sex discrimination, a violation of women's civil rights, the opposite of sexual equality."[45]

In modern liberal society, however, the protection of free speech is usually a common defense of pornography against the claim that it is a civil rights violation. To counter this view, MacKinnon, along with Andrea Dworkin, wrote an antipornography law that was passed by the Indianapolis city government. The law would have allowed a person who proved harm from pornography to seek civil damages from its distributor or its producer. As evidence of liberal priorities, however, the claim of freedom was enough to defeat the law, as the US Court of Appeals overturned this law on the basis of the First Amendment protection of speech.[46]

This example manifests a general tendency of the courts to view pornography as "only words," which may defame women but do not discriminate against them.[47] Words express ideas that can offend, but offensive words do not necessarily harm to the extent that the law recognizes. But in MacKinnon's view, this is a failure of the law because words, images, and ideas are not harmless; they can represent harmful social practices that deny women their full entitlements as citizens, and, moreover, these words promote and produce activities that brutalize and terrorize women. In short, pornographic language is an element in a system of power, just like the system of segregation in the old South, which renders women unequal and powerless to men.[48] If words and images discriminate and oppress, MacKinnon asks, should not women be protected from them by laws that are supposedly in place to guarantee protections of civil rights?

It is true that obscenity laws are currently in place regulating pornography, but MacKinnon argues that obscenity laws are only premised on prevailing moral standards. These standards stop short of banning the objectification of women in images and in words and, therefore, tend to favor the male's continued subordination of women. In consequence, obscenity laws only reinforce existing pornographic activities.[49] MacKinnon's argument is troubling for some because it is often difficult to determine what is pornographic and what is not.

Moreover, MacKinnon maintains that free-speech provisions should not protect pornography since, in doing so, the state permits discrimination based on gender.[50] Thus, MacKinnon advocates a new way of thinking about the freedom of expression. For her, various groups – such as Nazis, Klansmen, and pornographers – should not be accorded absolute freedom of speech, but their speech should be limited because it harms people who, in the context of the particular circumstances of our history, have been kept in subordinated positions.[51] In this case, the right to produce pornography would no longer be protected under the freedom of speech provision of a liberal civil society.

Still, there are many issues that some would raise about the threat to freedom of speech, with respect to both artistic matters and political matters, that MacKinnon's approach might raise. However, we put these matters to the side at this point. But even as we do, the question remains: would adopting MacKinnon's approach change the power relationships in society that cause severe harm to women? This is a question that MacKinnon seems not to address. As we discuss other theorists, however, the question remains on our agenda.

Elshtain on Feminist Ethics and the Discourse of Justice

Jean Bethke Elshtain's approach to challenging the role of women in civil society and rethinking the distinction between "public" and "private" is to consider the female person's understanding of what is important and meaningful about life. This means going beyond understanding women as the product of so-called external social forces, according to some abstract theory, and learning what constitutes, for them, the fundamental values that make their lives significant.[52] Knowledge of this sort comes from discussion and dialogue with women about their lives and about the way the existing circumstances in society are viewed as either helping or hindering their pursuit of what is important to them.

The dialogue Elshtain has in mind involves women discussing issues over which there is significant disagreement, such as abortion rights. To be productive, coercion and manipulation must be avoided in the discussion, and it would be marked by openness to views that some people may not share initially with others in the conversation. Central to this undertaking is the assumption that many views people have on matters of controversy need "probing and exploratory reexamination." This undertaking is designed to encourage people, through discussion, to examine "unreflectively" held positions.[53]

If this discussion took place, what would it tell us that would be helpful for reformulating a more just civil society? A main objective of this dialogue would be to realize the different points of view that women bring to issues of morality and politics. On this point, Elshtain embraces the views of Carol Gilligan who, in Elshtain's words, says that the moral lives of women are grounded in a "concern for others, responsibility, care, and obligation, and hence, a moral language profoundly at odds with formal, abstract models of morality defined in terms of absolute principles."[54] Elshtain's support of Gilligan suggests an ethics of care and of responsibility, which becomes foundational for many feminist political thinkers.

In Gilligan's view, women approach moral issues from the standpoint of an ethics of care or responsibility, and this orientation to social problems suggests that women form their identities through activities that seek to maintain affiliations to others.[55] In contrast, men typically approach others from the standpoint of a quest to realize equality, or a situation in which everyone is treated the same, in accordance with a shared conception of rights and basic moral principles. In doing so, men tend to approach others from the standpoint of intellectual objectivity and detachment, for without these qualities the system of rights and principles men seek to realize would be jeopardized by emotional bias. But to achieve detachment, it is necessary to deny centrality of place to values that women emphasize, such as caring for others. In consequence, men place less importance on retaining attachments to others, and thus male identity is more associated with separation and the absence of the deep connections to others that women seek.[56]

Thus, men and women speak in different voices; women speak in a language of care and responsibility, and men use a language of abstract rules and rights. Civil society would thus be more inclusive and politics, ultimately, would be more just if the differences of their perspectives were fully and equally allowed in public discourse. Following Gilligan, Elshtain would like to make certain that social discourse begins to include more fully the female voice, thereby encompassing all of civil society (men included) in the ethic of care and responsibility.

This viewpoint would be central, for example, to understanding why the family is such an important element in society. By providing loving care and nurturing, the family setting develops and nurtures the best human capacities and virtues in people. A childhood based upon love develops in children a sense of empathy, pity, and compassion. Individuals will lack their "capacity for human identification" when they become adults if these qualities instilled as children in the context of the special relationships of family life are neglected.[57]

Elshtain's feminist argument thus challenges the idea that the family is an exclusively private institution and recognizes that we all should take interest in strengthening families. To do this, it is necessary to support parenting throughout society by resisting the various social forces that "erode, impoverish, or preclude the flourishing of our most basic human ties."[58] Once we recognize the social importance of the family, the center of the "private realm," we can turn to improving the public realm.

Elshtain understands the public realm as consisting of a wide diversity of people shaping social policy and politics by engaging in a discourse with each other about what is best for the society. "Where any number of citizens is gathered in the name of acting together in common toward ends they debate and articulate in public, there is citizenship."[59] Rights have an important role here. Rights do not emanate so much from a (male) abstract conception of equality as from the need to protect people from the abuses of public authority so that each can share his or her views with others, during the course of defining common needs.[60] These needs can be commonly defined and pursued only in a context wherein everyone is protected by recognized rights.

Moreover, the experience of citizenship is also an experience of the transformative potential made possible by civic life. When men and women are engaged together in deliberation in which all are treated with dignity, it is likely that men and women will both undergo changes that enhance full participation in public life. A feminist outlook that is not open to "the possibility of transformation of men as well as women is deeply nihilistic," and the reason is that such a politics does not "believe in . . . the ideal of genuine mutuality."[61]

How would the discourse Elshtain urges achieve the transformations for which she hopes? Elshtain presumes that real discourse rests upon a possibility of mutual caring and respect, in which individuals willingly listen to each other and attempt to find ways to accommodate legitimate interests. In taking this approach, Elshtain maps out a "politics of compassion" that makes clear that "no good can come from the widespread dehumanization and destruction of others."[62] Indeed, she hopes for a politics that incorporates an ethic of caring and responsibility to create a public realm that rests upon ethical conceptions conducive to citizenship. This entails a desire on the part of people to support each other in maintaining those conditions that ensure fairness for all. In this context, all enduring political issues would thus be addressed from the standpoint of an ethic of caring,

> *a clear notion of what ideals and obligations are required to animate an authentic public, an ethical polity, must be adumbrated: authority, freedom, public law, civic virtue, the ideal of the citizen – all those beliefs, habits, and qualities which are integral to a political order.*[63]

Here, following Gilligan, the basis for restoring a civil society that is fair to all is a context in which people have genuine concern for each other, men and women.

An interesting problem naturally emerges from Elshtain's position. She nicely depicts the kind of dialogue, along with the consequences, of a politics that incorporates Gilligan's ethic of care. Such a politics would transform people so that, in a setting of mutual care and compassion, people would build spaces for citizenship, in which there was a common concern to protect the rights and to recognize the needs of others. But a major problem of this approach pertains to what comes first, the institutionalized acceptance of rights or an ethics of care and concern? Can we depend upon the latter to provide a setting that is capable of sustaining rights in a civil society? Or do we need first to have a well-established and well-maintained rights orientation, as manifested in Gilligan's depiction of the male voice? What if the ethics of care is not strong enough to sustain the transformation Elshtain hopes for in people? Then, is it not best to rely less on a dialogue of compassion and more on the (male, for Gilligan) machinery that abstractly and fairly, in a Hobbesian (male) way, upholds rights? Or is the cause of equality and a clear and protected space for the female voice denied from the start if we take this approach?

It is perhaps the case that the two dimensions, rights and caring, are intertwined and mutually reinforcing. As argued in Chapter 1, thinking about the best civil society, which is the backdrop for our discussion throughout this book, includes building it upon a foundation of respect for both rights, which secure individual choices, and basic civic virtues, such as toleration and mutual respect. It is likely that Elshtain would agree that both are simultaneously required for maintaining the basis of an inclusive and caring community.

Hartsock's Marxist Feminist Viewpoint

From an alternative feminist perspective, the work of Nancy Hartsock provides an economic and structural analysis of the situation in which women find themselves.[64] In developing this standpoint, Hartsock takes what she describes as a Marxist approach to analyzing society. In particular, she believes that, by looking at society from the standpoint of women in the same way that Marx viewed society from the standpoint of the working class, there emerges a "privileged vantage point on male supremacy, a vantage point that can ground a powerful critique of the phallocratic institutions and ideology that constitute the capitalist form of patriarchy."[65] What will this critique demonstrate? Hartsock believes that, as women analyze their experience, they will understand the way in which men structure their relationship of dominance toward women. In this context, not only will women understand these relationships as detrimental and inhuman, but women will realize, as a result of this understanding, the possibilities for liberation from their oppressive setting. Consequently, all ideological arguments used to justify this oppression can no longer be tolerated. In fact, the objects of the oppression, in this case women as for Hartsock, or workers as for Marx, will turn against those who use these justifications to continue the status quo.[66]

Hartsock's construction of the feminist standpoint takes place within the context of a capitalist society, within which women as a group must form a powerful political alliance that will radically change the existing structure of society. As we will recall from the description of Marxism in Chapter 13, workers find themselves forced to be producers of commodities for an owner class who monopolizes the profits from the worker's labor and uses these profits to enhance the owner's status and power in society. Like all workers in this analysis, a woman is a commodity producer in the society, but in addition to this form of exploitation, the woman is also a producer of various services in the family setting, such as housework, nurturing, and so on.[67] In consequence, women not only work more than men, but a large proportion of their work is devoted to tedious labor in the household.[68] (Here, the unrecognized and unpaid nature of "women's work" is an issue much as it is for liberal feminists like Okin.)

The differentiation of work roles is the basis for extreme conflict between men and women because women, unlike men, are able to develop close communal connections to others. The fact that men are so closely tied to commodity production and women to providing services in the family is a consequence of the reality that women are more prone to see themselves as relationally linked to others who depend on them. Traditionally, women's work in the home is essential to maintaining the lives of each of the members of the family. Therefore, women are tied directly to their families because of the work they must perform in the house. This is unlike the work of men, which produces goods in places that are primarily outside the home.[69] In their role as head of a family, women are better equipped to help members of society evolve into mature human beings and do this through an attitude of nurture and concern.[70]

These relational ties women have to their families are strongly reinforced in girls but not as much in boys. Girls learn their role from their mothers, who are always present. Boys do not learn their role from their fathers because the father is, for the most part, absent, and this fact has importance for the way males come to see the world. Boys, as a consequence of their socialization, are less likely than girls to define the world in terms of direct relational ties. In consequence, boys, unlike girls, tend to separate themselves from others.[71] This experience coincides with a young male's development of his sexual identity. Initially, the young male identifies closely with his mother, but society reminds him through the various institutions of socialization that maleness requires that he separate from his mother. He does so by constructing "barriers to femininity," as, for instance, when he sees his mother as an "evil creature."[72] Here, the boy constructs his sense of self by establishing a kind of hostile relationship to his mother, but this relationship becomes the prototype for the masculine relationship in general. A male's "construction of self in opposition to unity with the mother . . . sets a hostile and combative dualism at the heart of both the community men construct and the masculinist world view by means of which they understand their lives."[73] This experience is the basis for Hartsock's contention that the developmental paths of boys follow a course in which a boy's identity is a function of the need to define himself in opposition to others. Hartsock argues that this tendency "reverberates throughout the construction of both class society and the masculine world view and results in a deep-going and hierarchical dualism" in which there is a "we versus them" relationship.[74]

The masculine perspective of "us versus them" sets the terms for the way the dominant male voice organizes society. Men define their identities in terms of what they conceive to be a hostile world. "Masculinity must be attained by means of opposition to the concrete world of daily life, by escaping from contact with the female world of the household into the masculine world of politics or public life."[75] By the same token, the relational ties that women engender orient them to seek to break down the "us versus them" mentality and instead move to a situation in which there is a sense of connection and community among people. Indeed, this orientation is the basis for women's exposing the masculine perspective as perverse and in need of transformation.[76] The masculine response to the female aspiration for community is to reject this hope completely. The male has been socialized to separate himself from his mother and from any dimensions of community associated with family life, and this experience is the basis for a "profound lack of empathy and refusal to recognize the very being of another."[77] To prevent women from achieving their communal agenda, men try to isolate women from each other in the hope of stopping them from building natural communities. To this end, the male structures society so that women are left alone with their children, isolated from the rest of the society. Here, without the connection to and interaction with other women, women work alone in the house, serving others and denying themselves their connection to community. Ultimately, then, the male viewpoint becomes the dominant one, and the activities of women in the family as mothers "mark the transformation of life into death, the distortion of what could have been creative and community activity into oppressive toil, and the destruction of the possibility of community present in women's relational self-definition."[78]

From the Marxist feminist standpoint, then, men and women have different life experiences owing to their different work roles, and this difference becomes the basis for a conflict that leads to the denial of freedom and humanity to women.[79] Given these painful consequences for women, there is a need for "a vast and far-reaching social transformation" that would eliminate the conventional division of labor between men and women.[80] To accomplish this objective, private property itself, and the competition sustained in the capitalist system of economics, should be abolished, and there will be a need for "seizing the state's power" for a "lengthy post-revolutionary class struggle."[81]

Although Hartsock does not describe in detail the nature of the new society, she makes clear that she is imagining the need for an event akin to a socialist revolution. Her new society would not accept Mill's approach to change in which the workers end up managing their own factories. Instead, state power would be needed to eliminate the need for private property and to promote the objective of complete liberation for women. It is not clear how a new system of property ownership or a new "liberated" government would achieve these ends. What is clear is that the new world she hopes to realize will be one in which there are no longer any "institutionalized gender differences" between men and women. Associated with these changes would be a "transformation" of human relationships in society, in a direction that would liberate women from their subordination to men. Indeed, every human relationship would be transformed so that men as well as women would become involved in all the activities associated with maintaining human beings. Included here would be a need to institutionalize the participation of men and women in carrying out child-rearing responsibilities. In this new society, the old division of labor would be replaced with a new approach to work that would free men and women from past forms of class warfare that harmed mostly women.[82]

It is important for our discussion to note that Hartsock's reliance on the state and its control of the economy employs a "top-down" approach to the transformation of civil society. Unlike Elshtain, who advocates discourse in civil society that will ultimately transform society, Hartsock advocates an entirely institutional approach to "the revolution." From this perspective, then, Hartsock would also not accept Okin's liberal approach to civil society that stresses provision of equal rights for all in the current configuration of the economy and politics. For Hartsock, Okin fails to recognize that the liberal approach ultimately fails in a society in which women are always subordinated to the interests of men as a class. The effort to recognize rights, applied fairly and equally to all, could never be realized in a capitalist liberal society according to Hartsock. Until the system that places men and women into different and conflicting work roles is removed, there will be no liberation for women, nor, for that matter, will there be a chance for women to have equal rights to men.

Hartsock would probably accept MacKinnon's critique that requires redefining the nature of existing uses of rights, such as the freedom of speech doctrine, in light of the need to give to women social and political power they do not yet have. But to achieve this goal it will be necessary to go further than MacKinnon suggests is necessary. Hartsock would agree that women need more power to neutralize male domination, but she would argue that to attain this power it will be necessary to entirely transform the economic and social relationships in society. To achieve this objective will require not just localized efforts focusing on pornography but a thorough revolution that entirely changes the system of production and the division of labor in society.

Paglia's and Butler's Feminist Perspectives on Power and Will

Camille Paglia's views offer an example of a Nietzschean approach to feminism. To begin, we should make it clear that Paglia shares with her feminist colleagues a commitment to a society in which women can pursue the fullest range of life options possible. Equal opportunity is "a crucial ideal that all must support."[83] Indeed, a main objective of her undertaking is to eliminate the impediments to women's advancement in society.[84] Further, like many liberals, she is committed to permitting the broadest possible freedom of speech, and she takes this position to protect many lifestyles that otherwise might be denied full expression. In rejecting policies to police speech, she "respects and honors the prostitute," permits open availability of pornography, and advocates the fullest possible freedom for homosexuality.[85]

Unlike the feminists discussed thus far, however, Paglia does *not* define patriarchy as women's collective enemy. She argues that patriarchy symbolizes the larger culture that men and women share, a culture that has provided women a great deal of freedom. It is a patriarchal society, for example, that provided women the birth control pill, which, after all, "did more to free contemporary women than feminism itself."[86] Moreover, abuses of women, such as rape, have always been condemned as part of an ethics that is an integral part of a patriarchal culture. Indeed, throughout history, "men have protected women. Men have given women sustenance. Men have died to defend the country for women." Paglia argues, "We must look back and acknowledge what men have done *for women*."[87]

So, if patriarchy is not the real nemesis, what is? To understand her answer to this question, it is necessary to describe the general background conditions that, for Paglia, explain a central dynamic that rules and shapes the relationship between men and women. Paglia understands human life to be played out against the backdrop of a struggle between two opposing forces, each of which is integral to our personalities: Apollo and Dionysus. As we demonstrated in our discussion of Nietzsche, Apollo symbolizes a natural human disposition for order, and Dionysus symbolizes a natural counter-need to wreck Apollo's regimen. Paglia says, "Dionysus is energy unbound, mad, callous, destructive, wasteful. Apollo is law, history, tradition, the dignity and safety of custom and form. Dionysus is the *new*, exhilarating but rude sweeping all away to begin again. Apollo is tyrant, Dionysus a vandal."[88]

Paglia builds upon Nietzsche's argument when she suggests that the effort to subdue Dionysus is not always successful. The Western way of understanding views the world not only as Apollo suggests but often as Dionysus demands. Paglia refers to the latter tendency as pagan, and she argues that the Judeo-Christian tradition, which promotes Apollo, is unable to prevent the emergence of Dionysus.[89] The Dionysian impulses from within our own selves constantly seek to break away from a patterned consciousness and, in doing so, shatter the structures of ordered life by which we are supposed to abide.

The desire to live as our Dionysian passions require is best expressed in our sexuality. We cannot escape looking at others with sexual longing. The norms of Apollo, while trying to limit and to constrain, do not stop us from fantasizing sexual gratification with others. But we are often stopped from fulfilling these fantasies by an Apollonian-imposed regimen. Erotic torment, then, is inevitable because we cannot completely have what our fantasies point to, nor can we ever stop our desire for the things denied to us. This torment is depicted in various ways in both art and literature.[90] Thus, a tendency to look for what will satisfy our unending sexual yearnings always motivates the so-called Western way of viewing the world, irrespective of the ordering norms that orient us to do otherwise. The will to power is never choked to death, but it is always prevalent in our lives, directing, goading, and motivating us to triumph over an ordered, rational life.

For Paglia, gender differences arise not from conventions but from our biologic natures and hormones.[91] We create culture to control and subdue these hormones, but, owing to our Dionysian desires, there is an ever-recurrent need to overturn these cultural limits. Naturally, then, instead of being Jean-Jacques

Rousseau's peaceful individual in the state of nature, Paglia depicts us as filled with anger. Paglia follows the Marquis de Sade and not Rousseau, then, in arguing that deep within all of us is a tempestuous sea, with extraordinary explosive power and force, ready to cause pain and destruction to anything that stands in its way.[92] In this context, men become the natural aggressors. Paglia argues, "Man is contoured for invasion, while woman remains *the hidden*, a cave of archaic darkness."[93]

Why are men aggressors? In the procreative act, women are clearly the superstars, and men, by comparison, the minor, supporting role players. Women do the greatest and the most creative work in bringing new life into the world. But men are not satisfied with such a minor role in the life process. Thus, Paglia says, "Women have it. Men want it. What is *it*? The secret of life."[94] Women, who bear primary responsibility for reproduction, represent a "monumental challenge to our understanding."[95] For men, then, sex is a complicated undertaking. At first, it is an act designed to achieve a unique kind of satisfaction, but later it becomes associated with a sense of impotence and loss of significance. Sex signifies to men that they will never gain, through the act of sex itself, control of nature's mysteries. The latter is a domain that nature reserves for women alone. Yet, what is more important than the power of creation? Men cannot tolerate being made small players in the creation process, and as a result, they demand for themselves the power women have.

It is this experience, and the frustration and concomitant aggression, that explains why men commit violence against women. Rape must be understood not simply as a crime of violence as most feminists claim it is but as a symbol of "male power fighting female power," with the male wanting to appropriate for himself what only the female has: in particular, control over the mysteries of life.[96] This experience explains why men are potential rapists. Men face a continual and perpetual form of injustice that women never know. Yet, it is the protective character of Apollo, located in the laws of society, that seek to save women from the injustice of men who would commit rape.

From the foregoing, for Paglia, women, who are identified with nature, represent the Dionysian instinct.[97] Men rebel against this reality and create systems of order in which to place women and to control them. It is necessary to understand this classic and all-pervasive conflict as the foundation of our culture. Only when we do, can we begin to understand the problems with finding a way for men and women to live together in a setting that secures the fullest freedom possible for each.

How would this understanding or outlook affect our political judgments? For Paglia, we must design policies that respect both Apollonian and Dionysian dimensions by not moving so far in one direction that the other bursts forth with a vengeance that is destructive and harmful to the freedom of everyone.[98] A life that is too much geared to the Dionysian impulses overindulges these impulses, producing nothing but chaos and death. A life that is strictly Apollonian interprets natural desire as wrong and perverted, and it causes the objects of such desire, in particular women, to be treated with violence and hate. Moreover, the life of Apollo is a life of complete denial of our will, a life in which we do whatever we are told and, in the process, forfeit whatever freedom and creativity we may have. A Dionysian orientation must balance this way of life so that we can continue to retain some degree of spontaneity and feeling needed for creativity. For Paglia, then, the challenge is to find a proper balance between Apollo and Dionysus. She says:

> *We must learn how to make tiny corrections to avoid the uncontrolled swing of the pendulum [from Apollonian to Dionysian] that, over a generation, swept us from Fifties conformism to Sixties rebellion to Seventies excess and the cataclysm of AIDS. We now live with the smell of funeral pyres.*[99]

The feminist project must not, according to Paglia, wipe away the Judeo-Christian tradition that stands for Apollo. We also must not, however, allow the latter to deny completely the Dionysian dimension that she associates with pagan or pre-Christian tradition.[100] Nietzsche generally believes that we need to create a new order that allows the Dionysian impulses to thrive, and Paglia agrees. Thus, her language and mode of argument are often designed to pierce through the barriers of society and of modern ideology that stand against Dionysus. But, like Nietzsche, she is willing to recognize the need for Apollo to prevent the kind of extreme despair and destruction that, for instance, the AIDS epidemic typifies.

Paglia's view would suggest highlighting a way of life akin to one that Nietzsche professed: in this case, an ethic of extreme individualism. To break the bonds of Apollo, to allow one's instincts free expression, and to avoid destructive forms of self-imposed repression, it would be necessary to allow individuals to contemplate any life they want to engage in, and, subject to individuals not harming others (for Paglia, that is, and not necessarily for Nietzsche), pursue that way of life wherever it leads. This point of view makes pornography a necessary and natural part of life, according to Paglia. Unlike MacKinnon and Dworkin, who argue that pornography symbolizes rape and the male need to subordinate women, Paglia sees pornography as a need to get in touch with all the desires that nature generates. Nature, forever shrouded in mystery, allows an unruly imagination, which leads us to passionately embrace ways of life that are clearly not conventional. Continuous and nonconforming desires, as depicted in pornography, are inherent in life. Thus, "far from poisoning the mind, pornography shows the deepest truth about sexuality, stripped of romantic veneer."[101] Indeed, pornography suggests that we have "eternal fires of desire, without fatigue, incapacity, aging or death."[102]

Like Nietzsche, Paglia's approach means founding new values, values that help to give substantive meaning and purpose to life. To do this there needs to be an unusual, creative individual, who often stands by herself, defying existing norms, but who, in doing so, manifests the willfulness necessary to create the basis for new ways of seeing and understanding.

But what if the determinism of social forces and the power relationships we find ourselves within, prevent us from thinking outside current gender relationships? A feminist might ask this question, taking her lead from Foucault, who assessed the possibility for a radical transformation of society as being bleak. Judith Butler makes such an argument about gender, describing it as a consequence of social forces that are largely outside of our willful control.[103] Butler takes Foucault's lead in arguing that human beings do not exist on their own terms. Because of our entanglements with power there is no way for us to identify ourselves as separate from the social forces that constitute us and our identity. Accordingly, Butler argues that we have no independent means of describing value, justice, or social goods. Butler would be critical, then, of any feminist position that argues that we can easily transform society through simplistic political solutions.

In this view, civil society is a place in which gender identity is defined and formed. There can be no such thing as "liberation" or "rights" traditionally understood because these notions are also elements of the fabric of identity formation. When we take "free action," according to Butler, we are merely performing according to those roles and meanings that have already been determined before our decisions are made. It is not state action that is the primary source of restrictions to freedom, then, but society itself that has already determined our identities and sets of choices. Butler's primary argument is that gender is one of the primary examples of this social constitution. Our gender exists only in the context of its social meaning, and the formation of this social meaning is tied to a complex set of power relationships whose primary goals are to sustain themselves. There is no such thing as gender and thus no natural differentiation of male and female that can someday become "equal."[104]

On the surface, this deterministic account of gender identity seems to allow no room for anything we might consider to be free and reasoned action. Butler does, however, provide a description of how the individual can make decisions. Political agency – that is, action or assertion in civil society – occurs only when there are failures and contradictions within the forces of power acting on the self. The convergence and coexistence of forces on the constituted body "produces the possibility of complex reconfiguration and deployment."[105] As forces of power coalesce within and around an individual, they sometimes come into conflict or inconsistency with one another, and when these forces "rub together," they create a situation for the individual that manifests itself as a political action. It is, thus, conflicts in civil society that allow possibilities to change and reconfigure power relationships.

Within her account, Butler recalls the all-encompassing nature of power that Foucault described. In response to Butler one might wonder, however, if her analysis of the effects of power on the person presents the whole story of the problem of agency. Foucault himself recognized a possibility for a care of the self. If this is possible for Butler, where and how can it occur? We might answer that we often see examples of resistance to injustice within contexts that seem difficult. Paglia might argue against Butler that political agents often emerge and resist in novel and unpredictable ways despite what seems like deterministic contexts. In cases of severe oppression, for example, we find the significant examples of Martin Luther King Jr. and Mahatma Ghandi. That which certain social forces oppress seems to always lie below its surface. In the more optimistic view of several of the theorists discussed in this chapter, the hope for a free and equal society can be pursued even given the exclusion and oppression of women in the history of political life. We must only allow space for the voices and perspectives of the excluded to be heard and heeded. This may itself ultimately undermine the deterministic gendered meanings that Butler identifies.

Given this contrast between the Nietzschean and Foucualtian perspectives on feminism and the views that we have discussed in previous sections, what would Paglia and Butler likely say to the other feminist discussions of civil society touched upon in this chapter? In the first place, Paglia and Butler would likely argue that most feminists are victims of their own ideology. In attempting to make civil society into a setting that eliminates patriarchy and restores full rights to women, feminists fail to grasp the real sources of social oppression. Elshtain's and Gilligan's ethic of care would revive civil society by requiring women and men to constrain their needs so that all can relate together in communities of shared responsibility and concern. Paglia would ask whether this point of view does not tend to drown out the unique inner voices of people and force them, for the sake of being pleasant to each other, to subdue their Dionysian instincts. Butler would argue that the ethic of care, rather than a truthful source of liberation, is a social construction that operates as an element of the power that reinforces the fundamental difference between genders.

Okin's and Nussbaum's gender-neutral argument would create similar difficulties for Paglia and Butler. Whereas the idea of a gender-neutral approach as the basis for securing everyone the same rights may be laudable, it may be the case that to achieve this condition people would have to accept common standards and constraints. But to do so, many of the yearnings emanating from the Dionysian dimension of life would have to be suppressed. Would the truly unique individual be permitted any voice at all in this setting? Paglia would wonder, then, whether Okin's position would not reduce all people to the same level of mediocrity so that all can have the same rights. Butler would argue, in contrast, that a simple and formal "gender neutrality" would not solve any of the problems associated with the social construction of gender and would serve only to obscure the meanings and identities assigned to gender in society.

Hartsock's call for a Marxist revolution to overthrow the capitalist system is also the wrong turn for Paglia and Butler. Indeed, Paglia would have to defend capitalism for its encouragement of a full-bodied egoism, which exists at the center of all activities within the market setting. How else is one to manifest a will to power? Nietzsche's and Paglia's commitments to a will to power lead them both to support an extreme form of bourgeoisie individualism, the very type Marx identified as the source of all that is wrong with civil society. Butler would argue that economic relations were only a part of the problem of gender relations in society and are more appropriately considered a consequence rather than a cause of gender inequality.

We might wonder, however, how each of the writers addressed previously in the chapter would respond to the Nietzschean and Foucaultian feminists. In fact, to some degree, the previous writers have already responded to these more radical critiques. As we described explicitly when discussing Nussbaum's defense of liberalism, many feminist theorists who defend solutions to civil society are arguing not only on behalf of gender equality but also against other feminists who disagree with their intellectual standpoints and political tactics.

Elshtain's politics of compassion might tolerate Paglia and Butler, for example, but Elshtain would not consider Paglia's or Butler's descriptions of gender particularly useful for her political agenda. Elshtain would wonder how anyone professing Paglia's individualism or Butler's social constructivism would ever develop relationships of caring and concern that would ground a sense of responsibility on goals and objectives larger than one's own needs.

Okin and Nussbaum would respond to Paglia and Butler by arguing that the doctrine of gender neutrality would provide opportunities for individuals to enter areas of life that were formerly denied them. Included in this list of people with new opportunities awaiting them as a result of gender neutrality would be Paglia and Butler themselves. After all, most consider their arguments to be highly controversial and unconventional. Paglia and Butler probably would accept this positive dimension of liberalism as progress, but each would argue that this advance does nothing to fight the deeper social sources of patriarchy.

Just as MacKinnon would argue against Paglia's wholehearted support of individual rights (and her support of pornography), so she might also argue that Butler's argument takes the feminist critique too far. MacKinnon believes it is fully within the power of women to take social action within legal contexts. The social fight against pornography is an example of this. It would be a mistake to assume, according to MacKinnon, that women have the ability to take only a limited set of actions in the current social mode. Perhaps, MacKinnon (given her failure to achieve restrictions against pornography) would agree with Paglia and Butler, however, that a more thorough transformation of society is needed – in this case, one beyond the reach of simply changing laws.

Marxists such as Hartsock would respond to Paglia and Butler by arguing that the economic context of society needs to be changed before any gender liberation can take place. Hartsock might further criticize Paglia in particular for advancing destructive bourgeoisie individualism. The Marxist would argue that neither Paglia nor Butler allow for the possibility of creating communities in which workers together determine the basis for a type of work that allows for the full development of each person's potential.

IV. Feminism Beyond Gender?: The Expanding Scope of the Feminist Project

As is evident according to several of the thinkers we have already discussed in this chapter, the social concerns of feminism are increasingly moving beyond the mere consideration of gender. In line with the third wave of feminism discussed at the beginning of this chapter, there are many feminist theorists who argue that the feminist political project also requires a commitment to other struggles for equality and social justice. These theorists often argue that struggles for gender, racial, and economic justice are ethically, socially, and politically linked. This argument proposes that it is not enough to simply be a "feminist," and that the transformation toward a more just civil society, even from a feminist perspective, requires transformation with regard to other injustices as well.

In her book *Justice Interruptus*, Nancy Fraser emphasizes economic equality as a necessary condition to justice in a democracy. In it, she primarily deals with economics as it relates to the feminist project for liberation and inclusion, though she incorporates considerations of race and culture as closely related to the larger task of working toward a fully just society. For Fraser, economic justice is an integral aspect of the political project for inclusion, but she also points to other conditions of inequality that we must recognize in the struggle against oppression. Fraser centers her discussion on gender as an important focus for fighting against oppression in society but argues that this can be done only within a broader context of recognizing the other forms of social exclusion and oppression.

The first step in the "feminist" project, as Fraser understands it, is to eliminate the gender coding that takes place in society, which relegates women to a "lesser" existence than men. She says, "To dismantle those roles and their cultural coding is in effect to overturn that order."[106] She thus recognizes the power relationships that create the meanings of gender, but unlike Butler, Fraser argues that our awareness of the place of power in politics must not prevent us from attempting to identify and "dismantle" oppressive structures, such as the gender hierarchy. This goal requires not only a theory of power but also one that would foster liberation from oppression.

Along with considerations of gender difference, the multicultural challenge to politics also leads us to discussions of differences in politics. According to this challenge, theories of democracy often fail to consider alternative cultural viewpoints when describing and idealizing political reality. Instead, it is argued that the cultural assumptions of those in power are built into morality, therefore privileging those who hold those assumptions and excluding those who do not. We presumably want to correct for this exclusion with the assumption that other cultures may well add valuable insight to moral considerations in civil society or at least expose us to our own cultural bias. (We consider this multicultural challenge at greater length in the next chapter.)

Fraser believes the exclusion of gender and culture can be addressed when we conceive of civil society not as one single public sphere but as a collection of public spheres. It is in these "alternative publics" that a diversity of people can come to voice their experiences and debate public issues. Fraser's appeal for a "multiplicity of publics" is rooted in her understanding of what is required in a diverse world. She says, "We can conclude that the idea of an egalitarian, multicultural society makes sense only if we suppose a plurality of public arenas in which groups with diverse values and rhetorics participate."[107] Thus, for Fraser, when an exclusive discourse – in this case a discourse that excludes women – permeates the public sphere, other public spheres are needed in which alternative views are expressed. That is, to express themselves in civil society with the ultimate goal of equal consideration, women must initially have their *own* discourse and not be forced to conform to a single and comprehensive public sphere.[108] Fraser identifies an "alternative public" as useful because it allows marginalized groups to express themselves in ways that might not be possible in the most common modes of public discourse. They are also useful because they can function to challenge the prevailing public sphere, and sometimes expand so that they force their way into wider consideration. The successful social movements of both civil rights and women's rights might be identified as examples of this phenomenon.

In discussing the variety of publics in which women as well as other cultural groups live, Fraser makes clear the importance of "recognition" in according people a sense of dignity and self-worth, one of the most important achievements people can attain. But all too often, certain groups – in this case, women – have been denied recognition. What does it mean to be denied recognition? People's identities are defined in terms of core values and ways of life, which the groups and associations of which one is a member often protect. When society accords these groups respect and regard for their identities, they receive recognition and, through this, self-worth and dignity. Thus, recognition is denied to targeted groups when society denies them respect for their identity, and this circumstance takes place when society, or portions of it, denigrate in general the character and core values of the groups of which such persons are members.

But let us assume that society responds to a demand for recognition by providing it. Still, for Fraser, this important step is not enough to achieve justice for the group in question. And this is because the discourse about justice – what it means to have just treatment in society – is a concern that embraces an "inclusive" politics by which we define the important shared goods that each, regardless of their identities, are to possess. Here, Fraser echoes Elshtain's argument for the educational usefulness of inclusion that we have already discussed.

Thus, in line with others who take economics seriously, Fraser argues that it is not enough merely to struggle for recognition, but this must be linked to struggles for *redistribution*.[109] Besides recognition, then, people should be accorded those basic goods that all are entitled to have. In the context of the discourse that includes the concern for redistribution, all forms of inequality must be addressed for a feminist approach to politics to succeed. In this way, Fraser suggests feminists should orient the equality/difference debate to a consideration of multiple "intersecting differences."[110] She also argues against understanding difference as "natural" but that we still need some way of normatively evaluating different differences and their relation to inequality.

Another thinker who attempts to move feminism beyond mere considerations of gender is bell hooks. (hooks does not capitalize her name intentionally, she contends, to highlight the significance of the ideas she expresses rather than their author.) In her writing, hooks offers a critique of feminist theory as it has been historically conceived and applied to political discourse. Her discussion is useful to demonstrate not only the political uses and abuses of difference but also the interconnectedness of all forms of oppression and political inclusion. The central argument in hooks's *Feminist Theory: From Margin to Center* is that to overcome sexual domination, we must first overcome the contradictions and oppressions within feminist theory itself. According to hooks, these contradictions and oppressions take the forms of racism, the exclusion of men, misconceptions of power, visions of work, intellectualism, misunderstandings about the nature of violence, and inaccurate accounts of sexual liberation. As long as our assumptions regarding these issues remain entrenched in systems of domination and oppression, hooks argues, feminism itself will not be able to overcome the exploitation and discrimination within patriarchal society.

Agreeing with feminists like Hartsock and Fraser, hooks believes the advancement of feminism must include economic considerations. Contrary to many feminists who take up the theme of work, however, hooks criticizes the way in which some feminists have looked to work to serve a liberating function within society. Attempting to escape from the confines of housework, upper- and middle-class women believed the primary goal of the feminist movement was to get them into the workplace. The problem is that "as workers, poor and working class women knew from their experiences that work was neither personally fulfilling nor liberatory – that it was for the most part exploitive and dehumanizing."[111] One soon realizes that finding a "higher" place in the working world does nothing for liberation from patriarchal domination.

Hooks also describes the way in which the capitalist conception of work psychologically exploits women. Sexist ideology teaches that the only valuable work is work that directly generates economic gain. We value housework, for example, only if one gets paid for it (as Okin and others suggest). The feminist project, according to hooks, needs to recognize the value in all the work women do, doing away with the capitalist notion that the significance of work can be found only in its exchange value. In the context of a discussion about civil society, this may mean the development of a civic virtue that recognizes the value of contributions to civil society that go beyond financial considerations.

Hooks ultimately calls for feminism not to lose sight of the need for a total transformation of society. Her biggest fear seems to be that feminists might ignore the more important goals of social justice as they pursue localized efforts for liberation and equality. She realizes that "new social orders are established gradually,"[112] so she recognizes the need for feminism to engage in local projects of political action but always with the view that the overarching goal is the end to sexual oppression – and ultimately the elimination of oppression throughout society. We do this by doing everything we can to ensure that "the experiences of the people on the margin who suffer sexist oppression and other forms of group oppression are understood, addressed and incorporated."[113] Although hooks limits most of her analysis to ways in which the perspective of black women can offer insight into the feminist project, it is important to recognize that there are several other groups that may be able to offer similarly insightful perspectives of oppression. These include but are not limited to the poor, sexually marginalized groups, the handicapped, the elderly, and other marginalized races and cultures.

Fraser's and hooks's arguments, along with other feminists discussed in this chapter, draw attention to the fact that challenges continue to face civil society. In the next chapter, we consider the additional challenge of cultural difference as it relates to both local and global civil society. At their best, political thinkers like those discussed here remind us that the process of making civil society more inclusive, free, and equal cannot be one of noncommittal complacency. When we talk of the importance of inclusion, rights, and equality, we must also consider the fact that we are faced with a project that requires both ethical commitments and action. This is something that might be easily forgotten in theoretical discussions of democracy and civil society. It might be dangerous to take a simple live-and-let-live approach to civil society, because so much work needs to be done to bring about the *real* inclusion of marginalized groups in society. As political thinkers we may be able to frame an ideal vision of democracy, but this is only as good as we can put it into practice to further achieve justice in actuality.

Notes

1. Jennifer Purvis, "Grrrls and Women Together in the Third Wave: Embracing the Challenges of Intergenerational Feminism(s)," *NWSA Journal* 16, no. 3 (Autumn 2004): 93–123.

2. Jean Bethke Elshtain, *Public Man, Private Woman: Women in Social and Political Thought* (Princeton, NJ: Princeton University Press, 1981), 15.

3. Ibid., 15.

4. Ibid., 15–16.

5. Carole Pateman, *The Disorder of Women* (Stanford: Stanford University Press, 1989), 34–38.

6. Carole Pateman, *The Sexual Contract* (Stanford: Stanford University Press, 1988), 6.

7. Ibid., 129.

8. Ibid., 135.

9. Ibid., 136.

10. Ibid., 137–38.

11. Ibid., 138–40.

12. Susan Okin, *Justice, Gender and the Family* (New York: Basic Books, 1989), 128–29.

13. Ibid., 131–33.

14. Ibid., 90–91.

15. Ibid., 101.

16. Ibid.

17. Ibid., 102–3.

18. Ibid., 107.

19. Ibid., 103. To summarize, again, Rawls's principles of justice require that the basic institutions of society must be regulated, first by a commitment to equal basic liberty and second by a principle of equal opportunity that says all positions in society should be open to all persons and that when open competition leads to a situation where some people have greater wealth, authority, or responsibility, these differences must redound to the benefit of the least well-off members of society.

20. Ibid., 103–5.

21. Ibid., 175.

22. Martha Nussbaum, *Sex and Social Justice* (Oxford: Oxford University Press, 1999), 118.

23. Ibid., 33.

24. Okin, *Justice, Gender and the Family*, 175–76.

25. Ibid., 176.

26. The Family and Medical Leave Act includes measures that address these concerns. Debate continues about this and other laws that address concerns about gender equality and treatment in the workplace.

27. Ibid., 177–79.

28. Ibid., 180–81.

29. Nussbaum, *Sex and Social Justice*, 135–36.

30. Catharine A. MacKinnon, *Feminism Unmodified* (Cambridge: Harvard University Press, 1987), 8, 14, 22, 34.

31. Ibid., 16.

32. Ibid., 228.

33. Catharine A. MacKinnon, *Toward a Feminist Theory of the State* (Cambridge: Harvard University Press, 1989), 163.

34. MacKinnon, *Feminism Unmodified*, 166.

35. Ibid., 172.

36. Ibid., 173.

37. MacKinnon, *Toward a Feminist Theory of the State*, 140.

38. Ibid., 112–13, 128.

39. Ibid., 199; also p. 140.

40. MacKinnon, *Feminism Unmodified*, 172.

41. Ibid., 173.

42. Ibid., 179–80.

43. Ibid., 84–85.

44. Ibid., 189.

45. Ibid., 175.

46. Catharine A. MacKinnon, *Only Words* (Cambridge: Harvard University Press, 1993), 91–92.

47. Ibid., 11, 14.

48. Ibid., 38–41.

49. MacKinnon, *Feminism Unmodified*, 152–53.

50. MacKinnon, *Only Words*, 12–17.

51. Ibid., 109.

52. Elshtain, *Public Man, Private Woman*, 303–4.

53. Ibid., 312–13.

54. Ibid., 335–36.

55. Carol Gilligan, *In a Different Voice* (Cambridge: Harvard University Press, 1993; originally published in 1982), 73, 171.

56. Ibid., 161, 173–74.

57. Elshtain, *Public Man, Private Woman*, 329; also, pp. 326–30, 336–37.

58. Ibid., 337.

59. Ibid., 348.

60. Ibid., 343.
61. Ibid., 349.
62. Ibid., 350.
63. Ibid., 352.
64. Nancy C. M. Hartsock, *Money, Sex and Power: Toward a Feminist Historical Materialism* (New York: Longman, 1983), 232.
65. Ibid., 231.
66. Ibid.
67. Ibid., 234.
68. Ibid., 235.
69. Ibid., 236.
70. Ibid., 236–37.
71. Ibid., 238–39.
72. Ibid., 239.
73. Ibid., 240.
74. Ibid., 241.
75. Ibid.
76. Ibid., 242–43.
77. Ibid., 244.
78. Ibid., 245.
79. Ibid., 246.
80. Ibid., 247.
81. Ibid.
82. Ibid.
83. Camille Paglia, "Sexual Personae: The Cancelled Preface," in *Sex, Art, and American Culture* (New York: Vintage Books, 1992), 109.
84. Camille Paglia, "No Law in the Arena," in *Vamps and Tramps* (New York: Vintage Books, 1994), 30.
85. Ibid., 50, 57–58, 69.
86. Ibid., 38.
87. Camille Paglia, "The M.I.T. Lecture," in *Sex, Art, and American Culture*, 273. Italics in text.
88. Camille Paglia, *Sexual Personae: Art and Decadence from Nefertiti to Emily Dickinson* (New York: Vintage Books, 1990), 96–97. Italics are in the text.
89. Ibid., 33; also pp. 8, 10, 12.
90. Ibid., 33.
91. Paglia, "Sexual Personae," 107.
92. Ibid., 105–6.
93. Ibid., 108. Italics are in the text.
94. Paglia, "No Law in the Arena," 32. Italics are in the text.
95. Ibid., 30.
96. Paglia, *Sexual Personae*, 23.
97. Ibid., 12.
98. Paglia, "No Law in the Arena," 93.
99. Ibid.
100. Ibid., 40.
101. Ibid., 66.
102. Ibid.
103. See Judith Butler, *Gender Trouble* (New York: Routledge, 1999).
104. Ibid., 180.
105. Ibid., 184–85.
106. Nancy Fraser, *Justice Interruptus* (New York: Routledge, 1997), 61.

107. Ibid, 84.
108. Ibid, 83.
109. Ibid, 186.
110. Ibid, 187.
111. bell hooks, *Feminist Theory: From Margin to Center* (Boston: South End Press, 1984), 97.
112. Ibid, 159.
113. Ibid, 161.

19

Twenty-first Century Challenges for Civil Society: Culture, Religion, and Climate Change

I. Introduction

Any society that contains differences is bound to be filled with disagreements. Successful societies contain sufficient stability and common ground despite these differences to permit each person and group's way of life to flourish alongside others. The term "multiculturalism" is often used to refer to a political doctrine that aims to sustain a multicultural society in which a wide range of different cultural groups can flourish without harm to social stability. When used in the context of multiculturalism, difference is often construed broadly to include race, ethnicity, religion, gender, class, sexual orientation, region, and ability. Many contemporary theorists who engage in discussions about multiculturalism aim to expand notions of civil society to better account for the many substantive differences that inhabit it.

Debates about multiculturalism usually involve arguments about what kinds of cultural practices can be tolerated in a civil society and often involve claims that are made at local, national, and global levels. On the local and national levels, many argue that cultural differences should have no bearing on the recognition of citizenship, or the accordance of rights and freedoms to participate in civil society. Questions remain, however, about how to properly balance individual rights and the openness of civil society with the claims that certain cultures make against these ideals. At the international level, the question of multiculturalism becomes even more complex. Given the breadth and depth of cultural differences around the world, what are the possibilities for a flourishing and stable global multicultural civil society?

In this context, the challenge of multiculturalism raises anew perennial questions about civil society. For example, what kinds of beliefs and behaviors ought to be tolerated in the public sphere? How should politics be organized to allow the flourishing of all members of the polity? And from where do the virtues that sustain civil society come? In this chapter, we discuss some of the important thinkers who have played a role in theoretical discourse about the relationship between multiculturalism and civil society. We find that much of the concern about multicultural societies is about how different groups are able to speak to each other and about how decisions across differences ought to be made.

II. Multiculturalism and Civil Society

As we begin our discussion of multiculturalism, it is important not to misunderstand multiculturalism to mean a consistent set of principles or ideas. Many "multiculturalists" disagree with one another about how cultural claims ought to be dealt with in civil society, and even disagree about the meaning of multiculturalism itself. In the discussion that follows, we demonstrate one of these differences by emphasizing two major views of multiculturalism. The first view of multiculturalism reflects John Rawls's political liberalism, a term that can be used interchangeably with the idea of liberal democracy. The second view of multiculturalism is predicated on what Charles Taylor calls the "politics of difference."[1] At the conclusion of this section, we discuss the implications of each approach to multiculturalism for a civil society as a separate sphere of groups.

Rawls's political liberalism, as we saw in Chapter 15, seeks a civil society that permits people with diverse values and ways of life to live in peace and with mutual respect for each other's basic rights. To achieve this objective, Rawls promotes an overlapping consensus that people from diverse walks of life and with different core values could share. The overlapping consensus would include support by all people in society for a liberal democracy, one that guaranteed basic rights to each citizen within a setting of representative and democratic institutions. Rawls's view of multiculturalism thus suggests that societies with diverse cultures should permit a flourishing of these cultures but always within the context of a strong commitment to a shared *national community* built upon common standards and rules that protect the basic rights of each person. This priority of a national community would have to be upheld even when it might be necessary to limit the effect and hold of particular cultural traditions on the lives of individuals.

The second view, which we will refer to as a "politics of difference" view of multiculturalism, recognizes that society consists of a national community with common norms and rules for each citizen to follow but maintains that this national community cannot overwhelm or undermine the many different sub-communities that represent diverse ways of life within the community. At times, these sub-communities seek to uphold their own shared traditions and values as part of the effort to highlight the uniqueness that distinguishes them from other groups and other traditions. Taylor's politics of difference would find ways to support sub-communities seeking to maintain their unique identities, even when doing so clashed with the standards of the national community.[2]

To understand these two contrasting perspectives on multiculturalism, it is helpful to reference a concrete example of tensions that exist between a national community and a sub-culture within it. An example Taylor uses when discussing his view of multiculturalism is a case in Quebec, Canada. Among other efforts to claim a cultural identity distinct from the rest of the country, Quebec citizens sought to make French the primary language of the province, even though English is the predominant language in the Canadian national community. Thus, authorities passed legislation to forbid, generally speaking, citizens whose first language is French and immigrants from sending their children to English-language schools. The provision allows only Canadians in Quebec whose first language is English to send their children to English-language schools.[3] All other parents in Quebec are required to send their children to French-only schools. Many English-speaking Canadians, as Taylor points out, perceive this restriction as running counter to the basic rights granted to all citizens under the Canadian Charter of Rights and Freedoms established in 1982.[4] Indeed, Taylor recognizes that the Quebec law making French the primary language seems to favor French speakers over English speakers, and this reality might foster discrimination against the second. And even if discrimination does not occur, Taylor acknowledges that the "collective end" embodied in the education law "will probably involve treating insiders and outsiders differently."[5]

Nonetheless, despite the discrimination that seems inherent in these laws, and its limitations on parental choice, Taylor defends the Quebec laws on education, sanctioned by his "politics of difference" approach to multiculturalism. His argument on behalf of this position is that his politics of difference contains a view of liberalism that is more appropriate for the needs of Quebec than Rawls's brand of political liberalism.[6] That is, according to a politics of difference, some forms of discrimination that do not violate fundamental rights ought to be allowed in some cases in the interest of the rights of particular communities. Rights holders, according to Taylor's liberalism, can be communities as well as individuals.

To clarify this argument further, it will be helpful to now return to Rawls's defense of the ideal liberal state. In Rawls's political liberalism, the state – understood here as the national government – is to protect the basic rights of each citizen as its first and foremost obligation, and the state does so when it maintains a procedure that "insists on uniform application of the rules defining these rights without exception."[7] Furthermore, the state is not to impose onto any of the citizens "a particular substantive view about the ends of life."[8] The state upholds the right of the individual to choose his or her conception of the good life by treating people with equal respect through securing such basic freedoms as association, thought, religion, and conscience.

In political liberalism, then, the state remains "neutral" before the different conceptions of the good life that various members of the society might advance, and thus the state does not seek to impose any particular conception of the good life on society. Given this view, Rawls's political liberalism would not support the notion that citizens whose first language is French should be barred from English-language schools. All individuals in a liberal society, according to Rawls's liberal view, should have access to any school that is available to anyone else. The law is also troublesome for political liberals because it may promote an atmosphere of discrimination against English speakers, and this would facilitate a cultural schism between "insiders" and "outsiders." This means that the full effect of the laws makes the free exercise of parental choice for education next to impossible.

Taylor's politics of difference approach to multiculturalism, which would support Quebec's desire to maintain French cultural supremacy by upholding the school policy just cited, advocates a different type of liberalism. While Taylor maintains the liberal view that fundamental rights of individuals – such as freedom of religion, due process, rights to life and liberty, free speech, and so on – should not be taken away when promoting the interests of particular groups, certain other "privileges" (which might sometimes be confused for rights) can be compromised. For Taylor, people can be asked to forgo certain "privileges," such as the privilege of parents to send their children to the school of their choice without violating basic rights. Basic rights are not the same as privileges, and it is acceptable to violate the latter for public policies that promote and secure cultural identity.[9]

Thus, as Susan Moller Okin suggests, multiculturalist doctrines such as Taylor's believe that protecting the rights of individual members of a minority culture may not be sufficient to secure that culture's way of life. In these cases, added protections called "special *group* rights" must be extended to the minority culture in question.[10] A sharp tension between political liberalism and the politics of difference can be clearly recognized on this point. The tension centers around whether it is best to use rights on behalf of individuals, as Rawls seeks to do, or on behalf of groups, as Taylor would. The fear of political liberals is that the pursuit of group rights inherently conflicts with the fundamental commitment to protect the basic rights of individuals.

In the example of French-language schools, the dilemma is whether the ability of parents to send their children to the school of the parents' choice is a "right" that must always be preserved or a "privilege" that can be taken away for specified good public policy reasons. Taylor's answer is that because parental choice is a privilege and not a guaranteed basic right, it can be restricted in the name of a special group right designed to protect a minority culture. Others would argue, however, that parental choice for education is a right that is as fundamental as any other basic right. This view of basic rights, which expands the notion of "basic rights" further than Taylor does, is in line with Rawls's political liberalism that gives priority to a longer list of individual rights over group rights that may be recognized to preserve certain cultural communities.

This is not to say that political liberals are fundamentally opposed to group rights. Group rights may be allowable if it could be shown that recognizing the right of a group does not severely hamper the ability of individuals to make fundamental choices about the good life. Indeed, political liberals claim that an individual-rights approach actually protects the survival of various cultural identities. Within political liberalism, individuals are free to choose their own way of life, and part of this choice may include associating with a particular cultural lifestyle. Thus, cultural lifestyles must be secured for the sake of individual choice, not despite it. But what individuals cannot ask the state to do, according to the political liberal, is to give priority to any particular group's claims over and against any other particular group's claims. This approach is necessary to secure the basic rights and the freedom of choice of each person. For this outcome to occur, a civil society, based on the presumptions of political liberalism, is built upon the hope of finding a common ground (or what Rawls calls an overlapping consensus) and maintaining that commonality across the national community. For the political liberal, identifying that common ground should be the highest goal of each person in the civic arena; indeed, it should trump interests arising from group identity.

The common ground for political liberals includes, in addition to the agenda of basic rights and the freedom of individual choice, the hope that all people will learn about and respect difference. For instance, the common standards of the national community for political liberals should include teaching children about the different ways of life and diverse values that exist within any given society. Some people might prefer to have their children exempted from this requirement, however, fearing that if their children learn about difference, they may begin to question their own group's values.[11] But this is out of line with political liberalism because it contains the view that people should be able to engage in common deliberation that includes shared public reasons for resolving differences. For people to take part in common deliberation, it is necessary to understand the diversity of views that others bring to public deliberation. This goal cannot be met, according to the political liberal argument, if people refuse to learn about views different from their own. Those who support the position of political liberals and who advocate the teaching of different cultures argue as Stephen Macedo does that "a basic aim of civic education should be to impart to all children the ability to reflect critically on their personal and public commitments for the sake of honoring our shared principles of liberal justice and equal rights for all."[12]

Taylor's politics of difference would agree with political liberalism on this point. Respect for diverse cultures is a major public policy goal for Taylor. The major difference between Taylor's politics of difference and the approach to multiculturalism for political liberals centers on the *intensity* of the commitment to a wide range of individual rights. The political liberal would emphasize giving priority to national norms of individual rights, whereas Taylor is more willing to relax national standards of individual autonomy in deference to the traditions of particular cultural groups.

As might have already been noticed, this distinction is one that bears important consequences for civil society. In cases such as developing a national language or a common national curriculum, we are forced to make a choice between strengthening ethnic or group ties or reducing their influence in our lives. If we take the latter route for the sake of making individual rights the norm of a wider national community, we are free to maintain our group connections in the private sphere. But over time, an emphasis on a wide range of individual rights and participation in wider communities with shared values might cause us to weaken the group values that shape our identities. Here, as the place of liberal values is perpetuated across generations, decades of ethnic memory become reduced in importance.

Taylor would object to this result more than political liberals would because Taylor worries more about the survival of group identities.[13] In fact, it is the erosion of cultural identity in the modern world that justifies laws such as those in Quebec. Political liberals, on the other hand, are more concerned with teaching the standards necessary for a stable liberal national community rather than the particular cultural identities that inhabit it. Indeed, political liberals would be concerned that unless national standards are emphasized, people will not adapt well to the demands of citizenship, or to the demands of the economy and its requirement for highly skilled people. This circumstance may then lead to depriving some people of the conditions that secure basic rights and expand the opportunities for each individual in society.

Moreover, political liberals would further worry that, in emphasizing group recognition over individual rights, we might move to a more fragmented and conflict-filled society in which genuine communication among people from different backgrounds is less likely. In his comment on Taylor's *The Politics of Recognition*, K. Anthony Appiah reflects this concern as he criticizes some of the central features of Taylor's argument. Appiah agrees with Taylor that a liberal society must recognize and embrace cultural identity and difference but argues that a politics of difference must recognize the complicated relationships between identity, authenticity, and survival.[14] From a politically liberal perspective, Appiah cautions against the protection of certain collective identities in society at the expense of our commitments to equal dignity and autonomy.

Speaking of autonomy, Appiah agrees with Taylor that our identities are formed in our relationships with others, but in forming our identities we must give adequate recognition to individual choice.[15] Thus, when we describe our identity as "authentic," we mean "I have a way of being that is all my own." But this way does not come about without a context, which includes a variety of external factors. Not only do others around us shape our understandings of ourselves, but our society, religion, and state also provide the material for the content of identity. Thus, authentic identity formation is a confluence of choice and the inevitable influence of our circumstances. For instance, our circumstances contain givens such as our class background, sexuality, gender, race, religion, natural physical inheritance, and so on.[16] Many of these elements contain strong intimations that direct the development of our identities, but it is a mistake to assume that these exclusively determine who we are. It is also a mistake to assume, however, that we can simply make up any identity we choose. According to Appiah, "We make up selves from a tool kit of options made available by our culture and society. . . . We do make choices, but we do not determine the options among which we choose."[17]

Given this view of identity formation, many questions emerge. How do these collective identities develop from the context in which we live? Ought we to accept the collective and individual identities we have been given? Through philosophical reflection and historical understanding, we may also resist the cultures around us, and we might find identities radically separated from the identities we would expect from our immediate surroundings. This raises an important concern for Taylor's politics of difference. If we have a commitment to individual rights, and individuals can decide differently from their cultures, then there may be a point at which any support for cultural rights interferes with an individual's right to resist his or her culture.

Appiah also raises concerns about the problem of education in Taylor's view, as related in our earlier discussion of Rawls and Taylor. As we have already noticed, Taylor's politics of difference primarily is concerned about the survival of cultures within a liberal state. For a culture to maintain itself as an aspect of both collective and individual identity, it must be fostered, protected, and promoted from generation to generation. Education is important here because it is a cultural education that transmits values more substantial than liberal individualism. Appiah notices, however, that it is difficult to maintain this goal while at the same time respecting the autonomy of *future* individuals – the children of those who are "pushing" the culture forward through them.[18] Appiah, therefore, argues that the liberal state has a role in educating children toward a substantive view of the *liberal* good, in this case, protecting the autonomy of children against their parents based on ethical principles of equal dignity. Alongside the objections raised earlier about parental rights, Appiah raises the issue of a child's right to eventually make his or her own choices.[19]

Another problem for Appiah related to group rights and group identity relates to the way certain groups have been oppressed. He argues that, in a society that historically views an identity as negative, one who participates in this identity is obliged to affirm that identity as positive – a *reason* for respect. Appiah argues, for example, that since African Americans have been historically oppressed in America, in order to receive respect, they must affirm their identity as part of the group (rather than as an individual who deserves respect independent of the group).[20] The problem with this, for Appiah, is that we seem to have replaced "one kind of tyranny with another."[21] It seems as though a politics of difference requires that personal identity be organized around these superficial collective identities. The danger we must guard against, according to Appiah, is where the politics of recognition might become the politics of compulsion.[22]

In the debate between political liberals and multiculturalists like Taylor, the primary point of controversy is how individual rights and identity ought to be balanced against the important cultural meanings and values of cultural groups. Important questions that need to be answered thus include: can every cultural group survive within a liberal society? Is liberal society destined to turn every culture into a liberal culture? Which individual rights must be preserved in the face of cultural claims? These questions are becoming even more pressing as we move toward a global liberal society.

III. Civil Society and Religion

Religion is one obvious example of what many consider to be an essential cultural source of our identity. But what is the appropriate place for religion in a liberal democracy? In recent US presidential elections, much has been made in the media about the differences between red- and blue-state voters. Red-state voters are cultural conservatives who cast votes for Republicans and who emphasize that, all too often, secularists who vote for Democrats in the blue states they dominate have denied religion its proper place in society. Still, the divide is not so extreme that each side feels under dire threat for its very existence by the other. After all, there are plenty of cultural conservatives in blue states and probably just as many secularists in red states. Moreover, secularists do not deny that religion has an important place in American culture, where 87 percent of the people believe in God and nearly a majority of them attend places of worship. Nonetheless, so long as the division remains a central part of our national electoral politics, one side destructively stereotyping the other could mount in intensity, making it difficult to nurture the civic virtues of toleration and mutual respect so central to a civil society. It is precisely this unwelcome prospect that causes us to ask if there is a way to reduce, if not eliminate, the tension between the two sides.

Now, as Ronald Dworkin makes clear, realizing this goal depends upon identifying a common ground between the parties.[23] The common ground would, in our view, become the basis for a constructive discourse that would help to restore civic trust between the parties, even when agreement on the host of issues before them is not always resolved as one side or the other might wish. We have in mind issues such as embryonic stem cell research, gay marriage, teaching intelligent design in schools, displays of the Ten Commandments on public property, school prayer, and many others.

In this section, we contend that a basis for a common ground exists in the fact that both sides understand that human flourishing is possible only when individuals are accorded autonomy. Autonomy refers to the freedom and independence people must have to make their own reasoned judgments of private and public matters, without interference from either the state or any agency of civil society, including religious or secular groups.[24] In our view, each side gives high priority to autonomy, which means each side manifests toleration both for incorporating a prominent place for religion in society as well as for those who dissent from either secular or religious views. Indeed, it is the shared commitment to autonomy that is the foundation of each side's embrace of a broad toleration, and thus we agree with Dworkin who says that any discussion of the current cultural schism in our culture must start from the presumption that red- and blue-state voters are largely composed of tolerant secularists and tolerant religious believers.[25]

But because each side has different views of the best approach to achieving this common vision, there remains much difficulty resolving the host of issues we just enumerated. The source of the disagreement arises from the different intellectual frameworks that each side employs to advance their shared belief in autonomy.[26]

From the secularist perspective, the state must be walled off from any religious influence that could lead to a state-backed church. Were the latter to arise, sectarian strife would be inevitable because those who do not agree with the dominant religion that the state advocates would resist the state's effort to impose it on them. It is precisely this assessment of the implications of theocratic government that motivated Spinoza and Locke to construct their respective doctrines of toleration. Common to both doctrines is the understanding that the state is to advocate purely civic interests, which encompass only those shared goods – like the right of private property, freedom of thought and speech, and general security from domestic and foreign sources – that all people support, regardless of their religious identification.

In observing this principle, the state avoids entanglement with religion by never using its power to embody the interests of religious organizations into law and public policy. For instance, whereas the secularist would not allow Christmas trees and menorahs on public property, it would be acceptable to allow them in all the various private settings of civil society – from shopping malls to churches and synagogues – where people practice as well as celebrate religion.[27] Moreover, for secularists, it would not be acceptable to permit federal funding for social services that faith-based groups provide, but it would be acceptable to allow these practices to take place through private charities, which religious groups located in civil society often maintain. The effect of this approach is to allow the full practice of religion in the context of the many groups of civil society, while prohibiting the state from interfering with the practice of religion there and while not allowing the state to become a vehicle through which to advance the interest of particular religions or of religion in general.

What is the intellectual framework of religious believers? As Dworkin says, people who practice a "tolerant religion" do not want the state acting in a way to impose any particular religion on people. Still, the state should promote religion generally by declaring "religion to be an important positive force in making people and society better."[28] And there is a powerful reason for the state to take this position. After all, a major component of our society is American citizens' strong religious orientation. Religion matters profoundly to people. Furthermore, this characteristic of Americans is manifested not only in a pluralism of religions but in a strongly held belief that the state must respect the right of each person to determine their own relation to religion. Thus, the state must not allow a situation to develop where this freedom would be denied to anyone. When religion is kept out of the public sphere, however, the state is put in a position, whether it knows it or not, of thwarting the practice of religion, and this violates not just the strong sentiment in favor of religion in this society but also the commitment to support freedom of choice on religious matters.

Secularists would counter by saying that religious believers are often the ones that most abuse the freedom of religious choice. This is because people are born into families and traditions that inculcate from birth various religious values that people might never be able to cast off. But religious believers would respond that, in most cases, religious traditions encourage people to acquire both the ability and freedom to make their own choices with respect to the views they inherit, deciding if they wish to keep or modify them. As part of this undertaking, religious believers' traditions strongly encourage them to reflect deeply on the motives that govern their actions and to ask if they – both motives and actions – are in keeping with the moral teachings of their religion. Moreover, as part of pondering well and reflecting sincerely, believers are prone to ask if the traditions they hold contribute well to the moral improvement of society, and if not, people recognize that they have a responsibility to ask what in their traditions needs to change. But these undertakings cannot occur unless religious traditions teach people that a central part of human flourishing is the capacity for autonomous judgment and reasoning.

Secularists would be pleased with these accounts and certainly embrace them, but given the long history as well as the present-day reality of state-backed religious intolerance, secularists would argue that it is better to err on the side of being safe, and this means advocating a secular approach to law that builds a wall of separation between church and state. Thus, even as secularists allow a variety of religious expressions – all generally confined to the various associations and groups in civil society – they do not support government programs that advantage religious organizations, like school vouchers to pay for private-school education.[29] The core legal doctrine that sustains this view, as Dworkin points out, is the Supreme Court's Lemon test. Dworkin says that "this test forbids any state program that is either intended to or that does operate to the particular advantage of a religious organization."[30] Citing Justice Sandra Day O'Connor's opinion, which created this doctrine, the test makes clear that "what is crucial is that the government practice [under consideration] not have the effect of communicating a message of government endorsement or disapproval of religion."[31]

This principle profoundly troubles religious believers. As an example of why, Dworkin points to public-school prayer, which religious believers would support but with a caveat. In particular, because religious believers seek to practice tolerance of nonreligious people or of religious people uncomfortable with public prayers, the prayers should be ecumenical, and no child should be coerced into saying them. If children did not want to participate, they could avoid doing so without suffering a psychological stigma. So, the religious believer might ask if there is empirical data to demonstrate extreme discomfort for the children who choose not to participate.[32] If there is data to show psychological abuse of the non-participants, then a good case could be made for discontinuing the public prayer. However, based on the Lemon test, which embraces the view of a secular society, even this consideration is beside the point. As Dworkin says, "In a tolerant secular society . . . it would be seen as wrong in principle to make any state institution such as a public school the venue of any exercise of any religion."[33]

Of course, for secularists, public schools can teach about religion, but what they cannot do, based on this secular legal doctrine, is take part in activities that establish the great importance of religion to the lives of the students. But this is where the difference of opinion between secularist and religious people becomes clearest. Teaching about religion without establishing its fundamental importance will make it seem as just something that has been relegated to an interesting, but nonetheless useless, antique. Then, people would see no use in studying religious teachings among the important matters people should consider as they search for the guiding themes that clarify the arc of their lives, the values on which they stand, and the purposes for which they strive; in short, what they live for.

Thus, for the religious believers, secularists employ a concept of toleration that makes them second-class citizens. Wendy Brown critiques the practice of toleration in precisely these terms when she says that secular liberal views champion the notion that each person is the equal of the other and thus must be accorded the same rights as the other.[34] But the problem that arises is that very often the practice of equality leads to circumstances in which some people's rights have far less worth in terms of what people can do with them than is the situation for others, who, with the same rights, can do far more. For instance, as we saw with Rawls, in discussions of public issues grounded in public reason, people must – in deference to ensuring priority to the overlapping political values of a constitutional democracy – bracket their particular religious and ethical views, that is, not make them central to their arguments. Of course, religiously oriented people have the freedom of speech to propose their religious views in these discussions, but because their significance is negligible, the views of believers would not be given the same importance as those advocated by others. Religious people are thus tolerated but not treated as the full equals of others, especially in the context of important public discussions of law and policy.

And what is the secularist's response to this complaint? No doubt the latter would challenge the notion that the laws and policies of society reflect only secular viewpoints. Indeed, secularists would argue that, despite the Lemon test, one can point to a rash of policies where the state clearly has established support for religious institutions in law and policy. And the potential for this tendency to grow is what disturbs them.

For instance, in a *New York Times* series, the impact of religious influence on public policy was elaborated in a serious study.[35] Some of the findings include that the courts protect religious groups from many violations of civil rights laws against their employees in contrast to employees in secular settings. In addition, workers in religious organizations do not receive the protection of the Americans with Disabilities Act. For example, a US District Court in Ohio dismissed the claim of a nun who was fired from her religious order in Toledo after the church learned that she had breast cancer. Further, in Alabama, church day care centers are not subject to state licensing requirements, unlike nonchurch groups, and this practice was allowed even after regulations were tightened in the wake of nearly a dozen children dying in licensed and unlicensed day care centers over a two-year period.

The secularists would no doubt point to this information to make their case that the red states are likely to use state power to advance religious purposes, making a mockery of the Lemon test and ultimately overturning the wall of separation between church and state. Others, however, whom we call "moderates," might be more restrained in their assessments of what this cited evidence means. William Galston says that it is necessary in a liberal democracy to steer a course between a politics dedicated to imposing a single religious viewpoint on society and one that would allow religion only when it satisfies the "functional requirements of the polity."[36] This perspective seeks a hybrid legal doctrine that embraces some secularist and some religiously based policies, and all of this is undertaken to create a social space for people to pursue what Galston refers to as "expressive liberty," the freedom people should have to "live their lives in ways that express their deepest beliefs about what gives meaning or value to life."[37] Galston says that the practice of Rawls's public reason might "screen out the kinds of core beliefs that give meaning and purpose to many lives."[38] Still, for moderates like Galston, the state's support of a social space that permits different conceptions of life to flourish is not without the need for constraints. After all, the actions of people in this setting must not jeopardize vital state interests. As Galston says, in supporting a social space for diversity of views, including religious ones, "a free society is not a suicide pact."[39]

But locating the protection of religious belief and practice in a hybrid approach to law is risky because it often depends on a coalition of political actors, who may agree today but not tomorrow. When political coalitions shift, the bases for supporting previously agreed to hybrid legal approaches to religious belief and practice may disappear. Thus, today there may be an agreement among secularists, religious believers, and a host of third parties for laws that permit certain religious practices, like the posting of the Ten Commandments in public buildings. But tomorrow, because of a new coalition that includes a new group of people generally hostile to such a practice, it might be the case not only that the law allowing the posting of the Ten Commandments is rescinded, but, in addition, a new law is derived banning Christmas trees and menorahs in shopping centers!

Moreover, a complicating factor in predicating policies pertaining to religion on political balances is prejudice. Where prejudice against a certain group of people merely because of their religious beliefs is strong, a re-organization of a coalition that had previously protected these people's basic rights, including freedom of conscience, might, because of insidious bias, expose the affected parties to the loss of all their liberty. We have only to look at recent examples of just this very experience to demonstrate that these fears have a substantive basis. For years, Bosnian Serbs and Muslims lived side by side in a balance-of-power arrangement, but when the political balance was shattered, what resulted was a civil war that culminated in genocide against the Muslims by Bosnian Serbs. Underlying prejudice, which had never been eradicated, certainly helped to fuel this violence. A similar experience led to the mass murder of Tutsis by Hutus in Rwanda. Iraq, in the wake of the massive power shift there, became, at one point, a battleground between Sunni and Shiite Muslims, with thousands of people murdered. The classic case is pre–World War II Germany, where most Jews, prior to the Holocaust, believed they had fully assimilated into German society and considered themselves Germans first and Jews second. But anti-Semitic prejudice had never been eliminated – indeed, it was powerfully ingrained in German culture – and after power shifts took place with the emergence of Adolf Hitler, six million Jews were made victims (along with homosexuals, the Roma people, and political opponents) to Nazi barbarity.

Is America likely to remain an exception to these examples? If so, then a balance of power that protects people's rights today, even if it is changed tomorrow, will never lead to the decimation of anyone's basic liberty, including the freedom to practice one's religious views without fear. But this presumes we have no potential for destructive religious prejudice in this country, which, of course, is not true, given our history. Catholics were the targets of discrimination in public schools in nineteenth-century America.[40] Jews were subject to discrimination in admissions to many public and private universities in the early to mid-twentieth century.[41] Today, in the post-9/11 environment, including recent efforts by President Donald Trump to ban Muslim immigration to the United States in 2016, some Muslims complain that they have become targets for discrimination in a variety of settings.[42]

Examples such as these suggest that rather than basing religious toleration on hybrid legal policies that potentially shifting political coalitions sustain, it would be best to base toleration on a firm commitment to the principle of a Kantian-type respect for the dignity of all persons. Then, an obligation to tolerate all people, regardless of their religious perspectives, would be firmly established in the law. The government, especially at the federal level, in upholding the rule of law would thus compel compliance with the practices of religious toleration, regardless of the balance of political power in society. Dworkin advocates this approach, which we now consider.[43]

The specific design of the principle of respect for dignity of all persons has already been defined in terms of the common ground both red- and blue-state people support. As shown, both uphold treating individuals as equally worthy of being accorded freedom and autonomy of judgment in making critical choices about their personal lives and public issues. The question is what kind of environment needs to be created to help ensure that this principle is practiced in full and thus securely implanted into the law of the land? In general, we think it is necessary to establish, as a prominent part of civil society, a basis for public discussions that, even when they do not lead to agreement on important issues, they do at least lead to the view that the results of the discussions are reasonable and that all who participated can accept them because they have been treated as full equals in the society.

We list two approaches to this goal, one found in Michael Sandel's work and the other in a robust civil society. Regarding the former, Sandel would ensure that controversial but substantive moral and religious differences are placed squarely on the table of the public realm for argument and debate. These matters should not be bracketed out of the discussion because people are not likely to agree on them; rather, every effort must be made to find the best, most plausible arguments among those that are provided.[44] When morally controversial issues are joined and openly debated, suppression of moral and religious views is avoided, along with the intense frustration that arises from this circumstance and that culminates in enduring distrust among citizens.[45] Of course, at the end of the debate, disagreement may continue. Still, implied in Sandel's view is that dialogue is transformative because as people understand the reasons others provide for their positions, even if they still disagree with them, they tend to see others as human beings and not as beasts or demons. As such, these people become worthy of respect, too.

But we contend that this transformative feature of dialogue requires an important background condition, which is the presence of a robust civil society. This is a setting in which we live our lives across a field of people who manifest a variety of values and ways of life, and, in the process, we learn the importance of views and values that are different from our own. Amartya Sen made a similar point when he criticized the notion of "plural monoculturalism" by which people define themselves in terms of a single tradition and object to any interaction with people practicing other ways of life.[46] In this context, people from different traditions may live side by side, but because they have built impenetrable walls around themselves, they have no way of understanding each other or of responding to mutual needs and concerns. To be sure, the idea of civil society creates opportunities for people to *bond* together in groups with which they share common values and outlooks. But, in addition, a civil society is built on the premise that people learn to *bridge* across a variety of groups and learn to make space for many ways of life, including within their own primary groups.[47]

It is this experience that can provide an important background context for Sandel's public discussion. For as people learn to incorporate into their own thinking, as a commonplace practice, the values of diverse ways of life, they appreciate difference for the way it contributes to the richness and depth of their own reflections. After all, without being able to compare views that differ, it would be difficult, if not impossible, to know why and for what reasons one believes as one does. And then one would lose the reflective powers one needs to make autonomous judgments. But given that autonomy would forever remain important as a result of the experience in an authentic civil society, the demand for a principled and thus institutionalized legal commitment by the state to autonomy would never be allowed to waiver, however much the coalitions of power may shift.

In conclusion, one might ask if this view of dialogue – say, ten years from now – actually succeeded in reducing, if not eliminating altogether, the tension between red and blue states. What would this result mean? We can only hazard a guess. It is possible, indeed likely, that some secularists will interpret the outcome to mean that their views dominated. It is also likely that some religious believers will say the same thing. Moreover, it is just as likely that even when one side thinks its views have been subordinated to the other, the subordinated side still will accept the outcomes without bitterness but with a strong sense of civic respect for the others with whom they disagree. Both scenarios, especially when present together, are likely to diminish, and even possibly end, the tension between red and blue voters to the point that the chances of it ever turning into something that can cause deep fissures in society will be eliminated. Instead, civic trust will abound in a setting in which individuals are committed to making room for the diverse ways of life they experience in civil society. All of this, including the strengthening of the civic virtues of toleration and mutual respect – the cornerstones of civic trust – will have been made possible by the transformative powers of a civil society–based dialogue.

IV. Climate Change and Civil Society

As we saw earlier, Karl Marx wrote that capitalism so much favored the few who owned capital (the machinery, the factories, the raw materials, investment funds) that the workers the capitalists employed would be forced – for the sake of achieving a chance for a decent life – to bring down capitalism and replace it with socialism.[48] The latter, for Marx, represented an economic model that ensured that working people received back a fair share of the wealth they created, unlike in a capitalist society in which the capitalists exploit the workers by claiming that the wealth derived from their work is theirs and theirs alone. In which case, the capitalists have a strong interest in configuring the workplace in a way that allows them to extract more and more wealth from the workers' efforts.

But as David Wallace-Wells says, in *The Uninhabitable Earth: Life After Warming*, capitalism was fueled not just by the constant enhancement – typical of industrialization in the West – of worker productivity that has led to the profits over which both workers and capitalists fight. No, capitalism has been sourced not only by machines and well-organized – from the standpoint of efficiency – work but by the easy availability, especially over the past 30 years, of cheap energy in the form of fossil fuels, which is to say, gas and oil. This point is implied by Wallace-Wells when he says:

> *many perceive global warming as a sort of moral and economic debt, accumulated since the beginning of the Industrial Revolution and now come due after several centuries. In fact, more than half of the carbon exhaled into the atmosphere by the burning of fossil fuels has been emitted in just the past three decades.*[49]

This fact has created a different problem than the one Marx identified. The problem is not a matter of replacing capitalism with socialism on behalf of achieving a fairer distribution of wealth to the working class. Rather, the problem is to find the basis for a political will – shared by all sectors of society, from capitalists to workers, and involving all the nations of the world – to support actions and policies that substantially reduce the pace of planetary warming. Otherwise, neither workers nor capitalists will find themselves living in societies capable of sustaining the conditions that ensure the general happiness of their citizens.

In effect, the problem modern capitalism initially presented has morphed from a worker versus owner conflict into the need to stop the continued befouling of the atmosphere by the use of fossil fuels. Otherwise, it is quite likely that the planetary environment will become so degraded that the bulk of people on earth – workers and owners alike – will be plunged into deep and unending misery. The main political slogan in this case will not be as Marx wrote when he said at the end of the *Communist Manifesto*, "The proletarians [workers] have nothing but their chains. They have the world to win."[50] Instead, the main political slogan will be: "citizens, from whatever walk of life, we must act now to protect our earth, lest life becomes barely sustainable and mostly filled with unending misery for all people, everywhere."

Now, slowing – and in fact eliminating – the pace of global warming presents a clear choice for the present generation, which is to say, people reading this book! They – meaning you – can choose to act now on behalf of this goal, or you can choose, instead, to do nothing. You can choose to manifest a political will to fix this problem or, instead, choose to refuse to take a stand.

What is to convince people to make this choice on behalf of acting to eliminate warming? What, in other words, can be said on behalf of engendering among members of this generation a political will to terminate the warming of the earth largely for the sake of the happiness of both its current inhabitants and, but most significantly, for the welfare and happiness of future generations?

To answer this question, there is a need for a compelling moral argument. The latter gives powerful justifications for why people should override their natural self-interest to postpone action on warming. After all, the people largely to benefit from these actions are those who come after the people making the sacrifices for future generations have died. A moral argument makes clear the obligations of a conception of a decent personhood that individuals who seek such a standard for their lives must follow, even when doing so clashes with their immediate self-interest. What is the nature of that argument?

Before discussing the moral argument on behalf of ending warming – an argument that we sketch out later in this section – we first need to spell out the facts that supporters of the moral argument to end the warming would make the foundation of their actions.

To this end, we briefly discuss some of the findings in Wallace-Wells' book, and we do so in conjunction with the work of Bill McKibben, certainly one of the leading writers on this subject in our times.

Wallace-Wells makes clear the great magnitude of the disaster we will face if we fail to act in the present moment to protect the world's air and water resources. Warming is about the future and what scientists plainly describe will be our fate in the future if we do not act to change the trajectory of our warming planet. And that sketch of the future makes clear that if we are to make the world a decent place for future generations, we must act now – with great resolve – and accept the necessary sacrifices to ensure that the generations who come after us have the future they deserve.

But this sobering view is made all the more sobering by the fact that so much of what needs to be done has not been done. Past efforts to address warming have not been successful. For instance, the two major international agreements have failed to stop the pace of warming. The Kyoto Protocol of 1997 encompassed the view that increasing the earth's temperature more than two degrees Celsius put the world at the doorstep of major disasters, which would include terrible droughts and heat emergencies throughout the world.[51] But since Kyoto, the world has produced "more emissions than in the twenty years before."[52] Similarly, the Paris Agreement of 2016 also "established two degrees as the global goal," but "no single industrial nation [is] on track to meet its Paris commitments."[53] Moreover, to make matters worse, President Trump pulled the United States out of the Paris Agreement on June 1, 2017.

All of this is predictive of major disasters that are likely to befall us. Here, as recounted by Wallace-Wells, is a list of some of them.

Wallace-Wells says that at an increase of two degrees in the world's temperature, not only will massive ice sheets in the Arctic region collapse, there will also be 400 million people likely to suffer from "water scarcity."[54] At the same time, those who live in "major cities in the equatorial band of the planet" will find these areas "unlivable" due to increases in temperature.[55] Moreover, even in areas in northern latitudes, heat waves are likely to kill "thousands" of people during the summer.[56] Wallace-Wells further says that we should add to all of this the fact that India would experience "thirty-two times as many extreme heat waves, and each would last five times as long, exposing ninety-three times more people."[57]

Moreover, if the earth's temperature were to rise by three degrees Celsius, there would, according to Wallace-Wells, be a "permanent drought" in southern Europe, and Central America would find itself with droughts that lasted "nineteen months longer," whereas, in northern Africa, the droughts would last five years longer. In addition, the areas consumed by wildfires would double in the Mediterranean and grow by at least six times the number of previous wildfires in the United States.[58]

Further, if the earth were to warm by four degrees Celsius, worse calamities would occur. Wallace-Wells says that "there would be eight million more cases of dengue fever each year in Latin America alone and [this situation would push the world] close to annual global food crises."[59] Also, across the world there would be a nine percent increase of "heat-related deaths."[60] Further, "damages from river flooding would grow thirtyfold in Bangladesh, twentyfold in India and as much as sixtyfold in the United Kingdom."[61]

The impact of warming on the US gross domestic product (GDP) would be immense. Wallace-Wells says that each degree of warming costs the United States one percent of its GDP.[62] And if it happens that the world heats up 3.7 degrees, the damage this would inflict on the world would total $551 trillion. Keep in mind that this loss from warming should be seen in the context of the fact that the total wealth of the whole world is, by comparison, $280 trillion.[63] Now, this circumstance may be our reality in the future, given that, as Wallace-Wells says, by 2100 the current trajectory of our planet's temperature is due to rise by four degrees Celsius. As a result, there would be little possibility of economic growth, a reality that would create major hardships for people the world over.[64] The problem is made even starker, still, by the fact that 150 million more people would die from air pollution in a two-degree rise in the earth's temperature than in a 1.5-degree warmer world. That is the equivalent of 25 Holocausts, Wallace-Wells warns.[65]

Just as serious a problem is that with every half degree of warming, societies will find themselves between 10 and 20 percent more likely to become engaged in armed conflict.[66] Such circumstances are likely to be associated with mammoth movements of people – or climate refugees – toward areas considered more livable. These flows of people would be perceived as dire threats to the societies that climate refugees seek to enter. And to stop them, there would emerge among many societies an anti-globalization view in which societies everywhere would seek to exclude intrusions from refugees. In this, states would close their doors to each other and institute highly restrictive anti-immigration laws.

The notion of a globalized world – built on economic and political cooperation, sharing of knowledge, and maintaining mutual efforts to prevent war – would be lost. No doubt, this circumstance would advance a brand of nationalism that no reasonable person – especially with knowledge of the history of the twentieth century – could abide. In this case, nationalism would be based on the view that those not of one's nation are inevitably enemies who must be slayed before they slay us![67]

What is necessary to push against this tide then becomes the basis for a political will designed not just to slow down and eliminate warming but, in the process, to create the conditions for a global world order that makes peace among nations a continuing reality. Thus, a better basis for national identity than the old-style nationalism of the twentieth century is one built on shared ideals of advancing the civic equality and humanity of all people. An internationalism of this kind works to establish bridges across different nations, furthering an intention around the world for nations to accept a common commitment to act together for peace and prosperity.

Then, instruments like the International Declaration of Human Rights – formulated at the end of WWII – would have a better chance of becoming the norm. In which case, every person would be accorded the "right to life, liberty and security of person," and there would be rights to a host of other necessary goods, including equality "before the law;" freedom of thought, religion, and movement; peaceful assembly and association; a decent standard of living; and a right to education – an education that promotes tolerance among all groups and the "full development of the human personality."[68] But whereas the acceptance of this Declaration was a hard slog even before warming became an issue (the United States has still not ratified it), making such norms universal would be less possible in an increasingly warming world.

What will encourage people to adopt a political will to address, collectively, the problem of warming and by doing so move the world toward a globalization that embraces the ideals in the Declaration?

In our view, there needs to be a successful moral argument, one that convinces people that they must take the facts of warming seriously and act to stop it now. What is the nature of that argument, and could you support it? To start, let us explain the main obstacle that such an argument must address to win acceptance on a wide enough scale so that it can fuel a political will to stop warming.

It seems to us that a moral argument has to confront and successfully overturn the views of those who say, "yes, warming is a problem, but it will not affect us in the current generation with the full impact it will affect those who come after us, so why worry? More to the point, why should anyone in this generation sacrifice anything now for a cause that will only affect others who come later?"

What is the best way to counter this view? Or, in other terms, what is a "convincing moral argument" against this position?

In our view, the only way to sustain support for a political will that seeks to end warming is through an argument of fairness as opposed to an argument based on narrowly framed self-interest.

The argument for fairness starts like this. To the extent that each of us is a person with basic needs that no one can support by oneself – and thus without the help of others, or of society in general – then it follows that anyone receiving help from others, or from society, must accept an obligation to do the same for others and for society. To accept an obligation on these grounds is to do so from a sense of fairness. If others, or society in general, assist me to satisfy my needs, then I owe to them similar help in turn.

A fair society works on this principle. I contribute to others, or to our society, in general because both contribute to me in essential ways, just as you contribute to others, or to our society in general, because both do the same for you.

Fairness – described as reciprocity – is the basis for a decent society, as opposed to a society based solely on a narrowly tailored self-interest perspective alone. From the self-interest view, I can always ask why I should contribute to society, or to others, if I can get away with both receiving something I need from others, or from society, without contributing back to either? Here, the thinking from self-interest is clear: if I can play free rider by avoiding contributing to others, or to society in general, even when both contribute to me in ways that are necessary from my point of view, I get far more for myself. So, why not take this approach? Why practice fairness, instead? And, furthermore, what if it turns out that to get what I want I will not need the help of others or of society on all occasions? Yet, if I am bound to contribute to both anyway, I will find myself in situations where despite the fact that I do not need the help of others, or of society, I am contributing to both nonetheless, at great cost to my self-interest.

But, from a practical point of view, no one can maintain a singularly self-interested approach to life like this for all of one's life. The facts of life go against this view, entirely. Sure, some say otherwise, but they are either delusional, or they have the power to ensure that no one publicly critiques their views and exposes them for their mischaracterizations of what is really going on, namely, that for them to get what they want, most of the time they have to depend on the contributions of others or of society. Eventually, the fact is that I, like you, will need the help of others, or of society in general, to facilitate my needs. And, given that this is the case, then I do best for myself by maintaining reciprocal relationships of the sort that work both for others and for me. In consequence, self-interest as the basis for my contributing others is superseded by fairness.

But what is the fair, reciprocal relationship between generations living now and those that are to come? Addressing this question requires that we discuss further the claims of those who advance the self-interest argument. Again, as said earlier, they will say that they should not be asked to sacrifice for future generations because then they would get nothing in return.

But the fairness perspective counters this view. And it does this by asking us to use our *moral imaginations* to ponder how those in generations to come will think of us if we do not act now to stop warming. Clearly, if we fail in this regard, those who come later will look upon our generation with utter contempt. We can imagine their curses and their anger at us for not addressing the warming problem. If we put ourselves in the shoes of those who follow us, we will see them condemning our lives constantly. And to the extent that we take their condemnations seriously, we will gradually lose our self-respect. Instead of being the "Greatest Generation" – as the World War II generation who fought and triumphed over the Nazis was called – our generation will be called the "Contemptible Generation" because it cared only for itself.

Think of the issue this way: your grandchildren and all the others who come later will speak of you only in the most derisive of terms. So the question that must be asked is this: how can you know this to be the case and not think of yourself, now, as lacking in any redeeming qualities that undergird your sense of self-respect?

You might say, "who cares, if I have no self-respect?" But that is a recipe for plunging a person into the depths of utter, never-ending despair. Of course, we all care about losing our self-respect. Not having self-respect is a serious problem because without it our lives will lack meaningfulness. Yet, it is the latter that we crave the most. After all, we want to think of our lives as having some significance for advancing what is worthy and good, and failing to achieve such a prospect makes us small, unimportant, and, in fact, worthless. The depression and sense of meaninglessness into which we might be dropped as a result would suggest to us that if there is a way out of making this our fate, we should take that route.

And our way out of this misery is by acting from the standpoint of the norms of fairness. In which case, we would work to end warming now and thus give to future generations what they cannot give themselves without our help. But in exchange for what we give them, we can envision them in our moral imaginations providing us high regard for our contributions to their welfare. In this *quid pro quo*, we give them what they need to acquire a chance for a meaningful life, and we get from them what we need for self-respect and meaningfulness. If, on the other hand, we violate this arrangement in the name of our self-interest, then we end up being forced to think of ourselves as future generations will think of us, which is to say, as contemptible people with little to offer anyone not only in our own times but in their times, too. And then we would be thrust into the darkness associated with living a meaningless life, with all its incumbent miseries.

Will this moral argument win the day? That is your call. But McKibben thinks the moral argument may be in ascendency. He says that the next ten years may well be our "last chance" to prevent climate disasters. Still, the "good news" to note is that, in 2019, there were large mass demonstrations – across the world – focusing on climate change.[69] In this regard, we think of world leadership by people like Greta Thunberg, a teenage citizen of Sweden, whose calls on behalf of ending warming have captured the moral imaginations of millions of people from all cultures and nations. Moreover, when the Green New Deal advanced by US Congresswoman Alexandria Ocasio-Cortez and Senator Edward Markey (which seeks immediate solutions to reducing warming and which we discuss next) was initially introduced in Congress in 2019, there was widespread criticism of it. But the fact is that within months of that criticism, all leading Democrats running for president at the time ended up embracing it in one version or another.[70]

So, maybe the moral argument is at least gaining ground. Assuming it is, we can use it to substantiate a political will that orients us to act now to reduce warming in significant ways. If so, what are the concrete steps we should take with our political will to reduce warming?

The list of items on behalf of achieving a slowdown in warming includes the following. For McKibben, it is necessary to start with making the world more dependent on electric power emanating from the sun and the wind. This approach to renewable energy production is the least expensive way to produce power for a multitude of uses around the world.[71] Achieving this objective means continuing progress toward affordable batteries to store renewable energy and moving motor-vehicle owners toward electricity and away from gas and oil. It also means convincing institutions with a large amount of investment resources to not invest money in fossil fuel companies to produce oil and gas.[72] Indeed, McGibben says that during the recent past, a campaign for divestment from fossil fuels has caused endowment and portfolio enterprises to sell $12 trillion worth of their stocks in coal, oil, and gas businesses. And this effort has now been expanded to include banks and insurance companies in the hopes of getting them to stop lending money to fossil fuel businesses.[73] Overall, the goal is to shift investment to renewable energy.

Further, with civic pressure through activities like the Green New Deal, McKibben sees the possibility for working successfully on behalf of policies that slow warming in significant ways. The Green New Deal would link social programs – like universal health care and free college tuition – with efforts to make buildings more energy efficient, renewable sources of power more widespread, and the supply of electricity carbon-neutral by 2030.[74]

This linkage, on its face, may seem to make the job of stopping warming less easy, since it will be combined with other non-warming goals. But this view, says McKibben, is an alternative to the "libertarian hyper-individualism" of our times that has left in its wake "economically insecure communities" with wide social divisions the powerful can easily exploit to further degrade an already "degrading planet."[75] Seen in this way, then, the Green New Deal plan brings us closer to the moral argument from fairness – on behalf of marshaling our forces to end warming – that we outlined earlier.

The fact is that a fair society – as we argued with the moral argument from fairness – is predicated on reciprocal exchanges for the sake of improving the overall life prospects of all members. We rely on society for education and health care as major ways to overcome the social divisions now current in our society. In exchange for these public goods, the way is paved for achieving others, including our taking major steps to end the warming of our planet. This bargain is essential not just to us now, but for the sake of those who come after us, later. And we do best for ourselves by honoring this arrangement.

Otherwise, the citizens of the future will view us as having been perennially unable to understand that the moral argument based on fairness insists that each of us use the benefits of social cooperation, at critical times, to advance purposes larger than ourselves. On the other hand, if we do act now to end warming, we will certainly earn the admiration we so much want from subsequent generations – and as a result – protect our self-respect and sense of meaningfulness. Moreover, we can actually gain this great good without that much personal sacrifice. In fact, what is required of us today – in terms of changes in lifestyle – is a small cost to pay in comparison to what those who come after us would have to face, were we not to act now.

Explaining and advocating for this argument is a major task of writers like Wallace-Wells, McKibben, climate-change activists such as Greta Thunberg, and advocates of the Green New Deal. It is clear that they are securing from future generations their self-respect by advancing useful plans to end the warming of our planet in the immediate future. Will the rest of us respond similarly?[76]

V. Civility and Global Civil Society

Given the many conflicts that arise between groups and individuals in civil society over pressing concerns like culture, religion, and climate change, it is important to discuss the role of language and "civility" in the context of a civil society. Civility, as a way to address others, does not refer to a code of conduct common to an aristocratic European society of generations past. In that setting, civility signified an undemocratic deference on the part of the lower classes to their "betters," where the latter is defined in terms of inherited social standing and rank. Nor is civility merely politeness in speech and manners. Surely, in the context of civil society, civility means avoiding the slash-and-burn rhetoric of extreme partisanship that is common in political discourse today. But in addition, because civility is grounded in the main values of a civil society – including the civic virtues of toleration and mutual respect as discussed in Chapter 1 – civility suggests a particular approach to reasoning about public issues.

This approach requires us to first accept that civil society is a place to achieve agreement on a host of issues, despite the widespread differences of view encountered there. It is this aspect of civil society that makes it more than just a place for diverse ways of life to flourish side by side. But, additionally, because people from different perspectives seek in this setting a common ground to approach the issues that are of the highest importance to them, a civil society is a context for enabling people to become citizens. Consequently, a civil society is a location for devising, maintaining, and carrying out a public language that enables people who hold different value perspectives and manifest diverse ways of life to speak with each other and communicate across their differences. Such efforts may lead to discussions of how best to approach common concerns that affect not just the members of their groups but other groups as well, and, ultimately, the whole nation. Indeed, the public language helps people to stand in each other's shoes – to visit the minds of others whose views are different. And this enlarged perspective and understanding makes it possible for people to compare and contrast their opinions to the opinions of others. This experience is critical to enabling people from diverse backgrounds to identify public reasons that can stand as the bases for explaining the validity of various public policies, laws, and actions.

By contrast, using a private language – such as may be found in a particular ethnic group tradition – to discuss issues of shared concern with others would make it extremely difficult to establish public reasons for actions and judgments. A private language helps people from the same tradition communicate in intimate ways about personal matters, or a private language reinforces shared traditions with other members of one's group for the sake of maintaining the bonds of community with them. But, if while discussing public issues with others, people insisted on staying within the context of a language that solely represented a single cultural perspective, it would be difficult for people to understand as well as to communicate with others whose cultural perspective differs from theirs. In this case, people would be unable to work with others to find a way to discuss as well as to negotiate differences in perspective and from this experience achieve an accommodation that would be acceptable to all participants.

Securing civility is critical to achieving support for a national discourse and for the civic values that sustain it – what is at the heart of citizenship. Yet, achieving civility is a daunting task in the face of many group experiences that emphasize more the private language of particular group cultures than the values – like tolerance and mutual respect – of civil society that help sustain the language of civility. Nancy Rosenblum demonstrates that some groups accentuate a particular history and identity that frame the way all members interact with society.[77] When people are so thoroughly embedded in particular group settings that group perspectives completely determine the individual outlooks, individuals are less likely to reach toward other groups and work with them to find public reasons to resolve differences.

These kinds of *thick* ties promote a comprehensive and consuming unity. For groups who follow this path, there is a refusal to accept the larger influence of the national community and instead to stay only within the boundaries of one's own group. So, if bridging among different groups and ways of life is to take place, the bonds of group life must be eased somewhat and made *thinner* so that individuals can experience other ways of life and learn to communicate with people from different backgrounds. This approach to group life would permit individuals to manifest what Rosenblum calls a capacity for "shifting involvements," or the ability to move freely among different associations for the purpose of learning about and experiencing many different perspectives and ways of life.[78] Here, individuals move from one group context to another, and as they do, they are able to visit other minds – stand in others' shoes. In this milieu, individuals are not completely detached from group membership, but they are detached enough so that they can build bridges to other group contexts. Groups of this sort are thus able to welcome people from various walks of life, while at the same time maintaining a willingness to interact with other groups.

Just as important, from this experience, individuals develop important civic competencies, which permit them to search with others for the best way to address common needs, despite the many different approaches to them. In this way, the experience of civil society prepares people to search for the common policies that provide for the essential needs of all members of the society, regardless of their diverse ways of life. In effect, the experience of "shifting involvements" in a civil society enables people to regard themselves not just as members of particular groups but as citizens of the nation as a whole.

But how far and wide may individuals, who have "shifting involvements" with a variety of groups, range? Assuming it is possible for people in civil society to acquire a national scope to their approach to public discussions of important issues, the next question is if they can advance beyond the nation toward a more global perspective. In effect, will it be possible to create a good facsimile of the language of civility on a global level that civil society makes possible for the national level? And from this experience will it be possible for people to, in addition to becoming citizens of the nation, become citizens of the world?

Now, the need for a global civil society has been hastened by two major realities that contribute to globalization or the creation of linkages among nations across the world. First, there are the many authentic global problems facing the world, including matters pertaining to the climate change, to terrorism, to poverty, and to attaining a basis for a peace that will eliminate both war and the weapons that threaten mass destruction. None of these matters that seriously affect each nation can be solved without global cooperation. And second, the Internet enables people to travel virtually, that is mentally, anywhere and to learn about and to communicate with people from cultures the world over. Because we can know other ways of life so easily, it is unthinkable that we can deny their presence in our own lives. To be sure, nationalist sentiments remain strong in many settings, but it is the ready proximity, as well as reliance on the cultures of other nations, that makes it wrongheaded to define one's nation in exclusionary terms.

Globalization cannot be denied. We are linked to the rest of the world as the rest of the world is to us. All of which seems to hasten the need for the language of civility to extend from each society to all societies, in the hopes that, through civility, people can make possible something like a global civil society that will be the platform for solving the many problems that face the world. But is a global civil society possible? In other terms, is it possible for people to transcend private languages common to their own nation and create among the world's people a shared language of civility that can be used to find reasonable solutions to the problems that now vex us? Here, we can talk about only some of the obstacles that we would have to face and overcome if this goal is to be attained. The first is one Benjamin Barber discusses, and the second is Rawls's.

Barber discusses the competition between what he calls two leading approaches to understanding the world today, "McWorld" and "Jihad." McWorld, which is the view of the so-called modern world, shares the Enlightenment's attachment to freedom, its commitment to reason, its skepticism toward tradition, its faith in free markets, and its "disdain for parochial culture." Jihad, on the other hand, represents a still pervasive traditional worldview, built upon a fondness for communal hierarchies and for the mysteries of religion and the pull of habit. Naturally, Jihad stands in opposition to McWorld.[79]

How can a language of civility emerge in the face of two starkly different world views? Rawls in his *The Law of Peoples*, which is his revision of Immanuel Kant's quest for a universal peace among nations, affords an answer.[80] Kant argued, as we saw earlier, that the route to world peace is when all nations become republics. Republics let the citizens of a nation decide if they want to go to war, and because the people who fight wars do not find it in their interests to have them, republics will not go to war against each other but will find peaceful ways to resolve their differences. Now, Kant was right that republics would reduce the chances of war in at least one sense. The facts demonstrate that republics generally do not go to war with each other.[81] But republics have gone to war with nonrepublics many times, and because it is unlikely that all nations will become republics, the likelihood of war will thus remain. How, in the face of this fact, can a global civil society emerge?

Rawls' s *The Law of Peoples* is an important approach to achieving a global civil society. His view on this matter starts from the assertion that there are two sources of sovereign power: states (or governments) and peoples. States possess the machinery of power – such as the military and the police – to enforce their decisions. Peoples are each characterized by a moral character and a shared culture that distinguishes one people from another – French from Germans, Indians from Pakistanis, and so on. The people in a given region are thus bound together by sharing the same understanding of history, of religious practices, of norms, of language, and so on. This view of peoples, which defines the factors that unite one set of people but not another, emphasizes, as well, the differences between them. But it is possible that different peoples also share common values that facilitate cooperation among them. Indeed, Rawls believes that there are just and decent peoples who agree to an agenda that supports human rights and cooperative relationships.[82] And when this agenda is widely shared, it can provide an important set of norms to direct the use of governmental power across the world, ensuring that it is used for cooperative purposes productive of a global civil society.

Now, Rawls argues that there are two types of peoples likely to produce a foundation for peaceful interaction: liberal peoples and "decent hierarchical peoples," what he refers to, together, as "well-ordered peoples."[83] Decent hierarchical peoples do not share the values of liberal democracies because, in decent hierarchical societies, people "are not regarded free and equal citizens, nor [are they considered] as separate individuals deserving equal representation (according to the maxim: one citizen, one vote)."[84] Instead, decent hierarchical societies have a collective aim, which is to realize a substantive, "common good idea of justice." The latter refers to the all-embracing common culture, including religious and social values that individuals must uphold throughout their lives. Here, individuals understand that they have a duty to act in ways that will replicate the requirements of the culture, and by doing so, they can be said to act in keeping with the norms of justice pertinent to that culture.[85] In this context, then, individuals define their identities not in terms of rights granted them to be autonomous individuals who are able to stand toward one's own culture and critique and perhaps change it, as is the case in liberal societies. Instead, individuals define their identities in terms of the nation's dominant cultural reality to which each person is to dedicate his or her life in the expectation of reproducing the prevailing culture for future generations. Thus, decent hierarchical societies are formed as communities upheld by traditions, often religious in character, that have a firm hold on the minds and imaginations of each of the citizens. As such, individuals accept that the reigning cultural traditions and norms will fashion their life decisions, and the quest for achieving autonomy from them is not as important as upholding the duties and obligations associated with governing traditions.

Another important difference between liberal and decent societies is that in decent hierarchical societies, government is not transparent and directly accountable to the citizens. Still, there is a sense in which governments in these societies do permit different voices to be considered.[86] Of particular importance is that judges and public officials in these societies consider the views of those that dissent from positions prominent in government policy.[87] And, when people do not agree with the decisions of public officials, dissenters may continue their protest, "provided they explain why they are still dissatisfied, and their explanation in turn ought to receive a further and fuller reply."[88] As a result of this process, the various tendencies in society are represented.

Thus, decent hierarchical societies are not the same as societies that can be placed in the category of dictatorships that rule by terror and total control, where the main concern is not to protect the shared traditions that knit the society into a community, but the need for power by the ruling elite. Decent hierarchical societies do not fall into this category for two basic reasons. In the first place, these societies do not seek to subdue and dominate other societies for the sake of expanding their own range of power.[89] Second, these societies advocate an agenda of basic human rights for their governments to preserve. Included on the list of rights to protect is the "right to life," which makes possible security; liberty, which is freedom from slavery along with freedom of conscience, thought, and religion; ownership of personal property; and formal equality, which ensures that similar cases are treated equally.[90] Regarding religion, even though decent societies generally have a predominant religion, those with different religions are allowed to practice it freely and without fear. Still, because of the dominance of one religion, inequalities in religious freedom may arise in these societies, and thus, part of what is involved in being a decent society is to assist citizens affected by this circumstance to emigrate.[91]

Now in Rawls's view, these well-ordered liberal and decent hierarchical societies would support, because of their embrace of the values just referred to, a "Law of Peoples."[92] Rawls discusses a list of eight principles of justice that would be the basis for a Law of Peoples. The list includes matters such as respect for treaties and human rights, for a commitment to the noninterference and noninter-vention in the affairs of others, and for sense of duty to assist those people living under conditions that prevent them from having a decent regime.[93] It is precisely these rules that would enable commerce and trade among nations of either stripe, as well as buttress a combined effort to work cooperatively with each other to resolve world problems.

Could a global civil society emerge from these rules? Rawls hopes so. Three major problems stand in the way, however. Barber identifies one, and Rawls iden-tifies another. We will identify a third one.

First, Barber makes clear that globalization can be used as a tool to promote not a global civil society but corporate business interests the world over.[94] In this case, instead of teaching the language of civility as the basis for common deliber-ation, inclusion, and the pursuit of the common good, there is only the language of the business deal. Here, often major corporations' quests for the accumula-tion of material wealth – or greed – is the essence of all that is true and good in life. Thus, notions of inclusion and common deliberation – so essential to a civil society at the national or global levels – are pushed to the side in favor of those values that secure the triumph of corporate business. Further, a corporate-driven globalization is perceived often as a threat to local traditions and ways of life of Jihad cultures. These countries, however, worry not only that corporate globaliza-tion will erode their traditions, but in addition, that many political leaders in Jihad settings who might embrace elements of corporate globalization will not accept the democratizing aspect of a global civil society.

One of the obstacles Rawls identifies has to do with the fact that some advo-cates of liberal peoples think that treating decent societies equally is "inconsistent, or unfair" because these societies, owing to their commitment to hierarchy, main-tain an order that does not treat their members equally.[95] The force of the argument is that societies are owed equality of consideration only when they accord their members equality of treatment. But Rawls points out that many groups in our own society are run as hierarchies, and yet, these groups are accorded equal respect. This is as true for religious groups that are run as hierarchies as for many univer-sities, who, for instance, select presidents by "a kind of consultation hierarchy," which excludes an equal vote for each affected party.[96] Implicit in this view is that liberals should demonstrate the same regard for decent hierarchical societies that they manifest toward hierarchical groups in their own societies.

To this end, Rawls thinks that liberal societies must "tolerate" decent hier-archical societies. By tolerating these societies, Rawls means that liberal peoples should not subject decent societies to political sanctions, forcing them to make changes, including "military, economic or diplomatic."[97] Instead, liberal societ-ies must extend to decent hierarchical societies the chance to be participating members in a setting that accords all members mutual respect under a shared commitment to civility.[98] This prospect would help to establish mutually advan-tageous discussions that build a strong basis for a global civil society. And there is every incentive to move in this direction for liberal and for decent societies because what most threatens both are states that are neither liberal or decent but that are "aggressive and dangerous," and that, consequently, need not be tolerated by either and can be "forced to change."[99]

The third problem has to do with Rawls's view of the concept of peoples. Is it the case, for instance, that there is a uniform culture in the societies that Rawls refers to as representing a people? After all, many of the societies Rawls might have in mind as candidates for being decent hierarchical societies are fragmented by various conflicts over religion, poverty, and class, as well as over the sense that the government – owing to corruption or incompetence or just simply the weight of the problems it faces – is incapable of serving authentic public needs. It is precisely this circumstance that can become the breeding ground for terrorism, a factor that would make it difficult to invoke the language of civility as opposed to the language of war. Moreover, when liberal and decent societies agree to cooperate against terrorism, each may undermine the values that make possible the bases for cooperative relations that are productive of a global civil society. In particular, decent societies may become more hierarchical and less open to external interactions with other cultures, and liberal societies may become more prone to deny the principles of liberal conceptions of justice – including respect for basic rights – both to their own citizens and toward others in the world at large.

These factors, taken together or singularly, may make the creation of a global civil society difficult, not just across the world but even in liberal states that contain a great deal of diversity. We owe it to ourselves, and to the legacy of political theory detailed in this book, to take on this difficult task.

Notes

1. Charles Taylor, "The Politics of Recognition," in *Multiculturalism,* ed. Amy Gutmann (Princeton, NJ: Princeton University Press, 1994), 39.

2. Ibid., 38–39, 54–55.

3. Ibid., 55.

4. Ibid., 54–55.

5. Ibid., 55.

6. Ibid., 59–61.

7. Ibid., 60; also p. 56. In John Rawls, this approach is embodied in his notion of public reason, as discussed in Chapter 15.

8. Taylor, "The Politics of Recognition," 56.

9. Ibid., 52–59, especially p. 59.

10. Susan Moller Okin, "Introduction," in *Is Multiculturalism Bad for Women?,* ed. Susan Moller Okin (Princeton, NJ: Princeton University Press, 1999), 10–11. Italics are in the text. Also see Taylor, "The Politics of Recognition," 39–40.

11. Stephen Macedo, *Diversity and Distrust: Moral Plurality, Civic Education and American Liberalism* (Bloomington, IN: The Poynter Center, 1997), 11–12. He discusses the US Supreme Court case *Mozert v. Hawkins County Board of Education*, in which some families with fundamentalist religious views did not want their children involved in a public-school reading program designed to expose their children to a diversity of views, including religious diversity. The families sought to be permitted to opt out of the reading program while remaining in the public schools.

12. Stephen Macedo, *Diversity and Distrust: Civic Education in a Multicultural Democracy* (Cambridge: Harvard University Press, 2000), 239.

13. Taylor, "The Politics of Recognition," 61.

14. K. Anthony Appiah, "Identity, Authenticity, Survival: Multicultural Societies and Social Reproduction," in *Multiculturalism,* ed. Amy Gutmann (Princeton, NJ: Princeton University Press, 1994), 149–64.

15. Ibid., 149. Appiah comments that many of the arguments from the perspective of the politics of difference are "at odds with the individualist thrust of talk of authenticity and identity."

16. Ibid., 154.

17. Ibid., 155.

18. Ibid., 157.

19. Ibid., 159.

20. Ibid., 161.

21. Ibid., 163.

22. Ibid. Appiah recognizes, however, that "between the politics of recognition and the politics of compulsion, there is no bright line."

23. Ronald Dworkin, *Is Democracy Possible Here?* (Princeton, NJ: Princeton University Press, 2006), 1–23, Ch. 1.

24. Ibid., 9–21. The view of autonomy used here encompasses and is a version of the concept of human dignity discussed in Dworkin.

25. Ibid., 56.

26. Ibid., 57.

27. Ibid., 58–59.

28. Ibid., 58.

29. Ibid., 59.

30. Ibid.

31. Ibid.

32. Ibid.

33. Ibid., 59–60.

34. Wendy Brown, *Regulating Aversion* (Princeton, NJ: Princeton University Press, 2006), 70–71, 89–90.

35. Diane Henriques, "In God's Name: Favors for the Faithful," *New York Times*, October 8, 9, 11, 2006.

36. William Galston, *Public Matters* (New York: Rowman and Littlefield, 2005), 129.

37. William Galston, *Liberal Pluralism: The Implications of Value Pluralism for Political Theory and Practice* (Cambridge: Cambridge University Press, 2002), 28.

38. Ibid., 116.

39. Galston, *Public Matters,* 129.

40. Noah Feldman, *Divided by God* (New York: Farrar, Strauss and Giroux, 2005), 73, 77–85, 210–11.

41. Jerome Karabel, *The Chosen: The Hidden History of Admission and Exclusion at Harvard, Princeton and Yale* (Boston: Houghton Mifflin, 2005).

42. A report released by the Council on American–Islamic Relations for 2007 says that incidents of discrimination were up 25 percent from the previous year, including employers banning head scarves and not permitting a five-minute break for prayer. Cited in the *Cincinnati Enquirer*, June 20, 2007, B2.

43. Dworkin, *Is Democracy Possible Here?* 63–64.

44. Michael Sandel, *Public Philosophy* (Cambridge: Harvard University Press, 2005), 210–47, especially pp. 224–30.

45. Ibid., 246.

46. Amartya Sen, *Identity and Violence: The Illusion of Destiny* (New York: Norton, 2006), 156–61. Also, Amartya Sen, "Chile and Liberty: The Uses and Abuses of Multiculturalism," *The New Republic,* February 27, 2006, 27.

47. Sen, "Chile and Liberty," 29.

48. Readers may wish to review section IV in Chapter 13, which discusses the generation of surplus value by workers, and the owners' interest in usurping as much of it as possible.

49. David Wallace-Wells, *The Uninhabitable Earth: Life After Warming* (New York: Tim Duggan Books, 2019), 4.

50. Karl Marx, "Manifesto of the Communist Party," in *The Marx-Engels Reader*, ed. and intro. Robert C. Tucker, 2nd ed. (New York: Norton and Company, 1978), 500.

51. Wallace-Wells, *The Uninhabitable Earth*, 9.

52. Ibid.

53. Ibid.

54. Ibid., 12.

55. Ibid.

56. Ibid.

57. Ibid.

58. Ibid., 13.

59. Ibid.

60. Ibid.

61. Ibid.

62. Ibid., 27.

63. Ibid.

64. Ibid.

65. Ibid., 28.

66. Ibid., 125–126.

67. This history, which includes two world wars that cost the lives of millions, was propelled by nationalist creeds built upon the notion that one's own nation had to be exempted from the influences of other cultures, lest the ethnic and religious "purity" of one's own nation be sabotaged. This perspective motivated nations to see each other as threats to their own greatness and thus as dire enemies that had to be subordinated and ruled over.

68. See for the "Universal Declaration of Human Rights" the United Nations Website, www.un.org/en/universal-declaration-human-rights/index.html.

69. Bill McKibben, "A Very Hot Year," *New York Review of Books*, March 12, 2020, www.nybooks.com/articles/2020/03/12/climate-change-very-hot-year/?utm_medium=email&utm_campaign=NYR%20Tyranny%20of%20the%20Minority&utm_content=NYR%20Tyranny%20of%20the%20Minority+CID_280c2dddc79819de8500ecdbd5f0f55a&utm_source=Newsletter&utm_term=climate%20forecast.

70. Eric Klinenberg, "The Great Green Hope," *New York Review of Books*, April 23, 2020, 55.

71. McKibben, "A Very Hot Year."

72. Ibid.

73. Ibid.

74. Ibid.

75. Ibid.

76. See Jedediah Purdy, *This Land Is Our Land: The Struggle for a New Commonwealth* (Princeton, NJ: Princeton University Press, 2020), cited in Klinenberg, "The Great Green Hope." There, Klinenberg quotes Purdy as embracing the moral argument put forth here. Purdy says that we should support the idea of a commonwealth, which refers to an economy which "might be . . . [one] where no one gets their living by degrading someone else, nor by degrading the health of the land or the larger living world." This is a community in which "the flourishing of everyone and everything would sustain the flourishing of each person." Further, this is "a way of living in deep reciprocity as well as deep equality," p. 57.

77. Nancy L. Rosenblum, *Membership and Morals: The Personal Uses of Pluralism in America* (Princeton, NJ: Princeton University Press, 1998), 323–26.

78. Ibid., 350.

79. Benjamin R. Barber, *Jihad vs. McWorld* (New York: Times Books, 1995), 156–57.
80. John Rawls, *The Law of Peoples* (Cambridge: Harvard University Press, 1999), 10.
81. Ibid., 51. Here, Rawls cites the study of Michael Doyle, *Ways of War and Peace* (New York: Norton, 1997), 277–84, which provides solid evidence for this position.
82. Ibid., 26–27.
83. Ibid., 71, 62–65.
84. Ibid., p. 71.
85. Ibid., 71–72.
86. Ibid., 72.
87. Ibid., 61, 72.
88. Ibid.
89. Ibid., 64.
90. Ibid., 65.
91. Ibid., 74.
92. Ibid., 37, 69, 85.
93. Ibid., 37.
94. Barber, *Jihad vs. McWorld*, 280, 285.
95. Rawls, *The Law of Peoples*, 69.
96. Ibid., 69–70, 62.
97. Ibid., 59, 61.
98. Ibid., 61.
99. Ibid., 81.

20

Civil Society, Liberal Democracy, and Racial Injustice: A Political Theory Informed by the Black Experience in America

I. Introduction: Civil Society and Liberal Democracy

As we stated in the introduction, a "political theory is constructed as a response to enduring questions that hold the attention of the political theorist." The highly important question for us in this chapter is how does a political theory that is rooted in the experience of African Americans in this country contribute in a major way – as we think it does – to a liberal democracy? And what are the consequences for civil society?

Why is the first question so significant? Because a liberal democracy seeks to achieve civic equality for all, which means protecting the basic rights of each individual, regardless of status, race, gender, or sexuality.[1] There is no higher objective for a liberal democratic regime than to secure the civic equality (and, thus, the dignity) of all citizens. And, in our view, there is no higher purpose for politics, in general. For this approach to politics is the basis for an open, pluralist society in which all citizens agree – as part of what is required by the common good – to respect all others, no matter how different they may be from oneself.

It is also the case – as we know from history – that the public sphere (or what can also be called the national government) in a liberal democratic state has often failed to safeguard, and has instead worked to deny, civic equality for African Americans. And this reality has often worked against achieving an open, pluralist society. Why this has happened and why it often continues to happen, as well as what can be done to overturn such horrific injustice on behalf of ensuring civic equality for all, become the central concerns of a political theory that is both informed by the American experience of black–white relationships and grounded in a commitment to support a liberal democratic public sphere.

Moreover, these concerns inevitably are aired in civil society, where discussions designed to advance civic equality for all take place in the hopes of restoring in full measure a public sphere that can achieve civic equality for all citizens of whatever belief or color. A civil society, then, has a fundamental role in securing a liberal democratic public sphere, and without the former, the latter will be hard to achieve.

Before proceeding to explain this view more fully, we wish to do three things in the next five sections. First, our plan is to be more specific as to what we mean by the "public sphere of a liberal democracy." Included in this description is recognition of the factors that often contribute to the weakening, if not the destruction, of the public sphere. Second, we discuss civil society's relationship to the public sphere and, in particular, highlight the importance of a civil society as the location of the discussion that – when successful – makes the case for, as well as helps to safeguard, a liberal democratic public sphere. Third, we describe the significant role a political theory – impacted heavily by the experience of African Americans – has in civil society with respect to this goal. In this context, we introduce an idea of critical importance to a civil society that seeks to establish – through discussions there – a foundation for preserving a liberal democratic public sphere; in particular, we discuss what we call a "moral obligation to remember radical injustice toward blacks." Finally, in the sections that follow the first five, we discuss a few of the black voices that manifest in different ways a moral obligation to remember radical injustice.

II. The Public Sphere and Liberal Democracy

Starting with the first concern listed, we initially discuss the main achievement of a public sphere – or what, again, is also referred to as the national government – of a liberal democracy. In particular, the latter is predicated on obtaining majority backing for the resolution of all public issues before society but always within an unflinching commitment to protecting basic rights, which is to say, civic equality under the law for all citizens. It is never acceptable in a liberal democracy to advance majority positions when doing so threatens civic equality across society. In a liberal democratic public sphere that upholds the rule of law, the majority must not deny basic rights to any group or individual based on that group's or individual's cultural orientation, religion, social status, gender, sexuality, or racial identity. In effect, to protect the rule of law within the liberal democratic public sphere, bigotry – by which people do not tolerate others different from themselves – must never be used to justify the denial of civic equality for anybody.

Certainly, the abrogation of the rule of law on precisely these terms has been manifested over the long history of American society's relationship to black people. In the past, racist practices were considered by many to represent the majority white position that had to be honored by the society, even if in so doing blacks – as a consequence of racially based bigotry – were denied civic equality. A liberal democratic public sphere should always condemn this view of the majority-rules principle because it suggests that the majority has the authority to deny to some – merely for reasons of their skin color – the same rights all members of society are guaranteed under law. But when the liberal democratic public sphere does not censure this version of the majority-rules idea – as has been the case in the past with respect to blacks – then the public sphere is unable to protect the rule of law.

Now, of course, there will be times when the majority in posting its views makes the case that certain rights of *all* citizens may need to be limited, as when, for instance, it creates standards for public speech that deny the ability of citizens or newspapers – when discussing public issues – to refer to classified information, defined as such, by the national government. Or the majority may decide that health insurance should be the purview of *all*, even when doing so means that all individuals may lose some of the advantages they now receive in private plans. In cases like these – however the majority decides the matter before it – the resulting rights that are defined in consequence of that decision must not be denied to any single individual citizen. Otherwise, the commitment to civic equality for all would be abrogated. And that would violate a main tenet of the public sphere of a liberal democracy.

The public sphere – once again – signifies the national government in which matters, like those to which we just referred, are discussed and resolutions mandated for all citizens to support are achieved. As such, the public sphere is where citizens and duly authorized political leaders use different modes of public discourse to persuade other citizens and political leaders to adopt their views when discussing issues that affect all citizens, in general. Ideally, citizens and public officials who engage in discussions in the public sphere should rely – as the basis for convincing each other of their views – on reasoned and fact-based critiques of all issues.[2] This is needed to maintain the integrity of the public sphere as a place where citizens put, overall, the interests of all citizens above their own when the two are in conflict.

Practically speaking, however, the public sphere includes discourses that void reasoned, fact-based argument on behalf of raw appeals to various emotions, including those that target fear, distrust, and bigotry. Often, this approach to the public sphere turns it into a setting that favors an idiom of intensive and uncompromising hyper-partisanship. And when this happens, a discourse – based on fact-based, reasoned discussion – loses its place in the public sphere as the single uniting force of all citizens, regardless of partisan affiliation.

On better days, however, as just intimated, the public sphere may incorporate fact-based, reasoned views as the main coin of the political realm. Moreover, in this setting, diverse views and positions would become a standard part of the public sphere, and individuals would seek not just to respect differences from a variety of origins – including religious, cultural, philosophical, and, of course, political – but people would approach these differences from the standpoint of the strong need to find, among the contesting views, a basis for agreement. In this case, the realities common to political life – including intense partisanship – could be harmonized by efforts to achieve compromises acceptable to most citizens. And, by doing so, the give and take of compromise is likely to move the public discourse toward more reasoned and fact-based discourses as well as more respect for differences among citizens and their leaders, who, together, search for common ground on the issues before the society.

It is also the case that the public sphere of a liberal democracy on any day – good, bad, or in between – must always be grounded in, and thus must continuously uphold, core moral and constitutional principles. In effect, the idea of advancing the majority rules approach to public decisions but within the context of respect for and protection of civic equality of all citizens – and ideally within a setting characterized by fact-based, reasoned discourse as well – thrives only as citizens respect the rule of law by upholding core moral and constitutional principles.

What are the moral and constitutional principles that undergird the public sphere of a liberal democracy?

The main moral principle is to conduct politics – including the pursuit of majority positions – with a firm commitment to ensure that all citizens are accorded protection of the rights said to be for all. It is morally wrong – which is to say, it is unjust and unfair – to say that some have these rights but others do not and then to use arbitrary bases for this conclusion, including, most specifically, bigotry of any variety.

The main constitutional principle is for citizens and political leaders to uphold those institutions that ensure power is not vested in one single entity of the government but is shared across several. This notion is entrenched in a constitutional commitment that locates political power in different branches of the national government; one, the legislature, which makes the law; another, the executive, which enforces it; and a third, the courts, which act as neutral arbiters when there are differences between the first two branches. During times that the national government fails to follow this course, it – the national government – tends to gravitate toward allowing all its power to be in the hands of a few people, and these individuals would be likely to both undermine the quest for majority positions on issues as well as to torpedo the protection of basic rights for each individual citizen, under law.

To ensure that power is shared across several agencies of the national government, another essential constitutional principle is that citizens are accorded the right to vote, combined with the right of free speech. It is through these rights that citizens can hold those whom they elect accountable to their – the citizens' – collective wishes. Most specifically, citizens can use these core rights to ensure that elected leaders uphold the basic moral and constitutional principles. We thus follow John Lewis, an iconic civil rights leader, when he said in an essay that he left for us after his death, "the vote is the most powerful nonviolent change agent you have in a democratic society. You must use it because it is not guaranteed. You can lose it."[3]

All of which means that whatever supports the rights to vote and to free and open speech – including, surely, freedom of conscience and the right of citizens to publicly but peacefully protest government policies or proposals with which they disagree – are central elements in a liberal democratic public sphere.[4] Another element of the highest importance in this regard is the chance for an informed public through dissemination – as a result of the right to a free media – of accurate information that individuals use to analyze issues and to bring to bear on them reasoned and fact-based judgments. The rights just enumerated are critical in that, without them, it is likely that all the other rights listed on a "full rights "agenda provided in the liberal democratic public sphere would be under constant threat of annihilation.[5]

The moral and constitutional principles as just described are sustained and, indeed, reinforced in the public sphere by, among other things, symbols that are shared across society. For instance, the Constitution of the United States and the Declaration of Independence are national symbols that often evoke in both citizens and political leaders the need to protect the core moral and constitutional principles at the heart of a liberal democracy. Furthermore, civic education is designed to make clear not only the meaning of these symbols but the practices suggested by them, practices that all citizens should respect as part of what is involved in securing the public sphere of a liberal democracy. Finally, civic education encourages citizens and political leaders of whatever stripe to place the interests of the public sphere (or national government) ahead of their own when the two are in competition with each other.

Still, the public sphere – as mentioned earlier – is vulnerable to hyper-partisanship emanating especially from identity politics, which is discussed in the next section. And when this happens, people on either side of an intense partisan divide may so loudly and so dogmatically proclaim their partisan views that they turn the public sphere into a space that works only for them and that excludes all who are not them.

This is where civil society becomes critical in helping to safeguard the public sphere. It is within civil society that citizens and political leaders make arguments for shoring up the public sphere on behalf of it upholding the shared moral and constitutional principles, as well as on behalf of it supporting discourses based on facts and good reasoning and a commitment to finding common ground among a wide array of differences. When successful, then, a civil society bolsters the public sphere of a liberal democracy, a prospect we discuss in the next section.

III. Civil Society and the Public Sphere

To better understand this mission, it is well to review some central facets of what we have taken to mean by the term "civil society." As we have seen, a civil society is the space between the national government and the individual. This is a space in which individuals can find a variety of groups and associations through which to achieve their self-chosen ends. Without the social networks made possible by the many groups and associations in civil society, individuals might choose to do various things – from learning how to play the violin to studying philosophy to learning a particular trade – but have no concrete social framework by which to do them. These social networks thus enable persons to find out what they wish to do with their lives, and they provide the education and training needed to perform the various roles individuals may choose. It is because of civil society, then, that individuals manifest the *private freedom* to choose ways of life seen as providing them with the self-respect (and the meaningfulness of life) that all seek. Without civil society and the multitudes of social networks found there, the offer of private freedom in a liberal democracy would be empty and meaningless, and, as a result, the self-respect each seeks through the exercise of their private freedom would be impossible to acquire.

But this is not the only achievement of a civil society. It also enables individuals to take part in considering public issues of common importance to all citizens. Here, a civil society advances not so much private freedom but *public freedom*. As such, the discussions in civil society are often designed to enable people to understand and to respect differences that emanate from a variety of sources – including religious, cultural, philosophical, and, of course, political. But at the same time, a civil society is also the place in which individuals from diverse walks of life and cultures discover – via conversations of mutual respect (discussed in Chapter 1 and more fully later in this section) – what they share through their discussions of major issues. Conversations of mutual respect in civil society thus make it possible for individuals to both show regard for differences while finding among them a basis for shared approaches to issues of importance to all. As a result, the experience of a civil society provides a good foundation that undergirds – at least potentially – the public sphere of a liberal democracy.

However, it is also the case that citizens in a civil society may face grave challenges in their efforts to nurture the public sphere. And the reason why is clear. As mentioned earlier, there are immense pressures placed on the public sphere – pressures that cause it to function poorly on behalf of its ability to uphold its core moral and constitutional principles. Relevant to this chapter is that one origin of these pressures against the strengthening of the public sphere arises from differences in view within civil society over how best to approach the continuing threat of loss of opportunity and rights for blacks in a society that is obligated to provide civic equality for all citizens. Some – in this case, blacks – bemoan the denial of opportunity as unjust, and others argue in response that they should not be asked to shoulder full responsibility for ameliorating the situation about which blacks complain. Often enough, the two groups end up at loggerheads, unable to agree, and the public sphere – especially as a place to protect the shared moral and constitutional principles – is weakened, if not brought to the brink of its full destruction.

Indeed, this depiction of group conflict is a major source of what is today called "identity politics," now a resilient presence in our day. People practice identity politics when they embrace political identities that reflect their dominant perspectives on important political issues. And certainly the continuing impact of race on the fortunes of African Americans is one such issue.[6] For instance, to understand the concept of identity politics, ask yourself if your political identity mostly derives from your support of the demands of blacks for social and political justice or with those whose political identity is formed by having little patience with this view?

People who hold the latter position argue that, of course, everyone should be treated justly, but this can best be done when there are policies that, as Mark Lilla says, appeal "to Americans as Americans and emphasizing the issues that affect a vast majority of them."[7] This view of politics Lilla says, "would speak to the nation as a nation of citizens who are in this together and must help one another."[8] In other terms, Lilla wants an approach to political discourse that is fashioned along the lines of what is good for the working and middle classes, in general. These social classes represent the "vast majority of Americans," and the goal of politics should be to find the common good for this large group of people. Race should be deemphasized in determining the common good because members of various racial groups are to be included in the "vast majority" of people for whom the common good is fashioned.

Yet, this goal is hard to achieve where identity politics based on emphasizing the need to end racism and advance respect for diverse ways of life is a constant concern of numerous people today. In this regard, Lilla complains that many students enter college with a strong penchant for diversity, so much so, in fact, that they think promoting diversity is the only matter political discourse should emphasize. The fixation on diversity orients politics toward achieving justice for groups long denied it, which means, for instance, women, ethnic minorities, and most especially, in the context of this chapter, African Americans. But for Lilla, an emphasis on diversity in general, and thus on race in particular, may cause some groups to believe their interests are not as important as the interests of those groups that fall within the rubric of "diversity." People treated in this way are likely to feel that their voices are not given adequate consideration, with the result that it is much harder to focus as a society – encompassing all groups – on the great questions of politics, like "class, war, the economy and the common good."[9]

In contrast, those who view society from a concept of identity politics based on race argue that any approach designed to benefit the majority of Americans will fall short of this goal, unless there is strong focus at the same time on eradicating racist practices and attitudes in society. For it is the case that these practices often reappear and deny civic equality to blacks. This happens despite the fact that all people – including blacks – belong to the vast majority protected by the common good approach Lilla espouses. As Nicholas Kristof says, "the blunt truth is that America's most egregious failures have often involved identity" and, further, identity has frequently been defined in racial terms. Kristof cites higher frequencies of crib death and cancer among African Americans, suggesting significant "disparities in income and health care."[10] Moreover, we add to this judgment the fact that, today, data demonstrate that the black and Latino communities in the United States are "three times as likely to become infected [by the coronavirus] as their white neighbors."[11] Finally, Kristof says that "crime in America disproportionately involves blacks, as both victims and arrested perpetrators."[12]

Each identity group – one based on the needs of the working and the middle classes and the other more on the needs to overturn the continuing effects of racially based prejudice – thus holds a view that is seen as in intense competition with the other view. When this reality motivates our politics – as it often does – then neither group trusts the other. Political rhetoric between them thus becomes sharp, vituperative, and filled with resentment. And, consequently, people find themselves in protective silos from which they judge others – who do not believe as they believe – as dire threats to their own interests. Moreover, some political leaders use the resentment and distrust arising from this circumstance to win the support of the group to whom they direct their appeals. On behalf of this objective, political leaders urge one identity group to attack another in ways that deepen the sense of outrage and resentment on the part of both. In which case, the public sphere – or national government – slides away from being the place to discover the majority view on major issues, without sacrificing its commitment to protect civic equality for all.

Now, a civil society, as mentioned earlier, tries to counter this condition common in our current politics – and in the process protect core moral and constitutional principles of the public sphere – by enabling people to develop the capacity to discuss with diverse others their shared problems and to find a common ground, while at the same time respecting their differences. Here, silos are replaced by discussions that incorporate an ethos of mutual respect.[13] People who engage in discourses of mutual respect learn to see the world as others see it, and, in addition, individuals learn how to integrate their differences into a framework of shared understandings during the search for common ground. Further, people who practice mutual respect also approach the attainment of a common ground during discussions by employing facts and reasoned arguments as opposed to emotional or ideological harangues. When successful, the search within civil society for a common ground through a discourse of mutual respect is the basis for restoring, in some cases, or strengthening in other cases, the public sphere and, through doing so, protecting liberal democratic moral and constitutional principles.

But when the conversations in a civil society are unable to blaze a path to agreement among diverse points of view and understandings, civil society fails to create support for a liberal democratic public sphere. To be sure, there are many features that cause a civil society to be unable to achieve this purpose, including extremely elevated levels of intense partisanship emanating from clashes over identity politics, as just recounted.

Still, it is also the case that there are important elements in a civil society that can be used to counter this corrosive (to the public sphere) factor and, consequently, nurture – through the discussions in a civil society about a host of matters including those at hand here – the public sphere. And, among the most important of these elements is inscribed in a political theory that is built upon a shared recognition of the failure to secure civic equality on a regular and consistent basis to blacks across American history. A political theory that houses this memory encourages its holders to seek – through discussions in civil society of major issues – resolutions that never perpetuate past moments of injustice against African Americans by denying civic equality to them. When a preponderant number of citizens comes to embrace this view because of such discussions in civil society, upholding the moral and constitutional principles of a liberal democracy becomes such an important priority for citizens that factors intruding on the integrity of the public sphere – like intense partisanship – can no longer be allowed to interrupt the public sphere's commitment to protecting equal justice under the rule of law.

IV. Political Theory and Race: Core Argument

What is the way in which a political theory described along these lines formulates this view?

It is that citizens must come to accept a *moral obligation to remember radical injustice toward blacks.*[14] First, what is radical injustice? Radical injustice refers to times when basic rights (and, thus, civic equality) are guaranteed to all, but despite this fact, these rights are systematically denied to blacks for reasons that are morally reprehensible, such as to maintain racist worldviews and – in the context of the United States' origins – slavery. For instance, the Declaration of Independence advances a natural-rights-for-all-persons approach to securing the dignity of each citizen by saying that "all men are created equal."[15] But then the Constitution counts blacks as three-fifths of a person.[16] Moreover, despite the professions of equality in the Declaration of Independence, the Fugitive Slave Act of 1850 sought to ensure that slaves who fled slavery to freedom in the North were returned to their owners in the South.[17] Slaves were nothing more than the private property of the white owner class, and no free – which is to say, non-slave – state could be allowed to protect them. This view was actually embedded within the U.S. Constitution, in Article Four, Section 2, Clause 3, which required that runaway slaves had to be returned to their owner.[18]

Second, what justifies a moral obligation to remember moments of radical injustice to blacks? To answer this question, it is important to recognize a central truth of radical injustice; namely, that past instances of radical injustice toward blacks can – even in an age such as ours that formally rejects radical injustice – find their way back into society and once again undermine civic equality for blacks. In consequence, if we are to stop this cycle from continuing, we must – as a matter of a moral obligation – remember past instances of radical injustice. And from this memory, and thus as part of the moral obligation to remember radical injustice, we *must* devise a strong political will grounded in and directed by a steadfast commitment to ensure that the radical injustice of the past is not allowed to shape the present or re-emerge in the future.

In this context, then, it is understandable that the memory of radical injustice should always trigger a warning to people that, unless they act decisively against the past tendencies of radical injustice from re-appearing today, they – the tendencies that spawned radical injustice in the past – will in fact continue to work their way into the society. When this happens, the civic equality promised to all in the public sphere will be denied once again to blacks, even during a time, as today, when this view is said to be morally wrong and legally impermissible.

The poignant place of the memory of radical injustice – as something that continues to haunt us to this day – is evident in Toni Morrison's statement about her acclaimed novel, *Beloved*.[19] She speaks in her discussion of this novel about how slavery as an institution, though long gone, still plagues our society. In fact, there are many current issues that emanate from the past and haunt our lives today, most significantly the lives of black people. These are issues that suggest that the impact of the radical injustice of slavery remains alive – reaching out from the past and continuing to inflict severe damage on the lives of black people in the present – even though we know this situation is morally disgraceful. For instance, as we discuss more fully later, the mass incarceration of blacks has led to higher rates of imprisonment of blacks than for whites. Indeed, African Americans constitute 40 percent of those in prison, despite being around 13 percent of the US population.[20] Just as in the past – when blacks were disproportionately targeted for loss of their civic equality by the legal system – so it is the case that today blacks have been made subject to unequal treatment with respect to criminal justice policies. Thus, the radical injustice of the past reappears to install once again a racist tendency that works, unjustly, against the fortunes of blacks in the present and future.

But hasn't this tendency from the past been overturned by a recent bipartisan commitment to criminal justice reform? We have in mind the First Step Act, which is a major reform of the criminal justice system and which we discuss later in this chapter. But, as Michelle Alexander says, this new policy – which "benefits people of color subject to harsh and biased drug sentencing laws" – does not necessarily connote "major progress toward ending mass incarceration," given that, as she says, white nationalists have a large influence in our politics today.[21] And white nationalists seek to use this influence to advance the interests of white Americans, regardless of the cost to African Americans. Moreover, this perspective has been given strong support by President Trump, who Alexander says, "embraces the rhetoric and politics of white nationalism."[22] Alexander thus points out that we are in a difficult place as we discuss matters like mass incarceration "not because something radically different has occurred in our nation's politics, but because so much has remained the same."[23]

A major claim that can – and should, in our view – be inferred from Alexander's preceding statement is that past patterns of radical injustice toward blacks are often replicated in the present. We can end this practice only if we recognize it, and then after that, we must insist that it be terminated. In which case, if past tendencies against civic equality toward blacks are ever to be stopped from advancing into the present, it is necessary for people to share a "walk around civic memory" of a specific kind. Principally, this civic memory refers to those past moments of radical injustice that citizens have a moral obligation to remember. It is this memory that helps form among citizens the basis for a strong political will to prevent past moments of radical injustice from reemerging in society, and, through doing so, undermining the public sphere of a liberal democracy and its commitment to protect civic equality for all citizens.

Thus, the scenario Alexander described would be the foundation of warnings about the need – which is to say, the moral obligation – to be on the constant lookout for times when the radical injustice of the past continues to manifest itself in new ways in the present. Indeed, proponents of a political theory informed by the experience of race in American society would be prone to make warnings such as this within civil society. After the bulk of people in civil society took these warnings seriously, the public sphere could be made durable – and then it would ensure that civic equality is protected for all citizens. This is a regime dedicated to upholding the moral and constitutional principles discussed earlier – as well as a political discourse predicated on respect for differences and for facts and good reasoning.

V. Reconstruction, Jim Crow, and Memory

Now, the most painful memory embodied in a political theory based on the social reality of African Americans in this country is found in the relationship between the Reconstruction (1863–1877) and Jim Crow cultures (1877–1964). The former sought to stop the past existence of radical injustice created during slavery by establishing what Henry Louis Gates called a "biracial democracy" that extended to former slaves the protection of basic rights under the law.[24] This situation allowed blacks to move up the social ladder and to have prominent political roles. Gates says that, during this time, about "2000 black men served in office at every level of government, including two U.S. senators and twenty congressmen."[25]

Reconstruction politics – while taking major steps toward creating a public sphere of a liberal democracy that included blacks as full citizens – did not wholly achieve this goal because granting women the right to vote was not included in the Constitutional amendments of this era. What amendments do we have in mind? The 13th Amendment, in 1865, ended slavery. The 14th Amendment, in 1868, accorded "birthright" citizenship status to former slaves when it said that "all persons born or naturalized in the United States" are citizens of the United States. Additionally, the 14th Amendment prohibited former Confederate state governments from either "depriv[ing] any person of life, liberty, or property, without due process of law," or from "deny[ing] to any person within its jurisdiction [meaning the jurisdiction of US national government] the equal protection of the laws."

Finally, the 15th Amendment, in 1870, made possible equal voting rights for black males. Because the 15th Amendment did not include the right to vote for women of any color – a possibility that would materialize only with the 19th Amendment in 1920 – the public sphere during the Reconstruction – while making great strides in the direction of establishing a national government based on the moral and constitutional principles of a liberal democracy – did not, as of that time anyway, fully meet this goal.

But momentum to move in this direction was nonetheless advanced by various federal policies designed to help male freed slaves become full citizens. In this regard, the Freedman's Bureau was created in 1865. This agency – which was funded and maintained by the federal government – sought to provide former slaves (as well as poor whites) with help in matters pertaining to education, health care, contracts, various legal matters, and in securing land ownership, which was often difficult to achieve. All of this, as Gates says, allowed blacks to exercise "their right to marry and [to navigate] the transition to the contract-based free labor system."[26] In this environment, blacks succeeded in starting businesses, churches, and schools. Additionally, blacks developed their own art and literature to, as Gates says, "express the African-American experience . . . [an experience] that bonded them to generations of their ancestors for whom freedom was, in the words of Langston Hughes, the ultimate 'dream deferred.'"[27]

To support this endeavor, the federal government established five military districts in the South. These troops were used to protect the rights of black citizens, most especially against whites who resisted the 14th Amendment guarantee of the "equal protection of the laws" for blacks. Further, former Confederate states were required to establish constitutional conventions to write and pass new constitutions that accorded voting rights to black men.[28] Finally, the national government required the state governments of the South to ratify their support for the 14th Amendment.[29]

But so powerful were the tendencies of the (pre–Civil War) past against this vision of society that Reconstruction politics was overturned, and consequently, federal troops were removed from the South in 1877 as part of a deal for Rutherford B. Hayes to gain the presidency. Originally, as indicated earlier, these troops were there to protect black rights, but after they were forced to leave, no one was left to perform this essential function; thus, there was no federal – which is to say, national – government to prevent whites from totally denying civic equality to blacks in the South.[30]

And that moment of radical injustice – which was the centerpiece of what came to be called Jim Crow culture – was used to perpetuate a slave-like (and rights-denying) system of cheap black labor for the exclusive benefit of white landowners raising cotton in the South. As Gates says, cotton was a main source of economic prosperity in the South for many white landowners, and these planters needed cheap black labor to harvest cotton and prepare it for market. To this end, blacks were turned from slaves into sharecroppers.[31] As sharecroppers, blacks during the Jim Crow period rented land from the white landowners. Blacks then had to repay the owners for any costs that ensued. Because of this system, blacks were placed in a situation where their debt loads were so heavy, they had no recourse but to work under the continued domination of a white landowner class, just as in they had during slavery.[32]

In contrast, despite the "presence of anti-black racism in the North," says Gates, it is still the case that "many white Northerners" extended "legal and political equality [to blacks] as very few in the South were."[33] This included, in "a few Northern states, the [the extension of the] right to vote" to blacks."[34] Nonetheless, blacks in the North often were – because of anti-black white racism – relegated to live in segregated settings in the cities with many fewer public resources and opportunities than were provided to whites. To be sure, in the North, blacks were able to form – within major Northern cities – voting blocs from whom white politicians sought support in exchange for benefits that were helpful to blacks. This new circumstance for blacks helped to propel black migration from the South to the North on behalf of the search for better living conditions and jobs, as well as the chance for political power that could not be obtained in the South.[35] But black gains in political power in Northern cities never were of sufficient strength to offset the barriers to equality in rights and opportunities emanating from the prevalent racism there.

In this setting, whereas in the North during the Jim Crow period many whites supported civic equality for blacks in a legal sense, still, in a practical sense, because of white racist views aimed toward blacks, the latter's opportunity for achieving full civic equality with whites was very much constrained; the abject consequences of which we still struggle with today.[36] At the same time, during this period, Southern racism motivated many whites to manifest open contempt for blacks being granted civic equality. And overturning the consequences of this experience for black civic equality remains with us today as well.

In consequence, due to the strength of Jim Crow culture in both regions, the gains made on behalf of black civic equality during the Reconstruction were short lived. Nowhere was this more graphically displayed than in the South, where the Ku Klux Klan (KKK) maintained a regime of terror against anyone – white or black – advocating for black equality. The Klan was a general symbol for the commitment by whites throughout the South to draw lines of exclusion that blacks had to observe, lest they be treated with horrible violence. Thus, the Klan, as a stand-in for all of white society in the South, sought to use the fear they provoked in blacks and whites by their many acts of terror to ensure that southern society would remain segregated and that blacks – in the name of racist stereotypes – would never achieve civic equality with whites. To this end, various white terrorist tactics were employed, including the burning down of black homes and churches, lynchings, whippings, and other forms of public torture. The hope was to "convince" blacks, through terrorism, not to seek their full rights as citizens, rights that were guaranteed to them under the law.[37] Of special significance in this regard were white supremacists' successful efforts to use violence to prevent blacks from voting, thus ensuring that they would have no political power by which to protect their rights as citizens. It is in line with this perspective that whites invented many means, like literacy tests, to deny blacks the right to vote.

These actions were given legitimacy in the public sphere of the national government when blacks were legally denied civic equality under the separate-but-equal doctrine of *Plessy v. Ferguson* in 1896. This ruling reprised the vision of society that made blacks permanent outsiders and thus always subject to white racist attitudes that would deny blacks the hope of achieving civic equality with whites at any time in the future.[38] Despite the effort to achieve civic equality for all within a liberal democratic public sphere during the Reconstruction period, the tendencies of the pre–Civil War past that sought to avert this achievement became front-and-center influences in shaping the social and political norms throughout the Jim Crow period.

Moreover, the influence of Jim Crow thinking has not entirely died out in our times, despite the efforts of the modern civil rights movement – spanning the 1950s and 60s through to the present day – to end it. One of the main pieces of evidence for this view arises from the perception held by many blacks and whites that, too often, basic levels of security so necessary to making good use of the benefits of civic equality are regularly denied to African Americans. Specifically, we have in mind a spate of graphic videos that show unarmed African American citizens shot dead by police (or by white citizens taking the law into their own hands) in cities across the country. To many people, these shootings symbolize that black lives do not matter as much as white lives do.[39] This perception is reinforced by the phenomenon of mass incarceration, previously mentioned and discussed further in a subsequent section.

Or, as another example to show that Jim Crow still lives, take the issues of income and wealth disparities between blacks and whites. The medium household income rose for whites from $48,000 to $65,000 over the past 50 years, and, during that same time, from $28,000 to $40,000 for blacks. Moreover, the median household wealth during this period rose from $48,000 to $171,000 for whites and only from $2,000 to $17,000 for blacks. Further, the homeowner rate difference is telling as well: for whites, over the past 50 years, this rate rose from 66 percent to 71 percent, and for blacks, it stayed the same at 41 percent. Finally, the unemployment rate between the two groups rose during this period, from 3.2 percent to 3.6 percent for whites and from 6.7 percent to 7.5 percent for blacks.[40]

Or as further evidence of the radical injustice of the past locating itself in the present, take the issue of housing segregation in which blacks, through federal government–sanctioned policies like "redlining" and "restrictive covenants," were kept out of white suburbs and white areas in large cities and instead forced to live in low-income ghettos. Though these practices have been outlawed for many years, especially with the passage of the Fair Housing Act of 1970, the effects of racially discriminatory housing practices continue to negatively impact the fortunes of blacks. Consequently, blacks still lag behind whites in access to opportunities that are common in white neighborhoods, such as public goods like high-quality education, proximity to middle-class-income-paying jobs, and chances to build wealth through home equity increases. Moreover, racial disparities in the lending practices of banks in metro areas persist, much to the detriment of communities of color.[41] This situation is another clear manifestation of the way the history of separate-but-equal Jim Crow–style cultural politics continues to dish out drastic consequences for blacks.

Or, along these same lines, take the long history of voter suppression during the Jim Crow period with its poll taxes, literacy tests, and blatant intimidation that included discouraging blacks from voting through the threat of violence. Currently, there are efforts in various states to discourage blacks from voting but using different means from those employed during Jim Crow. For instance, during the 2018 election, the Secretary of State's office in Georgia purged voters from the eligible voters list for not voting in previous elections, and of the 53,000 residents purged, 70 percent were African American.[42] Alternately, voter ID laws that require photo identification to vote have reduced voter turnout according to the US Government Accountability Office by two to three percent. This happens, says the American Civil Liberties Union (ACLU), because IDs are an overly heavy financial burden to many individuals, and even when provided without cost, there are other expenses applicants must absorb to get their voter ID cards. For many individuals, these expenses make voting too expensive.[43] Or felony disenfranchisement laws in some states keep people from voting, and since there is racial bias in the criminal justice system, as we have pointed out earlier and will discuss further later, such laws disproportionately affect people from communities of color.[44] Many consider these devices as designed to reduce black voter turnout, just as was done in the Jim Crow past. In response, those who advocate these measures say that, without them, there will be many fraudulent votes. But this view is contradicted by a recent study from the Brennan Center for Justice, which says that in "elections that had been meticulously studied for voter fraud" the rate of voter fraud is between 0.0003 percent and 0.0025 percent.[45]

Had the liberal democratic public sphere been fully established throughout both the North and South – which was the hope of the Reconstruction – then Jim Crow culture and politics would never have arisen. Moreover, the Jim Crow manifestations of radical injustice of the type referenced in the previous four paragraphs would not have reappeared in our politics today.

Instead, a liberal democratic public sphere would have sought to secure its moral and constitutional principles – as well as the institutions that embrace them – on behalf of defining the shared, public good (as articulated by the majority) on a host of issues but only in the context of the full protection of civic equality for each individual, regardless of racial background. The political setting that achieves this goal includes – as mentioned earlier – political institutions that share power across the main branches of government, as well as a view of basic rights for the national government to protect for all citizens. Included in this case are the rights we have labeled as critical to securing a liberal democratic public sphere, including the rights of voting, speech, conscience, press freedom, and the chance to protest, non-violently, government policies and laws with which one disagrees. Without these rights – again, as argued earlier – all the other rights that are accorded individuals would be difficult to secure.

But, in addition to these dimensions, to achieve the objectives of a liberal democratic public sphere, citizens must guard against the return of historically grounded tendencies whose main purpose in an earlier time was to deny to some the civic equality that should have been accorded to everyone, regardless of skin color. And, this watchfulness is enshrined in the memory of radical injustice, especially the memory that makes clear that the return of Jim Crow must be a constant concern for citizens so that when any hint of its restoration is seen, it is stopped in its tracks and never re-authorized. This surely is the message of the civil rights movement that sought to end Jim Crow (especially as we recount that political movement in a later section on Martin Luther King Jr.'s "Letter from a Birmingham Jail"). And incorporated in this movement is the memory of what Jim Crow stood for and did (in both the North and the South), as the basis for ensuring that they are never allowed to re-appear in the present and become the basis for future forms of racist-based discrimination.

A successful argument for this view in civil society is a key way to establish this position within the public sphere of a liberal democracy. Then this perspective can become a fixture of the national government, which is to say, a main political norm that all citizens should respect, just as they respect – as pointed out earlier – symbols in the public sphere like the Declaration of Independence and the US Constitution. The latter two elements signify the commitment to secure equal rights for all within the framework of majority-rule governance. But the memory of radical injustice toward blacks cautions people that these ideals can be undermined and the tendencies from the past that advance radical injustice into the present may well replace them. The memory of radical injustice thus makes this admonition clear and, in response to it, people are put on notice that they must always approach shared issues in ways that advance a political will to resist radical injustice, lest the equal rights for all doctrine – symbolized by the Constitution and the Declaration of Independence – is seriously threatened, if not undermined completely.

And in achieving broad acceptance for this position in civil society, it is likely that the discourse of mutual respect of civil society could then be preserved as a normative standard against which to assess the quality of all political discourses, either in civil society or the public sphere. Now, partisanship would certainly continue in the public sphere but at much lower decibels than is common in a politics fueled by resentment. In consequence, not only are the moral and constitutional principles of a liberal democratic public sphere fostered, but so too is the hope of finding – through discussion among people of diverse views – the common good on many issues of shared importance to society.

The case for this position is given centrality of place in civil society by proponents of a political theory – located in the African American experience – that is found in whole or in part within various writers discussed here, including Frederick Douglass, W.E.B. Du Bois, Martin Luther King Jr., Michelle Alexander, Ta-Nehisi Coates, Ibram X. Kendi, John Lewis, and Cornel West.

We turn, in this regard, first to Frederick Douglass.

VI. Frederick Douglass, Radical Injustice, and Civil Society

It is Frederick Douglass who makes clear that the quest to place the prohibition against slavery as a central canon in the public sphere requires winning the argument for this position, first, in the context of civil society. But winning the argument in civil society necessitates gaining support from citizens there for giving a central place in civic life to the memory of radical injustice toward blacks, in the hopes of making clear that what happened in the past to deny blacks civic equality is forever prevented from returning to the societal mainstream.

Douglass approaches this task from the standpoint of having been a slave himself. He escaped to freedom and afterwards became the leading abolitionist voice against slavery not just for his age, but also for the ages. Now, in advancing the argument against slavery in civil society, Douglass said that slavery violates the Enlightenment-based idea that all people by virtue of being human beings – whether black or white – are to be accorded natural rights that no one is ever authorized to take from them.[46] Moreover, this view is always contained within authentic religion, too. Thus, in a speech delivered on July 5, 1852, in Corinthian Hall to the Rochester, New York, Ladies' Anti-Slavery Society, Douglass makes the case for building a citizen's movement to abolish slavery by demonstrating the way in which these two traditions reinforce each other.[47] Here, the point is clear: what the Bible commands of us is nothing short of what Enlightenment reason – as embodied for Douglass in the US Constitution – requires as well.[48] Both obligate us to upholding the natural rights of each person and thus to ending slavery.

David Blight calls the Corinthian Hall speech "nothing less than the rhetorical masterpiece of American abolitionism," and in keeping with this view, we provide some discussion of it in what follows.[49]

Who is Douglass's audience in the Corinthian Hall speech? He says his audience is not, as Blight says, "pro-slaveholder ideologues."[50] After all, Douglass "loved," Blight says, the Declaration of Independence and its Enlightenment-based natural-rights foundation.[51] In accordance with this doctrine, as we have just seen, all people by virtue of being human have these rights.[52] But, slaveholders do not believe that blacks are human, and it is unlikely that they will budge from this view. For Douglass, then, the question, as Blight says, is why "must he prove that the slave is human?"[53] Trying to convince slaveholders of this view is a waste of breath. Douglass, in this spirit, says in the speech, "What point in the antislavery creed would you have me argue?"[54]

For Douglass, the US Constitution and the Bible make clear that "the time for argument [with slaveholders] is passed."[55] Both documents, as just stated, reject the enslavement of blacks on behalf of the natural-rights-for-all-people argument. In saying this, Douglass also recognizes that he does not have to make the case for natural rights to people who already support this view, which is to say, the people to whom he is directly appealing in the Corinthian Hall speech. What he wants to do, instead, is to entice them to action against slavery by awakening in them a sentiment of justice (discussed more fully, later) that moves them to object strenuously to their becoming complacent in the face of this great evil. So, he says that the American public discourse now demands "scorching irony," which reflects a mode of discourse designed to arouse the consciences of those listening to him on behalf of encouraging his listeners to take action against slavery.[56]

In this context, then, Blight says that Douglass "had not come to Corinthian Hall for polite discourse."[57] People – especially those for whom the natural-rights-for-all doctrine is a principle of the highest importance – must be encouraged, which to say, compelled to do what is necessary to end slavery. Thus, he says,

> *O! had I the ability, and could I reach the nation's ear, I would today pour out a fiery stream of biting ridicule, blasting reproach, withering sarcasm, and stern rebuke. For it is not the light that is needed, but fire; it is not the gentle shower, but thunder. We need the storm, the whirlwind, and the earthquake. The feeling of the nation must be quickened . . . the hypocrisy of the nation must be exposed.*[58]

There is hypocrisy because the US Constitution does, in Douglass's view, support the idea of natural rights for all, but the practice of slavery undermines that constitutional principle. Douglass, Adam Gopnik says, did not agree, then, with William Lloyd Garrison – the leading white proponent of the abolition of slavery – that the "Constitution was so deeply implicated in slavery . . . that it could not be salvaged."[59] Rather, for Douglass, the Constitution was, says Gopnik, "a good document gone wrong," a fact perpetrated on the nation by the misdeeds of so many of its founders.[60] In his Corinthian Hall speech, Douglass says of the Constitution the following: "interpreted as it ought to be interpreted, the

Constitution is a GLORIOUS LIBERTY DOCUMENT. Read its preamble, consider its purposes. Is slavery among them? Is it at the gate-way? Or is it in the temple? It is neither."[61]

Now, for Douglass, all means necessary to end slavery and achieve liberty for blacks in keeping with the Constitution's guarantees of liberty for all should be considered. One approach sanctioned violence. Adam Gopnik says that Douglass "can readily be seen as the father of the most militant strain of resistance" to racism and to its most virulent manifestations of evil in the form of slavery.[62] As such, Douglass "believed in violent rebellion . . . when the face of racism became intolerable."[63] To this end, Douglass said – at a meeting in 1860 to advance free speech and to commemorate John Brown who had sought to instigate a revolt against slavery by raiding a federal arsenal in 1859 at Harpers Ferry – that "all methods of proceeding against slavery" should be employed, and this means supporting even the "John Brown way."[64]

But at the same time, Douglass always worked as a pragmatic politician supporting Lincoln in his efforts to end slavery and prodding him to move faster and further along these lines. In taking this view, he was like, says Gopnik, a "conventional party politician, a pillar of the Republican Party [the party of Lincoln]."[65] In this role, he worked with an "assemblage of minorities and progressives and city people . . . gathered in one baggy grouping, not too unlike what we find in the Democratic Party today."[66]

Douglass's approaches reflect both polarities: the fire of violence and the calming impact of politically constructive conversation within the context of civil society. In either approach, he pushed for a public agitated enough by the presence of slavery to take a stand against it. Unless people were strongly committed to act on this vision, the old world would forever undermine the new one that professed equal liberty and that was actually, for Douglass, embedded, once again, in the US Constitution. In this context, then, either through pragmatic politics or the threat of violence, Douglass sought to win the argument against slavery in civil society and through doing so to ensconce into the public sphere of a liberal democracy a dedicated commitment to protecting the civic equality of blacks.

Furthermore, to achieve widespread acceptance for the argument in civil society for civic equality, Douglass wanted to inspire – among decent human beings watching others living in the oppressive condition of slavery – a sense of deep moral revulsion, which is to say, a visceral feeling of disgust from which one can never be freed, so long as slavery continues to exist. For Douglass, the way to engender this disgust requires that white people confront their history and to read from it the fact that the founders departed from their own principles of liberty for all to ensure that there would be no liberty for blacks.

This fact is recorded, says Gopnik – referring to Douglass's address to whites in the Corinthian Hall speech – in "*your* history."[67] And Douglass is commanding his audience to *remember this history*. The latter consists of high moral values that, if applied to blacks, would have assured them civic equality. But just the opposite happened. Thus, Douglass says that "the existence of slavery in this country brands your republicanism as a sham, your humanity as a base pretense, and your Christianity as a lie."[68] Both Christianity and republicanism have supported liberty for all, in principle, but each ends up denying it to some for the sake of maintaining the vile institution of slavery. This history – the history that whites are commanded to remember – depicts the essence of what we define as radical injustice toward blacks. And, in being commanded to remember this history, whites are told that they must do so as a matter of moral obligation.

Following this course of conduct has two important consequences. In the first place, this memory will bring moral clarity as to the nature of the repulsive evil that must be ended. And, in the second place, as this memory accomplishes this purpose, it will also inspire – indeed, it will compel people to have – a political will dedicated to resist radical injustice, today and in the future.

Now, the memory of white radical injustice against blacks is – all too often – encapsulated in the words of white supremacists, as was the case with a writer against whom Douglass reacted when the writer said, in 1854, that "liberty is good for white men, but not for negroes."[69] Douglass called the political will emanating from the memory of radical injustice such as triggered in this statement, a "sentiment of justice." As cited by Henry Louis Gates, Douglass says:

> *If the negro has the same right to his liberty and pursuit of his own happiness that the White man has, [which the natural rights doctrines makes clear is demonstrably true] then we commit the greatest wrong and robbery to him a slave – an act at which the sentiment of justice must revolt in every heart – and negro slavery is an institution which that sentiment must sooner or later blot from the face of the earth.*[70]

Seen through the eyes of a sentiment of justice (or a steadfast political will to resist radical injustice), whites would find themselves in a position where they could never normalize slavery or desensitize themselves to its existence. No, they would have to react with loathing at the very sight of such an institution, and what would ensure that they did is a sentiment of justice lodged deeply inside their consciences.

But this sentiment arises, once again, only from a memory of radical injustice, which is to say, it comes from the recognition that, in history, republican idealism and Christian piety have been misused to support grave injustices. In this regard, Blight says that Douglass hoped to make his audience "feel, see, and hear" – with "aggressive language" – what Douglass called the "revolting barbarity" of slavery.[71] By using aggressive language in this way, he sought to enshrine the memory of radical injustice to blacks into the minds of his audience and, furthermore, by doing so, he hoped to arouse in his audience a continuing sentiment of justice or a political will that embraces this sentiment to resist slavery, racism, and the institutional and political corruption that embraces them.

To this end, Blight says that Douglass, in the Corinthian Hall speech, focused audience attention on what Douglass calls the "human flesh-jobbers" who run the markets for slaves. Douglass sought through his words to get his audience to hear the slaves' "savage yells and . . . blood-chilling oaths . . . the fetters clank . . . and the crack . . . sound of the slave-whip." Douglass wanted his audience to envision the mothers of children brought here as slaves and witness their "briny tears falling on the brow of the babe in her arms." Douglass thus compelled his audience to "attend the auction" and look at the "shocking gaze of American slave-buyers."[72]

In effect, Douglass forced the public to witness what was commonplace in an effort to expose the misery and terror of slavery.[73] And, as Blight said, no one could make clear the terror of slavery like Douglass could, and this is because he was informed by his own memories of having been a slave himself and of having to hear the "rattle of chains and the heart-rendering cries" from the long lines of slaves marched toward their plunge into the worst misery imaginable.[74]

Slavery is a violation of everything good and decent; everything housed in the conscience of every human being guided by a sentiment of justice. And it is on behalf of perpetuating this sentiment of justice across society to end slavery that we must – as a matter of a moral obligation – remember all of the humanity-denying realities of slavery (as Douglass describes them) and make them part of our shared civic memory.

In this, the past is a useful guide to the future. As Blight says, Douglass sought a "usable past," or a past that can be consulted to show us the best way to a prosperous future, one in which liberty abounds for all.[75] Thus, Douglass says in a speech given in the 1880s:

> *It is not well to forget the past. Memory was given to man for some wise purpose. The past is . . . the mirror by which we may discern the dim outlines of the future and by which we may make them more symmetrical.*[76]

Memory makes clear the radically unjust tendencies of the past that may well continue into the present and future, unless there is a strong political will – or sentiment of justice – to ensure that the past instances of radical injustice are killed for good.

Coincident with this view, Douglass, says Blight, wrote much about the "fight over the memory of the [Civil] war" so much so that "some critics accused him of living in the past."[77] But Douglass would never allow anyone to forget the significance of that war. He knew that if they did, then the past would be nothing but prologue for the continued denial of freedom for blacks. To counter this reprehensible possibility, Douglass, according to Blight, "would not forgive the South and he would never forget the meaning of the war as he saw it."[78] This memory of what the Southern way of life meant for blacks is best captured in a narrative – modeled on the Exodus story in the Bible – in which what is described is the long march, under God's authority, from tyranny in the South to freedom in a new world that respected the dignity of all people.[79] Blight comments that "for black Americans, Exodus is always contemporary, history always past and present."[80]

Douglass, in advancing this vision, became with Abraham Lincoln, says Blight, the two "voices of the Second American Revolution."[81] In consequence, the Lincoln Memorial in Washington, DC has become a major symbol – in addition to the US Constitution and the Declaration of Independence – of the public sphere's commitment to securing civic equality for blacks, or for anyone else for that matter. This powerful symbol in our view also makes clear – as Douglass would certainly want – that, to achieve this goal, it is of grave importance that no one ever again normalizes the return of the radical injustice of the past.

But there are so many forces afoot that make the normalization of radical injustice normal. And the chief culprit among them is (racial) prejudice. If the latter is not squelched, the normalization of the denial of natural rights will be accepted as a fact of life, justifying not only the past acceptance of the loss of these rights but their denial moving forward into the future as well. So he calls prejudice out as the tentacle with a long reach that advances radical injustice – in different forms, perhaps, from the past – into the present. He says, "The feeling (or whatever it is) which we call prejudice is no less than a *murderous hell-born hatred* of every virtue which may adorn the character of a black man."[82]

By understanding – as the moral obligation to remember radical injustice teaches – the many ways that past manifestations of radical injustice can perpetuate themselves into the present, especially through racial prejudice, we can mount an inspired political will – or a sentiment of justice – to resist this prospect. Winning the argument for this view in civil society – as was Douglass's hope – is the key factor in achieving the moral and constitutional principles that are central to realizing civic equality for blacks and for all others within the public sphere of a liberal democracy.

VII. W.E.B Du Bois, Booker T. Washington, and Memory

A subscriber to the memory of radical injustice would understand the warnings ensconced in this memory against the return of past forms of radical injustice. Jim Crow is a perfect example of a society failing to heed these warnings. And the consequence was severe: the restoration of pre–Civil War modes of radical injustice that were designed to forever deny in the public sphere – even after slavery ended – civic equality for blacks.

This circumstance was captured in the separate-but-equal doctrine described earlier. Separate but equal meant nothing more than the embodiment in the public sphere of the notion that blacks would never be accorded civic equality. To counter this view, and thus to return civic equality to blacks as experienced during the Reconstruction, it was once again necessary to win the argument for this position in civil society. After this job had been achieved in civil society, the way would be clear to establish a public sphere, a public sphere that in its embrace of discussions on behalf of defining the common good of the majority always works at the same time to protect the civic equality of all citizens, including blacks.

The writers we discuss in this section and the next are heavily involved in this endeavor. First, in this section, we discuss W.E.B. Du Bois, whose writings dominated the pursuit of justice for communities of color in the early twentieth century. And in the next section, we discuss Martin Luther King Jr., who similarly dominated the quest for justice for this group in the mid-twentieth century.

Du Bois says in his classic 1903 book, *The Souls of Black Folk*, that the "problem of the twentieth century is the problem of the color-line, – the relation of the darker to the lighter races of men in Asia and Africa, in America and the islands of the sea."[83] In taking this view, Du Bois implies that the memory of radical injustice is a constant fixture in the lives of blacks. Moreover, as long as that memory remains with blacks, the demand for blacks will always be the same: the provision and protection of the natural rights (which we refer to as civic equality) long denied them while, at the same time, long secured for others. Du Bois says:

> *by every civilized and peaceful method we must strive for the rights which the world accords to men, clinging unwaveringly to those great words which the sons of the Fathers would fain forget: "We hold these truths to be self-evident: That all men are created equal; that they are endowed by their Creator with certain inalienable rights, that among these are life, liberty, and the pursuit of happiness."*[84]

But during Du Bois's time, Jim Crow culture is dominant, and, as a result, liberty is totally and thoroughly denied to blacks. In this situation, a black person is always placed in a position where others, which is to say, white people, determine a black person's course in life. In this regard, Du Bois talks about a "double-consciousness," or a

> *sense of always looking at one's self through the eyes of others, of measuring one's soul by the rape of the world that looks on in amused contempt and pity. One even feels his two-ness, – an American, a Negro; two souls, two thoughts, two unrecognized strivings; two warring ideals in one dark body, whose dogged strength alone keeps it from being torn asunder.*[85]

Because of the social reality of double-consciousness, then, blacks are denied the most important fruit of liberty, which is the chance for autonomy. The latter enables people to form their own judgments and to make their own choices about matters of vital importance to their lives, like who to marry or befriend, what career to pursue, or what political and religious beliefs (if any) to hold.

Thus, where double-consciousness is preeminent for blacks, norms will remain in place that ignore the civic obligations that all citizens owe to blacks, considering a liberal democracy's penchant to accord each person their autonomy. This great achievement is possible only when the government ensures each person – regardless of color – equal liberty under the law.

And here is where memory of radical injustice toward blacks is so important. Unless that memory can become part of a civic memory that is shared by blacks and whites, there will be a weak commitment in the public sphere to secure blacks the autonomy that belongs to them as it belongs to all others.[86] Worse still is that when there is an active policy of forgetting radical injustice toward blacks, the past realities of radical injustice – as found in Jim Crow culture – will be given a green light to dominate the lives of blacks in the present and future. It is precisely this situation – the willingness to tolerate the forgetting of radical injustice toward blacks in the public sphere after the Civil War – that led to the creation of the systematic denial of rights to blacks during the Jim Crow South, which, as we discussed earlier, overturned the hopes of the Reconstruction for a biracial democracy.

So, for Du Bois, the question is if forgetting is to be allowed to overtake remembering.

This question permeates the conflict between Du Bois and Booker T. Washington. Washington was willing to put up with the injustices of Jim Crow on behalf of seeking for blacks the means to make a living by being provided with vocational educational opportunities. By following this course, what Washington was in fact doing from the standpoint of Du Bois was to invoke a policy of willful forgetting of Jim Crow radical injustice against blacks. It is in this context, then, that Du Bois calls out for extreme criticism of Washington's acceptance of the "old attitude of adjustment and submission [to Jim Crow-based racism] . . ."[87] By upholding this attitude, Washington showed that he would trade away – in the tradition of Jim Crow – not only political power for blacks but also civic equality for blacks as well as opportunities for higher education.[88] The latter type of education extends well beyond vocational training (or what Du Bois called "industrial education") so that people are able to transcend "the gospel of Work and Money" and move, instead, to "the higher aims of life [which certainly includes autonomy]."[89] For Du Bois, then, Washington "counsels a silent submission to civic inferiority such as is bound to sap the manhood of any race in the long run."[90]

In contrast, for Du Bois, whereas industrial education is necessary to provide many people with the work needed to support themselves and their families and to accumulate wealth, without higher education, blacks will not acquire political power. In which case, they will not be able to participate as full citizens in framing the public policy and laws of society. And their lives will then be forever divided and truncated by a double-consciousness that makes it impossible for them to attain their highest hopes and aspirations, which is the full autonomy that comes with liberty. For Du Bois, then, it is a mistake to deprecate "institutions of higher learning," as, in Du Bois's view, Washington does constantly.[91]

All of this makes the memory of radical injustice a central moral obligation of Du Bois's time, and he would hope for ours, as well. But in the midst, as Washington does, of forgetting radical injustice to blacks, the moral obligation to remember that injustice is overturned, and then the political will to resist the radical injustice that is described in this memory is lost as well. Here, black citizens would be asked – if not commanded – to acquiesce to the absence of civic equality for themselves, even as it is provided to whites.

This is the lesson gleaned from the actions of Booker T. Washington – at least as seen through the eyes of Du Bois – and it is a major teaching of a political theory that incorporates this experience. With Washington's approach to blacks in civil society firmly in place, we have become so prone to normalize an absence of justice to blacks that we end up legitimating the continuing place of this corrosive doctrine in the public sphere.

Du Bois seeks to counter Washington's view by making the memory of radical injustice a fundamental part of the public sphere. With this memory, then, blacks and sympathetic whites would recognize the need to stop the past tendencies of radical injustice – and its incumbent denial of civic equality for blacks – from being a continual reality shaping the public sphere. But to get to this place, the argument for this memory – as the basis for a political will to prevent the Jim Crow past from constantly undermining the public sphere – must be fully accepted in civil society.

Du Bois contributed much to this endeavor as a co-founder of the National Association for the Advancement of Colored People (NAACP) in 1909, wherein from 1910 to 1934 he was a member of the board of directors.[92] As such, he was part of an organization that, in civil society, insisted on equal rights for blacks in all areas of life, in the hope of eclipsing double-consciousness and replacing it with full autonomy for blacks. The argument Du Bois advanced in civil society on behalf of this goal made great headway through the actions of subsequent leaders of the NAACP. This happened, most notably, when the NAACP in 1954 brought the *Brown v. Board of Education of Topeka* case to the US Supreme Court. The Court found in favor of Brown and the NAACP when it ruled that segregation in public schools is illegal. This ruling overturned for good the aforementioned separate-but-equal doctrine in *Plessy v. Ferguson* and replaced it with the vision of a civil society dedicated to the integration of all citizens – regardless of background or color – into all institutions of American society.[93]

In consequence, the public sphere now had to embody – as one of its core moral and constitutional principles – civic equality under law for all citizens, including, in this case, African Americans. Thus, though during his time Du Bois did not fully win the argument in civil society for thoroughly eliminating legalized segregation, he set the stage for this achievement and, in the process, helped restore the Reconstruction-era liberal democratic public sphere lost to Jim Crow.

VIII. Martin Luther King Jr. and the Civil Rights Movement

Martin Luther King Jr. carried on this cause by way of his leadership of the civil rights movement in the late 1950s through the mid-1960s. His approach to this quest is summed up best in his "Letter from a Birmingham Jail." There, he seeks to nurture the previously mentioned sentiment of justice Douglass described. King's intention in so doing is to encourage people in civil society to act against all efforts to normalize radical injustice, which, in this case, is defined as Jim Crow–style segregation. Yet, the fact of the matter is that the Jim Crow laws and culture that King sought to end by leading a public demonstration against segregation in Birmingham, Alabama, in 1963 had been normalized not just by the diehard believers in segregation but also by many people who opposed it. The latter group represents those who, while against segregation (and presumably for civic equality for all), have nonetheless taken the view that the circumstances protecting it are simply too strong and encompassing to be reversed in the immediate future without encouraging social instability.

But King has no truck with this accommodationist approach, akin to Washington's view. So, he demands that the normalizers – those who wish to accommodate themselves to segregation but who nonetheless disagree with segregation in principle – help him create the social and political whirlwind that will bring an end to the reign of Jim Crow.

Now, in challenging the normalizers, King's letter is, in large part, a response to local white pastors who think his call for public protests, including civil disobedience to unjust laws, is mistaken. The pastors – whom he also refers to as white moderates – are worried that King will create social instability by seeking change through public demonstrations that directly confront the authority of those maintaining the laws of a segregated society.[94]

But for King, the argument for civic equality must be won on the streets of Birmingham through non-violent, civil disobedience. This is the only way to gain concessions from the white power structure on behalf of removing the many facets of Jim Crow's separate-but-equal doctrine, which serve only to continue to make blacks second-class citizens in their own country. In King's view, winning this argument in civil society – as a prelude to ensconcing civic equality for all in the public sphere – is a difficult undertaking. And this is because the pastors' call to slow down and not cause massive disruption as a result of public protests is nothing more than a sign of acquiescence to segregation. For King, then, the pastors – by asking him to not get involved in direct public protest, including non-violent, civil disobedience to upend unjust laws – are in fact likely to perpetuate the radical injustice that originated in the past well into the present and future.

In which case, the pastors are giving up on any attempt to make the case in civil society to end radical injustice, and then the public sphere will never be built in a strong enough way as to secure blacks their civic equality under the law. It is better, in King's view, not to accommodate the evil of Jim Crow in any way, lest people become so desensitized to it that they bolster radical injustice against blacks in the form of a segregated vision of society that always had and always will – if allowed to continue – deny blacks justice.

King is thus addressing his critics – once again, fellow pastors – who are telling him that, in pressing for more public demonstrations, he is likely to do more harm than good. But King has a ready answer to this claim. He says that waiting "340 years for our constitutional and God given rights" is enough time.[95] King, in fact – like all blacks and many whites – is tired of waiting. To wait any longer is to follow a course of accommodation – of acceptance of a moral wrong – even as those who pursue this course agree that that moral wrong needs to be ended. King says, in response, "Perhaps it is easy for those who have never felt the stinging darts of segregation to say, 'Wait.'"[96]

It is as though King's critics are telling him to wait patiently, and eventually the radical injustice of segregation will disappear by its own accord. But waiting patiently in this manner offers no hope to people who have seen their families murdered by racist mobs, who have seen police mistreatment on a regular and savage basis, and who experience their lives mired in poverty despite the fact, as King says, American society is affluent. Waiting does not even allow for the simplest of pleasures, like being able to go to an amusement park, which black children are prevented from doing because of the racist practice of segregation.[97] And these misfortunes are inflicted on a people merely because of the color of their skin.

Enough, then, is enough. King makes this point when he invokes – as we described in the previous two paragraphs – the memory of radical injustice. His intention is to clarify the nature of the tragedy brought on by Jim Crow, in the hope that by doing so, he can awaken peoples' sentiment of justice (or a political will that embodies this sentiment) on behalf of ending legalized segregation. Then, no decent-minded person will want to normalize the morally abnormal, but, instead, these people will work with him to eradicate it from society through public protest.

So, in the face of this injustice, King's call is for defying unjust laws that take away rights from blacks that belong to all people. And his approach to this goal comes by way of creating what King calls "constructive, nonviolent tension which is necessary for growth."[98] Through this process, people confront their own prejudices and bigotry and are, thus, challenged to show how they can be morally justified in the face of the radical injustice common to a segregated society that blacks must live with every day. King is confident that when individuals do this, they will conclude that change in the direction of justice for blacks must be undertaken here and now.

King's message, then, to white moderates – such as the pastors he is addressing – is that it is time to stop desensitizing people to the injustice all around them. People must see it in all its ugly facets to then be capable of asking how they may be contributing to it and what, in light of that question, they must do to stop perpetuating it. In this context, King says to the pastors that, whereas they are quick to condemn the demonstrations, they fail to take into consideration the many realities of Jim Crow–based segregation that have made the demonstrations necessary.[99]

There is good reason for whites to embrace King's message to the pastors. Actually, it is in the interest of whites not to do otherwise. Thus, King tells us that "injustice anywhere is a threat to justice everywhere."[100] To allow radical injustice – or the systematic denial of rights to all blacks, as was the case in the past and continued to be the case in Birmingham and in much of the South (as well as the country as a whole) during King's time – is to not just perpetuate injustice against blacks but potentially to inflict injustice against everyone. For the fact is – as we know from our own period – that unless the problem of race-based exclusion is resolved on behalf of securing everyone their civic equality, the problems that threaten social peace and justice will be experienced not just by blacks but by all members of society. This understanding, once adopted, would strengthen the political will – not just for blacks but for whites as well – that is dedicated to ending the radical injustice now manifest from the Jim Crow past in King's time, in the hope that it is never allowed back into society again.

In advocating this position in civil society, King embraces the rubric of being an "extremist for justice," similar in manner to many who came before him, including biblical figures.[101] As such, he expects that once the argument against segregation is accomplished in civil society through the campaign of non-violent civil disobedience, it – the argument to end segregation – can become a mainstay of the liberal democratic public sphere. In which case, all people – no matter what their racial background or status – would be ensured the freedom that the moral and constitutional principles of a liberal democratic state must protect.

IX. Mass Incarceration, Capitalism, and Reparations

Once again, a main objective of a political theory developed in relation to the American experience of blacks is to install in the public sphere – as a result of the successful argumentation in civil society – a moral obligation to remember radical injustice to people of color. By remembering radical injustice in this sense, individuals become dedicated to upholding a political will to ensure the past instances of radical injustice are never allowed to reappear in the public sphere – either in old or in new forms – and affect and even dominate the present and the future on behalf of denying civic equality to blacks.

Now, a political will motivated by the memory of radical injustice is manifested in various ways in the public sphere of a liberal democracy. In this section, we discuss several approaches to describing a political will that seeks, overall, to achieve civic equality for blacks and all others in the public sphere. But before going into more detailed discussions of each variant of the political will described here, in the first part of this section, we summarize them.

The first way to define the political will is that it is committed to making clear – and by making clear, eliminate – the implicit bias that people and whole cultures may maintain, unconsciously, with respect to their giving support to racist-based policies and laws. In fact, through the exposure in civil society of racially based implicit bias to public scrutiny, individuals can come to conclude that they have been acting unjustly to blacks without fully appreciating this fact and its coincident negative implications for furthering the quest for black civic equality. Once this understanding is both shared and accepted across civil society, the arguments won there on behalf of this undertaking can set the stage for a public sphere that works to recognize and then to exclude racially-tinged implicit bias. In consequence, the public sphere is better able to achieve civic equality for all citizens. This is one of the major intentions of Michelle Alexander in her book on the mass incarceration of blacks, *The New Jim Crow*, as we discuss later.

A second approach to defining the political will to prevent the radical injustice of the past from returning to society is to work on behalf of moderating capitalism and the consequent momentum it gives to racism. This argument – made by Ibram X. Kendi – is discussed in this section as well.

A third approach to defining the political will is contained in a policy of reparations for the massive, self-perpetuating harms to blacks from slavery and Jim Crow culture. These harms include, as we have already seen, large disparities (when compared to whites) in opportunities and protections of civic equality for blacks. Now, conversations about the feasibility and justness of reparations always bring to public awareness the question of how best to address a variety of practical challenges associated with ending these harms through a reparations policy. Indeed, there are many complex issues (as we describe them) that the call for reparations brings to mind within civil society. These issues at first appear so numerous and outsized that many people become discouraged from even entertaining a reparations policy. How can something as multifaceted as this matter ever be resolved to the satisfaction of most members of civil society? In which case, the argument for reparations in a civil society is unable to provide a basis for a consensus among all sectors of society. As a result of this failure to achieve agreement, what may also be lost is the ability of the public sphere to work on behalf of ensuring that the damage done to blacks through slavery and Jim Crow culture does not continue to manifest in the present.

In contrast, if there is, in a civil society, a strong political will – arising from the memory of radical injustice – to repair the damaging effects of slavery and Jim Crow culture on African Americans through a policy of reparations, the reparations question would not seem to be overly complicated and beyond the reach of individuals to address. In this setting, the public sphere would be able to foster a policy of reparations to blacks, a policy intent on fixing the damage that arises from the radical injustice of the past. Making the case for a political will in civil society that can achieve this outcome for the public sphere is ensconced in the writing on the topic of reparations by Ta-Nehisi Coates.

First, however, we discuss, in Alexander's work, the notion of implicit racial bias in relation to the mass incarceration of blacks, and this consideration is followed by a discussion of Kendi's take on capitalism, and Coates's views on reparations.

Democratic Party President Bill Clinton supported the Crime Bill of 1994 on behalf of taking the crime issue away from Republicans and, instead, making it a marquee issue for Democrats.[102] The Crime Bill of 1994, Alexander says, "created dozens of new federal capital crimes" and required "life sentences for some three-time offenders" and "authorized more than $16 billon for state prison grants and [the] expansion of state and local police forces."[103] And the result of this action was to inaugurate – as Alexander says, quoting the Justice Policy Institute – "the largest increases in federal and state prison inmates of any president in American history."[104] Clinton's get-tough-on-crime approach was further manifested, Alexander says, in 1996, when "the penal budget doubled the amount that had been allocated to AFDC [Aid to Families of Dependent Children] or food stamps."[105] He also supported policies that made it easier to exclude anyone from public housing who had a criminal history.[106] Alexander comments that this action was an "extraordinarily harsh step in the midst of a drug war aimed at racial and ethnic minorities."[107]

These factors – when taken together, as well as with others we do not name – contributed to an environment that created the mass incarceration of communities of color. To quote James Foreman, "blacks are much more likely than whites to be arrested, convicted, and incarcerated for drug offenses, even though blacks are no more likely than whites to use drugs."[108] Or, for the sake of clarity of perspective, it is worth pointing out as several writers on this subject recently do that "no other wealthy country puts as many people behind bars [than the United States] – and the prison population is disproportionately Black and Latino."[109]

Why did this happen? Mass incarceration happened because political leaders, like President Clinton, who supported the provisions that led to mass incarceration did so because these provisions were seen as race-neutral and, thus, as colorblind. In which case, unlike during the Jim Crow period, there was no intention of advancing a law that works to reinstitute a doctrine wholly intended to deny blacks civic equality. Indeed, in Alexander's view, for liberals like Clinton, a colorblind view tracks with the "dream of racial equality."[110] In a colorblind view, then, "race will be correlated with nothing; it will mean nothing; we won't even notice it anymore."[111]

But, for Alexander, colorblind policies often are grounded in implicit racial bias. What is implicit racial bias? Alexander says it reflects the following viewpoint:

> *you may honestly believe that you are not biased against African Americans, and you may even have black friends or relatives, [but these facts do] . . . not mean you are free from unconscious bias. Implicit bias tests*

may still show that you hold negative attitudes and stereotypes about blacks, even though you do not believe you do, and do not want to.[112]

And due to the implicit racial bias embodied in a colorblind approach, a race-neutral policy ended up instituting the mass incarceration of blacks.[113] In which case, blacks were treated by a different set of rules than what was applied to whites committing similar crimes.

Alexander makes clear that to recognize this fact, it is necessary to understand the criminal justice "system as a whole."[114] And, this means acknowledging "the racial and structural divisions that persist in society."[115] But by cloaking these structural divisions in a colorblind view, it is impossible to understand how they affect the fortunes of blacks. As a result, policies like those instituted under President Clinton – policies said to be colorblind – encourage people to become desensitized to the perpetuation of past patterns of radical injustice that used – just as in the days of Jim Crow – the criminal justice system to maintain blacks as a subordinate "racial caste in America."[116] Thus, due to the implicit racial bias embedded in the colorblind viewpoint, unjust norms of the past – defined in terms of "the segregated, unequal schools, the segregated, jobless ghettos, and the segregated public discourse – a public conversation that excludes the current pariah caste" – are not brought to public awareness as factors that must be eradicated to terminate the radical injustice of the mass incarceration of blacks.[117]

To further understand how implicit racial bias built into the colorblind perspective works to retain the realities of the Jim Crow past, it is well to examine the issue of stop-and-frisk laws in large cities, such as New York during the 1990s. There, blacks were profiled – which is to say, they were said to be more likely to be violent criminals – and so they were frequently stopped (far more often than whites), frisked (without authorization from a court), and, as was the case on many occasions, arrested.[118] Police often filled these moments with racist diatribe. James Foreman says that "police intrusions into the daily lives of black citizens . . . [were accompanied by] swearing and yelling, making belittling remarks, issuing illegitimate orders, conducting random and unwarranted searches, [and] demanding that suspects 'get against the wall.'"[119]

Stop-and-frisk laws are good examples of the implicit racial bias often found in community policing. Such laws gave police the authority to see blacks as far more likely to commit crimes than whites when in fact that was not true at all. But in taking this approach, and in allowing implicit bias against blacks to hold sway in police–community relationships, many blacks were "rounded up for drug crimes that are largely ignored when committed by whites [and this fact] is unseen."[120] Whites can accept this outcome – and normalize it – because the law is said to be colorblind.

However, in contrast to this point of view and as a means of overturning it, the political will to rid civil society of radical injustice can and must be defined in such a way as to expose implicit racial bias to public awareness – just as Alexander

has done in her work. And once exposed and then evaluated against the commitment to securing equal justice for all, a mutually respectful public discourse in
civil society may well follow, a discourse that seeks necessary reforms of the
criminal justice system and that by doing so achieves an end to mass incarceration
of communities of color as well as to stop-and-frisk laws.

This has happened slowly, and some minor reforms have been made of the
criminal justice system as a result. For instance, the First Step Act, as mentioned
earlier, commits to the following reforms: it provides judges with much greater
discretion in determining sentences; it allows prisoners to earn more time toward
release from prison for good conduct; it offers more recidivism reduction training to prisoners; it offers reduction in time served for prisoners' taking part in
anti-recidivism programs or other socially useful activities; and it provides for
more attention to placing inmates, once released, into either reentry settings or
home confinement.[121]

Still, as the name First Step Act implies, much more needs to be done to end
mass incarceration than is provided by this law. Perhaps, the most important form
of implicit racial bias that works against ending the mass incarceration of communities of color is the continuing refusal by many political and social leaders to
come to grips with the ways in which unfair deficiencies in opportunity – often
arising from racial prejudice – encourage people to take part in illegal activities
that make them susceptible to arrest, conviction, and prison. To be sure, a pattern
of victimization such as this does not excuse those who commit crimes, including,
most especially, crimes of violence. But society is not blameless either, especially
when it fails to afford life-enhancing opportunities to people who – because of
their history of victimization – are most likely to end up incarcerated.[122] Not recognizing this fact is itself a manifestation of implicit racial bias. Exposing and,
through exposure, ending this form of implicit bias would bring the system of
mass incarceration to its knees. This is where a political will to recognize and to
end implicit bias could lead us.

Thus, despite arguments such as those put forth by Alexander, and despite the
fact that these arguments have been accepted throughout civil society by many
individuals across the political spectrum, the fact is that these arguments have
not yet succeeded in establishing a public sphere that takes fully into account the
factors – in particular, implicit racial bias – that stand in the way of advancing
civic equality for all. It is because of this fact that the public sphere continues
to be weak in its ability to champion this objective. Nonetheless, as the discussion spurred on by Alexander continues on this matter, the hope is that the public
sphere can be strengthened with further reforms of the criminal justice system
brought to full fruition.

A second way to define the political will that stands against radical injustice is
to make it, the political will, foundational to working against capitalism's support
for racism. Kendi takes this view. And his starting point to explain this position
is his notion that to be an "antiracist," it is necessary to "think there is nothing
wrong with Black people, to think that racial groups are equal," and because they

are, each should be accorded civic equality.[123] His view of the need to extend equality to all racial groups is based on the truth that "no racial group has ever had a monopoly on any type of human trait or gene – not now, not ever."[124] And, when this view is contradicted, the only reason for doing so is a form of "racial discrimination" that would undermine the civic equality for members of the group made subject to this discrimination.[125]

Now, a major source of racial discrimination for Kendi is capitalism. Kendi says that, "To love capitalism is to end up loving racism. To love racism is to end up loving capitalism. The conjoined twins are the two sides of the same destructive body."[126] In which case, then, capitalism is not simply a force to create wealth for the world to share through markets and private ownership. The fact is that the wealth created by capitalism comes at a great cost to blacks. This is why, in Kendi's view, "capitalism is essentially racist; racism is essentially capitalist. They were birthed together from the same unnatural causes, and they shall one day die together from unnatural causes."[127]

What propels this reality forward? Simply put, the capitalist must divert attention away from himself as the source of blame for the loss of wealth that workers experience at his hands. It is precisely this tactic that breeds the black–white animus that capitalists count on to keep whites and blacks from uniting on behalf of a demand that the fruits of their collective labor be more fairly distributed to them than is currently the situation under capitalism. As Nicholas Lemann says in discussing this approach – "called racial capitalism" – in his discussion of Walter Johnson's book *The Broken Heart of America: St. Louis and the Violent History of the United States*, racism is a means for exploiting blacks while at the same urging whites to resent blacks in order to give cover to the capitalist's quest "to extract value" from blacks and whites alike.[128]

To be clear, Kendi would accept the view we have argued here that there is an obligation to remember instances of past radical injustice against blacks as a means of inspiring a political will to resist it in the future. But it is necessary, as this is done to focus on the main engine of this reality, which is the propulsive force of capitalism that constantly keeps racism alive and that, consequently, makes the radical injustice of the past a commonplace reality today. Thus, if the past experience of radical injustice is to be prevented from returning, then there must be a strong political will that works to galvanize all of society to limit, to moderate, and to prevent capitalism from continually fostering racism.

However, in taking this view, it is important to recognize – as Kendi surely would – that capitalism is not the sole environment in which racism flourishes. Indeed, there are many other settings than capitalism in which racism abounds. By not accepting this possibility, peoples' attention may be so focused on capitalism as the source of racism that they become incapable of understanding the other places in society – outside of the influence of capitalist institutions – that give support to racist views and practices.

In this context, it is well to address in civil society events like the "Unite the Right Rally" in Charlottesville in 2017. There, large numbers of people openly professed white nationalist views – which incorporated Nazi ideological thinking – when they chanted the words "Jews would not replace us." This chant also symbolized their hope to remove any hope of civic equality for blacks.[129] Here, racism lives on, and the reasons have little to do with capitalism but everything to do with the flat-out refusal of some individuals to accept a civil society setting that works tirelessly for a public sphere dedicated to protecting the rule of law on behalf of securing the vaunted goal of civic equality for all.

Moreover, to say that capitalism is *the* most prominent factor in maintaining racism is to focus attention away from the litany of reforms that have been made on behalf of ending racism's infliction of inequality on blacks. After all, there have been major achievements toward mitigating the effects of racial inequality, despite the overwhelming presence of capitalism. Included on this list are reforms like the 13th and 14th Amendments, the many lasting achievements of the civil rights movement led by Martin Luther King Jr., and Barack Obama's ascension to the presidency of the United States. Not recognizing the significance of facts like these for advancing civic equality for blacks – in order to maintain the position that capitalism will always defeat any progress toward civic equality – encourages, says Lemann (again in his discussion of the aforementioned book by Walter Johnson), "the hazards of defeatism" by "deflating and deriding the progress . . . made in the past and the promise [such progress] might hold for the future."[130] After all, as Lemann says, racial history in the United States "is necessarily messy, impure, and capable of producing no more than partial victories, and, even then, only when pushed hard by political movements."[131] But, nonetheless, there were substantive gains made in this context, and a sole focus on capitalism as the source of racism may cause us to not fully appreciate these achievements and, through doing so, strengthen their place in American society on behalf of a more just future.

To counter any hint of defeatism – in the name of building successful political movements for civic equality for blacks and everyone else – the political will must be shaped in civil society to resist racism in whatever form it takes. This means that racism in civil society can be located in any institution found therein and that each of us must be on the lookout for its appearance anywhere – on behalf of defeating it over and over again – everywhere. Then, we can protect the public sphere and ensure it lives up to its commitment to protect civic equality for all people, including, of course, blacks. And certainly, a political will fashioned in this way is a major factor in the protest politics movement – with all it challenges and its partial successes – which we discuss in the next section.

Finally, a third way to manifest a political will – which, again, arises from a moral obligation to remember radical injustice – is to focus on a discussion in civil society of how to repair the damage of radical injustice to blacks by way of a policy of reparations for slavery and for Jim Crow culture. That damage – which began in the past – continues into the present and is likely, unless stopped, to negatively affect blacks in the future. Understanding this fact and then seeking to correct it through a policy of reparations would recognize the many times when blacks were harmed by racist practices that were so powerful they have a continuing presence in contemporary society, and thus work to perpetuate radical injustice against blacks today.

The main hindrance to advancing this idea, however, is that there are so many parts that must be reconciled on behalf of achieving an effective reparations policy that it seems – at least from the outside looking in – to be hard to reach agreement on how best to implement it. But where there is a strong political will developed in civil society for a reparations policy, the sense of overriding importance of achieving this goal would be so significant a factor among citizens that the complexity of doing so would seem negligible, in contrast to what would be the case where a potent political will on behalf of this goal is nonexistent.

To explain this view further, it is well to take a look at some of the many issues involved with discussing reparations in civil society.

We have in mind questions such as the following:[132] should a policy of reparations give priority only to descendants of slaves, or should these payments be extended to African Americans who have – as migrants to this country from other nations – recently gained citizenship? And, further, should payouts to individuals in whichever category is chosen be linked to an income level? In other words, if you are above that level, you receive no reparations; if you are below it, reparations are justified. If so, what should that level be? Moreover, how much money should be placed in the reparations-payout pot? Should the size of the pot be justified on the basis of figures demonstrating the differences of black and white income that arise from past and present forms of discrimination? By some accounts, as Patricia Cohen reports, one economist estimated in 1983 a 40–60 percent difference between black and white incomes, a reality that arises from past and continuing forms of discrimination and which amounts to $500 billion.[133]

Or should the amounts of wealth lost to blacks from redlining – the practice employed in the twentieth century to keep blacks in segregated and poor neighborhoods – be determined and made the basis for distribution? Or what about the white riot against African Americans in 1921, which razed an entire black community, murdered 300 blacks, and caused injury to 800 others? This happened in the Greenwood neighborhood of Tulsa, Oklahoma, a prosperous place called Black Wall Street.[134] Should descendants of tragic incidents like this (and there were others) be compensated for their economic losses? Moreover, what kinds of things should reparation monies be spent on? Education, housing, businesses that create wealth, or all of the above? Or should other things be considered? And what might those other things be?

So many questions, so much complexity, so much, then, that seems to overwhelm the discussion of how to implement a reparations policy, thus making it, for some people, impractical and impossible to carry out. But this would not be the view if the argument for reparations was successfully linked, in a civil society, to a perspective demonstrating that a policy of reparations is an important and in fact leading way to heed the warnings of the memory of radical injustice. These warnings make clear that, unless past instances of radical injustice against blacks are disallowed space and life, these past moments may well be re-installed into society today. In which case – as discussed earlier – the existing differentials (that emerge from the experiences of slavery and Jim Crow culture) between whites and blacks in wealth, income, general opportunities, and assurance of rights – particularly in the context of mass incarceration as well as white supremacist and police violence – would not only *not* be ended, they would be made even more extreme!

In response, then, to the memory of radical injustice that underscores the potential contained in the radical injustice of the past against blacks to maintain itself in the present, many individuals – both white and black – would recognize the need to create a political will that supports a policy of reparations for blacks. Doing so represents an important way to repair, and thus provide restitution for, the harms to blacks (as mentioned in the preceding paragraph) that persist today and that result from the continuation of the radical injustice of the past. Further, a robust political will on behalf of this position in civil society would necessarily find its way into the public sphere. And once in place there, the complexity around this issue that at first looks daunting – and thus as an impediment to agreement on a reparations policy – would be seen as manageable and, in the context of mutually respectful discussions, the public sphere could find resolutions beneficial to all.

Now, this view of the public sphere is captured fully in what Coates – in his advocacy for reparations – calls "spiritual renewal." To this end, Coates says that

> *What I'm talking about is more than recompense for past injustices – more than a handout, a payoff, hush money, or a reluctant bribe. What I'm talking about is a national reckoning that would lead to spiritual renewal . . . Reparations would mean a revolution of the American consciousness. . . .*[135]

In our view, at the center of that "revolution of American consciousness" would be a moral resolve – a political will – to repair the damage done to blacks by slavery and Jim Crow culture, damage that will continue to harm blacks if not checked through a reparations policy. And then the public sphere would move to a more just place – nullifying the continuing pattern in the present of radical injustice from the past – and by doing so further securing the resiliency of the moral and constitutional principles of a liberal democratic form of national government.

Otherwise, what is today often referred to as "systemic racism" will continue without interruption. The term "systemic racism" is a concept suggesting that past tendencies of radical injustice are so embedded in social and political institutions that these institutions are unable to prevent earlier patterns of racist practices from constantly returning and harming communities of color. And then the disparities between whites and blacks in wealth and opportunity – as well as in the protection of black people's civic equality – are never repaired and, instead, these discrepancies continue to be made far worse. Systemic racism, thus, both draws and then polices hardcore racial boundaries between blacks and whites. This is done to protect the many privileges of "whiteness" that are denied completely to African Americans. To uphold a moral obligation to remember radical injustice, then, is to be strongly motivated to defeat the most salient, lasting effects of radical injustice, which is, in fact, systemic racism.

X. Protest Politics

Getting people to embrace a political will to resist systemic racism is a standard feature of the protest politics tradition in civil society. Now, protest politics, as Darryl Pinckney says, follows the model of activism manifested in the writing of Angela Davis. Pinckney believes, with Davis, that the "mass movements [in the 1960s and 1970s] could bring about systematic change [on behalf of overturning systemic racism]."[136] Given this view, the protest politics tradition – which manifested itself during the civil rights movement and is encapsulated in the "Letter from a Birmingham Jail" discussed earlier – is a main means by which the discussion of civil society is designed to appeal to a broad audience of whites in the hopes that they will be convinced to side with blacks on behalf of securing a public sphere that upholds the moral and constitutional principles of a liberal democracy.

There are two types of leaders of the protest politics tradition in civil society, what Cornel West calls "prophetic leaders" and what, in the context of the Blacks Lives Matter movement today, can be called grassroots activists. Take the first form, first.

West argues for the renewal of "prophetic fire" that manifests what he calls the "strong prophetic tradition of lifting every voice."[137] In advocating this view, West points by way of example to, among others, Frederick Douglass, W.E.B. Du Bois, and Martin Luther King Jr. – all people whom we have discussed.[138]

Now, West's view implies the need for a single leader who becomes, through his or her words and demeanor, an iconic figure, inspiring people to take to the streets in the name of confronting and overturning racist practices, and all of this is to be done on behalf of achieving justice not just for blacks but for all people. Implicit in this view of the prophetic leader is the continuing presence of a moral obligation to remember radical injustice to blacks. The past represents unjust tendencies that will always reoccur in the present and structure the future unless these realities are fully identified and then resisted and eventually extirpated by a political will to stop them. The latter arises from the memory of radical injustice that replaces a motivational orientation based on individualistic self-interest with an unselfish commitment to help others who are the continuing subjects of injustice. Black prophetic leaders embrace this perspective and work to achieve it as they connect themselves through their charisma and communication skills to masses of blacks and to many whites, who – along with blacks – are encouraged to support this cause.

Further, it must be said as well that this moral perspective that guides the political activity of the prophetic leader – which, as just stated, emanates from the memory of radical injustice and the need to prevent its continuation in the present and future – is not exclusive to such an individual. In a grassroots politics, a similar moral perspective arising from the memory of radical injustice is ever-present as well. Activists who orient themselves to work for justice are also motivated by a desire to recognize the radically unjust tendencies of the past that continue to weave injustice into the fabric of society on behalf of denying civic equality to groups of people and often based on skin color alone. Now, grassroots protest politics is characterized by the presence of a surfeit of leaders who arise to local prominence within communities all across America. Yes, there are chief spokespeople like Black Lives Matter's Alicia Garza, but, on the whole, the planning for action arises less from the inspiration of a single, iconic prophetic leader and more from the mobilizing skills of numerous community activists.[139] Thus, even though grassroots leaders may not attain the iconic status of a prophetic leader, it is still the case that they may help to maintain a popular movement from below that seeks to change society in such a way that the past never again manifests its Jim Crow self in the present and future.

Holders of both views – that of prophetic leaders and grassroots activists for justice – incorporate in their core commitments a political sensibility that is grounded in a moral obligation to remember radical injustice as the basis for stopping it from being perpetuated. Based on this perspective, protest leaders appeal to whites and blacks to support major changes in civil society on behalf of achieving civic equality for blacks and all others in the public sphere. Principally, then, whites are urged by protest leaders to envision a civil society that ends racist tendencies from the past – tendencies that prevent the achievement of justice for blacks in the present – as a major step in supporting changes in the public sphere that ensure civic equality for all. For instance, as we discuss more fully at the end of this section, protest politics – led by iconic leaders such as John Lewis – inspired discussion in civil society that was the basis for reconstituting the public sphere to embody the Voting Rights Act of 1965. The latter ensured that barriers long maintained in the Jim Crow culture against blacks voting, like literacy tests, were permanently eliminated in the public sphere.[140]

The underlying assumption of endeavors such as this in protest movements – whether driven by the prophetic leader or by grassroots leaders – is that many white people in civil society accept, on its face, the need to extend civic equality to all in the public sphere, including to blacks long denied it. Yet, winning over people in civil society to support in full measure what they already believe is, ironically, both the crux of protest politics and, at the same time, its most formidable challenge.

This dilemma was a core message contained in King's "Letter from a Birmingham Jail." There, as we saw earlier, King addressed pastors who presumably accepted the need to end Jim Crow segregation but also thought the pursuit of such a goal in the streets – through nonviolent civil disobedience – would create social and political instability. Implicit in the pastors' complaint, then, was that racism remains strongly in place and that to overturn its dominance through public demonstrations would inspire reactions that made many whites less tolerant of King's agenda, with the result that the hope of advancing the argument in civil society for civic equality would be dealt a significant setback.

In this context, many whites will say that it is best to have a public sphere that protects civic equality for all, but as a practical matter, this goal is an impossible utopian hope, one that can never be achieved, at least not in the immediate future. Here, numerous people who support the moral and constitutional principles of a liberal democratic public sphere end up resigning themselves to accepting a status quo based on what they know is opposed to these principles. And, further, such individuals are liable to justify this view by saying that there is little they can do – practically speaking – to redraw the contours of the public sphere. In consequence, these individuals who support civic equality for all help – ironically – to pave the way for the continuation of past tendencies of radical injustice into the mainstream life of society.

In response, the main goal of protest politics – whether led by the prophetic leader or the grassroots activist – becomes clear. It is within civil society to convince people – especially white people – who would otherwise support civic equality for all to resist any propensity to normalize what they know to be unjust from the standpoint of sustaining the moral and constitutional principles of a liberal democratic public sphere. Then the past tendencies that harbor radical injustice can be ended and no longer be allowed to continue. All of this means that the main question for protest politics to address is how the leaders of such movements – whether of the prophetic or grassroots type – are to appeal to people who both support civic equality for all but who are nonetheless skeptical that this goal is in fact feasible.

Now, this obstacle to nonviolent protest on behalf of advancing civic equality throughout civil society is far less a barrier to public protest for whites when the latter recognize that the continued practice of radical injustice will do great harm not just to blacks but to themselves as well by threatening liberal democracy. And this point has been made effectively in several ways. For instance, it is the case that, in the recent past, many social networks in civil society – from religious institutions to colleges and universities to various businesses and professions – encourage citizens to appreciate the way that past manifestations of radical injustice will return if allowed to do so. And once such moments find their way back into society, they will once again pose grave threats to civic equality for *all* Americans, as long as people do not – with a firm moral resolve – stop all manner of racist actions toward blacks.

Of special note in this regard, for instance, was the video in the spring of 2020 of a Minneapolis police officer who placed his knee on George Floyd's neck, causing his death by asphyxiation. All of this took place despite the fact that Floyd posed no threat to the officers involved. To a people schooled in the memory of radical injustice, such conduct is symbolic of the intention to deny civic equality to blacks in contradiction to the moral and constitutional principles of a liberal democratic public sphere. And it is in response to the need to protect that public sphere by stopping police practices, such as those displayed in Floyd's death, that millions of people across America took to the streets to engage in nonviolent public protests over a period lasting many weeks.

Like King in his "Letter from a Birmingham Jail," these activists – both black and white and led by the grassroots Black Lives Matter group – said that ensuring justice for black people had to be a primary goal, despite the potential for social and political instability that such protests might create. Otherwise, the public sphere of a liberal democracy will prove unable to protect civic equality – not only for blacks – but for *every* citizen, of whatever background or status. Just as King said in his "Letter from a Birmingham Jail," a key motivating factor on behalf of achieving justice for whites and blacks alike is the shared understanding that "injustice anywhere is a threat to justice everywhere." Demonstrators marching against Floyd's death channeled a similar view as they chanted in a firm, resolute voice: "No justice, no peace!"

Finally, it needs to be said that the protests in conjunction with Floyd's death arose, in part, from long-held memories of past efforts to protect blacks from radical injustice. Specifically, we have in mind the 1965 march from Selma to Montgomery, Alabama. Civil rights icon John Lewis – who, up until his death in 2020, was a long-time member of the House of Representatives from Georgia – led a march across the Edmund Pettus Bridge in Selma, Alabama, en route to Montgomery, Alabama, the state capital, on behalf of ensuring voting rights to blacks. But the marchers never got across the bridge. On that day – known as "Bloody Sunday" – Alabama state troopers descended on the marchers with batons and tear gas, and many protesters were severely injured, including Lewis, who suffered a fractured skull.

After a federal court permitted the march to Montgomery to continue, the protestors grew from 600 to 25,000 people, as a direct result of broadly shared public sympathy for those injured by the brutal nature of state trooper violence against the marchers, who were nonviolently demonstrating on behalf of acquiring an essential right.[141] Moreover, public sympathy for the civil rights marchers was given further support by the fact that Americans watched the violence on the bridge in close proximity to the televised viewing of the film *Judgment at Nuremburg*, which depicted Nazi war crimes against Jews. Christopher Klein says that "nearly 50 million Americans who had tuned into the film's long-awaited television premier couldn't escape the historical echoes of Nazi storm troopers in the scenes of the rampaging [Alabama] state troopers."[142] In this situation, reservations that many people might have had against the Lewis-led demonstration for voting rights never materialized in a broad-scale manner across the public. Consequently, the previously mentioned Voting Rights Act of 1965 was passed with the strong support of Congress, President Lyndon B. Johnson, and the American people.

The symbolic importance of this moment for securing a liberal democratic public sphere now has a permanent place in civic memory. As such, the memory of Lewis and his compatriots on the Edmund Pettus Bridge has become a rich resource to spur other actions on behalf of protecting and furthering civic equality during those times when it is under attack. It is likely, then, that those who embarked on demonstrating against morally abhorrent and unlawful police violence in the George Floyd case embraced and were motivated – at least in part – by the memory of Lewis's contribution to voting rights. In which case, the political will – arising from the memory of Lewis's resistance to radical injustice – is a constant reminder of the need, in civil society, to defend the liberty of blacks against radical injustice as an essential part of what is necessary to secure the liberty of all citizens in the public sphere of a liberal democracy.

No doubt, this is what Lewis meant when he said that "ordinary people with extraordinary vision can redeem the soul of America by getting in what I call good trouble, necessary trouble."[143]

XI. Response and Rejoinder

Finally, in the conclusion of this chapter, we discuss, once again, the schism central to our discussion of identity politics as manifested by Kristof and Lilla and described in section III of this chapter. Our question with respect to this schism is simply this: can the differences between these views be resolved so that our politics is not riven? Or, in other terms, what argument can be made in civil society – from the standpoint of political theory as discussed here – to end the conflict between these competing views of politics, especially on behalf of maintaining and strengthening the public sphere of a liberal democracy?

The answer from the standpoint of the political theory framed in this chapter is that Lilla's politics of the common good – which includes a prominent emphasis on satisfying the prevalent needs of the working and middle classes – cannot be achieved except if the members of these groups embrace a memory of radical injustice toward blacks, the broad outlines of which have been described in this chapter. This is because as long as this memory remains outside the scope of what is an acceptable political norm, the past realities that harmed blacks in earlier times will continue to manifest themselves in the present and future. In which case, the common good approach to our politics will always be shattered by its failure to build the political resolve from the memory of radical injustice to stop its continuing reintroduction into social and political life.

We can explain this view better by focusing on a major issue of the day: income redistribution. From the standpoint of a common good politics as Lilla might suggest, there is no question that the vast majority would be benefited if there was a fairer distribution of wealth in this country. It is no secret that the top one percent of households in America now own 40 percent of the nation's wealth, which is the largest gap since the early 1960s. In fact, the top one percent of American households in 2017 possessed more wealth than did the bottom 90 percent of households taken as a whole.[144] This situation, as we write, is likely to worsen with the current recession that is pulsating throughout the country because of the COVID-19 pandemic. In this setting, opportunities in education and career achievement for working- and middle-class Americans have been – and will continue to be – severely contracted. Surely, by fixing this problem and making wealth more fairly distributed, the overwhelming majority of people – regardless of color – will benefit.

Still, if the argument in civil society is about advancing common-good policies for all people, then the memory of radical injustice against blacks *must not* be denied centrality of place in that discussion. To understand this point better, it is well to remind readers of the conflict common to identity politics. Our treatment of this approach to political life described the tension between the working and middle classes as representing one identity group, and a competing identity group based on fears of continuing racial discrimination. Often, these two groups are at loggerheads with each other, and this creates mutual resentment that is hard to heal.

But with respect to income redistribution, there is a chance to transcend this conflict and unite the two identity groups behind a shared approach to this issue. What we mean in this regard is that, in discussing income redistribution, there is always a tension between plutocrats, seeking to protect their wealth, and ordinary citizens – both black and white – who seek to acquire some of that wealth for themselves.[145] A substantial portion of plutocrats – who hold, as described earlier, the bulk of the wealth and who want to keep things that way – inveigh against public programs designed to redistribute wealth across society, including programs for universal health care, federal government–backed college education for all, an increased minimum wage, government-subsidized day care, climate-change industries to avert the looming disasters of global warming, and so on.

The other side of this divide includes many citizens – both black and white – whose only recourse is to make use of liberal democratic institutions, as is done in the protest politics tradition, to more fairly distribute wealth across all groups in society. The challenge for such a politics is to protect the conditions that push plutocrats to embrace wealth redistribution. And, in fact, a resilient civil society can be a place in which the plutocrats experience strong pressures to support a plan for wealth redistribution that favors ordinary people over themselves.

What are the circumstances of a civil society that manifest this view? It is a civil society grounded in the memory of radical injustice toward communities of color. Here, we note that, especially on the income distribution issue, this memory is of great significance to all citizens, black and white alike. And this is because the memory of radical injustice toward blacks points to a reality that makes clear that one of the major dimensions of radical injustice is that it works to achieve its ends by keeping blacks and whites in a position where they are divided from, and in opposition to, each other. Regarding the wealth distribution question, we saw earlier that "racial capitalism" causes whites to resent blacks as part of a plan to ensure that the two groups do not unite to demand greater economic concessions from plutocrats.

Who benefits from this circumstance but plutocrats? Through a memory of radical injustice highlighting the dangers from racial capitalism, however, individuals – both white and black – are in a much better position to see the plutocrat/ordinary person divide as the basis for constantly perpetuating imbalances that favor plutocrats. In response, a political will – shared by blacks and whites – to resist this reality from repeating itself is the only way to move to a vision of the common good on the issue of income redistribution.

But to acquire this understanding of the political will also means that various other viewpoints that contribute in major ways to distrust between blacks and whites must be dismantled, including, most significantly, the systemic racism that prevents fair opportunity for blacks. Now, the memory of radical injustice toward blacks makes clear that past denials of civic equality to blacks live on today through systemic racism. Whites who share this memory and who take seriously its teachings understand that, if they are to find common ground with blacks on behalf of a policy for income redistribution, it is necessary to remove the barriers to civic equality for blacks that arise from systemic racism.

As such – and for the sake of the goal of a fairer income distribution in this nation – it is incumbent upon white and black citizens to work together to end systemic racism in all its various manifestations, from interactions of blacks with police and to disparities in income, wealth, and basic opportunities. Moreover, as part of this objective, any obstacles resulting from implicit racial bias – in particular, those justified by the colorblind perspective – must be exposed as well. And, once exposed, these obstacles must be removed, as Michelle Alexander made clear in her discussion of the mass incarceration of communities of color.

Once the impediments like these to forging agreements between blacks and whites are fully recognized and appropriately addressed, the schismatic pressures arising from identity politics, as we discussed earlier, would be reduced in poignancy. In which case, the differences arising from the competing views of identity politics would not stand in the way of both groups reaching common ground with each other in a discourse of mutual respect. And a civil society shaped, at least in part, by the memory of radical injustice to communities of color would facilitate this discourse by making clear the pathways (as mentioned in the preceding five paragraphs) that all must traverse successfully if plutocrats are to be forced to give ground in the name of achieving a fairer scheme for income distribution. In consequence, a redistribution of wealth could be advanced in a way consistent with protecting a public sphere that is dedicated to ensuring the permanence of the moral and constitutional principles of a liberal democracy, without which an open, pluralist society incorporating the discourse of mutual respect would be impossible to achieve.

Overall, then, a moral obligation to remember radical injustice to communities of color is an essential part of a civil society. And it is a political theory – rooted in the experience of African Americans in this country – that helps make the memory of radical injustice a permanent fixture of a civil society. There, arguments are made to resist the reach and power of radical injustice. And, by doing so successfully, it is possible to build an ever-stronger public sphere of a liberal democracy, here, there, and – it is to be hoped – everywhere.

Notes

1. These rights include, but are not limited to, the following: rights to speech, thought, conscience, religious choice, press freedom, education, public critique and protest of government policies, due process of law, and equality of citizenship, including most importantly, as we see later in this chapter, the right to vote.

2. See Steven M. DeLue, *How The Liberal Arts Can Save Liberal Democracy* (Lanham: Lexington Books, 2018), 27–33. An earlier version of this argument is presented there.

3. John Lewis, Posthumous statement entitled: "Together, You Can Redeem the Soul of Our Nation," *New York Times*, July 30, 2020.

4. What follows is based on the First Amendment in the US Constitution. We count, as stated there, freedom of religious choice and the freedom from the government establishment of religion as part of a larger commitment to freedom of conscience, which includes not just the liberty to determine one's views on religion but on many other social and political issues as well.

5. The other rights on a full-rights agenda include many not mentioned here, such as the right of privacy, the right to due process of law, and the right to an education at least through high school. And it is the right to vote, to free speech, to publicly criticize government, to freedom of conscience, and to receive accurate information through a free press that allow citizens to ensure that the full-rights agenda is accorded each citizen in the liberal democratic public sphere.

6. A similar argument is made with respect to women and homosexuals and members of various ethnic groups who have been marginalized in American society, but in this chapter, we only emphasize race.

7. Mark Lilla, "The End of Identity Liberalism," *New York Times*, November 18, 2016, www.nytimes.com/2016/11/20/opinion/sunday/the-end-of-identity-liberalism.html.

8. Ibid. An earlier version of this argument is made in DeLue, *How the Liberal Arts Can Save Liberal Democracy*, 61–62.

9. Lilla, "The End of Identity Liberalism."

10. Nicholas Kristof, "Identity Politics and a Dad's Loss," *New York Times*, December 8, 2016, www.nytimes.com/2016/12/08/opinion/identity-politics-and-a-dads-loss.html?ref=opinion.

11. Richard Oppel, Jr. et al. "Racial Disparity in Cases Stretches All Across the Board," *New York Times*, July 6, 2020.

12. Kristof, "Identity Politics and a Dad's Loss."

13. This discussion is based – as described in Chapter 1 – on the different implications for society of toleration and mutual respect. People who tolerate each other in a live-and-let-live way may build walls around each other in to maintain peaceful relationships. But by living in silos, as is implied here by the term "walls," individuals often are unable to develop sufficient trust to exercise their public freedom to find common ground among their differences. The doctrine of mutual respect and the sympathy discussed by Adam Smith, as discussed in Chapter 1, presume an ability on the part of people to transcend this circumstance through discussion to achieve a common ground without undermining respect for difference. This is one of the great achievements of civil society, especially one seeking to provide sufficient foundation to a public sphere.

14. This section benefits greatly from insights into modern liberalism provided by the now-classic work of Charles Mills in *The Racial Contract* (Ithaca: Cornell University Press, 1997). There, Mills makes clear that the Enlightenment liberalism advocated for a social contract that excluded blacks, despite its call for basic rights for all. He says that the "evolution of the modern version of the [social] contract, characterized by antipatriarchalist Enlightenment

liberalism, with its proclamations of the equal rights, autonomy, and freedom of all men, thus took place simultaneously with the massacre, expropriation, and subjection to hereditary slavery of men at least apparently human." (pp. 63–64) Mills makes clear that Enlightenment liberalism supported rights for all but ended up denying them to blacks, as was, of course, the case in this country. A political theory that seeks to secure liberal democracy on firm foundations must incorporate this view into its vision of the world through memory and, by way of that memory, ensure that the past instances of the denial of civic equality to blacks are not continued.

15. "We hold these truths to be self-evident, that all men are created equal, that they are endowed by their Creator with certain unalienable Rights, that among these are Life, Liberty and the pursuit of Happiness." Also, see DeLue, *How the Liberal Arts Can Save Liberal Democracy*, 167–70.

16. The Three-Fifths Compromise is found in Article 1, Section 2, Clause 3 of the US Constitution, which reads: "Representatives and the several States which may be included within this Union, according to their respective Numbers, which shall be determined by adding to the whole Number of free Persons, including those bound to Service for a Term of Years, and excluding Indians not taxed, three fifths of all other Persons." See *Digital History*, "The Three-Fifths Compromise," which says that, before the compromise, "The southern states had about 38 percent of the seats in the Continental Congress." But "because of the 1787 Three-Fifths Compromise, the southern states had nearly 45 percent of the seats in the first U.S. Congress, which took office in 1790." www.digitalhistory.uh.edu/disp_textbook.cfm?smtID=3&psid=163.

17. See Andrew Delbanco, "The Long Struggle for America's Soul," *New York Times*, November 2, 2018, www.nytimes.com/2018/11/02/opinion/the-long-struggle-for-americas-soul.html?action=click&module=Opinion&pgtype=Homepage.

18. Article 4, Section 2, Clause 3 says the following: "No Person held to Service or Labour in one State, under the Laws thereof, escaping into another, shall, in Consequence of any Law or Regulation therein, be discharged from such Service or Labour, but shall be delivered up on Claim of the Party to whom such Service or Labour may be due." See Andrew Delbanco, *The War Before the War: Fugitive Slaves and the Struggle for America's Soul from the Revolution to the Civil War* (New York: Penguin Books, 2018), 19.

19. Toni Morrison, *The Source of Self-Regard: Selected Essays, Speeches and Meditations* (New York: Alfred A. Knopf, 2019), 283.

20. David Cole, "Less Punishment, More Justice," *New York Review of Books*, July 23, 2020, 14.

21. Michelle Alexander, "The Injustice of This Moment Is Not an Aberration," *New York Times*, January 17, 2020, www.nytimes.com/2020/01/17/opinion/sunday/michelle-alexander-new-jim-crow.html?action=click&module=Opinion&pgtype=Homepage

22. Ibid.

23. Ibid.

24. Henry Louis Gates, *Stony the Road: Reconstruction, White Supremacy, and the Rise of Jim Crow* (New York: Penguin Books, 2019), 7.

25. Ibid., 8.

26. Ibid.

27. Ibid.

28. Ibid., 7.

29. Ibid.

30. Rutherford B. Hayes, a Republican, did not win the popular vote in 1876, and to win the electoral vote he made a deal with Democrats to pull federal troops out of the South. See "Compromise of 1876," *History.com*, March 17, 2011, www.history.com/topics/us-presidents/compromise-of-1877. The author states that "The Compromise of 1876 effectively ended the Reconstruction era."

31. Gates, *Stony, the Road*, 17.

32. Ibid.

33. Ibid., 13.

34. Ibid.

35. See Isabel Wilkerson, *The Warmth of Other Suns, the Epic Story of America's Great Migration* (New York: Vintage Books, 2010). This period took place between 1915 and 1970 in American history.

36. At the end of this section, we discuss several issues that demonstrate different ways in which civic equality has been denied blacks, long after Jim Crow officially ended, a fact that demonstrates that the effects of Jim Crow remain for many blacks. Also, we develop an important element of this reality in our discussion of systemic racism at the conclusion of our discussion on reparations.

37. Gates, *Stony the Road*, 35. Of special note is that, during this period, Gates points out that, in general, Southern states overturned their Reconstruction-based constitutions and denied blacks the right to vote as well as instituted separate-but-equal doctrines, which always meant the permanent denial of civic equality to blacks.

38. Gates, *Stony the Road*, 34.

39. "About 1 in 1,000 black men and boys in America can expect to die at the hands of police, according to a new analysis of deaths involving law enforcement officers. That makes them 2.5 times more likely than white men and boys to die during an encounter with cops." See Amina Khan, "Getting Killed by Police Is a Major Cause of Death for Black Men in America," *Los Angeles Times*, August 16, 2019, www.latimes.com/science/story/2019-08-15/police-shootings-are-a-leading-cause-of-death-for-black-men.

40. Fred Harris and Alan Curtis, "The Unmet Promise of Equality," *New York Times*, February 28, 2018, www.nytimes.com/interactive/2018/02/28/opinion/the-unmet-promise-of-equality.html?searchResultPosition=1.

41. Richard Rothstein, *The Color of Law: A Forgotten History of How Our Government Segregated America* (New York: Liveright Publishing Corporation, 2017), 64, 97, 109 for redlining and pp. 78–91 for restrictive covenants. Also, see, Kriston Capps, "How the Fair Housing Act Failed Black Homeowners," *Bloomberg CityLab*, April 18, 2018, for a discussion of racial disparities in lending practices.

42. Lawrence Goldstone, "America's Relentless Suppression of Black Voters," *The New Republic*, October, 24, 2018, https://newrepublic.com/article/151858/americas-relentless-suppression-black-voters.

43. American Civil Liberties Union, February 3, 2020, www.aclu.org/news/civil-liberties/block-the-vote-voter-suppression-in-2020/.

44. Ibid.

45. Brennan Center for Justice, January 31, 2017, "Debunking the Voter Fraud Myth," www.brennancenter.org/analysis/debunking-voter-fraud-myth.

46. David W. Blight, *Frederick Douglass: Prophet of Freedom* (New York: Simon and Schuster, 2018), 26, 228. Also, we rely on Blight's account of Douglass since it is the definitive biography of Douglass and has won acclaim across scholars.

47. Ibid., 229.

48. Ibid., 233.

49. Ibid., 230, 229–234.

50. Douglass cited in Ibid., 233.

51. Ibid., 233.

52. Ibid.

53. Ibid.

54. Ibid., 233.

55. Ibid.

56. Ibid., 234.

57. Ibid.

58. Ibid.

59. Adam Gopnik, *A Thousand Small Sanities: The Social Adventure of Liberalism* (New York: Basic Books, 2019), 205.

60. Ibid.

61. Douglass cited in Ibid., 206. The words in capital letters are in the text.

62. Gopnik, *A Thousand Small Sanities*, 209.

63. Ibid.

64. Douglass cited in Blight, *Frederick Douglass*, 330, also, see pp. 298, 301.

65. Gopnik, *A Thousand Small Sanities*, 208.

66. Ibid., 208–9.

67. Ibid., 206. Italics are in the text.

68. Douglass cited in Gopnik, *A Thousand Small Sanities*, 206.

69. Gates, *Stony the Road*, 65. Gates cites an editorial by the editor, John M. Daniel, in an 1854 editorial in the *Richmond Examiner*, which was a major defender of slavery.

70. Douglass cited in Gates, *Stony the Road*, 65. Italics were added.

71. Douglass cited in Blight, *Frederick Douglass*, 234.

72. Ibid.

73. Ibid. Douglass says that "the hypocrisy of the nation must be exposed."

74. Douglass cited in Blight, *Frederick Douglass*, 234.

75. Ibid., 531.

76. Douglass cited in Blight, *Frederick Douglass*, 531.

77. Blight, *Frederick Douglass*, 531.

78. Ibid.

79. Blight says that Douglass, like the Old Testament prophets he admired, sought a "story" or narrative that demonstrated, as in the Exodus account, the march from slavery to freedom. To achieve this prospect, people must heed the warnings inscribed in the past so that society, as in the Exodus story, moves from the worst possibilities for human beings of enslavement to the best possibilities of freedom. Blight, *Frederick Douglass*, 237–38.

80. Ibid., 238.

81. Ibid., 415.

82. Douglass cited in Gates, *Stony the Road*, 14. Italics are in the text.

83. W. E. B., Du Bois, *The Souls of Black Folk* (New York: Dover Publications, 1994), 9. Originally, published in 1903.

84. Ibid., 35.

85. Ibid., 2.

86. As referenced in the section on the Reconstruction and Jim Crow cultures, we pointed out that many Northern cities extended legal and political equality to blacks, despite maintaining a posture of anti-black racism. This circumstance suggests a weak commitment to civic equality, one not grounded in a memory of radical injustice and what follows from it, which is the need to reject its continuation through a strong political will.

87. Du Bois, *Souls of Black Folk*, 30. Also see, Darryl Pinckney, "The Afro-Pessimist Temptation," *New York Review of Books*, June 7, 2018, 51. Pinckney says, "White People took Washington to mean that blacks would accept Jim Crow and not agitate for restoration of the civil rights they had exercised during Reconstruction."

88. Du Bois, *Souls of Black Folk*, 30.

89. Ibid.

90. Ibid., 31.

91. Ibid.

92. See NAACP History, www.naacp.org/naacp-history-w-e-b-dubois/.

93. See https://en.wikipedia.org/wiki/Brown_v._Board_of_Education.

94. Kathy Lohr, "50 Years Later, King's Birmingham Letter Still Resonates," *NPR*, April 15, 2013, www.npr.org/2013/04/16/177355381/50-years-later-kings-birmingham-letter-still-reso natse. She says that the letter is a "response to eight white Alabama clergymen who criticized

King and worried the civil rights campaign would cause violence. They called King an 'extremist' and told blacks they should be patient." His response to them is represented in the letter as criticism of white moderates in whom he says he has been "disappointed."

95. See Martin Luther King's "Letter from a Birmingham Jail," African Studies Center, University of Pennsylvania, April 16, 1963, www.africa.upenn.edu/Articles_Gen/Letter_Birmingham.html Note that King is saying, with Douglass, that we have natural rights, rights granted by God, and thus religious traditions, in advancing their teachings, must protect these rights as part of their religious duty and as part of what reason commands reasonable people to do. Like Douglass, King makes clear that authentic Christianity must always provide a home for protecting the rights needed for liberty.

96. Ibid.

97. Ibid.

98. Ibid.

99. Ibid.

100. Ibid.

101. Ibid.

102. Michelle Alexander, *The New Jim Crow Mass Incarceration in the Age of Colorblindness* (New York: The New Press, 2012), 56.

103. Ibid.

104. Ibid.

105. Ibid., 57.

106. Ibid.

107. Ibid.

108. James Foreman Jr., *Locking Up Our Own: Crime and Punishment in Black America* (New York: Farrar, Straus and Giroux, 2017), 17.

109. David Leonhardt and Yaryna Serkez, "Why the U.S. Lags Other Rich Countries," *New York Times Sunday Review*, July 5, 2020, 5.

110. Alexander, *The New Jim Crow Mass Incarceration in the Age of Colorblindness*, 241, 243.

111. Ibid., 243.

112. Ibid., 107.

113. Ibid., 241.

114. Ibid., 185.

115. Ibid., 241.

116. Ibid.

117. Ibid.

118. Charles M. Blow, "The Notorious Michael R. Bloomberg," *New York Times*, February 13, 2020.

119. Foreman, *Locking Up Our Own*, 171.

120. Alexander, *The New Jim Crow Mass Incarceration in the Age of Colorblindness*, 241.

121. See Congress. Gov, www.congress.gov/bill/115th-congress/house-bill/5682/text; Also see https://sentencing.net/legislation/first-step-act-summary.

122. See, Danille Sered, *Until We Reckon: Violence, Mass Incarceration and a Road to Repair* (London: The New Press, 2019), 3–4.

123. Ibram X. Kendi, *Stamped from the Beginning: The Definitive History of Racist Ideas in America* (New York: Nation Books, 2016), 11.

124. Ibid.

125. Ibid.

126. Ibram X. Kendi, *How to Be an Antiracist* (New York: One World, 2019), 163.

127. Ibid.

128. Nicholas Lemann, "The Spirit of St. Louis," *The New Yorker*, May 25, 2020, 64. This view of "racial capitalism" is contained in Walter Johnson's book, reported by Lemann in his

review of this book, which is titled *The Broken Heart of America: St. Louis and the Violent History of the United States* (New York: Basic Books, 2020).

129. Jane Coaston, "Trump's New Defense of His Charlottesville Comments Is Incredibly False," *Vox,* April 26, 2019.

130. Lemann, "The Spirit of St. Louis," 66. This view of the need to avoid the "hazards of defeatism" is contained in Lemann's review of Walter Johnson's book titled *The Broken Heart of America.*

131. Ibid.

132. See David Brooks, "A Case for Reparations," *New York Times,* March 7, 2019; Patricia Cohen, "What Reparations for Slavery Might Look Like," *New York Times,* May 23, 2019. We have followed Cohen's statement in developing the views of the implementation of reparations. See www.nytimes.com/2019/05/23/business/economy/reparations-slavery.html?searchResultPosition=1.

133. Cohen, "What Reparations for Slavery Might Look Like."

134. Ibid. On the Black Wall Street riot, see Kimberly Fain, "The Devastation of Black Wall Street," *JStar Daily,* July 5, 2017, https://daily.jstor.org/the-devastation-of-black-wall-street/.

135. Ta-Nehisi Coates, "The Case for Reparations," *The Atlantic,* June 2014. Italics added by the authors, www.theatlantic.com/magazine/archive/2014/06/the-case-for-reparations/361631/.

136. Pinckney, "The Afro-Pessimist Temptation," 55. Pinckney cites Angela Davis, *Freedom Is a Constant Struggle* (Chicago: Haymarket, 2016).

137. Cornel West with and edited by Christa Buschendorf, *Black Prophetic Fire* (Boston: Beacon Press, 2014), 1.

138. Ibid., see Chs. 4–6. Moreover, West also sees the prophetic fire model of leadership manifested in icons of black politics, including Malcolm X, Ella Baker, and Ida Wells.

139. For a good account of Black Lives Matter, see, Jelani Cobb, "The Matter of Black Lives," *The New Yorker,* March 14, 2016 and reprinted July 27, 2020. Cobb discusses Alicia Garza's view that police brutality has persisted and continues to escalate, despite the election of a black president of the United States. This circumstance suggests that the radical injustice of the past continues in the present to do great harm to blacks and others, including all of those at the lowest rungs of society. And the only recourse for such people is a grassroots movement that organizes citizens on behalf of ending police violence by making reforms of police practices. See, pp. 20–21, the reprinted version.

140. See www.history.com/topics/black-history/voting-rights-act There, it is stated that "The act banned the use of literacy tests, provided for federal oversight of voter registration in areas where less than 50 percent of the non-white population had not registered to vote, and authorized the U.S. attorney general to investigate the use of poll taxes in state and local elections."

141. Christopher Klein, "How Selma's 'Bloody Sunday' Became a Turning Point in the Civil Rights Movement," *History Stories,* www.history.com/news/selmas-bloody-sunday-50-years-ago.

142. Ibid.

143. Lewis, Posthumous statement entitled: "Together, You Can Redeem the Soul of Our Nation."

144. Christopher Ingraham, "Economic Analysis," *Washington Post,* December 6, 2017, www.washingtonpost.com/news/wonk/wp/2017/12/06/the-richest-1-percent-now-owns-more-of-the-countrys-wealth-than-at-any-time-in-the-past-50-years/.

145. See Jacob B. Hacker and Paul Pierson, *Let Them Eat Tweets: How the Right Rules in An Age of Extreme Inequality* (New York: Liveright Publishing Corporation, 2020). The authors state that the "new superrich [whom the authors call "plutocrats"] have pulled away from everyone else." And this created a political dilemma for many in the Republican Party, which is "how to reconcile their [plutocratic] allegiance to wealth and power with the need to attract the electoral support of voters without much of either," p. 77.

Index